Language acquisition

Studies in first language development

Edited by

PAUL FLETCHER *and* MICHAEL GARMAN

Department of Linguistic Science, University of Reading

Second edition

CAMBRIDGE
UNIVERSITY PRESS

Published by the Press Syndicate of the University of Cambridge
The Pitt Building, Trumpington Street, Cambridge CB2 1RP
40 West 20th Street, New York, NY 10011-4211, USA
10 Stamford Road, Oakleigh, Melbourne 3166, Australia

First published 1986
Reprinted 1988, 1990, 1992, 1997

British Library cataloguing in publication data

Language acquisition: studies in first language
development. – 2nd ed.
1. Children – Language
I. Fletcher, Paul   II. Garman, Michael
401'.9   LB1139.L3

Library of Congress cataloguing in publication data

Main entry under title:
Language acquisition
Bibliography: p.
Includes index.
1. Language acquisition. I. Fletcher, Paul J.
II. Garman, Michael.
P118.L254   1986   401'9   85–15168

ISBN 0 521 25974 6 hardback
ISBN 0 521 27780 9 paperback

Transferred to digital printing 1999

For our parents

Contents

Contributors

MARTIN ATKINSON	University of Essex
WILLIAM J. BAKER	University of Alberta
RUTH A. BERMAN	University of Tel-Aviv
ROBIN N. CAMPBELL	University of Stirling
SHULAMUTH CHIAT	City University, London
DAVID CRYSTAL	University College of North Wales, Bangor
BRUCE L. DERWING	University of Alberta
HELEN GOODLUCK	University of Wisconsin, Madison
PATRICK GRIFFITHS	University of York
MAYA HICKMANN	Max-Planck Institut, Nijmegen
DAVID INGRAM	University of British Columbia
ANNETTE KARMILOFF-SMITH	Medical Research Council Child Development Unit, London
JOHN L. LOCKE	Massachusetts General Hospital
MARLYS A. MACKEN	Stanford University
LISE MENN	Boston University
PAULA MENYUK	Boston University
KATHARINE PERERA	University of Manchester
ANN. M. PETERS	University of Hawaii
RONNIE SILBER	Boston University
PHILIP T. SMITH	University of Reading
CATHERINE E. SNOW	Harvard Graduate School of Education
RACHEL E. STARK	The Johns Hopkins Hospital, Baltimore
URSULA STEPHANY	Cologne University
ROGER WALES	University of Melbourne
RICHARD M. WEIST	State University of New York at Fredonia
GORDON WELLS	Ontario Institute for Studies in Education

Preface

In the time elapsed since the first edition of this book, in 1979, the field
has inevitably altered. The fundamental requirement remains the same
– the description and explanation of changes in the child's language as
he or she gets older – but in our perception the responses to this task
in the mid-eighties are different in some important respects to those prevalent in the late seventies. There has been no dramatic theoretical advance,
it is true: no dominant theoretical framework has emerged to change and
unify our approaches to the data. Indeed it is as true now as it was in
1979 that there is no one theoretical position that seems adequate to explain
the range and complexity of data available to us. Nevertheless, there have
been fruitful theoretical developments. The learnability hypothesis has been
influentially expounded. Developments in grammatical theory have been
shadowed by energetic experimental work that seeks evidence of quite
specific language capacities in children. And by now traditional (i.e. Piagetian) cognitive accounts of language development have been supplemented by social-interactive views that owe more to Vygotsky. It is these
movements, together with developments in areas which were covered in
the first edition – child-directed speech, cognition and language variation –
that have persuaded us to augment the *Contexts and determinants* section,
and to move it to a more prominent place in this revised edition.

A second major change in the field that we want to reflect is the increased
interest in crosslinguistic studies. We do not, however, wish to depart too
far in the revised edition from the overall orientation of the first volume
to a roughly longitudinal account of the main features of the acquisition
of English. A reasonable compromise position, we feel, is the inclusion
here of two chapters specifically devoted to crosslinguistic perspectives,
one on phonological development, and the other on morpho-syntax.

The remaining differences that appear, in a comparison of this edition
with the initial volume, respond (again, in our perception) to changes of
emphasis in particular areas of inquiry within language acquisition research
over the last few years. Some of these changes mean that authors' statements

in the first edition can stand as they were in that volume. We believe that this is true of aspects of the transition from prelanguage to language, and of the functional characteristics of early utterances, both single-word and two-element. Other alterations in emphasis, however, have seemed to imply various types of revision.

Some specific topics seem to require a fundamental reappraisal in the light of new approaches – for example, early grammatical development. Other areas need expansion to reflect a rapid increase in interest and knowledge since 1979. A good example here is the replacement of the original chapter on the development of the verb phrase by two separate essays in this edition, one on modality, and one on tense and aspect. A further category of modifications concerns authorial revisions to many of the chapters that were represented in the first volume, to take account of developments in the interim. (Because of the pressure of other commitments, some authors who were invited to make revisions had to decline.) Finally, since there is so much more information on child language now generally available, particularly in the form of textbooks such as Eliot (1981), we have accordingly modified the editorial commentary that we contributed to the first edition.

As editors we owe a considerable debt of gratitude to our contributors in both editions – for the high standard of their essays, for their cooperation, and for their forbearance in the face of delays that seem to be inevitable in multi-authored volumes. We are grateful also to Penny Carter of Cambridge University Press for her encouragement and unfailing support and to Jill Lake for her meticulous copy-editing. Our thanks go also to Barbara Barnes, who performed all the secretarial duties associated with this volume with care and (necessary) equanimity.

PAUL FLETCHER

MICHAEL GARMAN

Reading, 1985

Part I

CONTEXTS AND DETERMINANTS

Introduction

The day when a monolithic explanatory theory of language acquisition could be elaborated and discussed in a section such as this is still a long way off. Nevertheless it is important to try to consider language learning as a whole in Part I, to set the scene for what comes later. Parts II and III of the book address important aspects of the development of phonology, morphology and syntax in English and, to a limited extent, in other languages. Part IV addresses changes in spoken language and its basis after 5 years of age, and the beginnings of literacy skills. It is appropriate, then, that we lay out here a number of different views of how explanation in language development might be approached, and how independent variables relevant to the learning of language might be delimited, and their effects examined. We have maintained here the part title of the first edition – 'Contexts and determinants' – which we interpreted there as the 'external' and 'internal' settings for language development. Three of the chapters from that part in the first edition appear here in a revised form: Snow on 'Conversations with children', Campbell on 'Language acquisition and cognition' and Wells on 'Variation in child language'. Part I of this edition also includes three new chapters: Hickmann gives a Vygotskian perspective on language development in 'Psychosocial aspects of language acquisition' and that is followed by two chapters concerned with the relationship between linguistic theory and language acquisition: Goodluck on 'Developing grammars' and Atkinson on 'Learnability'.

Let us consider first two chapters which in rather different ways are concerned with cognition and language development. First, Hickmann contrasts Vygotskian and Piagetian perspectives on the inferences to be made from children's language behaviour, as it changes, to cognitive and social development. A not untypical Piagetian way of considering the relationship between cognitive structures and language is the study by Corrigan (1978), which provides data on the relation between an infant's sensorimotor development and language ability by considering the two domains separately. As part of a longitudinal study, she used standardized scales of object

3

permanence and applied them to three children. She also videotaped linguistic interactions between the children and their mothers and analysed the language used. As it turned out, the relation between any child's degree of cognitive ability as measured by the object permanence scales, and his language ability as determined by, say, the age of onset of single-word utterances, was not straightforward. But the point at issue for Hickmann here would be how far one can accept a paradigm that treats cognition and language as separate entities, with language seen as a product of cognitive development; language on this view is one of a number of behaviours which follow from 'principles of organization and mechanisms of development which are themselves autonomous'. It is the separation of thought and language, and the priority of the former, which Hickmann challenges. Following Vygotsky, she emphasizes the interdependence of language and thought in development. On this view there are constant interactions between language development and cognitive development, and the uses of language are necessary for the development of certain higher mental functions. This theoretical view, it is important to emphasize, implies a different view of what the data relevant for child language study are. Those who insist on the independence and priority of cognition tend, when considering language, to be concerned with the formal-structural properties of sentence-like units, which are context-independent. The interactionist tends to be more at ease with functionally and / or pragmatically inclined accounts of language for which the context-dependent and social nature of language is primary. Often the unit for analysis, within this paradigm, will be larger than the sentence. Or, if the focus is on the child's use and development of a particular set of forms (pronouns, for example), the analyst will be concerned with how these forms are used in relation to the extralinguistic context and to the larger discourse in which they appear. Hickmann discusses recent research of her own, and of other researchers, which concentrates on functional analyses of the forms children use (particularly forms like pronouns and articles which are important for introducing and identifying referents). This work has identified important changes in development in the way such forms are used.

Campbell is initially sceptical, as he was in 1979, that a coherent theoretical framework exists to inform research on the relationship between cognitive and linguistic development. In an attempt to encourage progress towards what he would see as a useful (and non-nativist) framework, he also begins with Vygotsky, specifically with the assertion that 'the change of the interfunctional structure of consciousness' plays a crucial role in psychological development. To enable us to take the role of consciousness in cognition seriously, Campbell outlines a position involving a particular

sort of dualism, which distinguishes (from the point of view of the 'cognizer') *phenic* functions – those which are evident to the user, and which he can be aware (conscious) of, and *cryptic* functions – those which are hidden from the user: they are not conscious or reportable. The distinction allows Campbell to identify what he sees as problems in current approaches to cognitive psychology, for example in information-processing approaches, which blur the distinction between cryptic and phenic, and in experimental paradigms which change what would in naturalistic situations be phenic processes into cryptic routines.

The distinction is also constructively useful when it is extended to language. Campbell considers that the study of language development will also benefit from his dualist approach, which takes the system of communication, on the one hand, to be underwritten by phenic processes, and a system of language on the other, to which cryptic processes apply. Messages or intentions are not 'linguistic objects'; they are open to awareness and rational operation. The linguistic forms in which they are realized are *not* available to our awareness, and are not part of what Campbell wishes to recognize as cognitive psychology; the study of this, for him, must be limited to phenic processes. The remainder of his chapter considers the possible advantages of the dual representation approach in a number of areas, including lexical development and the development of linguistic awareness.

From an avowedly non-nativist position (see particularly note 8 to Campbell's chapter), we turn to two papers which explore in some detail nativist assumptions about language acquisition, particularly as they concern the development of grammars. Goodluck introduces her discussion of the relation between acquisition and current linguistic theory by considering some of the facts that a linguistic theory must account for: 'the complexity, orderliness and limited variety in human languages convinces linguists that language must be learned through a biological program that puts bounds on the possible grammatical system a child can postulate' (p. 49). In other words, limits are set on the class of candidate grammars to account for the data with which the child is faced, by a quite specific genetic endowment that the child comes to the learning task with. This program for language learning is given by *universal grammar* (UG). UG is determined by the linguist's examination of the complex of interrelations between components, and the rules within them, in grammars of existing languages. If languages demonstrate common 'core' features, and interlanguage structural variation can be seen to occur only along certain well-defined 'parameters', then a plausible and elegant hypothesis is that the child is able to screen out, from the start, a multitude of possible grammars, because

of his innate knowledge of the UG core and potential parameterization.

After considering a number of examples of structural principles which indicate the limits within which particular languages and groups of languages operate, Goodluck goes on to review a range of empirical evidence in support of the view that children learning language are sensitive to such principles.

Atkinson begins his chapter by drawing attention to an interesting separation in language development studies of two quite distinct groups of researchers. One, which he designates FLATs (for first language acquisition theorists), concentrates on empirical work with children, while the other group (antonymically labelled SHARPs) tend to avoid empirical work and concentrate on the logical problem of language acquisition. As with many convenient dichotomies, the impression conveyed by this division is not entirely accurate. Much of the work reviewed by Goodluck, for example, is concerned with providing empirical support for innate principles. And many FLATs are working within what they see as appropriate theoretical frameworks, even though these may be distinct from what a SHARP would consider respectable. Nevertheless Atkinson's labels do crystallize a distinct (if perhaps narrowing) gap in the field. One of the issues he addresses in this paper is whether the activities of either of the groups he identifies is of any concern to the other.

Learnability theory, narrowly defined, refers to formally specified principles of language acquisition to which the child has access. The theorems developed depend upon assumptions about the mental representation of the end-point of development, about the data to which the child has access in learning, and about the procedures with which the child operates on the data. Atkinson considers first this framework of assumptions. He goes on to review the Wexler and Culicover (1980) version of learnability theory based on Standard Theory transformational grammar, and then looks at implications for this version of learnability theory of the more recent Chomskyan grammatical framework, Revised Extended Standard Theory (REST). This represents for the linguist a *more* constrained theory, with a restriction of the transformational component to a single schema – move α, the requirement that base constituent structures rules are formulated within $\bar{X}$ theory, and comparable restrictions in other areas of the grammar. Atkinson points out that these proposals would strengthen the role of innate endowments and minimize that of the kind of learning procedure that Wexler and Culicover are required to set up within the Standard Theory procedure. Atkinson concludes by considering again his FLAT–SHARP distinction, and indicates some ways in which the divide can be bridged.

With the final two chapters we move away from approaches which concen-

trate on the resources that the child brings to the language learning task, to the environment in which the learning takes place and with which the child's resources interact. This environment can either be construed narrowly (as by Snow, where it means 'child-directed speech' – CDS) or more broadly, as a range of factors which could be relevant to the undoubted variation that exists among individuals, in both speed and style of language acquisition (Wells).

Snow begins by reviewing the development of CDS studies over the last fifteen years. She identifies various stages. The first group of (descriptive) studies, as a reaction to claims that input to children was ill-formed and complex, established that speech addressed to children who were language learners was quite different from adult speech, and was modified in such a way that it was appropriate to the child's linguistic level. These studies tended to concentrate on structural properties of CDS. The Stage II description of CDS extended its purview to the semantics of speech addressed to children: what were mothers talking about? It turned out that utterances addressed to young children were severely restricted in terms of the topics involved – mainly to the 'here-and-now'. It seemed that the structural simplicity found in the first group of studies could well be an artifact of semantic simplicity. Stage III research picks up on the finding of Stage II to consider the effects of semantic contingency (the mother elaborating or extending topics introduced by the child), on his language learning. Snow points out that even if we can demonstrate that semantic contingency facilitates language learning, we still need a theory of the learning mechanism that makes this possible. She concludes by considering the relevance of recent work on language acquisition and social interaction in non-Western societies, and the relevance of social facilitators other than semantic contingency for language learning.

Wells' Bristol Project has not only provided valuable information about the course of language development in British English-speaking children (see Wells 1984 for an account of the project and its major results) but, because of its design, allows a number of questions to be addressed concerning variables which might be presumed to be relevant to language development, in that they might affect the rate of learning, or the end-point that the child achieves. As Wells points out, the situation in which the child acquires language is complex and subject to a variety of influences. A range of the methodological difficulties in language acquisition studies are illustrated in his discussion of the variables involved. These cover inherent factors (such as intelligence and personality), social factors (such as the complex of factors referred to in the term 'social class'), features of the immediate situation of utterance, and the style of interaction. It is with

this last factor that Wells makes contact with the work reviewed by Snow: it is clear from the results of Wells and his colleagues that semantic contingency – paying linguistic attention to the meaning intention of the child and responding appropriately – is facilitating for the child. By contrast, variations in feedback from parents relating to the grammatical form of child utterances do not seem to account for individual differences in rates of development. Concerning social factors, it is intriguing that Wells finds little support for claims that have been made concerning a general effect of social class on linguistic ability. It seems that, as a source of variation, parental interactional style may be a more important variable.

1. Psychosocial aspects of language acquisition*

Maya Hickmann

1. Introduction

Language acquisition does not take place in a vacuum. As children acquire language, they acquire a sign system which bears important relationships to both cognitive and social aspects of their life. The issues involved in assessing the inter-relationships among social, linguistic, and cognitive processes in development are numerous, and no attempt is made here to present them exhaustively. As a starting point, this chapter considers the status of language in two developmental theories, Piaget's and Vygotsky's, in relation to cognitive and social-interactive processes. This brief contrast shows that the importance which is attributed to social interaction in Vygotsky's theory, and its relatively secondary role in Piaget's theory, result partly from the different ways in which they define language and interpret its development. More generally, the discussion highlights the implications of viewing language and its development as either intrinsically tied to, or as relatively autonomous from, its social-interactive context of use. It presents some of the issues involved in making inferences from child language about cognitive and social development, suggesting some implications of recent research on the functional properties of child language and on its contextual determinants.

Most theories of child development address in one way or another the question of how language, thought, and social interaction interrelate in the child's life. Depending on the particular focus of each theory, these three aspects of development can be defined and related differently. For example, it is possible to characterize some theories as relatively social: i.e. those which view social interaction as primary for development (e.g. Vygotsky, Mead, Baldwin, Rommetveit, Wallon, recent writings of Bruner and some contemporary writings in sociolinguistics), and some as relatively cognitivist: i.e., those which see individual cognitive processes as primary in development (e.g. Piaget, neo-Piagetian approaches, artificial intelligence, contemporary cognitive psychology and psycholinguistics).

Such a general contrast between social and cognitivist approaches captures one important dimension of developmental theories, but it overlooks others (for some discussion of the similarities and differences among some of these theories, see Kohlberg, Yaeger and Hjertholm 1968; Kohlberg and Wertsch in press; Hood in press). In order to illustrate how social and cognitivist approaches lead to different analyses of the inter-relationships among language, thought, and social interaction, it is useful to start with a contrast between two specific theories. A comparison of the theories of Piaget and Vygotsky concerning the relation of language and thought in development presents a particularly illuminating contrast.[1] This contrast can be fully understood only if we consider how these theories relate social interaction and cognitive development, and especially, how they relate social interaction and language.

2. Action, thought and language

An essential problem in developmental theory is to account for the relation between action and thought. Piaget and Vygotsky give complementary accounts of child development during the early sensorimotor period. However, Piaget emphasizes the later continuity between action and thought whereas Vygotsky sees the emergence of language as the source of a general discontinuity in development, in the sense that it introduces a new means of internal organization for the child.

For both Piaget and Vygotsky, child development before the emergence of language is characterized by a gradually more complex organization of means and ends in sensorimotor activity. Piagetian and neo-Piagetian research on the sensorimotor period has made a very rich contribution to our understanding of early child development, whereas Vygotsky did not directly study this period in any detail. However, Vygotsky's general account of early development, which is subsumed under what he calls 'the natural line of development', is compatible with Piaget's, since it focuses on the development of tool-use in infants (and in higher primates), and since this ability presupposes the kind of means–ends organization described in great detail by Piaget.

The two theories diverge in important ways with respect to later developments. Piaget focuses on the child's cognitive development, which he describes as resulting from the internalization of the means–ends organization of sensorimotor activity achieved in early development. Thus, the first cognitive representations are described as 'internal imitations' of external actions. The development of language is relatively peripheral to this theory, both as a content area in its own right (although many have later applied

Piagetian concepts to study language development) and in terms of the principal explanatory mechanisms from which cognitive development emerges. Children's use of language is merely one among many behaviours following from principles of organization and mechanisms of development which are themselves autonomous. In contrast, language development is for Vygotsky the principal motor of development, as it mediates the child's participation in both the intellectual and social life surrounding him. That is, the principles and mechanisms of cognitive development are not independent from the signs, particularly the linguistic signs, which the child confronts in his interactions with the world.

At the risk of oversimplifying these two theories (and their sometimes controversial interpretations), it is possible for our purposes here to summarize the ways in which they relate language development and cognitive development in terms of the notions of *autonomy* and *causal priority*. For Piaget, cognitive development is in principle both autonomous from language development and causally prior to it. Piaget and some researchers within Piagetian and neo-Piagetian paradigms have at times recognized the importance of language acquisition for cognitive development. The role of language appears particularly in discussions about the development of the symbolic function (Piaget 1946b), which characterizes the uses of all signs, including early imitations of actions (iconic signs) and later uses of language.[2] However, although linguistic signs are described as having particular properties, their uses are but one type among many sign-uses in the symbolic function and they do not play a central role for development within this theoretical framework.

The relative role of language remains a fairly controversial issue, as shown by the many discussions which focus on whether or not language is *necessary* for cognitive development. This theoretical issue has been particularly controversial with respect to the earlier stages of development ('pre-operational thought' and 'concrete operations'); Piaget's own position here was that language was neither necessary nor sufficient. However, it can also be found in discussions of the higher stages ('formal operations'), although Piaget himself has acknowledged that language may be necessary at this stage, at least for some forms of reasoning which require operating on symbolic forms themselves (e.g. Piaget 1963).

Empirically this issue can be found in research which compares the cognitive development of different populations of children, e.g., normal versus deaf or learning-disabled children. It can also be found in general methodological controversies about the extent to which children's uses of language should be (at least) one of the criteria for the diagnosis of children's operational stages. Thus, many discussions have focused on whether maximally

nonverbal responses, as opposed to question–answer sequences, verbal explanations and justifications of responses, should be elicited in experimental situations. An enormous body of developmental literature has been devoted to such questions (see, for example, some relevant empirical studies and/or reviews of the issues in Braine 1959, 1962; Oleron 1963; Furth 1966; Sinclair-de-Zwart 1967, 1969; Brainerd 1973; Sinha and Walkerdine, 1978; Stone and Day 1980; Kohlberg and Wertsch in press; Schneider 1984).

Even if we take this controversy into account, it is probably fair to say that although Piaget himself used a relatively verbal method of elicitation language clearly plays a relatively secondary role in his account of cognitive development, at least as far as his own metatheoretical writings on the subject are concerned. In these writings, the dynamic mechanisms that move cognitive development forward are the processes of adaptation which are clearly independent from language and which constitute explanatory principles ultimately defined in biological terms. These processes, namely the processes of assimilation and accommodation, allow the child to interact with his environment by adjusting reality to his cognitive organization and by adjusting his cognitive organization to reality, resulting in a gradual 'decentering' of his cognitive structures, which makes abstract reasoning possible. The development of children's decentering capacity is seen as underlying all changes in their behaviours, including their uses and interpretations of language, which in this sense have no particular status in relation to other behaviours. The nature of children's language at any particular time is explained as being merely one of the many symptoms which reflect a particular stage in their underlying cognitive structure.

In contrast, according to Vygotsky (1934/1962, 1978, 1981a,b) there are constant interactions between language development and cognitive development, such that thought is neither autonomous from language nor causally prior to it.[3] Furthermore, Vygotsky attributes to the uses of sign systems, and especially the uses of language, a privileged status in relation to other aspects of development. The uses of a sign system such as language are necessary for the development of uniquely human higher mental functions both in ontogenesis and in phylogenesis. More generally, language development is at the centre of what Vygotsky calls 'the social line of development' which interacts with 'the natural line of development' in ontogenesis and in phylogenesis. Whereas the natural line follows biological principles of explanation, the social line requires new explanatory principles that cannot be reduced to biological ones and that make ontogenetic development specifically human.

This view introduces in developmental theory what might be called semiotic principles of explanation, particularly the general explanatory principle

of 'semiotic mediation'. According to this principle, the properties and uses of sign systems, especially language, lead to new forms of organization in development that transform in fundamental ways other aspects of development. It is important to see that for Vygotsky semiotic principles of explanation interact with, but cannot be reduced to, biological ones. For example, as mentioned above, children's language acquisition is, for Piaget, one among many phenomena in ontogenetic and phylogenetic development that can ultimately be explained in terms of general, underlying, biological principles. In contrast, although Vygotsky sees language as a tool among other tools that participate in the organization of sensorimotor activity, he also sees language as a very special tool in comparison with others: by mediating the means–ends organization of sensorimotor activity, the uses of language transform this activity.

Semiotic mediation has enormous implications for what Vygotsky postulates to be the dynamic mechanisms of development and for how he describes the processes of internalization, in comparison to Piaget. For Piaget, thought emerges mostly as internalized action; i.e. its development is initially the result of internalizing the means–ends organization of sensorimotor activity. For Vygotsky, thought is mediated by inner speech; i.e. its development is initially the result of internalizing a new kind of means–ends organization which is imposed by speech and transforms the organization of all activities.

3. Social interaction and cognitive development

It is important to see these approaches to cognitive development, the one as relatively autonomous from language (Piaget) and the other as highly dependent on language (Vygotsky), in the light of how the two theories also relate cognitive development and social interaction. As implied by the preceding summary of Piaget's theory, cognitive development is for him relatively autonomous, not only independent of language but also of social interaction. As was the case with language, Piaget has at times acknowledged social interaction as a possible, albeit secondary, factor in development. For example, the child's participation in social interactions has been described by some researchers within this paradigm as a possible source of conflict confronting the child with other points of view, and motivating him to 'decentre' his cognitive structure in particular situations.

More or less explicit hints of such interpersonal factors in development can be found both in Piaget's early work, in which he observed children's interactions or their reasoning about social situations (e.g. Piaget 1923,

1924, 1932), and in other researchers' work inspired by his writings on moral judgement, moral argumentation, role-taking, the development of concepts of self and other etc. (Flavell *et al.* 1968; Kohlberg 1969, 1971; Selman 1976, 1980; M. Miller 1982, 1984). As was the case with language, the role of social interaction, as well as the very notion of conflict as a mechanism for awareness, has led to some controversy. Again, it is probably fair to say that within this paradigm, although some recognize the particular properties of social interaction, children's participation in such interactions (including their uses of language in them) is one among many behaviours and is in principle no different from their interactions with inanimate objects in various situations. That is, their social interactions are ultimately explained by the same principles which govern their logico-mathematical reasoning in situations where they are asked to comment on the properties of objects and on the results of actions performed on them.

In contrast, Vygotsky views children's participation in social interaction as a privileged kind of interaction with the world which is a primary factor for cognitive development. In this theory, patterns of cognitive activity and changes in such patterns cannot be understood independently of the social-interactive processes which shape them and from which they emerge. Vygotsky's relatively strong view on the relation between cognitive development and social interaction, particularly early interactions between children and adults or older peers, can be summarized by his claim that all higher mental functions appear twice in ontogenetic development: they first appear as social or interpsychological functions, during interactions with other social agents, and only later do they become individual or intrapsychological functions, through the internalization of social-interactive processes (Vygotsky 1978, 1981a).

It is useful to highlight at this point the different *units* of analysis that are used in these two theories to evaluate children's cognitive skills. Typically, the following methodological procedure is used in the Piagetian paradigm. Individual children are placed in various situations where their cognitive skills are evaluated as they interact with objects (social or inanimate) of various kinds. Whether verbal or nonverbal responses are elicited, children's reasoning is compared in various domains and/or situations, and consistencies or inconsistencies in their reasoning are evaluated (for example, conservation in one situation, but not in another). Inferences are made about the cognitive structures of individual children on the basis of such consistencies and inconsistencies. Social interactions, either between children and adult experimenters or among children, may be tools from which such inferences are made, but they do not enter the analysis itself, in the sense that in principle they are assumed not to affect signifi-

cantly the very nature of what is inferred. These interactions are interpreted in terms of the cognitive structures which are assumed to underlie individual children's behaviour.

Within the traditional Piagetian paradigm at least, the unit of analysis is clearly the individual child. Some researchers, either working within this paradigm or criticizing it, have begun to broaden this unit of analysis. For example, some have argued in various degrees that different patterns of adult–child interaction can affect significantly children's reasoning about social or nonsocial objects. Furthermore, some have argued that there exist reasoning processes in adult–child or child–child interactions that cannot be reduced to individual units (e.g. Rommetveit 1977; Cole, Hood and McDermott 1978; Stone and Day 1980; Selman 1980; Miller 1984; Hundeide 1985).

Vygotsky (1978) proposed to interpret children's cognitive skills in terms of the notion of the 'zone of proximal development', which he defines as the *relation* between two types of children's problem-solving behaviours: (1) their behaviours when they solve a problem in social interactions, particularly those in which adults provide them with some guidance, for example, if they structure the problem for them, solve parts of the problem, give them hints (potential level of development); (2) their behaviours when they can solve the problem on their own (actual level of development). As the child matures, and even sometimes over the course of a single experimental session, this relation between interpsychological and intrapsychological behaviours changes for a given task, so that children gradually come to solve on their own problems which they could earlier solve only partially, or not at all, except through interpersonal interaction with adults. The general point of contrast with Piagetian research is both methodological and theoretical: individual psychological processes are measured against interpersonal interaction and they are defined as necessarily emerging from such interactions.

It is not entirely clear how the notion of the 'zone of proximal development' should be operationalized in concrete empirical research. According to the writings left by Vygotsky, it can be generally described in terms of the processes of social interaction between adults and children which allow children to organize complex series of actions in problem-solving situations *before* they have the mental capacities to decide on the actions on their own. For example, adults regulate children's actions before children can represent the overall properties of the problem, organize their actions accordingly, and reflect on them. Gradually, the regulative behaviour of adults in these interactive contexts becomes a part of children's own behaviour.

This theoretical framework is similar in some ways to more recent proposals which have been made to account for developmental mechanisms that take place in adult–child interaction. For example, Bruner and his co-workers proposed the notion of 'formats' in development, i.e. patterns of social interactions in which adults scaffold children's verbal and nonverbal behaviours (e.g. Bruner 1975a, b, 1981; Wood, Ross and Bruner 1976; Bruner and Hickmann 1983). Such processes of scaffolding have been used to describe a variety of developmental phenomena, including not only the development of complex problem-solving behaviours but also the development of language itself.

Clearly, one of the most essential metatheoretical problems to be solved within this paradigm is to specify *how* the shift from interpsychological to intrapsychological functioning takes place. As will be discussed below, according to Vygotsky's principle of semiotic mediation it is specifically communicative processes, and most importantly the processes that involve language, which make this shift possible. (Note that this is not necessarily the case for other related proposals, and not even for some direct empirical applications of Vygotsky's zone of proximal development: see Rogoff and Wertsch in press.)

More generally, the ways in which cognitive processes are determined by social interaction, the kinds of cognitive processes which are so determined, and the extent to which they are so determined all need to be specified within this paradigm (also see Shatz 1981 for critical comments on similar issues concerning the role of social interaction in language acquisition). Although various kinds of evidence indicate that some cognitive capacities might be independent of wide variations in socio-cultural environments, ecologically inclined research has begun to show the importance of linguistic, social-interactive and cultural factors for the understanding of cognitive capacities that had been assumed to be autonomous and universal (e.g. the work of Bronfenbrener, Cole *et al.* 1971; Cole and Scribner 1974; Rommetveit 1977, 1979b; Cole, Hood and McDermott 1978; Donaldson 1978; Sinha and Walkerdine 1978; Hundeide 1985). I return below to this point, which requires a careful specification of what is meant by socio-cultural environment, by the role of language in this environment, and by the very notion of cognitive capacity.

4. Social interaction and language

An essential key to understanding Piaget's and Vygotsky's positions concerning the relation of cognitive development to language on the one hand and to social interaction on the other is to consider their different

approaches to language. In particular, they differ in how they relate social interaction to language and its acquisition.

For example, Piaget's view of language is explicitly inspired by a Saussurean framework (also see Bronckart and Ventouras-Spycher 1979). Piaget focuses on language as an abstract system of sign relations and on the propositional and context-independent properties of linguistic representation which make it a powerful tool for the development of abstract reasoning. He does explicitly refer to the 'social functions' of language, and even mentions some aspects of its context-dependence (e.g. Piaget 1923, 1946b), and some researchers have tried to integrate these aspects of child language more overtly into his theory (e.g. Bates 1976). However, it is not clear how far Piaget's framework can account for them without modifications. According to his own use of a Saussurean framework, these aspects are clearly secondary in how he defines this sign system and relates it to child development. This becomes obvious if we consider especially the ways in which the Piagetian metatheory accounts for the dynamic mechanisms of development in language acquisition itself and in other domains.

As noted previously, all developments in children's behaviour are explained within this paradigm in terms of the gradual decentering of children's cognitive structures. With respect to language acquisition, this decentering underlies a decontextualization of children's speech, allowing them, for example, to speak of displaced entities, events and relations among them which are not part of the here-and-now and/or to take into account the perspectives of their listeners. Although decentering is a very general concept that applies to perceptual, cognitive, linguistic, and social behaviours, its clearest impact on language acquisition within this paradigm is shown in the child's ability to use language as an abstract, context-independent system of signs (e.g. in logical reasoning).

In addition, although this model has been extended by some to account for social-interactive behaviours, it has been generally more concerned with logico-mathematical reasoning in domains of the child's life which (at least as they are explicitly treated) have relatively little to do with interacting social agents. A major exception can be found, of course, in research on children's moral judgements of role-taking skills (e.g. Piaget 1932; Kohlberg 1969, 1971; Selman 1976, 1980; Miller 1982, 1984). However, much of this work has focused on children's individual or collective reasoning *about* interacting social agents, the explanation of which ultimately depends on their logico-mathematical capacities. These logico-mathematical capacities in turn are rarely explained in terms of social-interactive and context-dependent properties of language. Thus, developmental stages in various domains are typically related to one another in a hierarchy, at the bottom

of which is the development of logico-mathematical reasoning (e.g. moral reasoning presupposes role-taking skills, which presuppose in turn logico-mathematical reasoning in nonsocial domains). Thus, whether we consider language acquisition itself or other content domains within a Piagetian paradigm, the social-interactive and context-dependent properties of language are somewhat peripheral to the essential mechanisms which set development in motion.

In contrast, the context-dependent and social nature of language is primary in Vygotsky's developmental theory. Vygotsky's approach to language is much more consistent with some functionally and/or pragmatically inclined semiotic and linguistic theories (e.g. Peirce 1932; Jakobson 1960) than with a Saussurean approach. Although his linguistic framework is not completely developed in his writings, its orientation is apparent in a number of ways: e.g., his focus on speech rather than language, a distinction which can be compared to (although not equated with) Saussure's distinction between *langue* and *parole*, his focus on the indicatory basis of communication in his discussion of both nonverbal signs (e.g. pointing gestures) and verbal ones, his distinction between *sense* and *reference* (especially Vygotsky 1962, 1981b; also see some discussion in Lee and Hickmann 1983; Wertsch in preparation). These points, among others, show Vygotsky's primary interest in what others have called in semiotic/linguistic terms 'deictic' or, more generally, 'indexical' aspects of language, i.e. aspects of language (whether referential or not) which are necessarily dependent on a relation of co-presence with the speech situation (e.g. Silverstein 1976, in press).

We return to some of these points below, in a more detailed discussion of recent approaches to language and its development. For the purposes of pursuing our contrast here, it is possible to summarize Vygotsky's approach as follows. Cognitive development is necessarily dependent on the fact that language is multifunctional, i.e. it is a sign system which is simultaneously used for abstract representation (e.g. internal logical reasoning) and for communication in social-interactive contexts. Furthermore, the context-dependent indicatory aspects of communication in social interaction are primary and constitute the foundation for the development of abstract reference-and-predication.

We can illustrate this approach by considering again Vygotsky's zone of proximal development. It is through communicative processes, mostly (although not exclusively) mediated by speech, that adults establish social interactions with children which play a role in the children's cognitive development. Such communicative processes are central for the zone of proximal development: in order to guide children's behaviours when they cannot

solve problems, adults use speech which, in conjunction with nonverbal gestures, simultaneously maintains social contact with them, directs their attention to different aspects of the context, and provides in a social-interactive context an overall regulation for their problem-solving behaviour.

A number of recent studies have, in fact, begun to document empirically Vygotsky's zone of proximal development by analysing patterns of mother–child and child–child interactions in problem-solving situations (e.g. Hickmann 1978; Hickmann and Wertsch 1978; Wertsch and Stone 1978; Wertsch et al. 1980; McLane 1981; Wertsch and Schneider 1981; see Wertsch in preparation for a review of these studies). The basic paradigm used in some of these studies consisted of presenting mother–child dyads in which children were approximately $2\frac{1}{2}$, $3\frac{1}{2}$, and $4\frac{1}{2}$ years old with a puzzle-completion task and asking each mother to help her child complete the puzzle in any way she saw fit. This simple puzzle task was made slightly too difficult for the children in a number of ways. For example, a model was used and the materials were prepared in such a way that in order successfully to complete the copy-puzzle in accordance with the model-puzzle, children had to organize a complex series of actions which depended on constantly comparing the copy and the model.

The analyses focused on how the verbal and nonverbal behaviours of mothers and children unfolded until the task was completed. They show that mothers systematically use a variety of utterance-forms in order to regulate the problem-solving activity. In particular, their directives vary along a number of dimensions: for example, how explicitly these utterances represent the overall goal of the task, whether they are accompanied by pointing gestures, where they direct the attention of the child, etc. Such communicative patterns vary as a function of the age and competence of the child, as a function of how the task unfolds, and as a function of socio-cultural factors. For example, the results show that younger children can only successfully sequence their actions when given an enormous amount of regulation on the part of the mother throughout the task, for example, by highly explicit directives and many pointing gestures, the combination of which directs the child's attention to relevant parts of the task and helps him organize his actions without requiring an understanding of goals and subgoals. In contrast, older children need little adult regulation to complete the task: mothers frequently use highly abbreviated directives with them and less nonverbal pointing.

Interestingly, some of these studies present evidence that children who are transitional, i.e. who need adult regulation at the beginning of the session but who then regulate their own behaviours towards the end of

the session, use utterance forms of the same type as their mothers. For example, toward the end of the session they themselves ask and answer question types which mothers used as directives early in the session. These studies propose a Vygotskian interpretation of such utterances, according to which they are examples of egocentric speech used by children to regulate their own problem-solving activity. As we shall see in more detail below, egocentric speech is here interpreted in the broader context of such functional analyses of mother–child interaction as an example of the transition from interpsychological processes to intrapsychological processes mediated by communication.

5. Structures and functions in development

This general, and somewhat oversimplified, contrast between the developmental theories of Piaget and Vygotsky presents a first illustration of the different descriptions and explanations which can be given of the inter-relationships among interpersonal, linguistic and cognitive aspects of the child's life. (For more details on some of these issues, see Lee and Hickmann 1983, Lee, Wertsch and Stone 1983; Kohlberg and Wertsch in press; Wertsch in preparation.) I have argued that an essential aspect of this contrast is how the two theories approach language, in particular: (1) whether or not they give language development a special status in relation to other aspects of development, and (2) what aspects of language they primarily focus upon, i.e., whether they see language as inherently social, or more precisely as multifunctional. This contrast raises some more general theoretical issues which cut across many other writings on child development. The issues summarized below revolve around the problem of specifying the relation between different interpretations of child language and the ways in which we attribute knowledge (linguistic, cognitive or social knowledge) to children.

A number of linguists, psychologists and philosophers have argued that there are systematic relationships between the types of models we use to account for communication (particularly language) and those we use to account for knowledge (see Bickhard 1980a,b; Silverstein in press, for some recent discussions of this issue). From a developmental point of view, let us consider, for example, approaches which focus strictly on the formal–structural properties of child language and those which focus on its functional properties, in relation to the kind of knowledge they attribute to children, to see how they describe this knowledge and how they explain its development. To my mind, the central issues which differentiate these two approaches to child language are whether they focus on the contextual

determinants of communicative behaviour and the extent to which they see them as primary.

The general tendency of developmental models focusing on the formal–structural properties of child language (whether these models are meant to characterize linguistic knowledge only or some other knowledge which might be inferred from language) has been to describe children's utterances in terms of their context-independent, syntactic–semantic–logical properties within sentential or propositional units of analysis. More generally, structural models infer from children's behaviours an abstract and ideal system of cognitive or linguistic competence, which is defined in terms of a formal and context-independent system (e.g. predicate calculus).

This ideal competence is seen as the primary (or only) principle describing and explaining children's behaviours across situations or domains. Various secondary factors are sometimes invoked to account for cases where particular actions deviate from this ideal system in particular situations. Contextual and functional parameters of everyday language are among such secondary factors. They are either ignored as performance factors having no important relation to competence, relegated to the periphery of the theory as unexplained phenomena which somehow interact in unspecified ways with the more central phenomena of competence, or acknowledged as relatively important and specified factors which, however, do not really affect the nature of competence (see Derwing 1973 for a detailed discussion of this issue as it applies to the developmental implications of generative grammar, and Stone and Day 1980 for a discussion of this issue in Piagetian theory).

In contrast, some recent approaches which focus on the functional properties of language have become concerned with the contextual determinants of child language (although see below for some important differences among different functional approaches). The growing interest in functional and contextual accounts of language has had important implications, the most obvious one being that the distinction between competence and performance has become blurred. This implication results from the fact that functional models are concerned with how and why a particular formal structure is used in particular contexts, with systematic variations among formal structures as a function of contextual determinants; and, in the more extreme cases, they have defined the very existence and characteristics of formal structures as deriving from such systematicity in contextual-functional variations. In this sense, functional models have questioned the distinction between competence and performance in various degrees, either redefining it so as to include knowledge of contextual-functional systematicity in competence, or rejecting it altogether (e.g. Rommetveit 1974, 1979a; Stone and Day 1980). Indeed, in strong versions of this approach, in which acquir-

ing a structure is defined (at least in part) as using it according to functional-contextual criteria, it becomes very unclear as to what could be meant by the statement, for example, that a child has acquired a cognitive or a linguistic structure but does not yet know how to use it.

A number of related implications follow from this approach, such as a greater focus on interactions among skills and on process (see Stone and Day 1980; Karmiloff-Smith 1983). For example, since structural approaches to both language and cognitive development look for regularities in behaviours independently of their particular context (or across many contexts), they are in principle not primarily concerned with how these behaviours unfold through time in any given context. In contrast, although process approaches to language and cognition are not restricted to functional ones, functional approaches which have been seriously concerned with the contextual embeddedness of structures are committed to account for process.[4] For example, a functional analysis of linguistic forms requires analysing their relation not only to the nonlinguistic parameters of the situation, but also to the linguistic context (within *and* across utterances) in which they are embedded. Utterances are preceded and followed by other utterances and, by virtue of the very nature of speech, this linguistic context always changes through time. A functional-contextual analysis of linguistic forms, then, must be time-bound and requires an analysis of where particular forms occur in discourse, how discourse unfolds up to that point, and how it proceeds after that point.

This kind of process approach to language tends to be closely related to a process approach to cognition and has consequences for how cognitive correlates are inferred on the basis of language use. More generally, process approaches have consequences for how one describes human (linguistic and nonlinguistic) action. For example, Vygotskian approaches to psychological development are clearly process-based, in comparison to Piagetian ones. Vygotskian descriptions and explanations of cognitive development do not focus on the structures of thought, but rather on thought as a goal-directed activity (see also note 3). This focus can be seen in microgenetic analyses of problem-solving behaviours, i.e. in analyses of how they unfold within the course of a single observation session (see Vygotsky 1978, and empirical applications in Wertsch and Hickmann in press. and Wertsch and Stone 1978). These analyses take into account how children initially define a problem-solving situation (e.g. the overall goal of the situation, the possible means to reach that goal, the objects involved in the problem) and how they gradually change their definition of the situation alone and / or through social interactions. More generally, the particular theory of activity which has derived from a Vygotskian perspective focuses not

only on the structural properties of activity but also (and most importantly) on how these properties result from the unfolding of activity in particular contexts (e.g. Kochurova *et al.* 1981; Leont'ev 1981; Zinchenko 1985).

6. Functions and contexts in language acquisition

Researchers have described the contextual embeddedness of language in various ways, in relation to different notions of function, and these have differing implications for the inferences we make from child language about cognitive and social development. After a period of child language research which primarily presupposed the theoretical and methodological premises of formal-structural models (e.g. Braine 1963; McNeill 1970), researchers began to look explicitly for contextual information which would provide clues to children's intentions and to the functions of the linguistic elements in their utterances.

Researchers focused at first on propositional units (e.g. Bloom 1970; Schlesinger 1971b; Brown 1973). For example, Bloom proposed to analyse child language using the method of 'rich interpretations'. According to this proposal, which has been used and extended by many researchers, the formal syntactic–semantic properties (e.g. 'agent-of', 'possessor') of linguistic elements in young children's utterances are determined (at least partly) from their contexts of use. The attribution of such syntactic or semantic functions to children's linguistic elements results in the attribution of a semantic intention to the child, i.e. of cognitive or linguistic knowledge pertaining to the representation of entities, events and relations among them in propositional form.

In comparison, different notions of contexts, functions and intentions have been used to interpret child language in other frameworks (see M. Miller 1979, for a critique of Bloom's interpretation). For example, one approach views language as a tool for the performance of social acts. This focus in developmental research has led to an emphasis on the development of a social or sociolinguistic competence: for example, the developing ability to perceive, to mark in speech, and sometimes to be aware of social distinctions or speech acts of various kinds (e.g. Andersen 1977; Ervin-Tripp 1977; Shatz 1978; Schieffelin 1979; Dore 1979). This second view has led to different inferences about child development. For example, the attribution of interpersonal functions to children's utterances within speech-act theory results in the attribution of illocutionary intentions to children and knowledge of the means–ends relations pertaining to the performance of socially significant events.

A third version of functional theory sees multifunctionality and context

dependence in language as two facets of the same problem. For example, some linguists have primarily focused on the context dependence of language and have defined the very notion of function in terms of the relation between speech and specific components of any communicative situation (e.g. Jakobson 1960). With a closely related framework, some developmental research has focused specifically on referential elements of utterances. There have been numerous studies of children's uses of referential expressions and an increasing concern for their indexical properties (e.g. Lyons 1975; Warden 1976; Karmiloff-Smith 1977, 1979a,c; Ninio and Bruner 1978; Atkinson 1979; Ochs, Schieffelin and Platt 1979; Hickmann 1980, 1982a; Wales this volume).

Some of this research has shown that the referential system of young children, although sometimes containing forms similar to those of older children or adults, can be functionally very different in two related ways. First, some studies have argued that young children's uses of referring expressions must be interpreted in the context of social interaction. For example, Ochs et al. (1979) have argued that referring expressions used as one-word utterances primarily have the deictic function of directing attention, and that propositions must often be inferred across sequences of utterances (e.g. Child: 'Horse', Adult: 'Horse', Child: 'Big').

Second, some studies have shown that children relate referential forms to different aspects of the context during language acquisition. For example, Karmiloff-Smith (1977, 1979a) has shown that young children use and interpret nominal determiners (a, the) and post-determiners (the same, another) in relation to the nonlinguistic context of utterance, whereas older children use and interpret them in relation to the linguistic context of utterance. Similarly, her analyses of referential expressions in narratives (Karmiloff-Smith 1979c) show that only older children systematically use pronouns and zero anaphors to maintain reference within discourse to highly presupposed referents (e.g. the protagonist). In contrast, younger children use definite nouns and pronouns deictically, i.e. in relation to the nonlinguistic context of utterance (pictures), rather than anaphorically, i.e. in relation to other linguistic elements in prior linguistic context.

These results are mostly consistent with other analyses of both indefinite and definite forms in children's narratives (Warden 1976; Hickmann 1980, 1982a), whether or not these narratives are elicited in the presence of relevant non-linguistic context. For example, Hickmann shows that young children have difficulties using indefinite forms to introduce referents in discourse, particularly highly topical *animate* ones: when such referents are not present in the speech situation the children frequently presuppose them on first mention, using definite nouns or even personal pronouns;

when the referents are present in the speech situation the children often use indefinite forms in particular constructions, e.g. predicating constructions (*It's a frog*).

This line of research on the contexts and functions of language use pertaining specifically to the referential aspects of language has implications for the kind of knowledge we attribute to the child on the basis of his language. Minimally, it suggests great care in making inferences about some underlying cognitive competence on the basis of speech forms independent of the contexts in which they are used. Karmiloff-Smith (1977) has argued along similar lines, suggesting that rich Piagetian interpretations about the cognitive stages which might underlie the uses of referential expressions should carefully attend to whether these elements are used functionally in the same way as adults (e.g. anaphorically rather than deictically).

Using a Vygotskian paradigm, Hickmann (1985) has hypothesized that the ability to use language as its *own* context, minimally, the ability to establish relationships among the utterances of continuing discourse (but also the ability to represent language in various ways through speech), should have great impact on both the cognitive and the social competence of children. In particular, even if we postulate some underlying cognitive competence which allows the development of this ability, once it is acquired, it should affect how the child plans and organizes his own uses of signs in problem-solving and / or social-interactive contexts. This hypothesis might lead (minimally) to revising some of the more traditional assumptions about the relation of language to other aspects of child development in order to take into account what Vygotsky has called a process of 'functional differentiation'. This notion can best be illustrated by contrasting it with the more traditional notion of decontextualization and by considering the implications of the two notions for the interpretation of 'egocentric speech'.

7. Egocentric speech, decontextualization and functional differentiation

The notion of egocentricity has frequently been invoked to account for very diverse phenomena, not only in child language but also in other (non-verbal) behaviours observed in children. It has been used in different ways, often in conjunction with the notion that young children do not take into account others' perspectives, but not always with a precise description of what the phenomenon might be. In fact, the term has been applied to explain and to generalize across so many behaviours and so many situations that it becomes difficult to define it other than as a very general principle. It then loses some of its explanatory power in accounting for specific phenomena, and particularly in accounting for language use.

Within the Piagetian paradigm, where the term as it is now generally used originated, the child's egocentricity is a general phenomenon, resulting from his lack of decentering; and it characterizes most of his behaviours which are not adapted to particular situations. With respect to language acquisition specifically, the general progression postulated within this model to account for egocentric speech is that children's language, having private characteristics, is at first not adapted to social communicative situations. It becomes socialized at a later point in development as decentering in the child's cognitive organization allows him to participate genuinely in social interactions. In his early writings on child language, based on observations of spontaneous conversations, Piaget (1923) described the private, relatively asocial nature of early speech in terms of the child's impulse to talk about what he is doing, with no real concern for being understood or even heard by others. It is as if he cannot prevent himself from commenting on his actions out loud, and his speech does not seem to have a real function.

The notion of egocentrism has been extended to account for specific phenomena in child language, all involving uses of speech in which the elements or the logical structure are relatively inadequate, e.g. referent-introductions (Warden 1976), spatial descriptions in route directions (Weissenborn 1981), moral argumentation (M. Miller 1982), explanations given about physical problems and temporal organization in narratives (Piaget 1946a), explanations given about games (Flavell et al. 1968), etc. In all these situations, children's speech is interpreted as being not adapted to the requirements of interpersonal communication.

In contrast, Vygotsky interpreted egocentric speech in terms of a different progression, according to which speech is primarily, and from the very beginning, social in nature, but at first undifferentiated from a functional point of view. That is, speech at first merely accompanies ongoing actions and perceptions in the context of utterance, serving as a means of social contact with others. At a later point, when speech has been differentiated, it forms a system which is multifunctional for the adult: when used externally it has a distinct communicative and social function; when used internally it mediates higher mental functions, for example in problem-solving situations where no interlocutor is present. Egocentric speech is a transitional phase between the initial undifferentiated phase and the later differentiated one. The child's use of speech at this point reflects his discovery of a *new* function of speech, namely an organizing function which regulates his non-verbal activities. These uses of speech do not yet have a *distinct* social communicative function for the child, i.e. they are not distinctly addressed to others.

On first reading, these two descriptions of egocentric speech may not seem different, in the superficial sense that neither of them interpret this speech as being specifically addressed to others for a communicative social goal. However, they differ in important ways with respect to their emphasis, the empirical predictions which can be made from them and, most importantly, the mechanisms which are used to explain language acquisition. As previously noted, the emphasis in Piaget's description is on the cognitive decentering which underlies a change from egocentric to social speech. In this view, egocentric speech is defined in relation to socialized speech either as not adapted to the communicative situation or as not having any real functions. In contrast, the emphasis in Vygotsky's description is on a change from speech which serves different functions (including a social function) in an undifferentiated way to speech which has distinct, though clearly related, social and cognitive functions.

Although little is known empirically about egocentric speech, some empirical findings follow predictions which can be made from Vygotsky's framework (see for some comparisons, Vygotsky 1934 / 1962; Kohlberg *et al.* 1968; Goudena 1983; Lee, Wertsch and Stone 1983; Kohlberg and Wertsch in press). For example, children use more egocentric speech in the presence of others than alone, and they use more egocentric speech when they are engaged in a relatively difficult task than when the task is simple. In addition, as previously noted, empirical studies of adult–child interactions in problem-solving situations have suggested that there is a striking formal resemblance between adults' regulative (verbal and nonverbal) actions which direct children's attention to relevant aspects of the problem and some children's self-regulatory actions during the task. Within a Vygotskian perspective, these formal resemblances provide preliminary evidence for the mechanisms postulated for development, suggesting a *functional* similarity between adults' speech to children and children's egocentric speech: children are using the communicative patterns established between them and the adult to direct their own attention to relevant aspects of the situation and to maintain social contact. These remarks are still somewhat speculative, and definite conclusions about developmental mechanisms must await further detailed analyses of egocentric speech. However, they do suggest that, at least when we observe in detail the unfolding of adult–child discourse in controlled situations, the interactive unit forms a system in its own right. Within this system, self-regulatory uses of speech have, at least in part, a social origin which cannot be ignored.

In the context of more recent research on language acquisition, it should be noted that the extent to which young children's speech is or is not adapted is not without controversy (see Hickmann 1982a,b for some aspects

of this controversy; also see Clark 1978a, for a wide review of early skills). For example, some research suggests that young children can adapt their speech as a function of their addressee (e.g. Shatz and Gelman 1973; Andersen 1977); or simply that they show concern that their interlocutor should pay attention to the 'topic' of conversation about which they want to talk (e.g. Keenan and Klein 1975). Thus, on the basis of child–child interactions, Keenan and Klein have argued that children's speech at 2 years is not egocentric, as shown, for example, by the fact that they seem able to introduce topics of conversation by drawing the attention of their interlocutor to a referent never mentioned before.

It is particularly interesting to consider this last piece of evidence in the light of other results previously mentioned. It is significant that Keenan and Klein's conclusion is based on evidence involving primarily the uses of speech in relation to nonlinguistic context. In this case, referent-introductions are typically deictic, e.g. nouns with or without determiners in predicative constructions and / or in successive repetitions. Such uses show that children are indeed concerned with directing the attention of their listener to an object which then becomes mutually shared. However, in situations where such deictic forms of introduction are not possible, either because no relevant objects are present or because their listener cannot see them, children must rely strictly on the linguistic context, *using speech to create the very context for speech*. In such situations their uses are seemingly egocentric, as primitive deictic uses cannot suffice for adequate referent-introductions. One might say, then, that in these situations egocentricity and decentering can be defined, at least partly, in terms of the child's functional–pragmatic repertoire. When the child discovers new functions of the signs he confronts in interacting with others, such a development in his repertoire allows him to rely *strictly* on a new, distinctly linguistic context.

This approach to egocentricity places more explanatory burden for cognitive and social development on the study of children's linguistic repertoire, particularly on its pragmatic and functional aspects, providing an alternative way of describing decontextualization. In this view, all activities unfold in some context and decontextualization, e.g. the ability to talk about displaced entities, events, and relations among them, is at least partly the product (rather than the cause) of the process whereby language becomes its own context. That is, decontextualization is redefined in this approach as the ability to use signs in new contexts, and particularly in contexts defined by language itself.

This broad review of general issues in developmental theory shows the complexity involved in interpreting child language in relation to cognitive and social development. Vygotsky's approach to the inter-relations of lan-

guage, thought and social interaction is to view language as a multifunctional and context-dependent system mediating simultaneously cognitive and social development. In other words, he makes language acquisition the *centre* of these inter-relationships. This approach, and its extension in light of recent developmental research, has the clear disadvantage of making generalizations across behaviours, domains and contexts in a formalized model of development much more difficult than a Piagetian approach. It has the clear advantage, however, of defining precisely, and relating at least some cognitive and social aspects of development, by describing regularities in cognitive and social interactive behaviours as regularities in sign-using activity.

2. Language acquisition and cognition*

Robin N. Campbell

1. Introduction

To explore the relationships between cognitive development and language development is to enter a very dark forest indeed! It is not so much a question of not being able to see the wood for the trees: one cannot even see the trees. Accordingly, the best advice one might offer to, say, a graduate student would be 'Danger, keep off'. For those with more leisure and securer positions it is perhaps possible to make an occasional foray without becoming entirely lost, but it should be emphasized that what is both desirable and possible in the study of language development at the present time is more facts, more flower-picking natural history. However, it is sometimes useful to make the attempt at a larger enterprise, if only as a source of ideas about where to look for new flowers.

The large mass of research with a bearing on this relationship has been reviewed by Bowerman (1976) and in a number of publications by Cromer (e.g. 1974, 1976a,b).[1] I think it can fairly be said that one thing missing from these reviews is any sign that a coherent theoretical framework informs current work on the relationship. Indeed, the same might be said of psycholinguistics in general. There *is* a coherent framework on offer, exposed in Chomsky's (1975, 1980a,b) and Fodor's (1975, 1983) writings and in their various contributions to Piattelli-Palmarini (1980). Whatever the virtues of this framework, it has become increasingly nativist with the passing years and has won few hearts and minds amongst those actively engaged in the study of language acquisition or cognitive development. Why then has so little progress been made towards an alternative framework? It is my firm view that a principal reason has been the failure all round to square up to the task of allocating a distinct role to *consciousness*, as it is involved in speaking, understanding, thinking and learning. Conscious mental processes are typically not distinguished from other cognitive processes either *structurally* (e.g. in terms of their temporal properties or the information that they manipulate) or *functionally* (e.g. in terms of what

kinds of purposes of the organism they serve). While the role of consciousness in these activities was a feature of European psychology until the mid-1930s (as may be readily seen in the works of Brunswik, Buhler, Piaget, Stern, Vygotsky and Werner), it failed to survive the flight across the Atlantic. In 1934 Vygotsky wrote in the opening paragraphs of his *Thought and language* (trans. edn, 1962):

> All that is known about psychic development indicates that its very essence lies in the change of the interfunctional structure of consciousness. Psychology must make these relationships and their developmental changes the main problem, the focus of study, instead of merely postulating the general interrelation of all functions. This shift in emphasis is imperative for the study of language and thought.

In this chapter I have chosen to explore some of the reasons why we find it difficult to satisfy Vygotsky's imperative and to attempt to persuade the reader that the effort is nonetheless worthwhile, in the hope that some genius will come forward to pick up the intellectual burden laid down fifty years ago by Vygotsky and just six years ago by that great European stay-at-home Piaget.

2. Cognitive development

What is cognitive development and how should it be studied? There is widespread disagreement about this. One can discern two clear positions, one represented in mainstream American psychology, the other in the genetic epistemology of Jean Piaget. In the first approach, cognitive structures and processes are identified with symbolic structures and processes (often called information structures and processes), which mediate the connection of outputs from sensory mechanisms with inputs to motor mechanisms. Thus every action of the organism beyond the simplest reflex is said to involve cognitive processes. In Piaget's system, cognitive structures and processes are identified with representations and operations upon representations that are tied in an intimate way to explicit knowledge and awareness; thus, only certain functions in certain organisms are said to involve cognitive processes. The use of the qualifier 'explicit' in the previous sentence will seem strange to those who are not accustomed to the peculiarities of the information-processing idiom. In that idiom it is commonplace to speak of 'tacit' knowledge in circumstances where the justification for calling something a cognitive event is noticeably lacking. Thus, Chomsky often speaks of tacit knowledge of rules of language. What is meant by this is of course that the rules in question are *not* known but merely observed.

There are several possibilities here. It might be that the rules of language are represented in the mind of the speaker in a fairly direct way, but are inaccessible to consciousness. This is what Chomsky means by 'tacit knowledge'. On the other hand, although falling apples observe the law of falling bodies they are not accused of having tacit knowledge of that law – but then, apples (falling or not) know nothing explicitly either. More to the point, apples are not capable of independent action; they contribute nothing to their fall beyond certain physical properties. Put another way. it is not *necessary* for them to know anything, tacit or not, about the laws of motion, in order to fall in the way that they do: they merely have to *be*. Most organisms, on the other hand, *are* capable of independent action. They are driven by motives the origins of which are remote and complex. The ape's controlled descent of a tree is mediated by something more than its physical properties. It seems to be necessary that the ape should *know* something about the shape of the tree, the disposition of its branches, the shape of its own body and the pull of the earth in order to descend in the way that it does. It is conceivable that we could, by considering possible trees, possible apes and actual dynamics, devise a theory of tree-descents amounting to a set of rules, which rules are followed by our ape in the course of his descent. Since common experience and the study of language tell us that (a) there are rules of language and (b) in using language we adhere to them but are not aware of them, it is possible that the ape is similarly unaware of the structures and rules that guide his progress down the tree and hence knows them only tacitly. It is, however, more likely that just as we know *something* about the rules of our language and exercise this knowledge on *some* occasions, the ape, too, has as a back-up some knowledge of the rules for descending trees[2] and sometimes employs it, for example, when in fog, in unusual trees, broken limbs (ape) or broken limbs (tree) (see, remarkably enough, Chevalier-Skolnikoff, Galdikas and Skolnikoff 1982).

So we may think of our tree user (or language user) as exploiting two kinds of knowledge, explicit and tacit, and functioning in two modes. Where action is governed by explicit knowledge I shall describe the organism as functioning in a *phenic* mode (characterized by phenic structures and processes); when not functioning in this way I shall describe the organism as functioning in a *cryptic* mode (characterized by cryptic structures and processes). Thus, in the phenic mode action is regulated by structures and processes accessible to consciousness; in the cryptic mode it is regulated by structures and processes inaccessible to consciousness. While certain other symptoms are typically clustered with consciousness, such as mental effort (cf. Kahneman 1973) and reportability (cf. Dennett 1978: ch. 9),

there are good grounds for introducing new terminology. Briefly, (1) the proposed terms have clear interpretations from the point of view of the experiencing subject – what is evident to the subject is *phenic*, what is hidden is *cryptic*; (2) it is central to my proposal that the distinction drawn should be *theoretical* and potentially applicable to infants and to. other organisms. Thus, *effortful / effortless* and *conscious / unconscious* fail, since these are simply the usual empirical marks of the distinction; *reportable / unreportable* is not only empirical but limited to language users; lastly, existing theoretical oppositions such as *higher / lower* and *inner / outer* have unfortunate anatomical implications. My strategy in employing this theoretical distinction will be to try to show that it solves problems for us, rather than to show that it has a direct empirical justification – since this latter route has been pursued long and hard without success. I should expect the distinction to turn out to be only conditionally associated with each of its usual empirical symptoms.

It might be wondered why I do not simply use the terms 'explicit' and 'tacit'. It seems to me best to reserve these for describing representations, since that has been their customary use. Moreover, mental acts which psychologists have described as governed by representations or involving computations in a representational system seem to be co-extensive with what philosophers, following Brentano, have called intentional acts – directed on some object. For the notion of mental representation – *qua* semantic entity which is the staple medium of cognitive processes – see Fodor's writings (1975, 1980b, 1981) and for some problems with it, see Dennett (1983b). For Brentano, intentionality was 'the mark of the mental'. Recently Dennett (1978, 1981a,b, 1983a) has pursued this line of attack with great patience and sophistication, seeking to characterize different sorts of intentional system and to explore the grounds for describing various organisms and devices as this or that sort of intentional system. Now, Chomsky's claim about tacit knowledge, echoed by many other psychologists and by Dennett, can be seen as a claim that many of our acts, though cryptic in my terms, are nevertheless intentional in the sense of Brentano, because they involve computations in a tacit system of representations. Chomsky describes such acts as involving 'cognizing' (1980a: 70) intending by that term to denote processes that appeal to knowledge, whether explicit or tacit, and to exclude processes which do not. This claim of Chomsky's and my linking of it to the notion of intentionality are extremely controversial (see Stabler 1983 and the commentaries by Rosenthal, Searle and Sober on Chomsky 1980b for discussion), and it may be that consciousness and intentionality will turn out to be more closely linked than they seem to be in the reading of the Chomskyan position just offered. For the moment,

however, it seems best to allow that consciousness (my suggestion) and intentionality may define quite different conceptions of 'the mental'.

We have arrived at a point where it is possible to frame what, for me at any rate, is the fundamental question of cognitive psychology. The question is 'What criteria determine the attribution of explicit knowledge?' Or, in the terms of the preceding paragraph, 'How can we know that we are dealing with a phenic process or structure?' For adherents of the information-processing approach to cognitive psychology this question is *not* fundamental: an answer will be provided, if at all, only when a theory is completed. For what an organism knows explicitly is regarded as epiphenomenal (i.e. devoid of causal significance).[3] However, for Piagetians and their like, the question *is* fundamental since it affects *description* of psychological events. Theory cannot *begin* until a way is found of deciding when to attribute explicit knowledge and what knowledge to attribute. It should be evident that there are no easy answers to this fundamental question. There is available neither a convincing refutation of epiphenomenalism nor a general method for determining criteria for explicitness; on the other hand, information-processing analyses are bedevilled by paradoxes and absurdities. For example, perceptual and inferential processes often receive identical treatments and manipulate structures with identical descriptions.[4] Again, no formal distinction (there is often some lip-service paid) is or can be made between an automatic routine process which carries out a certain function and a deliberate, conscious process which is 'called in' to carry out the *same* function when the routine process fails. The experimental/statistical requirements of reliability, replicability and low mean variance have led to widespread adoption of techniques which involve either lengthy periods of practice or many experimental trials per subject, with the result that the functions which are studied, though normally functions carried out – if at all – by phenic processes, are in fact observed only as cryptic routines.

This has had several disastrous consequences: (a) 'cognitive psychology' – which once had a clear meaning, denoting the psychology of phenic structures and processes – has slid through a period of ambivalence into its present appalling state, being now almost exclusively concerned with cryptic processes; (b) success in modelling these cryptic processes has given rise to the illusion that we have achieved some understanding of the (normally phenic) functions that they carry out; (c) valid work carried out within older or more peripheral traditions has been mistakenly called in question by robust mountains of data which in fact pertain to quite different processes. The most striking and unfortunate case of this is the persistent and breathtakingly insensitive impeachment of Genevan results in the field

of cognitive development by American and, lately, British psychologists; (d) onlookers from neighbouring disciplines encounter insurmountable difficulties in evaluating psychological research. Philosophers of mind, for example, who – to my mind correctly – often tend to discount the usefulness of 'images', 'concepts' and 'meanings' in epistemological contexts, are repelled and bewildered by the welter of such notions employed in cognitive psychology. In fact, of course, the notions (sometimes just the labels) have usually been misappropriated and applied to cryptic structures which have only some (at best) of the properties of the phenic structures to which these terms were originally applied.

In the case of models of the adult we are constantly reminded by our own nature of the need to be clear about which mode we are describing, and can often determine independently of any empirical criteria what sort of process or structure is being described. Thus, for example, in Forster's (1976) analysis of the lexical decision task as a massive search process we are sure that any such search is a cryptic process and that the role of the phenic mode in such a task (once initial orientation has been achieved) is simply to hold constant the *ad hoc* links established between perception, memory and action. Hence we learn nothing from such work about *cognitive* structures and processes (if the term cognitive is restricted to its traditional referential domain, as I am urging that it should).[5] However, in studying cognitive development we lack such empathetic guidance and are often at a loss. We thus encounter difficulties and paradoxes which, I believe, can only be resolved by adopting a framework of the kind that I am advocating and, ultimately, by discovering methods of investigation and descriptions which acknowledge such a framework. I will describe in detail only one such troublesome phenomenon – space perception in infancy – but similar difficulties arise in many disparate aspects of cognitive development, for example in perception of weight (Mounoud and Bower 1974) and classification (Campbell, Donaldson and Young 1976): for relevant reviews see Donaldson (1971) and Bower (1974b).

Brunswik (1956) elucidated a crucial distinction, originally due to Koffka (1935) and later elaborated by Heider (1939), between *distal* and *proximal* stimulus variables. To illustrate: the distance of an object from the eye (a distal variable – i.e. a goal of description) is partially specified by the values – strictly speaking, simple functions of these – of various proximal variables: retinal expansion, motion parallax, ocular convergence, lenticular accommodation, etc. Successful discrimination of variation in distance is thus achievable on the basis of sensitivity to variation of these proximal variables. *Which* proximal variable will vary in the appropriate way will depend upon the circumstances. However, successful discrimination does

not tell us *anything* about how such proximal variation is interpreted by the infant; still less does it tell us that it is interpreted as variation in the distal variable – in this example, distance. Various remedies have been proposed (see Bower 1974a: 79ff; Yonas and Pick 1975: *passim*). Bower makes two suggestions. First of all, it is known that infants habituate to any constant and regular stimulation. If their discriminations are based upon variation in distance rather than on proximal variation, then a slight change in the task which shifts the basis of discrimination from one proximal variable to another should not interrupt habituation. Otherwise, it should. Bower claims that methodological difficulties get in the way of attempting this ingenious experiment. His second suggestion is not accompanied by any argument: he states baldly (1974a: 80) that 'faced with problems of this sort, one feels that *natural* response methods are a refuge. If an infant reaches out for an object intentionally . . . there can be no doubt that the infant sees the object in the third dimension. This kind of simple certainty we just cannot get from discrimination experiments.' While one might well agree with this, the problem of determining whether or not a reaching movement is *intentional* (i.e. distally aimed) is not conceptually different from the problem (to be solved) of whether a spatial discrimination is distally based. Yonas and Pick likewise offer two suggestions, that on the one hand distally invariant stimulus presentations which have variable proximal outcomes and which elicit a common reaction (stimulus convergence, in their terms) and, on the other hand, proximally diverse response movements with an invariant distal outcome and a common eliciting stimulus (response convergence, in their terms) each indicate that perception is distally oriented, since other explanations of such convergence are grossly unparsimonious.

There are many things that remain unclear here. Is distal orientation a necessary or a sufficient condition for a claim about explicit knowledge? Do all or any of the suggested remedies constitute sufficient conditions for a distal claim? It seems to me that there is still room for doubt. Is there not in the behaviour of a butterfly landing on a flower a co-ordination and integration of sensory information and a flexibility of motor response that equally invites the inference that the butterfly has constructed a representation of space and objects in space with reference to which the sensory data and motor commands are interpreted? However, despite these uncertainties *some* things are clear. Able practitioners like Bower, Pick and Yonas evidently recognize the need to distinguish at least two qualitatively distinct levels of function of the organism, one which involves direct sensorimotor connections and another which requires an intermediate interpretative structure which gives *meaning* to the sensory data and *purpose* to the

motor commands. Moreover, there is a laudable reluctance in the field as a whole to fudge the issue by means of either of the two well-worn stratagems, (a) 'It's a complicated internal process; that's cognitive enough for me' or (b) 'Any criterion will do, so long as we stick to it' To return to the first point, a common reaction to the claim that levels or modes of function must be distinguished is simply to deny the possibility of doing so in an empirically principled way. My retort to this is that for sixty years or so we have tried to create a valid psychology without making such distinctions and in most important human functions we have failed. Likewise, philosophers of mind have attempted for centuries to found epistemology on analyses of different sorts of judgement and varieties of reasoning – all phenic functions – and have also failed. It is time to have a look at the foundations of this building which is always falling down.

If we had some clear idea of the special value of this higher level of functioning then we would be in better shape to attempt empirical determinations. Not altogether surprisingly, we have to dig fairly deep to find suggestions about its value. One of the more illuminating discussions is by Claparede (1917, 1918),[6] who argued that in microgenesis the higher level – which he identified with awareness – functioned as a catch-all standby procedure. Low-level processes which ran smoothly did not involve awareness, but if some breakdown or exceptional input occurred, the data were 'handed up' to the higher level and the process continued there. But this is surely just one role for awareness: it suggests a normally dormant organism which occasionally 'lights up' when things go wrong. Surely our intuitions tend in exactly the opposite direction – we are normally switched-on organisms which, when things go easily, switch off! So Claparede's 'law of awareness' explains only the movements of what Polanyi (e.g. 1968) has called 'focal' awareness. For example, it does not explain, except by means of trivializing extensions, why we are, on the one hand, constantly aware of our physical surroundings when we move around and, on the other hand, only rarely aware of the muscular adjustments involved in thus moving around. The few recent attempts to describe the function of awareness (e.g. Shallice 1972) seem to suffer from the same limitation. Alternatively, we might examine the empirical procedures of, say, Piagetians, to see what criteria are actually used in practice when phenic structures or processes are under investigation. If there *is* a single characteristic procedure, it is surely the employment of an interview method which has as its goal the discovery of the rational basis for judgements and actions, and as its principal technique the elicitation of verbal justification. Thus, this research tradition (and I seriously doubt whether other viable ones presently exist in cognitive development) has one great limitation from

the present point of view, namely that crucial evidence for the nature and course of phenic development consists of what children *say*, so, as Smedslund (1970) has pointed out, facts about the nature of the child's language are assumed in order to derive facts about phenic structure. Without some independent method it would evidently be ludicrous *then* to use facts about phenic development to explain language development. And yet it is a commonly held view that language development is explicable in terms of cognitive development. In fact, I do not believe that Piagetians have yet discovered a valid method for investigating cognitive development in the age range 1–4 years. Their investigations of sensorimotor intelligence provide a basis for speculation about the phenic framework governing very early language (see D. Edwards 1973 and Bates 1979)[7] and, of course, by 4 years child language is sufficiently adult-like to make it a plausible tool for exploring cognitive development. In the intervening age range, however, there has been little convincing progress. Indeed, Piagetian claims about some supposedly vital limitations of child thought during this period (e.g. inability to reason deductively, egocentricity) seem at best to be dubious now (see Donaldson 1978). So, even if we can justify causal links between cognitive and linguistic development, this is no panacea, since information about cognitive development in the important growth period of 1–4 years is either completely lacking or unreliable, and there is no obvious methodology available for securing such information.

3. Early language: the problem of perspicuous description

About fifteen years ago, a new approach to the study of early language development emerged in which attempts were made to investigate the properties of child language considered as a *system for communication*. To begin with (in accordance with the Wernerian developmental principle – that new forms (of investigation) first serve old purposes (of theory)) this shift was largely a shift of method, the goal being, as formerly, a specification of the set of sentences the child could produce or understand (in some limited sense of this word, e.g. 'assign a structural description to'). The most remarkable effort of this sort was Lois Bloom's (1970) thesis. The point of investigating the system for communication rather than the language *per se* was that it seemed plain that syntactic description was an impossibly arbitrary exercise unless some additional constraining data could be found. A natural step was then to examine not just the child's utterances but also the messages which were transmitted by these utterances. Assumptions about correspondences between message forms (i.e. meanings) and utterance forms (i.e. sentences) invoking bi-uniqueness could then be used

to constrain grammatical description of the child's language. In fact, Bloom made much less use of these putative correspondences than did other workers such as Schlesinger (1971b) and, later, Brown (1973) and Halliday (1975), preferring instead to follow the line urged by Chomsky (1965, 1968) and supported by McNeill (1970), in which arguments about adult English yield a ready-made apparatus for the description of child language. This may be regarded as an aberration from which Bloom (1973, 1974; Bloom, Rocissano and Hood 1976) made an admirable recovery.[8]

However little use Bloom may have made of the child's messages (as determined by adult interpreters), she established the fundamental methodological point, namely that this sort of analysis is possible. This method became known as the 'method of rich interpretation' – a misnomer, since it is simply the 'method of interpretation' – and its use has been a common feature of most subsequent work on early language. Its use has not gone unquestioned (e.g. Brown 1973; Campbell 1976; Howe 1976; Edwards 1978; Macrae 1979); but the questions have been concerned with details rather than general principles. For a rebuttal of Howe (1976) see Bloom, Capatides and Tackeff (1981) and Golinkoff (1981). However, there remains a difficulty. To me, at any rate, it remains an open question whether at any intermediate point in development these two constructions, the system for communication and the language, are to be given identical descriptions or not. Certainly it seems clear that in the adult they are not: attempts to describe the former construct (Grice 1967; Lewis 1969; Stalnaker 1972) have so far failed to make significant contact with attempts to describe the latter (*Linguistic Inquiry: passim*) as has been forcefully pointed out by Chomsky (1975) and Katz (1977). Equally certainly, the two constructs have distinct ontogenies (Vygotsky 1934 / 1962). In the case of the adult a good case can be made for pursuing investigation of each system independently; and it may even be the case (as Chomsky 1975 and Katz 1977 have argued) that it is better (easier) to begin with description of language. For the case of the child, this possibility does not exist. Gold (1967) has shown that languages of nonfinite cardinality cannot be identified on the basis of a text presentation, i.e. a sequence of sentences belonging to them. Since this is exactly (no more, no less) what is available to the child linguist who eschews study of the system of communication, it is clear that we cannot proceed with child language in the same way as we have with the language of the adult.[9] But here is our difficulty: we have not so far found a way of integrating knowledge about human communication with knowledge about human language. Indeed, in a way they seem to pass each other by. On the one hand, efforts have been made to extend structural linguistic analysis to larger and larger structures – from sound

to word to sentence to complete texts – and on the other hand, the rational analysis of communication lately initiated by Grice, Lewis and other philosophers has encouraged a downward extension into grammatical processes by functionally minded linguists such as Garcia (1975). From the point of view of this chapter, this is a clear absurdity: complementary explanations are being presented as if they were in competition! They are complementary, of course, because the rational processes at the heart of communication are at least potentially phenic, while the grammatical processes at the heart of language are normally cryptic – 'grammar is an underground process' (Seuren 1978). Naturally, each kind of process functions as a default for the other so that, (a) in contexts that are familiar and habitual, communication can proceed in a routine manner and (b) in contexts where deviant or unusual utterances are received, grammatical analysis can proceed under rational control. Thus, as I see it, the case for autonomy of grammar stands or falls with the case for psychological dualism! Further, Chomsky – though perhaps correct in claiming autonomy for grammar – errs massively in his view that linguistics is a branch of cognitive psychology; on the contrary, it has nothing to do with cognitive psychology (strictly conceived) but deals exclusively with cryptic structures and processes.[10] On the other hand, communicative processes, such as understanding, involve not just the autonomous language function but the whole being (see Ziff 1972 – easily the best and clearest presentation of this point of view; amongst psychologists, Herbert Clark's is perhaps the most congenial treatment – see Clark and Clark 1977).

The way in which grammatical and rational processes interlock in deriving a message from a text (i.e. utterance or inscription) is a matter of current speculation and need not be explored here. It is sufficient to note that, from this point of view, messages *qua* products of understanding are *not* linguistic objects. Thus, somewhat longwindedly, our difficulty is now clear: certainly it is possible to make defensible guesses about what messages are associated with which utterances in the speech of young children, but without knowledge of the structure of their message representations and the rational processes available to them we still have not radically improved our position as far as linguistic description is concerned. The point may be clearly illustrated with respect to the description of one-word utterances, where at least three distinct positions can be discerned. According to one common view (now less popular – for cogent criticism see Miller 1976, Barrett 1982b), such utterances transmit propositional messages which are initially encoded as a (cryptic) isomorphic structure which is converted via grammatical processes of reduction into a single morph (see model 1). A second extreme view, uncommon but perfectly viable (Campbell

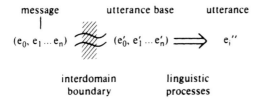

Model 1.

1976; E. Klein 1977), is that such utterances transmit nonpropositional, structureless messages which are encoded directly as single morphs (see model 2). A third, intermediate view (Bloom 1973), shown in model 3, is that such utterances transmit propositional messages by first selecting (by a rational process) a single message element and then proceeding as in model 2. A converse version of this third scheme is explicitly suggested by Sachs and Truswell (1978) as a means of accounting for comprehension of multiword utterances by children whose own utterances are limited to single words. It seems to me that the evidence favours a developmental sequence of model 2 followed by model 3 (see Bowerman 1976 for a thorough review).

As may be seen by inspecting the models, how the language of a child at this stage is to be described depends on (a) the complexity of the phenic structures that we think are involved, and (b) whether we think that the

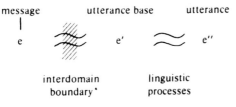

Model 2.

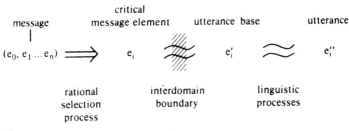

Model 3.

child can learn that a single message element (suitably encoded) will convey a complex message. Thus, analysis of a corpus consisting of pairings of messages and utterances must proceed on two fronts – cognitive and linguistic.[11] The discussion of cognitive development in section 2 should make it clear that there are few grounds for optimism amongst students of early child language. An adequate methodology seems more distant than ever.

4. Puzzles and prospects

In the preceding sections I have illustrated some of the difficulties encountered by the application of a particular theoretical framework, namely one in which consciousness is taken to be more or less constitutive of mental or cognitive activity, to cognitive and linguistic development. In this section I shall try to show some of the benefits that might result from adopting this theoretical scheme.

4.1. Concept development

One obvious degree of freedom introduced is the possibility of dual representation, for any structure may be represented *differently* at different levels. I shall argue that this allows resolution of some vexing problems concerning concept development and early lexical development. We can see, though, that it leads straight away to natural descriptions of concept acquisition. Consider first a case involving an *individual* concept. Piaget (1946b) describes an encounter (p. 225) between his daughter and a slug. She points at it and says 'There's the slug again!', mistakenly identifying it with a different slug encountered earlier at some distance (perhaps; see Karmiloff-Smith 1977 for a different account). Presumably, the slug's phenic representation was different for Piaget and his daughter. For Piaget, elementary reasonings about time, space and motion established distinct phenic representations for the two slugs; for Jacqueline the two slugs were assimilated to a single phenic representation. For an individual concept it seems clear that necessary and sufficient conditions cannot be given in terms of the perceptible features shared by successive appearances of the object denoted. Rather it is a causal criterion something like a path in space–time that determines the extension of such concepts.[12] However, for many objects (if not for slugs) a structure based on perceptible features serves as an indispensable *heuristic* for identification. In such cases it seems a natural guess that whereas the causal criterion is represented phenically (if at all), the heuristic identification procedure is cryptic.

Interesting cases involving *kind* concepts are afforded by such skills as plant identification and medical diagnosis: here the phenic representation (of species or syndrome) is determined by its place in a hierarchy, and identification ultimately depends upon serial examination of key characters and the making of inferences based on this hierarchy. However, the skilled botanist or clinician soon acquires a cryptic representation of these plants and diseases which permits rapid and reliable (although unjustified) identification. The representations are obviously quite different in character, since different information is employed at cryptic and phenic levels. That is, in the phenic process, microscopic characters may be employed: obviously these are unavailable for the cryptic process, supposing that this is based on the 'look of the patient or plant'. This example also shows that we must be careful not to confuse the method of acquisition of a skill with its eventual representation. For someone may learn to identify, for example, mushrooms with the aid of a phenic representation and a sequence of diagnostic tests. At the conclusion of this learning, however, he will have acquired an independent method of identifying mushrooms – 'by eye'. Of course, the phenic method is still potentially available as a back-up (and in medical cases one would hope rather more than just a potential back-up) technique, but if the cryptic method is more efficient, then knowledge of the phenic technique may lapse through disuse. Again, there are surely skills, e.g. swimming, bicycleriding, which do *not* have a phenic origin. Consequently, although grammar in the adult is an 'underground process', we need not suppose either that (a) all grammatical structures and processes have cryptic *origins* or that (b) those which *do* have phenic origins are isomorphic to the phenic structures / processes from which they derive. For example, syntactic categorization of early vocabulary may reflect simple early phenic distinctions of object, action, etc., although, of course, such distinctions cannot be noncircularly applied to later vocabulary, by which time related, but different, cryptic distinctions have taken their place. Again, if kinds of objects are initially distinguished phenically in terms of what actions can be carried out with them (as Piaget has maintained) then this need not deter us from supposing that a cryptic distinction is simultaneously developing on the basis of low-level perceptual variables. This seems to be the implicit basis of Nelson's (1973b, 1974) suggestion that early concepts have a functional origin despite the fact that identification of instances depends upon registering perceptual similarities.

In the case of both individual and kind concepts, then, there are grounds for distinguishing between what is criterial to the individual and the kind (the phenic content of the concept) and what information might be used heuristically to identify the individual or members of the kind (the cryptic

content of the concept). A similar suggestion has been made by Osherson and Smith (1981).

Questions concerning the origins of concepts have proved difficult for epistemologists and psychologists alike. Successful resolution of the long-standing problems in this area would therefore add greatly to the credibility of a dualist approach. An old guess about how concepts are acquired is the following: a series of denotata of the word in question, say *dog*, are ostensively presented to the child, who notices what features these denotata have in common. This set of common features, so abstracted, then functions as a dog-identifying-criterion and constitutes the meaning of the word *dog* and the child's concept of doghood. This is often regarded as an absurd story because in order to 'notice what is common' to the various denotata the child would have to have available a means for identifying each of the relevant criterial attributes, i.e. a system of concepts. According to this model of concept formation, all that the child learns in acquiring a new word is what particular logical function of existing primitive concepts is to be associated with that word. There are two, related, difficulties with this theory of concept formation. Firstly, where do the primitive concepts come from? Evidently they cannot be acquired in the manner just described. One answer (Fodor 1975) is that they are innate. How happy one is likely to feel about this rather depends on how rich the primitive framework is required to be. Fodor's notion is that it must indeed be very rich – in which case there is an obvious objection, namely that an ontogenetic mystery has been dispelled by postulating a phylogenetic one![13] But if the prior conceptual framework consists of a small set of very general concepts, then the second difficulty arises. As was noted long ago by Brown (1958) and recently confirmed by Nelson (1973a) and Ninio and Bruner (1978), the earliest predicates are words of *moderate* generality – denoting kinds of objects (attribute-clusters) rather than properties – and even as adults it is concepts of this 'weight' that we naturally employ (Rosch *et al.* 1976). So evidence from early lexical development suggests that the earliest kind concepts mastered define functionally significant categories of object rather than the elementary universal attributes needed to 'bootstrap' concept development.

To some degree these difficulties are avoided by the currently popular notion of stereotype or prototype.[14] Instead of the story given above, we would now say that kinds are identified by comparing each exemplar to a stored stereotypical individual (or, possibly, by comparison with a small set of such individuals). Words are then linked to their denotata via these stereotypes and similarity relations. This theory has many advantages. It relates early vocabulary acquisition in a natural way to the objects that

have functional importance for the young child, and the obviously spontaneous quality of these acquisitions is easily explained. The notion that such categories have a nuclear member or members, and that similarity to the nuclear member regulates membership, allows for the possibility that two individuals, sharing *no* salient properties, can belong to the same category – a frequently noted finding (Vygotsky 1934 / 1962; Bowerman 1978a).[15] Finally, overgeneralization – such a characteristic feature of early use of language – can be accounted for, either by supposing that *relative* similarity is what is involved (i.e. the 'nearest' stereotype determines what word is used) or that new individuals get added to a pool of stereotypes, each such addition stretching the boundaries of the concept.

This theory has numerous merits. However, the notion of similarity must be unpacked. What does it mean for an individual to be similar to some other individual? Surely, only that they share certain properties. So *this* theory of concept formation and semantic development, like the older one, makes an appeal to the notion of a primitive conceptual system, albeit in a less immediate and forthright manner![16] It does not seem likely that there is any escape from such a notion. Even Quine, not noted for ontological generosity, now talks of 'innate similarity standards' (1975: 69ff) as a basis of language learning.

Now what is problematic about this theory? A line of argument leads inescapably to the view that at the onset of language acquisition the child is armed with a primitive system of concepts which groups objects together on the basis of fixed attributes with elementary perceptual consequences. But there is a mass of evidence (Vygotsky 1934 / 1962; Inhelder and Piaget 1964; and see now Kemler and Smith 1979), derived from children's behaviour in matching and sorting tasks, which shows that young children have very great difficulty in grouping objects together on the basis of an elementary fixed attribute. Certainly, Ricciuti (1965) and Nelson (1973a) have shown that young children can perform well with such tasks when it is members of a kind (i.e. a complex cluster of attributes) that are to be grouped, but use of an elementary attribute as a basis for sorting or matching is a much later acquisition. Moreover, it is also clear (Nelson 1976) that the first attributive adjectives acquired by young children denote attributes which are *transitory* (e.g. *wet*, *hot*, *broken*) or *context-dependent* (e.g. *big*) rather than fixed and intrinsic.

So, on the one hand, we have evidence for the existence of a certain kind of concept and, on the other hand, evidence for its absence. The way to a resolution, it seems to me, is clear. The elements of the primitive conceptual system, Quine's 'innate similarity standards', are represented only cryptically and participate solely in cryptic processes: such concepts

have no phenic representation initially and their establishment at that level is a lengthy developmental process. Thus young children do not learn adjectives denoting fixed intrinsic attributes, since the content of such concepts is represented only cryptically. For the same reason, they cannot 'hold such attributes in mind' so as to regulate performance in matching or sorting tasks.

4.2. Metalinguistic development

A second difficult area where a dualist framework should prove helpful is the development of linguistic awareness. Experiments of my own (Campbell and Bowe 1978), and of Braun-Lamesch (1972) show that 3–4 year olds have enormous difficulty in making inferences about the meaning of nonsense words occurring in otherwise straightforward utterances which, *qua* utterances, have been accurately understood by them. An obvious guess about why this should be so is that individual words lack phenic representation at this stage of development (and so cannot participate in inferences). Likewise Karmiloff-Smith (1978) found that children of much the same age 'explained' gender assignment in French in terms of rules that they were plainly *not* following. Her explanation for this contradictory result, reformulated here in my terms, was that gender concord at this stage is determined by cryptic phonological processes except for a small number of exceptional cases which are decided by a phenic process involving determination of sex. The children's explanations, naturally enough, reflected this phenic process entirely and the cryptic process not at all. Other examples could be cited but the point is already clear enough. However, there is a residual puzzle here. While it seems obviously correct that 3–4 year olds lack phenic representations of words, this is odd in a way, since language learning *begins* with single words. Indeed, in section 3 I argued that there was a reasonable case for supposing that at certain early stages of acquisition (following Bloom and Sachs) inferences involving words were employed in the production of single-word utterances and in the comprehension of multiword utterances. It seems possible that it is wrong to think of the development of linguistic awareness as a one-way process (from cryptic to phenic).[17] Surely it is a common pattern of motor skill acquisition that the actions constituting the skill are first carried out in the phenic mode, with selection and coordination of elementary action segments consciously regulated. What practice seems to achieve – and how this happens is an utter mystery – is the gradual replacement of this phenic system by a cryptic system, proceeding from smaller to larger units. Indeed, the ancient study of Bryan and Harter (1897) claimed to show this pattern

of acquisition for typing skills: cryptic control (Bryan and Harter spoke of 'habits') is established successively at letter, word and phrase levels, eventually leaving the typist free to concentrate on the incoming text. Now the contemporary wisdom concerning the acquisition of word forms is that children initially use word forms without any awareness of them as semantically and auditorily distinct entities, and that with increasing age they become better able to attend to these forms and thereby attain some metalinguistic understanding. It is less clear whether there is any similar consensus regarding knowledge of word meaning. But what evidence is there for this view, admitting its general plausibility? I can think of nothing that rules out the possibility that (a) in the early stages of acquisition word selection and articulation are deliberate processes guided by the phenic contents of the concept associated with the word and by, say, a phenic sound image respectively; and that (b) in later stages word selection and articulation become automatic processes guided cryptically, leaving the learner free to concentrate on high-level tasks. Suppose this to be true. Why then does the preschooler have such manifest difficulties in bringing words *qua* semantic or auditory objects to mind? Earlier in this section I mentioned the possibility that phenic processes involved in the early stages of acquisition of concepts might lapse through disuse once mastery had been achieved. This is a familiar and comfortable notion and may possibly apply here also. But there is another possibility, equally familiar and comfortable. A characteristic symptom of cognitive development around 5 years is a difficulty in shifting perspective with regard to some problem or task. Piagetians have offered numerous hypotheses of this sort as explanations for the well-known systematic errors associated with the development of logico-mathematical knowledge. In my terms we might express this idea crudely in the following way: having plugged in one phenic system, children at this stage find it difficult to unplug it and plug in another. So it may be that they lack sufficient flexibility or versatility of consciousness to jump between the levels of sentence, phrase and word. Perhaps the late preschooler's attention in speaking and listening is 'locked' at the higher levels of control, and thus phenic monitoring of word selection and articulation is blocked. Some support for this view is provided by the sustained outbreak of late word-level errors which occurs and lasts throughout this period of development (cf. Bowerman 1982a). At any rate, the notion that children might pass from a stage where words are phenically represented to a stage where they are cryptically represented does not seem incoherent or unintelligible and presents the prospect of interesting explanations for a range of troublesome developmental phenomena.

In conclusion, I would like to emphasize the unoriginality of these propo-

sals: they are to my mind (at least) latent in the recent writings of Bloom, Bowerman, Brown, Karmiloff-Smith and Nelson.[18] It is, of course, difficult for psychologists trained in Britain or America to feel comfortable with psychological dualism, because of the strong empiricist / determinist traditions in these countries. However, in the European literature from the early part of this century until the outbreak of the Second World War there is the basis for an alternative approach. Because of the unsolved methodological problems associated with it, such an approach can hardly be said to challenge current scientific practice seriously. However, it seems to me that its considerable theoretical advantages recommend us to reconsider these methodological problems and seek solutions to them. At any rate, no one need be afraid of psychological dualism: our problem is not to distinguish 'the mental' from 'the physical' but to distinguish cognitive from other kinds of psychological process. Whether this distinction is drawn in the way I have urged or in other ways (such as Chomsky's), we need not be unduly nervous about the metaphysical consequences.[19]

3. Language acquisition and linguistic theory*

Helen Goodluck

Perhaps the best introduction to the topic of language acquisition and linguistic theory is a look at some of the facts that linguistic theory must account for. The complexity, orderliness and limited variety in human languages convinces linguists that language must be learned through a biological program that puts bounds on the possible grammatical system a child can postulate. The type of system that falls within the bounds of this innate learning ability is the matter of linguistic theory.

1. Some properties of human languages

1.1. Order and dominance

Sentences are strings of words. One of the ways in which languages differ is in the ordering relations and type of hierarchical structure that is imposed on words in sentences. Languages divide into so-called free word order languages and those that impose relatively rigid word orders on sentences, selecting one of the three basic word orders characteristically found in human languages. English has a basic Subject–Verb–Object (hereafter SVO) order (*Ants eat ants* etc.). The other two primary orders selected by languages are Subject–Object–Verb (SOV) and Verb–Subject–Object (VSO).

The choice of a system with relatively free versus fixed word order determines many important properties of a language's design. In free word order languages the words are concatenated with little superstructure; languages with more or less fixed word order in general permit the embedding of sentences and phrases one within the other, resulting in hierarchical structures of potentially infinite depth. So in English we can embed a sentence as the modifier of a verb, and that verb may itself have a sentence as modifier, and so on:

(1)   Mary believes that ants eat ants
(2)   Tom knows that Mary believes that ants eat ants
(3)   Alice believes Tom knows that Mary believes that ants eat ants . . .

49

In the above examples, the modifier sentences are hierarchically contained one within another, as illustrated by the structure for example (3):

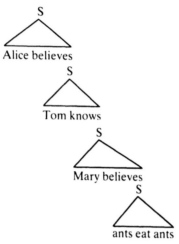

Free word order languages by and large eschew such hierarchical structuring of the word strings within a sentence. So we can distinguish *non-configurational*, free word order languages with little hierarchical structuring in the word string from *configurational* languages, which typically impose word order rules and permit hierarchical structuring within the sentence. The Australian Aboriginal language Warlpiri is an example of a non-configurational language, English of a configurational language.

Configurational languages have been far more widely studied by linguists than non-configurational languages, and we will concentrate here on properties of the former.[1] Configurational languages subdivide into distinct types that exhibit different kinds of regularities across the rules for organizing words into phrases and sentences. Languages such as English, with a basic SVO order in simple sentences, tend to build up modificational structure by placing the modifier to the right-hand side of the word or phrase it modifies – so the embedded sentences in the above structure are placed to the right of the verb they modify. Similarly, a relative clause such as *that the snake bit* in the following sentence is placed to the right of the noun phrase it modifies (*the doctor*):

(4)   Alice knows the doctor _S[that the snake bit]

By contrast, languages such as Japanese, with a basic verb-final order in simple sentences (SOV), generally place modifying material to the left of the phrase that is modified. So in Japanese a relative clause precedes the modified phrase.

English-type languages are known as right-branching, since in the internal structure of the phrase it is the right-hand side that is expanded for purposes of modification:

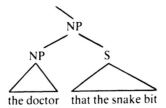

Japanese-type languages are known as left-branching, since the left-hand side of a phrase will be expanded for modification – a Japanese relative clause equivalent to the English relative *the doctor that the snake bit* will thus have a structure broadly the mirror-image of the English relative structure:

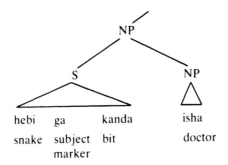

There is thus a chain of implicational relationships between language types and rules. This chain extends beyond the rules for specifying the basics of configurationality. In right-branching languages it is common to have rules for forming questions and other sentence types which dislocate a word from the position it would occupy in the corresponding declarative sentence, placing it at the front of the sentence:

(5)   John is eating something

       What is John eating?

Left-branching languages, on the whole, eschew such rules, often forming questions by marking the question word or phrase in the place it would

occupy in a declarative sentence; Japanese forms questions in this way. Thus, the basic phrase structure (right- or left-branching), which is itself correlated with the basic word order in simple sentences (verb-nonfinal or verb-final) affects the type of rule a language is likely to have for question formation.

1.2. Structure and constraints

The operation of rules for forming and interpreting sentences is constrained by the structure of the language. The English question-formation rule can link a question word to a position inside a sentence that is complement to a verb:

(6) Mary believes that ants eat something

What does Mary believe that ants eat?

It may not, however, lift a question word from within a conjoined structure, a complex NP (*the claim that* . . .) or a relative clause. All of the following questions are ungrammatical in English:

(7) Mary threw stones and something

What did Mary throw stones and?

(8) Mary believed the claim that ants ate something

What did Mary believe the claim that ants ate?

(9) Mary knew the doctor who killed something

What did Mary know the doctor who killed?

These constraints on question formation and other dislocation rules are structural – they refer to the grouping of words into sentences and phrases within the sentence.

Other types of structural constraint limit the interpretation of various types of referring words and phrases, such as definite pronouns (*he, she,* etc.), reflexive pronouns (*himself, herself,* etc.) and the reciprocal pronoun (*each other*). The reference of definite pronouns is constrained in such

a way that the pronoun may not refer to an entity within its immediate structural environment, whereas for reflexives and reciprocals the opposite is true – the pronominal form *must* refer to an entity in its immediate environment. The 'immediate structural environment' in the following examples will be the embedded sentence *the teacher(s) criticized X*:

(10) The parent said that the teacher criticized him
(11) The parent said that the teacher criticized himself
(12) The parents said that the teachers criticized each other

In (10), *him* may not refer to *teacher*, but may refer to *parent*. In (11) and (12) the opposite is true – *himself* and *each other* must refer to *teacher(s)*, the potential referent in the same domain, and not to *parent(s)*, which is the potential referent outside the immediate domain.

Domain conditions are only one part of the structural restrictions governing the interpretation of pronominal elements. Even outside its local domain, a definite pronoun such as *he* is not completely free to refer. Further conditions will be needed to account for the fact that *he* may refer to *Jones* in (13), but not in (14):

(13)   When he arrived at the airport, Jones saw Sue

(14)   He saw Sue when Jones arrived at the airport.

Nor is the requirement that a reflexive or reciprocal pronominal element refer to an entity within its local domain sufficient to account for the reference possibilities of reflexives and reciprocals. Inside the local domain the reference possibilities are further constrained; for example, in both (15) and (16) the reflexive must refer to *friend* rather than *John*:

(15) Alice said that John's friend washed himself
(16) Alice said that the friend of John washed himself

The local domain for the reflexive *himself* is the embedded sentence (*that ... himself*), yet the reflexive is not free to refer to any potential referent in that sentence, as is demonstrated by the fact that neither of the sentences can be taken to mean '... John's friend washed John'. As we will see below, the restrictions on pronoun reference outside the local domain, and reflexive and reciprocal interpretation within the domain, both make reference to the same structural relationship, which can be simply defined.

Conditions such as those governing question formation and the interpretation of pronominal elements are an important component in the design

of languages such as English. These conditions are structural: they apply to limit rules of sentence formation and interpretation in terms of the organization of words and phrases in the sentence. Their relevance in a particular language will depend on whether the rules and structures of the language are pertinent to their application. Thus, the condition that blocks questioning from within a complex NP or a relative clause is a condition governing the type of question rule that English has – a rule which dislocates a question word from its position in the equivalent declarative structure and places it at the front of the sentence. Languages that form questions by a different type of rule do not fall under the same constraint. Thus, the questions equivalent to *What did Mary believe the claim that ants ate? and *What did Mary know the doctor who killed? are grammatical in Japanese, which does not have an English-type question rule.

2. Universal grammar and language acquisition

What bearing does this medley of facts have on the question of how a child learns to speak his native language? The type of fact we have looked at allows a strong *prima facie* argument for an innate linguistic component. Many of the regularities that govern linguistic systems are plainly independent of cognition in any more general sense. There is nothing in 'logic' or the way in which humans categorize the world at a nonlinguistic level that dictates that the question *What does Mary believe the claim that ants eat?* is ungrammatical, as the fact that equivalent questions are grammatical in some languages demonstrates. Similarly, there is nothing outside of grammar that will explain why the pronoun *he* can refer to *Jones* in *When he arrived at the airport Jones saw Sue*, but not in the sentence *He saw Sue when Jones was at the airport*. The two sentences are identical with respect to their potential to describe real-world situations; they differ only in the way in which grammatical entities are matched with structure, and this difference bars a certain, logically possible, interpretation for one of the two sentences. Many facts of great intricacy could be cited to the same point.

In their spontaneous speech children do not appear to violate conditions such as those governing question formation and pronominal reference, although they do make other types of error (the most familiar examples being overgeneralization of regular rules to exceptional cases, as when children learning English overgeneralize the regular past tense form, producing *goed* for *went* etc.). The complexity of the rules that characterize the adult system, the independence of grammar from other cognitive systems, and children's apparent obedience to the dictates of linguistic rules, together argue for a substantial innate component. Children make errors,

but they appear to do so only within bounds. The pattern of occurring and non-occurring errors will be accounted for if the child's grammatical system is constrained by a language-forming capacity that sets limits on the shape of the system that will be acquired.

What is the language-forming capacity? Clearly, it must be flexible enough to permit a child to learn all kinds of human languages, since any normal infant can master any language, configurational or non-configurational, left-branching or right-branching, and so on, with equal ease. The biological program for language learning is envisaged as a set of innate blueprints for possible language types; these blueprints go under the name of *universal grammar* (see, e.g., Chomsky 1965, 1975, 1980a). Universal grammar is not a set of properties that are 'true of all languages' (although some universals will be of that type). Rather, it is a set of specifications for the shape of permissible kinds of languages; by spelling out the nature of the various types of grammatical systems observed in the world's languages, universal grammar will in effect also exclude all the non-occurring systems. If the child has tacit knowledge of the limits on possible language systems, the errors he makes on the path to adult knowledge may be expected to be constrained accordingly.

A strong version of the hypothesis that the child's development is constrained by innate blueprints is the claim that at each stage of development the child's grammatical system conforms to one of the patterns specified by universal grammar. That is, at every stage the child's grammar will correspond to a possible adult grammar, albeit not the correct grammar for the language he will ultimately master. On this version of the innateness hypothesis, there is thus a biological mandate against wild grammars.

The 'no wild grammars' mandate is not a necessary corollary of the thesis that language development is biologically programmed. It is logically possible that some properties of grammar in general, or of particular language types, are biologically programmed to appear only at a certain stage, after a period in which the child has got by with a system that to some degree does not obey the dictates of universal grammar. It is worthwhile, then, to consider how the child's performance corresponds to the patterns of adult languages.

3. Early grammatical knowledge

It is extremely difficult accurately to determine the child's earliest grammars. But it is plausible to assume that by the third year the child will be firmly on a particular language track (configurational, non-configurational; left-branching, right-branching etc.). The literature contains a range

of speculations concerning the nature of the child's earliest representations. There has been considerable interest in the role of grammatical relations in early stages of acquisition. Such relations as 'subject', 'object', and 'indirect object' are variously defined (see e.g. Jackendoff 1972; Bresnan and Kaplan 1982; Marantz 1983), but they are agreed to have a significant role in a number of areas of adult grammar. Some researchers propose a tighter correspondence for children between the categories of nonlinguistic perception and grammatical representations than is found in the adult grammar, where the mapping between cognitive categories, grammatical relations and structural categories (noun, verb, etc) is far from isomorphic. Thus, for example, Pinker (1982) points to facts such as the near identity of the semantic role 'agent' and the grammatical role 'subject' in early child speech as evidence for an early system in which there is close matching between categories at different levels. Such a system intuitively provides a natural stepping-stone to the more arbitrary adult system. Given the limited discourse environments of children, it is an open question at present whether such intuitions about early development are correct, or whether the observed correspondences between cognitive, grammatical and syntactic categories in child speech are only the products of what children happen to talk about (see Newport, Gleitman and Gleitman 1977 for discussion of the intricate relationship between discourse situation and grammatical development).

Neither is anything known about the way in which the child extracts from the speech around him knowledge of whether he is learning a configurational or non-configurational language. If the child is equipped with innate schemata for the specification of phrasal configurations and has somehow acquired the basics of word-category membership for his language, it is reasonable to assume that the choice of a configurational or non-configurational language track will be made with ease. A few instances of scrambled word order will signal the non-configurational track. Within configurational languages, exposure to a few examples of simple sentences will be sufficient to trigger a complex set of rules for various phrase types. Recall that verb-final languages are primarily left-branching, and languages which do not place the verb in final position are primarily right-branching. Linguists do not fully understand the principles that underlie this observation, but if we assume that children work within the set of systems defined in universal grammar, then it is clear that far-reaching decisions can be made on the basis of very little data. If his language is verb-final in simple sentences, the child can automatically project a modifier–head (S–NP) order for relative clauses, for example. (See Williams 1981a; Pinker 1984: ch. 3 for discussion of the acquisition of phrase structure schemata.)

It bears repeating that little is known about the structure of the child's system before the third year; but facts such as sensitivity to constructs governing the adult system in early speech (as in Brown's 1973 observations of the use of contractible and non-contractible *be*) and the spontaneous emergence of complex sentence look-alikes in children under 3 years (Limber 1973) are consistent with the view that the child quickly constructs a grammar that follows the broad outlines of the language he is exposed to. Some experimental work comparing the performance of children learning left- and right-branching languages supports this view (for example, Lust and Wakayama 1979; Tager-Flusberg, de Villiers and Hakuta 1982).

4. Sentence structure and proform principles

A clearer picture can be sketched of development beyond the earliest stages. We can use candidate principles of universal grammar as a probe of children's knowledge both of the principles and of the structures on which they are based. Some studies have used linguistic principles in this way, revealing a developed linguistic system by age 5. The grammar of definite pronouns and reflexives provides perhaps the best examples. We looked above at cases where definite pronouns are in complementary distribution with reflexive and reciprocal pronouns with respect to the possibility of a co-referent NP in their local structural domain: a definite pronoun may not refer to an NP in the same domain; a reflexive or reciprocal must refer to an NP in the same domain. A number of studies have shown that children are sensitive to these distinctions. Most of the studies use a comprehension task in which children act out sentences with dolls and other props (C. Chomsky 1969). Using this paradigm, Otsu (1981a), Jakubowicz 1984 and Solan (in press) have tested preschool children's understanding of the distribution of the different pronominal forms. Overall, children demonstrate knowledge of a distinction between definite pronouns on the one hand and reflexives and reciprocals on the other, correctly preferring to interpret *the pig* as the referent of *him* in sentences such as (17):

(17) The pig remembered that the dog hit him

and *the dog(s)* as the referent of *himself / each other* in sentences such as (18) and (19):

(18) The pig remembered that the dog hit himself
(19) The pigs remembered that the dogs hit each other

Otsu was able to achieve a considerably higher success rate on children's

performance with reciprocals than Matthei (1981); Otsu attributes this to a paring down of the complexity of the materials in his experiment as compared with Matthei's.

More striking than sensitivity to local domain conditions is children's knowledge of the role of dominance relations in interpreting definite pronouns outside their local domain and reflexives and reciprocals inside their domain. Within the hierarchical structures that characterize configurational languages, some elements are intuitively 'higher on the tree' than others. It is clear from the structure below that NP_1 is higher on the tree than NP_2, since it is closer to the root of the tree (S):

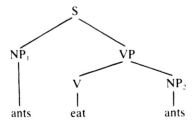

The notion of relative height can be made precise:

> Node A (NP, VP, etc) is higher on the tree than another node B if all the branching nodes that dominate A also dominate B[2]

A branching node is simply a phrase node that forks into two or more subordinate nodes. In the tree above, the only branching node that dominates NP_1 is S, which also dominates NP_2, so NP_1 is higher than NP_2. (Note that NP_2 is not higher than NP_1, since it is dominated by a branching node, VP, that does not dominate NP_1.)[3] This definition of height forms the basis for an explanation of the facts of pronominal reference above and beyond domain restrictions. Two principles will be needed, one for definite pronouns and one for reflexives and reciprocals; in each case, children's performance fits reasonably well with knowledge of these principles and the structures to which they apply.

In general, reference between a definite pronoun and another NP is quite free where the pronoun follows that NP. A structural restriction is imposed only where the pronoun precedes the NP it potentially refers to – that is, where the pronoun and NP are in the linear order . . . Pronoun . . . NP . . . The principle required is the following:

> A definite pronoun may not both precede and be higher on the tree than an NP it refers to

Going back to our earlier examples, it is easy to see from a look at the structures for the two sentences (13) and (14), given again here:

(13) When he arrived at the airport, Jones saw Sue
(14) He saw Sue when Jones arrived at the airport

that the pronoun is higher on the tree than the following NP *Jones* in (14) but not in (13)

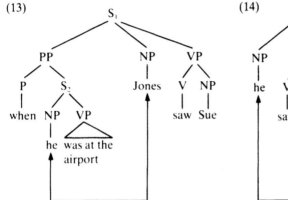

Pronoun *he* not higher than NP *Jones*:
Co-reference permitted

Pronoun *he* higher than NP *Jones*:
Co-reference blocked

In (14) the first (and only) branching node above *he* is S_1, and S_1 also dominates the NP *Jones; he* is thus higher on the tree than the NP *Jones* and co-reference is blocked. In (13) the pronoun *he* is dominated by the branching node S_2 and this node does not dominate the NP *Jones*; so *he* is not higher than *Jones*, and co-reference is permitted.

Children are aware of this distinction in co-reference possibilities. In toy-manipulation experiments in which an actor not mentioned in the sentence is made available to the child, that actor is chosen as referent of the pronoun most often when the pronoun is higher on the tree than the noun that follows it (see Lust, Loveland and Kornet 1980 for a study with 3–7 year olds, and Solan 1981, 1983 for a study with 5–7 year olds). That is, in acting out sentences such as (20) and (21):

(20) He hit the pig when the dog ran around
(21) When he ran around, the dog hit the pig

children will select an actor other than the dog as the referent of the pronoun significantly more often in the first sentence type than in the second. Solan

shows that children's sensitivity to the pronominal reference possibilities defined by the pronoun principle is not confined to these two sentence types, but generalizes across a range of constructions and accounts for subtle distinctions in children's responses.

The same definition of dominance that governs children's interpretation of definite pronouns outside their local domain also enters into the domain-internal restrictions on the interpretation of reflexives and reciprocals. We noted above the following facts: the reflexive must refer to *friend* and not to *John* in both (15) and (16), given again here:

(15) Alice said that John's friend washed himself
(16) Alice said that the friend of John washed himself

The following principle will account for this restriction on the interpretation of the reflexive (the same principle can be applied to the interpretation of reciprocals, which, for simplicity, are omitted from the discussion):

A reflexive pronoun must refer to an NP that is higher on the tree

From the structures for the sentences above, we can see that under our definition of relative height the entire circled NP *John's friend* or *the friend of John* is higher on the tree than the following reflexive, but that the NP *John*, which is a subpart of the larger NP headed by *friend*, is not higher on the tree than the reflexive. As the reflexive searches around for a referent in its local domain (the S node in the structures below), it will thus find only one NP to which it may be co-referential – the circled NP. The entity picked out by that NP is *the friend*, not *John*.

Using a picture-identification task, Deutsch and Koster (1982) demonstrated that 6 year olds are aware of the reference possibilities for the reflexive in sentences such as *John's friend washed himself*, and *The friend of John washed himself*, correctly preferring *the friend* as referent of the reflexive in both cases. (Deutsch and Koster's experiment was with children learning Dutch as their first language; the structural properties of Dutch are identical to English in the critical respects.) In a toy-manipulation experiment, Jakubowicz (1984) has demonstrated that English-speaking children's interpretation of the two sentence types is adult-like with respect to the referent of the reflexive; her subjects were as young as 3 years.

The definition of relative height, the pronoun principle and the reflexive principle are putative principles of universal grammar; children's sensitivity to these conditions supports the view that the child quickly develops a language system that is adult-like in its organization and governing principles, consistent with the 'no wild grammars' mandate. The case of pronominal interpretation is not an isolated example. Studies that have drawn on

(15)

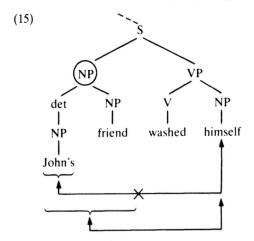

(16)

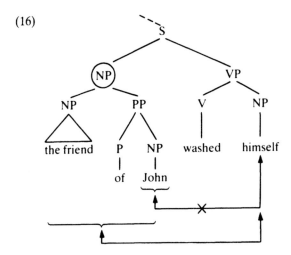

constructs of linguistic theory have revealed a highly structured grammatical system on the part of the child in a number of areas of grammar, including: complement subject interpretation (Maratsos 1974; Goodluck 1981; Hsu 1981; Goodluck and Tavakolian 1982; Roeper 1982a; Hsu, Cairns and Fiengo 1985); phrase structure configurations (Solan and Roeper 1978); relative clause formation (Goodluck and Tavakolian 1982; Hamburger and Crain 1982). Additional studies of children's proform interpretation may be found in Lust (in press).

5. An update

The 'no wild grammars' mandate can be interpreted as a reasonable, and conservative, null hypothesis for child language studies. Wild grammars increase the burden of explanation for a theory of language development by increasing the gap between child and adult abilities, for which transition mechanisms must be found. Yet such grammars have frequently been posited in the acquisition literature. Carol Chomsky's (1969) study of the development of complex syntax pursued the idea that some parts of our grammatical knowledge may be slow to develop. She gathered some of the first experimental evidence concerning children's rules for complex sentence interpretation, and analysed her evidence in terms compatible with grammars quite unlike the adult system. In the general context of Carol Chomsky's work, it is easy to see how researchers were willing to propose child grammars that did not conform with the dictates of adult systems. Two examples will illustrate ways in which such candidate child systems have been shown to be inadequate or unmotivated.

The first example originates in Chomsky's (1969) study. Chomsky found that children aged around 5 years correctly interpret the missing subject of an infinitival complement to *tell* as referring to the main clause object – thus, *Donald* will be the one who is made to lie down when a child acts out with dolls a sentence such as (22):

(22)   Bozo tells Donald to lie down

Chomsky accounted for children's performance by a linear distance principle in which the child makes the subject of the complement verb refer to the most immediately preceding NP – *Donald* in the example.[4] Such a rule can be shown to be inadequate for the adult grammar, in which the rules for complement subject interpretation must refer to levels of representation other than surface order of words (see, for example, Williams 1980; Chomsky 1981a; Bresnan 1982a, for differing, and partially competing, accounts). Consider, for example, the passive version of the *tell* sentence above:

(23)   Donald is told by Bozo to lie down

In the passive *tell* sentence, *Donald* is the subject of *lie down*, just as in the active. *Donald* is not the nearest NP to the complement verb in the passive sentence; thus a simple 'nearest NP' rule will not work for complement subject interpretation in the adult grammar.

That such a rule is insufficient to account for children's behaviour was demonstrated by Maratsos (1974). He showed that children aged 4–5 dis-

tinguish between active and passive *tell* sentences in terms of the interpretation of the complement subject, correctly picking the main clause object (the nearest NP) as complement subject for active sentences and the main clause subject (the furthest NP) as complement subject for the passive sentences (provided the main clause is correctly understood as a passive). No linear distance rule that picks out the immediately preceding NP as complement subject can account for children's performance with passive *tell* sentences, as Maratsos observed. The more recent studies of children's rules for complement subject interpretation cited above have confirmed that children work within a highly structured, if not fully adult, system in this area of grammatical knowledge.[5]

A second example of a candidate child system that has become implausible in the light of recent studies is Lust's (1981) proposal that children start off with a grammar in which the rules and constraints governing pronoun interpretation and conjunction reduction are collapsed at some level. Such a proposal amounts to positing a wild grammar, since no adult language collapses rules for pronominalization and conjunction reduction in the way that Lust proposes.

The evidence Lust presents for such a collapsed system is that in sentence-repetition tasks children experience difficulty both with sentences in which a pronoun precedes its potential antecedent and with reduced sentences in which the site of a missing (null) element in a conjoined construction precedes the element to which the null element must be linked. For example, both sentences of the type:

(24)   When he was at the airport Jones saw Sue

and sentences of the type:

(25)   Jenny baked and Sue ate a cake
         (= Jenny baked ∅ and Sue ate a cake)

are difficult ones for children to repeat (the latter sentence type deriving from a kind of conjunction reduction operation ('right node raising') that leaves a reduction site (∅) in a position preceding the element to which it must be linked – the NP *a cake* in the example sentence). The common difficulty of sentences in which a pronoun precedes its potential antecedent, and of sentences in which a reduction site precedes the element it must refer to, doubtless reflects children's sensitivity to structural configurations, but does not constitute positive evidence of an under-differentiated rule system on the child's part with respect to pronominalization and conjunction reduction. Recent work on children's knowledge of the grammar of pronouns renders such an interpretation implausible. Studies such as those

summarized in the preceding section (including some of Lust's own work) show that children make fine-grained distinctions with respect to pronominalization in various sentence types, distinguishing between, for example, *When he was at the airport, Jones saw Sue* and *He saw Sue when Jones was at the airport* in terms of the potential for co-reference between *he* and *Jones*. Such results argue that the fact that constructions which are governed by distinct rule systems in the adult grammar (pronominalization and conjunction reduction constructions) are difficult for the child is best interpreted as showing no more than that these constructions are indeed difficult ones. The child's rule system may be adult-like, with distinctions within it untapped by our observations.

6. Developing grammars

The 'no wild grammars' mandate does not preclude the possibility of a developing grammar; it merely says that each developing grammar will fall within the bounds of adult language systems as characterized by linguistic theory. At that level, Carol Chomsky's idea that language development is a process that extends into middle and even later childhood may well turn out to be correct. Linguistic theory does not necessarily tell us what the shape and ordering of the sequence of non-adult grammars will be, but it provides some pointers and a frame of reference.

It is generally agreed that within particular language types there are central properties that characterize that type. These are the rules and conditions that form the 'core' of a language, and define the normal, or *unmarked*, state (for discussion see, for example, Chomsky 1981a,b). Variation between languages of basically the same type will be largely a matter of conditions and rules that fine-tune the application of core rules and principles, and of peripheral constructions idiosyncratic to particular languages. Included in these language-particular specifications will be atypical, or *marked*, rules and forms. The commonsense first hypothesis for a theory of language development is that there will be a progression of developing grammars that represents a series of adjustments away from the core, and towards whatever marked, language-particular specifications the child must learn. Whether it is in fact the case that grammars develop over time in this way is quite moot, and the question may lend itself to different answers in different areas and sub-areas of grammatical knowledge.

In the phonological (sound) system, the available evidence fits quite neatly with the notion that the earliest mastered forms are the unmarked, normal forms. For example, the sound [æ] (the vowel in *cat*) is a frequent vowel in the inventory of English words, but it is mastered late (Jakobson

1968). This vowel is a relatively rare sound in languages of the world, so its late emergence fits the view that rare, marked forms are late acquired. Similarly, Smith (1973) observed his child simplifying initial sequences of the three consonants *str* to *tr* and *sr* but not to *st-* : *strawberry* was pronounced 'trawberry' or 'srawberry' at a certain stage, but not 'stawberry'. So the child avoided a sequence that does occur in English (English has words beginning with *st*, such as *sting*) but produced a sequence that does not occur (English has no words that begin in *sr*). The child's performance can be accounted for in terms of markedness. The normal order for sequences of consonants at the beginning of a word is to put the least vowel-like sound first. The *t* is least vowel-like of the three consonants in question, *s* is more vowel-like than *t*, and *r* most vowel-like of the three. The cluster *st(r)* violates the general rule that least vowel-like consonants are placed first in clusters. The child's use of 'tr' and 'sr' simplifications for the cluster *str* is thus a choice of the two possible simplifications that conform to the unmarked situation in which least vowel-like sounds are placed first. The child avoids *st* clusters, although he hears words with such clusters in the speech around him; he avoids exactly that simplified cluster that is the marked case.

In syntax the role of markedness in developing grammars is rather less clear-cut, perhaps because we lack knowledge in depth concerning what the unmarked and marked situations are; perhaps also because the relation between data (the speech the child hears) and learning may be different in syntax and phonology. In some of the studies cited above there are patterns in the data that suggest the child's syntactic performance is governed by markedness factors. Although in many experiments children have been shown to draw adult-like distinctions with respect to the operation of grammatical principles, nonetheless errors are made by children. Children's handling of, for example, definite pronouns and reflexives is not completely adult in terms of the absolute level of correct responses. What is of interest is that in a number of studies there are more errors in the direction of treating definite pronouns such as *he* as if they were reflexives such as *himself* than the other way around. It is notable that where the local domain conditions are (exceptionally) relaxed in the adult grammar, they tend to be relaxed in the direction of using a definite pronoun where the domain conditions would lead us to expect a reflexive – as, for example, in the sentence *John saw a snake near him*, where the local domain of the pronoun is the whole sentence, and we would normally expect a reflexive (*himself*). Children's performance is thus most variable with the form that admits exceptions in the adult grammar and most adult in the form that is less prone to exceptions. This is at least suggestive of some role for

a metric of markedness that allows domain restrictions to be relaxed for definite pronouns more readily than for reflexives (see Otsu 1981b; Solan 1981, in press; Jakubowicz 1984, for pertinent data and discussion).[6]

In other areas of syntactic development, the order of developing grammars may run counter to the predictions of markedness. Anita Gallucci and I have been studying the development of English-speaking children's ability to comprehend preposition-initial and preposition-final relative clauses:

(26) John sees the donkey to which the camel pushes the zebra
(27) John sees the donkey which the camel pushes the zebra to

The preposition-initial form (*to which* ...) is generally considered to be the unmarked, normal form and the preposition-final form (*which* ... *to*) to be marked. Many languages admit only the preposition-initial form. Nonetheless, modern English favours the marked, preposition-final form. Preposition-final forms are certainly the forms that a child will hear most frequently in the speech around him – perhaps almost exclusively. Preschool and young school-age children in our study vary considerably in their ability to comprehend preposition-initial forms, with the preposition-initial forms being more difficult for many children than the marked, preposition-final forms. Thus, in this case, the acquisition sequence may follow the dictates of the speech forms the child hears around him rather than the order predicted by a progression from unmarked to marked forms, in contrast to the late emergence of the sound [æ] cited above.

Perhaps this type of contrast reflects a general distinction in the relation between our perceptual systems and the organization of our grammatical abilities. Although both the phonological and syntactic systems of human languages are organized by principles that are biologically given and independent of logic or necessity, it could be argued that there is a sense in which the rules of phonology are governed by our physiological and perceptual makeup in a way syntactic rules are not. The unmarked values of phonological forms and rules may originate (albeit at some long-past evolutionary stage) in a correspondence to ease at the level of perception and production. The unmarked nature of some syntactic forms may also be related to a balance of tension between the rules of grammar and the mechanisms for sentence production and comprehension that subserve the grammar – so the unmarked status of the preposition-initial form may be related to the fact that the preposition-initial form provides the processor with an early clue to the fact that an oblique, prepositional object, and not a direct object, is the focus of the construction. But the putative source of the 'ease' of the unmarked form may be quite different in the cases

of phonology and syntax – ease in the former case deriving from the tuning of the human perceptual device to the immediate speech stream, in the latter from the language analyser's ability to map the input onto an accurate representation of the syntax, and then ultimately onto a semantic interpretation of the sentence. This difference may contribute to a closer match in phonology than in syntax between markedness and developmental sequences.

7. Summary and conclusion

The points I have tried to make in this chapter are easily summarized. Language systems exhibit variation within highly constrained bounds; it is the business of linguistic theory to characterize those bounds. A comparison across languages shows many conditions governing particular language types that cannot be put down to general, nonlinguistic constraints on human cognition. The prohibition on questioning out of a conjoined construction, or a complex NP in left-branching, configurational languages, or the structural restrictions on various types of pronominal interpretation are examples of such constraints. Such conditions are plausibly part of a biological program that limits the types of grammar a child can postulate. From studies of children's development to date, there is every indication that the child's development is rapid and follows an adult-like system from the earliest stages. We do not need to assume that there is no such thing as language development in order to maintain the hypothesis that there are no wild grammars in the course of language learning; we need only assume that each child grammar falls within the bounds of the set of possible human languages dictated by principles of universal grammar.

It is worth stressing how little is known about the course of development, even within the framework of constrained grammar formation that I have suggested. Constraints governing question formation and other rules of dislocation have a central place in linguistic theory and in some theoretical modelling of acquisition (see Wexler and Culicover 1980); yet experimental work on children's knowledge of such constraints is only just beginning (see Otsu 1981b; Phinney 1981b,c; Roeper 1982b for some suggestive results and discussion). We know that even within languages of broadly the same type, the block on question formation from within a conjoined construction appears to be solid, and relatively immune to exceptions; the block on questioning from within a complex NP, by contrast, is rather more variable, and subject to pragmatic and discourse conditions in some languages (see, for example, papers in Engdahl and Ejerhed 1982). Nothing is known to date about how these variables relate to sequences of grammars in development.

Similarly, although there has been a good deal of speculation concerning the role of knowledge of individual words in the development of both lexically restricted and lexically unrestricted rules of grammar, little is known concerning the way in which the child maps back and forth between his word store and grammatical rules in the course of development (for discussion and pertinent data, see, for example, Tyack and Ingram 1977; papers in Baker and McCarthy 1981; Roeper *et al.* 1981; Bowerman 1982b, 1983; Pinker 1982; Randall 1982; Mazurkevich and White 1982).

The essential point is that we are very far from an adequate theory of language development at the linguistic level; that is, from an account of the ordering of the child's grammars that relates the sequence of development to overgeneralization and under-differentiation of linguistic constructs within the bounds permitted by universal grammar. One point is, however, plain. Linguistic theory comprises the most sophisticated attempts to characterize human languages, and the constructs of linguistic theory have proven effective probes of the child's knowledge. Recent studies drawing on linguistic theory have shown that children work with an adult-like system in many areas of grammar. The most interesting developmental question thus becomes 'What *don't* children know about their language?'

4. Conversations with children

Catherine E. Snow

Only ten or fifteen years ago it was thought possible to study language acquisition without studying the language addressed to children. All the research done before the late 1960s on the nature of linguistic input to children was carried out by linguists and anthropologists studying 'baby talk'. They collected data on the special lexicon used with babies, and several noted that the baby talk words could be analysed as simplified forms of adult words (reviewed in Ferguson 1977). They also noted the characteristic prosodic features of baby talk – high pitch and exaggerated intonation contours (e.g. Blount and Padgug 1977). This research on baby talk was done primarily with the purpose of describing a certain speech register, not with any specific interest in the relevance of baby talk to language acquisition (though several papers noted that the informants justified using baby talk with a didactic motive, 'to make the language easier to learn'). Much more recently the nature of the speech addressed to children has been studied by psychologists and linguists interested in language acquisition. They have concentrated on syntactic and semantic rather than lexical or phonological aspects of that speech, and have tended not to use the term 'baby talk' to refer to their object of study. Other terms have been coined, such as 'motherese', which gives the misleading impression that only mothers talk in a special way to children. In this chapter I will avoid both such neologisms and the term 'baby talk', and will use the term 'child directed speech' (CDS) instead.

This chapter will be primarily concerned with the relationship between CDS and language acquisition. Until very recently, children's acquisition of language was studied without considering CDS because it was assumed that the nature of the CDS made very little difference to the course of language acquisition. It was thought that there was a large innate component in linguistic ability which buffered language acquisition against sparseness, complexity and confusion in the primary linguistic data. Two positions on the nature of this innate linguistic component can be identified: the notion that the innate component supplied knowledge of linguistic universals such

as the existence of word classes and the importance of order of elements (McNeill 1966a), and the position that the innate component supplied procedures for discovering the grammar of the language to be learned (Fodor 1966). Under the assumption of either innate grammatical knowledge or of innate grammar discovery procedures it could be argued that only a minimum of linguistic input was adequate to enable the child to learn language, and that both a high level of complexity and a large amount of misinformation (e.g. ungrammatical utterances, slips of the tongue) in this linguistic input could easily be tolerated.

In this chapter I will attempt to present the current position regarding the relationship between the linguistic environment of the language-learning child and language acquisition. Since the present position is the result of several major shifts of emphasis within a relatively short time, it is perhaps useful to review historically the research which has been done in this topic.

1. Stage I: Simple, well-formed, redundant

The first analyses of speech addressed to children were undertaken in response to the claims that such input was ill-formed (characterized by mistakes, garbles, ungrammaticalities, false starts, mispronunciations and stutters; see, for example, Miller and Chomsky 1963; McNeill 1966a) and that it was very complex. This description assumed that CDS did not differ in any important way from the language used among adults (Fodor 1966). It was a fairly simple matter to disconfirm that view. Various investigators collected and analysed samples of speech addressed to children in the age range 18 to 36 months by their mothers (Drach 1969; Kobashigawa 1969; Broen 1972; Snow 1972a; Phillips 1973; Remick 1976; Sachs, Brown and Salerno 1976). Every measure used in these studies for grammatical complexity (mean length of utterance, incidence of subordinate clauses, mean preverb length, incidence of conjunctions, etc.) or for well-formedness (incidence of hesitations, disfluencies, within-constituent pauses, false starts, etc.) revealed that the speech addressed to children aged 18 to 36 months was both simpler and more grammatical than the speech addressed to adults. Furthermore, CDS was also found to be highly redundant. Mothers frequently repeated phrases and whole sentences and paraphrased their own utterances (Snow 1972a). Individual mothers used certain 'sentence frames' (e.g. *That's* NP; *Where's* NP; *See* NP) quite frequently (Broen 1972).

The general conclusion drawn from the Stage I studies of mothers' speech was that the speech addressed to children of language-learning age was very different from adult-directed speech, in ways that seemed to constitute adaptations to children's linguistic level. In view of the nature of CDS,

it was concluded by many that the burden of explanation for language acquisition could be shifted away from the sort of innate language acquisition device envisioned by Chomsky (1965), McNeill (1966a) or Lenneberg (1967), toward a more general learning procedure that made use of the rather simple, orderly and redundant data available in the CDS.

Two additional bits of information which became available at about the same time as the results of the early CDS studies supported this conclusion. First, it was found that not only mothers, but also all adults and even children aged 4 to 5, produced simplified, redundant speech when addressing 16 to 36 month olds (Andersen and Johnson 1973; Shatz and Gelman 1973; Sachs and Devin 1976). This finding meant that such speech could be assumed to be universally available to language-learning children; and not just children growing up in middle-class North America and cared for by their mothers, but also children in other cultures who live in extended families, who are cared for by older siblings or cousins, and who may have little opportunity for dyadic interaction with their mothers, could be assumed to have access to a modified speech register. Second, it was found that children can play an active role in selecting which sentences they hear. Adult sentences which were far more complex than the child's own utterances, and those begun with an unfamiliar word, were less likely to be attended to than simple sentences begun with familiar words (Shipley, Gleitman and Smith 1969; Snow 1972b). This finding helped explain why children did not become confused and misled by the complex utterances overheard from adult–adult conversation or from radio and television. Not only was much of the speech available to young children adapted to their linguistic level, but speech not adapted to their level could simply be filtered out.

The findings of the first set of studies on CDS were purely descriptive. No one had undertaken to sort out what it was about children that caused CDS to be simple, grammatical and redundant – whether their age, their inability to speak correctly, their low status, their size, their cuteness, or their unwillingness to do as they were told was the relevant variable. An indication that feedback from the child played some role in influencing the adult to talk simply and redundantly came from a study in which mothers were asked to make tapes which would later be played to their children (Snow 1972a). Although the mothers in this situation did speak more slowly, simply, and redundantly than they would have done to an adult, they did not speak as simply or redundantly as when the child was present with them. This finding suggested that the characteristics of CDS could be explained at least partly as adjustments made in response to cues from the child. If the adult speech were too complex, the children would tend

to become inattentive and would fail to comply with requests or respond to questions. These cues would cause the adult to simplify her speech until it reached a level of complexity at which the child would be optimally compliant and attentive. An implication of this model is that CDS would be quite well adapted to the child's linguistic level. The characteristics of CDS would also be expected to change abruptly in the direction of simplicity, well-formedness and redundancy at 12 to 14 months, when the child first showed signs of understanding, and then gradually over the next three to four years to re-approach the normal adult values.

Oversimplification 1: Mother's language lessons. One possible interpretation of the findings discussed above was that the mothers were providing their children with ideal 'language lessons' – a carefully graded curriculum of information about the structure of their mother tongue (Levelt 1975). Such an interpretation was, of course, an unwarranted extrapolation from the findings. Although mothers do often teach children about language by training them in politeness forms, answering questions about the meanings of words, correcting errors with irregular forms, explicitly teaching labels, etc. (see, for example, Moerk 1976, Ninio and Bruner 1978), what mothers are doing most of the time is simply trying to communicate with their children. A side effect of their attempts to communicate is the set of modifications described. These modifications are not the result of attempts by the mothers to teach their children to talk: rather, they are the result of attempts to communicate effectively with them. See Garnica (1977) for comments from mothers about why they talk to young children as they do.

Oversimplification 2: No innate component. Another misinterpretation of these early findings was the conclusion that there was no innate component to language ability. It is, of course, absurd to argue that any complex behaviour is entirely innate or entirely learned. Innate and environmental factors always interact in the development of complex abilities, and both are of crucial importance. It is not, however, absurd to ask what proportion of the developmental variation in some complex ability like language is attributable to innate as opposed to environmental factors, for it is certainly the case that environmental factors can be relatively more important in determining an individual's achievements for one type of ability (e.g. solving arithmetic problems) than for another type (e.g. singing on key). Chomsky's position regarding language was that it was more like singing on key than like arithmetic; anyone with an innately good ear can learn to sing on key, with only minimal practice and exposure to music, and any human being (i.e. any possessor of the species-specific innate linguistic structure) can learn language on the basis of minimal exposure to even complex and

ill-formed utterances. The correct conclusion to be drawn from the Stage I studies was that Chomsky's position regarding the unimportance of the linguistic input was unproven, since all children, in addition to possessing an innate linguistic ability, also receive a simplified, well-formed, and redundant corpus. Thus, the relative importance of the innate and the social factors could not be determined. The prediction was made that children without access to such a simplified, redundant corpus would be unsuccessful or retarded in learning language. If such could be proven to be the case, then it could indeed be concluded that an innate, species-specific, linguistic component was relatively less important than Chomsky had hypothesized. But the conclusion could be drawn that the innate component was of no importance only if the provision of a simplified, well-formed and redundant corpus enabled nonhumans with human-like cognitive capacities, e.g. young chimpanzees, as well as human children, to learn language.

1.1 Is CDS really simpler?

It has been suggested that the results of the CDS studies actually support Chomsky's position, by demonstrating that the speech addressed to children is really syntactically quite complex (Newport 1977; Newport, Gleitman and Gleitman 1977). The basis for saying that such speech is complex, despite the short utterance length and absence of complex sentences, is that questions and imperatives are used very frequently in addition to declaratives. Newport *et al.* argue that a well-designed curriculum for second language learners starts with the 'basic sentence type', the sentence type in which the order of elements in surface structure shows the least deviation from deep structure. In English this is the declarative, which maintains the underlying order of elements Subject NP–Aux–V–Object NP, and in which none of these elements is deleted. In questions, the order of the Aux and the subject NP is inverted, and in the imperative the subject NP is deleted. How could a child learn the underlying order, argue Newport *et al.*, from a corpus which has about 40–60 per cent of such deformed sentence types? It is clear that English-speaking children do operate with a general SVO rule, since not only their declaratives but also their early questions show this order of elements.

The fact that children hear a mixture of surface orders would indeed be confusing if there were no basis for distinguishing among those orders or for noting that they are used for different functions. In such a case one would expect that the child might pick the most frequently offered order and use that as his basic order of elements. Evidence from children learning Italian and Finnish suggests that this does indeed happen. In Fin-

nish, declarative sentences have a free order for subject, verb and object, although the SVO order is most frequent. One child studied chose the order her mother used most often, SVO, and used it almost exclusively (Bowerman 1973). Italian mothers most often use the emphatic VOS order, rather than the normal SVO, to their children, and Italian children are relatively late in acquiring correct word order (Bates 1976). Why, then, do English-speaking children not start using verb-first orders in their declarative sentences, since imperatives and questions, which show a verb-first order, are more frequent than subject-first declaratives? One reason is certainly that the three sentence types are well distinguished in English by intonation contour. Imperatives and questions addressed to children usually have a final rise in intonation, whereas declaratives show a falling intonation. There is evidence that mothers use, and even very young children interpret, sentences which end in a rise as signals that some response is required (Ryan 1978). Thus, children do have a salient acoustic basis for separating out declaratives, imperatives and questions, rather than treating them as one class of utterances. Furthermore, declaratives, imperatives and interrogatives are used in quite different conversational and situational contexts, and the contextual cues combine with the acoustic differences to distinguish quite easily the classes of utterance. One ability which children are very precocious in is the ability to understand social acts – to distinguish among directives, descriptions, prohibitions, offers, and requests for information. This ability, demonstrated even by the prelinguistic child, means that the child in the early stages of language acquisition will have no trouble using pragmatic differences among utterances as one basis for sorting out their formal differences (see Ninio and Snow in press, for further discussion of a pragmatic-based language acquisition theory).

We are still left with the question of why children choose the less frequent declarative rather than the more frequent question form as a model for their word order. Perhaps they don't in the beginning, since in fact both declaratives and almost all questions show the same order of subject and main verb. It is the auxiliary which is preposed in questions in English. If no auxiliary is present, one is introduced by the rule of *do*-support. There are various sources of evidence suggesting that children may not attend to such auxiliaries, since they are unstressed (Van der Geest 1975) and unfamiliar (Shipley *et al.* 1969). Thus, the child presented with the questions:

> Is daddy going?
> What's the doggie doing?
> Who is eating the cookie?

may in fact be hearing:

> Daddy going + rising intonation
> What doggie doing + rising intonation
> Who eating cookie + rising intonation

In every case, the SV order is maintained. This specific explanation only holds, of course, for languages like English in which questions are formed by subject–auxiliary inversion. A much more common pattern is subject–verb inversion, which would present the problem envisaged by Newport *et al*. More study of languages which form questions by subject–verb inversion is needed in order to determine whether children learning such languages start forming utterances using an order of elements not frequently modelled in the input language. In French, for example, it may be the case that mothers more often use questions of the form:

> Est-ce qu'il va?

which maintain the declarative SV order rather than forms like:

> Va-t-il?

There is evidence that Dutch-speaking mothers very often use modal or other auxiliaries in their utterances, which cause the lexical verb to be placed in the final position in questions and imperatives as well as in declaratives (R. Klein 1974). Thus, Dutch children hear utterances which almost all show the surface order SAuxOV (declaratives), AuxOV (imperatives), or AuxSOV (questions), corresponding to the generally accepted underlying order SOV. The general conclusion from the available evidence must be that the basic order of elements is modelled for children more frequently than the distribution of utterances across sentence types might suggest, and furthermore that children's early utterances use the order most frequently modelled in the CDS.

1.2. Is simpler really better?

In a more recent paper, Gleitman, Newport and Gleitman 1984 argue that the simplest CDS may not be the best basis for learning language. They derive this conclusion from the sort of learnability model (see Wexler and Culicover 1980) that presumes the child uses the input to formulate hypotheses which are revised only when disconfirming evidence becomes available. The child is assumed to operate without benefit of negative evidence, i.e. without ever being told 'That rule is wrong' or 'Here is an incorrect sentence'. It is, thus, impossible for a hypothesized rule which generates

all the correct sentences but which also generates some incorrect sentences ever to be revised, since the system never receives information that those incorrect sentences are incorrect. Such a rule can be thought of as 'too simple', in the sense that it fails to incorporate some limitation or condition that the correct rule does incorporate. Gleitman *et al.* argue that such over-simple rules are likely to be hypothesized by the child if the CDS does not display the full range of complexity in the language.

The Gleitman *et al.* paper was motivated by a set of seemingly contradictory results in the literature, i.e. their own findings (Newport *et al.* 1977; Gleitman *et al.*, 1984, confirmed also by Barnes *et al.* 1983) that the complexity of maternal utterances correlates positively with children's language growth, and Furrow, Nelson and Benedict's (1979) finding of a negative correlation. Gleitman *et al.* argue that the Furrow *et al.* finding must be spurious, since it is theoretically inexplicable, in light of the considerations outlined above. However, the two sets of findings are based on children of different language levels – Furrow *et al.*'s in the one-word stage whereas the Gleitman *et al.* and Barnes *et al.* subjects were in stages I to III. (Oddly, Gleitman *et al.* did not find the positive correlation between complexity of the CDS and speed of acquisition they would expect for their older, and linguistically slightly more advanced, group of subjects.) The kind of learnability model Gleitman *et al.* based their argument on presupposes, further, a learning process which is identical across age and stage. Consider an alternative possibility, that the task of learning language is quite different in different stages of acquisition. If the task in the earliest stages is to learn a basic vocabulary and to learn effective ways of expressing simple semantic forms and pragmatic functions, then very simple CDS might well be the most facilitative. Subsequently, as the child's task shifts to the acquisition of morphological and syntactic rules, it might be the case that more complex input is required. Furthermore, such learning models generally assume that the formal properties of the CDS are the only ones that influence speed of acquisition, whereas such properties as interpretability in context might be equally, or more, important.

Another issue which arises out of learnability models is the claim that children receive no corrective feedback. This claim is based on one study (Brown and Hanlon 1970) which noted explicit parental corrections or failures to comprehend in response to child utterances. Explicit corrections occurred in response to child utterances that contained errors of fact, but not in response to child utterances that were grammatically incorrect or incomplete, leading to Brown and Hanlon's identification of a major paradox in child rearing, that children nonetheless end up speaking grammatically but not truthfully. Brown and Hanlon's conclusion concerning the

	Qty
	1

Sales Order
F 19016090 1
Cust P/O List
54.99 GBP

Ship To:
UK 18589001 F
LIVERPOOL JOHN MOORES UNI
GROUND FLOOR RM RF07, ACQ
MARYLAND STREET
LIVERPOOL
MERSEYSIDE
L1 9DE

Volume:	
Edition:	1997
Year:	
Pagination:	xii, 613 p. :
Size:	24 cm.

Routing	1
Sorting	
Y14A05X	
Inpro	
RFID	
Covering — BXAXX	
Despatch	

ISBN
9780521277808
Customer P/O No
283327
Title: Language acquisition

Format: P (Paperback)
Author:
Publisher: Cambridge University Press
           STOCKDEV2-2015
...nd: NONE
...tion: NONE
...Type: 1775596
...CN:

...cific Instructions
...OTE: WEB — BRP # GW,
...UPLICATE

existence of negative feedback to grammatical error may, however, be based on too narrow a definition of what constitutes negative feedback. I have argued above that children are more socially than linguistically precocious – they come to language learning with a good understanding of what constitutes communication. Accordingly, children are capable of interpreting many adult responses other than explicit correction or total failure of comprehension as negative feedback. Any response that reflects a need to negotiate about the exact meaning of the child's utterance is negative feedback. No data concerning the frequency of negotiation of meaning in parent–child interaction are available.

2. Stage II: The here and the now

The Stage I descriptions of speech addressed to children showed a curious oversight: no description was given of what the mothers were talking about. This oversight becomes more comprehensible if one realizes that the Stage I studies were done in the late 1960s, at a time when analyses of child speech were primarily concerned with children's acquisition of syntactic knowledge. It seemed, thus, most relevant to analyse maternal speech so as to determine how it could provide information about syntactic structure. The child's task was seen as one of testing many different innately supplied hypotheses about the syntax of the language being acquired against the patterns observed in the input, and thus eventually eliminating the incorrect hypotheses. Under this view, the acquisition of semantics was seen as a separate task facing the child.

In 1972 Macnamara argued that this view of language acquisition was incorrect, that the acquisition of syntax could be explained only if it is recognized that children collect information about the relationship between syntactic forms and semantic structures. Similar views were expressed by Schlesinger (1971a) and have been incorporated into more recently developed learnability models (Pinker 1979; Wexler and Culicover 1980). In other words, children figure out the rules underlying syntactic structure by using the cues provided by the meaning of an adult's utterance. This implies that children must be able to determine what an utterance means on the basis of nonsyntactic information – since the syntax is precisely what must be learned. Macnamara suggested that knowledge of the meaning of the important lexical items, plus knowledge of what is likely to be said about those entities or actions given the situation, must enable the child to guess correctly what the utterance means. This implies, of course, not only that the child must be a good guesser, but also that the adult must say the kinds of things the child expects to hear, that adult and child share

a way of looking at the world. Greenfield and Smith (1976) have argued that such a shared view of the world does exist, and that this is what enables adults to interpret children's early, presyntactic utterances. Macnamara's argument goes the other way around – that adult utterances have no syntactic structure as far as young children are concerned, and that children in the early stages of language acquisition must, therefore, interpret adult utterances in the same way as adults interpret children's utterances, by relating the words used to aspects of the situation being described. After many thousands of chances to observe that the word referring to the agent precedes the word referring to the action in adult sentences, the child can start to induce a rule about the order of those semantic elements. Much later, after the child starts to hear sentences in which words which obviously do not refer to the agent stand in the first position (e.g. passives like *The cake got eaten*) he will be forced to abandon this simple semantic rule for a syntactic rule incorporating the notion of sentence subject.

This model of how language acquisition proceeds rests on the presumption of *semantic* limitations on adult utterances – that they describe those aspects of the situation at hand which are most obvious to the child, and that the adult utterances are limited to those topics about which the child has extralinguistic information.

If one re-analyses maternal speech keeping this model of semantic matching in mind, then it becomes clear that the semantic content of speech addressed to young children is indeed severely restricted. Mothers limit their utterances to the present tense, to concrete nouns, to comments on what the child is doing and on what is happening around the child (Phillips 1973; Snow *et al.* 1976). Mothers make statements and ask questions about what things are called, what noises they make, what colour they are, what actions they are engaging in, who they belong to, where they are located, and very little else (Snow 1977b). This is a very restricted set of semantic contents, when one considers that older children and adults also discuss past and future events, necessity, possibility, probability, consequence, implication, comparison and many other semantic subtleties. This limitation on the semantic content of maternal speech can to a large extent explain the syntactic simplicity commented on above. Propositions of name, place, state and action can be expressed in short utterances without subordination or other syntactic complexities. It may, then, be the case that the syntactic simplicity in CDS is an artifact of semantic simplicity.

The question of whether CDS is 'finely-tuned' to child language level has aroused considerable controversy. Newport (1976; Newport *et al.* 1977) and Cross (1977) found no significant correlation between maternal and child MLU or other measures of syntactic complexity, and concluded that

there was no syntactic fine-tuning in CDS. Nor have analyses of the semantic relationships expressed in CDS revealed any fine-tuning at a semantic level (Snow 1977b; Chapman 1981; Retherford, Schwartz and Chapman 1981). Rather, it seemed that a fairly nonspecific limitation on topics and syntactic complexity characterized CDS.

More recent, more detailed analyses have, however, revealed evidence of fine-tuning, both at the semantic and at the syntactic level. An increase in the MLU of CDS with the child's age or MLU has been reported by Fraser and Roberts (1975), Longhurst and Stepanich (1975), Bellinger (1979, 1980), Furrow *et al.* (1979) and Stern *et al.* (1983). Shaffer and Crook (1979) found a positive correlation with age for directive speech acts, though not for attention-directing utterances. Clarke-Stewart, VanderStoep and Killian (1979) and Cross (1978) found a correlation with child's comprehension level. The correlation with child age or language ability holds true, as one might expect, only during the early stages of child language production; studies which start too young (before 14–18 months) or go on too long (after Brown's Stage V – Brown 1973) attenuate the correlations.

The correlations found between child variables and complexity of CDS may be attenuated for a variety of reasons; it is, in addition, crucial to examine them during the right stage of development:

1. Individual differences among adults, in the level of complexity they typically use, lower correlations computed on cross-sectional data. Two parents may be very finely-tuned to their own children, increasing complexity by small steps as the children get older, but nonetheless they may use different styles, such that the older child hears simpler speech.
2. The nature of the fine-tuning may differ for different communicative acts. Averaging MLU across descriptive, directive, playful, and peda-gogical speech may obscure the correlations that exist within each speech style (see Shaffer and Crook 1979).
3. The fine-tuning may be situation-specific, and thus not measurable if situations are mixed or randomly chosen. For example, Snow and Goldfield (1982) analysed the speech of one mother–child pair reading one book over a period of 13 months. The mother's speech became more complex in terms of semantic content with time, especially for those pictures which were discussed recurrently.
4. The fine-tuning may be content-specific. Sachs (1979, 1983) described the way in which parents of one child introduced reference to past events into the conversation at fairly low and constant levels until

27 months, when the child showed appropriate response, after which the frequency increased dramatically. The early parental uses of past tense could be seen as 'not tuned in', but Sachs suggests they functioned as probes which enabled fine-tuning to occur for this content area.

5.   Fine-tuning may need to be assessed within conversational exchanges rather than across all the output of one speaker. Adults shorten their utterances after child responses that indicate non-comprehension (Bohannon and Marquis 1977; Van Kleek and Carpenter 1980; Bohannon, Stine and Ritzenberg 1982; Stine and Bohannon 1983). Thus, fine-tuned utterances are produced, but may constitute a minority of adult utterances.

It seems clear that fine-tuning, to the extent it occurs, is more sensitive to the child's comprehension level than to productive language level (Cross 1978; Clarke-Stewart et al. 1979); is stronger for word choice and content than for syntax (Chapman 1981); and is multiply determined. Chapman (1981) suggests, furthermore, that fine-tuning is unnecessary to provide the child with language input of graded difficulty, since the child's comprehension abilities in any case automatically filter out complexity beyond a certain level (see also Shipley et al. 1969; Snow 1972b). Thus, child listener and adult speaker both function in such a way that the speech that is processed is finely tuned to the child's comprehension level.

3. Stage III: Talking to one another

Assuming that the semantic component of maternal speech is finely adjusted to the child's linguistic ability, how does this happen? By what mechanism do mothers keep their speech content pitched at the right level?

The answer to this question is quite simple, as soon as one attains the seemingly obvious (but for researchers in this field, long awaited) insight that mothers do not talk at children, but with them. A large proportion of maternal utterances are responses to child utterances, and almost all maternal utterances are directly preceded and followed by child utterances. In other words, mothers and children carry on conversations with one another. These are, in fact, very special kinds of conversations, in that the partners are very unequal. The mother can speak the language much better, but the child nonetheless can dominate the conversation, because the mother follows the child's lead in deciding what to talk about. A very common pattern is for the child to introduce a topic and for the mother to make a comment on that topic, or for the child to introduce a topic

and make a comment and for the mother to then expand that comment. Thus, at a semantic level, the mother's speech is very much shaped by the child's linguistic abilities, his cognitive abilities, his ideas and interests.

Interestingly, the above description of child-directed discourse accounts for the occurrence of expansions, the characteristic of maternal speech which was first commented upon by Brown and Bellugi (1964). Expansions are full, correct expressions of the meanings encapsulated in children's telegraphic utterances. They are, thus, the ultimate example of a maternal utterance which is semantically related to the preceding child utterance. It was hypothesized that provision of expansions might greatly aid the acquisition of syntax, since the expansion gives information about the full, correct realization of the child's intended meaning at the time the child wishes to communicate that meaning. Considerable evidence for positive effect of expansions has been found (Malouf and Dodd 1972; Nelson, Carskaddon and Bonvillian 1973; Schumaker 1976; Nelson 1977; Cross 1978; Howell, Schumaker and Sherman 1978; Wells 1980), though provision of extra conversation with the child even without including expansions seems to have an equally beneficial effect (Cazden 1965; Nelson et al. 1973), and the provision of semantic extensions (incorporating the child's topic, but adding new information) seems even more facilitative than simple expansions (Cross 1978; Barnes et al. 1983). It may well be that expansions can provide crucial bits of information about syntax or morphology, but that this information if not available from expansions will be picked up from other sources, especially from utterances related to child-selected topics.

The conversational model proposed briefly above explains a good many of the characteristics of CDS, and seems furthermore to be useful in understanding how CDS can facilitate language development. Seeing children as relatively incompetent conversational partners helps us to understand why CDS is so full of questions (attempts to pass the turn to the child), clarifying questions and expansions (attempts to clarify and upgrade child turns), and limitation to topics of interest to the child. Shugar (1978), for example, refers to mothers and children interacting dyadically to 'create text'. She has described how mothers produce utterances which create context within which very simple child utterances become meaningful parts of the rather complex whole. For example, if the mother says 'Who's just coming in?' and the child answers 'Dada', then the child utterance can be interpreted semantically as referring to an agent of a presently occurring action, whereas the same utterance without the linguistic context might be uninterpretable. Cross (1978), Barnes et al. (1983) and Wells and Robinson (in press) have found that the percentage of maternal utterances which are semantically related to preceding child utterances is the best predictor

of the child's linguistic ability, and Snow, Dubber and DeBlauw (1982) found a high correlation between the percentage of adult speech related to child activities and the child's vocabulary. This implies that children who learn to talk quickly and well have considerable, if not constant, access to semantically related maternal utterances, such as in the following break-fast-table conversation between a 29 month old and his parents:

Child:	pancakes away
	duh duh stomach
Mother:	pancakes away in the stomach, yes, that's right
Child:	eat apples
Mother	eating apples on our pancakes, aren't we?
Child:	on our pancakes
Mother:	you like apples on your pancakes?
Child:	eating apples
	hard
Mother:	what?
	hard to do the apples, isn't it?
Child:	more pancakes
Father:	you want more pancakes?
Child:	those are daddy's
Father:	daddy's gonna have his pancakes now
Child:	ne ne one a daddy's
	ne ne one in the plate
	right there
Father:	you want some more on your plate?

In accord with the findings that semantically contingent utterances promote language development, Bates (1975) has suggested that second children, twins and institutionalized children may learn language more slowly than children whose input comes mainly from adults, because egocentric peers do not provide enough interpretable, semantically relevant messages. But Lieven (1978a,b) has described one mother–child pair where well-constructed dyadic texts were extremely rare: a high proportion of child utterances were not responded to by the mother at all, and the responses which did occur were very often semantically unrelated to the child utterance. They were very likely to be comments like 'Oh, really?' Despite receiving very little semantically relevant speech from her mother, the child in question did eventually learn to talk normally, though her speech at the time Lieven was studying her was highly repetitive, uninformative and difficult to interpret. Thus, though it seems clear that the provision of much semantically relevant speech is advantageous for language acqui-

sition, it has not been proven that access to such speech is crucial to normal language acquisition.

Mothers are able to provide semantically relevant and interpretable speech because they follow up on topics introduced by the child. It seems clear that some mothers will be better at doing this than others, but also that some children will be better at eliciting semantically relevant and interpretable speech than others. Children with poor articulation, for example, will produce fewer interpretable utterances for the mother to expand upon. Children whose speech is highly repetitive, such as the little girl studied by Lieven (1978a), are less interesting to converse with than children who frequently introduce new topics. It is also possible for mother and child to be focused on different aspects of the world, in which case the kinds of comments made by the mother do not match the child's intentions or interests. In such cases, the child's language acquisition can be slowed down (Nelson 1973b).

The kind of semantically relevant and interpretable speech described above begins long before the children themselves begin to talk. This indicates that it is not produced purely in response to utterances from the child. Mothers talking to babies as young as 3 months show many of the same characteristics of CDS as are present in speech to 2 year olds. Some of the characteristics, such as questions, occur with even greater frequency in speech to younger children. The most striking similarity between speech to very young babies and speech to children aged 18 to 36 months is the extent to which the mother's speech is directed by the child's activities. Infant behaviours such as reaching for something, changing gaze direction, laughing, smiling, vocalizing – even burping, coughing and sneezing – can often evoke specific relevant responses from the mother. At 3 months the majority of maternal utterances refer only to the child. By the time the baby is 6 to 8 months old, and is showing many clear signs of interest in objects and activities about him, the maternal utterances also refer to those objects and activities (Snow 1977a). Thus, the semantic steering of maternal speech by the child begins very early, and may be the basis for the child's discovery of some predictable relationship between utterances and events.

It has been suggested that semantically contingent speech to prelinguistic infants is crucial to the infant's discovery of his own potential for communicative intentionality. Trevarthen (1977), for example, has suggested that attribution of intention to infants is prerequisite to infants' intentional action, and furthermore, that infants cannot discover their own capacity for intentionality without the demonstration by adults that their behaviour can be interpreted as intentional.

The mechanism by which semantically contingent speech contributes to language during later stages of development is unclear. The intuitive attractiveness of the finding that semantic contingency promotes language development has somewhat obscured the absence of any hypothesis concerning exactly how it might work to promote language development. For some reason information about the structure of language is more usable by a child if it is presented in utterances which express the child's own intentions or which are related to topics of the child's choice. Adult utterances on adult-selected topics provide information which is in some way less useful, perhaps because children attend to it less fully or comprehend it less well.

The finding that semantically contingent adult speech facilitates language acquisition is a powerful and robust one, but its importance is limited unless it can be linked to an explanation of precisely how and why semantically contingent speech has its facilitative effect. If we wish to claim that language is *learned* as a result of specific experiences the child has, rather than simply triggered by those experiences, then a theory is required in which the functioning of some postulated learning mechanism is made possible by the presence of the facilitative experience. Such a theory has not yet been offered for experiences of semantic contingency, to explain their effects in terms of the working of a learning mechanism. However, consideration of what social experiences facilitate language acquisition may be the best source of clues as to the nature of the language learning mechanisms available to the child. Thus, the importance of the findings concerning the facilitative effects of semantic contingency has not yet been fully exploited.

4. Stage IV: Other ways to do it

Belief in the importance of semantic contingency as the major social facilitator of language acquisition has been somewhat mitigated by research reports of two kinds: (a) ethnographic descriptions of language acquisition and social interaction in non-Western and non-middle-class settings, and (b) postulations of language acquisition mechanisms that rest on social facilitators quite different from semantic contingency. We will discuss each of these in turn.

4.1. Language acquisition in other cultures

The nature of social interaction with children in the cultural contexts most intensely studied (North American and Northern European urban, mostly middle-class families) is highly child-centred. Parents adjust their speech

(and their other behaviour) to their children, both in terms of complexity and in terms of topic. Children are, furthermore, treated as conversational partners and their functioning as conversational partners is encouraged and supported.

Such a willingness to adapt adult speech to children, and such a high regard for the verbal precocity of children, is not, however, universal. In some societies, for example among the Kipsigis of Kenya (Harkness 1977) and rural Blacks of Louisiana (Ward 1971) children's comprehension skill is valued much more highly than their verbal production, and most of the speech addressed to children consists of directives and explanations, rather than questions or comments on their activity. Among the Kaluli of Papua-New Guinea and among Samoans, semantically contingent responses to children are extremely rare, and indeed would be considered inappropriate within the cultures, for a variety of reasons (Ochs and Schieffelin 1984).

Needless to say, Kipsigis, Kaluli and Samoan children, like American and European children, learn to talk, and as far as anyone can tell, learn just as quickly and with no greater rate of failure than those children. They learn without the benefit of semantically contingent speech, clearly demonstrating that semantically contingent speech is not crucial to the language-learning child.

4.2. Other social facilitators

Although Kaluli mothers do not provide their children with semantically contingent speech, it would be incorrect to conclude that they pay no attention to language learning. In fact, the Kaluli believe that quite explicit help and teaching is required if children are to develop beyond their immature language forms into competent speakers. Their techniques for teaching children involve a considerable amount of direct modelling, with instructions to imitate. The utterances presented for imitation are meant to be effective social acts, and are not simplified or otherwise adapted to the child's language level (Schieffelin 1979, 1984). Such models need simply to be uttered by the child, not comprehended. Consider the following conversations (cited in Ochs and Schieffelin 1984), in which the mother directs 27-month-old Wanu in talking to his 5-year-old sister, Binalia, who has been taking too much food:

Mother (to Wanu): Whose is it? Say like that
Wanu (to Binalia): Whose is it?
Mother: Is it yours? Say like that

Wanu:	Is it yours?
Mother:	Who are you? Say like that
Wanu:	Who are you?
Mother:	Did you pick it? Say like that
Wanu:	Did you pick it?
Mother:	My gramma picked it! Say like that
Wanu:	My gramma picked it!
Mother:	This *my gramma* picked. Say like that
Wanu:	This *my gramma* picked

Presumably Wanu does not fully understand the rhetorical force of the utterances he is producing. Nonetheless, he is learning how to use rhetorical questions so as to influence (as in this case) another's behaviour. Samoan children are engaged in very similar sorts of triadic interactions, in which caregivers tell them what to say to a third party (Ochs and Schieffelin 1984).

Although elicited imitation is not generally considered to be an important teaching device by American parents, many children discover imitation as a strategy for expanding their communicative competence (reviewed in Snow 1983). The usefulness of imitation is promoted by the recurrence of events in children's lives, such that utterances previously produced during the event by the adults can be 're-used' by the child (Snow and Goldfield 1983). The recycling of adult utterances in such predictable, recurrent situations is presumably a language acquisition mechanism used even more extensively by Kaluli and Samoan children.

The importance of recurrent situations in promoting children's language development has been emphasized most strongly in work on games and on book reading during the very early period of language acquisition (Bruner 1975a; Ninio and Bruner 1978; Ratner and Bruner 1978). For example, Bruner (1975a) describes how infants can come to communicate effectively using some minimal signal in the course of games like 'Ride a cock horse'. In such games, the mother bounces the baby with a regular rhythm while reciting the first lines of the verse, but gives a 'big bounce' on the last line. After a number of repetitions the mother often pauses before the 'big bounce' until the baby jiggles expectantly. The mother interprets the jiggle as a message to go on. This interpretation probably has two effects: (a) the mother receives the satisfaction of feeling that her baby is communicating with her, and (b) the baby learns that his own behaviours function as communicative signals. Clearly, the recurrence of the game, engineered by the mother's persistence in playing it, is prerequisite both to the effectiveness of the child's signal and to the child's being

able to learn what signal to produce and when. At later ages children learn to take over the adult behaviours that occur at predictable points in the game, also to adopt adult behaviours and utterances in routinized events such as book reading (see Ninio and Bruner 1978).

Semantically contingent adult speech and highly predictable situation-specific adult speech are very different in terms of the cultural norms that underlie them and in terms of the nature of the interaction in which they are embedded. They are identical, however, in terms of a major feature which may be the crucial one: both types of utterance are highly comprehensible even without a complete grammatical analysis. Learnability theories (Pinker 1979; Wexler and Culicover 1980; Braine in press) have postulated that utterance–meaning pairs must be the basis for children's discovery of the rules of grammar. The successful language teaching environment, in this view, is any one that provides sufficient numbers of utterances in contexts such that their meaning can be accurately ascertained from the context. Both semantically contingent and predictable, context-specific utterances have the characteristic of being comprehensible in the absence of a complete linguistic analysis, and both therefore could be expected to promote language acquisition skill.

4.3. Other ways

We have argued that both semantically contingent adult speech and predictable adult speech in recurrent situations can contribute to children's language acquisition, perhaps even through the same mechanism. We do not mean to suggest, however, that these are the only social facilitators in the child's linguistic environment, nor that there is only one language learning mechanism. On the contrary, when a highly complex skill is acquired with a very low failure rate, as language is, one can conclude either that an innate ability essentially accounts for the acquisition, or that there are a number of different mechanisms which all contribute to the acquisition, such that no single one is crucial. We believe that the picture of social facilitation of language acquisition better fits this second explanation than the first – a variety of cognitive mechanisms subserve the acquisition process, each one of which is enabled to function with maximum efficiency by a different aspect of the social-linguistic environment (see Snow and Gilbreath 1983). This explanation seems better because it can account for the facilitative effects found for various features in CDS – for example, syntactic simplicity, use of nouns rather than pronouns, use of utterances with short preverb constituents, offering acceptance of children's attempts at speech, withholding correction, etc. – without suggesting that any of

these features might be crucial. Furthermore, this view makes it easier to understand how language acquisition can occur in such a wide variety of settings (suggesting that it is indifferent to the nature of the social environment) and yet show facilitative effects of various features of the social environment (suggesting paradoxically that it is not at all insensitive to environmental effects).

Research in Western, middle-class settings has concentrated our attention on semantic contingency as the acquisition-facilitator par excellence, to the extent that we know very little about routes to language acquisition other than the formation of sound–meaning pairs. The descriptions of Kaluli children (see above) and some observations of how children use spontaneous imitation (Snow 1981, 1983) suggest that acquiring unanalysed utterances with a conversational (rather than a propositional) meaning and subsequently segmenting and analysing one's own output of those utterances constitutes an alternative route to language. Although the sound–meaning pairs route emphasizes the child's need to achieve an understanding of semantic relations, it seems very likely that some children acquire and work with syntactic frames whose semantics are not fully filled in (e.g. Van der Geest's 1977 subject, who produced utterances like *I am being jumped off it* with the meaning *I am jumping off it*). Imitation and the use of empty syntactic frames are only two of the possible routes to language; there are undoubtedly others which will become evident as studies of language development become less ethnocentric.

5. Conclusion

Research on CDS has too often been of limited value to language acquisition theory because it has been purely descriptive, or because it has been assumed to be relevant only to the theoretical question of nativism versus empiricism. In our view the greatest potential value of research on CDS, and on facilitating features in CDS, is to constrain hypotheses concerning the nature and variety of language learning mechanisms. The finding that any particular feature in the CDS facilitates the speed or ease of language acquisition should be taken as a starting point for hypothesizing a language acquisition mechanism that operates better because of that feature. In the past, research that has emphasized the social aspects of language development has been too little integrated with (has perhaps even been seen as opposed to) research on the cognitive mechanisms relevant to language development. It is, of course, a commonplace to point out that both a functioning organism and an appropriate environment are prerequisite to

normal development, and that consequently the social and the cognitive explanations are complementary rather than opposed.

Beyond this, though, hypotheses about the cognitive mechanisms subserving language acquisition have not taken into account data about facilitating features in the child's social environment – surely a rich source of information about constraints on the learning devices which are available. To cite only a few examples: (a) evidence that children can perform immediate and delayed imitations of complex adult utterances in situationally appropriate ways provides information about the size and the nature of the memory capacities young children use in learning language; (b) evidence that sentence forms which prepose auxiliaries contribute to the learning of the auxiliary system more than sentences with non-initial auxiliaries suggests that initial elements are more salient, easier to understand and / or remember; (c) evidence that certain forms which are modelled primarily, but not exclusively, within a single speech act category are acquired for use only to express that speech act implies that children operate with pragmatic, speech act-based categories during the early stages of language acquisition; (d) evidence that children acquire and generalize regular forms even when many irregular forms are also modelled in the input suggests that the language learning mechanism is frequency-sensitive. Similarly, information that certain features of the CDS have no effect on language acquisition, or can facilitate its acquisition only during a restricted stage of development (for example, extreme syntactic simplicity seems to be facilitative only during the one-word stage) also constrains hypotheses about the nature of the language learning mechanisms. A variety of facilitative effects implies a variety of learning mechanisms, all operating whenever the enabling conditions hold. Such a picture is consonant with the most remarkable fact about language acquisition – its reliable occurrence in a wide variety of social settings.

5. Learnability

Martin Atkinson

1. Introduction

The publication of Wexler and Culicover's *Formal principles of language acquisition* (1980) signified the arrival of learnability theory as a central concern for those interested in constructing explanatory theories of language development. Before this, Wexler and his associates had produced a series of papers (Hamburger and Wexler 1975; Wexler, Culicover and Hamburger 1975; Culicover and Wexler 1977) which, while demonstrating the feasibility of the formal study of language learning, had conclusions which were hardly arresting for the student of child language. Since 1980 learnability has been located firmly at the centre of a constellation of related concepts which has come to dominate much discussion in linguistics and language acquisition. This constellation includes the logical problem of language acquisition, the nature of the data available to the learner, restrictiveness in linguistic theory and parameter setting and markedness. One purpose of this chapter is to map out this area of enquiry, drawing attention to some of the major conclusions and, more importantly, methods of argumentation. This involves construing learnability broadly, so as to encompass considerations which do not arise in the context of a fully formalized theory. Additionally, in the final section of the chapter I shall discuss what seem to me to be the most serious reservations about the significance of the achievements of learnability theory for the traditional study of first language acquisition.

In an earlier paper (Atkinson 1983) I drew attention to what some might regard as a puzzling phenomenon in language acquisition research: the existence of two, largely disjoint, sets of scholars both professing a deep interest in language development but having nothing in common as far as research goals, strategies of procedure and conclusions are concerned. Most strikingly, the two groups are distinguished by the fact that the more populous one devotes a good deal of its energy to conducting empirical work with children whereas the other eschews such enquiry entirely. I

referred to members of the former group as First Language Acquisition Theorists, acronymized to FLATs, and antonymic considerations suggested the label SHARPs for the latter group. Given this position, it is natural to enquire whether the activities of the two groups are, as it might appear to some, of no mutual concern, or, indeed, whether the concerns of one group are somehow improper from the alternative perspective. I hope to be able to throw some light on these issues.

It is useful to begin by establishing the limitations of the discussion that follows. Most generally, learnability theory can be viewed as working within the abstract framework schematized as (1):

(1) (i) assumptions are made about the mental representation of the end-point of some organism's development in some domain
(ii) assumptions are made about the data to which the organism has access in its development in this domain
(iii) assumptions are made about the procedures with which the organism operates on the data and manipulates its mental representation of the domain

Significant and interesting problems arise when it can be demonstrated that a set of assumptions of this kind is not adequate, in the sense that mental representations of the specified kind cannot arise in an organism equipped with the stated procedures and having access to the assumed data. In such a situation, a number of strategies are available to the theorist: modifications of the assumptions under (1ii), leading to a richer view on the nature of the available data; modifications of the assumptions under (1iii), leading to the postulation of a more powerful learning procedure; a reduction of what the organism has to learn regarding the representation in (1i) by restricting the set of alternatives it needs to consider, so that a representation of the required kind can still arise with the original assumptions of (1ii) and (1iii) intact. This third possibility has been the one most eagerly followed by workers in this field, as the subsequent discussion will make clear. A further option, which is not usually considered, is that the assumptions under (1i) are simply wrong.

This framework is perfectly general and, while it has only received significant attention in the context of the study of language, there is no principled reason why it should not be extended to other cognitive domains and, indeed, to nonhuman development.

Within the study of language, the vast majority of relevant arguments have appeared in connection with syntax and have taken for granted that the end-point of syntactic development is best characterized in terms of the possession of a mental representation of a generative grammar. The

details of this generative grammar have differed from one study to the next and this has led to corresponding differences in the learnability problems considered. In what follows, in section 2 I shall restrict myself to exposition of the theory developed in Wexler and Culicover (1980) and based on the Standard Theory transformational grammar of Chomsky (1965). Section 3 will be concerned with the role of learnability in the Revised Extended Standard Theory and its progeny; we shall see problems with a quite different complexion arising in this framework. For reasons of space, I shall not discuss lexical-functional grammar (but see Pinker 1982), nor generalized phrase structure grammar (for some preliminary remarks, see Gazdar 1982: 132–3; Wexler 1981: 48). Phonological and semantic development also fall outside the scope of this chapter. Again, there is no issue of principle here and every reason to believe that these domains could be approached in terms of the schema in (1). However, the existing literature is slight and, in my view, unexciting; for phonology, see Dresher (1981a,b) and McCarthy (1981a), and for semantics, Hornstein (1981).

2. Learnability and Standard Theory transformational grammar

Gold (1967) distinguishes two modes of data presentation corresponding to distinct assumptions about the data to which the learner has access. The first, text-presentation, sees the learner as confronted at each moment with only grammatical strings from the language being learned; this corresponds to the popular assumption that the learner's primary data contain no negative information. In informant-presentation, on the other hand, the learner is presented at each moment with either a grammatical string or an ungrammatical string and is also informed as to which category the string belongs. Of course, this is equivalent to the assumption that negative information occurs in the primary data. Gold further assumed that learnability should be equated with identifiability in the limit, and a class of languages was said to be identifiable in the limit if the learner could be guaranteed after a finite time to guess the language to which he was being exposed and thereafter maintain his guess through subsequent presentations of data.[1] With this minimal framework Gold established some rather surprising results. In particular, he was able to show that with text-presentation all the familiar classes of languages from the Chomsky hierarchy (Chomsky 1963) are unlearnable. With informant-presentation things are rather better, the classes being learnable up to the class of primitive recursive languages; but a large body of opinion has it that informant-presentation is not a sound assumption, i.e. the child does not, in fact, benefit from expo-

sure to ungrammatical strings labelled as such.[2] Thus, it is the first of these results which has been viewed as more significant, and what this result appears to show is that a learner, equipped with the knowledge that he is being exposed to, say, a context-free language, cannot be guaranteed in a finite time to guess a context-free grammar which weakly generates the input language. The only class of languages which is learnable under Gold's assumptions is the class of finite cardinality languages.[3]

It is important to emphasize that Gold's results obtain, not because some of the languages in the relevant classes are of infinite cardinality, nor because there is an infinite number of languages in the classes. What is vital is that there should be certain algebraic relations between languages in unlearnable classes and these relations exist for the well-known classes referred to above. For an example of an infinite class of infinite languages learnable according to Gold's criterion, and for a characterization theorem for classes of unlearnable languages, the reader can consult Wexler and Culicover (1980: 43–6).

Given the algebraic nature of the difficulty, it immediately follows that any superset of a set of unlearnable languages is also going to be unlearnable on these assumptions, and it is from this point that Wexler and Culicover develop Gold's ideas. Standard Theory transformational grammar assumes a context-free base and a relatively unconstrained transformational component. If, counter to what was actually the case, we allow the base to be any context-free grammar, and if we accept that a context-free grammar with no transformational component is degenerately a Standard Theory transformational grammar, it immediately follows that the class of languages which can be generated by Standard Theory grammars is unlearnable; this class will be a superset of the set of context-free languages. Confronted with this conclusion, as pointed out in section 1, there are several options open to the theorist. First, assumptions about the data available to the learner may be revised. A radical move in this direction would reintroduce negative information but, as already mentioned, workers in this area have seen no justification for such a step. Wexler and Culicover themselves do eventually subscribe to a different view of the data from that necessary for Gold's demonstrations, but this is a consequence of their redefining the nature of the problem rather than a direct response to it. Second, it might be possible to revise assumptions about the learning procedure. Unfortunately this is not true in the case of Gold's negative results, as these results obtain even if the learner is equipped with an enumeration procedure for the relevant class of languages.[4] Opposed to enumeration procedures are heuristic procedures which, while they may be more likely to make the correct choice earlier, are also not guaranteed to succeed,

if, indeed, success can be guaranteed (see Pinker 1979 for a critical discussion of heuristic learning procedures). Gold's criterion of identifiability in the limit requires a guarantee and the fact that enumeration cannot provide such a guarantee is proof that no other procedure can. The third possible response to the unlearnability of the class of transformational languages being considered is somehow to constrain the set of hypotheses available to the learner and, as we shall see in the next section, this is the direction in which Chomsky's own work and that of his recent co-workers has developed. It is also a characteristic of the theory of learnability that Wexler and Culicover go on to advance, although here, just as with their views on the data available to the learner, this appears to be in part a consequence of their reconstrual of the problem. Note further that once it is admitted that constraints could be placed on the set of hypotheses the learner might consider within a transformational framework, the same point could be made regarding, say, the class of context-free languages. As pointed out by Lasnik (1981a) and Berwick and Weinberg (1982), the class of possible human languages is not only bounded from above but also from below, since, to make the point most obviously, the finite cardinality languages are not possible human languages. It follows that attempts to identify the class of possible human languages with some concentric circle in the familiar doughnut represented in figure 1 is misguided. Additionally, Wexler's (1981) suggestion that Gazdar's (1982) theory of generalized phrase structure grammar does not have the desirable properties Gazdar claims for it in terms of learnability is not clearly correct. It would only be correct if Gazdar did not recognize that there are context-free languages which are not possible human languages and claimed his theory to be extensionally equivalent to the unconstrained theory of context-free grammar.

How, then, do Wexler and Culicover respond to the problem of unlearnability? They do not contemplate radically restricting the transformational component of grammars, as they believe that this would involve too considerable a change in the role of transformations; restrictions do play a role in the theory, but, as mentioned above, this is a consequence of other decisions. The first move is to exploit the fact that a Standard Theory grammar consists of a base and a transformational component by assuming that learning the base presents no problems (perhaps it is universal) and pursue the learnability of transformational components. The fundamental idea is that a transformational component can be viewed as a function mapping base-generated structures to surface structures (in fact, Wexler and Culicover's work has always related to surface strings, not structures). Consideration of functions gives rise to the notion of function-learnability

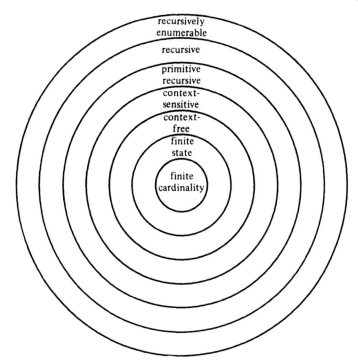

Figure 1. Classes of languages and their relationship

and we say that a set of functions is function-learnable if a learning procedure exists which can guarantee choice of the correct function from the
set after a finite number of argument-value pairs from the function have
been presented to the learner.

Given this definition, any enumerable class of functions is function-learnable. This is easy to see: assume that the learner has a particular function
as his guess at a certain point in the learning sequence and that he is presented with a new datum in the form of an argument-value pair. Either
the new datum is consistent with the current function, in which case no
action is taken, or it is not, in which case the learner continues through
his enumeration of the functions until he finds one which is consistent
with the new datum and all previous data. This function becomes the new
guess. As the set of functions is enumerable, the correct one appears somewhere in the enumeration and the learner will eventually get to it. From
this point onwards there will be no inconsistency between the guessed function and data and the learner will retain the correct function as his guess.

The next step in the argument is to show that the class of transformational components defined on the presumed base is enumerable, and this is achieved by first showing that the class of possible transformations is enumerable and by then using properties of this enumeration to effectively index sets of transformations, i.e. transformational components. Accordingly, the set of transformational components is function-learnable on the assumption that the learner is presented with data consisting of an argument of the function (a base structure) and a corresponding value (a surface string). Such data are referred to as (b, s) pairs. It would appear, therefore, that we have an easily accessible and positive answer to our enquiry into the learnability of transformational components. Why not stop here?

An interesting mode of argumentation has been pioneered by learnability theorists in answer to this question. In the above discussion of function-learnability no attempt was made to take account of limiting characteristics of the learner. In particular, the presumed enumeration procedure is going to place an intolerable strain on the memory mechanism; not only must the learner match the current datum against his transformational component, but, if he gets a mismatch he must run through the enumeration and have available all previous data against which to test transformational components. There is, therefore, a strong case for weakening the learning procedure; but this may carry a price, in that the transformational components may cease to be learnable with more realistic assumptions of this nature. As another illustration of this type of argument, we can note that there are those (e.g. Levelt 1974) who have argued that simplification of the data available to the learner will facilitate learning. However, if simplification is identified with less exemplification of complex structural principles, it should be clear that such simplification would make the learning of systems which manifest such principles even more puzzling. For a clear discussion of this point, see Wanner and Gleitman (1982: 39–40). The consequences of making assumptions more realistic in this fashion are illustrated by Wexler and Culicover's degree-2 learnability proof.

The modifications in the learning procedure away from enumeration are as follows. For any (b, s) datum for which the learner's current component works, there is no change in the component, i.e. there is no learning from such data. If, however, the learner's transformational component yields s' when applied to b and $s' \neq s$, a modification will take place in the component which will consist of either the rejection of a current transformation or the hypothesization of a new one. Wexler and Culicover provide explicit criteria for deciding which transformational rules are available for rejection and hypothesization for any datum and ensure that the two sets are finite. Choices between rejection and hypothesization of any available rule are

then equiprobable. It should be clear that such a procedure differs from enumeration, not only in terms of its implications for the learner's memory and processing capacity but also in terms of what gets changed in a developmental sequence. For enumeration, whole transformational components are rejected and hypothesized on the basis of a single datum; in the Wexler and Culicover proposal, single rules get changed and some notion of gradualness enters the system.

There is one further modification in the model which it is necessary to introduce in order to comprehend Wexler and Culicover's major result. Recall that learning only takes place when the learner's transformational component makes an error on a (b, s) datum. Now, suppose that there is an incorrect transformation in the learner's component but that it only leads to an error on inordinately long and complex sentences. As a matter of fact, adults do not expose their children to such sentences and, therefore, if the system is not to retain the mistaken transformation, there must be some assurance that erroneous hypotheses will be exposed on relatively simple data (additionally, the probabilistic model of data presentation assumed by Wexler and Culicover requires some finite upper bound on the complexity of sentences on which errors are revealed).

Thus, there are two ways in which Wexler and Culicover appear to be making their theory more readily compatible with the facts about learners and their linguistic environments. The consequences of weakening the learning procedure and making the data less rich are that the set of hypotheses available to the learner has to be reduced if learnability is still to be guaranteed, and what this amounts to is that transformational rules are no longer assumed to operate in an unconstrained fashion. Learnability can only be preserved if the rules obey a number of principles, the most important of which are the *binary principle*, a close relation of *subjacency* (Chomsky 1973), and the *freezing principle*. Wexler and Culicover go to great lengths to provide independent linguistic support for these principles, seeing the convergence of learnability arguments and traditional linguistic arguments as a particularly attractive outcome (for further work along these lines, see Williams 1981b). The major result of their study can now be stated: the class of transformational components on a universal base satisfying a number of principles including the binary principle and the freezing principle is learnable by a rejection and hypothesization learning procedure on the basis of exposure to data which do not involve more than two levels of sentential embedding – this is degree-2 learnability.

It seems to me that the argumentation leading to the above result is demonstrative, although many controversial assumptions are made along the way. Some of these are raised and honestly discussed by the authors

themselves (see also Pinker 1979; Atkinson 1982: ch 10). From the perspective of this chapter, the most important of these are that the learner is exposed to (b, s) pairs as primary data and that his primary data contain no negative information. This second assumption is shared by those working within a more restricted syntactic framework.

3. Does learnability require learnability theory?

In the previous section I noted that Wexler and Culicover explicitly reject a vastly attenuated role for transformations. However, such an attenuated role is commonplace in a number of contemporary approaches to syntactic theory and with it has come a concern with learnability in the context of the study of the logical problem of language acquisition. General attempts to constrain the form and functioning of rules are now fairly commonplace (see, for example, Emonds 1976; Lasnik 1981b); but in this section I wish to consider arguments which are quite limited in scope and very direct in their consequences for acquisition. Typically, they can be illustrated by schemas (2) and (3):

(2) Premise 1:   The learner's primary data suggest generalization G
     Premise 2:   The learner does not make G

     Conclusion: The learner must be initially informed in such a way that he will never consider a hypothesis permitting the formulation of G

(3) Premise 1:   To decide that rules of grammar allow a particular option, it would be necessary to have access to certain data
     Premise 2:   The learner does not have access to the data in question

     Conclusion: The learner does not consider the option of Premise 1 in his hypotheses

I shall now illustrate these argument forms. Baker (1979, 1981) provides some of the best-presented instances of (2). In the earlier paper, he considers primary data such as the following:

(4) a. Gordon gave a present to Halcyon
     b. Gordon gave Halcyon a present

(5) a. Gordon sent a present to Halcyon
     b. Gordon sent Halcyon a present

If we assume that the learner's primary data include such sentences, and

if we further suppose that he is capable of formulating transformations in a fairly unconstrained fashion, we might expect the hypothesization of a transformation (dative movement) along the lines of (6) to express the apparent generalization:

(6) $NP - V - NP - to - NP \Rightarrow 1 \quad 2 \quad 5+3 \quad \emptyset \quad \emptyset$
      $\quad\quad 1 \quad\;\; 2 \quad\; 3 \quad\;\; 4 \quad\; 5$

But, of course, as is well known, the generalization is too powerful, as is demonstrated by the following data:

(7)   a. Gordon said something horrible to Halcyon
      b. *Gordon said Halcyon something horrible

(8)   a. Gordon donated his letters to the library
      b. *Gordon donated the library his letters

The linguist has access to such judgements as those contained in (7b) and (8b) and can begin to think of ways of patching up his analysis. Baker, however, subscribes to the standard view that the primary data contain no negative information. If this is correct, the child receives no information about (7b) and (8b) and could be expected to maintain the too powerful generalization expressed in (6). Demonstrably the child does not maintain this generalization, as he grows into an adult who shares Baker's feelings about (7b) and (8b). How can this puzzle be resolved?

There are two questions to consider. Is there an alternative analysis to the transformational one which is not too general? If there is, how is it possible to ensure that the learner opts for this rather than the transformational one?

With regard to the first question, not surprisingly in a climate in which transformational rules are playing a less important part in linguistic analyses, Baker adopts a lexicalist analysis which, in order to answer his point, has to be extremely conservative. According to this analysis, the learner gradually builds up subcategorization frames in his lexical entries and does this solely on the basis of being exposed to lexical items appearing in the appropriate frames. So, a verb like *send* would have a partial entry, as in (9):

(9)   *send:* (____NP *to* NP), (____NP NP)

whereas a verb such as *say* will have only one of these frames in its lexical entry, as in (10):

(10)   *say:* (____NP *to* NP)

From our present perspective, the second question is more interesting: assuming the learner's initial assumptions allow the formulation of hypotheses such as those expressed by (6) – and we should note that Baker is not wishing to rule out transformations entirely – what is to stop him formulating such a hypothesis rather than developing his lexical entries along the lines of (9) and (10)? The answer is: nothing. Accordingly, Baker has to legislate to rule out (6), and the way in which he does this is to disallow transformations which delete lexically specified material (in this case *to*) except under identity. This constraint is then built into the learner as part of the solution of the logical problem of language acquisition.

Turning now to (3), we can illustrate this using the vexed question of optionality and obligatoriness of rules. Consider a situation in which a learner can formulate hypotheses including both optional and obligatory rules, and suppose that a linguist puts forward the view that R_1 is optional and R_2 obligatory. The linguist might motivate this by drawing attention to the following pattern:

(11) a. A derivation including an application of R_1 terminates in S_1
      b. The same derivation not including an application of R_1 terminates in S_2
(12) a. A derivation including an application of R_2 terminates in S_3
      b. The same derivation not including an application of R_2 terminates in *S_4

If we now make the standard assumption that the primary data contain no negative information, the learner will not have access to the crucial piece of information in (12b), i.e. that S_4 is ill-formed. To avoid this problem it is necessary to assume either that all rules are optional or that all rules are obligatory. The usual course of action has been to assume optionality, although with either assumption the dilemma of (11) and (12) cannot arise. An argument with identical structure can be constructed against the theory of grammar permitting extrinsically ordered rules.

The sort of argumentation I have exemplified above can be extended to lead us into the area of the theory of markedness. A straightforward example appears in Chomsky and Lasnik (1977). They consider NPs like those in (13):

(13) a. the book which you bought
      b. the book that you bought

Within the framework they are assuming, all rules are optional including *wh*-movement and deletion in the complementizer. Consistent with this

framework is the fact that (14) is well-formed:

(14) the book you bought

However, it would also appear to follow that (15) is well-formed, with none of the optional deletions having taken place:

(15) *the book which that you bought

This is now problematic, as the usual assumption about primary data demands that the learner does not receive negative information about the status of (15). As a consequence, we would anticipate the formulation of generalizations consistent with the assumed rule system, and such generalizations would predict that (15) is well-formed. How are we to prevent this transparently incorrect prediction from arising? So far there is nothing here to distinguish the argument from that of Baker considered above; and Chomsky and Lasnik's solution, while not amounting to a general constraint in the manner of Baker's, has the same logical force in that it legislates against certain possibilities. This solution amounts to the formulation of a set of filters, one of which is the multiply-filled COMP filter along the lines of (16):

(16) $*_{\text{COMP}}[wh\text{-phrase} - \text{complementizer}]$

According to this proposal, the rules of grammar are kept maximally simple at the cost of the introduction of (16) as a constraint on the learner's hypotheses. However, there is a further problem in this case.

If (16) has the status ascribed to it by Chomsky and Lasnik, it ought to follow that wh-phrase–complementizer sequences are universally ill-formed. But this is not so, and Urdu (Radford 1979) and Middle English (White 1981) are known exceptions. It would appear, then, that nothing has been gained by the postulation of (16), as negative evidence will be necessary to learn it because of its language-specificity. Now comes the additional layer of the argument. Chomsky and Lasnik continue to maintain that (16) constitutes a constraint on the set of hypotheses entertained by the learner, but it is a constraint which can be shown to be inoperative in the learner's language by *positive* evidence; it represents the unmarked case. Thus, the child learning Modern English will never be provided with evidence to show that the filter does not operate in the language and will continue to assume that it does. What we find, then, within this approach is a set of inviolable constraints, and alongside this a set of constraints which constitute unmarked options and which require contradiction from positive data in order to become inoperative.

One might at this stage pause for a moment and consider the sense of markedness which is being employed in this type of argument (for further examples see, among others, Lasnik 1981c). White (1981) maintains that the relevant sense of markedness is captured by noting that the learner needs more complex information to suppress the operation of (16) than if he is acquiring a language which abides by it. Given the way the argument has been constructed, this is splendidly unilluminating. Furthermore, one might suggest that at variance with the above usage of markedness is the proposal that exceptions to general rules are marked. On this interpretation it ought to follow that the *presence* of (16) in the grammar of a language represents the marked case, since (16) is motivated by a desire to deal with exceptions to a perfectly general set of rules. The extent to which this tension exists between different senses of markedness in other cases is, perhaps, a topic worth looking into.

The above arguments constitute only a small sample of those which have appeared in the literature in the last few years. I believe that they are reasonably representative and convey something of the attempt to construct a simple and general theory of grammar with a very restricted set of options for the learner. The learning of a transformational component remained a significant task within Wexler and Culicover's approach as the complexity of their theory amply testifies. Restriction of the transformational component to the single schema *move α*, and comparable restrictions in other components of the grammar, have led some to the conclusion that the learning procedure part of the overall model is straightforward and uninteresting. This attitude also demands, of course, that more information has to be provided for the learner as part of the solution of the logical problem of language acquisition. To be a little more specific, Koster (1979) has suggested that within the approach being discussed here the learner has to select a system of core grammar from a finite and possibly very small number of alternatives. The base will consist of some variety of X-bar ($\bar{\mathrm{X}}$) theory and variability across languages here will be minimal. The transformational component only permits variation in the identity of $α$. Conditions on logical form will be near universal, variation perhaps being allowed as far as the set of bounding nodes is concerned (Chomsky 1981c). The variation which is allowed amounts to the specification of a set of parameters the values of which are to be set by experience. Furthermore, there may be implicational relations between such parameters so that fixing the value of one of them has automatic consequences for the values of others.

Roeper (1981), following Williams (1981c), provides a clear example based on the correlation between Verb–Object / Object–Verb order and whether a language is prepositional or postpositional, the idea being that

experience of either VP or PP order will be sufficient to fix the other. Again, of course, markedness considerations might upset such implicational parameter fixing, but this would be consistent with the suggestion that more complex experience is necessary to fix marked alternatives. The correlation itself can be seen as following from higher-order choices within the $\bar{X}$ system and, once these are made, the unmarked word order characteristics of the language will follow (see Huang 1982 for an insightful analysis of Chinese word order along these lines). Of course, this is all extremely speculative, but I am less concerned here with correctness than with style of argumentation.

I hope that enough has now been said for the reader to have a feel for the major differences between a theory of learnability like Wexler and Culicover's which includes a significant learning procedure confronted with an infinite set of alternatives, and the proposals of Chomsky, Koster and others which point to the triviality of learning procedures within a very restricted theory of grammar. Both approaches are nativist, and it seems perfectly appropriate to see the latter as more strongly nativist than the former, to the extent that the former does admit a substantial role for learning. Incidentally, the extent to which it is appropriate to regard what goes on in the Wexler and Culicover model as learning as opposed to the inductive fixation of belief (Fodor 1975, 1980a) is not at all clear. An undoubted advantage of the Wexler and Culicover approach is that they have developed a complete theory, whereas it remains for those working within the attenuated model of syntax to provide a detailed specification of varieties of triggers (see Roeper 1982a for some very preliminary remarks), the way in which parameters are fixed and possible implicational relations between parameters (although, see Berwick 1981, Berwick and Weinberg 1983, for an implemented developmental parser which incorporates many of the features we have been discussing here).

4. Evaluation

The reader who has always believed that the study of language acquisition necessarily involves empirical work with small children may be rather puzzled by the content of this chapter so far; very far-reaching claims are being considered about the nature of language acquisition but empirical work of the traditional kind has not figured in the discussion at all. In terms of the distinction I drew in section 1, it is SHARP literature and SHARP arguments that we have been considering. What are FLATs to make of all this?

It seems to me that there are two very negative lines that one could

adopt on this, neither of which I would want to support. The first, echoes of which can be found throughout the SHARP literature (e.g. Baker 1979: 533n; Wexler and Culicover 1980: 12) simply recognizes the existence of the two groups and makes more or less categorical recommendations that SHARPs need not bother themselves with whatever it is that FLATs are up to. Whether FLATs are doing anything interesting does not get systematically discussed in these sources, although it is not difficult to discern attitudes ranging from tolerance to indifference (see, e.g. Hornstein and Lightfoot 1981: 23). Thus, FLATs and SHARPs might continue to live their separate lives.

The second attitude, which I have not been able to locate in print, is to maintain that the success of the SHARP enterprise would have the effect of rendering FLATs superfluous. To see the cogency of this view one has only to note that most FLATs would claim to be in the business of studying the learning of language in some significant sense of 'learn'. But the more SHARPs succeed, the fewer learning problems there are, and, as we have seen in the previous section, these might be quite trivial. Even when a theory has a significant learning component, it may not be appropriate to talk about what goes on as learning and, courtesy of Fodor, this may go for everything we have been used to thinking of as learning. Such a prognosis suggests that developmental FLATs everywhere should, perhaps, turn to the situations vacant column. I must now say why I do not wish to subscribe to such gloomy predictions, while at the same time I do feel that FLATs have to pull their socks up.

Consider the first perspective. Can FLATs and SHARPs just go their own ways? I believe that FLATs have to take seriously the sort of work we have been looking at in this chapter. In Atkinson (1982) I insisted that a criterion of adequacy which has to be imposed on (FLAT) developmental theories was that proposals representing particular 'stages' of development had to be constructed with some appropriate general theory in mind. I also complained repeatedly that this criterion was not satisfied by a large number of the proposals I considered there. Now, while in this chapter we have not been considering developmental theories as such, we have been discussing proposals which identify themselves firmly with some reasonably explicit theoretical position. Of course, with such works as Tavakolian (1981), there appears to be a growing number of FLATs who can get away with being SHARPs and I propose that this is a good thing. Note that this is not to subscribe to any single claim or interpretation appearing in such work, nor, indeed, to the correctness of the presupposed theory. On the whole, it is difficult to formulate FLAT predictions on SHARP arguments and even more difficult to offer findings which SHARPs would

recognize as significant. In addition to the papers in Tavakolian's book, I might mention Phinney (1981a), Roeper (1982a) and, as somewhat distantly related to the Wexler and Culicover framework, Hamburger (1980). FLATs have to keep trying, I feel. Can a converse responsibility be argued for?

In the course of our discussion I have tried to draw attention to the assumptions which are vital to the sort of argument we have considered. Firstly, Wexler and Culicover assume that the data available to the learner consist of (b, s) pairs, b being a base structure and s a corresponding surface string. Both aspects of this assumption are problematic, s because it takes for granted a good deal of unspecified pre-analysis, and b because its availability depends on the learner being able to work out the meaning of an utterance from the situation in which it is used and then project the base structure from the meaning. Koster (1979) is one commentator who finds the suggestion that meanings are determinate on the basis of situations totally implausible on conceptual grounds. Yet most workers in the field are convinced that something like this must be the case at least some of the time, and a summary of empirical work relating to this mapping from situation to meaning can be found in Wanner and Gleitman (1982). Suffice it to say here that a great deal of FLAT research remains necessary before the plausibility of this aspect of the assumption can be assessed with confidence. Wanner and Gleitman also cite evidence relevant to the pre-analysis problem, citing work on the extraction of phonetic information from the acoustic waveform (see also J. Miller and Eimas 1983) and suggesting that stress may be an important variable in understanding how the input to the learner gets segmented into words and phrases. As the authors admit, there are profound difficulties to do with the generality of this suggestion, but clearly they are addressing the right question from the standpoint of learnability theory.

Common to all arguments and, therefore, especially significant, is the assumption that the learner receives no negative information. Justification for this assumption is often seen by SHARPs as coming from Brown and Hanlon (1970), in which the authors showed that parental expression of approval was not contingent on the syntactic well-formedness of the child's utterances. Additional support is sometimes adduced by citing McNeill (1966a) on the non-efficacy of correction on the speech of a child, and Brown, Cazden and Bellugi (1969) who reported a similar lack of potency for parental expansion. It seems to me that neither of these two studies address the point directly enough to carry much weight. What is at issue is first the *existence* of direct or indirect correction and second, some recognition by the child that he is being corrected. Correction could exist and could be seen as correction by the child without having any short-term

effects on particular structures (McNeill) or long-term effects on syntactic development in general (Brown *et al.*). The important study, then, remains Brown and Hanlon's.

I believe that at the moment the most one can say is that some caution is justified. Most importantly, perhaps, Brown and Hanlon's study was concerned only with young children (samples from Stages II and V of the Harvard project were analysed). This may not seem important until one takes account of the fact that a large number of arguments of the type considered in section 3 refer to fairly complex structures which would not appear anyway in the Brown and Hanlon materials. It is possible that in the later development of the child, particularly in school, there is much more syntactic correction. Furthermore, Moerk (1983) and Platt and Mac-Whinney (1983) have recently argued, from quite different perspectives, that the preschool child may receive rather more negative information than was previously suspected. Again, it seems to me that neither of these studies attacks the problem directly enough for anything to be concluded. If they are correct in claiming that exposure to negative information exists, nothing necessarily follows; as mentioned above, it has to be seen as negative information by the child and, presumably, it has to relate systematically to the sort of problems SHARPs have considered. This latter requirement is not met. Despite the inconclusiveness of this discussion, I believe that there will have to be further FLAT investigation of this area in the future.

It is, perhaps, also important that FLATs should curb SHARP excesses in certain respects. Baker (1979), having offered his lexicalist alternative to the transformational analysis of dative movement verbs, claims that his analysis does not suggest the incorrect generalization and that children do not produce instances of the incorrect generalization, e.g. such utterances as (17):

(17) I said mummy night-night

But I have attested (17) and I would be extremely surprised to be unique in this respect. More worrying, however, there is no reason not to expect the incorrect generalization on the basis of the lexicalist analysis. The model of morphological / syntactic development recently advanced by Maratsos depends upon the child generalizing across syntactic frames in exactly this way (Maratsos 1979, 1982; Maratsos and Chalkley 1980). It would be perverse to deny the child's propensity to generalize in just this situation. If this much is admitted, Baker's solution is no better off than the transformational analysis he starts by opposing.

Chomsky (1980a), in a discussion of the specified subject constraint, says categorically that children never interpret (18) as well-formed with

the interpretation that 'each of the candidates wanted me to vote for the other':

(18) The candidates wanted me to vote for each other

But, insofar as I have investigated this informally, this is precisely what children do do without hesitation round about the age of 11. There is, of course, a standard response to such an observation, to the effect that the 'understanding' that such children are achieving is not a result of the exercise of just the language faculty but of its interaction with other cognitive systems. This may be true, but it does ring rather hollow if it is not accompanied by at least an outline of how such systems might interact to give the described outcome. It is also the case that Chomsky's discussion contains no hint of such an interaction.

Another interesting issue concerning *each other* interpretation is raised by Matthei's (1981) study in which he asked children (4;2–6;6) to act out sentences like (19):

(19) The chickens wanted the pigs to tickle each other

Over 60 per cent of his subjects made the chickens tickle the pigs and *vice versa*, suggesting to Matthei that here we have a violation of the specified subject constraint with *the chickens* acting as antecedent for *each other* over the specified subject *the pigs*. As the specified subject constraint is part of Chomsky's solution to the logical problem of language acquisition, it ought not to be learned, and markedness considerations are no use here. Matthei claims that his evidence shows that it is learned. Chomsky, cited in White (1981), points out in response that Matthei's subjects are not treating *the chickens* as antecedent of *each other*; if they were, asymmetrical tickling from pigs to chickens should result. Rather, the children's behaviour is more consistent with them interpreting (19) as if it had a conjoined subject and no embedding, as in (20):

(20) The chickens and the pigs tickled each other

If this is correct, there is no violation of the specified subject constraint as far as the child's interpretation of the stimulus sentence is concerned. The moral is clear: a great deal more attention needs to be paid to understanding how the child interprets his linguistic environment, as sensible discussion of the nature of the data available to the learner only makes sense in the context of such understanding.

Clearly, the stance that Chomsky and some of his associates have recently adopted on the status of language as an epiphenomenon resulting from the interaction of core grammar with a number of other systems can be

viewed as insulating the theory from traditional psychological enquiry. This is not a stance which I find objectionable, but it does have a consequence which is, I believe, of some importance to this chapter. Koster (1979), in his discussion of the nature of primary data, has the clearest statement of what concerns me. Since core grammar does not generate a language directly, it would appear to follow that instances of a language, even if all positive as the standard assumption has it, are not directly relevant to the construction of core grammar. As Koster so revealingly puts it (p. 13):

> In conclusion, we may say that the primary data form an intriguing, but relatively mysterious aspect of the learnability concept. *We simply do not know what to look for*, and we will never know unless we are willing to give priority to the development of richly articulated and narrowly constrained hypotheses about the initial state of the language learning organism [my emphasis – MA]

But, as section 3 has argued, the development of the hypotheses Koster talks about depends upon making assumptions about the primary data. One has to be careful, but this circle looks a bit vicious![5]

In conclusion, I can return to the second prognosis for FLAT futures – that the dole queue awaits. Clearly, so long as the type of uncertainty voiced by Koster exists, there is little prospect of this. However, I would hope that FLAT research can, in the future, align itself with SHARP issues rather more than has recently been the case. Generally, it should not be concerned with theoretically unmotivated empirical procedures, and, insofar as it focuses on the characteristics of the data available to the learner, it should go beyond the counting of superficial characteristics of caretaker speech.

6. Variation in child language

Gordon Wells

One of the most significant developments in recent work on child language has been the increasing number of studies which report the existence of individual differences: differences not only in rate of development but also in characteristic patterns of use and perhaps also in patterns of learning. Since the existence of such differences could have far-reaching implications for the design and use of language programmes in clinical and educational settings, and for policy decisions more generally in the fields of early child care and education, it is important carefully to examine the claims that have been made and, in particular, to evaluate their theoretical and methodological foundations. The first part of this chapter will therefore be devoted to a consideration of these issues, before going on to discuss the main areas in which research on variation has been carried out. Inevitably, no more than an overview can be presented here but, where appropriate, references will be made to books and articles in which specific issues are more fully discussed.

1. Types of variation

Let us imagine that we pick a group of children and attempt to describe them – their personalities, the sorts of homes they come from, their favourite activities, who they spend their time with, and so on. We shall quickly find that they are all different – different, probably with respect to each of the headings that we consider, and certainly different in the combined profiles that we might attempt to construct. Let us now imagine that we also record one, or a number of, samples of speech from each of these children in the course of their everyday activities, and without anyone being aware that we are making the recordings. When we come to describe these speech samples we shall even more quickly realize that each one is different, and that a large part of this difference is directly related to the differences that we have already observed in the activities, preferences,

109

etc. of the children, and in the situations in which the speech samples were recorded.

The researcher into child language is thus faced with a dilemma: either to reduce the problem to manageable proportions by strictly limiting the number of variables that are taken into account, or to attempt to take account of as many as possible, at the risk of being overwhelmed by the complexity of the task. The dilemma, of course, arises from the fact that, in order to take the first course, the researcher needs information about the full range of sources of variation so that he can control those that he does not wish to investigate; but this is only possible if the full range of variation has already been investigated and a theory developed which provides a basis for the principled control of unwanted variation.

In practice, most researchers have attended to only one or two sources of variation, usually those that are most amenable to description, making the simplifying assumption that the remaining variation is arbitrary or coincidental. Such a strategy has had the effect of leaving completely unexplored such pervasive parameters as the situation in which speech occurs (Cazden 1970), and of reducing to polarized dichotomies such parameters as social background (e.g. Bernstein 1971), which are in reality made up of a cluster of interacting parameters, each varying continuously over the total population. As a result, there is as yet no overall theory of variation, merely a number of relatively unrelated findings that still await integration. Given this situation, it may be helpful to start by making a number of broad distinctions between different types of variation, and by considering the ways in which they may be related.

Firstly, there is the child's actual language behaviour. Of course, this itself is not a unitary phenomenon: there are many aspects of language behaviour which display variation and these change with increasing maturity. The problem, therefore, is to know which aspects to attend to. Until quite recently, researchers have tended to concentrate on global measures such as Mean Length of Utterance (MLU) (Brown 1973). The validity of this measure has been the subject of a considerable amount of critical discussion (e.g. Crystal 1974; Peters 1983; Wells 1985), but because of its apparently general nature and the ease with which it can be calculated, it still continues to be widely used. Other global measures that have been used include vocabulary size (Nelson 1973b), vocabulary comprehension (Brimer and Dunn 1963; Huttenlocher 1974), sentence comprehension (L. Lee 1969; Reynell 1969), and a variety of measures based on spontaneous speech, including syntactic complexity (Menyuk 1969) and range of options acquired within particular linguistic systems (Wells 1985).

Investigators using these general measures of development have usually been interested in variation in *rate* of development. This has been approached either by obtaining scores on a particular measure from a sample of children all of the same age, or by equating children for level of development, irrespective of age, and measuring the gain made on a particular measure between this first point and some later point in time. The first approach has typically been adopted when the interest is in investigating the range of variation in children's linguistic ability at particular ages (e.g. Brimer and Dunn 1963; Reynell 1969); the second has been the one most favoured by those interested in evaluating the effect of differential treatment (e.g. studies of parental input by such as Furrow, Nelson and Benedict 1979; Barnes *et al.* 1983).

Substantial variation in rate of development has long been recognized by lay people as well as by students of child language. The interest in variation in *route* of development, however, is much more recent. To some extent this has a rather simple methodological explanation. Until a fairly detailed account is available of the common trends in development, it is difficult to make any systematic assessment of the extent to which there are significant individual differences. But, as several investigators have pointed out (Horgan 1981; Peters 1983), the lack of interest in individual differences has also been due in part to the universalist assumptions strongly associated with the descriptive apparatus of transformational generative grammar that was so widely adopted in the 1960s and early 1970s. However, as the empirical base of child language study has become both wider in the range of children studied and more comprehensive and detailed in the descriptive systems that have been used, it has become apparent that there are recognizable differences between children in the relative emphasis that they give to different aspects of language at particular stages of development. It has also been suggested that these observable differences in behaviour may result from different learning strategies and correspond to differing routes on the way to linguistic maturity. The nature and possible significance of these differences will be discussed more fully below.

Variation in either rate or route of development is of limited interest in itself, however. What is of greater interest is the reason for the existence of these differences, their correlation with subsequent developmental indices (such as school attainment) and the extent to which they are open to modification. To study these questions it is necessary to investigate patterns of covariation between linguistic indices and other attributes of children and their experience which vary across the population. Systematic studies of this kind are still in their infancy, so it is too early to draw

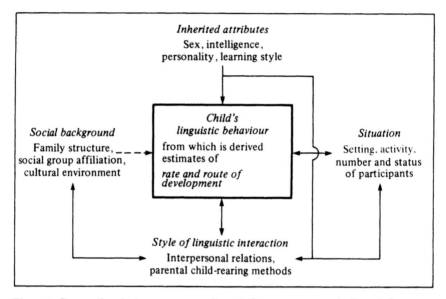

Figure 1. Types of variation: ⟶ direct influence; - - - → indirect influence

any firm conclusions. However, it may be helpful to suggest a framework within which to consider those findings that have been reported. This is set out schematically in figure 1.

At the centre of the diagram is the children's linguistic behaviour, for it is variation in this that has to be explained. Around the sides are four broad groups of factors which have, in various studies, been proposed as potentially causative influences. Only one group is, strictly speaking, concerned with attributes of the children themselves, those that might be described as biologically *inherited*: intelligence, personality, learning style etc. The remaining three cover different aspects of the children's environment: long-term characteristics of children's *social background*; factors in the social and physical *situation* in which the children's linguistic behaviour occurs; and the style of *linguistic interaction* which provides the context for their acquisition and use of language. All except social background are suggested to have a direct influence on the child's linguistic behaviour.

Clearly, such a classification is no more than a matter of convenience for purposes of exposition. Variation in children's linguistic behaviour or in rate or route of development is not caused uniquely by any one of these groups of attributes, but is the outcome of an interaction between all of them, as the diagram attempts to indicate. Variation is also reciprocal: for example, as will be discussed in a later section, the style of interaction

that the child experiences depends on his own inherent attributes and on attributes of his own language behaviour, as well as on the characteristics of those with whom he interacts and on the situations in which these interactions occur. At least this degree of complexity must be attributed to the patterns of covariation that characterize children's linguistic development, and this should be borne in mind in interpreting the research findings that are already available. Before discussing the separate groups of factors, however, I shall look first at some of the difficulties that beset those trying to investigate linguistic variation and its correlates.

2. Methodological problems of data collection and analysis

2.1. Obtaining reliable data

Labov (1972) refers to this problem as the 'Observer Paradox': in the absence of an observer it is difficult to obtain interpretable data, but the very presence of an observer may so alter the situation that the speech that is observed lacks the qualities of spontaneity and naturalness which are essential for the investigation. Child language researchers, rightly convinced of the need for the richest possible contextual information to assist in the interpretation of the child's utterances, have usually convinced themselves that the effect of their presence is minimal; but we should remain sceptical. I have suggested elsewhere (Wells 1982), on the basis of our own recorded data, that the frequency of 'expansions', for example, may owe a great deal to the presence of an adult who is relatively unfamiliar with the child, for whose benefit the mother, quite unconsciously, expands or interprets all the child's utterances that may be difficult for the visitor to understand. There are probably other systematic changes in parents', if not in children's, behaviour when an observer is present. What is incontrovertible, I believe, is that the presence of an observer, however well-known to the family, will have effects on the speech that occurs, and that these effects will differ according to the type of home, thus introducing a form of interference that makes it difficult to study the linguistic interaction between the child and other members of the family, which provides the most important context for the child's linguistic development. A second problem associated with reliability concerns the child's physical and emotional state when the speech sample is obtained. Even when there is no bias introduced by an observer, it is important to ensure that the data are not distorted by the child being ill or upset or in any other way not 'on form'. Whilst it is probably not possible to measure this in any very

precise way, the mother will usually be able to say whether or not her child is behaving as usual.

The same problems arise, but in an even stronger form, when the data for study are obtained in experimental or test-like situations. Labov (1977) has vividly described the way in which many children respond to the questioning of unknown adult research workers by a stubborn refusal to utter anything more than monosyllables; and Donaldson (1978) and Rose and Blank (1974) have shown how children may be led to produce apparently illogical or inappropriate responses as a result of their misperception of the artificial testing context in which the questions or instructions are presented. The problem is that the language behaviour that is called for in such test or experimental situations is likely to be artificially divorced from a meaningful context in the child's experience, and thus the behaviour that occurs does not provide reliable evidence for the question under investigation, namely, his ability to use language to communicate with the familiar members of his home environment.

2.2. Obtaining representative data

As well as being reliable, the data for analysis should also be representative. This issue needs to be considered on two distinct levels. First, there is the need to sample from the child population in such a way that variation within that population is adequately represented. Where there are *a priori* theoretical grounds for distinguishing particular subgroups, this is relatively straightforward; but in the absence of theoretically motivated distinctions, it is necessary to draw a sample of randomly selected individuals which is large enough for significant groupings within the population to be empirically determined from a *post hoc* analysis of the data. Although this issue is well understood in the field of experimental psychology, it has frequently been ignored in child language research, presumably because of the dominating interest in the universal characteristics of language development.

On a second level, there is a need to sample from the population of situations in which speech occurs. However, except perhaps in laboratory-like conditions, it is difficult to control the kaleidoscopic shifting from one context to another that makes up a typical child's day; and even if it were possible, we do not yet know enough about the significant parameters of situations to sample from them in such a way as to maximize the chances of obtaining a speech sample that represents a child's range of control over all aspects of language. Some long-term social and situational sources of variation which have linguistic repercussions are quite outside the control of the researcher. For example, in a study of the emergence of early seman-

tic relations within the sentence I found that the expression of possession was likely to emerge earlier in children with older siblings (Wells 1974). Of course it is possible to control this particular source of variation by studying only firstborn children (although this would make the study unrepresentative in other important ways), but the example is indicative of the enormous range of differences in the patterns of organization of family life which subtly influence the range of experiences, and through them the specific structures, meanings and functions of language, which provide the context for the child's acquisition of language as a means of communication and reflection.

2.3. The quantification of linguistic data

Even when the researcher has satisfactorily resolved the problems of obtaining reliable and representative data, she or he is still faced with the problem of quantifying them in some appropriate way. In his introduction to his study of the copula in Black English Vernacular, Labov writes:

> The study of variation is necessarily quantitative, and quantitative analysis necessarily involves counting. At first glance, counting would seem to be a simple operation, but even the simplest type of counting raises a number of subtle and difficult problems. The final decision as to what to count is actually the solution to the problem in hand; this decision is approached only through a long series of exploratory manoeuvres.   (Labov 1977:82)

It is just such a series of exploratory manoeuvres that is necessary when analysing children's speech. First, there are problems in the allocation of tokens to types. For example, in the relatively unstructured speech of an 18 month old, is the 's in *What's that?* to be counted as a token of the contracted copula or is it to be treated as an inseparable part of an unanalysed question-asking utterance type (Peters 1983)? If it is recognized as a copula, is the contracted copula to be treated as a separate type from the uncontracted copula, as in *What is that?*, or are instances of contracted and uncontracted equally tokens of the same type – the copula? Similarly, with somewhat older children it has been observed that relative clauses occur almost exclusively in relation to verb complements (Limber 1973; Wells 1985). Is it necessary, therefore, to set up more than one relative clause type, one for complements, another for subject relative clauses, and so on; or should it be argued that there is only one type, with the imbalance in position of occurrence being attributed to pragmatic factors, such as

the tendency for the subject of a sentence to express 'given' information, with a consequent lack of necessity for it to be fully specified linguistically?

Having resolved such problems, a decision still has to be made as to whether it is the occurrence of types that will be treated as significant or whether some frequency of tokens will be treated as the measure of control. When a particular element is well-established, it may well be that it is variation in frequency that is of interest (as in the preference for nouns or pronouns discussed below). On the other hand, where the focus is on the point at which a particular element is acquired, one single token of the type may have to be taken as the appropriate evidence, because a criterion set in terms of a greater token frequency would seriously underestimate the number of children having control of the type in question. In the case of certain items, such as the morphemes studied by Brown (1973), the frequency of obligatory linguistic contexts may be high enough to set a criterion such as 90 per cent presence, below which the child is judged not yet to have attained mastery. But for other items, the frequency in the language as a whole may be so low that the probability of actually observing them in a speech sample of a particular size may be too small for presence or absence to be reliably informative (Wells 1985). For example, in a sample of approximately 18,000 utterances that we have obtained from 60 children, each recorded three times between 36 and 42 months, 30 children used a passive verb a total of 50 times, no child producing more than three tokens, and several children producing one token on the first occasion but none on the two subsequent occasions. Here, there is no obligatory context in which to look for proportional frequency of occurrence, and given so low an absolute frequency, there can be no certainty that children who are not observed to use a passive do in fact lack control of this item. A possible solution here is to use cumulative frequency over a number of observations.

2.4. Problems of size

As will be apparent by now, the biggest problem facing research on child language that tries to take systematic account of even one or two of the multiple sources of variation whilst at the same time obtaining data amenable to detailed linguistic analysis, is the sheer size of the sample required. Early research, such as the normative studies reviewed by McCarthy (1954) and the later study by Templin (1957), was based on a substantial number of children (480 in Templin's case), but the corpora obtained were neither reliable nor representative in terms of the above criteria,[1] and the linguistic analysis was extremely crude. Some of the more recent research, in the

tradition inaugurated by Brown (1973; Brown, Cazden and Bellugi 1969) and Miller and Ervin (1964), has succeeded in obtaining corpora of data large enough to allow a detailed linguistic analysis, but at the price of restricting the number of children to a handful, and by ignoring most of the social and situational causes of variation.

The Bristol Study,[2] with a sample of 128 children, representative of the urban child population in terms of sex, month of birth and class of family background, and with recordings made of each child once every three months at frequent intervals over a normal day at home without an observer present, has attempted to overcome the problems of reliability and representativeness; but the quantity of child speech obtained at each recording (120 utterances on average) and the intervals between recordings still pose problems for certain types of quantitative analysis, as suggested above.

Thus, if it is an essential prerequisite of work on variation in child language that the data for study should be obtained in such a way that they meet the criteria that have just been discussed, it must be concluded that there is as yet little or no research in this field that will support any confident generalizations. Yet the nature and extent of this variation is a subject of considerable importance, not only because an understanding of it is needed as a basis for sampling decisions, whatever the focus of the research, but also because of the educational significance that has been attributed to certain aspects of linguistic variation, although in the absence of adequate empirical evidence. Because of the limitations of almost all of the studies to be referred to below with respect to at least one of the issues discussed above, few of the findings can be taken as conclusive, though many of them are suggestive of fruitful hypotheses for further evaluation. In the remainder of this chapter I shall consider these findings in terms of the major factors distinguished in figure 1.

3. Individual differences in language development

The evidence for substantial variation in rate of development has already been mentioned. At 42 months, for example, in the representative sample of 'normal' children (i.e. with no known handicap) investigated in the Bristol Study, the difference between the most and least advanced children was equivalent to 30 to 36 months (Wells 1985). The existence of this variation in rate has long been recognized and has, in fact, been one of the major spurs to the investigation of nonlinguistic correlates. More recently, however, evidence has begun to appear of variation of a different kind – in what I have called route of development. As this work has been

admirably reviewed in two recent articles by Nelson (1981a) and by Brether-ton *et al.* (1983), only a summary will be attempted here.

One of the first indications of differences in route of development – or at least of difference of emphasis in language use – appeared in Nelson's (1973b) study, in which children were found to differ in the proportion of general nominals in their first 50 'words'. Whilst, for the majority of her sample, more than 50 per cent of these words fell into the general nominal category, this was not true for a sizeable minority, who had a more diverse vocabulary including a large number of sentence- or phrase-like social routines. Nelson labelled the two ends of this continuum, respec-tively Referential and Expressive.

Since that time evidence of other dimensions on which children differ has appeared. Some of the better attested are shown in table 1, with refer-ences to the publications in which they are reported, together with the number and ages of the children investigated.

At a fairly general level, several of these dimensions are clearly quite similar in showing a preference for nouns. This is most strikingly portrayed in Horgan's (1980) characterization of children as either noun 'lovers' or 'leavers'. In several of the studies cited this preference has also been found to be correlated with one or more of the other dimensions. This has led to a tendency to try to assimilate all the dimensions to two distinct 'styles' which have then been variously opposed in terms such as 'referential' versus 'expressive', 'semantic' versus 'syntactic', 'cognitive' versus 'pragmatic', 'analytic' versus 'holistic' (or 'gestalt'). However, whilst such a reductionist strategy clearly simplifies exposition and may be fruitful in the generation of hypotheses for further investigation, it is certainly not warranted by the evidence actually available.

In the first place, to talk about two styles is to imply a dichotomy, whereas from the data available it would be more appropriate to think of continuous variation along one or more dimensions. Secondly, there is as yet no evi-dence that all the dimensions *do* converge on one single continuum. When Bretherton *et al.* (1983) attempted to test this hypothesis, using the tech-nique of cluster analysis to reduce the wide variety of variables they had derived from observation and maternal interview, they failed to find the anticipated opposition between the two styles. Whilst there were indeed two clusters that could be identified as, respectively, referential / nominal and expressive / pronominal, not all the other dimensions mapped on to these clusters. Moreover the two clusters were themselves significantly cor-related with each other, thus undermining the argument for distinct styles. As the authors conclude (p. 312): 'many children balance both strategies; none use one to the exclusion of the other'. Finally, sample sizes have

Table 1. *Dimensions of individual differences reported in early language development*

Dimension	Reference	Number in sample	Age
Proportion of general nominals in early vocabulary	Nelson 1973b	20	14–24 months
	Starr 1975	18	10–30 months
	Leonard et al. 1979	12	1–2½ years
Relative preference for nouns or pronouns in encoding sentence meaning relations	Bloom, Lightbown and Hood 1975	4	19–26 months
	Nelson 1975	18	10–30 months
Proportion of NPs per utterance	Starr 1975	30	2–4 year
	Horgan 1980, 1981	12	1–2½ years
Range of combinations of the categories S, V and O in the early stages of syntax learning	Bloom et al. 1975	4	19–20 months
	Ramer 1976	7	13–27 months
Amount of imitation	Nelson 1973b	6	18–25 months
	Bloom et al. 1975	3	11–24 months
	Ferguson and Farwell 1975	20	14–24 months
	Leonard et al. 1979	18	20–30 months
Use of long 'unanalysed' units	R. Clark 1974, 1977	1	2–6 years
	Peters 1977, 1983	1	7–27 months
Functional emphasis: referential or expressive	Nelson 1973b	2	1–2 years
	Dore 1974	2	18–25 months
	Starr 1975	18	10–30 months
	Lieven 1978a	12	1–2½ years
Attention to segmental or suprasegmental phonology	Dore 1974	3	11–22 months
	Branigan 1977	2	1–2 years
	Ferguson and Farwell 1975	3	1–24 months
	Peters 1977	1	7–24 months

on the whole been small and socially homogeneous (barely more than 100 children in total contributed data to all the studies referred to in table 1). It is therefore not yet possible to assess how representative the observed differences are of the range of variation in language learners generally.

At present, therefore, I would suggest a more cautious interpretation of the evidence. Certainly there are differences between children in their linguistic behaviour which suggest that they may be adopting different strategies in working out the complex relationships between the functions, content and form of language. Since some of the differences, such as the tendency to emphasize nouns, seem to persist over quite extended periods of time, there is clearly also some degree of divergence in developmental route.[3] It would, however, be unwise to foreclose investigation at this stage by too ready an acceptance of a simple global opposition between two overall styles, strategies or routes.

4. The effect of situation

It is now many years since Cazden (1970) drew attention to the way in which child language researchers have tended to neglect the importance of the effect of situational factors on the language use that is observed; the methodological implications of her warning have already been briefly touched upon in this chapter. However, as Cazden pointed out, situational variation is an important issue in its own right, and in the last decade there have been a number of attempts to investigate some of the more salient dimensions of this source of variation.

The activity in which the participants are engaged is one obvious place to start. Snow (1977b), for example, reports a number of studies by herself and her associates in which differences in mothers' speech were observed across different activities, such as freeplay, bookreading and caretaking. Although she does not discuss the effects on the children's speech, it seems reasonable to suppose that there were concomitants of the substantial differences observed in the length and complexity of maternal utterances. This was certainly the case in the comparison reported by Dore (1978) of conversations between nursery teachers and 3 and 4 year olds when visiting a supermarket and when talking about the visit later in school. Similarly, Wells (1985) reports substantial differences in the relative frequency with which children used different utterance functions across 10 contexts of activity, from 18 months onwards. This variation is not at all surprising and, in itself, is chiefly of interest in underlining the importance of pragmatic considerations in early language use. However, if children also vary substantially in the amount of time they habitually spend in different activities,

we may expect to find this reflected in the differential frequency of particular forms and functions in their speech when this is obtained from randomly recorded samples or from continuous diary records.

We may also find differences developing in their expectations about what language is chiefly used for, and perhaps, as a result, in the strategies they employ in acquiring it. To take a specific example, does the emphasis on general nominals in early vocabulary learning, noted by Nelson (1973b), result from a greater than average amount of time being spent playing the naming game whilst looking at a picture book with an adult? Or, more generally, do differences on the 'stylistic' dimensions discussed in the previous section have their origin in children's differing hypotheses about the major functions of language, resulting from their differential experience of the activities in relation to which language is used? As yet, there is no firm evidence on this issue, but it is one that seems likely to repay further investigation.

Similar arguments could be advanced with respect to the status of the participants with whom the child habitually interacts. The most obvious contrast here is between adults and other siblings as the most frequent conversational partners, but we might also stretch the notion of status somewhat and distinguish between experience of the same adults in their different roles as caretaker / controller, instructor or companion. Where variation in rate or route of development has been found to be associated with the child's position in the family (Nelson 1973b; Lieven 1978a; Wells 1985), this may well have resulted in part from differences in the relative frequency with which they experienced interaction of these different kinds, as Nelson (1981a) observed (see also section 6.2, below).

5. Inherited attributes

5.1. Sex

References to the superiority of girls with respect to almost all aspects of language development abound in the literature, although it is extremely rare to find such extreme differences as those reported by Ramer (1976), in whose sample of seven children all the girls but none of the boys were characterized by a style of acquisition associated with rapid development.

Reviewing the literature in 1954, McCarthy wrote:

> The vast accumulation of evidence in the same direction from a variety of investigators working in different parts of the country [USA], employing different situations and methods of observation, and

employing different analyses and linguistic indices, certainly is convincing proof that a real sex difference in language development exists
in favor of girls . . .   (McCarthy 1954: 580)

However, only a few years later Templin, summarizing her own findings,
had this to say:

> When the performance of boys and girls is compared over the entire
> age range, girls tend to receive higher scores more frequently than
> the boys, but the differences are not consistent and are only infre-
> quently statistically significant

and she went on to suggest that:

> It may be that the differences which have appeared in the literature
> have been overemphasised in the past. It may also be that over the
> years differences in language ability of the two sexes have actually
> become less pronounced in keeping with the shift towards a single
> standard in child care and training in the last few decades.   (Templin
> 1957: 145–7)

A similar conclusion is reached in more recent reviews by Cherry (1975)
and Macaulay (1978), and our own research strongly supports the view
that what differences there are between the sexes are in rate rather than
in style of acquisition, but that they are rarely significant and do not consistently favour either sex.

However, it is the last sentence of the quotation from Templin that is
most interesting, for it heralds a new trend in studies of sex differences,
towards an investigation of the differential treatment of the two sexes as
an explanation of what had previously been taken to be a genetic superiority. Under this hypothesis, the relatively greater loquacity and fluency of
girls (Smith and Connolly 1972) would be attributed to differential expectations of, and communication with, the two sexes by their parents. There
is some evidence to support this hypothesis in the responses in our maternal
interview when the children were aged $3\frac{1}{2}$ years (Wells 1985).

In this context another finding from the Bristol research is of particular
interest. Using the corpus of speech collected at $3\frac{1}{4}$ years, sequences of
conversation were distinguished according to whether they were initiated
by the child or by another person. All sequences were also categorized
according to the context in which they occurred and the dominant purpose
of the conversation. Of those sequences whose initiator could be determined, 70 per cent were initiated by the child, and for these sequences
there were only small, and mainly insignificant, differences between boys

and girls with respect to context or purpose. In the remaining 30 per cent of sequences, the vast majority of which were initiated by the mother (and a few by the father), there were substantial sex-related differences in the contexts in which adults chose to initiate conversations with boys and girls (table 2). The most striking contrasts were in the contexts of 'Play with adult participation', 'Helping and non-play activities'.

This suggests that adults emphasize more useful, 'domestic', activities in their interactions with girls, whilst the emphasis with boys is towards a more free-ranging exploratory manipulation of the physical environment. What is not clear, however, is who establishes this differential preference – the children or their parents. Given that there is this sex-related difference in activity contexts for talk, it is rather surprising that the only differentiation that is apparent in the children's own speech is in the proportional frequency with which they choose particular linguistic options. As yet, no resulting differences have been found in either rate or route of development.

5.2. Intelligence

If sex differences turn out to owe as much to environmental factors as to biological differences, the same is probably even more true of the relationship between language and intelligence. Interpretation of the undoubted correlations between intelligence and linguistic development reported in the studies reviewed by McCarthy (1954) is made more difficult by the fact that most tests of intelligence, even those purporting to test nonverbal intelligence, require certain minimal skills in communication, usually through language, for their administration – if only so that the subject can be made aware that a response is required and that it should take a particular form. Furthermore, neither intelligence nor language is a unitary phenomenon and developments in the two domains interpenetrate each other in an interactive way. This suggests that any effort to establish a global, unidirectional, causal relationship, in whichever direction, is almost certainly misguided. It seems much more plausible, instead, to hypothesize a continuum of causality extending in both directions, on which observed correlations between particular tests and linguistic subskills might be located. The relationship between size of vocabulary and a test of intelligence such as the English Picture Vocabulary Test (Brimer and Dunn 1963), which depends on the comprehension of pictured objects and events, for example, would probably fall at the language → measured intelligence end, whilst the relationship between the ability to recognize spatial or temporal sequences or configurations, as measured by Raven's Progressive Matrices, and rate of acquisition of the hierarchical structure of syntax, particularly

Table 2. *Proportions of conversations initiated by adults with boys and girls in different contexts*

	Toileting, dressing and meals	Playing alone	Play with other child	Helping and non-play activities	Play with adult	Talking and reading	Watching TV	Total %
Boys	14.4	8.1	2.7	28.8	18.1	22.5	5.4	100%
Girls	12.1	3.4	2.6	56.8	5.2	19.0	0.9	100%

$\chi^2 = 25.037; p < 0.001$

subordination and embedding, would probably fall towards the intelligence → language end.

Mention has already been made of the variation between children in the extent of their experience of test-like situations and the effect that this can have on test performance. Attention has also been focused on the problems of cultural bias in tests of intelligence and in many of the instruments that have been used to assess linguistic skills and maturity (Labov 1970). It is clear, therefore that covariation between intelligence and language must also be firmly related to environmental variation, and particularly to social and cultural differences in the valuation that is put upon different types of intellectual and linguistic performance.

5.3. Personality and learning style

These two potential sources of variation are considered together for two reasons. First, they are almost certainly inter-related; and second, although likely to be of considerable importance, they have as yet received very little attention. In addition, to the extent that personality and learning style are learned through interaction with a social environment, the direction of causation is likely to be complex (Hardy-Brown 1983).

In the literature on first language learning, there is little reference to personality differences as such, although the behavioural differences described in some studies might well be seen as having their source in differences of this kind. Lieven (1978a), for example, notes that of the two children she studied one was much more concerned in her use of language to attract her mother's attention while the other seemed to be more interested in talking about the objects and events around her. Nelson's (1973b) study also makes reference to certain cognitive style attributes of mother and child that are appropriately considered in this section. She reports (p. 113) that the degree of match or mismatch between mother and child on this dimension was 'most potent in accounting for the child's progress during the second year'. However, the findings from both these studies might equally well be considered in terms of style of interaction.

Only two studies, to my knowledge, have made a systematic attempt to study the relationship between personality and language learning, and in one of these, the Bristol study, no clear results have yet emerged. In the other, by Bretherton *et al.* (1983), the Colorado Child Temperament Inventory was completed at 28 months by mothers of the 30 children whose language had been assessed by maternal interview and direct observation at 20 months. Of the five subscales of the inventory (sociability, emotionality, soothability, attention span and activity level), only the first was asso-

ciated with clusters derived from the language measures and these were confined to the clusters from the observations. However, as both style clusters were found to be significantly correlated with sociability, the authors interpreted the result only as evidence that the children's scores on the observational measures may have been affected by such temperamental factors as nervousness and reluctance to talk with an unfamiliar adult.

Whilst this interpretation seems entirely reasonable, given the lack of correlations between sociability and the *style* clusters derived from the maternal interview, it may nevertheless hide a real relationship between temperamental or personality differences amongst children and their rate of language learning. On the face of it, it seems likely that the differences between an active, out-going child and a placid, retiring child will influence many aspects of the interactions in which they participate, and that this in turn will have an effect on the speed and ease with which they acquire the linguistic resources for interaction. Certainly, in the spontaneous learning of a second language sociability has been found to be a major influence on rate of learning (Wong-Fillmore 1979). On the basis of her longitudinal study of five 5- to 7-year-old Spanish-speaking children as they acquired English during the course of one school year, she rates active involvement in interaction with speakers of the target language as a major determinant of success, and offers (p. 209) as the most important strategy: 'Join a group and act as if you understand what's going on, even if you don't.' Whilst the situation of first language learners is somewhat different, in that they do not need to seek out a group to join, it is probably still the case that those who are temperamentally inclined to join in and communicate, using whatever resources they have available, will make the most rapid progress.

As far as learning style is concerned, there is little to be added to what was said in section 3, where the notion of different styles was discussed. On the basis of recent work on cognitive development (e.g. Kogan 1976), there are grounds for believing that there may be inherited differences between children in language learning style, but the effects of these differences have not as yet been clearly distinguished from the effects of other factors, such as those associated with situation (section 4) and with quality of interaction (section 6, below). In particular, as Hardy-Brown (1983) points out, where children are brought up by their biological parents it is difficult to separate the effect of genetically-transmitted differences from those that arise from interacting with an environment provided by genetically-related parents and siblings. A further problem for the interpretation of most of the studies that have so far addressed questions of style is that the same samples of observed behaviour that have been used to describe differences in route have also provided the basis for the ascription of one

or other of the proposed styles. An essential next step, therefore, is to make a clear theoretical distinction between learning style and route of development.

With respect to rate of development, on the other hand, there does seem to be quite strong evidence of a relationship between variation in style / route of development and rate of learning. 'Referential' children acquire their early vocabulary more quickly (Nelson 1973b); 'noun lovers' are six months or more ahead of 'noun leavers' in reaching the same MLU level (Horgan 1980); children who exploit the full range of two constituent combinations on the way to control of the full SVC (subject, verb, complement) structure acquire that control more quickly (Ramer 1976). It should perhaps be added that this relative precocity is to some extent dependent on the measures used in making the comparisons: referential children did not seem to have as wide a conception of the functional potential of language as their expressive counterparts; noun leavers at a given MLU had superior comprehension; the children who mastered the SVC structure quickly were also more inclined to take risks and make errors.

Despite these reservations and qualifications, however, it now seems incontrovertible that there are a number of dimensions on which individuals differ in their patterns of language learning. There remains a great deal of work to be done to clarify the nature of the relationships involved, but without doubt this is one of the most exciting areas of current work on child language.

6. Social background

This is probably the most controversial of all the dimensions of variation in child language and more has certainly been written on this subject and its supposed implications for educability than on all the other dimensions of variation added together. For this reason, only selected aspects will be considered in this chapter; for a comprehensive and critical review of the literature, the reader is referred to Dittmar (1976), A. Edwards (1976a) and J. Edwards (1979).

Since the formal organization of language and the meanings and purposes it serves to communicate are learned chiefly through social interaction, it seems self-evident that insofar as this varies from one social group to another there will be variation in children's language which can be related to group membership. And on this point there is very little disagreement. Where the disagreement is to be found is on: (1) the nature and size of the variation; (2) whether the major differences between groups are in the resources available or in the uses made of those resources; (3) the

parameters that should be used to distinguish significant social groupings; and (4) the mechanisms responsible for the relationship between social group membership and linguistic variation.

Historically speaking, the debate has for the most part been conducted with socioeconomic status, or social class, as the point of departure (they are usually treated as if they were equivalent), thus pre-empting a serious consideration of possible alternative parameters. Research findings were initially presented in terms of rate of development, with children from lower SES groups showing a developmental lag, frequently at a statistically significant level (McCarthy 1954; Templin 1957). An evaluative element was soon added, and the developmental lag became a linguistic deficit (Loban 1963; Deutsch 1965). Then, under the influence of Bernstein's formulation of the class–code relationship, a difference in style of acquisition was introduced, the middle class being said to develop an exploratory and explicit use of language in contrast to the expressive and implicit use of the lower class (Bernstein 1960, 1965).

At about this point, in reaction to the extreme 'deficit' claims, two new strands entered the debate. On the one hand Labov used evidence from his studies of nonstandard English to point out that many of the characteristics of lower-class speech that were being treated as indices of deficit were in fact systematic differences of dialect. In a now famous polemical article (Labov 1970), he dismissed the supposed superiority of middle-class speech and argued strongly that although working-class Negro children differed in the form of English that they spoke and in the value that they placed upon particular uses of language they were just as linguistically proficient as the middle-class white children who had been taken as the point of comparison.

On the other hand, and at about the same time, Bernstein reformulated his theory in terms which made it clear that the codes regulated habitual 'performance' and were not to be taken as a description of underlying 'competence', or if so, only of 'communicative competence' (Bernstein 1971: 146). However, this reformulation is less radical than might appear, for being limited to a restricted code is still seen as the probable cause of cognitive deficit:

> for this code orients its speakers to a less complex conceptual hierarchy and so to a lower order of causality . . . Thus the relative backwardness of many working class children who live in areas of high population density or in rural areas may well be a culturally induced backwardness transmitted by the linguistic process. Such children's low performance on verbal IQ tests, their difficulty with 'abstract' concepts, their

failures within the language area, their general inability to profit from the school, all may result from the limitations of a restricted code. (Bernstein 1971: 151).

It is true that the distinction between speech variant and code, and the introduction of the notion of critical socializing contexts, gave greater precision to the theory, but the results of the empirical studies carried out by his research team continued to be presented in terms of the relative inferiority of working-class children's speech: shorter utterances, less syntactic complexity, greater use of pronouns than of nouns and particular reliance on exophoric reference – all realizations of the restricted code user's orientation to particularistic, context-dependent meanings.

These two new developments have been seen by many to be in direct opposition to each other. But this is not the case. Labov's argument, that nonstandard dialects are as adequate for the development of logical thought as any other dialect of English, is surely correct. Bernstein's thesis, however, is not concerned with differences between dialects, rather with underlying code orientations to different orders of meaning, particularistic and universalistic, in whatever dialect, standard or nonstandard. In principle, therefore, it is perfectly possible for there to be standard dialect speakers whose speech is regulated by a restricted code, and speakers of nonstandard dialects whose speech is regulated by an elaborated code. The main reasons for the assumed incompatibility of the two arguments are, firstly, the fact that the majority of the nonstandard dialect speakers considered by Labov are working-class and, secondly, that Bernstein has persistently argued that the restricted and elaborated codes have social origins in orientation to the means of production: the restricted code both springs from, and transmits, the social structure experienced by the working class. The working class are, almost by definition, restricted code speakers.

If we now recapitulate the various arguments that have been developed, there appear to be two main hypotheses concerning the relationship between social class and language development:

(a)   that lower-class children are relatively retarded in acquiring control of the dialect of their community
(b)   that lower-class children are more likely to use restricted speech variants and to have restricted code orientation towards context-dependent, particularistic meanings.

The evidence for and against both hypotheses is, as might be expected, difficult to disentangle. In the case of the first, dialect differences have certainly clouded the issue, for in some of the earlier studies, which claimed

to find substantial class differences, nonstandard departures from Standard English were treated as evidence of a developmental lag in acquiring the standard form. The conditions under which the speech samples were collected may also have affected children from different social classes differentially, as Labov (1972) argues. In a number of studies, also, the samples have been drawn from the population in such a way as to maximize the chances of finding the expected class differences (e.g. Adlam 1977; Tough 1977).

In the Bristol Study we have tried to guard against all these forms of bias: by representing the full range of family background; by sampling from the naturally-occurring contexts in which speech takes place in the children's daily lives (with no researcher present during the recording); and by treating local dialect forms, where they occur, in the same way as the equivalent standard forms. From our observations, there is no evidence of significant class differences with respect to the amount of speech produced in the time-based samples, the types of context in which child speech occurs, or the range of pragmatic functions realized. It seems, therefore, that in very general terms spoken language plays the same sort of role for children of all social classes.

When we look at the evidence with respect to rate of development, however, the picture is somewhat more complex. In selecting the children to be studied a stratified random sampling design was used, with an equal number of children being selected from each of four divisions of a continuous scale of family background based on information about the occupation and education of both parents. When these four groups were compared in terms of the distribution of their scores on the Bristol Scale of Language Development, using the χ^2 test for independent samples, they were not found to differ significantly. This suggests that children's rate of oral language development is not associated with their class or family background. On the other hand, when each child's score on the scale of family background was used rather than his / her membership of one of the four classes, a significant correlation ($r = 0.40$; $p < 0.001$) was obtained between family background and rate of development. The explanation for these apparently discrepant results seems to lie in the contribution of the extreme scorers on both the language and the family background scales. Extremely fast developers had a strong tendency to be found in families with high scores on the scale of family background; conversely, extremely slow developers had a strong tendency to be found in families with low scores on the scale of family background. The contribution of these two small groups of children was sufficient to produce an overall significant correlation when individual family background scores were considered. On the other hand, because

within-class differences were greater in the sample as a whole than between-class differences, the between-class differences were not statistically significant. On the basis of these data, therefore, it must be concluded that there is not a consistent relationship between family background and rate of language development during the preschool years (see Wells 1985).

On the second hypothesis the evidence is less conclusive. Much of the relevant research has been carried out by Bernstein and his colleagues, and although many of their results lend support to the hypothesis of a relationship between class and code, the contexts from which the speech data were obtained were both nonspontaneous and highly specific, so it is difficult to assess how far the results were distorted by the differential responses of the two groups to the task situations and by their differential perception of the task demands, as Adlam (1977) admits in her discussion of these investigations. Hawkins' (1969) study of the different uses of the nominal group in telling a story from pictures is a good example of the problem. The restricted code stories that were typical of the working-class group, with their high proportion of exophoric reference, could be taken as entirely appropriate in the situation, since child and researcher were both able to see the pictures. Furthermore, the relationship between the hypothesized underlying code, with its somewhat speculative cognitive implications, and the speech variants actually observed in specific situational contexts has continued to elude really satisfactory articulation. Although the speech of working-class children frequently is less syntactically complex and lexically less specific than that of middle-class children in the contexts chosen for examination, the fact that, under what they consider to be appropriate circumstances, working-class children can be explicit, producing utterances of appropriate grammatical complexity and lexical specificity to achieve their communication goals (Francis 1974; A. Edwards 1976b), makes it inappropriate to continue to characterize the differences in terms of a binary distinction of either class or code, and must cast doubt on the usefulness of the construct 'code' itself. Or, if the concept is to be retained, we should allow for a plurality of codes, in the same way as we do with registers. Certainly, much greater attention must be paid to aspects of context than has typically been the case in such studies (but see Adlam 1977 for an attempt to relate code and context).

It is in relation to education that the putative relationship between class and restriction in the uses of language has assumed the greatest importance, for large-scale policy decisions (e.g. Plowden 1967; Halsey 1972) have been based on evidence such as that produced by Bernstein's Sociological Research Unit, and by similar research in the United States (e.g. Deutsch 1965; Hess and Shipman 1965, 1968). In her research in this tradition into

class differences in the use of language, Tough (1977) even labels her two contrasted groups of 3 year olds in terms of predicted educational 'advantage' and 'disadvantage', although the chief criterion for selection was parental status: professional as opposed to unskilled or semi-skilled occupation. In this research it is not code as such which is the focus of investigation, but the relative frequency with which children from the two groups make use of different functions of language. The major functions distinguished were self-maintaining, Directive, Interpretative and Projective, with distinctions of uses within these categories being arranged in a notional order of complexity. Comparing samples of speech recorded in a play situation, Tough found marked differences between the two groups, to the point that only one child in the disadvantaged group 'had scores on some measures that were better than the scores of one or two children in the advantaged group' (1977: 85). Although the meaning of 'better' is not defined, 'these results lead her to conclude (p. 87) that 'these children, coming from differing home environments, had established different priorities for expressing meaning, and different orientations towards the use of language'.

Once again, however, these conclusions were reached on the basis of data that failed to meet the criteria discussed in the opening section of this chapter. The speech samples were obtained from only one situation, with the observer present and taking notes, and the frequency data were not submitted to statistical analysis. In an attempt to carry out a partial replication of Tough's research, I carried out a similar analysis of samples of spontaneous speech at home for a subsample of the Bristol children, who were drawn from the full spectrum of family background (Wells 1977). After applying statistical tests to both sets of data, I found that the Bristol sample showed a much less clear-cut picture. In the first place, the frequency of uses considered to be most complex by Tough was so low for both samples as a whole that no statistical significance could be attached to differences between groups. In the second place, although there were still some significant differences between classes with respect to the more frequently occurring categories, there were few of the linear trends indicative of simple correlation, and some of those that did occur were in the opposite direction from that predicted by Tough. As with the first hypothesis, therefore, the evidence is conflicting and certainly does not allow firm conclusions to be drawn on the relationship between class and language use.

Nevertheless, one point of very general significance does emerge from the comparison of these two studies, and that is the distorting effect that is produced when social variation is reduced to an opposition between two monolithic classes and claims made that ignore the very large degree of variation that certainly exists within these classes. There is a persistent

tendency to reduce variation to dichotomy and nowhere is this tendency more prevalent than in discussion of class and code differences.

Class, or occupational status, which is the index most frequently used to identify it, is not the only form of social variation, however, nor even a very informative one in trying to account for variation in rate or style of language acquisition. At best it is correlated with a variety of other characteristics of children's homes – income, type of neighbourhood, size and composition of family, level of parents' education, and parental attitudes to society in general – any one of which is likely to have more influence on the child's learning environment than class membership as defined by the Registrar-General's I–V scale.

Although class, defined chiefly in occupation terms, is central to Bernstein's exposition of primary socialization, it does not seem to me to be a necessary component of a theory which seeks to explain the role of language in the social transmission of knowledge and values. On the other hand, if class membership were treated as just one among a number of group affiliations, which would include membership of groups organized around religion, sports, politics, etc., all of which influence a family's values and orientations to other members of the family and to larger groupings within society, then Bernstein would surely be right in arguing that these values and orientations are largely embodied and transmitted through interpersonal communication, and that their realization in particular, contextualized, conversations constitutes the means whereby the child learns both his language and the social structure of reality that both includes and is expressed by language.

7. Experience of linguistic interaction

Given this emphasis on the social context of language acquisition, it is natural that attention should have come to focus more and more on characteristics of caretakers' conversations with their children. The qualitative modifications of mothers' speech to young children are now well documented (Snow and Ferguson 1977) and have been discussed in chapter 4 of this book. Most of this research has been searching for the universal characteristics of the linguistic input to the child. In this section, however, I shall examine the evidence for variation in input.

7.1. Amount and type of conversational experience

The conversations in which a child participates simultaneously provide a model of the language to be acquired and an opportunity for him to try out his existing language system in a context where shared experience makes

it possible for his partner to provide feedback that should be optimal for further acquisition. Variation in amount of conversational experience might be expected, therefore, to be related to variation in rate of development.

In the Bristol Study, the amount of conversational experience was found to vary quite widely as a result of differences in domestic arrangements and individual differences in loquacity. The most talkative children regularly produced five or six times as many utterances per observation as the least talkative and the differences between the adults talking to the children were even more substantial. As might be expected, therefore, there was a significant relationship between amount of conversation and rate of progress (Barnes *et al.* 1983; Wells 1985). As well as differences in the sheer quantity of conversation with adults, there were also differences in the distribution of this conversation over different contexts, which seemed to result from the number of siblings in the family. In the earlier pilot study (Wells 1975) a comparison was made between three groups of contexts in which conversation occurred: *Mothering* (which included such contexts as bathing, dressing, feeding and cuddling), *Independent* (all contexts where the child was alone, with other children only, or receiving no more than sporadic and divided attention from an adult) and *Joint enterprise* (contexts of shared activity, such as doing the housework together, play with adult participation, looking at books together or just talking). Comparing the proportion of speech that occurred in each of the three groups of contexts, a significant relationship was found between rate of development at $2\frac{1}{2}$ years and proportion of speech addressed to the child in contexts of Joint enterprise. It also happened that, of the eight children compared, the four faster developers were all firstborn children, and it was suggested that it was the greater opportunity that the mothers of these children had to engage in talk in the context of shared activities, compared with the mothers of the children with one or more siblings, that account in large part for the firstborn children's more rapid development. In the main study, when the age interval between siblings as well as their position in the birth order was taken into account, a significant relationship was again found between *Position in the family* and rate of development at $3\frac{1}{2}$ years ($r = 0.29$; $p < 0.001$). As before, this was interpreted as resulting from the greater opportunity available to the only child, or the child with no siblings close in age, to talk with her / his parents in contexts where she / he had their undivided attention.

7.2. Qualitative differences in adult–child interaction

The systematic modification of adult speech to young children has already been mentioned and, at least in mainstream European and North American

linguistic communities, has been found to involve almost all aspects of speech: length of utterance, grammatical complexity, intonation, range of sentence meaning relations, vocabulary and interpersonal and discourse function (see Snow 1977b for a review). There is also a considerable amount of evidence that the modifications that adults make are progressively adjusted in response to the child's own development, as evidenced by his comprehension and production and by various aspects of his nonlinguistic behaviour (Cross 1977; Snow 1977b; Wells 1985). Adults, then, in general have a tendency to modify their speech when talking to young children. However, there are also substantial individual differences between them in the manner and extent to which they do so (Olsen–Fulero 1982). Are these differences associated with differences between their children in either rate or route of development?

Let us first consider influences on rate of development. One hypothesis that has been investigated by Cross (1977, 1978) is that it is the extent of modification that is of significance or, more precisely, the extent to which the modifications are 'finely-tuned' to the child's current stage of development. In a cross-sectional comparison of 'accelerated' and 'normally-developing' children, she found that the accelerated group received speech that was more finely tuned to their linguistic level, particularly their level of comprehension, on quite a variety of linguistic measures. What characterized the mothers of these accelerated children was that in the adjustments that they made they were both sensitive and responsive to the cues provided by their children. Starting from a consideration of the functions that conversation served, Nelson (1973b) also stressed the importance of matching between the strategies of mother and child at different stages of development. Taking the three dichotomous variables, *match/ mismatch* between the child's cognitive structure and the semantic structure of the lexicon used by the adult, selection by the child of a *referential/ expressive* hypothesis concerning the central function of language, and *acceptance / rejection* as the mother's dominant feedback to the child's utterances, she identified eight interaction patterns and examined the relationship between these and rate of vocabulary acquisition. Match–referential–acceptance was found to be most strongly associated with rapid acquisition and, as might be expected, mismatch–expressive–rejection with slowest acquisition. Of the three variables, cognitive–linguistic match / mismatch appeared to be most powerful in accounting for progress during the second year, but the parental feedback variable was considered to have the greatest long-term effects.

Quality of feedback – its contingent appropriateness – is what is central to the second hypothesized facilitating characteristic of adult speech. Under this rubric can be included findings by a number of investigators that

children who make rapid progress are likely to receive a greater frequency of utterances which are contingent on their own previous utterances in the form of imitations, expansions, extension and various combinations of these types of incorporation (Cross 1978; Barnes *et al.* 1983; Hardy-Brown 1983).

McDonald and Pien (1982) approached the same issue from a functional perspective and analysed mothers' speech to 11 children aged 2;5 to 3;0 in terms of mothers' interactional intent. Two polarized clusters emerged from their analysis, which they characterized as a concern to control the child's behaviour as opposed to a concern to facilitate conversation. Only the latter motivation, they suggested, was likely to facilitate children's linguistic and intellectual development. In a study of similar-aged children, Olsen-Fulero (1982) found that variables associated with these same two broad interactional intentions showed differences between individual mothers that were both substantial and stable across two occasions. However, she took the differentiation a stage further by using the relative proportion of characteristics from the two clusters to delineate three styles: controlling, conversational and didactic: 10 out of the 11 mothers in her study could be characterized in terms of these three broad types. The eleventh mother shared the heavy emphasis on the conveying of information of the didactic mothers, but without their frequent use of test questions; she also showed the same degree of 'warmth' as the mothers who appeared to want to influence their children, but without the emphasis on directives shown by the controlling mothers and with a smaller emphasis on questions than the conversation-eliciting mothers. Like McDonald and Pien, Olsen-Fulero speculates that it is the conversation-eliciting mothers whose style is most likely to facilitate their children's linguistic development.

This speculation is certainly supported by the results that are so far available from the Bristol Study (Ellis and Wells 1980; Barnes *et al.* 1983). On the basis of these results and those of other researchers, Wells (1985) suggests that, apart from varying degrees of concern to control their children's behaviour, parents' styles when interacting with their children may realize one or more of the following intentions:

1.   to secure and maintain intersubjectivity of attention
2.   to express their own meaning intentions in a form that their less mature partners will find easy to understand
3.   to ensure that they have correctly understood the meaning intention of their partners
4.   to provide responses which extend, or invite the child to extend, his/her contribution to the construction of shared meaning

5.   to instruct their partners so that they may become more skilled performers, both linguistically and referentially

An analysis of the relationship between variables in the parents' conversational behaviour and the children's rate of progress suggests that, whilst there is little difference between parents with respect to the first two intentions, there is considerable variability with respect to the last three. Children whose parents were more prone to instruct made less than average progress, whereas those whose parents were more concerned to ensure mutual understanding and, above all, to extend the children's topics through related questions, comments and explanations, were likely to make faster than average progress. These parents, it is suggested, as well as providing clear evidence from which the child can construct his control of the language, also increase his motivation to communicate and to acquire the means to do so more effectively.

Whether these different 'styles' – that is to say, different emphases – in parental speech are associated with different routes of development in their children is much less certain. On the face of it, Nelson's (1981a) argument seems reasonable that 'if children adopt different hypotheses about what language is used for, obviously such hypotheses must be based on their experience with language in use' (p. 181). However, apart from the somewhat inconclusive results of Della Corte, Benedict and Klein's (1983) comparison of the input to groups of 'referential' and 'expressive' children, there is as yet little evidence to support this claim and, as argued above, it is by no means clear that it is appropriate to reduce individual differences among children to a single dimension, let alone to a dichotomy. Furthermore, even if a consistent association were to be found, it does not seem to me self-evident that it should be interpreted as resulting from a unidirectional causal influence of parental style on children's style. Studies cited earlier make it clear that there is a considerable measure of adjustment on the part of parents to the level of their child interlocutor's control of language. It seems at least possible, therefore, that if there are differences between children in the strategies that they most frequently use in learning and/or using language, their parents will also adjust to these characteristics when interacting with them. This seems to be implied, at least, in the possibilities of 'match' or 'mismatch' between mother–child pairs in the study by Nelson (1973b) that was discussed earlier in this section.

Several of the studies of parental input that have been referred to in this section have found indications of an association between parental style and parents' level of education or class membership. Much more important, though as yet barely investigated, are differences between whole cultures

in the values that are placed on different types of language use in interaction with young children and, indeed, on whether adults converse with young children at all. Brice Heath (1982) shows that even amongst native English speakers in one town in the United States there are very clear differences in values and expectations with respect to children's learning and use of language between 'mainstream', educated town-dwellers, poor white manual workers and poor black manual workers. As the studies of Blount (1977) and Schieffelin (1979) indicate, the differences are even more pronounced when the child-rearing practices of non-Western cultures are observed. From these investigations it is clear that variation in patterns of language learning and in style of interaction with young children is very much wider than is suggested by the majority of studies reviewed in this chapter. This being so, it is clear that the only firm conclusion that can be drawn at present is that the relationships between experience of linguistic interaction and patterns of language learning are both more complex and more variable than we have so far been willing to recognize.

8. Conclusion

In this chapter I have attempted to review the major dimensions of variation in children's language behaviour and to evaluate the significance of other covarying factors that have been proposed as possible determinants of differences between children in either rate or route of development. From the evidence considered, it is apparent that there is a wide range of variation in rate of development and probably also in the use of the linguistic resources that have been acquired. The evidence for different routes or styles of development is more equivocal, but here too there is evidence of variation in fine points of detail. Whether or not there are clearly differentiated styles leading to different routes or merely an indefinitely large number of interactions between relatively independent dimensions still remains to be investigated on a large enough scale to permit firm conclusions to be reached.

What is clear is that on each of the dimensions considered the distribution of scores derived from observations is continuous rather than dichotomous, which should lead us to be wary of setting up hypothetical categories which are discrete and mutually exclusive. In any case, in many cases where such oppositions have been proposed the categories identified by the two ends of the continuum will both be required if the child is to develop as a normal language user. Both nouns and pronouns are necessary in mature speech, as are the functional uses indicated by such terms as 'expressive' and 'referential'. The same is true of the strategies labelled 'analytic' and 'holistic'.

Both are necessary if the child is to construct his language on the evidence of the speech addressed to him. Differences of these kinds between individuals, therefore, can only be relative: a matter of timing and emphasis rather than of presence or absence.

These qualifications seem to me important, for the picture is neither as clear nor as simple as some writers seem to suggest. Nevertheless, on the basis of the evidence reviewed in this chapter, it is clear that variation should be as central a concept in thinking about language development and language use as are the concepts of regularity and universality. In many respects, however, the first concept is much the more difficult to research by means of empirical investigation. Linguistic behaviour – what a person says or understands on any particular occasion – is influenced by many factors: the immediate context of activity, the expectations of the participants, the way in which they are negotiating their intentions as the interaction proceeds, and so on. And these situational and inter-actional variables are influenced by longer-term factors such as personality, interactional style, linguistic resources available and so on. To give due weight to all these factors in designing a piece of research is clearly extremely difficult.

Not surprisingly, therefore, much of the evidence that has been reviewed in the preceding pages has had to be qualified because of methodological weaknesses in the investigation through which it was obtained. There is thus a need for further research which attempts more satisfactorily to meet the criteria of validity, reliability and representativeness discussed in the opening section. Furthermore, whilst small-scale studies are invaluable for the generation of hypotheses, these can only be tested on relatively large and carefully constructed samples. The difficulties involved in carrying out such studies are substantial, but without them we shall remain at the level of little more than unsupported conjecture.

Equally important, however, if there is to be a real advance, there must be a sustained attempt to develop a theory or theories that will integrate observations and results already obtained and also provide a framework for more systematic empirical investigations in the future. Clearly, several of the writers referred to in this chapter are already engaging in just such an attempt. We may therefore expect the next decade to see a considerable refining of our understanding of the nature and causes of variation in child language.

Part II

THE DEVELOPMENT OF LINGUISTIC
SYSTEMS: PHONOLOGY

Introduction

Four of the chapters in this section are revised versions of essays that appeared in the first edition – those by Stark, Crystal, Menyuk, Menn and Silber and by Ingram. The chapters by Locke and Macken are new, and represent developments since 1979 in the areas of the child's phonological perception, and crosslinguistic perspectives on language development. In this volume, all the chapters on the child's phonetic and phonological development, segmental and nonsegmental, are here brought together within one section.

The child's vocal behaviour in the first year or so is dealt with in the chapters by Stark and Crystal. Stark concentrates on recognizably segmental aspects of production, and Crystal on the antecedents of prosodic development. Stark, after a historical review of work in the area of prespeech segmental development, concludes that while it is now generally agreed that there are levels or stages in the child's vocal behaviour over his first year, we still do not understand the processes underlying the shift from one kind of behaviour to another in the early part of life. After reviewing specific findings from both studies using auditory-impressionistic transcriptions and those which rely on instrumental analysis, Stark details the stages through which children seem to pass, successively: reflexive crying and vegetative sounds, cooing, vocal play, reduplicated babbling, and non-reduplicated babbling. She concludes by relating these behaviours to what is known of the changing anatomy of the infant vocal tract and his developing central nervous system.

In a chapter that is complementary to Stark's, Crystal also identifies descriptive 'stages' in the child's prosodic development. His elaboration of this aspect of the child's development is, however, preceded by a discussion of issues which have to be addressed, in the relatively unfamiliar area of nonsegmental features of language, before characterization of the child's behaviour can be attempted. The first and most important of these questions concerns the domain of a prosodic theory. What phenomena does it address? Crystal points out that the conventional distinction between segmen-

tal and nonsegmental phonology defines the latter as a kind of residue of the former – those linguistically contrastive sound effects that are *not* characterizable in terms of vowels, consonants and the higher order phonological units in which they appear. For the purposes of the chapter, Crystal generally limits the discussion of acquisition to aspects of pitch, loudness, speed and rhythm (including pause) in the child's speech, with various features of pitch patterning receiving most attention. Some space is also devoted to the range of functions which prosodic patterns may be claimed to perform.

The stages which children pass through in developing their prosodic capabilities begin with very early 'cry' and other continuous, though more differentiated, vocalizations. Where there is variation in this behaviour, it can be attributed to the baby's sex or surroundings. The next stage Crystal identifies is perceptual: children at or about 3 months of age are reported to demonstrate an awareness of prosodic contrasts in adult utterances directed to them. Stages III and IV of Crystal's account document the way in which the child's 'increasingly varied vocalizations' come to resemble, in their prosodic characteristics, the language of their environment. A final stage, for the purposes of his essay, examines the interaction between prosodic features and early grammatical development. Crystal emphasizes, throughout his chapter, the methodological problems that beset the study of this area, and the extensive research that remains to be done.

The chapter by Menyuk, Menn and Silber considers both the perception and production of segmental phonological contrasts in the transition from babbling to early language. The perspective within which this account is given is that of the child as active problem solver, both as hearer and speaker (the two aspects of his role as a language user presenting rather different problems). In much of the literature on phonological development (and, incidentally, phonological disability) the role of perception has been played down or ignored. One reason for this is undoubtedly the difficulty in obtaining data from very young children on their perceptual capabilities. But, particularly in the early stages, it seems clear that the perception of sounds deserves very close scrutiny. The emphasis given to it by Menyuk *et al.*, and the chapter by Locke devoted to it, should serve as useful correctives to the relative neglect of perceptual factors. In a detailed review of what is known about early perception, Menyuk *et al.* emphasize the likely reliance by the child on the recognition and storage of larger units (syllables, words), rather than analysing what he hears down to individual segments or distinctive features. Their account of both perception and production can be seen as a reaction against the universalist, segmental approach to even the earliest phonological development, an approach which dominated

the field following the publication of Jakobson (1968). The first cracks in this edifice were engineered by Ferguson and Farwell (1975), whose study of the variable pronunciations of words and segments in early production vocabularies indicated considerable inter- and intraword variation in the pronunciation of individual segments. This in turn suggested that a purely segment-based characterization of early pronunciations, which assumed early phonemic differentiation, would be inappropriate. At this stage of development, it seemed unfruitful to consider the child's segmental phonetics/phonology independently of the lexical items in which these segments appeared. Menyuk *et al.* explore the implications of the idea that syllables and words play a major role in the child's perception and production, in the transition from prelanguage to language, and relate an impressive range of apparently disparate empirical findings to their problem-solving theory of the acquisition of phonology.

In the initial stages of establishing a lexicon, the child may be able to get by with relatively inaccurate pronunciations, with a highly limited phone set. As his vocabulary increases during the end of the second and the beginning of the third year, the child's strategies must provide, fairly rapidly, an increasingly differentiated set of phones, which need to be organized within the phonological structure of the language he is learning. The remaining chapters in this section deal with the problems faced by the child in this aspect of development (and those presented to the analyst in characterizing it).

In trying to make sense of what Ingram calls 'the phonology of the simple morpheme', between approximately 18 months and 4 years of age, we are faced with an apparent paradox. On the one hand, we can find quite young children striving to maintain phonemic distinctions: for instance, Fey and Gandour (1982) report on a child not yet 25 months, who consistently maintains a distinction between voiced and voiceless stops by representing the former by a post-nasalizing of the stop, so *feet* and *feed*, say, would be distinguished as [viːtʰ] and [viːdŋ]. We can thus find early evidence of systematicity so far as contrastiveness is concerned. On the other hand, we have Olmsted's (1971) finding, from a study of errors in pronunciation in 100 children between 1;3 and 4;6, that there was a high degree of variability in the phonetic realization of adult phonemes in spontaneous speech. The children in the sample did not learn phones 'across-the-board' – there was little evidence of instantaneous change in their surface realizations – nor did they, in the substitutions they made, always substitute the same phone for the adult target. Admittedly, younger children make more mistakes, but it seems as if children well beyond the stage of 50-word vocabularies evince inter- and intralexical variation in their pronunciation.

The variability displayed goes well beyond allophonic variation. Successful phonological contrastivity depends on the deployment of a limited set of allophones, conditioned by the relevant environments. How do we reconcile these apparently distinct tendencies that appear in the data, to systematicity on the one hand and variability on the other? And how do we resolve the problem of the considerable individual variation that children show in their convergence on an adult phonological system?

These are issues that the remaining three chapters are concerned with. Ingram describes the phonological patterns that can be found, in production, in the acquisition of English and other languages, by a consistent description within a phonological process framework. The success of the framework in handling disparate data suggests that the notion of phonological process may have explanatory value. Ingram does, however, point out the problems caused by non-isomorphic processes (i.e. child forms that it is impossible to relate segment-by-segment to adult targets) and the range of individual variation. The development of any single child can be seen as an amalgam of common phonological processes and 'unique phonological preferences' that may take quite distinct forms in different children.

Locke's chapter is concerned with auditory representations – with the child's interpretation of the adult spoken form and how this affects his pronunciation. An example (not one used by Locke: see Braine 1976b) will help to underline Locke's concerns. Suppose a child at a particular stage in development represents adult /nt/ clusters by [t], and adult /nd/ by [n]. How do we explain the difference? If we assume that the child's lexical representation is the same as the adult's spoken form, we simply have to assume he has distinct production rules for nasal clusters with voiceless and voiced consonants. But (as Braine pointed out) there is a plausible perceptual explanation for such behaviour. It is well-known that vocalic elements are longer before voiced than before voiceless stops in English. Thus the [n] preceding [d] would be more salient than the [n] preceding [t], and this is perhaps what the child has latched on to in his initial attempts to interpret the phonetic sequences he hears. The pronunciation errors we note are, on this hypothesis, not the result of production problems but of inadequate perception (or rather inappropriate interpretation of the perceptual data presented). Locke's chapter is a plea for us to take seriously the child's problems of the interpretation of perceptual data.

Macken's paper begins by underlining the 'central challenge' for those studying phonological acquisition – the one we have already referred to: 'the coexistence of extensive diversity – across time, languages and children ... and striking similarities – patterns that must seemingly derive from

some set of invariant properties of the language capacity'. The chapter synthesizes information from both perception and production in addressing the issue of how the child learns the phonological structure of his language. With the added dimension of crosslinguistic material to inform consideration of the interaction between the learning capacity and the structure of the language being learned, this chapter serves as a fitting finale for the section.

7. Prespeech segmental feature development*

Rachel E. Stark

1. Introduction

In the first part of the twentieth century, investigators who studied infant vocal output had two quite different aims in mind. One group wished to trace the development of the adult spoken language system, usually German or English (Stern and Stern 1928; Leopold 1947); the other group was concerned with scales for measuring psychological development in infants and was, therefore, concerned with infant behaviour *per se* (Cattell 1940; Gesell and Amatruda 1941, and others). Both groups, however, lacked the tools for adequate description of infant vocal behaviour. Their observations are of interest, but the findings yielded little understanding of the developmental processes which might be involved.

Although it was contrary to some of the evidence already accumulated, particularly in the work of Gregoire (1939), the view was expressed that prespeech vocal behaviour was a completely random activity, subject to no developmental laws. In this activity, the infant was said to produce 'all possible sounds'. Jakobson (1968) is most widely quoted in support of this view but others have espoused it also (Osgood 1953; Lenneberg 1962; Rees 1972). This view also implies that there is a sharp discontinuity between the period of random articulatory activity and the production of first words which is subject to developmental laws having certain universal aspects (Jakobson 1968).

In subsequent work, interest in the developmental processes that might be reflected in prespeech vocal behaviour began to be manifested. Bever (1961) re-analysed phonetic transcription data, obtained by Irwin and his colleagues in the 1940s (Irwin and Chen 1946), in terms of magnitude and rate of change in production of phonemes throughout infancy. Bever identified three distinct developmental periods: 0 to 3 months, 4 to 11 months and 12 to 18 months. He showed that there was a cyclic pattern of segmental feature development in each of these periods, with a peak of activity in the mid portion of each cycle and a decline thereafter. Patterns of vowel

149

and consonant acquisition were found to differ from one another in a number of ways, thus suggesting that 'vocalic activity does not emerge by the same process as consonantal'. The developmental periods, and the cycles of activity within each, correlated well with other aspects of neurological development and in Bever's view reflected central nervous system maturation.

Menyuk (1968) reviewed data obtained by Nakazima *et al.* (1962) and concluded that the rank ordering of mastery of distinctive features in the babbling of the infants studied by these investigators was similar to that shown by a somewhat older group of American children in their word productions (Templin and Darley 1960). The data suggested a 'hierarchy of feature distinction which might be a linguistic universal, probably dependent on the developing and productive capacities of the child'.

Other studies conducted in the 1960s were based upon the Jakobsonian view that the sounds of all languages are present in the infant's output. These studies were concerned with the factors which govern the infant's selection from his repertoire of those phonemes which are appropriate for the language he is to learn. Some were concerned with hypotheses about the role of imitation (Webster 1969). In others a shaping process was hypothesized in which the phonemes of the language spoken by the child were selectively reinforced by the adults in his environment (Siegel 1971).

Studies of vocal conditioning have indeed shown that rate of vocal output may be brought under control by appropriate contingent rewards (Rheingold, Gewirtz and Ross 1959; Weisberg 1963; Sheppard 1969) and that, over the short term, the relative frequency of occurrence of particular utterance types may be influenced in the same manner (Routh 1969; Wahler 1969). In the most exhaustive study of its kind, Wahler identified vocal behaviours appearing in the output of an individual infant throughout the first year of life. He found that, by selective reinforcement, the frequency of occurrence of new vocal behaviours could be increased at the expense of old and *vice versa*. However, the form of each new vocal behaviour was not under experimental control and was not predicted by the experimenters. Wahler concluded that a shaping process was not responsible for the changes in vocal behaviour which were documented.

At the present time, investigators using acoustic-phonetic approaches to the study of infant vocal behaviour agree that there are levels or stages in the development of this behaviour. We are still far from understanding, however, the processes which motivate shifts of the infant from one level to the next. It is not clear to what extent the development of vocal behaviour may be continuous and to what extent discontinuities may appear. Resolution of these questions may depend in part upon greater deployment of

the techniques of analysis that are now available. Additional techniques, for example, the use of ultra sound to examine articulatory activity, may also be required.

In this chapter we will describe a variety of methodological approaches that have been used in the study of infant vocal behaviour and will review the findings yielded by each. In addition, we will examine the relationship of these findings to information at present available with respect to the changing anatomy of the infant vocal tract and to the development of those parts of the central nervous system that are likely to be involved in the control of vocal behaviours.

2. Phonetic transcription

Phonetic transcription began to be used for the purposes of description of infant sounds in the 1930s and 1940s (Irwin and Chen 1946, 1947; Leopold 1947; Lewis 1951). Irwin and his colleagues used a limited transcription system in which few vowel or consonant items other than those of American English were represented. They studied a large number of infants, some on a longitudinal basis, and were able as a result to draw up an inventory of vowel and consonant types present at each age level. This inventory, which was based upon group means, indicated that vowels predominated in the infant's output in the early months of life, both in terms of overall frequency of occurrence and of the ratio of vowel to consonant types produced. Consonants showed more rapid growth than vowels throughout the first two years of life. These data also indicated that consonant types produced at the back of the mouth were acquired first and those produced more anteriorly were acquired later. Vowels appeared in the opposite direction, that is, from front to back. A later study in which taperecordings were employed confirmed these findings in general (Fisichelli 1950).

Lewis (1951) studied only one infant's vocal output but made extensive longitudinal phonetic analyses. He was one of the first to try to account for the developmental sequence in acquisition of consonants and vowels, which he found to be similar to that reported by Irwin. He noted that the early appearing back consonants usually transcribed as /ç/, /g/, /x/ and /k/ were produced in comfort; the later appearing front consonants /m/ and /n/ were first associated with discomfort but as the infant accumulated experience of relief from discomfort the sounds became associated with that relief and were produced in comfortable states also. Lewis further believed that other front consonants, for example, /p/ and /b/, produced in the second six months of life were associated with the experience of feeding.

In subsequent studies, problems with the use of phonetic transcription quickly became apparent. Some infant sounds eluded all attempts to transcribe them by this means. Acoustic analyses revealed differences between infant and adult productions which were not accounted for by the phonetic transcription system (Lynip 1951); and the problem of establishing interjudge reliability, which became more apparent after taperecordings began to be used, proved difficult to resolve. More recent studies have employed narrow transcription by means of a modified version of the International Phonetic Alphabet (Smith and Oller 1981; Smith 1982). Modifications were in the form of diacritics added to capture more accurately nuances of vocalizations produced by infants and young children. Only vocalizations judged to be 'speech-like' were transcribed by this system, however. Reliability studies showed that independent listeners agreed with one another between 80 per cent and 90 per cent of the time in transcribing these vocalizations. Reliability increased with the age of the infant.

The findings of Smith and Oller were substantially in agreement with those of Irwin and his colleagues. Back consonants dominated in early productions and front consonants increased in frequency of occurrence toward the end of the first year. The opposite trend was found with respect to vowels. In addition, a surprising result obtained in these studies was that Down Syndrome infants were not significantly different from normal infants with respect to order of emergence of sound types, nor with respect to the onset of babbling (at 8½ months on the average in Down Syndrome infants as opposed to 8 months in the normal infants). Hearing-impaired infants were delayed in the onset of first words and in aspects of earlier vocal development also, but demonstrated similar trends to those of normal infants with respect to frequency of occurrence of back and front consonants. All three groups (normal, Down Syndrome and hearing-impaired) showed a predominance of front and central vowels of mid-to-low tongue height throughout the prelinguistic period.

Later phonetic studies were concerned with issues of continuity of development. Oller et al. (1976), for example, showed that there are certain commonalities of phonetic structure from babbled utterances produced in the prelinguistic period to the child's first attempts to produce meaningful speech. These investigators predicted correctly that babbling would, in continuity with meaningful speech, show the following characteristics:

(i)   reduction of consonant clusters
(ii)   deletion of final consonants
(iii) devoicing of final consonants where these were present
(iv)   a greater number of initial stops than initial fricatives and affricates

(v)   a greater number of /w/ and /y/ glides than of liquids in the prevocalic position
(vi)   a greater number of apical than of velar consonants

These findings also implied a relationship between babbling and phonological universals. It would appear that those sounds which the infant is capable of producing at the end of the prespeech period are the sounds most likely to find their way into adult phonological systems (see also Cruttenden 1970).

Subsequently, de Boysson-Bardies *et al.* (1981) presented phonetic data suggesting that children in French- and American English-speaking environments may share the phonetic preferences, such as cluster reduction, described by Oller *et al.* However, de Boysson-Bardies, Sagart and Bacri (1981) also reported differences in the late babbling of a French child (18–20 months of age) which might be ascribed to corresponding differences in his target language. They compared the phonetic repertoires of French, English and Thai with this child's late babbling corpus and concluded that there was a closer similarity of the corpus with French than with the other languages considered. They hypothesized on the basis of these results that a selective, language-specific phonetic acquisition may take place in the late babbling period.

3. Acoustic-phonetic studies

In a number of studies, acoustic analyses have been employed in addition to phonetic transcription. The acoustic analyses in these studies were applied to phonetic features upon which listeners agreed or which could be abstracted from the transcriptions of a number of listeners on the basis of an acceptable level of consensus. The earliest of these studies focused upon crosslinguistic data. Nakazima (1966) first showed, by means of phonetic transcription and spectrographic analysis, that infants raised in an American English- and a Japanese-speaking environment produced similar sound types throughout the prelinguistic period. In subsequent studies, measures of voicing in stop consonants were obtained from spectrographic data. It was shown that voice onset time, i.e. the time interval between release of a stop consonant and the onset of voicing, was very similar for infants of 10 to 12 months raised in an Arabic- and an American English-speaking environment (Preston *et al.* 1969; Kewley-Port and Preston 1974). The same voice onset time results were later obtained for infants raised in a French-speaking environment (Enstrom and Stoll 1976).

Acoustic-phonetic studies have also been carried out with the aim of

identifying characteristics of mature languages in the vocalizations of infants. One such characteristic was the final-syllable lengthening found in English and other languages. Oller and Smith (1977) found that the final syllable of a babbled series in infants of 8 to 12 months showed significantly less lengthening in comparison with nonfinal syllables than is the case for adult speakers of English in their regular speech or in their imitations of infant babbling. Laufer (1980), on the other hand, in an extensive study of four infants in the first six months of life, found a consistent final 'protosyllable' lengthening in two-protosyllable utterances. Laufer defined the protosyllable as a 'relative peak of sonorance characterized by a rise in fundamental frequency, amplitude and duration'. Base phonetic structures, e.g. consonant + vowel, vowel + glottal stop + vowel, vowel + aspiration, etc. were subsequently derived from these protosyllables by judgement of both auditory and acoustic data. Laufer concluded that final-protosyllable lengthening reflects a type of central programmed regulation of vocal behaviour.

A second characteristic that has been described in acoustic-phonetic studies is that of vowel quality. Lieberman (1980) and Buhr (1980) have studied the development of vowel production in a small number of American infants. Vowel utterances for which satisfactory agreement could be reached in transcription by a panel of three phonetically trained listeners were subjected to spectrographic analysis. The authors showed that formant frequencies are higher in infants than in older children or adults, as would be expected on the basis of their shorter supralaryngeal vocal tract. Formant frequencies fall as the infants increase in age and with vocal tract growth. An approximation of the acoustic vowel space of English appeared to take place during the babbling stage: that is, analysis of formant 1/formant 2 plots over time revealed the emergence of a well-developed vowel triangle, resembling that of older children and adults. The authors suggest the presence of a perceptual mechanism that 'normalizes' vowel sounds in terms of the speaker's presumed vocal tract length. Thus infants, if they are imitating adult vowel sounds, do not mimic the absolute formant frequencies of the adult speech they hear (as in theory they could for certain vowels). Instead they produce a vowel sound that is perceived as the equivalent of an adult / i / , for example, but that has formant values appropriate for an infant vocal tract. There is no evidence of discontinuity in Lieberman's data. However, data from George (1981) and from Stark, Heinz and Wright-Wilson (1976) have suggested that there is a greater increase in use of the vowel space in the production of infants after 3 months than at any time prior to that age. This finding may reflect acceleration in the overall growth of the supralaryngeal vocal tract from approximately 3 months of age.

4. Descriptive feature systems

Auditory and spectrographic features have been identified and studied primarily by investigators who have had to deal with the output of very young infants. Phonetic transcription is least appropriate and useful in the age range 0 to 3 months. The feature systems developed for the purpose of description of the vocalizations of these young infants are shown in table 1. It should be noted that the features listed are considered to be descriptive and not in any sense distinctive. Truby and Lind (1965), Wasz-Hockert et al. (1968) and Vuorenkoski et al. (1971) employed spectrographic features to describe vocalizations produced in quite rigidly defined circumstances. Kent and Murray (1982) have developed a coding system based upon acoustic features of vocalic utterances but have avoided the use of auditory judgements other than those pertaining to the vocalic or consonantal nature of an utterance and the exclusion of non-speech-like sounds, i.e., vegetative or reflexive sounds such as breathing noise and cough. Zlatin (1975) and Stark, Rose and McLagen (1975) employed auditory and spectrographic features to describe utterances produced in certain broadly defined states (e.g. cry, noncry, laugh). Zlatin (1975) used a segmental transcription system and then examined spectrographic data in order to find out how well the listeners' judgements correlated with acoustic features which she had previously identified as indicating the presence of an articulatory event, such as glottal stop or glottal aspirate. However, this procedure does not necessarily establish the validity of the system. The articulatory gestures implied cannot be observed directly, and it can only be assumed that they were made.[1] Oller also examined both phonetic and acoustic infant vocalization data in order to derive a set of descriptive features.

Stark et al. (1975) allowed listeners to examine the spectrographic representation of an utterance and to listen to it at the same time. This procedure has the advantage of increasing intra- and interjudge reliability. The units for which judgements are to be made may be defined more clearly in terms of interval and segment duration and the system improves the judges' ability to detect features in both modes. It will be noted that certain features, namely place of articulation for consonants, tongue height and position for vowels, and nasality of vowels, have been omitted from this system. These features could not be judged reliably in either mode.

In spite of the differences in methodology employed, there is considerable agreement among investigators employing feature systems with respect to the development of segmental features in infancy. This agreement makes it possible to trace segmental feature development through the first year of life at least in a preliminary way, and to relate that development to the acquisition of early forms of spoken language acquired in the second

year of life. As indicated above, this development is thought to take place in a series of stages or levels.

5. Stages of vocal development

The descriptions of the stages of vocal development in all infants studied thus far are remarkably consistent with one another. Six stages have been identified. It should be pointed out, however, that these stages overlap to a considerable extent: the behaviours from early stages, for example, only gradually decline in frequency of occurrence as new stages emerge.

5.1. Stage I: Reflexive crying and vegetative sounds (0 to 8 weeks)

In Stage I only reflexive sounds (e.g. crying, fussing) and vegetative sounds (e.g. burping, swallowing, spitting up) are produced. Crying and fussing have certain features in common. Their segments, i.e. vocal units separated from one another by at least 50 msec of silence, are:

(i)   predominantly voiced – breathy voicing may be present but completely voiceless portions, which seem always to be associated with forceful expulsion of air, are brief and relatively infrequent

(ii)   predominantly egressive in breath direction – expiration is prolonged and voiced inspiratory (ingressive) segments, which may sometimes be produced immediately following a cry, are relatively brief

(iii)   predominantly vowel-like – the vowels are judged to be mid or low front vowels (Lieberman et al. 1971); nasal and liquid consonant-like elements are found in low-level crying and fussing, and glottal stops are often observed to initiate or terminate a cry segment; however, the major portion of each cry–discomfort segment is vocalic

On the average, cry segments are 500 to 1000 msec in duration (Ringel and Kluppel 1964; Truby and Lind 1965; Stark and Nathanson 1974). They occur in long series which may occupy as much as five minutes with only brief pauses. Discomfort (fussing) sounds are 500 msec or less in average duration, and they tend to occur in shorter series than cry sounds (Stark et al. 1975). Extremely high pitches and sudden shifts in pitch are more common in pain than in hunger cry; a reflexive hiccoughing motion of the diaphragm, which is associated with forceful expulsion of air, is more characteristic of hunger or other spontaneous cries. The expulsion of air gives rise to rapid alternation of voicing with voiceless breath noise in these types of cry. Wasz-Hockert et al. (1968) refer to the phenomena as 'glottal pulses'. Other voice quality features such as vocal fry (creaky

voice), harshness and subharmonic break, are very common in all types of cry.

The class of vegetative sounds may be subdivided into grunts and sighs associated with activity, and clicks, stops and other noises associated with the management of nutrients (air and liquids). They are:

(i)   equally likely to be voiced or voiceless – about 25 to 30 per cent of all vegetative sounds are voiceless throughout and thus barely audible

(ii) equally likely to be produced on an outgoing or ingoing breath – ingressive portions are not more prominent in terms of frequency of occurrence than egressive

(iii) equally likely to be vowel-like or consonant-like – the consonant elements are clicks, stops, friction noises and trills

(iv) very brief (330 msec on average for egressive vegetative sounds, mostly grunts and sighs, and 140 msec for those which are ingressive)

5.2. Stage II: Cooing and laughter (8 to 20 weeks)

Cooing (comfort) sounds are produced in comfortable states, often in response to smiling and talking on the part of the mother. These sounds are sometimes referred to as vowel-like, but in fact they contain brief consonantal elements also (Lewis 1951; Nakazima 1962; Oller *et al.* 1976; Stark *et al.* 1976). They usually appear between 6 and 8 weeks of age. According to Murai (1960), Nakazima (1962) and Oller (1976), early comfort sounds have a quasi-resonant nucleus, that is, they take the form of a syllabic nasal consonant or a nasalized vowel. The lack of resonance probably reflects the fact that the mouth is less widely open than during cry. The consonantal elements, usually transcribed as $/ç/$, $/g/$, $/x/$ and $/k/$, are all produced at the back of the mouth, where the tongue and palate are most likely to resume contact with one another during vocalic sounds.

When cooing sounds first emerge they tend to be produced as single segments only, each one of approximately 500 msec duration. Subsequently, these segments enter into series with one another, series which may have as many as 3 to 10 segments within them. In some infants there is typically an intake of breath (usually voiceless) between each segment, while in others more than one segment is likely to be present in an expiratory vocal unit. Glottal stops and voiceless intervals separate these within-vocal unit segments. Vowels may become more fully resonant and more diversified in quality in later-appearing cooing sounds (Lieberman *et al.* 1976); however, although listeners agree in hearing a greater variety of vowels in

the older infant's output, there may be less agreement after than before the onset of cooing in their transcriptions of any given vowel sound (Stark *et al.* 1976). Changes within vowel nuclei, which may be heard as either diphthongs or glides, begin to be recorded more frequently and re¹ ·bly in the output of some infants. Zlatin (1975) refers to the production of longer series of comfort sounds as 'early syllabification', although the segments produced are not like the syllables of adult speech in their timing or their feature content.

From 12 weeks of age onward, the frequency of occurrence of crying drops markedly and in most infants primitive vegetative sounds begin to disappear. At 16 weeks of age sustained laughter emerges (Gesell and Thompson 1934). In the earliest laugh sounds a rapid alternation of voiced and voiceless portions initiates laughter. This alternation, which might be transcribed as /hahaha/, resembles the glottal pulses of spontaneous crying. The series usually terminates with a segment which resembles the infant's cooing sound segments.

5.3. Stage III: Vocal play (16 to 30 weeks)

Oller refers to this stage as the expansion stage. There may be some overlap of the end of Stage II with the beginning of Stage III. The essential characteristics of Stage III are that longer series of segments are produced than in the cooing stage and that the infant produces prolonged vowel- or consonant-like steady states in these series. The rate of transitions within the segment, for example, in pitch, voicing, or degree of constriction of the vocal tract may be much slower than in child or adult speech. At the same time, however, extremely abrupt transitions in pitch, voicing and constriction of the vocal tract are also found. Segments are of greater duration (700 to 1500 msec on the average) than in Stage II. Consonantal elements are produced more anteriorly.

In Stage III the infant repetitively produces primitive segment types characterized by:

(i)   high pitch and extreme pitch glides
(ii)   low pitched growling, pharyngeal friction, or, less frequently, vocal fry
(iii)   voiced and voiceless egressive friction noises and trills (the friction noises and trills are produced by approximating tongue and pharyngeal palate, tongue and both the alveolar ridge of the palate and the lips, or the lips with one another, and by blowing air, saliva, or food through the constriction formed by these structures) and, in some infants, prolonged fricatives

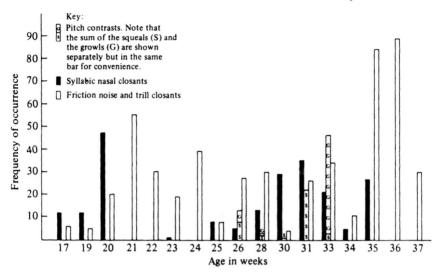

Figure 1. The frequency of occurrence of different segment types in the production of Infant VW from 17 to 37 weeks

(iv)   voiced inspiratory sounds
(v)   syllabic nasal consonant sounds (/ m / and / n /)
(vi)   exaggerated voiceless clicks, e.g. lip smacking and affricate clicks
(vii) vowels in which tongue height and position are more varied than in Stage II.

All of the features of these segment types except (vii) are present in Stages I and II. In Stage III, however, they are employed repeatedly, prolonged and elaborated. They are also divorced from their previous cry, vegetative or comfort sound contexts, and are used in a variety of communicative situations. Notice that many of these segment types (e.g. lip smacking and voiced inspiratory sounds), although found in adult spoken languages, are not phonological universals.

The above segment types show different orders of appearance in the vocal output of different infants. One infant may use the first two types of segments (high pitch and / or extreme pitch glides and low pitched segments) alternately for many weeks and then abruptly switch to the third type (voiced and voiceless friction noises and trills), engaging in the practice of the latter sound types for a brief time only, perhaps as little as a portion of one day. Another infant may show these behaviours in a completely different order. This lack of uniform order of appearance of segment types is illustrated in data from two different infants shown in figures 1 and 2.

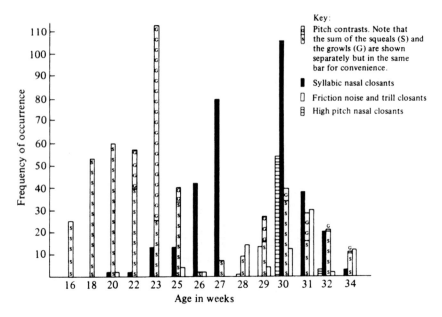

Figure 2. The frequency of occurrence of different segment types in the production of Infant MV from 16 to 34 weeks

Towards the end of Stage III the above features enter into increasingly complex combinations with one another in still longer vocal units and segments. For example, a vocal play sound unit may be initiated with a high pitched vowel and/or pitch glide, shift to a vowel of normal pitch and terminate with a voiced trill, the entire unit occupying from 2 to 3 seconds without pause. These complex segments are also produced in long series. Imprecisely articulated stop–vowel syllables may appear in these series. In these syllables, a brief trill or friction noise may occur as the stop is released into the vowel. The vowel format transition is likely to be irregular and may be highly variable in duration, often extremely long. Oller (1976) refers to these series as 'marginal babbling'.

5.4. Stage IV: Reduplicated babbling (25 to 50 weeks)

Reduplicated babbling has been defined as the production of series of consonant–vowel syllables in which the consonant is the same in every syllable. Examples are /nənə/ or /ədada/. Quite often, as indicated, a brief vowel initiates the series. Thus, the series of syllables in reduplicated babbling are relatively steretyped in content. The degree of precision of consonant

production may vary over a babbled series, at the onset of Stage IV. Thus, the apical stop /d/ may predominate in the syllables within a series but glides or brief friction noises at the same place of articulation may also be present, initiating one or more of the syllables within the series. Labial and alveolar stops and nasals, and /w/ and /y/ glides are the most frequently appearing consonants in babbling. Listeners may still have difficulty in agreeing upon the place of articulation. Inspection of videotapes indicates that in the case of stops and nasals, because the tongue is still relatively large in relation to the oral cavity, the tongue blade may approximate the alveolar ridge but may also be resting against the lips, which are partially closed around it. Thus, some of the acoustic cues are likely to be intermediate between those of bilabial and of alveolar consonants of adult speech. The vowel nuclei are almost all fully resonant.

The consonant–vowel transitions are smooth and regular, occupying 100 msec approximately. The tongue no longer separates from the palate as though the constriction so formed were forced open by the air pressure building up behind it, with an abrupt tap as in earlier nasals, or with a trill or friction noise as in earlier stop–vowel syllables. The opening of the constriction now appears to be relatively well controlled. Fine control of timing, e.g. of the onset of voicing in the stop–vowel syllables, may be different from that found in adult speech, however. There is some evidence that all possible values of this voice onset timing are equally likely when stop–vowel syllables first appear. However, as indicated above, by 11 months of age infants of different language communities strongly favour a simultaneous release of the stop and onset of voicing, or values which are very close to synchrony of these two gestures (Preston *et al.* 1969; Kewley-Port and Preston 1974; Enstrom and Stoll 1976). Adult languages are likely to show more than one modal value of voice onset time. (These adult values correspond to the categories of voiced, voiceless, voiceless unaspirated, and voiceless aspirated stops.)

Reduplicated babbling is not used in communication with adults but rather in a self-stimulatory manner at the onset of Stage V. Towards the end of this stage, however, the babbling may be used in ritual imitation games with adults.

5.5. Stage V: Non-reduplicated babbling

In Stage V, reduplicated babbling is replaced by babbling in which vowel, consonant–vowel and consonant–vowel–consonant syllables may all appear within a given series. Within these series, the consonants as well as the vowels may be different from one syllable to another. The consonants

already found in reduplicated babbling are present in this variegated babbling (Oller's term, 1976). To these are added new elements, and in particular the fricatives (/s/, /x/, /g/ and /ç/) and high front and mid and high
back vowels, both rounded and unrounded. Towards the end of Stage V,
a variety of stress and intonation patterns may be imposed upon non-
reduplicated babbling so that, according to parents, the babbling 'sounds
like a foreign language', hence the term 'expressive jargon' (Gesell and
Thompson 1934). Some infants spend several months in this activity; others
proceed more rapidly to Stage VI, the production of first words, which
will not be described here. Dore (1973) refers to the former group as 'intonation babies' and suggests that they are more socially adept, better able
to express their attitudes and perhaps to manipulate adults than the latter
group whom he refers to as 'word babies'; 'word babies' are more interested
in naming objects. Nelson (1973b) finds that children who are developing
meaningful speech may also be classed as 'referential' or 'expressive',
according to the strategies they use in learning how to put words together.
It is not at present known whether the same infants are likely to be 'expressive' or 'referential' in both developmental stages.

Dore *et al.* (1976) identify a transitional period between babbling and
first words in which certain phonetic forms are used consistently to express
primitive groupings of experience and in play rituals. These utterances
may resemble the sounds accompanied by the gestures of reaching, pointing, grasping and rejection that are described by Bates (1976) as protowords
and by Carter (1979) as sensorimotor morphemes. Their production may
correspond also to Nakazima's (1970) first step of the reorganization of
babbling.

6. Developmental processes

The stages of development of vocal behaviour were previously thought
to be hierarchical in nature. It was believed that each new stage incorporated
previous stages and built upon them. Thus, an apparent discontinuity from
one stage to the next was thought to reflect a quantal jump in development
rather than a lack of relationship between the adjacent stages. Such views
of developmental stages are based upon Piagetian constructs and have
recently been subject to controversy. They may well be partly true. However, a number of different accounts have been suggested (e.g., Brainerd
1978; Fischer and Corrigan 1981). Some aspects of vocal development may
be recombinatory in nature, such that features of vocalization are progressively co-ordinated with one another; other features of prelinguistic vocalization are not incorporated into the child's meaningful speech but are

dropped. In addition, certain aspects of vocal development appear to be quite novel at the time of their appearance, i.e., they cannot satisfactorily be explained as representing recombinations of previously existing skills, but must reflect other developmental processes.

6.1. Anatomical development

Oller (1976) suggests that the earliest productions of infants provide a matrix of primitive metaphonological features from which some of the most important aspects of speech derive. One of these metaphonological features, for example, is phonation, over which Oller believes that the infant begins to gain control very early in life, probably in the third or fourth week. Other features are added sequentially as different stages or levels of vocal behaviour emerge. The consonantal feature of velar or uvular constriction is added, for example, at the onset of cooing.

Kent (1981) suggests that these new acquisitions parallel related changes in the anatomy and physiology of the vocal tract. The neonatal vocal tract is not a smaller replica of the adult's, but is quite different in overall configuration, resembling the vocal tract of the adult nonhuman primate more closely than that of the adult human. Thus, in early infancy phonated sounds, especially noncry sounds, tend to be nasalized because of the relative height of the larynx and close engagement of larynx and nasopharynx. The tongue is large in relation to the inner dimensions of the oral cavity and is capable of back and forth motion only.

The features of the cry sounds and vegetative sounds produced in Stage I, the reflexive stage (see figures 3 and 4), reflect both the configuration of the infant vocal tract and its physiologic manifestations (Bosma, Truby and Lind 1965; Bosma 1972, 1975). The young infant is a compulsive nasal breather except during cry. The mouth is filled by the tongue which rests against the lower lip and maintains apposition with the soft palate. During cry this apposition is given up. The soft palate and pharyngeal wall move dorsalward. The jaw is lowered and with it the tongue, which shows median grooving. The opening of the mouth gives rise to the vowel-like character of most distress sounds. However, the tongue tends to resume apposition with the soft palate in low-level crying and discomfort sounds and when it does, a nasal or liquid consonant-like sound results (Stark and Nathanson 1974).

In addition, active crying alters the respiratory pattern observed at rest (Langlois and Baken 1976). The expiratory phase of respiration is greatly increased in duration; cineradiographic data indicate a generalized constriction of the pharyngeal area and the opening to the larynx (Bosma 1975).

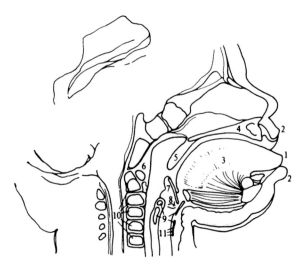

Figure 3. Sagittal section through the head of the newborn infant in midline (after Bosma 1972; original figure drawn by H. Bartner). Notice that the larynx is high, at about the level of the first to the third cervical vertebrae. It is very closely suspended from the hyoid cartilage. The tongue is large, filling the oral cavity and resting upon the lower lip. The oropharyngeal area is the only portion of the vocal tract in which the tongue may change its position, except when the mouth is opened. Adjustments in vocal tract configuration take place in this area in response to cry, sucking and swallowing, and possibly also to changes in the head position. These adjustments are necessary to maintain patency of the airway and to ensure adequate ventilation. *Key:* 1, tongue blade; 2, lips; 3, body of tongue; 4, hard palate; 5, soft palate; 6, posterior pharyngeal wall; 7, epiglottis; 8, vocal and ventricular folds; 9, cartilages of larynx; 10, cervical vertebrae; 11, trachea

The pharynx and larynx are elevated above the rest position. During the very brief inspiratory phase the pharynx is expanded by outward movement of the pharyngeal walls and sometimes also by extension of the head and neck. The soft palate moves towards the tongue so that breathing is at least partly through the nose during inspiration.

The class of vegetative sounds is associated primarily with maintenance of the patency of the airway for respiration and its defence against penetration by substances which might choke the infant; it is also associated with intake and output of fluids. Vegetative sounds include coughing, belching, and sneezing which persist into adult life. In the very young infant, however, the positioning of structures in the pharyngeal area of the vocal tract is highly unstable. Sensory receptors in the pharyngeal region are of great importance for maintaining airway patency. Thus, respiratory

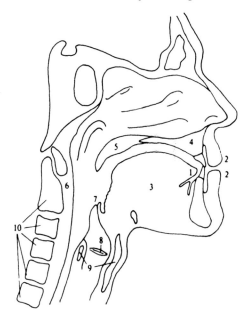

Figure 4. Sagittal section through the head of the adult in midline (from Zemlin 1968). The larynx has descended to the level of the third to the fifth cervical vertebrae. Downward and forward growth of the face has increased the size of the oral cavity in relation to the tongue. The tongue is now capable of assuming positions at different heights in front, mid and back of the mouth, and also of a considerable range of motion within the mouth (for Key see figure 3)

movements are exaggerated and are constantly required to adapt to reflexes such as rooting reflexes, swallowing and stimulation to the nostrils. Many of these adjustments give rise to brief stops, clicks and other noises which occur without voice and may be expiratory or inspiratory. They can only be recorded with the aid of a sensitive air microphone or a throat microphone.

A new combination of features is formed in cooing sounds, of the voicing and egressive breath direction typical of cry, and the stops, trills, and friction noises previously present in vegetative sounds only (see figures 5 and 6). Careful listening suggests that this new combination emerges primarily because, as the infant gains control over voicing, he becomes able to express pleasure as well as discomfort vocally (Stark 1978). He is, however, unable at this time to inhibit vegetative activity of the vocal tract. This activity, which leads to constriction in the oropharyngeal region, is frequently superimposed upon pleasure voicing, thus giving rise to the brief nonsonorant

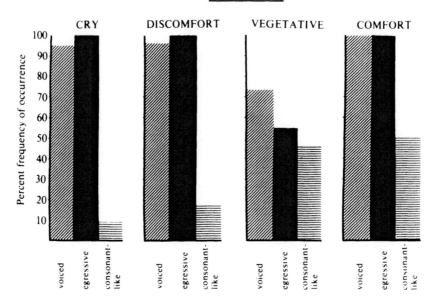

SOUND CLASS

Figure 5. Percent frequency of occurrence of the features voiced (in whole or in part), egressive (in whole or in part) and consonant-like, in cry, discomfort (fussing), vegetative and comfort (cooing) sounds. Notice that the comfort sounds resemble cry and discomfort sounds with respect to voicing and breath direction; but resemble vegetative sounds with respect to frequency of consonant-like elements

consonantal elements which are present in many cooing sounds. The nasal consonants are similar to those found in cry.

Thus, cry–discomfort sounds have some of the characteristics of speech, namely prolonged vowel sounds, nasal and liquid consonant-like sounds, predominance of expiration, and temporal organization of output over a prolonged vocal episode, which are not present in vegetative sounds; and vegetative sounds have other characteristics of speech, namely voiced and voiceless nonsonorant consonant-like elements, which are not present in cry. Some of the characteristics of these two different sound types are combined with one another in cooing (see also Wolff 1969).

During Stage III the infant begins to adopt oral tidal respiration (Sazaki *et al.* 1977). Downward and forward growth of the facial skeleton increases the size of the oral cavity and thus gives the tongue more room to manoeuvre within it. Also, specialization and changes in concentration of mucosal sensory receptors are taking place in the pharyngeal region as a result

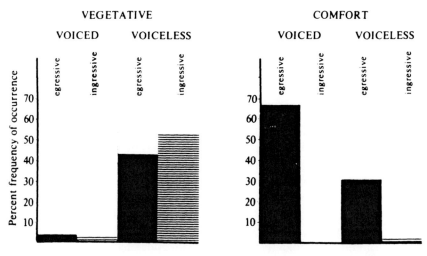

Figure 6. Percent frequency of occurrence of the features of breath direction (egressive vs. ingressive) and voicing (voiced vs. voiceless) in the consonant-like elements found in vegetative and comfort (cooing) sounds. Notice that these elements are predominantly voiceless in vegetative sounds, where they are equally likely to be ingressive or egressive. In comfort sounds on the other hand they may be voiced or voiceless but they are hardly ever ingressive. Thus, a combination of the features of consonant-like, egressive breath direction, and voicing has become prominent and acquired new importance in comfort sounds. Many of these new consonant-like elements are stops, or brief friction noises or trills

of enlargement of surface areas, and also possibly actual reduction in the number of receptors present. The capacity for discrimination of touch, pressure and movement at the apical portion of the tongue and at the lip margins may assume greater importance than before (Bosma 1975). These changes may all contribute to the diversification of place of consonant production and to the increase in number of vowel types that are thought to be characteristic of Stage III.

It has further been suggested that in vocal play the infant explores and maps the vocal tract at a time when its spatial co-ordinates are changing rapidly (Mattingly 1973). Thus, the infant updates sensory information about oral and pharyngeal spaces by touch, pressure, and activity within these spaces. The activity has also been viewed as a secondary circular reaction according to Piaget's (1952) description of Stage III of sensorimotor development.

Further influences on the infant's rapidly changing vocal tract structure, according to Kent (1981), may be the following: (1) maturation of the

intrinsic muscles of the tongue permitting refined adjustments of tongue shape in vowel production; and (2) increased influence of the supralaryngeal muscles upon the vocal folds as the larynx descends, possibly giving rise to heightened contrasts of vocal pitch.

6.2. Neurophysiological development

If nervous system mechanisms above the brainstem level are of primary importance for vocal development, then one might expect to see discontinuity of vocal development as higher-level structures within the system mature and begin to exert control over lower-level structures. Each new level of organization should possess unique properties of structure and behaviour. At birth, vocalization is controlled at the brainstem level. Respiration and phonation in crying are co-ordinated through nuclei in the dorsal midbrain-pons region (the periaqueductal grey area having special importance), and the nucleus ambiguus. Cry phonation also is co-ordinated with sucking and swallowing activities at this level (anencephalic infants, for example, are capable of cry and vegetative activity of the vocal tract).

Two major landmarks of vocal development (cooing, Stage II and reduplicated babbling, Stage IV) follow the initial reflexive sound-making period. The onset of meaningful speech (first words) constitutes a third major landmark. Landmarks may reflect discontinuities of vocal development and of neural development. They may be referred to as 'hardware' developments. It also seems probable, however, that periods of expansion of vocal skill (in Stages III and V) intervene between the major landmarks of vocal development. These expansions may be accompanied by continuing maturation within the functioning components of the vocal motor system. However, they may also reflect vocal learning as a result of social conditioning, and inventiveness on the part of the infant as he experiences his own vocalizations through the auditory modality. These expansions of vocal skill may be referred to as 'software' developments.

Accounts of neural development in the human vocal motor system are still very incomplete. Ontogenetically, maturation of the central nervous system proceeds outward from the brainstem, i.e. both cephalward and caudalward (Bosma 1975). The onset of the first vocal landmark, i.e., cooing (Stage II), at 6 to 8 weeks of age, appears to coincide with beginning functioning of the limbic cingulate area (Ploog 1979). This area has been associated with initiation of vocalization, and the limbic area in its entirety with emotional expression, in nonhuman primates and in man (Jurgens and Von Cramon 1982). It is noteworthy that the emotional expression

of laughter appears toward the end of Stage II, at approximately 16 weeks of age.

Following the cooing period, elaboration of lower motorneuron systems as well as of limbic structures must take place. If improvisations and inventions are introduced in the first expansion period (Stage III), the expression of individual neurophysiological variation might be found in these improvisations, i.e., in the sound types produced, in their order of appearance, or in the manner in which they are combined with one another in sequences. The sound types may be limited by both anatomic and neurophysiologic constraints.

On the basis of the limited data accumulated thus far, it is believed that only a small number of sound types are produced in Stage III and that their emergence is not closely related to chronological age. The sequences in which they are acquired may vary across infants.

Primate vocalization does not appear to offer a parallel for expansion or improvisation in vocal learning. In the species studied thus far, sound types employed by the adult are already present early in infancy and may be innate. For example, the 'isolation peep' (which is considered to be analogous to infant cry, see Newman in press), the comfort sounds and shrieks and trills that are produced by squirrel monkey infants appear to be genetically determined. Some of these sound types, moreover, may be acoustically similar to those produced by human infants in Stage III, the first expansion period. Different structures within the limbic system appear to be involved in the control of production of each of these calls. It is possible that analogous structures develop at different rates from one human infant to another. They may do so in response to the infant's 'discovery' and practice of different sound types.

Auditory feedback may also be essential to vocal learning and improvisation. Sound types that are characteristic of Stage III are produced by hearing-impaired infants to a limited extent only. They are not elaborated by infants with severe to profound hearing impairment until these infants are provided with amplification (Stark 1972, 1983). Auditory feedback appears to be crucial to the emergence of reduplicated babbling also.

Pathways have been discovered extending from the cingulate cortex of the squirrel monkey to the auditory association area. Cell nuclei within the auditory association cortex have been found to respond differentially to self-produced calls and similar calls recorded from other individuals in this species (Muller-Preuss 1978). Similar mechanisms may become effective within the human infant in Stages III and IV of vocal development.

The emergence of the second major landmark of human vocal development, reduplicated babbling (Stage IV), at 6 to 9 months of age may coincide

with maturation of one or more layers of the cortical mantle in the motor face and larynx area and / or of the analogous areas of the supplementary motor cortex (see Milner 1976: 58, for proposed maturational schedules in this age range). Striatal and cerebellar circuits may also undergo extensive maturation at this time.

Ploog (1979) has suggested that the highest level of the motor system (around the cortical larynx and face areas) is not engaged in vocal development until the onset of meaningful speech. These cortical areas are involved in the vocal signalling process in humans only. Ploog points out that the articulatory gestures of babbling, i.e. 'marginal babbling' (Oller's term), late in the Stage III period and in reduplicated babbling (Stage IV), are often produced in the absence of a social partner and independently of internal needs. He concludes that these vocalizations are devoid of communicative or social function and states that 'all observers of infant babbling agree that this behavior resembles play with buccopharyngeal muscles . . . and is obviously an exercise of the phonatory apparatus'.

It is also possible that the vocal behaviours of babbling have a higher-level 'recognitory' function with respect to objects toward which the infant's gaze is directed. In normal infants the alternating opening / closing movements of tongue and jaw in reduplicated babbling may be strongly associated with visual inspection and / or manipulation and mouthing of objects (Stark 1980), activities with which infants in these vocal developmental periods are intensely preoccupied.

Maturation of primary auditory association areas and of the tracts linking auditory and primary and secondary cortical motor areas is not achieved until early in the second year. The best known of these auditory-motor tracts is the arcuate fasciculus. This maturation may be essential to imitation of the segmental features and intonation contours of adult speech. It is noteworthy that visual association areas develop in advance of auditory association areas in the human infant. The infant is able to imitate silent gestures of the mouth very early in life in response to visual input. Imitation of speech sounds, however, requires that the infant is able to co-ordinate a variety of oral gestures with phonation, and also that he can make use of auditory templates in doing so. True imitative ability may not be acquired until the onset of Stage V, i.e. non-reduplicated babbling or expressive jargon, the last stage before the emergence of referential words.[2]

7. Summary

As the above descriptions indicate, there is a lawful developmental sequence in segmental feature production from reflexive sound making

to first word production. In spite of individual differences, the progression may have certain aspects which are universal. These aspects may be genetically determined and may be related to anatomical and neurophysiological development.

It has been suggested that the earliest productions provide a matrix of primitive metaphonological features from which babbling, jargon and speech ultimately derive (Oller 1976). Most, if not all, of the articulatory features of speech are present in the earliest sounds of infants in a remarkably well-organized form. For example, the feature stop, produced at the glottis, initiates many cry segments and the feature bilabial place of articulation is present in the brief clicks of sucking. The appearance of these gestures under given circumstances is highly reliable; they are executed with great rapidity and are co-ordinated with one another in the sense that crying reactions will pre-empt some vegetative behaviours (e.g. sucking) and other vegetative behaviours (e.g. coughing) will pre-empt crying.

These gestures, and the pattern of auditory and spectral features resulting from them, are not organized in a manner that resembles speech. The features do not form compact bundles but simple and quite limited associations with one another in primitive segment types. Certain feature combinations are not present at all – for example, there are no bilabial stops. Also, there are few transitions from one articulatory gesture to another involving different structures of different parts of the vocal tract in a continuous pattern of movement. Thus, it may be the sets of features within vocal segments which strike the listener as 'primitive', rather than the features themselves.

Subsequent vocal development may take place in a series of stages or levels. The beginning of each stage may be thought of as a landmark of vocal development, the major landmarks being the onset of cooing, of reduplicated babbling and of meaningful speech. The term 'landmark' may suggest a discontinuity in vocal development; indeed the major landmarks of vocal development may reflect marked changes in vocal tract configuration resulting from downward and forward facial growth or from the descent of the larynx into the neck. They may also reflect discontinuities of neural development within the speech motor system.

At the onset of a new stage, new segmental feature combinations are brought under control. Nasals, friction noises and stops may be produced at a more anterior place of articulation; supraglottal stops and fricatives may develop from friction noise and trills. There may also be a concomitant loss of previously acquired abilities at the onset of a new stage as new abilities are acquired: for example, the ability to move rapidly from open (vowel-like) to closed (consonant-like) positions of the vocal tract within

a segment may be temporarily lost. Regression to a simple overall organization of series of segments may also be observed, for example in the transition periods between Stages I and II (onset of cooing) and between Stages V and VI (single-word production or the beginning of meaningful speech).

Vocal behaviours that are characteristic of one stage, however, may persist into succeeding stages and new landmark behaviours may have their antecedents in preceding stages. Thus discontinuities of vocal behaviour, although the most salient aspect of vocal development, do not describe that development completely.

In addition, Stages III and IV, described above, may be characterized by expansion. More complex feature sets may evolve as a result of expansion. Once new segment types are mastered they may also be incorporated into more complex series of segments as a result of expansion. Prosodic features, e.g. rhythmic patterns and intonation contours, may be elaborated within expansion periods. Thus, there may be cyclical aspects of vocal development that reflect an underlying developmental continuity.

Expansion of vocal skills may be subject to learning. Mountcastle (1978) and others have stated that the development of central control systems may be subject to modification on the basis of learning and experience, especially during critical periods of development. If learning and experience are important for vocal development, aspects of continuity as well as of discontinuity in vocal behaviour might be predicted across developmental levels. It is possible, for example, that there are continuities with respect to the development of the vowel system and of pitch control from Stage III through to and including Stage V.

Finally, it is important to recognize the importance of auditory learning and of cognitive and social development to prespeech segmental feature development. Auditory learning is essential to the forming of auditory-motor linkages and the development of speech perception (Eilers 1976; Kuhl 1976; Aslin and Pisoni 1980b). Cognitive and social development are reflected in vocal communication.

In intentional prespeech communication, vocal signals are used to attract adult attention or to engage adult participation in an activity. Eye-to-eye contact and gesture directed toward adults accompany these vocalizations and contribute to their interpretation. As such new forms of vocal communication appear, new replications of local neural circuits may be generated, first at midbrain and limbic levels and then in the neocortex. In this manner, new connections may be formed between and among neural control systems, e.g. those controlling manipulation of objects, gaze, and vocalization. As these connections are established, new forms of communication may emerge, e.g. cooing, intentional vocal communication (as in the production

of pre-words) and the use of referential words. As knowledge of the development of segmental feature production in infants increases, it will become possible to ask still more interesting questions about the ways in which these stages are influenced by other aspects of infant development, such as the development of speech perception and of nonverbal cognitive abilities.

8. Prosodic development

David Crystal

1. The nature of prosody

Unlike the well-established fields of grammar and segmental phonology, the field of prosody requires a certain amount of exposition before one can talk about its development in children. What range of data is to be subsumed under this heading? For present purposes, it will be useful to select three main themes from the prosodic literature, reviewed, for example, in Crystal (1969, 1975): (a) What is excluded from the domain of a prosodic theory? (b) What variations in prosodic form may be identified? (c) What range of prosodic functions may be established?

The first question may be answered briefly, as its purpose is solely to relate prosody to other areas with which it is often confused. Given a specification of semiotic behaviour as 'patterned human communication in all its modes' (Sebeok, Hayes and Bateson 1964), then prosodic features can be identified as one component of the auditory–vocal dimension of communication, i.e. excluding the visual ('kinetic'), tactile ('proxemic') and other communicative modes referred to globally under the general heading of 'nonverbal communication' (see Argyle 1975). Within the auditory–vocal area, a distinction is conventionally made between *segmental* and *nonsegmental* phonology, the latter usually being defined as the 'residue' of the former – what is left *after* one has studied the vowel / consonant / syllabic system of sounds. More positively, one can define nonsegmental phonology as any linguistically contrastive sound effect which cannot be described by reference to a single segment (phoneme), but which either (i) continues over a stretch of utterance (minimally, a syllable), e.g. extra loudness; or (ii) requires reference to several segments in different parts of the utterance, e.g. the use of breathy voice on vowels. Within this field, prosody is a term which traditionally has referred only to certain aspects of this variability, namely linguistic variation in pitch, loudness, speed and rhythm (including pause) of speaking. Other aspects were either ignored, or grouped loosely together under the heading of 'paralanguage' (e.g. nasal,

husky, or whispered vocal effects). In the language acquisition field, the term 'prosody' has tended to follow this orientation, though one sometimes sees it used where it plainly has a more general meaning, namely, for all aspects of nonsegmental variability. Certainly, with few exceptions, the attitude adopted to prosody is very much that of the 'residue' referred to above. It is regularly assumed that segmental phonology, grammar and lexicon can be analysed without reference to prosodic features, which may, if at all, be mentioned only in passing. The methodological fallacy here is particularly worrying with reference to grammar at the early stages of development, but its implications cover all aspects of language structure and function. There are signs, particularly in the recent literature on the interactional analysis of early language, that the importance of prosody is becoming increasingly realized; but this literature also illustrates the difficulty of working precisely within this domain, as will be discussed below.

Turning now to the second question raised above: what prosodic variability to recognize? A traditional misconception here is to talk of a child's 'prosody', implying that this is in some sense a single, homogeneous phenomenon. The linguistic literature shows very plainly, however, that several different kinds of patterning are involved in prosodic analysis, and it is important to distinguish these in order to specify precisely what it is that is being acquired. The present chapter will be restricted to those aspects of prosodic patterning the importance of which is generally agreed among the various approaches (the terminology and particular theoretical emphasis used is that of Crystal 1975).

(i) The primary focus must be on the way in which the several prosodic characteristics of the speech signal are integrated to produce a totality, which expounds meaning. The linguistic use of pitch, or *intonation*, ultimately develops into the most complex of all the prosodic systems, and for the adult it can to a considerable extent be studied formally as an autonomous system. But from a semantic point of view, intonation is merely one factor in communicating a meaning – as is clear when we consider what range of vocal characteristics enter into the definition of such tones of voice as sarcastic, angry, parenthetic, etc. Particularly for the first two years of life, non-intonational features (such as variations in loudness, duration, rhythmicality) are of considerable importance in the expression of meaning. This is so not only for attitudes but also for grammatical patterning. For example, when one tries to decide whether a sequence of two lexical items constitutes one sentence or two, one must listen out for far more than pitch contour and pause (the two features usually referred to): they may be linked by extra loudness, longer duration, marked rhythm, or with some shared paralinguistic feature (e.g. marked tension, or nasality)

– all of which requires one to place intonation in its proper perspective. Intonation nonetheless has attracted most attention in the developmental literature, and the following discussion reflects this emphasis.

(ii) A basic distinction is postulated between pitch *direction* and pitch *range*. A pitch may fall, rise, stay level, or do some combination of these things within a given phonological unit, e.g. fall–rise on a syllable; and these directional *tones* are usually isolated as one system of intonational contrastivity. But any of these tones may be varied in terms of range, seen as a separate system of contrasts, e.g. a falling pitch used relatively high, mid or low, or being widened or narrowed in some way.

(iii) Features of pitch direction and range, along with features of rhythm and pause, are organized into prosodic configurations, or *tone-units* (or 'primary contours', 'sense groups', etc.), which expound meanings over and above the accompanying 'verbal' meanings. Tone-units provide the most general level of organization that can be imposed upon prosodic data, equivalent in status to the notion of 'sentence' in grammatical analysis.[1] For example, the normal tone-unit segmentation of the utterance:

When he comes / tell him I'm out /

is as indicated by the slant lines. In general, the assignment of tone-unit boundaries seems motivated by syntactic reasons, e.g. to mark the boundary between clauses (see further, Crystal 1975: ch. 1). We might accordingly expect such a fundamental notion to be an early characteristic of prosodic development (see below).

(iv) The prosodic feature which seems to carry the next most important linguistic contrastivity is the placement of maximum prominence on a given syllable (or, occasionally, on more than one syllable). This is primarily a matter of pitch movement, but extra loudness is involved, and duration and pause may be used to heighten the contrast between what precedes and follows. The prominent, or *tonic* syllable may be seen capitalized in the utterance:

Because we stayed until MIDnight / we got in TERribly late /

This is the focus of most of the discussion on intonation in the context of generative grammar (e.g. Bresnan 1971), where the aim was to demonstrate that tonicity (i.e. tonic syllable placement) had a syntactic function, being used to disambiguate sentences or signal a distinction between grammatical and ungrammatical. While this sometimes happens, the alternative view (which I share) is that of Bolinger (1972), who argues that the factors governing tonic placement are primarily semantic, e.g. the signalling of new information in context.

(v) The next most noticeable prosodic characteristic is the specific direction-range of the tonic syllable, e.g. whether the *tone* of the syllable is high–falling–wide, low- rising–narrow, etc. These tones seem to signal primarily attitudinal information, though certain tonal contrasts can expound grammatical meaning, e.g. the 'asking' versus 'telling' distinction in tag-questions:

> You're CÒMING / ÁREN'T you /
> You're CÒMING / ÀREN'T you /

The third question raised at the beginning of this chapter concerned the range of functions which these prosodic patterns might be said to perform. Here five roles need to be distinguished.

(i) In a *grammatical* function of prosody, the prosodic feature(s) signal a contrast, the terms of which would be conventionally recognized as morphological or syntactic in a grammar, e.g. positive / negative, singular / plural, statement / question. These contrasts are common in tone languages, such as Twi, but some of these may also be found in English, where tone-units, tonic syllables and tones can all perform grammatical roles (cf. the tag-question contrast above). In a related sense, prosody may be used obligatorily to mark a grammatical distinction already overt in word order or morphology, as in co-ordinated utterances such as:

> I'll ask the FÍRST question / and you ask the SÈCOND one /

(ii) The *semantic* function of prosody subsumes a speaker's organization of meaning in a discourse, whereby he signals which parts of what he is saying are most important, which parenthetic, etc. This includes the emphasizing of a relatively unexpected lexical item in an utterance, as Bolinger argues (1972), as well as reflecting the presuppositions about subject matter or context when focusing on a specific item, as when, for example *There was a* BÙS *in the road* implies a context where someone had queried whether this was in fact the case.

(iii) The *attitudinal* function of prosody is usually distinguished from (ii), cn similar grounds to the classical distinction between denotation and connotation. Personal emotions are signalled concerning the subject matter or context of an utterance, e.g. anger, puzzlement, surprise. It is unclear how far such emotions use prosodic features specific to a language and how far they rely on universal characteristics of emotional expression (see Bolinger 1964).

(iv) The *psychological* function of prosody is evident from the several experiments which have shown that performance in short-term memory recall, perception and other variables is affected by the prosodic character

of the utterance, e.g. words containing tonic syllables are more readily recalled (Leonard 1973).

(v) The *social* function of prosody signals information about the socio-linguistic characteristics of the speaker, such as sex, class, professional status, etc. (Crystal 1975: ch. 5). The importance of this function in facilitating social interaction in dialogue is being increasingly recognized, e.g. when the intonation of a stimulus sentence prompts someone to respond, or implies that no further comment is needed. The role of prosody in expressing the illocutionary force of speech acts, such as persuading or commanding, is also now seen to be significant – though whether one might refer to this as primarily a social, attitudinal, semantic or grammatical role is very much an open question!

This last point raises a principle of fundamental importance, which needs to be emphasized in view of the extent to which it is neglected in child language studies – namely that there is no one-to-one correspondence between the above categories of prosodic form and prosodic function, nor between any of the individual features subsumed within these categories. A rising tone, for example, signals far more than a questioning meaning, and a grammatical question may be uttered using other tones than rising ones (for discussion and references, see Crystal 1969: ch. 1). It is accordingly fallacious to assume that a child who uses rising tones is thereby 'asking a question', 'making a questioning speech act', or the like: everything depends on the careful analysis of the accompanying behaviour and situation before one can be justified in ascribing such an interpretation to the utterance.

2. Prosodic acquisition

Given the limited empirical study which has taken place (almost entirely within the first two years of life), talk in terms of clear stages of development in this area may well be premature. On the other hand, the evidence which is available does agree so far on several points, hence the following progression. Five stages can be distinguished, of which the last two are particularly important.

Stage I. There have been many studies of the prelinguistic antecedents of prosodic features, usually under the heading of 'infant vocalization'. On the whole, these studies recognize a period of biologically determined vocalizations (e.g. the 'basic cry' pattern, underlying hunger, pain, etc. states described in Wolff 1969: 82), and a period of differentiated vocalizations which permit general attitudinal interpretation only (e.g. 'pleasure', 'recognition'). Systematic variation in these vocalizations can be ascribed

to such factors as the baby's sex or environment. There seems to be little difference in their physical characteristics and attitudinal function across languages. This stage, from birth until around 6 months, is reviewed in detail in Crystal (1975: ch. 8).

Stage II. The first sign of anything linguistic emerging is the awareness of prosodic contrasts in adult uttei ces directed to the child. This has long been known to be present in children from about 2 to 3 months, as the reports in Lewis (1951) testify. But this literature is rather anecdotal, and experimental studies are lacking which attempt to separate prosody from other semiotic features of the stimuli, and to identify the roles individual prosodic features might play within the adult utterance (e.g. whether pitch or loudness is discriminated first). Nor is it obvious whether prosodic features are discriminated before segmental ones (cf. Kaplan 1970; Kaplan and Kaplan 1971), though infant speech perception studies have made it clear that both these aspects of speech can elicit responses by as early as 6 weeks (Morse 1972; Spring and Dale 1977; Chang and Trehub 1977; Jusczyk and Thompson 1978; Mehler *et al.* 1978; Nooteboom, Brokx and deRooij 1978; Kessen, Levine and Wendrich 1979; see also Sullivan and Horowitz 1983, who use an auditory preference paradigm). Here, as elsewhere in prosodic studies (see below), a great deal will depend on the recognition that there are different levels of prosodic organization to be distinguished within the adult stimulus, some of which are likely to be discriminated before segmental features, others of which are likely to overlap. The research field is much in need of an appropriately general phonological perspective to integrate the range of experimental observations already made and to indicate those areas of prosodic contrastivity so far neglected.

Stage III. The increasingly varied vocalizations of children around 6 months have begun to be studied in detail, using a combination of acoustic, articulatory and auditory criteria, and it is possible to isolate a wide range of nonsegmental parameters in terms of which the patterns of crying, babbling, etc. can be classified. Stark, Rose and McLagen (1975), for example, cite breath direction, pitch, loudness, and several kinds of glottal and supraglottal constriction; within pitch, they distinguish contrasts of range, direction and continuity.

Gradually, these nonsegmental features come to resemble prosodic patterns of the mother tongue – from as early as 6 months, according to most scholars (see the review in Crystal 1975: 136). Initially, the resemblance is only hinted at, by the occasional use of a language-specific prosodic characteristic within a relatively long stretch of nonlinguistic vocalization. Such instances are very striking when they occur on a tape, as they stand

out as something much more familiar, discrete and transcribable than the general background of utterance. Increasingly, at this time, babbling patterns become shorter and phonetically more stable: accordingly, when a babbled utterance of only one or two syllables is used in conjunction with a language-specific prosodic feature, the result is going to be very much like an attempt at a meaningful utterance. Such combinations are quickly focused on by parents, who will comment on what they think the baby is 'saying', often providing lexical glosses. It is, however, very difficult to be precise about the nature of the development at this stage, and there is some disagreement about the facts. For example, Atkinson, MacWhinney and Stoel (1970) were unable to confirm the observations of Weir (1962) in relation to the early emergence of language-specific prosody; and Olney and Scholnick (1976) found that adults were unable to differentiate samples of Chinese and American children aged 6, 12 and 18 months. On the other hand, de Boysson-Bardies, Sagart and Durand (1984), after reviewing several methodological problems in previous work, found that adults *were* able to distinguish French, Arabic and Chinese children of 8 months on the basis of their intonation patterns. There are evidently several methodological and theoretical problems which remain to be clarified in this area. Small numbers of subjects have been used and only certain prosodic variables examined; the examples of contrastive prosody have been highly selective and we have no information concerning the incidence of these patterns in the child's vocalization as a whole. Nor has there been an appropriate range of multi-listener studies, to control for individual adults' perceptual biases, parental 'reading in', and so on. Moreover, to say that a language-specific feature has been detected is to say very little: recognition of language-specificity involves both phonetic notions (e.g. the 'community voice quality' or characteristic 'twang' of a language) and phonological notions (e.g. the selection of contrasts which produce an identifiable accent), and it is by no means clear how to distinguish these in the child's vocalizations at this stage, or whether some more general level of analysis needs to be invoked (such as the 'metaphonological' parameters, affecting both segmental and nonsegmental features, recognized by de Boysson-Bardies, Sagart and Durand 1984). The boundary area between the phonetic use of pitch, loudness, etc. during the first 6–9 months of life, and the phonological use of these features which emerges towards the end of the first year, is totally uncharted territory (but see de Boysson-Bardies *et al.* 1981 on variations in temporal structure – specifically, in syllable durations – which indicate a transition between vocalization and language in the late babbling of one child).

Stage IV. However the transition to phonology takes place, it is evident

that learned patterns of prosodic behaviour are characteristic of the output of the child during the second half of the first year. These patterns can be studied both formally and functionally. From the formal viewpoint, the increasingly determinate and systematic character of these patterns is readily statable: a configuration of features is involved, using primarily pitch, rhythm and pause. This configuration has been variously labelled a prosodic 'envelope' or 'matrix' (Bruner 1975a: 10) or 'frame' (Dore 1975). Weir (1962) had previously talked about the splitting up of utterances into 'sentence-like chunks', at this stage. Lenneberg (1967: 279) describes the process thus:

> The first feature of natural language to be discernible in a child's babbling is contour of intonation. Short sound sequences are produced that may have neither any determinable meaning nor definable phoneme structure, but they can be proffered with recognizable intonation such as occurs in questions, exclamations or affirmations. The linguistic development of utterance does not seem to begin with a composition of individual, independently movable items *but as a whole tonal pattern*. With further development, this whole becomes differentiated into component parts . . . [my emphasis]

The important point is that these primitive units have both a segmental and a prosodic dimension, but it is the latter which is the more stable, and the more readily elicited. In one child studied at Reading, aged 1;2, the phrase *all-gone*, regularly said by the parent after each meal, was actually rehearsed by using the prosodic component only: the child hummed the intonation of the phrase first, viz. ‾‾ ▪— , only then attempting the whole, producing an accurate intonation but only approximate segments ([ʌʔdʌ]). The phrase could be easily elicited after any meal, but it was not until a month had gone by that the child's segmental output became as stable as his prosodic. Menn's Jacob (1976a: 195ff) also produced 'proto-words' with a distinctive prosodic shape – the ones reported being used at 1;4 for a peekaboo game, an item with demonstrative function (êsɑ), and, later, a name-elicitor (zɨ). Dore (1975) refers to the formally isolable, repeated, and situationally specific patterns observed at this stage as 'phonetically consistent forms', whose 'protophonemic' segmental character is complemented by a distinctive prosody, which is the more stable.

From a functional point of view, these prosodically delimited units can be interpreted in several ways – semantic, syntactic and social 'explanations' have all been mooted. The latter view is perhaps the most widely held: here, prosody is seen as a means of signalling joint participation in an action sequence shared by parent and child. This view, emphasized particu-

larly by Bruner (1975a), is part of a developmental theory wherein vocalization is seen as one component in a communication activity alongside such nonvocal behaviour as reaching and eye-contact. In a peekaboo game, for instance, both the utterance and the activity of hiding-and-reappearing are obligatory, interdependent components (as the absurdity of attempting to play the game without either indicates). And when adults play these games, the lexical character of the utterances regularly varies ('Peep-bo', 'See you', etc.) whereas the prosodic features display much less variations. Another example is in action sequences such as nuzzling the child or jumping him up and down, where there are parallel prosodic patterns. The development of 'turn-taking', either between parent and child (Snow 1977a) or between children (Keenan 1974) also involves prosodic delimitation and interdependence. One Keenan twin, for example, would regularly take the prosodic character of the other's utterance and 'play' with it. Another child, studied at Reading, marked the end of a jargon sequence with a distinctive two-syllable pitch movement (• .), which was openly described by his parents as 'their cue to speak'.

Several attempts have been made to describe the social or 'pragmatic' functions of such utterances, especially using the metalanguage of speech act analysis. Dore, for example (1975: 31ff), argues that prosodic features provide crucial evidence for the development of speech acts. Primitive speech acts are said to contain a 'rudimentary referring expression' (lexical items) and a 'primitive force indicating device' ('typically an intonation pattern', p. 31), as in labelling, requesting and calling. The distinction between referent and intention is pivotal: 'whereas the child's one word communicates the notion he has in mind, his prosodic pattern indicates his intention with regard to that notion' (p. 32). Likewise, Menn says about Jacob (1976a: 26–7), 'he ... consistently used certain intonation patterns in conjunction with actions that communicated particular intentions, so we can ascribe meaning to his use of those contours'. The difficulty with all such approaches, of course, is empirical verification of the notion of 'intention'. As has been argued in other areas of child language, the fact that parents interpret their children's prosody systematically is no evidence for ascribing their belief patterns to the child's intuition. At best, one can argue as does Menn (1976a: 192) that 'consideration of adult interpretation of intonation contour on vocalization does give us information about what the child *conveys*, if not what he/she *intends*'. It is difficult to go beyond this, and know that a child at this stage intends a distinction between, say, 'calling' and 'greeting' (two of Dore's categories). Searching for one-to-one correlations between prosody and other aspects of the child's behaviour is unlikely to be successful, because the situations in which the language

is used are often indeterminate, and the gestures and other kinesic features accompanying are usually ambiguous. There are also fewer pitch patterns available in a language than there are situations to be differentiated. It is possible that more detailed behavioural analyses will give grounds for optimism, but these ought to begin with the most concrete, determinate and replicable of situations (e.g. the daily, ritualized settings referred to in Bruner 1975a and R. Clark 1977). Attempting to establish developmental speech act theories using as sole data a sample of unstructured, spontaneous play interaction is liable to produce a set of unfalsifiable interpretations about what went on. The intuitive plausibility of interactional approach to the study of utterances at this stage is thereby much reduced.

As an alternative to a social approach, it is possible to see these prosodic frames – or primitive tone-units, to use the terminology above – primarily as having a formal or grammatical role. Bruner, for instance (1975a), at one point describes the function of these frames as 'place-holders': a mode of communication (such as a demand, or a question) is established using prosody, and primitive lexical items are then added. In a stretch of jargon, from around 12 months, it is often the case that one will recognize a word within the otherwise unintelligible utterance (cf. also several of the utterances in Keenan 1974). And the transitional stage between one- and two-element sentences also contains uninterpretable phonetic forms which may perhaps be interpreted as remnants of a primitive prosodic frame (cf. Bloom 1973; Dore et al. 1976). Dore et al. (1976: 26) in fact suggest seven transitional stages at this point:

(i)   prosodically un-isolable, nonphonemic units ('prelinguistic babbling')
(ii) prosodically isolable, nonphonemic patterns ('prelinguistic jargon')
(iii) prosodically isolable, nonphonemic units ('phonetically consistent forms')
(iv) conventional phonemic units ('words')
(v)   word plus 'empty' phonetic forms in single prosodic pattern ('pre-syntactic devices')
(vi) chained conventional phonemic units forming separate intonation patterns ('successive single-word utterances')
(vii) prosodically complex patterns ('patterned speech')

The phonological and phonetic details of the development of these frames into determinate tone-units with a definable internal structure are, however, not at all clear, so little empirical work having been done. In particular, it is unclear whether tonicity or tonal contrastivity develops first, or whether they emerge simultaneously. The suggestion that the development is simultaneous is based on the observation that tonicity contrasts are early evi-

denced in jargon sequences (in which sequences of rhythms are built up which resemble the intonational norms of connected speech), whereas tone contrasts are early heard in the use of lexical items as single-word sentences. Menn, for instance, finds her child's semantic control of certain tones on 'babble carriers' and their contrastive use on words to be almost simultaneous (1976a: 186). If one ignores jargon, however, as being both less central to communicative development and less systematic in its patterning, then it would seem that tone develops before tonicity. Polysyllabic lexical items at this stage tend to have fixed tonic placement (Atkinson-King 1973), though they may vary in terms of pitch direction and range, e.g. *dàda* (said as daddy enters the room), *dáda* (said when a noise was heard outside at the time when daddy was expected). Of the two, range seems to become contrastive before direction, especially high versus low, but also wide versus narrow. Most of the contrasts noted by Halliday (1975), for example, involve range rather than direction – mid versus low first, later high – e.g. the distinction between seeking and finding a person, signalled in his child by high versus mid–low range, from around 1;3. Eight pitch range variations are in fact used by Halliday in his transcription (very high, high, mid high, mid, mid low, low, wide, narrow), as well as four directions (level, fall, rise, rise–fall). The notion of high versus low register is discussed further in Konopczynski (1975), and a great deal of early child data can be interpreted in this way, e.g. in Keenan (1974) and Menn (1976a).

Based on Menn (1976a), Halliday (1975), and my own study, a tentative analysis of early tonal development – the contrasts involving both direction and range – emerged as follows:

(i) Initially, the child uses only *falling* patterns. Menn states that – except for imitations of adult rises – her child used rises on words only after these words were first used with falls (1976a: 195). Halliday's range contrasts are all on falling tones (1975: 148).

(ii) The first contrast is *falling* versus *level* tones (high level in Halliday (1975: 150–1)), the level tone often being accompanied by other prosodic features, e.g. falsetto, length, loudness variations.

(iii) This is followed by *falling* versus *high rising* tones, the latter being used in a variety of contexts. Menn's special study of rising tones brought to light a large number of contexts between 1;1 and 1;4, including offering, requesting, attention-getting, and several 'curiosity' noises (e.g. when peering). Several of these notions, moreover, are complex – e.g. 'request' includes requests for help, recognition, permission, to obtain an object, etc., all of which are distinguishable in the situation (1976a: 186ff, 198–9). The 'natural' distinction between fall and rise is characterized as 'demanding' versus 'request / offering' (p. 193). Halliday's high rises are first used in association with falls, as compound tones (1975: 151).

(iv) The next contrast is between *falling* and *high falling* tones, the latter especially in contexts of surprise, recognition, insistence, greetings. Halliday reports a high falling contrast between 1;1 and 1;3, and further distinguishes a mid fall.

(v) A contrast between *rising* and *high rising* tones follows: the Reading study suggested a particular incidence of high rises especially in playful anticipatory contexts. Menn notes the latter mainly in 'intensification' contexts: the child gets no response to an utterance with a low rise, and repeats the utterance with a wider contour – the extra height, according to Menn, is the 'essential information-carrying feature' (1976a: 193–4). Halliday's mid versus high rise emerges at 1;3 to 1;4.

(vi) The next contrast is between *falling* and *high rising–falling* tones, the latter being used in emphatic contexts, e.g. of achievement (e.g. *thêre*, as an extra brick is placed on a pile) or impressiveness (e.g. *bùs* versus *bûs*, the former being used by one child studied to refer to 'any' vehicle, the latter to a *real* bus). Menn reports a mid–high–low contour at 1;4; Halliday has a similar contrast from as early as 1;1, but regularly from 1;3.

(vii) Next appears a contrast between *rising* and *falling–rising* tones, the latter especially in warning contexts, presumably reflecting the *be cãreful* pattern common in adults; cf. Halliday (1975: 154), between 1;4 and 1;6.

(viii) Among later contrasts to appear is that between high and low rising–falling tones, especially in play contexts.

These features appear on isolated lexical items to begin with, and for a while cannot be distinguished from a prosodic idiom (i.e. an invariant prosodic pattern accompanying a fixed lexico-grammatical utterance, as in a nursery-rhyme line). Only later, when the same lexical item is used with different prosodic characteristics, can we talk with confidence about the patterns being systemic and productive. At this point, too, the tones come to be used in juxtaposition, producing the 'contrastive syntagmas' and prosodic 'substitution games' reported by Weir (1962), Carlson and Anisfeld (1969: 118), Keenan (1974: 172, 178) and others.

We may compare, at this point, the conclusions of some recent work on the acquisition of tone languages: Kirk (1973), Hyman and Schuh (1974), Li and Thompson (1977), Westermeyer and Westermeyer (1977), Tuaycharoen (1977, 1978), Tse (1978), Clumeck (1980) and Rūkė-Dravinā (1981). These studies agree that phonetic accuracy in the production of lexical tones is learned earlier than in the production of segments. Kirk's study of imitation ability in 2- and 3-year-old Gã children found that there were fewer tonal errors than other types. Westermeyer and Westermeyer studied 43 Lao children between 3 and 15, finding no tonal errors, though segmental errors continued until age 9. Tuaycharoen's study of a Thai

child found evidence of lexical tones at 0;11, and correct usage in the language the child had learned by age 2. Rūke-Dravina's report on Latvian found tones present at 1;2, though some errors were still being made at age 4. The period between 1;0 and 1;6 seems to be especially important for the early development of lexical tone, but the studies are too few for generalizations on matters of detail to be safely made. In some children, tonal learning seems to precede segmental learning, but in others there seems to be considerable overlap. In some children, falling tones precede rising; in others, rising precede falling. Pitch range does, however, seem to be more important than pitch direction, as in the intonation studies: high level versus low (Tse's Cantonese study), high level versus falling or high / rising versus low (Mandarin case studies by Li and Thompson, Clumeck), and high (rising) versus (low) mid (Tuaycharoen's Thai study). Later stages of development are obscure, due to individual differences among the children, the differences among the linguistic systems being acquired, the complex phonotactic factors which affect the learning of tones (the so-called 'tonal sandhi' rules, which continue to pose problems for children at age 5 and beyond), and the increasingly complex interaction between lexical tone, intonation and other prosodic variables (such as duration and rhythm). Clumeck, for example, finds variability in phonetic accuracy, depending on whether the tones occur in utterance-final position or not, which is perhaps due to the child's difficulties in controlling his timing of syllables. Similarly, given the importance of segmental length in Latvian, distributional factors might account for the persistence of tonal errors until age 4 in Rūke-Dravina's study. It is therefore difficult to find anything other than vague parallels between the acquisition of lexical tones and intonation contrasts. The above literature does contain some discussion of the point in terms of perceptual and production constraints; but without far more studies it is not possible to draw detailed conclusions. The only matter on which there is general agreement is that (lexical) tonal contrastivity appears later than the first use of intonation contours.

Particularly with the intonational studies, one must remember that the situational interpretations used cannot be taken at face value. In much the same way as has been argued for syntax and segmental phonology (Howe 1976; Lenneberg 1976), it is necessary to free the mind from the constraints of adult language analyses, where situational notions such as 'question', 'request', 'permission' etc., are normal. As already agreed, it is insufficient to show that adults can differentiate these patterns and give them consistent interpretations, as several studies have succeeded in doing (e.g. Menyuk and Bernholtz 1969): as Bloom points out (1973: 19), this is no evidence of contrastivity for the children. Detailed analysis of both

the phonetic form and the accompanying context of utterance, moreover, readily brings to light instances of contrastivity which have no counterpart in the adult language. Halliday's child, for example, for a while used rising tones for all 'pragmatic' utterances (those requiring a response, in his terms), and falling tones for all 'mathetic' utterances (those not requiring a response; see 1975: 29, 52; also Furrow 1984). Menn's child between 1;0 and 1;8 used a class of non-adult rising tones, e.g. between 1;1 and 1;3 he used a low rising tone (peak 450 Hz) to 'institute or maintain social interaction' (the 'adult-as-social-partner' function) and a high rising tone (peak 550 Hz) for 'instrumental use of the adult' ('obtaining an object or service') (1976a: 184). Tuaycharoen's child used high / rising tones for asking, demanding or pointing out unusual things, and mid / low tones for acknowledging or for indicating familiar things (1977). Clumeck's child used rising / high / level tones for wants or requests for action, and falling tones to indicate something found, to accompany his own actions, or to express contentment (1980). In the case of a child studied at Reading, the falling–rising tone was initially used only in smiling-face contexts, with a generally 'playful' meaning, and never to express doubt or opposition, as it frequently does, with frowning or neutral face, in adults.

There have also been a few studies which try to establish the child's communicative intent at a more abstract level than that illustrated by the above functions. For example, Sachs and Devin (1976) reported the use of higher pitch and wider intonation patterns when 3- and 5-year-old children talked to a baby or doll, or role-played a baby, but the relevant information was introduced only informally. Leder and Egelston (1982), in a study which showed that interrogative intonation by 2 year olds facilitated adult responses, argued that this contour performed a social-conversational function – a means of holding on to an end in conversation when nothing else was available. Delack and Fowlow (1978) carried out a spectrographic analysis of selected pitch contours used by children in their first year, when they were alone, with their mother, with another adult and involved with various objects. They observed several points of contextual differentiation – in particular, the use of rising-type contours when alone, contrasting with the use of rising–falling contours when with the mother. Furrow (1984) also investigated the effect of an audience on prosody, using older children (2 year olds) and a broader prosodic measure (a composite of pitch direction, range and loudness), related to whether the children made eye-contact with the adults, exhibited various forms of social behaviour, or showed no interactive behaviour at all. His main finding was a differentiation in the children's use of prosody, depending on whether speech was being directed to themselves or to others. When eye-contact

was being made, utterances were louder, higher and more variable; when there was no interaction, the reverse was the case.

These are all examples of a relatively familiar form conveying an unfamiliar function. The converse also applies. Throughout this stage of development, the range of phonetic exponents of the prosodic frame increases markedly, to include contrasts in loudness, duration, muscular tension and rhythmicality, not all of which are used in the adult language. At around 1 year, contrasts have been noted between loud and soft, drawled and short, tense and lax, and rhythmic and arhythmic utterances. Weeks (1971) reported the emergence of a wide range of nonsegmental characteristics with a variety of functions, in children between 1 and 5 years: exaggerated intonation, loudness, high pitch and 'clarification' (slower, carefully enunciated speech) characteristics were of particular importance. Halliday (1975) noted, in addition to the pitch direction and range contrasts already described, several other prosodic and paralinguistic features: slow, long, short, loud; sung, squeak, frictional and glottalized. Contrastivity involving two or more prosodic parameters emerges, e.g. the use of a low, tense, soft, husky, spasmodic voice (a 'dirty snigger'). Carlson and Anisfeld (1969) distinguish loud and soft, and staccato and drawled articulations, amongst others. Other examples are the use of marked labialization, falsetto voice for whole utterances, and spasmodic articulations (lip trills, 'raspberries', etc.). It is regrettable that a more comprehensive phonetic description of this stage of development does not exist.

Stage V. Tonic contrastivity (or 'contrastive stress', as this area is often, misleadingly called) appears as sentences get more complex syntagmatically, with the appearance of two-word utterances at around 1;6 (Bloom 1973; R. Clark, Hutcheson and Van Buren 1974: 49).[2] The general developmental process seems clear. Lexical items which have appeared independently as single-element utterances, marked thus by pitch and pause, are brought into relationship (whether syntactic, semantic or collocational need not concern this chapter). At first, the lexical items retain their prosodic autonomy, with the pause between them becoming reduced, e.g. daddy / . garden /. Often, long sequences of these items appear, especially repetitively, e.g. dàddy/gàrden/sèe/dáddy/dáddy/gàrden/dàddy/gàrden/sèe/. (Such sequences of course defy analysis in terms of the usually cited grammatical–semantic relations.) The next step is the prosodic integration of sequences of items, usually two, into a single tone-unit. How general a process this is, is unclear, but in several English combinations studied it was the case that one item became more prominent than the other; it was louder, and had an identifiable pitch movement. There was a rhythmic relationship between the items (anticipating isochrony), and intervening

pauses became less likely in repeated versions of lexical sequences. This step is considered to be of central theoretical importance, because it is claimed to be the main means employed by the child for formally expressing grammatical–semantic relations within a sentence – 'the simple concatenation under one utterance contour of the words which interact to create a compositional meaning that is different from the meanings of the two words in sequence' (Brown 1973: 182). Unfortunately, the process of concatenation is not so 'simple' as Brown suggests. All the following sequences have been observed (. = short pause, - and — = pauses of increasing length).

DÀDDY / — ÈAT /	DÁDDY / — ÈAT /
DÀDDY / – ÈAT /	DÁDDY / – ÈAT /
DÀDDY / . ÈAT /	DÁDDY / . ÈAT /
DÀDDY / ÈAT /	DÁDDY / ÈAT /
daddy ÈAT	DÁDDY eat /
DÀDDY eat	DÁDDY EÀT / [3]

It is accordingly often difficult to decide whether we are dealing with one sentence or two – especially if the context is unclear, e.g. the child is looking at a picture. In the above example, the subject–verb relation, so 'obvious' to the adult observer, may motivate one set of decisions. However, in the following examples (each of which may be found with any of the above twelve patterns), the 'compositional meanings' are by no means so clear:

DÁDDY / CÀR / (child is looking at daddy in a car)
DÁDDY / MÙMMY / (child is looking at a photograph of both)
DÁDDY / NÒ / (daddy has left the room)
DÁDDY / DÀDDY (said while being held by daddy)

Prosody, it seems, cannot be used by the analyst as a primitive discovery procedure for semantics or grammar – just as it cannot be in the adult language. It is one factor, and only one, in the simultaneity of language, behaviour, situation and adult interpretation which constitutes our analytic datum. In certain settings, prosody will be a primary determinant of meaning; in other settings, it will be discounted. The way in which these factors operate upon each other in these various settings is, however, by no means clear (see further, Eilers 1975).

However it is arrived at, it is plain that around 1;6 in most children two-element sentences within single prosodic contours are used, and tonic prominence is not random. In adult English, the prominence in a sentence consisting of one tone-unit is in 90 per cent of cases on the last lexical item (Chomsky and Halle 1968: 17ff; Crystal 1969, 1975: ch. 1). Bringing

the prominence forward within the tone-unit is possible, for both grammatical and semantic reasons. In the former case, one may be constrained by rules of cross-reference within the sentence (e.g. *Jack saw* JÍM / *and* HÉ *said* ... /); in the latter case, one may be making a (referential or personal) contrast between lexical items (e.g. *the* RÈD *dress* / *not the* GRÉEN *dress* /). The presuppositions and attitudes of the speaker also promote marked tonicity (e.g. *I* WÀNT *a red dress* / , *he* ìSN'T *coming* /). At the two- to three-word stage in children there will obviously be little to note in relation to the prosodic marking of grammatical or lexical relations – such contrasts are likely to be more apparent when clause sequences appear. The most fruitful way of analysing variations in tonicity at the two-element stage, as a result, is therefore to establish a relationship between the changes in the child's environment and his prosody. Wieman (1976), for example, attempts to show that new information in a sentence affects tonic placement, whereas old information does not (see also Gruber 1967). If a child is given a marble, he might say / *got* MÀRBLE / , but thereafter he is likely to say / SÈE *marble* / , because *marble* is old information the second time. It is not difficult to hear examples which do not confirm this hypothesis, however; and plainly, there are difficulties in working with notions of 'information', 'presupposition' and the like with young children. How does one know that what is 'new' to the observer, interpreting the situation in terms of adult expectancies, is also going to be new to the child? How does one establish the emergence of personal, attitudinal contrastivity, equivalent to the emphasis an adult might give, quite out of the blue, to the following sentence: I LÌKE *Bartok* (I've decided!) (where it is not necessarily the case that this had previously been in doubt – 'I didn't know you DÌDN'T like him', one might respond).

The literature on the acquisition of rhythmical contrastivity is sparse. We have already referred to the importance of rhythmical coherence entering into the identification of language-specific contours in the second half of the first year; but this is a simple, undifferentiated notion (presence versus absence of language-specific rhythm). During the second year we encounter the emergence of rhythmical contrasts which play a structural role in identifying words and phrase. Chief amongst these is the contrast which is variously labelled *stress* or (if pitch prominence is the focus) *accent*. The development of these contrasts overlaps with, but should not be confused with, the learning of intonational contrastivity – in particular, the notion of tonicity referred to above. Of course, the two dimensions – rhythmical and intonational – often coincide, as in the sentence 'I see a *cab*bage', where *cab* is simultaneously the carrier of primary stress in the word *cabbage* and the tonic syllable of the tone-unit *I see a cabbage* (assuming normal,

unmarked intonation). But the separability of the dimensions can be readily shown, by introducing a contrastive intonation: in 'I *see* a cabbage', the tonic syllable has shifted to *see*, but *cab* is still the primary stressed syllable of *cabbage*.

The few studies of the acquisition of rhythm and stress are in general agreement that, while the first signs of learning in this domain are quite early – before age 2, the mastery of the whole system, to include full perceptual and productive control, does not take place until around age 12 (Atkinson-King 1973; Malikouti-Drachman and Drachman 1975). Several features of this process have been noted. Blasdell and Jensen (1970) found that stress facilitated the imitation of nonsense monosyllables in 2–3 year olds. Risley and Reynolds (1970) found a similar imitation effect with accented words in 5 year olds. Atkinson-King (1973) found that 5 year olds were unable to consistently differentiate noun phrases from compound nouns on the basis of stress alone. Allen (1983) introduced a cross-cultural dimension to the topic, by studying the ability of 4–5-year-old French, German and Swedish children to discriminate stress patterns in pairs of nonsense words. He found that 5 year olds did better than 4 year olds on most of the distinctions presented, apart from the interesting result that the French children apparently began to *disregard* lexical stress distinctions not relevant for French at around age 4. On the basis of this and previous studies, Allen concludes that age 3–5 is a particularly important period for the acquisition of a language's stress system.

Allen and Hawkins (1978, 1980) have presented a more general account of the acquisition of what they call 'phonological rhythm'. In their view, the early utterances of children are best described as a form of syllable-timed rhythm, which is most noticeable in the reduplicated forms characteristic of early word learning. They see the main problem facing the child as one of learning the rules for reducing full syllables so as to produce the diversity of unstressed syllables in a language. They note certain trends in this process – for example, that unstressed prenuclear syllables are dropped in early productions more frequently than postnuclear syllables (*raff* for *giraffe*, rather than *ta* for *table*, etc.). Their general view is that the underlying trend in development is towards the establishment of a trochaic rhythmic pattern (i.e. one in which a stressed syllable is followed by an unstressed one). On the other hand, they note a great deal of variability amongst children in the 2–4 year old range.

H. Klein (1984) is also concerned with the analysis of variability in the learning of stress patterns, but her study focuses on the different patterns encountered in a single child. She found no general rule which could explain the range of stress patterning manifested by the 2 year old she studied.

Rather, there seemed to be different stages of ability to use stress simultaneously present. Klein explains the variability in terms cᶠ a combination of lexical and (segmental) phonological factors – in much the same way that other researchers have done in order to explain variation in the acquisition of phonemes. She found that her child's use of stress seemed to be lexically based in that words he used spontaneously had a more consistent stress pattern than those produced in an imitation task (which were less familiar). Moreover, within the productive class of words, articulatory difficulty also had an effect in misplacing stress.

Myers and Myers (1983) introduce the further factor of task variability into the discussion. They studied the ability of a wide age range of children (kindergarteners to 6th grade) to detect same / different patterns on nonsense words, and to evaluate the appropriateness of certain contrastive patterns in linguistic contexts. They found that older children were more able to handle the contrastive patterns, but that there was still evidence of development taking place at age 12 or 13. In particular, they noted a differential effect between the two tasks, performance always being poorer on the linguistic task. In their conclusion, accordingly, they emphasize the need to allow for the variable effects introduced by such task differences as the use of nonsense versus meaningful stimuli, or spontaneous versus synthesized stimuli, in future research into the learning of stress.

One general conclusion from these studies must be to emphasize the very gradual nature of the acquisition of stress and associated contrasts. Another must be to reinforce the view, strongly represented in phonological theory, that there is an integral relationship between the units of the segmental system and aspects of the nonsegmental system – stress, in particular (see Chomsky and Halle 1968, etc.). From this point of view, stress, seen as the point of intersection between segmental and nonsegmental word-level phonology, and between nonsegmental word-level and sentence-level phonology, takes on an especial significance as a focus for research in child language studies.

3. Motherese

The first studies of motherese drew attention to the distinctive role of prosody as part of this variety (Ferguson 1964, 1977; Remick 1976; Blount and Padgug 1977; Garnica 1977; Sachs 1977). Pitch was particularly implicated: adults talking to children were said to use a higher pitch level and a wider pitch range – a phenomenon which was felt to be universal. However, for some time little attempt was made to define the nature of the effect in precise acoustic or auditory terms, or to investigate its variability

between different mothers, other adults, and in different settings. A major trend in recent research has been to begin the systematic study of the factors constraining the phenomenon, much of the early work being anecdotal, selective in its coverage (usually only terminal pitch contours are studied), and related to older (after age 1) children.

It should first be pointed out that the prosody of adult baby talk is a complex feature of the variety, involving all the variables recognized by theories of nonsegmental phonology (Crystal 1969). Not only is there distinctive use of pitch direction and range, but also of loudness (overall level, as well as specific stress patterning), tempo (of whole utterances, as well as of the duration of individual syllables), rhythmicality, pause, and the range of paralinguistic features (labialization, creaky voice, resonance, etc.). The involvement of these variables has been especially noticed in relation to studies of maternal speech to infants in the first year, which has been a neglected period in motherese research despite the experimental findings, referred to above, that infants can discriminate pitch and other changes in speech at a very early age. It is now plain that mothers make adjustments to the prosody of their speech as soon as their babies are born (Fernald 1978; D. Stern *et al.* 1983). For instance, Stern *et al.* studied maternal prosody to children at birth and aged 4, 12 and 24 months, examining the variation in pitch (terminal contour change, transitional change between utterances, overall utterance range and highest utterance level), timing and rhythm. They found that lengthened pauses were most noticeable at birth, exaggerated pitch contours and higher levels at 4 months, and longer utterance durations at 2 years. They suggest the need to consider adult prosody to children in terms of a series of *phases* of development, arguing that during a particular phase of interaction a mother increases her use of a subset of prosodic features and decreases her use of others. Different subsets will be in use at different temporal periods and in different contextual settings (play, feeding, etc.). Stern *et al.* draw particular attention to the role marked pitch and pause might play as end-of-utterance cues in the mother's speech, thus facilitating smoother conversational turn-taking on the part of the child. However, their paper does not systematically examine functional differences.

In the absence of appropriately detailed studies of the form of maternal prosody when talking to children, discussion of functions is inevitably premature – though, as is regrettably all too common in language acquisition research, this has not stopped scholars speculating at length about the range of functions involved, and about their developmental significance. Thus, in relation to the exaggerated pitch characteristics noted, several theories have been proposed – that adults are trying to adapt themselves to the

pitch level produced by the child; that the children themselves prefer exaggerated pitches, demonstrating their preference through their orientating behaviour; that these features are a sign of adults' increased affective involvement with the child; and that they are used by adults as a means of obtaining the child's attention. None of the theories is unequivocably supported. Any adaptation theory is much weakened by the prosodic similarities between adult male and female speech, in talking to children (e.g. Tuaycharoen 1978; Jacobson *et al.* 1983), and by evidence suggesting that, if anything, females introduce more variability than males (e.g. Jacobson *et al.* 1983). There is insufficient clear data to determine the relevance of the orientation theory: it is difficult to isolate prosodic variables in such a way that unambiguous infant responses can be obtained. The affective theory does not explain the variability in patterning noted by D. Stern *et al.* 1983, nor the fact that not all languages use exaggerated pitch characteristics even in the context of parental interaction where affection is plainly demonstrated (Pye and Ratner 1984).

The attention-attracting theory is the one which has attracted the most attention, being frequently cited in the early literature on motherese (Garnica 1975, 1977; Brown 1977; Sachs 1977, etc.), and being most in tune with the sociolinguistic thrust of much of the recent research in this area. Stern, Spieker and MacKain (1982), for example, analysed maternal speech to 2-, 4- and 6-month-old infants, and found five contours commonly used by the mothers. The rising contour (with a broadly questioning function) was the most frequent (accounting for 22 per cent of the analysed utterances in their study), and they judged this to be associated with an interactional context where the mother seemed to be trying to gain the child's attention. They drew a contrast between the use of this contour and that of a contour which they identified as sinusoidal, the latter being used to elicit affective responses (such as a smile) from an already attentive baby. The possible attention-getting function of the rising contour has been noted by others (e.g. Chapman 1981). However, the situation is not entirely clear-cut. Sullivan and Horowitz (1983) used an auditory preference paradigm to assess 2-month-old infants' differential attention to both naturally-produced and synthetically-generated rising and falling contours, hypothesizing that they would attend more to rises than falls. The infants did attend more to the rising contour when it was naturally produced by females; but they attended more to the synthetically-produced falling contour, and responses to male stimuli were split. Moreover, linguistic information is slowly accumulating to show that rising contours are not universal. In Tuaycharoen's (1978) study of a Thai child from around 3 months, falling pitch was the adult feature to which the child most readily responded. Even more striking

is Pye and Ratner's (1984) study of Quiché Mayan baby talk, where high pitch characteristics seem to be totally lacking – a somewhat lower-than-normal pitch range being used instead. It would thus seem that there is a certain language-specific arbitrariness involved in the explanation of adult prosody when talking to children, which can perhaps be further clarified by referring to the sociolinguistic traditions of communities, in which such factors as age, sex and social status may exercise an influence on the speech form.

Future research on the prosody of adult talk to children, then, needs to adopt a more detailed and systematic formal and functional frame of reference than has previously been the case. Under the heading of *form*, proper attention needs to be paid to the range of phonological variables (at least a dozen) which seem to be affected, namely:

> pitch height of utterances (and utterance sequences)
> pitch height of parts of utterances (e.g. individual words)
> terminal pitch contour (bearing in mind that a simple fall versus rise distinction will not suffice to capture the range of variation which exists)
> contour of whole utterances (and utterance sequences)
> pitch range of utterances (and utterance sequences)
> loudness level of utterances (and utterance sequences)
> stress patterns of words / phrases
> tempo of speech (noting inter-pause syllable rate, and vowel / consonant durations)
> duration of pauses
> rhythm of utterances (and utterance sequences)
> paralinguistic features, e.g. secondary articulations (labialization, nasalization, etc.), laryngeal effects (whisper, creak, etc.), singing

Under the heading of *function*, we need to introduce a fuller specification of the range of sociolinguistic variables known to influence language use in general, including such factors as sex of the adult, whether the adult has had much previous experience of children (Jacobson *et al.* 1983), the nature of the adult–child activity, and so on. What needs to be explained is not why adults introduce marked prosodic contrastivity into their speech when talking to children, but why they do not do so all the time. The amount of variability, both within and between adults, has been much underplayed in the above literature – and indeed there does not even seem to be a general estimate available of the incidence of these features in adult–child interaction.

4. Future research

Once grammatical patterns and lexical sets develop, then the tracing of prosodic patterns becomes a much more straightforward task. What is important here is for researchers to remember the important role prosody has in the adult language in relation to the delimitation and integration of such structures as relative clauses, co-ordination, adverbial positioning, direct / indirect object marking, etc. (see Quirk *et al.* 1972; Crystal 1975: ch. 1). Very little research seems to have been carried out on the later development of such patterns in speech production (but see Menyuk 1969; Wode 1980). Correspondingly, relatively little work has been done on the comprehension of these features (but see Cruttenden's 1974 study of certain aspects of intonation in a restricted class of co-ordinated utterances – football results – which showed that awareness of the rules involved was still in the process of developing between 7 and 10 years; Cruttenden (1985), which confirms this late development for a much wider class of utterances; and also Carol Chomsky 1969, Maratsos 1973, on the late awareness of co-referential pronouns in certain contexts of co-ordination). These examples make it probable that intonational learning continues until puberty (and, of course, when one thinks in terms of one's stylistic control over prosody, as in dramatic speaking, well into adult life).

Finally, it is particularly important to focus on the specific role prosodic variables (especially tonicity) play in psycholinguistic experimentation, e.g. in experiments on memory or attention, or on paraphrase and imitation. Varying the prosodic input does influence response patterns, as has been shown both for normal children (e.g. Du Preez 1974) and adults (e.g. Cutler 1976), and in the context of disability, for example by Goodglass, Fodor and Schulhoff (1967), Stark, Poppen and May (1967) and Crystal (1981: ch. 3). Du Preez, for instance, shows very plainly that children have a predilection to imitate tonic syllables: words occurring finally in a tone-unit are imitated first, and those earlier in the tone-unit are imitated only when they are given marked tonicity, the tonic apparently 'act[ing] as a signal to notice what to follow' (1974: 71). Bonvillian, Raeburn and Horan (1979) examine intonation, rate and length in presenting 3–4-year-old children with a sentence-imitation task. They show that sentences presented at the child's own rate (two words per second) were better than those presented faster or slower, and that normal (as opposed to flat) intonation helped imitation when sentences were long. They suggest that children may rely on intonation as an aid to comprehension when their cognitive capacities are being stretched (as in the processing of lengthy sentences). On the other hand, it must not be forgotten that the demonstration of psycho-

linguistic effects is very dependent on exactly which aspects of prosody have been selected for study. If too much of the prosody is eliminated from consideration, for example, effects may disappear (e.g. Johnson, Leder and Egelston 1980, who find that recall of single-word sequences is not facilitated when the words are intonated simply as a series of falling tones, rising tones or level tones). The question of what 'counts' as intonation is raised by such studies. And similarly, the common strategy of 'leaving the prosody out' in experimental work, by presenting a series of stimuli in identical tones of voice, involves assumptions which themselves require investigation (such homogeneous sequences are abnormal in parent–child interaction; how far might such unfamiliar stimuli affect responses?). Here, as in the other research areas listed above, the problems are urgently in need of systematic study.

9. Early strategies for the perception and production of words and sounds

Paula Menyuk, Lise Menn and Ronnie Silber

1. Introduction

Not until this past decade has the notion of the development of perceptual and productive phonemic contrasts during the so-called 'prelinguistic' period been taken seriously by linguists. Previously it was held that during this period infants engaged in playful sound making. The sounds produced were held to be largely a product of the random exercise of the human infant's vocal mechanism for sound making, and, therefore, the sounds produced were universal. Further, Jakobson (1968) suggested that there was a silent period between the production of babbled utterances and the production of first words. This silent period indicated the discontinuity between the two periods. Some behaviourist researchers, in contrast to this, suggested that this prelinguistic period was one during which the child's perception and production of sound contrasts was 'shaped' by parental input to take on gradually the characteristics of the adult's perception and production of sounds in the native language. This shaping occurred through the principles of conditioning (i.e. observing stimulus–response–reward relations). These sound generalizations were then chunked into words and the words into sentences. The most perceptually salient sounds were those mastered earliest. Therefore, no discontinuity could be said to exist between so-called prelinguistic and linguistic behaviour (Olmsted 1966; Staats 1967).

Recent data on the discrimination and production of speech sound contrasts by infants, and studies of the behaviour of their caretakers over this period, indicate that both these positions are questionable (Ferguson 1976). That is, contrary to the Jakobsonian position, the child is actively engaging in linguistically important behaviour during the first year of life, not merely producing random vocalizations (Menyuk 1971), and no silent period exists between babbling and first words. Contrary to the behaviourist position, there is no indication in the data that caretakers systematically isolate and contrast speech sound categories for their children or reward in some systematic way approximations to the contrasts presented. What

does occur is a reduction in the number of utterances that are long babbled strings, and an increase in the number of utterances that appear to be transitional between babble and words in various respects, or that appear to have the characteristics of words. In this chapter we will review current data on the phonological linguistic abilities of children (not their morphological or syntactic abilities) during this reduction in babbling to beginning of word acquisition period. We will suggest some of the ways in which earlier developments are a prerequisite to development during this period and in what important ways developments during this period are markedly different from previous and later periods. We will discuss some differences in language processing strategies, perceptual and productive, used during this period, comparing them with others, to account for the language behaviour observed. Finally, we will suggest some much needed research in order adequately to describe the development of phonemic contrasts during this period.

2. Perception of phonemic contrasts

It should be stated that although there are a number of studies of speech sound discrimination by the infant and by children approximately 3 or more years of age, there are comparatively few studies of this behaviour during the latter months of the first year of life until the beginning of the third year of life. This age period is the most pertinent one for our discussion. Any conclusions reached concerning the development of perception of phonemic contrasts during this period must be highly tentative. We shall review those studies which have direct bearing on the issue of developmental changes in speech processing before and during this period.

2.1. Development of speech processing

Before this period the infant gives evidence of a capacity to discriminate between speech sound syllabic segments that contrast the features of initial consonants (± voice as in /pa/ versus /ba/; coronal as in /ba/ versus /da/) or those that contrast the fundamental frequency pattern (steady versus rising or falling) (Morse 1974). Vowels, liquids, and glides can also be discriminated (Morse 1978). The paradigm most frequently used, at present, to study speech sound discrimination in children is the visually reinforced head-turn, introduced by Eilers, Wilson and Moore (1976) and developed by Kuhl (1980). As well as being able to discriminate, the infant appears to be developing the ability to categorize. Kuhl (1980) was able to demonstrate perceptual constancy for vowels (the ability to identify the

same vowel across different speakers, pitches and other changing environments) in children aged 5.5 to 10 months, and also constancy for consonants
when represented in different vowel contexts. This provides evidence that
infants have the potential for categorization rather than simply syllabic
discrimination, at least under optimal training circumstances. It had been
suggested that the human infant is neurologically preprogrammed, in terms
of feature detectors, to be sensitive to those acoustic features which mark
speech sound differences (Eimas 1974). However, further research indicates
that this ability should be viewed as not being limited to speech, but, rather,
extended to all acoustic events that share certain features; and, further,
that the ability to discriminate among speech sound syllables is not limited
to human infants (Morse 1978).

Two studies have been carried out during the age period of 10–21 months
(Shvachkin 1973) and 17–22 months (Garnica 1973) which test children's
ability to learn to associate nonsense syllabic sequences, that differ only
in one feature of initial consonants or of vowel and consonants, with objects.
These studies, unlike those of infant speech sound discrimination, indicate
that there is, to some extent, a developmental progression in the child's
ability to make these distinctions. That is, some distinctions or feature
contrasts are learned before others by all children, and, therefore, presumably, some distinctions are easier to detect than others in these association
experiments. In the infant discrimination studies no such developmental
progression in feature distinctions between consonants has been observed.
Further, the ± voice discrimination found with infants as young as 1 month
is the latest distinction observed by children in the association studies.
In addition, in the Garnica study, unlike the Shvachkin study, it was found
that although all children learned some feature distinctions before others
(i.e. a developmental progression was observed with all children), and that
although some feature distinctions were more likely to be acquired before
others by the population as a whole, there was considerable variation among
the children in the exact sequence of acquisition of differentiations.

Two studies have examined the 2 year old's ability to discriminate
between + and − voice segments when the stimuli are either computer-
edited natural speech or synthetic speech (Zlatin and Koenigsknecht 1975;
Simon and Fourcin 1978). The overall finding of both studies was that
2 year olds only label extreme values of VOT consistently. Intermediate
values are labelled randomly. By the age of 4 responding is clearly categorical and remains so. The preceding set of results gives rise to some questions
that are still unresolved. We need to account for the fact that infants whose
perceptual systems are presumably less mature than those of 2 year olds
apparently do better on a speech discrimination task. The answer may

lie in developmental differences in what is attended to when processing the speech signal.

In addition to the above experimental studies there have been some detailed observational studies of the child's comprehension of words during the latter part of the first year of life and the beginning of the second (Lewis 1963; Nakazima 1970). These data indicate that the child understands a set of words in relation to certain contexts and expectations. That is, the environment in terms of the communicative behaviour of the addressor (gesture, facial expression and prosody of the utterance) plus the objects and actions in the situation appear to cue the child to the content of the utterance heard and to produce appropriate behaviour. Barton (1976, 1980) found that children between the ages of 27 and 35 months were able to discriminate between minimal pair words that contrast most of the English late-acquired speech sounds, including the ± voice contrast of stops in final position (*log* / *lock*) and the two liquids in consonant clusters (*clown* / *crown*). He noted, however, a strong response bias among these children in favour of familiar words. Error rates were highest when both the words in a pair were unfamiliar. These findings, Barton argues, indicate that studies of phonemic contrast acquisition using nonsense syllable stimuli probably underestimate children's actual ability to discriminate between minimal pair words.

Finally, it has been suggested, although not tested, that by the time the child is well into the word production period her perceptual categorizations are those of adult surface phonemic forms (Smith 1973). Another suggestion is that the child has perceptually categorized the phonological segments in the word as a sequence of identified segments (equal to those of the adult) and unidentified noises (Ingram 1974), or, as Wilbur (1980) suggests, partially identified noises. Both these suggestions concerning perceptual categorizations are based on what the child produces en route to adult-like production of words, and on the child's ability to distinguish similar sounding words in discourse. Menn (1976a) argues for the same position as Wilbur, on the ground that avoidance and exploitation strategies (see section 3.3 on the origin of phonological rules) could not be used by children under 24 months of age unless they were able to differentiate between the favoured and disfavoured sounds. It seems entirely reasonable to suppose that perceptual representations underlie productive realizations. The problems are the differing interpretations of perceptual representations that experimenters give based upon productive data, and the lack of data on the relation between perception and production.

The above pieces of evidence indicate the following: the human infant at age 1 month is capable of discriminating between some acoustic para-

meters that mark speech sound differences; by age 9–13 months the infant appears to be able to comprehend the meaning of phonological sequences in certain contexts, that is, gestalt comprehension of phonological sequence plus context rather than phonological differentiation of sequences; the child is able to learn to associate objects and nonsense syllables that contrast many of the initial consonant features during the period of 10–22 months; by 35 months the child can distinguish between minimal pair words that contain most English singleton phonological contrasts. Added to these findings are those which indicate that there are individual differences among children in the sequence in which they observe phonemic contrasts in the abstract domain of nonsense syllables and it seems that familiarity of lexical items plays a role in the ability to observe phonemic contrasts. If this is the case, one might assume there are individual differences in the sequence of development of contrasts observed in words, since different children might be exposed to different sets of lexical items with varying frequency.

Although the data are sparse and also confusing, if we try to outline what the child does developmentally in order to recognize words and begin to talk in a manner similar to an adult, the following seems to occur. First, shortly after birth the child distinguishes between sound patterns that come from different sources: human versus other animate and inanimate objects, or, in other words, displays the ability to differentiate between speech and nonspeech. The child at this time is also capable of discriminating between speech sound categories and of producing phonated sounds. Second, the child observes recurring patterns in human sound sequences and recurring patterns in nonlinguistic events, and begins to categorize these patterns. Third, the child recognizes that recurring patterns in human sound sequences occur in conjunction with recurring events, and learns to reproduce aspects of these sound patterns in certain specific situations. During this period acoustic patterns of human sound sequences may be stored as wholes or gestalts, just as visual or motor patterns may be stored as gestalts. No further analysis of the dimensions of the acoustic, visual or motor image occurs. Fourth, the child begins to analyse the contents of these speech sound patterns and the situations in which they are produced. The analyses of the speech sound sequence are translated into articulatory gestures. Each of these developmental changes on the way to listening and speaking like an adult reflects developmental changes in the competences available to the child for analysing and translating the phonology of the language, analysing and translating recurring nonlinguistic events and, finally, relating the two.

Much of what occurs phonologically during the first year of life appears to be based on the biological readiness of the human infant to acquire

language; that is, the psychophysical parameters of the mammalian auditory system (Aslin and Pisoni 1980b). Thus, at a very early period of development the infant behaves differentially to signals that are human speech or speech-like as compared to those that are not. Also, at a very early age the infant displays sensitivity to, and can discriminate between, speech signals on the basis of acoustic parameters that the adult also uses to discriminate between speech signals. We do not have a complete picture of what these parameters are, but they appear to include voicing onset time, locus and rate of change of second formant transition (Miller and Eimas 1983) and changes in fundamental frequency pattern. Differences in vocalization patterns occur during this early period which indicate that there is a sequence in the production of phonological segments which may, in part, be accounted for by increasing control of the output of the vocal mechanism. It is also during this period that the infant indicates discrimination between different prosodic patterns, produces babbled strings that have different prosodic patterns and appears to categorize these patterns, at least in terms of affective communicative intent. In summary, the child during this period can discriminate between sounds, produce syllabic strings that are marked prosodically and use prosodic patterns in communications. All of these abilities seem necessary prerequisites to listening and speaking like an adult. However, it does not seem to be the case that the capacity to discriminate between segments on the basis of feature distinctions, or to produce the phonological segments in the language on this basis, is used in the beginning to recognize and reproduce recurrent phonological sequences.

Given the evidence of the studies we have reviewed on the development of perception of phonemic contrasts, some basis other than the distinctive feature appears to be used initially. Although the distinctive feature has long been held to be the basis of speech sound discrimination in both children (Menyuk 1971) and adults (Miller and Nicely 1955; Wickelgren 1966) the role of the distinctive feature in speech perception (storage and retrieval of phonological information) has been questioned. Data on response time in a recognition task indicate that the syllable is much more accessible to the adult perceiver than the segment and feature. The latter are focused upon with greater delay. This also appears to be the case developmentally.

At the end of the first year of life, or the beginning of the second, children more frequently select to listen to word-length utterances than to connected speech and more frequently produce word-length utterances or so-called 'jargon' phrases than babbled strings (Menyuk 1972). During the transition from babbled utterances to word approximations or compressed sentences (Branigan 1977) the child appears to recognize most recurring patterns

in sound sequences only in conjunction with specific events. Some exceptions to this are the child's own name or the word *no*, which are repeated very frequently in varying contexts. Only later does the child indicate recognition of sound patterns in a variety of situations. This, the word or phrase or sentence, depending on the chunking strategy of the child, appears to be initially stored as phonological sequence plus situation. Later the child may recognize the word in a variety of situations and, still later, when it is presented in isolation. It is suggested that phonological contrasts are first observed between words, then syllables and finally in terms of distinctive feature contrasts between segments.

Evidence for syllabic decoding as preliminary to feature analysis has been suggested by several researchers and is reviewed in Menyuk (1972, 1976). The role of the syllable in generative phonology has recently been explored (Kahn 1976; Clements and Keyser 1983), and substantial evidence is given that the syllable is a necessary element in phonological descriptions that claim psychological reality. Further, there is now evidence of distinct acoustic patterns of formant transitions from stop Cs to V (rising transitions, or falling transitions, or both rising and falling), and these may form the basis of perceptual categorizations (Stevens 1972). Thus, resolution of a category requires information that exceeds the segment or features of a segment (see also Fujimura and Lovins 1978).

However, analysis in terms of the contrastive features of syllables probably does not occur at the initial stage of this period of development. We would suggest, rather, with Ferguson and Farwell (1975), that words are contrasted and identified as wholes, and, indeed, are identified not only in terms of a phonological event but also in terms of the context in which they occur. Thus, *cup* in the child's lexicon may at the beginning stages of its identification represent only the cup that he drinks milk from and not any cup in the environment. Is it feasible to suggest storage of phonological contrasts in terms of whole words plus meaning at this initial period? Certainly the productive lexicon of the child is small at the beginning of the word production period. Children in one sample population achieved a lexicon of 50 spoken words at a mean age of 19.6 months (Nelson 1973b). How far the recognition vocabulary of children exceeds their spoken vocabulary when it consists of 1 to 10 words is not clear, but one would assume by not too great an amount for storage of words as wholes. However, it is also clearly the case that this strategy will not carry the child very far as the lexicon increases.

Does this mean that the distinctive features of sound segments cannot be employed by the child? The evidence of minimal pair studies indicates that these contrastive elements can be used in test circumstances by the

child, but only with effort and training. That is, the distinction is not readily available to the child. The following is an outline of the development changes in speech processing proposed:

1. *Readiness in processing speech*
    A. Distinction between speech and nonspeech
    B. Discrimination between speech sound categories and prosodic patterns
    C. Production of CV sequences marked prosodically

2. *Analysis of meaningful unit(s)*
    A. Phonological sequence and situation
    B. Phonological analysis and situational analysis
    C. Analysis of syllabic features of phonological sequences
    D. Analysis of distinctive feature content of sequences

2.2. Processing strategies

The above conclusions are highly tentative and are based on the slim data of studies of perception during this period, the early production of phonological sequences, some notions about the course of development in all aspects of the language which seems to proceed from generalization to differentiation to abstract generalization, and the speech perception strategies of adults. The data indicate that the hierarchy in speech perception by adults is that represented by steps 2B, C, and D above. The distinction between young children and adults is that the adult, unlike the child, (a) has easy access to all steps, and (b) has the ability to keep all aspects simultaneously in mind during processing (Menyuk 1977).

Two models of processing, among others, have been discussed in the literature on adult perception of speech. One is analysis by synthesis and the other is synthesis by analysis (Fodor, Bever and Garrett 1974). If the synthesis by analysis strategy is employed by the child, then it might be the case that phonemic contrasts are categorized first in terms of feature contrasts or bundles of features of segments and then that bundles of features are chunked together for recognition of words. An analysis by synthesis strategy would lead to determination of the largest meaningful unit, and then further analysis of this unit in terms of its content and context of occurrence. This latter strategy seems to account for the data much more adequately than the former. We further suggest that the first subanalysis in terms of acquisition of phonemic contrasts is the syllable. As we have stated, this is just a suggestion. There are some data, however, which bear on the question of whether or not early analysis is in terms of features.

Barton (1976) investigated the ability of children age 20–24 months correctly to discriminate between words which contrasted initial stop voicing (*pear* / *bear, coat* / *goat*). He found that although most of the children were able to do it, many of them required considerable pre-training. Thus, even though infants are capable of discriminating between minimal pairs of syllables on the basis of voicing onset time, this strategy is not spontaneously used by young children when the domain of analysis is the word. Under these conditions children seem initially to use some lexical look-up procedure to determine similarity or difference (i.e. the meaning) before they attempt a phonological analysis. Adults apparently do the same (see Brown and Hildum 1956). The fact that some children preserve the initial voicing distinction in their production of words with initial stops (Hildegard Leopold, for example), long before children can be shown to observe this distinction in nonsense syllables or words, need not imply that the perceived distinction is on the basis of the $\pm$ voice distinction of segments but, rather, that these lexical items might be stored and retrieved as unsegmented wholes.

Can one speak of the development of the perception of phonemic contrasts as a universal sequence of development? Although an analysis by synthesis strategy might be universally employed by all children, there are several factors which might lead to individual differences in the sequence of development. A factor that was touched upon previously is the chunking strategy of the child. Some children appear to chunk together larger units than words (compressed sentences) and work on these for further analysis, whereas others work on words or on a combination of the two (Branigan 1977; Peters 1980; Thomas 1981). These different strategies would obviously lead to differences in sequence of acquisition of phonemic contrasts. A second factor is lexical repertoire. If it is the case that a lexical look-up procedure is used in minimal pair discrimination tasks before further analysis, as it is by adults, then those pairs that contain familiar lexical items will be distinguished before those that do not. Since children will vary to some extent in their lexical repertoires, individual differences will be observed.

We are still left trying to account for both universals and individual differences in studies of discrimination of minimal pair words and nonsense syllables. We make the following, again tentative, suggestion. First, perceptual saliency of phonemic contrasts of the syllable may account for whatever universality exists in the order of phonemic distinctions observed. Thus, for example, the distinction between /la/ and /wa/ might be less perceptually salient than that between /ga/ and /da/ because of the nature of the acoustic differences between the pairs. However, this may be the

case only with nonsense syllables. In attempting to determine perceptual saliency of contrastive syllables one would need to take into account different vowel contexts (i.e. co-articulation effects on acoustic outputs), and this has not systematically been done. Individual differences in minimal pair nonsense syllable tasks might be accounted for by the child attempting to use a strategy of analogy for recall. That is, when attempting to determine the difference between, and to recall, nonsense syllables, reference might be made to lexical items that are similar. No attempt has been made to probe for the strategies used by children in these experiments, for example by asking them what they have done or by providing known word analogies and examining rate of acquisition of distinctions under the latter circumstances.

Still another factor which may lead to individual differences in sequence of development of phonemic contrasts is the state of knowledge of the child at the time of sampling. Just as production of a phonemic distinction in a particular case might not imply an awareness of the phonemic status of the contrast involved, but only of the difference between the particular words, so some phonemic contrasts that are collapsed by the child in production might coexist with an awareness of distinctions (Eilers and Oller 1976). Since different children may be working on different problems at different times in the acquisition of phonemic contrasts, they may be attending to different aspects of the phonological system and, therefore, be more or less aware of certain contrasts at given times. Experiments systematically examining the relation between perception and production of phonemic contrasts in the same children in the domain of words over this developmental period need to be carried out.

These comments are being made to suggest that choice of stimuli in any study of the perception of phonemic contrasts (nonsense versus real sequences, consonantal plus vowel composition of sequences) and the state of knowledge of the child (lexical repertoire, productive strategies) may all affect the child's perceptual processing of 'phonemic' contrasts, and, thus, the competence the child displays at any given time.

3. Production of phonemic contrasts

A traditional question in the study of child language has been 'When does the average child acquire each of the phonemes of English?' Years of data-gathering and advances in linguistic theory have shown that while this question can be given rough normative answers, it is simply the wrong question to ask if we want to understand the way in which an individual develops

the ability to pronounce the words of his / her language. We do not have the space to expose all the false assumptions that make this a bad question, but we will begin this section by discussing two of the important ones.

The first assumption is that norı. children resemble one another sufficiently in acquisition of phonology that information about the 'average' child will predict the development of the individual. This is not the case. Normal children can vary widely in the age at which they become able to produce the various sounds of English, and in the order in which they acquire the ability to produce each of those sounds (Irwin and Wong 1983). A second false assumption is that a phoneme is a well-defined object for the purpose of study of acquisition of phonology. Leaving aside the lively and highly relevant controversy about the nature of the phoneme within linguistic theory, it is still clear that the phoneme is not a 'unit' for acquisition. There are two important groups of facts which contradict this false assumption. The phoneme does not generally correspond to a single phonetic target, nor to targets which are grouped in similar ways for all phonemes. In English, some phonemes are represented by single, narrowly defined phonetic targets (/f/ seems to be an example), while others have allophones which vary greatly in sound. Furthermore, these allophones may be in free variation (usually subject to positional restriction, e.g. 'optional' use of released or unreleased final stops), stylistic variation, or variation conditioned by neighbouring sounds (palatal pronunciation of /t, d/ before /r/). What degree of mastery of allophonic variation should then be counted as 'acquisition'?

Besides the variation in the number and diversity of the target phones that 'belong' to a phoneme, there is considerable variation in the difficulty that each phone presents to the child, depending on the neighbouring sounds in the word in which it occurs and on its position in the word. Even if it is the case that there is a single target phone /f/, for example, which is essentially invariant across content in the adult language, children will still have differing degrees of difficulty in producing it, depending on such factors as whether it occurs initially, medially or finally, whether it is part of a cluster, and what other consonants occur in the word. While some of these factors have been known and taken account of in the literature for a long time (Templin 1966; Olmsted 1971), others have been brought out only in recent work. For example, it seems that position in a word affects the difficulty of different sounds differently; fricatives are sometimes acquired first in final position, while stops fare best in initial position for most children. It should, however, be remembered that individual variation across children may affect these general tendencies in any particular case.

It is now known, furthermore, that if there are two consonants within the same word which are formed with different positions of articulation,

the combination presents problems which neither consonant alone would present (see Vihman 1978 for a review of the literature on this topic). A child who can say *do* and *egg* correctly may still say [gɔg], [dɔ], [dɔd], or possibly even [ɔg] for *dog* in the earlier stages of the acquisition of phonology. Other contextual effects are also found in individual children's speech; many of them are idiosyncratic phonotactic rules, but even these fall into general groups from which we can make generalizations about how the context of a phone affects its difficulty. Many such rules are exemplified in chapter 10, this volume. Altogether, it has become clear that both the Jakobson picture of successive splitting-off of contrasts and the structuralist model of the acquisition of phonemes are inadequate as theories of the acquisition of the ability to produce the phonemes of one's language. The theory which has been evolving to replace these older models is generally called a 'cognitive' or a 'problem-solving' theory (Menn 1979b, 1983; Macken and Ferguson 1983). The problem-solving theory of the acquisition of phonology views the child as making trial and error attempts at perceptual classification and production of sounds and sound sequences, and as developing strategies for production in the attempt to bring adult words within the limited range of existing production abilities.

It is useful to begin with a task analysis of what is involved in the acquisition of phonology, for in that way our thinking about it is less apt to be constrained by previous theory. To even begin to talk, a child must be able to say a recognizable word at an appropriate time. Furthermore, he or she must produce it not as a solo game or in sociable imitation but spontaneously, when it is socially and / or pragmatically opportune – *bye bye* at parting, *cookie* when a cookie is really desired and when there is someone around who might be able to produce a cookie. To do this requires the ability to recall both sound and meaning, and the ability to produce some approximation of the sound, all within a few seconds' time.

If instead of looking at the skilled language user we focus on the development of language production in children, we can construct the following rough sequential task analysis:

Production tasks
(i)   to learn to produce a variety of vocal sounds
(ii)   to learn to produce vocal sound patterns so that they more or less match sounds which are heard (imitation)
(iii) to learn to remember certain sound patterns well enough to produce them without just having heard them (delayed imitation)
(iv)   to learn to produce specific sound patterns in situations where they have been produced by others or by oneself in the past (situation-bound word use, to be discussed below as 'signalling' use of words)

(v)   to become able to produce a word in a novel setting as a means
      to an end (beginning of 'symbolic' use of words – see below)

Each of these tasks is first accomplished by a child for just a few sounds or sound patterns. Furthermore, wherever we have evidence of what the child is going through, we find that it is carried out laboriously and clumsily. Then, for each task level, greater degrees of skill develop. Instead of being able to handle only one or two special cases, the child develops routines which become both more general and more automatic. For example, on task level (iv) a child at a certain age may be able to imitate one or two well-known sound patterns, but at a later time he / she may be able to imitate a large variety of unfamiliar words: some general routines for trans-ducing 'what one hears' to 'what one says' have been developed during the elapsed time. It should be noted that the existence of such routines on level (ii) (imitation) carries no implication that any general routines have been developed on the next level (delayed imitation). That is, a child who can imitate new words with a particular degree of skill may be unable to produce them as well after a time lapse.

In this section we will survey the following issues concerning the beginning of children's language use: (a) what is the relationship between babbling and speech? and (b) what is the origin and the nature of rules of child phonology?

3.1. Transition from babbling to speech

During this period the child continues to learn to produce vocal sound (task i); improves his / her ability to imitate and to imitate with delay (tasks ii and iii); begins and becomes adept at learning to 'signal' with particular words (task iv) and, finally, starts to use a few words in a symbolic way (task v), thus making the major cognitive breakthrough required of the early period of language. Detailed longitudinal studies show that the bound-ary between late babble and speech is in general a fuzzy one. It is not merely that there is normally a temporal overlap between what were once thought to be disjoint stages of 'prespeech' and 'speech'. The fuzziness is much more serious than that. There are also individual recurrent entities in a child's production that cannot be classified unequivocally as either 'babble' or 'speech', and in some children these forms are quite prominent. They seem to occupy a pivotal position in language development in such children, and careful consideration of their form and function illuminates the nature of the transition from babble to speech in the general case.

Some of these transitional terms, which we shall refer to as 'proto-words'

(see Menn 1976a), are well-defined, meaningful sound patterns that are apparently not modelled on any adult word; as their functioning becomes more word-like, in ways in which we shall discuss below, they can be regarded as words invented by the child (see especially Halliday 1975). Other proto-words are in origin adult words which have become subjects for the child's sound play. Menn's subject Jacob (1976a) was fond of wandering about producing vocal variations on two themes, his name and the word *okay*. Other transitional items, not counted as proto-words because they lack identifiable articulated sounds that recur across instances, are the jargon stretches which are uttered with communicative intent and with eye-contact, gesture and intonation patterns appropriate to that intent (Menn and Haselkorn 1977). However, in some children these jargon stretches have 'real' words embedded in them (Jones 1967; Branigan 1977). Thus, proto-words, words and jargon stretches containing real words can all be produced during the same period of development.

We can find, among proto-words, phonologically interesting kinds of variability across instances (tokens) which would be anomalies from the adult point of view. These anomalous variations are very important for constructing a model for the acquisition of phonology, because they help us see more clearly what it is the child needs to learn, and to look at it in a way less coloured by our knowledge of mature linguistic behaviour. Menn's Jacob had two prominent proto-words, one modelled on the adult word *thank you* and the other apparently his own creation, which showed very striking variation across tokens. Within his lexicon these were among the most variable items, but he had present during the same period less variable items and items that were produced without much variation. Jacob's own creation, [ioio] as we referred to it, appeared randomly in a great variety of phonetic shapes, which can be unified by saying that Jacob was varying the timing of front-back articulations against the timing of lowering and raising the tongue. Depending on the way in which he co-ordinated these orthogonal gestures, his output was variously heard as [ioio], [wiʌwio], [wejaweja], [iʌiʌiʌ], [ajaj], [ajʌajʌ], etc. Division of these sequences into 'phones' obscures the simple unity of the underlying pattern which we describe in words and which also can be captured within the formalism of autosegmental phonology (Clements 1976; Goldsmith 1976; Menn 1978; Clements and Keyser 1983).

Thank you also exhibited wild variations on an underlying pattern. Unlike [ioio] it can be segmented into a CVCV sequence without violence, but there was evidence that two consonants formed a prosodic unit of a peculiar kind. Each could appear as virtually any nonlabial stop, from dental to velar (including palatal); the medial one usually but not always voiced,

the initial one voiced. The vowels were also variable: the first one was usually less back than the second. Examples include [geika], [dɛjdʌ], [gaita], [dɛgʌ], [gigu], and a few with vocalic [m] in place of the second vowel.

These variations are explained in terms of the problems posed by the adult model word, which has neither vowel nor consonant harmony and was Jacob's first word; the point of the example is not that the reason for Jacob's treatment of it is hard to find, but that the notation and conceptualization of a traditional theory are inadequate to the description. One does much better in this case to work with prosodic units and underspecified (archiphonemic) elements. Here we have been focusing on phonological rather than semantic–functional aspects of the transition from babbling to speech. The two, however, are richly connected (again, see Halliday 1975) and therefore, even in a chapter on the acquisition of phonology, there are aspects of semantic–pragmatic development which it is not possible to leave out.

The major thread in semantic–pragmatic development during the transition from babbling to speech is the gradual freeing-up of proto-words from the narrow pragmatic circumstances in which they almost always first appear. Halliday (1975) and Clumeck (1977), among others, concur with Menn and Haselkorn (1977) in finding that the first word-like objects, whether self-created or derived from an adult model, are tightly bound to specific functions – some accompany particular actions, some are greetings or farewells, some accompany pointing, some are used as labels, others as demands. They are, at this early stage, essentially vocal signals, and may be compared to adult words which have very limited pragmatic range, such as greetings and cries of *ouch*. The meanings of such items, for both adult and child, are best characterized as 'what you say when you do X'.

Proto-words do not remain restricted in this fashion, however, for more than a few months. They develop what is called 'symbolic autonomy' – the potential for being used for a variety of ends. Even the most impoverished word of the adult language (e.g. *ouch*) has some degree of symbolic autonomy, for an adult can use it in reporting what he / she or another said as well as when actually communicating present pain. A child's vocable has developed symbolic autonomy if he / she can use it for a variety of pragmatic ends. For example, children may start by using *hello* only as 'what you say when you pick up a telephone', and then develop the ability to use it (along with gesture) as a request to get an adult to talk on a toy telephone. Or, a word like *down* or *boom* may begin as action accompaniment to dropping, throwing, or pushing objects over, and then later may be used to describe the fall of an object or to request permission to cause an object to fall. As a proto-word develops the full degree of symbolic

autonomy possessed by a word of the adult language, it must become able to be used with a variety of intonations – rising, falling and more complex contours as well. In this way, the semantic–pragmatic development is interwoven with the suprasegmental aspect of phonological development.

3.2. Distinguishing between phonetics and phonemics in production

At some point, we have inferred, phonetic and phonemic analysis across words begins – quite possibly via an intermediate stage where the atomic units are syllable-length or consist of syllable-onset units and syllable-nucleus-plus-coda units. It is still impossible with present techniques to assess the course of development of the child's ability to subdivide and compare words in perception. We can, however, work out some of the aspects of this transition for speech production, the beginning of the acquisition of target phones and the acquisition of phonemic contrast in production. The process of bringing articulation of segments under control in the production of a variety of words, and the intertwined but distinct process of constructing the set of phonological oppositions of a language, both take place gradually. The two developments are not always in step with one another. For example, a child who cannot yet produce the consonant clusters /sn/, /sm/ may represent them by [hn], [hm] or by the voiceless nasals N, M. The contrast between the singleton nasals and the /s/ + nasal clusters is preserved, but the articulation is incorrect and the child's appaent target has only some of the features of the adult cluster. Assuming the child's production of these incorrect clusters is stable, then both contrast and control are good, but the target is wrong.

Another kind of developmental pattern occurs when the child has difficulty in controlling his production of similar sounds, perhaps to the extent that two phones which are distinct in the adult language seem to be confused and yet an analysis of the child's error patterns reveals that he is indeed aiming at distinct and appropriate targets. Menn's Jacob, for example, for several weeks (1:7:29 to 1:8:22) had great difficulty with /ɔ/. In the speech around him this phoneme had two allophones, a higher and more rounded one before / r / and a lower, more centralized one in other environments. Even though Jacob seldom hit either of these targets correctly, producing [o], [u], [a], [ɔ], and [æ] during the weeks in question, a plot of his attempts at *door, more, horsie* as compared with *on, off* shows that the two allophones were distinct targets (see figure 1), more or less accurately located in the vowel space, and also distinct from the other vowels with which they overlapped in production. Contrast with other phonemes was correct, and so was location of phonetic target; but control, also a phonetic matter, lagged behind.

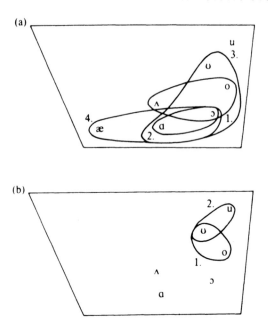

Figure 1. Distribution of attempts by a subject to produce ɔ and ɔʷ during the 21st month

(a) ɔ
1. *on*, 8 tokens
2. *off*, 4 tokens
3. *ball*, 16 tokens
4. *walk*, 3 tokens

(b) ɔʷ
1. *more*, 2 tokens
2. *door*, 6 tokens

On the other hand, a child may control a sound nicely, and yet fail to preserve the contrast between that sound and similar sounds. This is the commonly reported case, as for example when a well-articulated [ts] is used to represent /č/ and /ts/, or /f/ and /p/ are rendered by a clear [p]. It should be added that instrumental results, such as those of Chaney (1978) and Macken and Barton (1980a) are likely to force re-examination of all conclusions when those conclusions are of the form 'child X does not make the distinction between phones a and b', 'child X has a target identical with adult target c'. These instrumental studies indicated that some children make reliable productive distinctions which adults cannot hear. Macken and Barton, for example, have shown in four children followed over a number of months that the first stage of acquisition of initial voicing contrast in English is the maintenance of a contrast imperceptible to adults. During this stage the voicing-onset time distribution

for initial C +voice targets and C −voice targets were distinct, but the voice onset time means for the +voice and for the −voice targets lay quite close together, and both within the range perceived by English-speaking adults as voiced (short lag).

It should be noted that this result alone is sufficient to make an external reward theory of the acquisition of phonology completely untenable. Adults cannot 'shape' the child's pronunciations to produce this imperceptible differentiation of, say *big* from *pig*, since they cannot hear the differences. The child herself must somehow be making the differentiation in the attempt to match the adult model.

3.3. Origin of phonological rules

Ingram (1976a) suggests that at or around a certain point in a child's speaking life, he gets control of a system for learning to say most one- and two-syllable adult words on a few hearings. We might say that at this point the child has developed a method for transducing some auditory patterns to sequences of articulatory gestures. Some of these transductions result in the production of relatively faithful renditions of the model word, while others result in considerable distortion. Although the notion needs some elaboration (see Ingram 1974 and ch. 10 this volume; Kiparsky and Menn 1977; Menn 1978), a child's transduction system for getting from model to production is essentially his set of child phonology rules. Notice that this formulation treats /a/→ [a] as a rule, just as much as /f/→ [p]; ways of saying sounds which are accurate and ways of saying sounds which are inaccurate, we hold, are the same sort of thing for the child. Both the accurate rules and the inaccurate ones may change as the child develops.

Ingram has noted that in several cases children's rate of acquisition has taken a rapid upswing at the point where about 50 words have been acquired; before that time, 'the child does not seem to have a productive sound system' (1976a: 22) – or, in our terms, a transduction system. He therefore refers to it as the 'period of the first 50 words'. However, the '50' is only an approximation (Nelson 1973b, for example, observed such an upswing in many of her 16 cases, but usually somewhat before 50 words were attested), so we prefer to call this early period the 'exploratory period'. The upswing which Ingram describes is in some cases a very well-defined occurrence, appearing in one such case (Menn 1971) to be the consequence of the invention of a single powerful simplifying rule. On the other hand, the transition from the exploratory period to the following period (Ingram's 'period of simple morphemes') may happen much more diffusely. Jacob, who used few simplifying rules, still showed a modest rate of output vocabul-

ary growth at 80 words, and could not be said to have passed from a rule-inventing 'stage' to a rapid-acquisition 'stage'.

This brings us to the necessity of dealing with individual strategies during the exploratory period. There are two groups of strategies which have been described in the literature. The first group may be characterized as *selection* strategies. These have been identified as *avoidance* and *exploitation*.

Normal children must have some kind of knowledge of the phonetic quality of their own productions, or they would never learn to talk. Without auditory feedback they would, of course, be in the same situation as deaf children, who have to rely on signals from others as to whether they have got a word right. However, this knowledge derived from auditory feedback need not be conscious. Indeed, one way to account for children's receptive behaviour when adults imitate their mismatches ('I didn't say fiss, I said fisss!') has been to assume that children's conscious ability to monitor their own productions is faulty, and that a child who say· [gʌk] for truck or [beit] for plate is unaware of doing so. In general, this does seem to be the case, and it might seem far-fetched to credit any under-2 year old with enough metalinguistic awareness to choose to attempt or not to attempt words of the adult language on the ground of the sounds they contain. However, it has been shown that some beginning speakers do in fact behave in just this fashion; they select on phonetic grounds which words to try. In cases of avoidance the child avoids attempting to say words containing certain sounds; in cases of exploitation the child shows a great bias towards words with a particular sound or natural class of sounds and produces that set of sounds rather well. These phenomena may indeed be common, but simply hard to document, because in order to prove that a child is behaving in such a fashion one needs a corpus large enough to be sure that the observed biases of distribution are not random. The case for avoidance is strengthened if it can be shown that the child understands a fair number of words containing the sound which she fails to say (Ferguson and Farwell 1975; Farwell 1976; Menn 1976b). Further, Schwartz and Leonard 1982 were able to show avoidance in a laboratory study with sufficiently young children; the phenomenon seems to disappear as children become more skilled.

Avoidance is the antithesis of rule formation, of course, while exploitation is an example of the use of non-distorting rules (/a/ → [a]-type). Much more familiar, since they are more obvious in operation, are rules which yield mismatches between the model word and the child word. These rules are the result of the other group of strategies, the modification strategies.

Either some children are not very aware of which sounds they can match, or they want to talk so badly that mismatches are not in ortant to them. During the exploratory period, many children, perhaps most, have created a fairly large set of child-phonology rules, which may be regarded as highly systematic routines for reducing the complexity of adult words to a pronounceable level. In his chapter in this volume Ingram discusses such rule systems in detail; here we will discuss the available evidence on how such rule systems arise in the first place.

The child's earliest attempts at adult words usually do not show such rules operating. Instead, rules gradually come into play after the first few adult-modelled words are established, either by a process of the assimilation of a new adult word to forms which the child has already learned to say or by the collapse of two similar-sounding words towards one another. An excellent example of the first type of rule formation is given by Vihman (1976) for a child learning Estonian as her first language. This child initially showed a great deal of selectivity in her production, and among the constraints which her words obeyed was the following: if the word contains two vowels of differing heights, the first one must be more open (lower). Now it happens that the Estonian words for 'father' /isa/ and 'mother' /ema/ both violate this constraint. For a short time the child tried just /sa/ for 'father', and used no word for 'mother'. Then, for almost four months, she used no word for either, despite the fact that 'both father and mother made earnest attempts to elicit the words /ema/ and /isa/'. Finally at 15½ months, the child invented a metathesis rule to solve the problem: '/ema/ emerged as [ami] or [ani] ... at which time /isa/ also reappeared, now pronounced [asi], and the word /liha/ 'meat' was reproduced, following the same rule, as [ati]'.

Less spectacular rules also originate in the same way. New words are modified so that they comply with sound patterns already existing in the child's speech. We shall say that when a sound pattern found in some words of a child's speech is extended to a word in the adult language which does not comply with that pattern, the new rules, which are formed thereby, have been created by the carryover of the old sound pattern to the new word.

The other process of rule formation which has been distinguished, consolidation, is one in which two or more words of similar sound patterns, both of which the child can initially articulate, coexist as distinct in the child's speech for some time (although one or both may be unstable in form). Then the patterns collapse together in production – one of the patterns is used for both words. At this point, then, at least one of the adult patterns has been modified by the child, and we express this fact by saying

that the child has created one or more rules that relate (his percept of) the adult form to his output form. Jacob, for example, had a period of time in which [tei] from *table* and [ti] from *tea* were both produced for both words; then *tea* stabilized to [ti], and shortly (but not immediately) afterwards [ti] became the form also used for *table*. At this point, an /ei/→[i] rule had been created, and it later generalized to some other words, for example giving [kiːk] for cake. Such cases again show that child-phonology rules are neither of purely articulatory origin nor are they automatically available to the child as he begins to speak.

4. Some conclusions

The data on the development of phonemic contrasts during the period when lexical morphemes are not being stably and consistently produced (from babbling to word(s)) are quite limited. We will, nevertheless, attempt to come to some tentative conclusions. To begin, we will discuss some general developmental trends. We will then discuss these trends in the light of what we think the phonological acquisition task is and how processing constraints might explain these developmental trends.

4.1. General developmental trends

The child's most important comprehension advance during this period is learning that sequences of phones can carry distinct meanings, meanings which remain (roughly) constant in spite of changes in their situational and linguistic context. The corresponding advance in production – the ability to use at least some words in novel situations – also may start to take place during this time. This development is obviously dependent on the ability to observe consistencies in phonological sequences (i.e. to categorize in some way morphological units) and therefore is dependent on earlier discrimination abilities. However, the development during this period is remarkably different from the previous period in that it is not simply a case of sounds being discriminated and perhaps categorized, but rather that sequences of sound and meaning are being simultaneously categorized.

Second, the initial categorization of phonological sequences appears to be based on the auditory images formed by word gestalts. Initial analysis of these gestalts may be based on the syllabic patterns of these units rather than segments or features. Third, and very important, individual differences both in the sequence of development of phonological contrasts and in the utilization of strategies for the acquisition of these contrasts can be observed. Contrary to previously held notions, children apparently achieve

the ability to discriminate between particular phonemes in somewhat different orders and to reproduce variation using different strategies. Some children organize their output on the basis of a word, others on the basis of phrase plus word (compressed sentences), and still others on a combination of both. Different children use the different strategies of avoidance, exploitation, and at least two sorts of modification strategies (rule formation).

Finally, the previously held notion that the order of development of productive contrasts faithfully follows the order of development of perceptual contrasts is not supported by the data, even in studies which are limited to examination of discrimination of minimal pair words or reproduction of these words. This seems reasonable, given that not only are the task requirements different but also that strategies employed by individual children in the perceptual task may vary from those employed in the productive task. Pure application of logic tells us that the child cannot reliably match specific targets in his language without being able to hear what they are (except for the trivial case of accidental coincidence between a favourite syllable and a real word of the language). In this sense, production cannot precede perception. On the other hand, if the child cannot handle a task involving deciphering a syllable without semantic support and yet can produce that same syllable as the name of an object, then for the tasks involved, production, trivially, certainly will be 'better'.

At this point, what we can do is suggest that the great task-dependency of perception and production in itself is evidence for the active nature of the processing of speech. Therefore it involves many kinds of knowledge. The psycho-acoustic substrate of perception and the facility of articulator movement, which are likely to be determined by maturation, are so far from determining what is 'perceived' and 'produced' that great individual differences are to be expected.

4.2. Processing constraints on phonological acquisition

Speech is a patterned event, occurring over time, which conveys meaning. The child's task, therefore, is two-fold; discovery of the pattern and determination of meaning. However, the nature of the pattern is by no means transparent: it is encoded, so the task is not an easy one. Making it even more difficult is the fact that the environment rarely, if ever, provides consistent examples of a pattern. To give an example in the perceptual domain, the child is unlikely to hear an utterance such as 'Put the coat on the goat' which would put the voicing distinction in relief and put the two target words in similar phonological contexts.

Continuing with the voicing example, the problem becomes even more aggravated in production. It is not possible to show the child how to vary the timing between vocal fold vibration (with all its attendant muscular adjustments) relative to the opening of the upper articulators. The difficulty is compounded by the fact that in any given instance the child must produce syllables and words to convey meaning. The acoustic and articulatory specifications that the child needs to know in order to succeed are highly integrated. Having framed the issue in this way, it is now reasonable to view the child as an active problem solver. As such, errors early in the transitional period could be viewed as accidents, resulting from trial and error attempts to gain purchase on the pattern. Once systematicity begins to emerge in production and perception it seems reasonable to consider deviations (relative to the adult) as initial approximations to the adult model, rather than merely as errors. The imperfections in these attempts arise from two sources. First the child's auditory and articulatory apparatus or 'hardware' is physiologically immature (see Aslin, Pisoni and Jusczyk 1983, and Kent 1976, for consideration of the two areas respectively). The second reason is lack of sophistication in the child's knowledge at any given point. This can be due to the aforementioned hardware constraints and, more important, to general processing limitations. These include attention, manifested in both reduced attention span and, perhaps, channel-switching capabilities. As a result of these limitations the child can only deal with small amounts of information. This information is, therefore, incomplete (and, by definition, incorrect). For the child, however, his specification may be the best one possible.

On this account, the rules and strategies we have been discussing are not processes in and of themselves but emerge from the limited processing abilities of the child. A linguistic rule, or any rule for that matter, can be considered to be a description of a specific sequence of acts that is directed toward achieving some goal. A strategy is a general plan or collective action for achieving that goal. Thus, rules particularize and order the individual actions necessary to effect a plan for attaining some goal. A strategy, in turn, may be a means to further an end. For example, consider consonant harmony as a strategy. We have a variety of means, in the way of rules (act sequences) that can be implemented to gain this end. These include omission, substitution and metathesis. Using these rules we have achieved our strategy, attained consonant harmony. Consonant harmony, in turn, becomes a means (one of several that might be chosen) to achieve a general end, that of reducing the complexity or information load.

Some pains have been taken to discuss processing constraints and to define rules and strategies, as a caution to those who would explain the

deviance in a child's output by saying that it occurs because she had this rule or that strategy. A statement of this kind, we believe, carries with it the implicit assumption that rules and strategies are synonymous with processes such as attending and remembering. It is our opinion that they are not. Rules and strategies are themselves the result of processing. Therefore, they are descriptions, not explanations.

Earlier in the chapter we noted that the child's perceptual representations of adult sounds may be underspecified. Her problem in production is, as we said, one of translating or transducing the words she hears into recognizable utterances. The child's rule provides her with a way to say what she hears. Given the processing and knowledge constraints discussed, perception will be limited and will in turn constrain articulation, since the rules derive from the child's current state of perceptual and general knowledge. In addition, particular children may develop particular realization rules. Using consonant clusters as an example, a particular child who does not have the CCV canonical form may choose to avoid words with clusters, another may delete one of the consonants, and a third child may reduce the cluster to a single consonant but preserve some features of both consonants in this single segment.

On this account, while phonological development entails the development of individual features and the overcoming of so-called natural processes, these notions prove to be of limited value in explaining the course of phonological acquisition. Instead, the majority of the young child's efforts are best seen in motor control terms as: (1) learning to increase the number of variable parameters (C / V options) that can be freely assigned to a word; (2) learning to increase the number of values (features or phones) a parameter can take; and (3) learning to link up shorter programs to make longer ones. All of these increases in control lead to increases in the *number* of variables observed within segments, syllables and words in both perception and production.

This description can not only account for the specifics of phonological development but can explain the fact that although there is a general pattern of development across children there is also considerable individual variation existing within a child and across children. This individual variation arises from a number of sources: early trial and error learning, and, later on, differences in the origin, type and concatenation of rules and strategies used by particular children.

The orderly and universal development of phonemic contrast suggested by earlier researchers does not seem to be supported by the data of the more detailed studies that have been carried out recently. This is a challenge rather than a confounding. The task for future researchers in this aspect

of linguistic development appears to be two-fold. Since the product of these developments is similar (i.e. all children achieve the ability to distinguish between and reproduce all the patterns of phonemic contrasts in the language, and appear to do so by approximately age 6 or 7), one task is to determine the limits on the *range* of strategies that may be employed by children to achieve this product. A second task might be a determination of which aspects of the range of strategies employed are indeed universal and when these occur developmentally. It seems unreasonable to suppose that perception and production of phonological units are unrelated to each other; and it is also seems unreasonable to suppose that the strategies employed are infinitely variable. However, it is also unreasonable, given the findings of recent studies, to approach the task by asking children to distinguish minimal pair words or nonsense syllables and by asking still other children to reproduce these differences during this period of development. These recent data indicate that this is not what the children conceive of as their task when acquiring phonemic contrasts. For them the task is 'How do I solve the problem of learning how to communicate with others in my linguistic community?'

10. Phonological development: production

David Ingram

1. Introduction

Between the ages of 1;6 and 4;0 the young child undergoes considerable development in phonological ability. Starting with a small vocabulary of approximately 50 words, the child proceeds from single-word utterances of very simple phonological form (see Menyuk, Menn and Silber, ch. 9, this volume), to multiword utterances that are relatively high in intelligibility. Phonological ability improves through an increase in the ability to produce adult sounds and combine them into more complex phonological structures. Elsewhere (Ingram 1976a), I have referred to this stage as one in which children acquire 'the phonology of simple morphemes'.

Years ago Jespersen (1922) noted the distinctness of this stage of phonological acquisition from the one that precedes it. In characterizing it, he emphasized the regularities that occur in the child's words (pp. 106–7):

> As the child gets away from the peculiarities of his individual 'little language', his speech becomes more regular, and a linguist can in many cases see reasons for his distortions of normal words. When he replaces one sound by another there is always some common element in the formation of the two sounds ... There is generally a certain system in the sound substitutions of children, and in many instances we are justified in speaking of 'strictly observed sound-laws'.

For example, Jespersen mentioned the observation that children in different linguistic communities show a tendency to replace velar stops with alveolar ones. The child who says [tæt] for *cat* will also say [do] for *go*. This general pattern would then qualify as a sound-law for this stage of development. A child's words at any point could be described within this approach by specifying the sound-laws that are operating in the child's speech.

In recent years, sound laws as described by Jespersen have been referred to as *phonological processes*, a term used by Stampe (1969). Stampe sees these processes as consisting of a universal set of hierarchically ordered

223

procedures used by children to simplify speech. They are universal to the extent that every child is born with the facility to simplify speech in a consistent fashion. They are hierarchical in that certain processes are more basic than others. Stampe sees phonological development as a gradual loss of these simplifying processes until the child's words finally match their adult models.

The establishment of various phonological processes in the speech of young children has been the goal of much recent research (see Ingram 1976a and the references cited there). This research consists basically of attempts to propose generalized statements to describe common substitutions in the speech of young children. This chapter will attempt to describe the phonological patterns found in the words used by children between 1;6 and 4;0 through the establishment of phonological processes. It will begin with a description of the more common processes found thus far, with evidence provided from children learning diverse languages. Once the utility of process analysis has been shown, the chapter will then briefly discuss the limitations of this approach. Specifically, the process approach does not explain the striking fact that there is also tremendous individual variation from one child to another. The discussion will conclude with evidence showing that development during this stage also needs to take into account phonological preferences that vary from child to child.

2. Phonological processes

2.1. Substitution processes

A common characteristic of the phonological analysis of the speech of young children is the determination of *substitutions* in the child's words. This is done by comparing the child's word to the adult model and noting the correspondences between the two. Take, for example, the child who says [bɑt] for *book*. The correspondences between the first two segments in the child's form and those in the adult model are a match, so that no substitution has taken place. For the final segment, however, adult [k] has been replaced by [t]. The postulation of processes not only describes substitutions, but attempts to explain them. In this case, the difference between the two segments is one of place. The process involved can be described as one which tends to replace velar stops with alveolar ones.

By examining samples of children's words from several children both within and across languages, it is possible to isolate the more common substitutions that occur and subsequently to postulate general processes. The first major type of processes are those that result in the replacement

of one segment by another. Below are five of the more common *substitution processes*, with examples from a variety of children. (For data taken from published work references follow the first mention of the child's name. Otherwise, data are taken from the author's own files. Also, phonetic transcriptions have been altered to conform to those used throughout this book.)

Stopping. Fricatives, and occasionally other sounds, are replaced with a stop consonant.

English
A (N. Smith 1973) 2;9   *sea* [tiː]; *sing* [tiŋ]; *say* [tʰei]
French
Suzanne (Deville 1890–1) 1;9   *fleur* 'flower' [pø]; *chaud* 'hot' [tɔ]; *seau* 'bucket' [tɔ]; *sel* 'salt' [te]
Hungarian
(Examples from Kerek 1975) / viraːg / 'flower' [bijaːg]; / faːzik / 'he is cold' [paːzik]; / saija / 'his mouth' [taːja]

Fronting. Velar and palatal consonants tend to be replaced with alveolar ones.

English
Joan (Velten 1943) 2;0   *shoe* [zuˑ]; *shop* [zaˑp]; *call* [taˑ]; *coat* [dut]; *goat* [dut]; *goose* [duˑs]
French
Suzanne 1;11   *chaise* 'chair' [sɛ]; *chat* 'cat' [sa]; *cassé* 'broken' [tase]; *cou* 'neck' [tu]; *gâteau* 'cake' [tatɔ]
Polish
Hania (Zarębina 1965) 1;11   / dzʼeŋkuje / 'thank you' [dzʼekuje]; / tʃasu / 'time' [tsʼasʼu]; / dzembi / 'If I were' [zʼembi] (but note: / koniki / 'pony' [kaniki])

Gliding.
A glide [w] or [j] is substituted for a liquid sound, i.e. [l] or [r].

English
Jennika 2;1   *lap* [jæp]; *leg* [jek]; *ready* [wedi]
Estonian
Linda (Vihman 1971) 1;9   *raha* 'money' [jahaˑ]; *Rosbi* 'Robert' [joˑbi]; *ruttu* 'fast' [jutˑu]
BUT *French*
Elie-Paul (Vinson 1915) 1;9   *lampe* 'lamp' [ãp]; *la* 'the' [a]; *lapin* 'rabbit' [apɛ̃]
Suzanne 1;10 *lapin* [apɛ̃]; *laver* 'wash' [ave]; *lire* 'read' [i]; *lune* 'moon' [um]

Vocalization. A vowel replaces a syllabic consonant, a process particularly characteristic of English.

> Philip (Adams 1972) 1;9   *apple* [apo]; *bottle* [babu]; *bottom* [bada]; *button* [bʌtʌ]; *dinner* [dindʌ]; *hammer* [mænu]

Vowel neutralization. Nasal vowels tend to be changed into oral vowels and vowels in general are often centralized, i.e. [a] or [ʌ].

> Joan V. 2;0   *back* [bat]; *hat* [hat]; *yard* [zaːd]; *hug* [had]

The stopping process is widespread and is one of the more established patterns in children's speech. Fricatives are the most commonly affected group of sounds, although resonants will also occasionally be affected. While stopping is common, the actual patterns of its application by individual children are not. Children typically will not necessarily change all of their fricatives into stops, and it is not possible to predict which ones individual children will select (see Ingram *et al.* 1980 for a more complete discussion).

Fronting is also quite common across children, although some children prefer it more than others. It is important to realize that there are actually two processes involved here, fronting of palatals and fronting of velars, and children may show one and not the other. Also, the process interacts with stopping, so that it is not unusual to find an English or French child replacing [ʃ] with [t].

We know less about the process of gliding, although it is well-documented in English. An examination of data from seven French children did not reveal any cases of it. Interestingly, French does not use word-initial [j] and has also restricted use of [w], suggesting that English children may be substituting glides because they are available in other words in the child's language. This suggests the possibility that the substitutions used in phonological processes may be highly influenced by the child's phonological system, not just by universal tendencies.

Vocalization is common in English, where syllabic consonants often occur. For the velarized [ɫ], the most frequent substitution is a back rounded vowel, either [o] or [u]. In other cases, an [a]-like vowel occurs, although the substitution may also be affected by the tendency to assimilate unstressed vowels to stressed ones.

The last process, vowel neutralization, is an especially early one and is normally not characteristic of this rapid period of development. Joan Velten (Velten 1943) appears to be highly atypical in this regard. Also, nasal vowels appear to be acquired quite early by French children. Other processes do affect vowels, however, for example, the tendency to unround

front rounded vowels and the occasional tensing of lax vowels. Since vowels develop quite rapidly, the processes which affect them seem to be lost earlier than those for consonants.

2.2. Assimilatory processes

Another general group of processes that will result in mismatches between the child's form and the adult model is the one that is composed of tendencies to assimilate one segment in a word to another. Even if the child has acquired a particular adult sound in some words, there may be certain contexts where its production may be altered. While detailed research is necessary on this topic, the following processes are relatively common.

Voicing. Consonants tend to be voiced when preceding a vowel, and devoiced at the end of a syllable.

> *English*
> A *paper* 2;3 [beːbə]; 2;7 [beibə]; 2;7 [peːpə]; 2;8 [pʰeipə]; *tiny* 2;4 [daini]; 2;7 [taini]; 2;8 [tʰaini]
> Kristen 1;5 *pig* [bik]; *paper* [bɛpi]; *toes* [doṣ]
> Jennika 1;6 *bed* [bɛt]; *bib* [bip]; *bird* [bit]; *egg* [ek]
> *French*
> Jacqueline (Bloch 1913) 1;7 *popo* 'chamber pot' [bobo]; *pelle* 'shovel' [beː]; *poule* 'hen' [bu] [buː] [bubu]

Consonant harmony. In $C_1VC_2(X)$ contexts, consonants tend to assimilate to each other in certain predictable ways. Three frequent patterns are:

(i)   Velar assimilation. Apical consonants tend to assimilate to a neighbouring velar consonant.
       Jennika 1;7 *duck* [gʌk]; *sock* [gʌk]; *tongue* [gʌn]
       A   2;2 *tickle* [gigu]; *truck* [gʌk]; *taxi* [gɛgiː]
(ii)   Labial assimilation. Apical consonants tend to assimilate to a neighbouring labial consonant.
       Daniel (Menn 1975) *tub* [bʌb]; *table* [bʌbu]; *steps* [bɛps]; *tape* [bejp]
(iii) Denasalization. A nasal consonant will denasalize in the neighbourhood of a non-nasal consonant.
       French
       Elie-Paul 2;1 *mouton* 'sheep' [potɔ̃]; 2;2 *morceau* 'piece' [baʃo]; *mouchez* 'blow nose' [bøʃe]; *monsieur* [poʃø]
       Fernande (Roussey 1899–1900) 2;1 *malade* 'sick' [balaːd]; *mange* 'eat' [baʃ]; *menton* 'chin' [baːtoː]; *marcher* 'walk' [base]

Progressive vowel assimilation. An unstressed vowel will assimilate to a preceding (or following) stressed vowel.

> *English*
> Joan V. 2;0   *bacon* [búːdu]; *birdie* [búːdu]; *flower* [fáːwa]; *hammer* [haːma]; *table* [duːbu]
> *French*
> Fernande 1;7   *oiseau* 'bird' [pogʸo]; *pomme de terre* 'potato' [tɛtɛt]

Voicing as described actually refers to two separate but related processes. One of these, the devoicing of final consonants, is well-documented as a characteristic of languages. The other, voicing of prevocalic consonants, requires some discussion. To date, this process has been predominantly observed for English. There is the possibility, as mentioned in Ingram (1974: 60), that what transcribers have recorded as voiced consonants are actually voiceless unaspirated ones, since English speakers hear voiceless unaspirated consonants as voiced ones. While it may be true that transcribers have made some errors in hearing voiceless unaspirated segments as voiced ones, there is evidence that suggests voicing does take place. First, Smith (1973) made this distinction in his data, and they show a gradual shift from a voiced substitution to a voiceless unaspirated to the correct voiceless aspirated. Second, there is evidence in Bloch (1913) that his French-learning daughter voiced prevocalic consonants at the beginning of her phonological development. Since French [p] is voiceless unaspirated, it is highly unlikely that Bloch was making errors in judgement. Lastly, recent evidence (e.g. Gilbert 1977) shows that voice onset time for voiceless stops is less stable and takes longer to develop than for voiced ones.

Young children show various kinds of consonant harmony or assimilation (see above for three frequent patterns). This is an area that is not particularly well documented, and one that requires more research. One problem is that some children appear to assimilate more than others; also, the various possibilities for assimilation are quite numerous. It may be that phonological preferences (to be discussed below) determine a great many of the variations that occur. Menn (1975) has proposed that there is a strength hierarchy that determines the direction of assimilation, in which weaker consonants become homorganic to stronger ones. The hierarchy, from strongest position to weakest, is velar, labial, dental. This means, for example, that dentals will assimilate to both labials and velars, with the latter being a stronger tendency. She uses this hierarchy to explain patterns in her son Daniel's speech which fell into four types:

1.   b–d, t   e.g. *bed* [bɛd]; *boots* [buts]
2.   k–p, d   e.g. *cup* [kʌp]; *cuddle* [kʌdu̧]

3.   t – b → b – b   e.g. *tub* [bʌb]; *table* [bʌbu̜]
4.   b – g → g – g   e.g. *big* [gɨg];   *back* [gæk]

She states (p. 295): 'The rule is that C_1 assimilates to C_2 if C_1 is weaker than C_2 on the strength hierarchy.' Further analyses such as this one are required to establish more general observations on consonant harmony.

The denasalization process is quite characteristic of French and shows how a specific language may have phonological characteristics that bring out particular processes. The process is not as operative in English, presumably because of the tendency to have initial stress. I have observed one English child, Daniel, who at 2;10 said [bən'ík] for *Monique*, his babysitter, and [bíʃél] for *Michelle*, a neighbourhood acquaintance.

Since vowels develop rapidly, progressive vowel assimilation is a process that is usually lost early. Children begin quite early in development to differentiate vowels within a word, although isolated cases of assimilation occur for several months.

2.3. Syllable structure processes

While it has not been explicitly mentioned, it is clear that the notion of syllable is quite important in understanding all the processes discussed so far. Substitution processes will vary according to the place of the sound in the syllable. For instance, stopping of fricatives is usually lost for final fricatives before it is for syllable-initial ones. Stated differently, fricatives are easier to produce postvocalically than prevocalically. The notion of syllable is also important in assimilatory processes. The voicing of consonants varies according to the place in the syllable. For consonant harmony, it is known that children often have an early restriction that the consonants in CVC structures must be homorganic. With vowel assimilation and denasalization, the important factor is that a segment in an unstressed syllable is likely to 'weaken' or assimilate to a segment in the stressed syllable.

Besides these syllabic influences, there are specific phonological processes which are directly motivated by the tendency of young children to simplify syllable structure. For most children, the direction is toward a basic CV syllable. Some of the more basic *syllable structure processes* include the following:

Cluster reduction. A consonant cluster is reduced to a single consonant.

English
   Philip 1;11 *clown* [kaʘn]; *play* [pe]; *train* [ten]; *dress* [dɛs]

French

Elie-Paul 2;1   *bleu* 'blue' [bø]; *clef* 'key' [ke]; *grand* 'big' [gã];
prends 'take' [pã]

Estonian

Linda 1;9   *klaun* 'clown' [kaum]; *kleit* 'dress' [kit·]; 1;8 *prillid* 'eye-
glasses' [pil'·a]; 1;9 *kruvi* 'screw' [kup·]

German

Dorothy 2;2   *fliegen* 'fly' [fiːkən]; *trinken* 'drink' [tikən]; *grosse*
'big' [gosə]; *schreiben* 'write' [saibən]

Deletion of final consonants. A CVC syllable is reduced to CV by deleting
the final consonant.

English

Jennika 1;5   *bib* [bi]; *bike* [bai]; *more* [mʌ]; *out* [aʊ]

French

Suzanne 2;0   *air* 'air' [ɛ]; *allumette* 'match' [me]; *assiette* 'plate'
[asɛ]; *autruche* 'ostrich' [ɔsu]

Deletion of unstressed syllables. An unstressed syllable is deleted, especially if it precedes a stressed syllable.

English

Jennika 1;9   *banana* [nǽnʌ]; *bicycle* [báikʊɫ]; 2;3 *Granola* [ówʌ];
1;11 *Jennika* [géŋkʌ]; *potato* [dédo]

Romanian

Eileen (Vogel 1975) 2;0   *maşina* 'the car' [ʃína]; *prosopol* 'the
towel' [sʌpʊ]; *lumina* 'light' [ninːə]; *papuşă* 'doll' [puʃa]

Reduplication. In a multisyllabic word, the initial CV syllable is repeated.

English

Philip 1;9   *Anne-Marie* [mimi]; *cookie* [gege]; *Rogers* [dada]; *TV*
[didi]; *water* [wawa]

French

Jacqueline 1;11   *asseoir* 'sit' [sisi]; *bavette* 'bib' [vɛvːɛ]; *bouche*
'mouth' [bubu]; *poupée* 'doll' [pepːe]; *serviette* 'napkin' [üɛüɛ];
vache 'cow' [vava]

The reduction of clusters is one of the most widespread processes
observed. The direction of the deletion is also predictable in many instances.
One of the most regular patterns is the deletion of sonorants when they
occur in combinations with stop consonants. The deletion of [s] is also
common, although there are cases where [s] has been retained instead

of the stop. This situation may result if the child has an [s] preference, a point that will be discussed at the end of the chapter. In nasal and stop clusters, stops are usually retained, although the nasal will often be kept if the stop is voiced.

The deletion both of final consonants and unstressed syllables is also frequent, although the latter seems to persist longer than the former. When final consonants do begin to appear, they develop gradually, with certain sounds appearing before others. Although conclusive data still needs to be collected, there does appear to be a tendency for the appearance of final nasals to occur early. Also, fricatives tend to be easier in final position than initially, although there is individual variation. Some suggestions for the order of appearance of final consonants are presented in Renfrew (1966).

The last process mentioned above, reduplication, occurs quite early in children's speech and is often lost by the time the stage under discussion begins. Some reduplications persist, however, and other partial reduplications continue to occur, e.g. [babi] for *blanket* where the consonant is reduplicated. Of some interest is the fact that children vary greatly in their tendencies to reduplicate. Some seem to like to do it a lot, whereas others rarely do it. There is also a relation between this process and the deletion of final consonants. Some children acquire their final postvocalic consonants through the use of reduplication, e.g. *bag* [baga] (based on Ross 1937; see also Schwartz *et al.* 1980 and Fee and Ingram 1982).

3. Other aspects of phonological development

The establishment of phonological processes in the speech of young children is itself an advance in the description of phonological development between 1;6 and 4;0. Given just the small number of processes mentioned in the previous section, one could say a great deal about any random phonological sample of a child. To do this, however, does impose certain limitations, some superficial but others of a more substantive nature, which should be pointed out. This section will briefly discuss a variety of these other aspects of phonological development that are also important in understanding this stage of acquisition.

3.1. Dynamic considerations

In studying a young child's speech, one is constantly confronted by the fact that the system being observed is one that is constantly under change. That is, it is not static but dynamic, at any time showing both older and

newer developments. This is highly important in the study of phonological development, and is manifested in a variety of ways.

One of the most striking of these consequences is the *phonetic variability* that children show in their pronunciation of words. Examples from a variety of children were presented above, along with the impression that these were the only ways that children said these words. In reality, children will often show a variety of productions for the same words. Jennika, for example, produced the following forms for *blanket* on the same day, 1;6 (24): [bwati], [bati], [baki], [batit]. Works in English have often avoided the mention of phonetic variability (e.g. Velten 1943), although the French diarists (e.g. Roussey 1899–1900) were usually very careful to record alternant forms. Bloch (1913: 39), for example, found this to be very characteristic of the period of development being treated in this chapter.

> This mobility is much less noticeable during the early months than in the later ones … it seems that during the months preceding 1; 9, when the vocabulary was limited to around 40 words and language was used less frequently, pronunciation was more fixed than after this time, when the vocabulary grew every day and the linguistic work of the child ᴗecame more active.

Whether or not this stage has more mobility than the previous one needs to be studied, but the fact that it exists is well-established (if often ignored).

This aspect shows that one needs not only to isolate phonological processes but to state also their percentage of operation. Presumably, one reason for phonetic mobility is the fact that children are gradually going from one pronunciation of a word to another. Stated differently, phonological processes are lost not suddenly but gradually. Thus, the analyst must state both the processes that children use and their percentage of occurrence both within and across words. Stating this percentage with the forms for a single word is important because it appears that some words are more phonetically variable than others. The reasons for this are not well understood, although likely ones are phonetic complexity and novelty of the word. That is, how complex a word is and how recently it has been acquired appear to contribute to higher variability in pronunciation (see also Leonard *et al.* 1982).

Another aspect of phonological development is that the notion of *word* is highly important (Ferguson and Farwell 1975). At any point, children will usually have *frozen forms* in their speech, which are pronunciations that occur early in development and persist during a time when the child should show better pronunciation. Philip, for example, at 1;9 was still saying [gege] for *cookie* even though his production from other words suggested

that he should have been able to say *cookie*. Also, children will produce occasional *advanced forms*, which are productions that are better than what would be expected, given the child's phonological abilities. Jennika, for example, used [bwati] for *blanket* at 1;5 although her form settled into [bati] and [badæ] at 1;8. The advanced use of a cluster was not representative of her system.

The simultaneous occurrence of advanced and frozen forms with more typical forms of production shows the dynamic nature of the child's system. In terms of processes, phenomena like this indicate that processes cannot always be stated generally; rather, it is also necessary to take into account the words which they affect. The fact that a particular process may not occur in all instances may be because of certain peculiarities of individual words, not because the process is necessarily being lost.

The importance of words leads to a significant claim about the structure of a child's phonological system. Within process analysis (as described in section 2), there are two aspects that are important as describing a child's system.

adult form + phonological processes = child's form

Evidence of the sort mentioned about words suggests that this description is inadequate. As I have argued elsewhere (Ingram 1974, 1975, 1976b), it is necessary to consider the possibility that children actively operate on adult forms to establish their own phonological representations of these words. That is, there is (1) the adult form; (2) the child's representation of the word; (3) the child's spoken form. For example, Philip's form of [gege] for *cookie* persists because he has established this form as the representation of this word, and this representation becomes resistant to phonological processes. With new words that show advanced form, we can say that the child has not yet established a representation, so that the form has not yet conformed to the child's system. The claim that the child has a system of his or her own is controversial (see the discussion in Ingram 1976c), yet it appears to account for some otherwise inexplicable aspects of young children's phonological patterns.

Since the young child has a small phonetic inventory, it is not surprising that the first few months of phonological development are also characterized by relatively extensive homonymy. By homonymy I mean the production of one phonetic form for several adult target words, e.g. Joan Velten's [bat] at 22 months for 12 different words such as *bad*, *bark*, *bent*, and *bite*. The actual causes proposed for the early existence of homonymy are somewhat controversial. Priestley (1980) has pointed out several problems in the study of homonyms. For example, they may result from the fact

that the child perceives the adult words as the same – or at the other extreme, that the adult perceives the child's productions as the same – when they actually have subtle phonetic differences. Vihman (1981) has even proposed a 'homonym strategy' whereby the child actively seeks out homonymy.

There seem to be at least two important facts that need to be considered in examining children's use of homonymy. First, longitudinal data indicates that the rate of homonymy decreases consistently over time (Ingram forthcoming). Second, the extent of occurrence becomes minimal for most children by age 2 (Ingram 1981). In Ingram (1975) I proposed that such facts suggest that the decrease in homonymy may reflect the unconscious awareness of the principle of phonemic contrast. Interestingly, the sharp decrease in homonymy does not appear to be a direct result of a rapid increase in the size of the child's phonetic inventory. Rather, the child seems to use the sounds available to create new phonetic forms to avoid homonyms. The treatment of specific words under the pressure to avoid homonyms demonstrates from another perspective the lexical dimension to phonological development.

The existence of phonetic variability and lexical influences shows that phonological processes are not simple to state. Even if one had a complete list of possible processes, one would need to deal with problems that concern their degree of operation and effects in certain words. The inclusion of these factors into process analyses, however, provides a broader description of early phonological development.

3.2. Non-isomorphic processes

Thus far, phonological processes have been assumed to be isomorphic in relating the adult form to the child's production: that is, there is a one-to-one correspondence between each element in the adult form and each one in the child's. The child who says [gɔg] for *dog* has an isomorphic relation between the initial segment of the output and the adult model's initial segment [d]. In this case the substitution is [g] for [d] with velar assimilation as the process involved. These individual isomorphic processes then are grouped under more general titles, such as cluster reduction, voicing, etc.

While these processes help to explain most of the substitutions children do, there are cases where non-isomorphic processes are involved. These are cases where the relevant process cannot be explained by referring to one-to-one correspondences between the adult and child forms. To explain these, a broader view of the notion of process needs to be developed.

One example of this kind comes from a young German child, Dorothy. At 2;2:26, she was recorded several times producing the word *Flugzeug* /fluktsɔik/ 'aeroplane' as [suktɔix]. Within a typical process analysis, we could propose that initial f → s and k → x by substitution processes. Although none of the processes mentioned earlier covers these, we could propose that these are possible, but not necessarily widespread, processes. However, a more direct explanation is possible. Notice that both syllables of her word have similar place relations of alveolar, then velar. We could say that the f → s change is triggered by the t __ k sequence in the second syllable (there are no other cases of f → s in the data). The change of k → x appears at first sight unusual, but can be accounted for by proposing that she is balancing the syllables by having one fricative in each. The juxtaposed elements of the two syllables are both stops [k, t], and the outermost are both fricatives. The pattern is caused by a combination of factors which are far from isomorphic.

While one could possibly incorporate the above data into syllable structure processes, this becomes even more difficult for the case described by Priestley (1977). Around 1;10–1;11, his son Christopher showed a number of words that all had the following shape:

(a) *banana*   [bajan] 1;10
    chocolate [kajak] 1;10

(c) *carrot*   [kajat] 1;11
    peanut   [pijat] 1;10

(b) *Brenda* [bɛjan] 1;10
    panda   [pajan] 1;10

(d) *streamer* [mijat] 1;10

Group (a) was by far the predominant pattern. The processes the child seemed to follow were these:

(1) Change all multisyllabic words into the structure C_1VjVC_2
(2) After cluster reduction, place the initial consonant of the adult word into the C_1 position
(3) If the second consonant of the adult word is an obstruent, place it into the C_2 position   (Group a)
(4) If the second consonant of the adult word is a sonorant, drop it and place the next consonant into the C_2 position   (Group c)
(5) If the second consonant is a sonorant, but there is not a third consonant, place the sonorant into C_2 (Group b: the [d] in these is presumably deleted previously by cluster reduction)

Some cases are simply inexplicable, for example *streamer*, which by the above rules should have been [tijam], was produced as [mijat]. There is still another peculiarity in Christopher's pattern. The only final consonants

in his words are [m, t, s, n, l, ŋ, k]. Of these, [s, n, l] never occur word-initially. Thus another principle is to produce these finally but avoid them initially.

Regardless of how one would like to analyse these data, it is clear that current analyses by processes would fail. Instead, one will need to resort to the notion mentioned in the last section about the child's capacity to construct a system of its own. In many cases, this system may not be obvious; with Christopher, however, there is a very specific way the child has organized the adult forms and this varies a great deal from the adult models. Children in this stage of development will use both phonological processes of the sort discussed and others that result from the child's active organization of the representation of words.

3.3. Phonological preferences

Much of this chapter has shown very general processes children use to simplify the words of the adult language. In the last few subsections, observations have been made which show ways that children may differ from each other, despite choosing from a similar (perhaps universal) set of processes. There is another striking way in which children construct a phonological system that results in marked differences between children. This is the result of individual *phonological preferences* from child to child.

A phonological preference is used here to refer to a preference by a child for a specific articulatory pattern. This preference may be for a particular class of sounds, such as fricatives or nasals, or for a particular kind of syllable structure. The result is that the child will produce an unusual number of words that show the preferred sounds or syllable structure. The data from Christopher is an example of a phonological preference for a particular syllable structure.

It is not particularly unusual to find children who have a preference for a particular sound or group of sounds. Philip, a child mentioned in several examples so far, for several months had a phonological preference for nasal consonants. This preference showed itself in a variety of ways, for example, using many words with nasals and showing a tendency to assimilate non-nasal consonants to nasal ones. The following examples from his sample show this:

candle	[naɲu]	1;7	[naŋu]	1;9
candy	[ɲaɲi]	1;7	[naŋi]	1;9
cream	[mim]	and	[miŋ]	1;9
down	[naɷ]	1;7	[naɷn]	1;9

hammer   [mænaʊ] 1;7 [mænu]1;9
meow (cat cry) [memaʊ] 1;7
plane   [me]   1;7
sandwich   [nanu]   1;7 [nænu] 1;9

Notice that nasal assimilation does not account for the medial [m] in *meow*. When a child has a preference such as this, several processes will usually be involved.

The fact that preferences like these can lead to individual variation among children can be shown by looking at data from three French children in the production of fricatives. French has the following word-initial fricatives: [f, v, s, z, ʃ, ʒ]. These can be divided into three distinct places of articulation – labial, dental, and alveo-palatal. Table 1 presents the substitution patterns for these fricatives for three French children as reported by their fathers (a dash indicates that no words were used with the sound).

Table 1. *Substitution patterns for French fricatives by three French-learning children*

Adult sound	Substitutions		
	Elie-Paul 1;11	Fernande 2;4	Suzanne 1;11
/ f /	—	s	f
/ v /	—	s	v
/ s /	ʃ	s	s (t)
/ z /	ʃ	—	z
/ ʃ /	ʃ	s	s
/ ʒ /	ʃ	s	ʒ

As shown in table 1, Elie-Paul has a marked alveo-palatal preference, illustrated by his use of [ʃ] for several of the fricatives. Some examples are: *casser* /kase/ 'break' [ʃe]; *chaud* /ʃo/ 'hot' [ʃo]; *jus* /ʒu/ 'juice' [ʃü]. Fernande, on the other hand, has a dental preference, using [s] throughout her language, e.g. *baiser* /bɛse/ 'kiss' [bɛse]; *bonjour* /bɔʒür/ 'good morning' [busu]; *bravo!* /bravo/ 'bravo!' [basoː]; *café* /kafe/ 'coffee' [kase]; *fil* /fil/ 'thread' [sil]; *manger* /mãʒe/ 'eat' [base]. Both Elie-Paul and Fernande had a difficult time with [f], and neither acquired it before age 3. Suzanne, on the other hand, found the labials quite easy and acquired both by 1:11, even though both adult [s] and [ʃ] still were not acquired. Even though labials did not occur for other fricatives, we could still describe Suzanne as having a labial preference of sorts. The more striking differences between these three children can be described as the result of different preferences for particular places of articulation.

While the above preferences show preferred sounds, there may also be differences dependent on the place of a sound in a word. Concerning consonants, one can speak of three basic positions: initial, medial, and final. Children may vary concerning their preferences for each of these positions. Christopher Priestley had definite preferences for initial and final consonants, using only [j] in medial position, with a preferred structure C_1VjVC_2. Padmint Ross, however (based on Ross 1937), preferred initial and medial consonants; to avoid final consonants he would reduplicate vowels: e.g. 1;8 *bag* [baga]; *book* [buku]; *brick* [biki]; *dog* [dɔgɔ]; *pot* [pɔtɔ]. Lastly, Stern and Stern (1928) report that their son Günter from 1;11 to 2;4 had a preference for medial and final consonants. Initial consonants were either omitted or replaced by [h] and occasionally the palatal fricative [ç]. As with the French fricatives, there are children who show preferences for each possible form.

While discussing preference, it is also necessary to mention avoidance. Not only do children over-use certain preferred sounds, they also may avoid words that contain sounds that they cannot currently produce. The possibility of avoidance was first mentioned by Ferguson and Farwell (1975). More recently, Schwartz and Leonard (1982) have pursued the issue experimentally. Following twelve 1 year olds longitudinally, they attempted to teach children nonsense words that fell into two groups. One group of words were IN words, in that they consisted of sounds that were part of the child's phonological system. The other group of words were OUT words containing sounds not yet produced by the children. They found that the children were more apt to produce the IN words than the OUT words, both in imitated and non-imitated contexts. Thus an individual child's words will demonstrate both preference for certain sounds and avoidance of others.

Data like these show that the use of a highly common set of phonological preferences does not mean that the phonologies of individual children will necessarily look very similar. As a result of distinct preferences that each child has, the outputs from child to child may be quite different. Even though children have similar possibilities to choose from, they appear to choose in very different ways.

One further observation needs to be made about individual children. Not all children show the kinds of unusual or interesting changes that have been exemplified above. That is, some children keep very close to the adult models and use only the most familiar phonological processes. This in itself results in individual variations among children, and yet this topic has rarely been discussed in the literature. It may even be that these children constitute a majority, and that the cases most often cited in the literature are atypical in their phonological development.

4. Summary

This chapter began with a proposal that much of the rapid phonological development that takes place between the ages of 1;6 and 4;0 can be described by looking for general phonological processes. These are essentially statements about how children simplify adult words. After a brief description of some of the more general processes in children's speech, two cautions were given about the description of a child's speech in this way. One dealt with the problem that the child's language is dynamic in nature, so that any analysis needs to take into account both old and new developments, as well as the gradualness of phonological change. The second caution was that one has to consider the child as an active organizer of its own system. The processes that a child may exhibit in these cases look very different from those more commonly found in the literature, and they show a willingness on the child's part to break down the more frequent isomorphic relation that is maintained between adult forms and the child's production. The use of different organization principles can account for some of the individual variation between children. Specific suggestions were made that the phonological preferences individual children have will also contribute to marked differences. Phonological development at this stage can be seen to consist of both very general phonological processes and also the child's unique phonological preferences shown through various productions of speech forms for the language he / she is acquiring.

11. Speech perception and the emergent lexicon: an ethological approach*

John L. Locke

1. Introduction

If the phonology of an established language includes a set of rules which relate internal representations to surface forms, to understand a developing phonology one must infer the child's stored lexical forms from observations of his physical expression of those forms. Child phonologists would then seek to determine the relationship between stored and articulated forms, hence, the nucleus of the child's phonology. Those wishing to understand deviant utterances would additionally look for discrepancies between the child's internal representations and the prevailing forms in his environment.

As all phonologists need to know something of children's internal representations, it is embarrassing that most of us know nothing substantive about them. Even those who have diligently studied children's perception of speech know little of their internal representation of words. In the face of this, are phonologists hesitant to make statements about children's rule systems? Are developmental phonologists busily applying the techniques of cognitive psychology to reconstruct children's stored lexical forms? These would seem to be appropriate behaviours under the circumstances, but in fact many phonologists have suggested – and still appear to assume – that children 'have the adult form as their internal representation'.

Peters (1974) has asked what it means to say 'the adult form' when there are lots of surface forms for any given word, within and across adult speakers. Many of us would like to believe that if a child responds appropriately to the speech of others his internal representations must correspond to their produced forms. This seems entirely reasonable; for even children with phonological disorders may judge standard English forms to be correct forms (Locke 1980). But how can we be sure such judgements do not represent a *failure to discriminate* others' correctly produced forms from their own (perhaps incorrect) stored forms?

In this chapter, I will explore the child's perception of speech as a process crucial to his acquisition of language. Rather than treat speech perception

as an ability or skill, independent of its linguistic significance, I will ask what role perception plays in the development of the child's beginning le con.

Others have reviewed the rather remarkable perceptual abilities of the neonate for isolated speech-like sounds in the laboratory (Jusczyk 1983) and it is not my purpose to go over this work here. Suffice it to say, when various phonetic features are presented in quiet, most infants respond differentially. My concern is therefore the infant's perception of oral language in his natural habitat.

In the development of language, infants do not 'start from scratch' either perceptually or motorically. As a consequence, I suspect it is rare for infants just to scoop up auditory patterns, withholding speech until they know enough about environmental patterns to achieve an imitation. Rather, there is evidence to suggest that infants more prevalently attend to particular patterns, and consult their store of available articulations in search of the closest matches.

2. The available articulations

Numerous studies show that infant vocalization, far from being random play, is characterized by oral motor behaviours which are patterned both segmentally and syllabically. Table 1 shows the consonant repertoire of infants reared in 15 different linguistic environments, as reflected by parent diaries (see Locke 1983). Note that [m] and [b] are common to all infants and environments, [ʒ], [tʃ] and [dʒ] to none of them. Overall, stops, nasals and glides comprise 82 per cent of all consonants in the records. Fricatives, affricates and liquids comprise just 18 per cent. Other studies indicate that consonant singletons exceed clusters by a ratio of 9 to 1, and that syllable-initial consonants exceed final consonants by a margin of 2 or 3 to 1 (Oller *et al.* 1976; Oller and Eilers 1982).

Studies of the deaf suggest that infants need not hear themselves or others in order to babble, and that hearing infants do not derive their articulatory patterning from what they hear. From a review of published and unpublished literature, Locke (1983) found that children born and reared deaf continue to babble until at least 6 years of age, and have a repertoire of consonant-like sounds that closely resembles that of hearing infants. In Carr's (1953) group of 48 5 year olds, stops, nasals and glides made up 72 per cent of the babbled consonants while liquids, fricatives and affricates constituted just 27 per cent. This suggests that infants have a preference for stop, nasal and glide *movements*, and indeed, both Koopmans-van Beinum (personal communication 1982) and Labov and Labov

Table 1. Consonant-like sounds in the babbling of infants reared in 15 different linguistic environments

	b	m	p	d	n	h	t	k	g	w	j	v	l	ŋ	s	r	f	θ	ʃ	z	ð	ʒ	tʃ	dʒ
Afrikaans	*	*	*	*	*	*									*	*		*	*					
Mayan	*	*		*	*	*																		
Luo	*	*	*	*	*	*			*				*	*										
Thai	*	*	*	*			*	*	*		*													
Japanese	*	*	*	*	*		*	*	*	*	*	*												
Hindi	*	*	*		*	*	*	*	*						*									
Chinese	*	*	*		*	*	*	*	*		*			*										
Slovenian	*	*	*	*					*	*			*											
Dutch	*	*	*	*	*	*	*			*				*										
Spanish	*	*	*				*	*																
German	*	*	*	*		*				*	*	*	*			*								
Arabic	*	*		*	*	*	*	*	*	*	*	*	*	*	*					*				
Norwegian	*	*	*	*	*	*	*	*	*	*	*	*									*			
Latvian	*	*	*	*	*	*	*	*	*	*	*	*					*							
English	*	*	*	*	*	*	*	*					*											
Total	15	15	13	12	11	11	10	9	9	7	7	5	5	4	3	2	1	1	1	1	1	0	0	0

Note: Phonemically non-English sounds have been eliminated from this tabulation. Original sources and population details are available in Locke (1983).

(1978) have observed hearing infants to make silent labial movements (for the feeling?) just before or during the period in which labial *sounds* are more frequent in their vocalization.

There seems to be no evidence as to when hearing children become aware of the spectral or temporal properties of the sounds produced by their oral movements, though they are evidently aware of their voices within the first week of life (Cullen *et al.* 1968). One might suppose that infants are aware of their own vocal pitch by 4–6 months, for at that age investigators have observed systematic pitch matching (Kessen, Levine and Wendrich 1979). Whether pitch imitation requires awareness of one's own vocal frequencies has not been established, and though it makes a certain 'common sense' to suppose that it does, there is evidence that neonates who have never seen their own faces are capable of imitating facial gestures (Meltzoff and Moore 1977).

3. Phonetic inventory of the early lexicon

It is evident that early lexicons are expressed in phonetic features which coincide broadly with the feature classes observed in infant babbling. According to my count, 85 per cent of the consonants used by 10 children to express their first 50 words (from Leonard, Newhoff and Mesalam 1980) were stops, nasals or glides. The other feature classes – the fricatives, affricates and liquids – are those which also are conspicuously absent in infant babbling. Elsewhere (Locke 1983) I have argued that this similarity is no coincidence, and is due to the child's use of the motor–phonetic patterns of babbling in word construction.

4. Babbling frequency, speech availability and word admissibility

Essentially, my hypothesis is that movement patterns that are frequent in babbling are available for speaking. As such, the patterns are useful in constructing early words.

The child, to start with, must know something about his own system, for in large measure he *selects* words for reproduction that even in the standard language are like his own babbling forms. Thirty-five per cent of the consonant-initial words in T's 50-word vocabulary (Ferguson and Farwell 1973: app. 1) begin with bilabials, while only 26 per cent of the English monosyllables begin with bilabials (Moser 1969). Of course, the child's environment undoubtedly does some selecting for him too, but from Leonard *et al.* (1981) it is evident that the child makes selections of his own.

So we have a child who made lots of bilabials in his babbling, and now we see him selecting /b/ words for his early lexicon, and also overextending [b] sounds where they are not welcome (for example, T's occasional use of [b] to represent standard /r/; Ferguson and Farwell 1973). The perceptual questions in this are: (1) whether the sounds heard in standard words are sufficiently like sounds that are in the child's current repertoire that any will be lexically useful; (2) which repertoire sounds may be so employed; and (3) for which standard units might the child's repertoire sounds be used? According to Labov and Labov (1978: 849), observing their daughter:

> Jessie's phonological inventory was only a small subset of her babbling inventory. But phonological development was hardly an independent process. Her selection of phonetic realizations was the product of her perception of the fit with adult forms, the canonical shape of her syllable, and some fortunate matches between articulation and meaning. To this we must add our own perception and recognition of these forms.

As there is precious little evidence of phonetic drift in babbling (Locke 1983), I would argue that the first time an infant seriously addresses the phonetic values of either his environment or himself is when he becomes interested in producing words. As he recognizes the admissibility of his own repertoire sounds it becomes important for the infant to know more about what sounds he currently can make in relation to the sounds he hears others making. This will permit him to appropriate for lexical service the most closely matching sounds.

5. Internal representations of the early lexicon

Though young talkers produce a variety of words which resemble adult words, children's forms may derive from internal representations quite unlike the internal representations of adults. Rather, there is reason to suppose that children's internal representations are more motorically structured, are less completely analysed auditorially, and are segmentally reduced relative to adult versions of the same words. I will take up each of these cases in greater detail, but first it is necessary to say more about what is meant by internal representation: I mean by it what Linell means by 'phonetic plan'.

> ... for each word form there is one *phonetic plan* which is psychologically central and defines the phonological identity of the word form in question. In speech production the speaker intends to realize this plan [which is] the most *careful pronunciation* that the speaker is acquainted with. (Linell 1979: 47–8, 54)

Linell went on to suggest that phonetic plans were basically auditory in nature, encompassing 'lexicalized information about *sound* structure', and requiring for their expression 'fully specified articulatory plans' which contained prosodic and allophonic details. Internal representations are, then, basically auditory in nature, implemented by motoric plans.

6. The motoric structure of early lexical representations

How well does the child have to be able to perceive speech – others' and his own – to develop his first words? Not well. At or before 12 months a number of children have been observed to say [da]- or [dae]-like syllables in reference to 'daddy'. Since [d] is of considerably greater frequency in the babbling of 11–12 month olds than the other stops (Irwin 1947), one might hold that all the children *have* to perceive is [+stop]; if they were to produce their most frequent stop their replicas would 'automatically' be alveolar and voiced. In other words, I am not sure one can credit the child's perceptual system for all the matching features in the child's response if some can be motivated extra-perceptually.

If infants are predisposed to project innate movement patterns onto standard words (as they perceive them), only *contradictory* information may be needed from perceptual analyses for the child to avoid unintelligible results. A fairly crude analysis of his own sounds in relation to environmental sounds would be sufficient, and there would be, therefore, a motor basis to speech perception – and internal representations – from the very start.

Since I argued earlier that the infant's babbling has a largely motor or sensorimotor basis (recall that deaf infants have a similar consonantal repertoire), and as there is considerable overlap between the phonetic features of babbling and of speaking, it follows that when the young child draws upon his phonetic experience he is drawing largely upon his articulatory motor experience. The infant learns that his prelexical [dada]s and [mama]s are admissible as representations of standard *daddy* and *mommy*. Though they will become auditorally enriched through experience, the earliest representations or phonetic plans of children may be primarily motoric in nature.[1]

7. The 'to be perceived': *umwelt* of the English child

I have argued above that the yearling has access to certain articulatory patterns, is grossly familiar with their acoustic correlates, and is disposed to use these behaviours to represent (and to contrive) words. But what is the phonetic form of these words, and how might early word forms

Table 2. *Phones of conversational American English in three word positions (from Mines, Hanson and Shoup 1978)*

Rank	Phoneme	Per cent of consonants	Initial	Medial	Final
1	n	11.49	867	2,861	3,246
2	t	9.88	1,242	1,804	2,953
3	s	7.88	1,777	1,406	1,473
4	r	6.61	588	2,541	886
5	l	6.21	896	1,961	918
6	d	5.70	872	850	1,731
7	ð	5.37	2,945	276	41
8	k	5.30	1,108	1,346	766
9	m	5.11	1,177	871	1,054
10	w	4.74	2,536	333	4
11	z	4.70	17	306	2,467
12	b	3.24	1,286	646	36
13	p	3.07	890	670	298
14	v	2.97	190	711	902
15	f	2.65	1,016	378	207
16	h	2.23	1,250	106	0
17	g	2.02	835	292	96
18	y	1.87	894	236	0
19	ŋ	1.85	1	346	778
20	ɾ	1.76	75	600	394
21	θ	1.19	417	149	155
22	ǰ (ʤ)	0.95	284	182	111
23	š (ʃ)	0.95	189	336	48
24	ʔ	0.85	82	107	321
25	č (tʃ)	0.85	96	149	270
26	t ~ ʔ	0.21	0	9	118
27	ž (ʒ)	0.15	9	75	5
28	t ~ ɾ	0.13	14	36	28
29	ʍ	0.07	43	0	0
Total		100.00	21,596	19,583	19,306

be related to sounds produced in the presence of infants and young children? When adult Americans speak to each other they produce phones of the type listed in table 2. It is evident from this table that conversational American English includes many sounds not commonly associated with American English. For example [ɾ], [ʔ] and a dental-glottal [t ~ ʔ] have a higher incidence in some word positions than many 'standard' sounds such as [ʃ], [g], and [ð]. Such a 'common' sound as [b] had a word-final frequency of just 36 out of 19,306 (or 0.2 per cent).

Where 'nonstandard' phones creep in, of course, some very standard ones also creep out. Neu (1980) has documented a very high rate of consonant deletion in words such as *and* and *just* when adults speak casually. Zwicky (1972) has created an elaborate taxonomy to catalogue the many

segment omissions and other changes that occur in normal adult conversations. Labov (1966) has observed that when New Yorkers speak casually they are considerably more likely to omit /r/, and to stop of affricate /θ/, than when they read words or word-pairs.

It is understood, of course, that speakers read in temporally regular ways – fluently – while speaking conversationally in temporally sporadic ways – frequently with hesitations and other forms of nonfluency. What I am suggesting is that the bulk of what we know about speech comes from studies in which adults read isolated words or short phrases, and that such studies tell us very little about the phonetic elements and patterns to which children might be exposed.

8. The child's phonetic environment

When we study the child's phonetic environment we must concern ourselves both with the speech which occurs within earshot of the child and with the speech which is directed to the child himself. To my knowledge, no studies have been done to determine whether adults speak differently to other adults when they know children are listening. We also seem not to know the influence of overheard adult–adult speech relative to adult–child speech. Therefore, when we examine so-called 'motherese' it is not clear that we are getting a sufficient view of the phonetic values which effectively reach the child. And even when we restrict our attention to motherese the picture still is not a clear one. For example, some studies suggest that mothers make little or no adjustment at the phonetic level when talking to children (Baran, Laufer and Daniloff 1977); other studies suggest that mothers enhance (Bernstein 1982) or – perversely – reduce their phonetic distinctiveness (Shockey and Bond 1980; Bard and Anderson 1983).

There is a knotty cognitive problem side-stepped by all the motherese studies. MacKain (1982) pointed out that there is a difference between linguistic exposure and linguistic experience. In order to perceive speech well enough to reproduce it, a measure of selective attention is necessary. Apart from the transmission of lexical meaning, it is difficult to see what the child's need for such focal listening might be. If adult-generated words evoke certain perceptual responses – and not others – in the child, then it becomes important to assess whether such words – and not others – are used selectively (and perhaps repeatedly) in his presence. For it is the phonetic patterns of these words that the child would analyse and store, and toward which the child's own articulations would be extended. According to Schwartz and Terrell (1983), the words used most frequently by

adults – other things being equal – are more likely to be attempted by children.

9. Segmental reductions

If frequently produced words are likely to form the core of the child's emergent lexicon, it is important to ask if frequent words – as produced by adults – have any special properties that could be perceptually significant.

According to Zipf (1932, 1949), frequent words may be predicted to be of phonemically shorter duration than rare words, and there is confirmation of this in the literature. Neu (1980) found that adults delete the /d/ in 90 per cent of their productions of *and*, compared to a 32.4 per cent rate of /d/ deletion in other monomorphemic clusters; at 49 per cent, /t/ deletion is just exceeded by that of other -*st* clusters. Fidelholtz (1975) has observed less in the way of perceptible vowel reduction for frequent words, and Koopmans-van Beinum and Harder (1982 / 83) have confirmed this in the laboratory. The frequency-reducibility effect evidently holds even where syllabic and phonemic length are equated (Coker, Umeda and Browman 1973; Wright 1979), and as the effect apparently has little to do with differences in the information content or predictability of high and low frequency words (Thiemann 1982), their differential reducibility suggests that frequent (i.e., familiar) words may be stored in reduced form.[2]

10. Rephonologization

From the above account one might suppose that some children – indeed, some adults – have for standard *and* an internal representation of /aen/. More generally, a case can be made that for all words ending in voiceless stops many normally developing children, for a period, have vowel-final internal representations. There are several sources of evidence for these developmental restructurings – or 'rephonologizations' as Jakobson (1972) and others have called them in an historical context. One kind of evidence is acoustic measurements of children's speech, which shows that where final voiceless stops are perceptibly omitted, the preceding vowel obeys the English rule and is of short duration, and also may be abruptly terminated, as are vowels prior to /p,t,k/. A second kind of evidence comes from children's patterns of mis-spelling. Read's (1975) data reveal that children omit in their *spellings* more *p*, *t*, and *k* letters, overall, than *b*, *d*, and *g* letters. They also omit more *t* letters than *p* or *k*, which accords well with the fact that children glottalize more final /t/ sounds than any of the other voiceless stops (Locke 1983).

11. Memorial 'processes'

Children's restructurings may be even more pervasive than the final deletion evidence suggests. Consider, for example, the study by Aitchison and Chiat (1981). They introduced to 90 British children between the ages of 4 and 9 years the names of nine animals (for examples, armadillo, bandicoot, cuscus, kudu). Following correct repetitions of the animal names initially, the children were tested for their ability to recall them. Aitchison and Chiat found that the standard forms, repeated correctly at input, frequently were reproduced erroneously. Errors were not random, however. Rather, they were phonetically highly patterned (perhaps reminiscent of adults' recall patterns of CV syllables; see Wickelgren 1966), and could be classified according to 'natural' phonological processes previously identified with children's developmental output errors (see Stampe 1973; Ingram 1976a). For example, there was final obstruent deletion in *bandicoot, cuscus* and *mongoose*. There was a great deal of consonant harmony on *kudu*, with 10 productions of 'kuku', seven of 'kutu', five of 'kugu' and five productions of 'gudu'. As this was a completely naturalistic study, one must conclude (and indeed Aitchison 1972 and Aitchison and Straf 1981 found) that in 'real life' children frequently store or develop forms which differ from standard ones, regardless of whether the original input was perceived correctly. And when these nonstandard forms are expressed faithfully, sounds will be produced which many phonologists would like to link by an elaborate set of rules to an assumed adult-like internal representation. But it seems that children who have relexicalized in this way probably consider the standard form as an acceptable variant (as in Locke 1980: 454–5), or have the standard form as an alternative phonetic plan (H. Andersen 1973; Linell 1979). In such cases as these, phonological rules are necessary to account for the child's behaviour. But their function would be to transform adult-like internal representations not to child-like surface forms but to child-like internal representations.

12. Long units

Peters (1983) identified the formulaic nature of many of children's early words, defining formula as a 'multimorphemic phrase or sentence which, either through social negotiation or through individual evolution, has become available to a speaker as a single prefabricated item'. Though all speakers produce idioms such as 'kick the bucket', etc., children produce many additional ones such as 'fall down', 'so big', and, from Peters, 'open the door' and 'I carry you.' I once came across an account of a child who

asked at the family breakfast table where the 'jamminit' was. This request evidently made no sense to the parents until they recalled that when the child was given toast he was routinely asked if he wanted some 'jam on it'.

As there usually is independent evidence that the child perpetrators of formulas are unable in other utterances to handle the same complexity of syntax, or do not use formulaic words in other utterances, Peters chose to call such phrases 'long units', unanalysed wholes. Their producers seem not to be aware that they are producing more than one word, not to be aware of word boundaries. To the extent that young speakers' expressions are formulaic, so their internal representations are likely to differ from those of adults. When children seem at some later age to slide back, producing a regressive phonological idiom (as when Hildegard's [priti] deteriorated to [piti]; see Leopold 1949a), it may be that such 'recidivism' actually marks a developmental advance, indicating the first correct perceptual analysis and consequent revision of internal representations.

13. Concluding remarks

Though speech perception has been treated as a phenomenon or a process in and of itself, I have tried to show here that the child's perception of speech must be viewed in relation to its linguistic and biological function, namely, the acquisition of the units which permit lexical communication. When the approximate form of these words is known, the child in turn knows which of his currently available phonetic segments are lexically admissible, and in what sequence they ought to be deployed. It follows from this that the early internal representation of words may contain less phonetic detail than the child's speech might suggest, and that the early phonetic plans may contain a fair amount of motoric information.

Regardless of the efficiency of children's perceptual processes, there are reasons for supposing that some of the early non-adult internal representations will continue and that other nonstandard representations will develop. As speech of its very nature is variable and redundant, the child listener–speaker may misapprehend the cue structure of certain words, or even mistake a short phrase for a word. In other cases, certain phonetic information perceived well at input may for memorial reasons become altered or deleted, perhaps causing or creating the impression of misperception on subsequent occasions.

12. Phonological development: a crosslinguistic perspective

Marlys A. Macken

1. Introduction

A central challenge for a theory of language acquisition is the coexistence of extensive diversity – across time, languages and children – and striking similarities – patterns that seemingly must derive from some set of invariant properties of the language capacity. Not only these general patterns, but also the speed of development and the relative uniformity of the final state seem to require invariant properties behind the child's convergence on what is, in all respects, a highly complex system. In child phonology, as in phonology generally, the last several decades have been dominated by the search for invariance, for universals of acquisition. We are indebted largely to Jakobson (1968) for two fundamental premises of our field: first, that the utterances of the young child constitute 'language' in the sense of being rule-governed at all stages (save perhaps babbling); and second, that the governing principles are consistent with those principles that define and constrain phonological systems generally.[1] Yet the universalist character of this period is not without prominent exceptions (see, for example, Olmsted 1971, for acquisition, and proponents of the British prosodic school for general phonology); and it has been suggested that many details of acquisition are random or result from ephemeral details of input or experience (McCawley 1979). In its commitment to a universal system that defines the primary characteristics of phonologies and of acquisition, this paper falls within the universalist tradition; yet much of it will be devoted to variation, in the belief that constraints on that variation are important concomitants of an adequate theory of universals, and, moreover, that the form of that variation provides a crucial window through which the process of acquisition can most clearly be seen. The focus is the universal structure of phonology that defines both the form of phonological systems and the principled freedom exhibited in those systems crosslinguistically and therefore also in the individual.

Acquisition examples will be taken from the crosslinguistic research of

the last several decades that casts some light on the causes and nature of variation and the structure of universals. While much of the non-English data come from Spanish, a number of studies of Spanish-learning children will not be used, primarily because crucial differences in methods and goals complicate interpretation in the present framework. For example, there are three large-scale 'normative' studies of Spanish: Linares' (1981) of 97 3- to 6-year-old children from Chihuahua, Mexico plus a sample of bilingual children from New Mexico; Mason, Smith and Hinshaw's (1976) of 424 4- to 9-year-old children from San Diego near the Mexico border; and Melgar de Gonzalez's (1976) of 200 3- to 6½-year-old children from Mexico City. These could, of course, be profitably used in comparison with similar studies on English (e.g. Templin 1957). As for acquisition issues, this paper deals with only the earliest stages of acquisition and primarily the acquisition of consonants; it is hoped, however, that these restrictions do not seriously distort the picture of acquisition that emerges.

2. Preliminary considerations

2.1. Universals

The phonologists who accept the view that the goal of linguistics is the description of universal properties of language divide roughly into two groups, and we will, to some extent, draw on the work of each in our discussion of acquisition. For the 'formalists', linguists who owe allegiance or intellectual indebtedness to generative phonology, issues of concern are the universally-given constraints on phonological rules and on the set of elements that may figure in phonological representations. The original theory was based largely on the extensive analysis of a single language (English; see Chomsky and Halle 1968); but diversification within this tradition has been partially a function of the wide variety of crosslinguistic phenomena that have come under consideration. Examples include the introduction of two levels of phonological representation (segmental and nonsegmental 'tiers') to handle tonal systems ('autosegmental phonology', e.g. Goldsmith 1976) and the splitting of the segmental tier into three separate and autonomous tiers (the vowel tier, the consonant tier and the 'syllable skeleton') to handle problems in Semitic phonology and morphology (e.g. McCarthy 1981b). Further work in this tradition, representing even more radical departures from the standard generative theory, has focused on units larger than the segment: 'prosodic theory' recognizes a set of categories (the prosodic or accentual word, the foot or stress foot, and the syllable), analyses 'prosodic structure' as the hierarchical arrange-

ment of these units, and claims that this structure is crucial to the analysis not only of stress or prominence relations but also of phonotactics – a previously largely neglected area (e.g. Liberman and Prince 1977).[2] Crucially, each tier, or alternatively each prosodic unit, can be affected independently by rules specific to that tier or unit, and languages differ as to their exploitation of these different levels of representation. Broadly speaking, this formal approach seeks to derive limits on language and language types from formal properties of the system, as for example in the set of stress systems yielded by the tree geometry allowable under the theory of metrical structure.

The work of the 'typologists' is in contrast less theory-driven and more directly based on examination of phonological data from a number of languages.[3] Universals here include: statements such as 'all languages have vowels' (which would also be a substantive universal in the Chomskyan tradition); 'implicational universals' such as 'the existence of front rounded long vowels implies that of back rounded vowels but not *vice versa*'; and 'statistical universals' such as 'nearly all languages have nasal consonants' (where, for example, Salishan languages do not). (Note here that 'language' refers to spoken languages.) In child phonology, many 'universals' are actually statistical universals – that is, patterns that have a high probability of occurrence but need not be exceptionless. Work done in this tradition takes care to analyse a representative set of languages in order to rule out similarities that result from areal, genetic or typological bias (see Comrie 1981b: ch. 1 for a good introduction to this research). Current acquisition theorizing (and this paper is no exception) is based largely on studies of the acquisition of European languages (a notable exception is the crosslinguistic work on morphology and syntax done by Slobin and colleagues); caution is accordingly appropriate.

2.2. Variation

The types of variation are many, as for example, that due to the social setting, the style of speech, the type of task; or that variation due to dialects, borrowing, or a sound change in progress; or even that variation introduced merely by way of analysis or measurement error. Most of these factors apply also to child speech, where, moreover, there is generally only one source of information – what the child produces. This problem is two-fold: first, the process of inferring the child's intent (or 'underlying representation') on the basis of production alone is risky; and second, output alone notoriously underdetermines the system. Different types of child-produced variation are summarized in Ingram (1979), Menn (1979a) and Macken

(1980a). The latter article also discusses variation artifactually introduced by the analysis imposed by the adult listener / researcher.

3. The child's task

A currently widely held view of the organization of the phonological component recognizes two basic levels of representation, one phonological and the other phonetic, and a set of rules mapping the two levels. As previously discussed, there may be further levels of structure within each basic representational system; in addition, it should be noted that these basic 'formal' levels are included in, but are not necessarily identical with, 'processing' levels (see section 3.4). In essence, this (oversimplified) demarcation assigns language-particular organization to the phonological level and language-independent, presumed invariant structure to (the lowest) phonetic level. An examination of a subset of the properties of these two levels (and the controversy over their proper formulation) will demonstrate the complexity of the task faced by the child (and the researcher) and will show why variation is inherent in the process. We will return below to several of the points raised, for explanations in those cases where the child data seem accurately to reflect, and / or derive from, fundamental principles of language.

3.1. Phonological level

The phonological level is inherently relational, hierarchical, abstract and relatively arbitrary. Crucial to the phonological status of an element is its semantic function as a contrastive element (rather than its phonetic content *per se*) in what is a relatively arbitrary system relating sound to meaning. While there is a definable relation between a phonological unit (such as a phoneme) and its phonetic substance, the two levels are essentially independent: two languages with the same phonetic inventory may have very different phonologies, and the converse is in principle possible. A phonological unit is, then, a set of physically distinct elements that nonetheless count as the 'same' in a given language. A fundamental premise of phonology is that speakers construct hierarchies, for example by abstracting a single representative as the 'basic' or prototypical member of each set (in effect the 'name' of the set). A phonological 'rule' states the relations or correspondences between the physically distinct elements that count as the same. Much of the phonological literature can reasonably be described as arguments over which element is basic to a particular set in a given language (and why), or arguments over which type of unit is basic

to the phonological component (and why). (Units include the feature, segment or phoneme, and supra-word units, in addition to those mentioned in the previous sections.) To take a simple example involving a segment: Spanish treats the following sets as being the same set-internally and different across sets: [b... β], [d... ð] and [g... γ].[4] For a variety of reasons, the basic member is said to be [b], [d] and [g], respectively. The rule involved – usually called the Spanish spirantization rule – states, for example that postpausal, word-initial [d] corresponds to intervocalic [ð] and to post-vocalic, word-final [ð]; thus, [deðo] and [ðeðo] are the 'same' (two contextual variants of *dedo* 'finger'). The rules for defining phonological similarity and establishing hierarchical relations must clearly be learned, even where the rules have substantial acoustic and / or articulatory underpinnings. Moreover, if there are interim stages at all, one variant or a particular subcomponent of a given element will have to be learned / used by a learner before others. In principle, then, wherever two languages vary as to 'same' or 'basic' for any given group of elements, language learners may vary also.

3.2. Phonetic level

The phonetic level, on one view, consists of a linear sequence of units or segments, each of which decomposes into a set of features that characterizes the significant and articulatory properties of that segment. As is well known, however, the physical waveform is quasicontinuous, and the research tasks of segmenting it into linear units and defining the crucial constituent features have proven to be quite difficult. The physical form of each segment varies quite radically by context (say, [d] in [di] versus [du], or [da] versus [ad]) and by speaker. In fact, no two productions of the same word by the same speaker are identical. Yet speech is perceived by listeners who presumably extract criterial information to form perceptual categories from the continuous and highly varied physical stimulus. The phenomenon of recognizing segments produced in different contexts or by different speakers as exemplars of the 'same' category is called 'perceptual constancy' (Shankweiler, Strange and Verbrugge 1977). The structure of those categories is partially modelled by the phonetic features, in that they are intended to capture both what all tokens of a particular segment crucially have in common (for example, what makes a [d] a [d]) and how that segment both resembles and is different from other segments (for example, why [d] and [n] are more similar than either is to [s]). The latter is important to the definition of the segment and also to the classificatory function of features: segments that are similar in certain ways participate in the same

or similar ways in rules of different languages; features characterize the basis for such interactions. In the example, crucial to [d] are, minimally, its alveolar place, noncontinuancy and its voicing; [n] shares all these features with [d] (and additionally has a nasal hum) while [s] is neither voiced nor noncontinuant. Each language employs only a subset of the available features, and the segments of a given language will typically vary by more than one feature; this redundancy is a fundamental property of language. In the Spanish example previously given, the sets given contrast with the voiceless, noncontinuants [p], [t] and [k]; if [voice] is the crucial or distinctive feature, then [noncontinuant] is the redundant feature (or *vice versa*). Clearly the language learner must analyse stimuli at the feature level and learn which features are crucial; the redundancy in the system helps distinguish segments (by increasing the contrast between segments) but also permits alternative analyses. At issue also, though, is the extent to which basic phonetic categories are learned: do speakers 'construct' each category by comparing a large number of exemplars and extracting criterial properties across many different contexts, or are there invariant acoustic properties that provide the learner with an automatic segmentation?

3.3. Acoustic substrate

Early research on the acoustic correlates of phonetic features assumed there was a one-to-one correspondence between the acoustic and phonetic levels; however, what was found was not simple invariance but, rather, evidence for a highly complex mapping. In fact, more than thirty years of highly sophisticated research have not unravelled the complexities. We will take voicing as an example. Lisker and Abramson (1964) claimed that voice onset time (VOT) is the single most reliable feature separating voiced/voiceless stop cognate pairs in languages of the world, regardless of the conventional feature designations used in descriptions of those languages. For stop consonants, three modes of voicing can be distinguished by VOT: voiced (voicing begins before the stop release, as in Spanish /b,d,g/); voiceless, unaspirated (voicing starts at or very shortly after stop release, as in Spanish /p,t,k/ and as typically in English initial /b,d,g/); and voiceless aspirated (voicing starts considerably after the release, as in English /p,t,k/).[5] Pisoni (1977) suggested that these three voicing types were a function of limits on the resolution of temporal sequentiality: if the timing interval between two events was less than 20 milliseconds, those events would be perceived as simultaneous; only with intervals greater than 20 ms could the order between, for example, the onset of voicing and the burst

release be perceived. But it was known that a number of cues covary with VOT and that each can be used to discriminate voiced / voiceless tokens. In English initial tokens it was found that, for example, the spectral characteristics of the release burst, the intensity of the aspiration, the timing of the first formant relative to higher formants and its frequency at voicing onset, plus small pitch perturbations in the following vowel, all contribute to the perception of voicing in English.[6] There also is no absolute value or form for any of these cues: their interpretation may vary by the place of articulation of the stop, the vowel environment and other factors such as contextual speech rate.

One solution to the lack of single cue invariance was to posit more complex models of the integration of cues (see Stevens and Blumstein 1981 on spectral 'templates'). It has also been suggested (Stevens 1975) that invariance exists in the form of 'prototypical' acoustic cues – a set of 'primary' cues optimized in certain contexts, for example, in [b,d,g] in syllable-initial position before [a]; these cues are primary in that they occur in most contexts. In addition, there are 'secondary' cues that are more salient in other contexts, as for [b,d,g] in syllable-initial position before high, front vowels. The hypothesis is that infants initialize a phonetic category on the basis of primary cues and then by association learn the secondary cues and the category's other members in those contexts where the primary properties are not present. Thus, while some cues can be used, say, from birth, it may be that some aspects of even the basic phonetic categories must be 'constructed' by learning the patterns of similarity evidenced by a large number of exemplars. This requires that perceptual sensitivity be directed to each of many parameters (e.g. each of the cues to English voicing noted above). If so, then, 'the roles of learning and linguistic experience may be to attach an importance to each parameter appropriate to its distinctiveness in the listener's particular language', in which case 'the development of sensitivity of the constellation of parameters should have different characteristics for children acquiring language in different linguistic communities' (Summerfield 1982).

We will be returning to many of the points in this section when we take up the infant and child data, but at least the following should be clear: even when we consider the simplest notion of phonological structure (the relation between phonological unit, phonetic feature / segment and acoustic feature property), we encounter enormous complexity in the structure of the 'level' and the mapping between them, and we find that there is considerable freedom (of different degrees at different levels) in the alternative ways in which that mapping can be done.

3.4. Processing factors

In the preceding sections, three 'levels' of analysis were discussed: the phonological and phonetic levels, and the acoustic substrate. In constructing real-time, processing models of language, we must deal with a different notion of level. As a minimum, there is a single level – the lexical representation of, say, a word – that is recognized during perception by a set of perceptual decoding rules and transformed during production by a set of articulatory rules. Models of child phonology are sometimes elaborated to account for possible differences between a stored representation that is closer to the adult model and one that is closer to the child's output form – a sort of 'two lexicon' model that is perhaps similar to the model hypothesized to account for the fact that some readers can read correct spellings but write the same words in a consistently wrong way. The relationship between production and perception in a processing model is as complex and controversial as any topic so far discussed, but again a few points must be introduced before turning to the child data.

Much current work on speech perception utilizes information-processing models. In these, perception occurs in part via temporally ordered stages in which information is transformed and stored in successively more abstract levels of representations, and in part via a *parallel* processing function in which decisions at higher levels of processing strongly influence processing at lower levels (e.g. Neisser 1966). Levels here correspond, on some analyses, to the traditional divisions of linguistics and also subdomains of knowledge within each division. On one view, there are two interactive components: a more-or-less direct analysis of the incoming waveform, and an active synthesis component that takes the output 'feature matrices' of the first stage, generates a hypothesis, given several kinds of available information, then checks this hypothesis against a stored representation of the incoming waveform. What kinds of phonologically-related information does the listener use to restrict hypotheses?

In the model of lexical access described by Forster (1978), to take one example, different types of phonological / phonetic structure can correspond to different 'bins' of the phonological 'peripheral access file': these bins in effect group phonetically similar lexical entries together, and entries within each bin are listed according to frequency. (See Marslen-Wilson and Welsh 1978 for a lexical access model that, unlike Forster's, allows different types of information to *jointly* determine access.) For example, word stress is an important retrieval cue, and it appears that there are different access bins corresponding to different word stress contours (see Engdahl 1978), such that a particular contour can be used to retrieve words

that have the same stress contour but differ on some or all other phonetic parameters. The number and nature of the different access bins will depend on the number and nature of different phonotactic patterns in a given language. This model of lexical access is compatible with that acoustic research which shows that at least some aspects of word recognition depend on the identification of acoustic patterns of units larger than segments and features – namely, on the extraction of an entire acoustic pattern for a syllable or word as a gestalt without subsequent analysis into constituent segments or features (e.g. Klatt 1980).

Although the information-processing model for language is not uncontroversial, the higher order, top-down influences on phonetic perception advocated by some (and explored in a variety of studies on adults) appear to play an important role during acquisition. We will also draw on cognitive, information-processing theories in discussing individual differences and a general learning mechanism. Many important processing factors are, however, omitted here (for example, the roles of attention and memory), while still others receive only passing mention (for example, the important and equally complex topic of production-driven constraints, and the interaction of production and perception in delineating sound categories).

4. The child's early abilities

Beginning with Moffitt (1971) and Eimas et al. (1971), many studies have shown that very young infants have an impressive facility for processing acoustic stimuli which when processed by adults are perceived as language: these infants respond to changes in the waveform which correspond to phonetic features used in languages and, moreover, they do so in a discontinuous manner that resembles categorical perception in adults.

Infants have been shown to discriminate acoustic cues that underlie stress, pitch contours, voicing, place of articulation, certain fricatives, liquids, glides, nasals, the stop:glide and stop:nasal contrasts, certain vowel contrasts (e.g. [aːi], [iːu]; and [iːɪ]) and a few contrasts in syllable-final position (note that there is substantially less data on prosody and multisyllable stimuli). There are some negative findings as well, including contrasts between certain fricatives (e.g. Eilers, Wilson and Moore 1977) and, more importantly, stimuli in complex syllables ([atapaːataba], [mapaːpama], Trehub 1973; but see the medial position discriminations reported in Jusczyk and Thompson 1978). The crosslinguistic data are incomplete, but similar in general outline. Infants from an English-speaking environment can discriminate nasal:non-nasalized vowels contrastive in French, the Czech contrast

[řa:ža] (Trehub 1976), and the Hindi show [retroflexed:non-retroflexed] and [aspirated:breathy voice] contrasts (Werker *et al.* 1981). Infants from Spanish-speaking environments (Lasky, Syrdal-Lasky and Klein 1975; Eilers, Gavin and Wilson 1979) and from a Kikuyu-speaking environment (Streeter 1976) can discriminate the [voiced:voiceless unaspirated] contrast phonemic in those languages.[7] In addition, these infants also show enhanced discrimination of the English unaspirated:aspirated contrast which does not occur in their language. However, infants from English-speaking environments generally are reported to fail to discriminate the Spanish and Kikuyu contrast (e.g. Eimas *et al.*1971).

There is considerable controversy over some of the negative findings, and in particular over whether or not the crosslanguage data are evidence for learning or the effects of linguistic experience / exposure (see Eilers *et al.* 1979, 1980; Aslin and Pisoni 1980a; MacKain 1982; and the lucid discussion of problems in disentangling innate, maturational or learning aspects of the infant data in Aslin and Pisoni 1980b). Assuming that the negative findings correctly imply constraints on infant processing, we can say that it appears that not all contrasts are equally discriminable even in simple CV stimuli (e.g. fricatives and the [voiced:voiceless unaspirated] contrast), and that certain types of phonetic complexity appear to make difficult the discrimination of contrasts that would be easy in the simplest CV stimuli (where, for example, complexity is measured in syllable length or phonotactic diversity of particular kinds). Nevertheless, it is clear that infants can discriminate a wide range of acoustic stimuli.

It also is clear that infants not only discriminate, but also recognize the equivalence of, certain physically distinct stimuli. For example, when presented with tokens that vary in 20 millisecond steps along the VOT continuum from zero to +120 ms, infants will respond as if the stimuli were not six different types but rather only two. This 'discontinuous' discrimination function resembles closely that found for adults on similar stimuli. The adult function is called 'categorical perception', meaning that adults can only discriminate as many categories as they can label.[8] It is important to note that the adult data come from both discrimination and labelling experiments, while the infant data are from only the former. Two important observations can be made. First, infants can effectively deal with one of the two general classes of acoustic variability – that due to inherent variability of a particular segment (or category) in a given context by a particular speaker (e.g. aspirated stops with VOT values ranging from +60 to +120 ms). Second, while these data show that infants *extract* relevant, distinctive acoustic information, they do not show that infants *segment* the stimuli into constituent units (say, [p] and [a] from the syllable [pa]), or

that infants *categorize* a segmented stimulus in a way similar to adults (where, for example, the [p] of [pa] is the 'same' as the [p] in [pe] or [ap]).[9] This latter problem – categorization – is the second major type of variation that infants will have to deal with – variation due to phonetic context and also to speaker.

The problem of categorization – or perceptual constancy – has been studied most notably by Kuhl (e.g. Kuhl 1979, 1980). Her work suggests that infants can recognize certain similarities among members of a stimulus set that share phonetic features and, in that sense, can form categories that correspond to some adult perceptual categories: for example, infants appear to recognize similarities in tokens of [a] or [i] produced by different speakers or with different pitch contours. As to whether the infant is recognizing complex configurations or evidencing a simple sensitivity that does not require complex explanation, Kuhl notes 'we must simply reserve judgment ... until we have tested a fair number of speech-sound categories in a constancy format, it is difficult to say how configurational the infant's responses really are, and impossible to attribute their precise nature and origins to special mechanisms' (Kuhl 1980: 63). It is important to note that the research paradigm used in these constancy studies is essentially a learning one; thus, the results do not show that infants have innate perceptual categories, but rather that infants can be trained to ignore, for example, changes in speakers' voices. Still, the ability to learn the task probably rests on some prior ability to recognize similarities across tokens of a given category.

This research shows that infants can discriminate a number of cues that differentiate phonetic categories. This innate or early activated system[10] structures the input and no doubt facilitates language acquisition. There is probably a predisposition towards speech-like characteristics on the production side that is similar to the predisposition to process acoustic stimuli in a speech-like way. Such a predisposition would provide the infant with a basis for linking articulatory and auditory configurations, and – since such a linkage is necessary to language – any such predisposition would likewise facilitate language acquisition. The work done on prespeech production of infants from English-speaking environments strongly suggests some such universal base (see Kent 1981; and chapter 7 of this volume). However, there is even less crosslinguistic work on this topic than on infant discrimination; the work that is done often employs quite different methods and analysis techniques (in contrast to the far more unified field of infant discrimination), and the findings (not surprisingly) appear to be more contradictory (e.g. Atkinson, MacWhinney and Stoel 1970 versus de Boysson-Bardies, Sagart and Bacri 1981, for evidence against and for a drift in

babbling toward greater phonetic similarity with the language in the infant's environment). (The two fields cover different development periods, in that the infant discrimination research tests infants up to about 6 months old, while the babbling studies follow infants up to approximately 1 year o.

While it is clear that infants possess impressive, probably innate discrimination abilities, it appears that learning (or 'tuning') of some sort is necessary at least for contrasts that rely on few or difficult cues (e.g. the Spanish-type voicing contrast and fricative contrasts generally), and for extracting cues from complex syllable shapes.[11] There is little evidence so far that infants segment and categorize the input, but our hypothesis is that even basic phonetic categories must be learned or constructed, at least insofar as they depend on secondary cues and the integration of cues that can be differently weighted in different languages.

Let us assume for the moment, however, that infants can use these cues to recover phonetic segments fairly directly. If that is the case, then we face the puzzle of why the child's earliest 'phonological' unit is not the segment but a much larger unit, namely the 'word'. The solution seems to rest (at least partly) first on integrating the simple discrimination model used in infant studies with an information-processing model for perception (one that is partially top-down), and second, on combining the simple feature analysis with other phonological units, such as the accentual word from prosodic theory. The extensive crosslanguage differences found in child phonology can also be explained in part by this integration.

5. Learning the phonological system

Below, we will examine children's production for evidence bearing on the topics of segmentation, analysis and categorization. A prior issue is the child's perceptual system and the relationship between production and perception. On one view, the child's perceptual system is adult-like, and the errors in output are due to production difficulties (e.g. Drachman 1973; Smith 1973). The opposing view shifts the weight of explanation to an incompletely developed perceptual system (e.g. Waterson 1971; Klein 1978). The intermediate position recognizes perceptual difficulties as one of several problems the child must overcome (M. Edwards 1974; Braine 1976b; Macken 1980b). The data on children's perception and its relationship to production are contradictory; this no doubt is due in large part to the complexity of the domain and attendant methodological problems (see Barton 1980; chs 9 and 11 in this volume). If, however, children's perception of voicing in English is any indication, then even 3-year-old children appear to require several cues and / or large differences in cues

to discriminate certain contrasts, and the perception skills of even 6 year olds are not completely adult-like (Zlatin and Koenigsknecht 1975; Greenlee 1980). It also appears that the more complex the stimuli or task, the greater the difficulty for children (Cole 1981).

The position here is that perceptual factors play an important role in the early stages of phonological development. On the one hand, the adult system itself is complex, interactive and free from rigid deterministic control of the lowest levels. Moreover, it is probable that the child's perception is not adult-like in the early stages and that children must learn to segment and categorize. Most studies which take this position – that the development of the perceptual system is crucial – deal (as we do) with younger children, children up to approximately the age of 2 years. In such studies, perception is generally taken to mean perception of features or segments; we additionally hypothesize that top-down processing is also crucial.

Returning now to the infant discrimination data of the previous section: if we were to assume that that data 'solved' the phonetic problem by demonstrating innate or early maturing perceptual / phonetic categories, and if perception were a bottom-up process, then we would expect great similarity at the beginning of language acquisition. Additionally, we would expect crosslinguistic variation to occur later, when the child began learning higher-level patterns.[12] (These expectations also require the additional assumptions that production units correspond more-or-less directly to perception units, and that the acoustic / articulatory link-up rules and the actual production rules are as early maturing and homogeneous across children as the infant discrimination skills.) But do we find such uniformity? If we go beyond the earliest stage where variation between children is largely due to a very small lexicon and its somewhat random phonetic properties, we still encounter less uniformity than the simple model would predict. In addition, we encounter some crosslinguistic variation from this same early point. The question is why?

5.1. Segmentation

Most studies of child phonology employ a segment-sized unit as the unit of analysis (e.g. Smith 1973). Such studies describe the child's output in terms of segment-to-segment rules (as, for example, deriving a child surface form from an underlying segment, typically the adult phoneme), or in terms of 'processes' or general descriptive statements which, like segment-to-segment rules, define correspondences between elements but which, unlike such rules, do not imply a derivation (see chapter 10 in this volume). In contrast, some studies (e.g. Ferguson and Farwell 1975; Menn 1978; Chiat

1979; Macken 1979) have demonstrated that a more appropriate unit of analysis for the corpora from very young children is the 'word'. In these studies, phonological rules are not segment-to-segment rules, but rather formalizations of the strategies that a particular child has adopted to represent words and classes of phonetically similar words. While the 'phone tree' analysis of Ferguson and Farwell (1975) groups together similar segments that occur in the same position across several words, Macken (1979) found that the entire word was a 'prosodic unit': each target word was assigned to a particular 'word pattern' based on its general features; words, not segments of the traditional kind, were the building blocks of the early period.

The 'word' in the data from Macken (1979) was a grammatical unit indistinguishable from the morpheme. Part of its function in the analysis was quite traditional: a grammatical unit was needed to describe constraints on sequences of smaller units, to specify the domain of phonological processes and to block and to condition rules. However, the data suggested that the word and associated word structure constraints played a much more important role, in that the child appeared to formulate hypotheses about Spanish phonology on the basis of global similarity between words, by abstracting 'word patterns' which were then expanded and generalized to handle new words. For this child, the word was a basic organizational unit, and the learning of smaller units was influenced by the higher-level unit: without considering the word as a unit, some phonological phenomena (particularly at the segment level) would have appeared quite arbitrary and the frequency and consistency of other phonological phenomena could not easily have been explained. Although the learning of word patterns, segments and features was occurring simultaneously during the early period, the evidence for the centrality of the word had largely disappeared by 2;1, and the data from 2;2 to 2;5 could be adequately described in terms of more traditional segment rules.

This child appears to be unusual in the extent to which global, prosodic patterns affected her phonology and the duration of the word-based period. Several phenomena seemed to suggest a particular processing mode, and the data accordingly were related to an information-processing model for individual differences. Under this analysis, this child would differ from more 'detail' or 'analytic' children in a number of ways, including how early or how frequently the larger units were broken down into segment-sized units.

One source of variation across children, as is also true across languages, is the *extent* to which different units, provided by the universal grammar, are exploited. We assume that the differences between children and

between languages are of degree, not kind. (While it is significant that children employ a word pattern phonology and languages like Semitic may similarly exploit the consonantal tier, it is not the case that these cases or their shaping factors are the same.) It is as if the phonologies of languages and of individuals were plotted in a multi-dimensional space defined by a number of points along a number of parameters, where no phonology is an extreme (as, say, in a purely segmental language or a purely prosodic one).

The combined evidence suggests that all children start out with the prosodic word as a basic unit; that they form phonotactic and accentual 'generalizations' (e.g., word patterns), and that the learning of segments is partially determined by the development of rules at the word level. The research done on formal, prosodic theory and on lexical access models both point to the importance of word-level phenomena. These phenomena may be incorporated in a processing model by attributing additional structure to the lexical representation of individual words (the traditional approach within phonology) and / or by postulating, say, correlated accessing bins à la Forster (e.g. one per word pattern). If such word-based patterning enters into the developmental process from the beginning, as appears to be the case, then language-particular phenomena like phonotactics have an effect from the beginning. This then is a major source of crosslinguistic variation. For example, the prevalence of word-initial labial word patterns in the speech of the Spanish-learning child just discussed was hypothesized (Macken 1979: 47) to be related to properties of Spanish phonotactics (particularly the structure of the syllable). These same properties may similarly account for the special status of labial consonants in Spanish child phonology reported in a number of other studies (e.g. Montes-Giraldo 1970, 1971; Macken 1980a; Macken and Barton 1980b; Fontanella de Weinberg 1981). Early top-down effects of word-level properties also should account for much individual variation insofar as individual lexicons differ systematically (e.g. the range of early word patterns reported for children learning English discussed in Macken and Ferguson 1983).

Two important questions remain. First, how are words themselves segmented from the speech stream? The problem of isolating words and the contribution of phonology to this problem are two areas too frequently neglected (but see the cogent discussion in Chiat 1979). Second, how do bottom-up analysers (say, feature detectors) and the top-down pattern recognition mechanisms (parsing word patterns) interact during the development of segmentation and categorization? Since the child's knowledge at any given stage crucially affects the learning process (see Macken and Ferguson 1983), word patterns must play an important role in lexical devel-

opment (thus interfacing phonology with syntax), and in the simultaneous developments of phonetics and phonology.

5.2. Analysis and categorization

Recall that for any given feature of a segment, a number of acoustic cues covary, and that each phonetic segment decomposes into several features. When a child operates at the segmental level, s/he must extract from the set of covarying cues those that are crucial for the identity of a given segment in that language and then learn to produce those differences. What evidence do we have for this learning? First, it should be remembered that many factors affect the child's output – failure to perceive, a reweighting of criterial features, an inability to produce a feature, etc. Second, in those cases where a child does not rank the features in an adult-like way and / or produces the noncrucial feature only, adults of that linguistic community may fail to hear the contrast the child is making; sometimes only instrumental analysis of the child's speech will reveal the child's categories. Several instrumental studies have discovered such non-adult categories, for example, Kornfeld (1971), Macken and Barton (1980a), Maxwell and Weismer (1982).

Some English-speaking children first distinguish initial position voiced/voiceless stop phonemes by small VOT differences, all of which fall within the adult perceptual boundaries for the voiced phoneme:[13] productions for voiced and voiceless phonemes may average from +5 to +10 ms and from +15 to +25 ms, respectively. Some time later (typically after a period in which the child has slowly lengthened the VOT of the voiceless phonemes to around +35 ms), there is a sudden, dramatic change in the voiceless phonemes and they are now produced with very long lag (from +100 to +150 ms) – longer values than the adult norm. The obvious question is whether this discontinuity is simply due to a sampling bias (i.e. due to a time period of more rapid change) or due to a qualitative change in the child's system reflecting the sequential development of two skills (Macken and Barton 1980a). The latter is an intriguing possibility.

Recall that the cues covarying with VOT in English voicing include the spectral characteristics of the burst and the aspiration component; and that Korean contrasts two unaspirated stops not on VOT but on 'tenseness', where the presumed acoustic cue is the spectral characteristics of the burst (note that the third voiceless stop is aspirated, about +90 ms VOT). Interestingly, whereas VOT does not reliably separate the two unaspirated Korean stops, they typically differ in VOT, with the tense stop values falling around +35 ms and the lenis stop values around +10 ms (note that the latter

stop has both voiced and short lag allophones with some voiceless ones being slightly aspirated) (Kim 1965). The similarity between the English-speaking children's first contrast and the Korean lenis:tense, unaspirated contrast tends to support the two skills hypothesis. If the children's production directly reflects perception (a large 'if'), then we can interpret these data as evidence that English-speaking children first attend to the burst spectra (a decidedly secondary cue for adults) and later to the aspiration cue (or long lag cues). This hypothesis has *prima facie* plausibility in that the learning mechanism with which English-learning children are endowed must in principle allow such an option to those children learning Korean. Further, similar type re-analyses are fundamental to sound change. A third covarying cue to English voicing is vocalic pitch perturbations: the pitch of a vowel is higher following an aspirated stop than an unaspirated one (and, note, lowest of all following a voiced stop). While no English-learning child has been reported to first mark the voicing contrast as a pitch contrast, many languages have developed tonal contrasts from just such an originally redundant property of a voicing contrast.

Different analyses or weightings of cues presumably account for many child rules. A number of different solutions to English final voicing have been reported: epenthetic schwa syllables (Macken and Ferguson 1983); contrastive preceding vowel duration (Hooper 1977); and nasally-released segments (Fey and Gandour 1982). In the latter case, the child is not building on a redundant property in the adult input but rather matching voicing with an acoustically similar feature (cf. our earlier discussion of [d] and [n] and the classificatory function of features within phonological theory). A frequently cited and similar case is the retention of nasal consonants before voiced, but not voiceless, consonants (e.g. by children learning Spanish, see Macken 1979; and English, see Smith 1973; but apparently not Telugu, see Chervela 1981).[14] Here, the duration of the nasal differs markedly in the two contexts (at least in Spanish and English), and children mis-analyse, mis-segment, or misperceive the differences (see Greenlee and Ohala 1980, for several examples of such 'faulty acoustic imitation').

A particularly clear case of the effect of a language-particular phonological pattern on acquisition comes from Spanish. Children acquiring Mexican-Spanish first signal the adult voicing contrast by producing the adult voiced stop phonemes as continuants (Macken and Barton 1980b). In this case the children have 'analysed' the supposedly redundant feature as being the distinctive one (see section 3.1). This is all the more striking in that children as old as 4 years who show some ability to produce the voicing features still rely more on the continuancy feature. These findings may be dialect-specific (cf. Eilers, Oller and Benito-Garcia 1983 for Miami

Cuban-Spanish data) and may partially reflect the inherent difficulty of fully voiced stops. This latter point is problematic: while French-learning children also have difficulty with these stops (G. Allen, personal communication), children learning Telugu and Hindi appear not to experience such difficulty (Srivastava 1974; Chervela 1981).

It is likely that language-particular phonological and / or phonetic factors are at the root of many puzzles such as the following: [tʃ] is learned unusually early in Spanish (Macken 1979; Eblen 1982); English [ð] is produced as [d], as is common crosslinguistically, while Spanish [ð] interacts with the liquids (Stoel-Gammon 1974); nasal consonants – typically highly stable crosslinguistically – are produced as voiced stops by children learning French (Ingram 1979).

For a learning mechanism that can account for the variations between children learning the same language and different languages, researchers have turned to cognitive, information-processing theories (see Macken and Ferguson 1983 and the references cited therein). While the data from children no doubt result from a number of factors, including general development or maturation of perceptual and articulatory skills, some learning mechanism is required. Insofar as the language capacity itself is sufficiently free to account for the known diversity between languages and for language change, it likewise requires a similarly flexible learning mechanism. In arriving at an explanation of linguistic variation, we can derive constraints from a theory (as in formal approaches to phonology) or, given a range of data from many different languages, construct constraints (as in typological approaches). Child phonology has neither a learning theory nor the necessary crosslinguistic data. The theory that accounts for phonological development will ultimately incorporate a complex, interactive model like that sketched here. A predictive and explanatory theory must wait until considerably more is known about how those interactions between levels in the processing model and between types of information take place.

Part III

THE DEVELOPMENT OF LINGUISTIC SYSTEMS: GRAMMAR

Introduction

In Part III we look at the developing grammatical system, from its earliest beginnings up to (roughly) the point at which the child can be said to have acquired 'the basic tools of language' (see Karmiloff–Smith in Part IV). Understanding what this might mean in detail is an issue that we shall postpone to the next Part. Our immediate task is to look at how the grammatical system gets started, and how it then begins to develop over time.

First, by 'grammatical system' we understand a highly differentiated entity comprising vocabulary, morphology (derivational and inflectional), syntax, and the communicative functions which are expressed by these aspects of language structure. So, in reality, we are dealing with rather different subsystems, having their own structural properties and calling ultimately for some developing executive control which is distinct from them but accessible through study of how they interact, over time, in what we are calling the larger grammatical system. Secondly, what we might recognize as general grammatical functions also appear as rather different subsystems – modality, aspect and deixis, for example. These also may appear to interact, and, most importantly, to bear no simple relationship to well-defined structural subsystems. Thus, deixis may be studied in the personal pronoun system, in verb contrasts such as *come* versus *go*, and in the adverbials, e.g. *here* versus *there*; modality is expressed in the English auxiliary verb system but also in a subsystem of adverbials; and so on.

It is accordingly difficult to design a section on such a vast topic in a volume of this kind in sufficient detail and with due regard for comprehensiveness. In approaching this problem for the second time, in this edition, we have kept to our original developmental perspective in placing new chapters on early vocabulary (Griffiths) and syntax (Peters) and Derwing and Baker's revised chapter on early morphological development first; but we have tried to elaborate the treatment of particular grammatical areas with new chapters specifically on the personal pronoun system (Chiat), on tense and aspect (Weist) and on modality (Stephany). Wales' revised

chapter on deixis highlights, as in the first edition, the cross-cutting nature of structure–function relationships in a particular area of grammar, from the earliest stages onwards. Finally, we have commissioned a new chapter on crosslinguistic issues in grammatical development (Berman). In part, this has been in response to the need to reflect current interests in the field of child language studies; but, more importantly, crosslinguistic research offers the best chance of examining how far the heterogeneous subsystems within the area of grammatical development interact, both in terms of how one linguistic subsystem trades off against another within the same language, and also in respect of the long-standing issue of how far development is to be seen as 'purely linguistic' or 'cognitively determined'. In addressing such issues in a crosslinguistic fashion, Berman's chapter complements and extends many points raised in earlier chapters in this Part.

The first issue that Griffiths deals with is how children get started as users of verbal language in the period before they begin producing their own linguistic expressions. He emphasizes (a) the general behavioural framework for early adult–child interaction, within which, by the end of the child's first year, a mini-linguistic system starts to emerge based on just a few stable forms in the child's productive repertoire; (b) the asymmetrical sharing relationship between adult and child, in which the adult shares more but may select less, and demonstrates to the child which of the child's attempts to express meanings are successful in that they are understood by the adult; and (c) the nature of the constraints which operate to shape the child's progression from early, 'ritual starters' to more mature control and sequencing of linguistic behaviours. The second issue he addresses concerns the sort of mental representations that are acquired by the child for the important lexical type of nominal expressions. For these, he mounts arguments against criterial attributes theories, and supports the view that children work from prototypes which, to begin with, may be too scene-specific. He concludes by pointing to possible morphological and syntactic developments as prerequisites to later, hierarchical, structuring of the developing vocabulary system, and hence of associated mental concepts.

Peters' discussion of early syntax recognizes, as Griffiths does, a distinction between (a) an early process of item learning and (b) a later one of system building, involving hierarchical reorganization of linear structures.

As far as the early items are concerned, the distinction between 'vocabulary' and 'syntax' is a moot one: these are scene-specific expressions, extracted out of discourse contexts from the child's linguistic environment, and they may represent anything from more-or-less grammatically relevant

syllables to whole formulae. What happens to them is either that they come to be used in sequence with other units of acquisition, or are analysed out into their constituent units, or both – depending on the strategies of individual children and on the nature of the initial expressions. The early attempts at sequencing Peters wishes to call 'combinations', thus distancing them from the more truly syntactic nature of the hierarchically organized sequences that are increasingly characteristic with expressions involving three or more units. Peters cites some interesting research on the issue of how 'flat' grammars might become hierarchical (unfortunately, the necessary prosodic information is presently lacking), and concludes by making contact again with vocabulary in the matter of the development of *word classes*. Here, the opposition between acquired distinctiveness ('fission', out of an initial 'fused' category) and acquired similarities ('fusion', out of an early situation in which there may be as many word classes as words) may prove to be as confoundable for individual children as, Peters argues, such other putative distinctions as referential versus expressive, analytic versus holistic. It appears that individual differences in developmental 'style' require more subtle delineations than these rather gross dichotomies can provide.

When the child comes to analyse out the internal components of early expressions, one of the layers of language structure to be revealed will be morphological, i.e. where the complex is to be described partly in terms of syntax-like sequencing (stem and affix, in fairly discrete linear relationship) and partly in terms of vocabulary relationships (*builder* and *build* are related words). Derwing and Baker argue that the child can analyse out wholistically-acquired expressions quite early – and observation of apparently productive use of typologically distinctive word shapes by the age of 2;0 accords with this view. They endorse Bybee and Slobin's (1982) view that there is an intermediate development between unanalysed and fully analysed forms, of 'schemas' where children appear to be sensitive to tendencies towards form – function parallels, for example, that an English past tense verb typically ends in -/t/ or -/d/. They also support Clark and Hecht's (1982) view that a complex of factors underlies the child's developing abilities to structure the internal constituents of words, and they provide their own data to suggest that this development continues steadily through adolescence. One of their main concerns, however, is with the methodological basis of empirical investigations of such abilities, and with quantifying the concept of 'stage' of development (also one of Peters' concerns). They anticipate much of the discussion in later chapters in this Part by laying emphasis on the integration of naturalistic with experimental data, on the use of crosslinguistic information, on longitudinal as opposed

to purely cross-sectional studies (which Peters also calls for), and on the establishment of more truly performance-based groupings of children's behaviour than the criterion of age can yield.

Chiat's chapter on personal pronoun development takes us into that part of this section which deals with relatively well-defined formal-functional subsystems of grammar. The basic puzzle here is why it should be that the earliest pronouns, 1st person, 2nd person and inanimate 3rd person, do not represent a natural class in terms of their formal linguistic attributes (recall Griffiths' criticism of criterial attributes as an account of early vocabulary representations). Like Peters, and Derwing and Baker, Chiat recognizes a complex of factors, pragmatic, semantic, syntactic and morphological, underlying the development of pronominal use, and argues that it is necessary to study this development in the context of the noun phrase system as a whole. Here again, segmentation becomes an issue, with pronouns emerging out of the child's gradual analysis of linguistic expressions encoding adult/child speech roles (Chiat, and later on Wales, makes reference to Charney 1980, and Wales discusses how pronouns fulfil deictic function by acting as referential place-holders in whole expressions). Chiat suggests that this analysis starts to yield productive pronoun use, albeit in a limited way, at an age younger than standard experimental methods of investigation can reliably explore.

The two chapters which follow deal with what is arguably at the heart of the developing grammatical system in the 2- to 3-year-old child, the verb and associated elements. Concentrating primarily on the inflectional categories, Weist first argues for a fairly specific developmental pattern for the emergence of tense, where first event time, then speech time and finally reference time become independent components within the increasingly complex temporal system. He traces the earliest use of formal tense marking back to a truly temporal (rather than an aspectual) function, in contradistinction to the claims of the 'defective tense' hypothesis, which he finds to be crosslinguistically suspect. In this there is a directly related observation in Wales' chapter also, to the effect that the available evidence does not commit us to postulating (as the defective tense hypothesis requires) a nondeictic (aspectual) stage of acquisition preceding a deictic (tense) stage. Weist's crosslinguistic emphasis is evident also in his discussion of aspect. He calls into question the so-called fundamental status of the contrast ± Punctual, observing that in Polish the earliest distinction is perfective versus imperfective. He sees aspect and tense as evolving independently yet interacting as part of the developing temporal system of a language. When children break out of the restricted system of the here-and-now, they can make the distinction between ongoing events during

speech time and complete events prior to speech time. Weist concludes his crosslinguistic survey by observing that where linguistic devices for marking a particular category are similar across languages the emergence of that category is crosslinguistically stable; hence, it is possible to relate precociousness or lateness of emergence of categories to observable linguistic properties, or to cognitive factors, in a much more principled way than is possible from a monolingual perspective.

In her chapter on modality, Stephany, like Weist, concentrates on the grammatical rather than the lexical marking of the category. This takes her into the verb inflections of Greek and the modal auxiliaries of English. As with English pronouns, English modals appear to develop in piecemeal fashion; as Stephany points out, they represent a semantic rather than a syntactic problem area for the child, and their sensitivity to contextual factors probably accounts for the divergent orders of emergence noted for them after the early forms *can* / *can't* and *will* / *won't*. What seems clear, though, in both English and Greek, is that deontic functions (and their associated forms) figure dominantly over epistemic in the early stages; thus English *can* is used, typically with 1st or 2nd person subjects, to express physical ability, social possibility, and also (in questions) for permission and requesting. In the case of 2nd person subjects, these early deontic utterances are frequently directive in function, with future orientation. The later emergence of epistemic functions, sharing forms as they do with deontic functions, is therefore attributed to cognitive development – Stephany specifically relating them to the concept of (logical, or nonsocial) possibility, developing in Piaget's preoperational stage. There may, however, be a continuum of development between social (deontic) and logical (epistemic) possibility, which may help to explain the coincidence of forms for both functions.

Wales' revised chapter, like the original, is a wide-ranging survey of deixis as expressed in a number of different formal subsystems of grammar: determiners, adverbs, pronouns, prepositions, lexical verbs and tense. It thus makes contact with many of the issues raised in other chapters in this Part, as we have already had occasion to note. Wales looks in particular at two aspects of *that* / *there* deixis: (i) the attention-directing function (see Griffiths' observations on the early importance of this); and (ii) their contrastive spatial function. A wealth of crosslinguistic evidence supports the view that deictic terms are among the earliest vocabulary items in the first of these functions. Wales notes that they may be peculiarly effective in providing the cues or frames within which much early language input is set; and that neither children nor mothers seem much concerned about the spatial contrasts to start with. Neither is there much evidence of egocen-

tricity. Instead, early use of these terms seems to be scene-specific, in ways that other authors in this section have stressed, and from this stage to later, mature, use takes about five years. Such a long developmental progression, Wales suggests, cannot be explained simply on the basis of children acquiring the ability to mark spatial contrasts in the absence of gestural support; rather, the children must be seen as moving from an earlier stage of 'fused' deictic terms, which encode not just proximal/distal features but also animacy and other 'high' deictic characteristics of objects. Prepositions receive extended treatment in Wales' revision, especially since locative terms (*there, here*) seem to be dominant over, for example, demonstratives (*that, this*) in many of the studies referred to earlier in the chapter: what is *this* or *that* depends on whether it is *here* or *there*. Recent studies indicate that locative prepositions are interpreted together with the elements they serve to relate, in ways that show the interaction of linguistic with conceptual factors. What remains is to determine rather more precisely how language-specific acquisitions interact with general cognitive constraints. Temporal deixis is also revised and expanded. Wales suggests that it is correct to see temporal expressions as derived developmentally from spatial interpretation, in terms of children's performance on these terms. In particular, children appear sensitive to the amount of spatial information available for terms like *before* and *after*, even where they are required to make temporal decisions. 'Time-line' models fit the data quite well for children's use of temporal expressions, except for the conceptions of the future: this evidence fits with views of this category, for English at least, that it has more to do with mood than with tense.

Finally, Berman's chapter provides a succinct survey of the state of the crosslinguistic art. Many of the chapters in this section illustrate the second of her categories of crosslinguistic research, where data from essentially similar types of investigation, on given topics, are compared; and they address two of her recognized concerns, the separation of linguistic and cognitive factors in language development and the discovery of trading relations between subparts of the same linguistic system in development. As Berman notes, the fact that there has been relatively little of this sort of work until recent years must reflect the difficulty in doing it properly; in particular, it seems essential to base crosslinguistic comparisons on rich naturalistic data from the languages concerned, so as to take account of developmental factors as well as the more purely formal linguistic properties of the systems. As a framework for her discussion, Berman recognizes three phases of development: (a) initial access to the system, largely context-based; (b) structure-based grammaticization of knowledge; and (c) discourse-sensitive manipulation of the developing system. The latter phase

clearly looks towards the sort of abilities that Karmiloff–Smith deals with in the first chapter in Part IV; Berman concentrates her attention on the first two. As far as the first phase is concerned, the universalist nature of Slobin's (1985a) concept of Basic Child Grammar is based on shared features of early utterances 'despite great differences in the actual forms used by different languages'. However, the boundary between the first and second phases may be regularly breached by units of language acquisition that contain within them the sorts of language-specific grammatical properties that get unravelled in the second phase. Hebrew-speaking children, like their English counterparts, acquire causative expressions first as periphrastic constructions or as derived transitives; but whereas these types are the most productive in English, they are not part of the genius of the Hebrew language, and Berman observes Hebrew-speaking children having to proceed from this stage to mark causality in terms of the rich verb morphology of the language. Once this is mastered, she notes that these constructions then get overgeneralized, which is a typical phenomenon of phase (b) control. Such observations relate to what Berman calls the 'typological imperative', by which certain formal features are so much part of the linguistic system that they must be marked 'in order to speak the language even minimally'. Recall here Stephany's remarks about the non-avoidable nature of inflected verb forms for the Greek-learning child. Berman's main point about the second phase is that it is the point at which children come to attend to the dominant formal patterns of their language; from this point on, the language learning task is differentiated into the English, French, Turkish, etc. learning task, characterized by selective allocation of resources to different subparts of the grammatical system.

13. Early vocabulary

Patrick Griffiths

1. Introduction

Before children put together their first two-word sentences, at very approximately 18 months of age, their language acquisition *appears*, in terms of what strikes the investigator's ear, to consist mainly in amassing a stock of words. The period from the child's first 'word', at very approximately 9 months, to the first sentences is then a conveniently delimited one for an essay on early vocabulary.

A child of 18 months has accumulated a vocabulary of 'words' attested in *production* that numbers about 45. This figure is derived from Benedict's (1979) quantitative study of eight children. The 18 children in Nelson's (1973b) monograph would give a slightly lower average at 18 months; the average for the six children studied by Rescorla (1980) is higher. The inventory for *comprehension* begins earlier and increases more rapidly (see e.g. Valentine 1942: 400; Leopold 1949b: 162–7; Snyder, Bates and Bretherton 1981). An impression of how many 'words' are understood at age 18 months may be gleaned from the fact that Benedict's (1979) sample reached cumulative comprehension totals of 50 at a mean age of 1;1.5; had up to that point been gaining, on average, 22 'words' a month; and were at that point still all evincing upward trends. Twenty-two new expressions a month would, if the same rate were continued for another 5 months, add 110 items, to give a total of about 160 by 18 months. (Three of Benedict's sample were already at or near 200 by age 16 months.) Thus I shall be dealing with a period during which a (middle-class, English-speaking) child acquires cumulative vocabulary totals of roughly 45 items in production and perhaps four or more times that number in comprehension. The usual pattern of development is a slow start followed by acceleration towards the end of the period (see Nelson 1973b: fig. 6; Benedict 1979: figs. 1, 2; Nelson (1973b: 36) notes that advance in a minority of her subjects was more nearly linear). It should be stressed that there is wide individual variation in acquisition rate.

279

Vocabulary counts depend strongly on the criteria employed in deciding whether to credit a child with knowing an item. The sensible course – followed in the studies cited above – generally involves accepting an expression as comprehended only when there is clear evidence in support, and accepting it as being in the child's production repertoire only when it is used spontaneously and is both phonetically and semantically reasonably consistent (regardless of whether it is relatable in sound or meaning to any adult word). Leopold (1939: 149f) and Nelson (1973b: 13f) provide good discussions of criterion problems. Grieve and Hoogenraad (1979) give examples to show how difficult it is to identify recurring 'words' in children's early utterances. The totals offered above are *cumulative* ones, which is to say that once an expression had been entered into the record of a child's vocabulary it was kept there for the count even if it was not subsequently observed. Both Leopold (1939: 159f) and Bloom (1973: 66ff) note that some early forms are lost, and Rescorla (1980: 325) observes that 5 per cent of the total corpus had, at the end of his study, not been detected in use for at least two months.

At the beginning of this section I stated that children in the period under consideration *appear* mainly to be acquiring words, and 'words' has subsequently been put into single quotes. My motive for doing so was that the distinction between *word* and *sentence* is essentially inapplicable to speech output during the early part of this period. A *word* is a sentence constituent, but 1 year olds speak in *holophrases* ('word-sentences'). A holophrase is an utterance that is about as long as a (short) adult word – and is, indeed, often modelled on an adult word – but which is used in ways comparable to the uses of a whole adult sentence. That is, it is used to perform 'illocutionary acts' such as requesting and greeting (see Griffiths 1979 for further discussion).

By the time the child is about 18 months old, however, many holophrases have evolved into true words that are ready to be slotted into sentences. In the four or five months preceding the appearance of two-word sentences, it becomes increasingly reasonable to talk of children's *words* and to distinguish between different classes of words in their vocabularies. This is because the onset of sentence-making is not abrupt. That all manner of 'transitional phenomena' form a bridge from the stage of exclusively holophrastic speech to the stage of two-word utterances is clear from the work of Leopold (1949b), Bloom (1973), Dore *et al.* (1976) and Scollon (1976); see also chapter 14 in this volume. Furthermore, children's comprehension points to some grasp of syntax at ages rather younger than 18 months. Leopold (1939: 29) states of his daughter Hildegard in her 13th month that 'By the end of the month she followed complex directions like *Gib Klaus den Spiegel* or *Lass den Wauwau Papa beissen.*'(In translation: 'Give

Klaus the mirror' and 'Make the doggy bite Papa'.) See Huttenlocher (1974) for similar examples presented in greater detail, and see Valentine (1942: 419).

The remainder of this chapter focuses on two issues. Section 2 is concerned with how children get started as users of verbal language. Section 3 deals with 'nominals', a class of words that will often include more than half of a child's vocabulary items at age 18 months. Section 2, on beginnings, covers the period up to about age 1 year, a time when the child's language is manifested principally through comprehension. From an examination of the kinds of meanings transmitted in the first few months I infer a number of constraints that surround the start of verbal language. In Section 3 I adduce data and arguments in support of a version of 'prototypes' theory as a plausible account of how children mentally represent the meanings of their nominals. I also attempt to show that this account is compatible with the proposals of section 2. In the final part of the chapter (3.2) I argue that *linguistic* meaning, properly speaking, is a matter of interword relationships ('sense relations') and I turn to a consideration of semantic structure within children's vocabularies of nominals. Section 3 ranges up to age 2½ years, simply because some of the points discussed there, though applicable to the first half of the second year, are more readily exemplified with data from 2 year olds.

2. The beginnings of verbal language

If a 6-month-old child could articulate a view on the nature of speech it would probably add up to: (1) speech noise is highly predictive of the presence of humans (when you hear it there is bound to be someone about); (2) the effects of speech on the hearer vary along a single scale from frightening to comforting / amusing; and (3) speech can form a turn in conversational interaction (e.g. I smile, then you make some speech noise, then I smile again or make some speech noise myself, then you ...). The 6-month-old child is faced with having to discover what talking is all about, not just with having to acquire an inventory of meaningful expressions. See the first two chapters of M. Lewis (1963) for a sensitive discussion of this big step.

In her abstract, Benedict (1979: 183) dates the start of vocabulary in *production* as age 1;0. Examination of figure 2 in her paper suggests that this is an impressionistic rather than a statistical statement. However, it will serve as a convenient – though somewhat arbitrary – upper age limit for an early, comprehension-dominated part of the holophrase period. Leopold (1939: 29) notes that by the end of her 13th month his daughter Hildegard had reached the point 'when it proved impractical to continue

recording everything that she understood'. In table 1 I present information extracted from what Leopold (1939: 16–28) recorded of Hildegard's linguistic development up to the end of her 12th month. This diary material has been cross-checked with commentary elsewhere in Leopold's first volume (1939) and third volume (1949b) for clarification and supplementation. All the expressions noted by Leopold are included in the table. I have used glosses, quotation and summary to reflect as nearly as possible everything that he offers relevant to the meanings of these forms. For present purposes, the fact that Hildegard was growing up bilingual may safely be ignored when discussing her first year (except for the minor matter of paraphrase mentioned below). Leopold (1949b: 174) says of the first year: 'We may assume that the phonetic perception of the child was still dim and coarsely differentiated. She may not even have taken cognizance of the differences between German and English stimuli ...' He surmises, for instance (1939: 25), that *Nein, nein!* and *No, no!* were recognized simply by their shared 'falling intonation' (and I have accordingly linked these two expressions, in the 11th month entry in table 1, by means of a slash to suggest that they were a single item from the child's point of view).

Leopold's material was chosen for presentation because it was very carefully collected and is probably as complete a record as one can hope for. That it may be regarded as representative is suggested by comparison with other authors. I now list a few such comparisons to give an impression of the similarities. In relation to the 7th month entry *Hildegard* in table 1, consider the following interesting observations given by Valentine (1942: 404):

> B, 0;5½. Faint signs of recognition of his name 'Baba'. When he was on M's knee I stood in corner of room where he could not see me and spoke a series of names all in same tone – e.g. London, Taylor, Pitlochry, interspersed with Baba and Dada. Only 'Baba' produced a smile three times and 'Dada' once: but they failed to do so two or three times ...

When the test was repeated at 0;6½ only *Baba* resulted in smiling, and it did so every time.

Carter (1974: 86, 1979: 75f) reports a 'general want expresser' [ɔː] or [ɔ̃ː] that was used to gain attention and was sometimes used with pointing too (see [ʔaǃ], 9th month, in table 1). The child in the diary abstracted by Sully (1896: 405) 'would look towards a particular picture, Cherry Ripe, when the name was uttered' (see *Where is the baby? / Wo ist das Baby?* in the table). Halliday (1975: 19f, 149) glosses his son's [dɛə] (0;10½–1;0) as 'look (a picture)!' and speaks of 'meanings of an interactional kind involving the focusing of attention on particular objects in the environment, some

favourite objects of the child which are used as channels for interacting with those around him' (see *Bild*, *pretty* and *there* in the table). M. Lewis (1963:28) recounts of his son in his 10th month that 'when he was about to put a piece of paper into his mouth and someone said *No!* he desisted; when someone said *Say Goodbye!*, he waved his hand' (see *Nein, nein!* / *No, no!* and *Byebye*). Bloom (1973:90): 'From 11 to 14 months, Allison would vehemently protest unwanted events by saying something like "nə nə nə nə nə", with appropriate gesture and emphasis' (see [nenene]). Many more parallels could be cited, but the foregoing must suffice.

A linguistic communication system is, minimally, a selection of expressions from which a speaker can choose one to utter and can then with reasonable confidence expect that the utterance will transmit to the addressee a meaning different from that carried by any other expression in the system. Table 1 comes close to summarizing such a system. It is not quite what I have just described: (a) because of a few cases of paraphrase (e.g. *Backe, backe Kuchen* and *Patticake* subserve the same meaning); (b) because the table exhibits a system that developed over time (e.g. the meanings of *No, no!* and *Ticktack* changed and [nenene] replaced the loud [da da da]); and (c) because for a few of the expressions we cannot be confident that their utterance resulted from choice-with-the-intention-to-communicate on the part of the child (e.g. [mama]). In the role of *speaker*, the child and the adults had differential access to the system: the adults could select utterances from a set about three times the size of that available to the child. The adults also did not avail themselves of all the expressions in the system: Leopold (1949b:116) asserts that 'Hildegard's environment tried to avoid baby-talk . . .' Nonetheless, it was a shared communication system for sharing meanings. I believe that table 1 offers strong indications as to how children manage to make a start in talking and in understanding what is said to them, but it is first of all necessary to examine what kinds of meanings are available in the system.

2.1. Meanings in the early system

Halliday (1975:10), talking of children's first meaningful utterances, says:

> these meanings are not something which can be glossed in terms of the adult language, something which we can enter into a dictionary and which correspond to the meanings of words and phrases and structures in the adult language. They are meanings which we can best interpret if we begin with some kind of functional hypothesis
> . . .

Table 1. *Expressions comprehended and spoken by Hildegard up to age 1;0 (Observations extracted from Leopold 1939, 1949b)*

Comprehension	Function[a]	Production	Function[a]
7th month			
Hildegard '... it usually induced her to turn her head expectantly toward the speaker. There was no doubt that she referred these sounds in some way to herself' (1939: 20)	√Att		
9th month			
Daddy possibly 'made her pay attention, stop crying, and look around' (1939: 21)	Att	[ʔaː] to gain attention	√Att
No, no! possibly produced a 'similar reaction' to that for *Daddy* (1939: 21f)	Att	After about a month, also used with pointing gesture, as a demonstrative (1949b: 16)	√AttD
Where is the baby? / Wo ist das Baby? Orientates towards a particular picture (of herself) on the wall and laughs	Rit		
10th month			
		[da da da] satisfaction	?
		[da da da] said loudly Disapproval (1939: 72)	Att
Wo ist das Bild? Orientates to other pictures (1949b: 148)	Rit	Possibly *Bild* Picture '... often accompanied by pointing' (1949b: 159)	AttD
Wie gross bist du? Smiles and puts her hands on her head	√Rit		
Backe, backe Kuchen & Patticake Puts her hands together. Initially often confused with *Wie gross ...?*, above (1939: 23f)	√Rit		
Peekaboo & Guck, guck Hides using blanket etc.	√Rit		
Hopp, hopp, hopp Makes hopping motion	√Rit		

	11th month		
Presumably *pretty* (see right) was understood in some sense	AttD	*pretty* 'an expression of admiration, especially when pointing toward a picture; sometimes admiration was merged with desire to have the object' (1939: 24)	AttD
Presumably *there* (see right) was understood in some sense	AttD	*there* 'a demonstrative interjection uttered while pointing with her right hand at objects, also usually pictures' (1939: 25) 'No wish component is, however, recorded for this word' (1949b: 16)	√AttD
		[mama] 'means food' (1939: 181) '. . . uttered also without any reference while she was playing . . .' (1939: 101)	?
(Call the) squirrel Makes palatal clicks, to call squirrels. 12th month: calls to a canary in the same way when told *Call the birdie* or *Ruf den Vogel* (1939: 128)	√Rit	Palatal clicks, for squirrels (see left)	?
Nein, nein! / No, no! Desists from whatever she is doing	Att	[nenene] Disapproval 'Successor' to loud [da da da], above (1939: 112)	Att
Gib mir das Hands over what adult wants; 'the extended hand being as much an incentive as the words' (1939: 25)	Rit		
Patsch, patsch! 'the stimulus for making her clap my palm with hers' (1939: 118) Often confused with *Gib mir das*, because of adult's extended hand in both (1939: 25)	√Rit		
	12th month		
Papa Her father	√AttD		
Ticktack Looks at her father's watch. By end of month, looks either at his watch or at the wall clock (1939: 124)	√AttD	*Ticktack* 'It was always an objective statement of the fact that she recognized an object as falling within the classification covered by the term' (1949b: 17)	√AttD
Hoch, hoch! Raises her arms to facilitate dressing	Rit		
Prost! Tilts back her head and makes a gesture of drinking, with a cup or any other object in her hand	√Rit		

Table 1. *Contd.*

Comprehension	Function[a]	Production	Function[a]
Komm her! / *Come here!* Crawls towards speaker	Rit		
Nicht in dem Mund! Desists from putting things in her mouth. '"Finger aus dem Mund!" she understood, but rarely obeyed . . .' (1939: 27)	Att		
Wo is der Vogel? Orientates towards canaries kept in the house	√AttD	Possibly *piep, piep* (modelled on *Piepvogel*, 'birdie'). Canary. *Birdie,* for a canary, was reported to Leopold by relatives in the previous month (1939: 118f)	AttD
Look 'made her pay attention' (1939: 27)	√Att or √AttD		
Bye bye and 'less dependably so the German equivalent "winke, winke"' (1939: 17) Waves her arm	√Rit		
Shoes / *Schuhe* Her shoes	√AttD		
Mama Her mother	√AttD		
Opa Her paternal grandfather	√AttD		

[a] Att = attention getting; AttD = attention directing; Rit = ritual triggering; √ = author, PG. regards classification as uncontroversial (see text, 2.1).

For comprehension also, I can see no other sensible way of classifying the meanings in table 1. We have to ask what the speaker – adult or child – could do by means of the expressions in that system.

In the columns headed 'function' in table 1 I propose a three-way classification of the items in the table: those that served to grab the interlocutor's attention (Att), those that seized the interlocutor's attention and directed it to some entity in the situation (AttD) and those that set the addressee off into performing a ritual (Rit). This doubtless seems an outrageously undifferentiating and indeterminate classification, but I hope to show that it is an illuminating one.

For many of the entries marked Rit there will surely be no quarrel with my regarding them as expressions which triggered rituals (see *Prost!* for example). The ones I take to be uncontroversial are embellished with a tick (√Rit). There are two possible objections about Rit elsewhere in the table: that other items also deserve to be labelled Rit, or that Rit is not appropriate for some to which it has been applied. As an example of the first type of objection, consider the expression *Hildegard*. The word 'usually induced her to turn her head expectantly toward the speaker'. Is that performance not a ritual too? Well, I am prepared to grant that it *is* one, in a sense (though a ritual should really perhaps lack significance outside the system). However, it is so basic an orienting 'ritual' that it deserves a separate category: Att. And, if this is accepted, then I beg to be allowed a subspecies of Att, namely AttD, in which the 'ritual' response amounts to focusing one's orienting on to some entity other than the interlocutors themselves. Notice how [ʔa!] establishes a developmental relationship between Att and AttD.

What about the objection that Rit has encompassed too many items? (Problems with Att will be taken up shortly.) *Where is the baby?* and *Wo ist das Bild?* have been marked Rit. Are they not cases of AttD? Well, yes, they are; and the very similar items *Ticktack* and *Wo ist der Vogel?* have indeed been put into the AttD class. The reason for the equivocation is that I see AttD as evolving out of orienting-to-something ritual triggers, such as *Where is the baby?* Leopold calls the latter item a 'game', and that seems to me to be correct – hence the classification Rit for it – but it is a game from which there arise very numerous variations. The progeny of this game are what we call *acts of referring*, in which it no longer matters whether you physically turn to look at a particular something as long as you turn your mind to it. Greenfield (1973: 41) observes that from 0;11 her daughter no longer regularly oriented for the expressions *Baba*, *Mama* and *Dada*. It had by then become possible for the child 'to "understand" a sound pattern without necessarily turning to look at its referent'. Reading

Leopold convinces me that the physical ritual aspect had been submerged in later acquisitions such as *Ticktack* (see the quotation appended to this item in the table), and that here we have an expression used in genuine acts of referring (see Atkinson 1979; Griffiths 1979: 115–17). Somewhere between *Where is the baby?* and *Ticktack* I had to switch from Rit to AttD; the actual point chosen is pretty arbitrary and the difference signified is more a matter of degree than of kind.

Now, what about the ritual triggers *Gib mir das*, *Hoch, hoch!* and *Komm her!*? Surely these are *requests*? Again, I concede the point. They *are* requests. But they are also rituals. In fact, to make matters worse, all ritual evokers are requests of a sort. For instance, if Leopold wanted his daughter to tilt back her head and pretend to drink from whatever she had in her hand, he had only to say *Prost!*; and does that not amount to requesting? The distinction hangs on the 'sincerity condition' (see Searle 1969) to the effect that the speaker of a request must truly want the specified action carried out. Did the Leopolds truly want their daughter to perform the actions associated with the Rit items in the table? Almost certainly for some cases of *Gib mir das*, *Hoch, hoch!* and *Komm her!* the answer is Yes: compliance would make childcare that much easier. But a parent can also keenly want a child to perform an empty ritual (or to perform an otherwise useful act that is not currently necessary), just to be able to know that the child understands and is growing to be a communicating social being (Berko-Gleason and Weintraub 1978). As far as describing the communication system in table 1 goes, the distinction between Rit and request is irrelevant: it is through playing along when adults use ritual triggers that the child *ipso facto* learns how to comply with requests (M. Lewis 1963: 27f). Leopold (1939: 27) notes that near the end of her first year Hildegard often reacted to *Komm her!* 'by running away on hands and feet, with a roguish squeal, challenging people to catch her . . .'; and this is perhaps a sign of the dawning of awareness of sincerity conditions.

There is a related problem with Att. *Nein, nein!*, *Nicht in dem Mund!* and the child's disapproving (loud) [da da da] and [nenene] look like requests – requests to stop doing something. Notice, however, that human beings have only a limited amount of attention. If one can draw that attention to oneself there is a fair chance that they will not have enough left to spare for whatever they were doing up to that point. Furthermore, having got their attention one can show displeasure through facial expression or gesture, or even signal the same thing through paralinguistic modulation of the voice in the very act of uttering the attention getter. A little experience at the receiving end will enable the recipient to deduce the connection between his or her acts and the speaker's displeasure, and then read this displeasure into the attention-getting utterance itself. The change between

the 9th month *No, no!* and the 11th month *Nein, nein! / No, no!* shows that Hildegard patently made this connection. I submit a parallel explanation for the request force lurking in *pretty*: the adult on looking at the child, to see what she wanted to direct attention towards, would notice a grasping gesture or any yearning there might be in her face and would come to pin this to the word (and since Hildegard used *pretty* to point out things she liked, the yearning would often be there).

Additionally, it must be accepted that all cases of Att and AttD are just special kinds of request; the speaker uses them to request the addressee's attention *per se* or attention to something. Also, Att is a precondition for everything else: one cannot communicate that a ritual performance is desired or that attention should be directed to something until one first has addressee's attention (Atkinson 1982: 166–70).

Finally, the child's palatal clicks for summoning squirrels have not been classified because they were, at this stage, still simply part of a response to a Rit. The expression of satisfaction [da da da] and the expression [mama] have been left out as they are assumed to be 'comfort sounds' (M. Lewis 1963: ch. 1) which could inform an adult that all was well with the child, though Leopold offers no grounds for believing that these were intentionally uttered by Hildegard to convey that message. Note the second quotation attached to [mama] in the table, and observe that [da da da] was so much part of the babbling background that it could become a vehicle for a modulation (loudness) that signalled disapproval, the opposite of contentment.

Through the perhaps unconventional device of a critique of my own classificatory system, I hope by now to have persuaded the reader that verbal language first manifests itself in the use of expressions, in request-like fashion, to get the addressee to perform a 'ritual'. At first the 'ritual' is as simple as just orienting towards the speaker (Att), but this is so fundamental a basis for any other linguistic communication that the single quotes on 'ritual' are justified for it. Pointing once attention has been gained (AttD) develops into the earliest acts of referring. Display of wish or displeasure, once attention has been gained, imports true request force into the system. And, along another path, as Rits become more diversified, some of the acts evoked are genuinely useful to the child's caretakers, and again we have true requests. Bruner (1975a) and, especially well argued and illustrated, Ferrier (1978) have also claimed a foundational role for rituals.

2.2. Constraints surrounding the start

Now it is time to ask what the content of the early system tells us about how a start is made in building it. Notice that all the communications repre-

sented in table 1 (except for the two 'comfort sounds', which have been discounted) required an *act* as a response. Notice too that, particularly near the start, these response acts were highly specific (an adult who is asked *Wo ist der Vogel?* can respond in many ways other than just turning to look at the canaries). It was partly this specificity that suggested the term *ritual*. But a ritual is more than just a repeatedly performed specific act; ritual also involves fixed sequencing of acts. If I frequently turn off the kitchen light, that on its own is not a ritual, but if I frequently turn off the kitchen light after putting out the empty milk bottles and before brushing my teeth and going to bed, then we have a ritual: the ritual of turning off the light *after* ... or *before* ... What comes after or before could be other people's acts, including speech acts; the sequence of acts does not have to be performed all by one person.

The principal constraint on what can figure in the beginnings of a verbal communication system is that expressions can only come to have meaningful signalling value to the extent that addressees, adult and child alike, can *show* the speaker what meaning his or her utterance is understood as transmitting; and of course the speaker has to show that this interpretation is accepted.[1] Private meanings that a speaker might intend but which fail to evoke signs of appropriate receipt are private meanings. They cannot be presumed, by either the speaker or the observing linguist, to have any role whatever in the communication system. See M. Lewis (1963: ch. 2) and Halliday (1975: 24); Wells (1980) is a good statement of an interactional theory of language acquisition.

Even though it is often a convenient shorthand to talk of 'child language acquisition', we should not think of the child as engaged in a lonely task of acquiring a stock of meaningful adult expressions. Rather, child and adults are together building a communication system, by making their understandings known to their partners. Of course, adults have the social backing of being members of a wider speech community, while the singleton child in the early years has no society, other than family and family friends, to support his or her contributions to the shared system. Adults can also be clever: noticing that the child is about to perform part of a ritual that *could* become the displayed meaning for an expression, they can supply the expression. Anticipation is possible because the steps in a ritual are sequenced (see Snow 1977a). It is thus not surprising that the adult–child system comes to be more and more like the adult system that has currency beyond the home.

Most of the other constraints mentioned below follow from the first one. Let them be numbered and italicized:

(1) *Expressions become meaningful items in the system through adult*

and child displaying to each other how the other's expressions are understood.

For a link to be made between speaker-expression and addressee-display, representations of both expression and display must be simultaneously in the addressee's mind. (Whitehurst, Kedesdy and White 1982 found that learning of new nouns in 2 year olds was best when 'name' and thing were presented simultaneously; even a 10-second interval was detrimental.) People use their minds to control their actions and this provides the only confident route we have for guessing what is currently in another's mind. 'Actions' here includes cries and facial signals as slight as flickers of recognition, interest, pleasure and disapproval.

Therefore: (2) *Early meanings centre around actions.* See Leopold's accounts (1939: 22, 26f) of how *Where is the baby?* and *Prost!* were added to the system. Benedict (1979: 197f) and Tracy (1893: 126) offer supportive comment. Motion is attention catching; so there will be many opportunities for developing language via this path – and indeed Nelson (1974) has founded a theory on it. 'Ostensive definition' (definition by concurrent naming and pointing) is not enough: it only works when the recipient's mind is attending to what is being ostended. That attention is only shown to the speaker through actions, and the speaker has to be guided by these to avoid confusion.[2]

Vocabulary counts (usually extending into the second year; so do not be tempted to quantify table 1 for comparison) have often shown that 'nominals' (= AttD minus demonstratives) constitute more than half of the items in the list and 'action words' are rather fewer (Nelson 1973b; Benedict 1979; Rescorla 1980; Tracy 1893).[3] Does this cast doubt on constraint (2)? No. Vocabulary counts are counts of *types*, not text frequency counts of tokens. Except for names of habitual interlocutors, 'nominals', though they may dominate in the listed vocabulary, seem not to be used as often as other types of expression (Bloom 1973: 66ff; Carter 1974: 177; Tanouye 1979). Further support for the centrality of action comes from the frequent observation that words such as *up*, which have both a dynamic directional sense and a static locative one in the adult language, enter the holophrastic child's speech first in their dynamic sense, and only later come to bear the static meaning too. See Leopold's (1939) vocabulary entries for *in, off, up,* etc., Bloom's (1973: 85f, 88) observations on *more* and *up*, Ferrier (1978: 307), Griffiths and Atkinson (1978) and Gopnik (1982). Farwell (1975), however, voices doubts on this interpretation of the data.

(3) *The child's perceptual and cognitive abilities are a constraint on what meanings can enter the system,* because children cannot display an understanding of what their minds are incapable of conceiving. Piagetian theory

has it that mental representation is in terms of action during approximately the first 18 months of life (for two perspicuous expositions, see Flavell 1963 and Donaldson 1978: 129–46). Ingram (1978) and McCune-Nicolich (1981a) have demonstrated relationships between language development and stages in the development of sensorimotor intelligence. Bloom (1973) has argued that certain facets of sensorimotor development are necessary precursors for certain aspects of language acquisition (see also Brown 1973; D. Edwards 1973). If 1 year olds do think solely in terms of interiorized action, they are obviously well suited for a language curriculum that is initially action centred. However, my argument above approached the matter from a different angle: I argued that no other course could possibly lead to the construction of a shared communication system.

Keil (1979) has undertaken an ambitious attempt to investigate 'ontological knowledge', our conceptions of the basic categories of existence. Regarding most of the youngest children whom he studied, 3 and 4 year olds, Keil (1979: 109) concludes that 'all things appeared to be physical objects of two kinds: living and nonliving'. Other categories, such as functional artifacts, events and abstract objects, were not yet part of their 'theories' about the nature of existence. If Keil's conclusions are correct, then the child's 'world view' must be a powerful limitation on what can be talked about in beginning language.

(4) *The beginnings of verbal language are influenced by the communication system that antedates it ontogenetically.* Children are already able to communicate with their parents before they begin to contribute to the construction of the kind of system illustrated in table 1 (see Wells 1980 for a persuasive statement of this position). The prior communication system is one of cries and gestures signalling desires and emotions (see e.g. Bühler 1930; M. Lewis 1963; Wolff 1969; Lock 1978). This earlier system cannot but be relevant in the display of understandings. It is part of what provides the necessary redundancy to enable a display to be communicated without using the communication system that is itself under construction.[4] Carter (1974, 1979) describes how, between 12 and 16 months in the child she studied, gestures were initially obligatory parts of communications (vocalizations being optional additions), but later in the period became increasingly optional as the vocalizations stabilized phonetically. Ferrier (1978) provides similar evidence. The confusion between *Gib mir das* and *Patsch, patsch!* noted in table 1 points to the child's reliance on gesture. Observe too the importance of pleasure in *Where is the baby?*, desire in *pretty*, and displeasure in [nenene] and *Nein, nein! / No, no!* – carryovers from the meaning potential of an earlier system. The continuing importance of affect is probably shown in the well-attested phenomenon that negation is used by children to express rejection before it is used for truth value

denial (Bloom 1973; Ito 1981; Gopnik 1982). I have observed a parallel phenomenon in two children: their affirmations (*yes*, *yeah*, *OK*, etc.) were initially expressions of acceptance and compliance, only later being used to affirm the truth of propositions.

If meanings have to be displayed to become part of the system, then: (5) *Meanings that involve objects can only be established if those objects are present to be acted upon in the context.* This is in harmony with the frequently mentioned restriction of early conversations to here-and-now topics and to the, equally commonly noted, concreteness of early vocabulary.

(6) *The personalities of the child and the adults are bound to affect rate of acquisition and the relative proportions of Rits and AttDs in the system.* Meanings, I asserted, have to be displayed, and people differ in how 'demonstrative' they are (see Lieven 1978a for a convincing small-sample study). Nelson (1973b) originated this idea: 'expressive' versus 'referential' children. Della Corte, Benedict and Klein (1983) have demonstrated a relationship between mothers' speech styles – presumably in part a function of personality – and type of vocabulary acquired by their infants: 'referential' children (in effect those with higher proportions of AttDs in their vocabularies) have mothers who speak more during caretaking and provide more descriptions and fewer prescriptions.

Table 1 shows, if my classification is accepted, that uttering Rits was an exclusively adult prerogative during Hildegard's first year. Many of the Rit expressions are multiword ones, whereas AttDs are generally reduced to a single noun towards the end of the period. Children who emphasize the exchange of social pleasantries and the use of language to manipulate people (rather than overindulging in reference) have been called 'expressive'. They have also been held to be more willing to gabble a longer string of sounds – modelled on a whole adult sentence – than 'referential' children (e.g. Peters 1977). However, I argued in section 2.1 that AttDs are just a special kind of Rit. This means that a child with a vocabulary of mainly AttDs could also be 'expressive', by using these items mainly as gambits to prolong interactions with adults. On the other hand, a gabble as long as a sentence is unlikely to be understood by adults as a mere act of reference to an object. Bretherton *et al.* (1983: 311) have, in an exemplary study, come close to demonstrating this:

> while it is true that a strategy favouring the acquisition of unanalysed or partially analysed utterances may only be compatible with the expressive function (because it is hard to refer without [nominals, PG]), the reverse does not hold. In our view, the expressive function does not REQUIRE a non-nominal style.

They also caution that no child is exclusively 'referential' or 'expressive'.

(7) *The child's developing phonological abilities, in both perception and production, are a constraint on the expressions that can be used in the early communication system.* This is the only one of the constraints that I do not regard as deriving from (1). When Hildegard first succeeded in discriminating the sound of her own name, that was a major step forward. Children much younger will orient towards a voice without regard to the particular speech sounds uttered (see e.g. Bühler 1930; Valentine 1942; M. Lewis 1963). To begin to do so selectively for a particular pattern of sounds is an impressive advance: from voice = Att to *Hildegard* = Att. See again Valentine's (1942) observations on *Baba*, cited earlier in section 2. Hildegard's mother had 'repeatedly' (Leopold 1939: 22) to say *baby* in relation to the baby picture before *Where is the baby?* was incorporated into the system, and even then, *Where is daddy?* 'tended to produce the same reaction'. Quite evidently, it is difficult at first for the child to identify a particular expression in the stream of adult speech. The first clear instances of Hildegard succeeding in this without the support of a ritual situation and the full ritual incantation appeared near the end of her first year (Leopold 1939: 27f). One of the examples given is that Hildegard reacted by raising her arms when the word *gross* just happened to occur in an adult conversation (i.e. she reacted in the same way as to *Wie gross bist du?*).

As children start to develop a phonological *system* for their own speech production (as distinct from a mere set of phonologically unrelated expressions) they begin to show predilections for expressions that fit their nascent systems (Ferguson and Farwell 1975; Vihman 1981; Schwartz and Leonard 1982). The fact that production lags behind comprehension is perhaps partly attributable to it being hard for beginners to achieve reasonably consistent articulation of a target expression. However, there are other possible explanations available: *recognition* (all that is needed for comprehension) is an easier mental process than *recall* (needed for production); parents are more astute teachers than children. See Huttenlocher (1974: 364–7) and Thomson and Chapman (1977) for discussion of possibilities in this area.

3. Nominals from the latter part of the holophrase period onwards

It might seem bizarre to classify the presyntactic child's words into parts of speech (nouns, verbs, adjectives, etc.). After all, the child's utterances lack the overt distinguishing characteristics for such a classification: there is no inflectional marking, there are no accompanying grammatical function words and, before the child makes sentences, word order is not available

as a criterion (see Leopold 1939: 166ff; Bloom 1973: 112). However, although the parts of speech in an adult language are tied up with syntax, they are to some extent also founded in semantics (Lyons 1966b, 1977: ch. 11); and my distinction between Rit and AttD can be viewed as a claim that the outline of a semantic basis for the distinction between verbs and nominals is already present in the data of table 1. More importantly, the adult parties to early child–adult communication systems already speak a language with syntactically relevant parts of speech categories, and many of the expressions in the adult–child system are based on adult words. This must influence adult interpretations of what the child says; and adult interpretations (as displayed to the child) are, I argued above (2.2), an important factor in the creation of the child–adult system. The child's expressions are thus being inexorably sorted into syntactically-relevant semantic categories: entities versus actions, processes and events versus relations versus qualities. Most investigators would accept that there is, towards the end of the holophrase period, a genuine difference between, at least, entity-denoting expressions (nominals) and the rest of the child's vocabulary. Lock (1978: 8) goes so far as to say that object naming has 'a totally separate history'. The most intensively researched class of words in this period has undoubtedly been nominals and (forced to choose for want of space) I confine myself to them in what follows. See Bloom (1973: 65–112) for a wider ranging discussion; Gentner (1978) for some suggestions on how 'relational' words might differ from nominals in child language; and Gopnik (1982) for a discussion of 'action words'.

3.1. The nature of children's mental representations for nominals

Over the past decade, the literature on children's semantic development has been dominated by rival hypotheses as to the nature of the mental representations children have for their nominals. (Even when authors have not confined their hypotheses to nominals, that has been the category from which the bulk of the evidence has come.) The available alternative hypotheses are ably discussed by Bowerman (1976), Anglin (1977: ch. 1), Atkinson (1982: ch. 3), Barrett (1982a) and Greenberg and Kuczaj (1982). In brief summary, the possibilities fall into two camps: a *criterial attributes* account and a *prototypes* account. The criterial attributes view in its strongest form holds that the child's recipe for the application of a nominal is a set of *separately necessary and jointly sufficient* (i.e. each of them must be present; and when they all are, that is enough) criteria that entities must meet for a word to be applied to them. Clark's extremely influential (1973b) contribution may be taken as the epitome of this position, supplemented

in her case with the assertion that perceptual attributes, e.g. shape and size, are the ones that figure most prominently in the beginning.[5] It is slightly simplistic, but not grossly misleading, to say that Nelson (1974) presents a theory of the criterial attributes type, at least with regard to 'functional' characteristics (what an entity does and what can be done with it). She sees 'function' as the true cement for the young child's conceptual categories. Barrett (1978) regards Nelson's theory as being of the criterial attributes kind.

Prototypes theories, deriving from ideas put forward by Rosch (e.g. 1973), hold that the child employs internal representations of 'best examples' as the basis for applying nominals. Entities are candidates for being labelled with a word if they are sufficiently similar to the stored prototype(s) for that word. Theoretical proposals that make at least some use of the notion of prototype include those advanced by Griffiths (1976), Anglin (1977), Bowerman (1978a), Greenberg and Kuczaj (1982), Barrett (1982a). They differ amongst each other in what supplementary mechanisms are invoked, and according to whether prototypes are deemed to be internalized facsimiles of experience or some kind of abstraction of a 'central tendency' from such facsimiles. See Greenberg and Kuczaj (1982) for discussion of differences.

As in other areas of child language research, a good deal of the evidence against which these theories have been tested has come from observations of disparities between the child–adult system and the adult language. One type of disparity that has attracted a good deal of attention is the kind that Clark (1973b) called 'overextension'. Table 2 provides an example of 'overextension', taken from three successive weekly taperecorded play sessions with a little girl, R.[6] The table lists all of the situations in which she was observed using the word *shoe* spontaneously. Up to the end of the period represented in table 2, R had a cumulative production vocabulary of 41 different items attested on taperecordings or in parental questionnaire entries. From a parental questionnaire entry earlier than table 2, we know of one further situation in which R chose to say *shoe*: with reference to her own shoes.

An approach to these data in the spirit of Clark (1973b) would ask what perceptual attribute (or limited number of them) is common to the doll's shoes, socks and arms, the beetle and the shoes in the pictures, the teddy bear's feet and R's own shoes. Could it be some kind of curved shape manifested by all of them? It evidently is not colour, for that varies across the objects (the doll's socks were white). Furthermore, the criterial perceptual attribute(s) must not be one (or a set) that is found in objects to which R applied any of her other 40 words. This latter point has sometimes

Table 2. *All the situations in which R spontaneously said 'shoe' on three taperecordings made over a two-week period*

1;7.4
Pointing at shoes on doll
Picking up doll's shoe
Handing doll's shoe to adult
Adult putting a shoe on doll (on three separate occasions)
Handling her teddy bear's (shoeless) feet
Putting sock on doll
Passing second arm of doll to adult (adult has just refitted doll's other arm)
1;7.11
Looking at picture of pair of red shoes (twice)
Holding up doll's shoe
Putting shoe on doll
Looking at picture of a brown beetle
1;7.18
Looking at picture of pair of red shoes
Receiving doll's sock from adult
Picking up doll's arm

not been made sufficiently explicit – see Barrett (1978, 1982a) and section 3.2 below. R was first noted to say *sock* at 1;8.8 and *feet* at 1;8.22. The Clark (1973b) account would assert that R applied *shoe* to entities over and beyond ones that adults call *shoe* because she had not yet accumulated 'the full adult set' of criterial attributes. If she was using 'curved shape' as a single necessary and sufficient criterion then she needed to add, say, 'semi-rigid sole' in order to pare away arms, socks, feet and beetles.

Looking from Nelson's (1974) point of view, one would ask what 'functional' unity there was in R's shoe category (that is absent from non-shoe situations / things). Perhaps it is that shoes for her were things that get put on to bodies. This accommodates the doll's arm, shoes and socks, and probably R's own shoes, but what about the pictured objects and the teddy bear's feet? The Nelson (1974) response would be that children abstract from their 'functionally'-unified categories some perceptual characteristics that may be used as rough guides to the possible 'functional' potential of objects. The teddy's feet and pictured beetle and shoes then perhaps exhibited one or a few perceptual attributes that R had abstracted from the put-on-to-body-able category as predictors of likely membership in that category.

For anyone's theory, some data from later parts of the holophrase period can be plausibly discounted by arguing that the child's utterance of word *X* with respect to object *Y* is not really being used by the child to mean '*Y* is a / the *X*' or to point out *Y* as 'a / the *X*'. Rather, the child is, in effect, saying '*Y* looks like an *X*' or '*Y* belongs to *X*' etc. (see Bloom

1973: 98–101; Nelson 1979; Rescorla 1980). For instance when R fingered her teddy's feet and said *shoes*, this might have been tantamount to a wish for teddy to be given shoes, or a comment that it lacked shoes, or that if only it had had shoes they would go on the feet she was touching (the more fortunate doll and its shoes had been the topic of conversation immediately before). The holophrastic child lacks the syntactic resources needed to express these distinctions; the two-word-sentence child of a little later can distinguish *want shoe* from *no shoe* from *shoe here*.

Prototypes theory will be examined soon. First notice a difference between the contents of table 2 and the forerunners of nominals in table 1. For the younger child the denotata of a word are very tightly circumscribed: *baby* initially related to a unique picture; *Ticktack* at first signified only her father's watch; *Papa* was only W. F. Leopold (at the end of Hildegard's 15th month, however, she was using *Papa* 'indiscriminately for any man in the street . . .' – Leopold 1939: 43). The generalization from ritually-restricted denoting to using a word to cover a wide range of entities is a noteworthy advance, whether it matches adult norms (as in the case of *Ticktack* coming to include the wall clock) or violates them (as with *Papa*); a point emphasized by Bowerman (1976) and Rescorla (1980: 334). So-called overextensions, for example, R's application of *shoe* to the beetle picture and the doll's arm, are interesting because they are good evidence that the child herself is making creative generalizations. Hildegard's parents might have offered the word *Ticktack* for the wall clock too: this association of expression and 'meaning' might therefore have been a separately rote-learned 'item' (see Cruttenden 1981). On the other hand, it would be incredible if R's adult interlocutors were knowingly responsible for bringing arms, socks and beetles into the ambit of *shoe*. The example from Hildegard *might* illustrate a creative generalization by the child; the examples just given for R almost certainly *must* have been.

My version of prototypes theory (Griffiths 1976) would attribute to R's mind something like videotape recordings of one or more shoe-involving episodes from her life, filed in association with a representation of the pronunciation *shoe* – the associations having been established, I now believe, in the manner proposed in section 2.2.[7] Other nominals in R's vocabulary would have had their own episodic recordings (Anglin 1977: 253n also invokes Tulving's 1972 notion of 'episodic memory' as an original basis for meanings). When R wanted a label for the beetle (or the doll's arm or socks, or indeed for a shoe), I claim that she compared what she was currently experiencing with episodes in her mental 'video' library and found that current input was closer to something in the *shoe* collection than to anything else.[8] For the beetle, the similarity was probably

visual appearance (the beetle in the picture did somewhat resemble a shiny brown shoe); for the arm, the relevant similarity was probably the action of being fitted on to a body; for the doll's socks and shoes, it was probably similarity in both appearance and action. I now turn to a rehearsal and updating of arguments presented in my thesis (Griffiths 1976) in favour of this version of prototypes theory and against criterial attributes theories.

The following lettered and italicized statements are a set of five reasonably firmly established generalizations about the development of the meanings of nominals in the holophrase period, and for about a year thereafter (up to, say, $2\frac{1}{2}$ years).

(a) *It is in practice very hard to discern what the sets of necessary and sufficient criteria are that children are using, if that is what they are doing.* Clark (1973b: 77) proposed that: 'By considering the actual categories that result from an overextension, one should be able to infer which features the child has used criterially.' Thomson and Chapman made a careful attempt to do exactly that, on data from five children, 1;8 to 2;3. They conclude (1977: 373f): 'In our data there was seldom a consistent featural basis for a child's word use ... Detailed aspects of shape appeared to be particularly important in the picture-naming tasks, but the shared perceptual feature usually varied from one instance to another.' Rescorla (1980) reports a higher level of success, but also many cases in which a tidy list of necessary and sufficient criteria cannot be found. See also Press (1974).

Major (1906: 265f) had the ingenious idea of showing his son, starting shortly after age 1;7, 'divided pictures', e.g. 'a shoe cut in two at the instep leaving the "upper" in one piece and the foot and heel in the other ...' He reports that 'The two halves of the shoe were named as "shoe" or "shoos" every time.' If, say, the perceptual attributes of a sole had been criterial, then only one half of the picture should have been identified. If there were criterial perceptual attributes, they must have been ones such as colour or texture that spread across the dividing line, but Clark (1973b: 83) found no evidence that colour is ever used criterially by young children. I leave it to readers to judge the plausibility that Major's child identified the halves of the shoe in the picture by texture alone.

In Griffiths (1976: 26f, 172–5, 191ff) I described a number of my own observations concerning sets of denotata which seem similarly irreducible to criterial attributes. There was, for instance, J, who (2;0 to 2;2) called a toy crane *boat* and called a picture of a simple wooden toy ocean liner with nothing on its decks *boat* too. His mother explained that he had taken an interest in the derricks on the deck of a boat seen while on holiday. If J's prototype for *boat* was founded on this experience, there would be no problem for a prototypes theory: the toy crane matched one aspect

of the prototype and the pictured liner matched a different aspect. Or consider J calling table salt *soap* during the same period, but also applying the word to a picture of a bar of pink soap. What common attributes could be shared by these two denotata (that are not also in things he did not call *soap*)? I cannot guess, but a prototype bar of white soap would provide a perspicuous link: the salt would be like it in colour and the pink soap would qualify by virtue of its shape. Or there is K (2;4) calling a wooden rod *penny* as he tried to push it into the money slot of a toy telephone. He had often pushed plastic pennies into this slot and *penny* was his word for these toy coins, but not only when they were going into the slot. Again, I cannot infer the criterial attributes, but if the prototype was a plastic penny entering the slot, the rod could have been related through similarity in action, and pennies in isolation via their shape. Likewise, an episodic image of a telephone, recording both its appearance and its noise, gives a straightforward account of how G, when he acquired the word *phone* (2;1), could apply it to both a picture of a telephone (which obviously did not ring) and to the noise of the telephone ringing, unseen, in the next room. These examples could be multiplied.

(b) *Cases of 'underextension' have been reported.* These are instances of a word in the adult–child system not applying to the full range of denotata for the corresponding adult word. A celebrated case is Reich's (1976) report on his son's comprehension of *shoes*, starting at age 0;8. Initially, only shoes in his mother's closet counted as *shoes* for him. He would even crawl past a pair of his mother's shoes placed near him on the floor, when responding to *Where's the shoes?* Reich (1976) and Anglin (1977: ch. 4) have both pointed out that 'underextension' is less likely to be observed in spontaneous conversation than is 'overextension'; 'underextension' does not overtly violate adult norms and may pass unnoticed. Anglin (1977: ch. 4) investigated the matter experimentally and found 'underextension' to be perhaps even more prevalent than 'overextension' (the youngest children in his sample were $2\frac{1}{2}$ year olds). Stross (1973: 124) reports a $2\frac{1}{2}$-year-old Tzeltal child who could correctly name the species of a particular tree growing next to her home but could not give this name for other trees of the same species growing elsewhere.

(c) In fact, *the characteristic early path is for nominals to be 'underextended' first and only later to apply to a wider range of entities* (perhaps then going as far as 'overextension'). See Anglin (1977: 260) and Cruttenden (1981). Clark (1973b: 78) herself dates the first appearance of 'overextension' to about 1;1. Snyder, Bates and Bretherton (1981) suggest approximately the same age for the advent of 'contextual flexibility', the first signs of words not being ritually restricted to particular contexts. Rescorla's

(1980) study covered the age range 1;0 to 1;6–1;8. In the 7th and 6th months before the six children in this study individually reached cumulative vocabulary totals of 75 (i.e. about 1;0 to 1;2) only one-tenth of their words were 'overextended', whereas in later months the proportion was between a quarter and a third (1980: 329). Gruendel (1977: 1575) observed that the two children whom she followed through the second year of life 'showed many instances of first naming a specific object, for example, one ball, and then extending the word to reference many representations of the object, as in the class of balls'. (Gruendel also reports contrary cases of a narrowing down of denotational range, but speaks here of 'several instances' rather than 'many'; and it is possible that her recording schedules caused her to miss earlier 'underextended' phases for these words too.) See also Rescorla (1981: 229).

(d) *'Overextension' is relatively infrequent and happens mainly in production rather than in comprehension.* Rescorla (1980: 325) found that only 33 per cent of 445 vocabulary items from six children, 1;0 to 1;8, were ever 'overextended', even once. Griffiths (1976: 167–71) also noted that very many words of the three children in that investigation were never 'overextended' and, furthermore, that even for words that were sometimes 'overextended' this usually occurred infrequently. For example, up to 2;6, G had been recorded using the word *car* 240 times, but in only 5 of these instances did he apply the word to something adults would not regard as a car (a toy bus, a toy train, and pictures of a tricycle, a boat and a lorry). Gruendel (1977: 1569) found no instances whatever of 'overextension' in comprehension from her two subjects, though Mervis and Canada (1983) do report some cases. Thomson and Chapman (1977), in a detailed examination of a small number of words that five children, 1;8 to 2;3, 'overextended' in production, found a statistically reliable tendency for these same words not to be 'overextended' in comprehension. One of Rescorla's (1981) subjects 'overextended' the word *car*, in production, to a fair range of different denotata, but could correctly distinguish between the same objects in response to the words *motorcycle, bike, truck, plane, helicopter* (and *car*).

(e) *A particular 'overextension' of a nominal in production usually ceases as soon as the child's production repertoire includes what adults would deem to be a more appropriate word* (Anglin 1977: ch. 4; Barrett 1978, 1982a; Rescorla 1981 provides similar observations).

The moral from (a) was drawn in the presentation of that generalization, above. From (b) and (c) we can also conclude that a developmental version of criterial attributes theory is misguided.[9] Development of a nominal's meaning cannot usually consist in starting with one or a few criterial attri-

butes and then subsequently adding more criteria to the list: that would fail to predict 'underextension' and would falsely predict a progressive decrease in the incidence of 'overextension' during the relevant period. If we assume, instead, that children start with too specific a mental representation (see Reich 1976: 120) – a detailed prototype – then the norm for development is predicted to be what it in fact is: nominals tend to be treated initially as if they were proper nouns. Notice that this is also exactly what would be expected from the origin-in-ritual that I argued for in section 2.2.

Rarity of 'overextension' (d) also points to detailed prototypical representation rather than sparse checklists of attributes. A list of one or a few criteria would be satisfied by many different objects. Together, (c) and (d) suggest that children are cautious over straying far from what is licensed by comparison with detailed prototypes. I argued in 2.2 that child meanings need to be endorsed by display of adult acceptance. Perhaps children's caution with respect to 'overextension' is a reflection of adult reluctance to accept nonstandard overinclusiveness. Sometimes a child will know full well, as shown by comprehension, that a word is not appropriate, but will nonetheless be forced by performance exigencies to try using it in production, through inability to retrieve anything more suitable, possibly because a more suitable word is simply not yet part of the child's production repertoire. (See the end of section 2.2 for a brief discussion of possible reasons why production lags behind comprehension.) I will admit, though, that some cases of 'overextension' are possibly not ones in which the child is knowingly using 'the wrong word'. Sometimes inadequate knowledge of the world seems to be responsible. For instance, Griffiths (1976: 53) reported a child of 2;3 calling a red-roofed barn in a farmyard scene *bus*. What was visible of the barn was indeed remarkably like the top of a bus, but an adult would avoid the 'mistake' by knowing that buses are not usually found in farmyards.

If Nelson's (1974) proposals are correctly regarded as a version of criterial attributes theory, then they too are cast in doubt by the reasoning offered in this section. The fact that Anglin (1977: ch. 6) and Bowerman (1978a) have adduced copious data to show that children rely more on perceptual characteristics than on 'functional' ones seems to me less damaging to Nelson's position. After all, she holds that children will use static perceptual attributes as a clue to what an object might do or what one can do with it (its 'function'). And though she views 'function' as the final arbiter of category membership, she makes no claim about how frequently children will resort to this final arbitration. My 'videotape' prototypes allow for both static perceptual and action similarities to be brought into play; and Griffiths (1976: 191ff) did report some cases in which a common action

was apparently the link. I have no noncircular explanation for the preponderance of static perceptual characteristics among the similarities that children seem to rely upon in applying their nominals.

The relevance of generalization (e) will be taken up in section 3.2, below. Before doing so, I should like to mention two further types of observation that favour the prototypes view. First, a rigid criterial attributes position would make the set of entities denoted by a word homogeneous: all and only those entities that meet the criteria should equally well be members of the category. Rosch's prototypes theory (e.g. 1973) was founded on demonstrations that the members of a category denoted by a word are not uniform: some (those that are closer to the prototype) are 'better' members of the category than others. What Leopold reports about Hildegard's words *choo-choo* and *Auto*, during her second year, fits this aspect of prototypes theory rather well. Both words were applied not only to trains and cars but also to a fair range of other vehicles and machines, for example, she used both for wheelbarrows. However, 'Cars were never called *choo-choo*. Trains were never called *Auto*' (1949b: 133). Cars and trains were evidently close to prototypes for these two words, respectively; wheelbarrows were poor relatives hovering near the edges of the two categories.

Secondly, my version of prototypes theory makes it possible that, in comparing perceptual input with the stored prototypes, different similarities may come to the fore at different times and sometimes the input will be equally similar to the prototypes for more than one word. This should lead to vacillation in the labelling of objects, and Griffiths (1976: 54, 175–80) reported cases in which children appeared to be torn between more than one prototype. Here are two of the examples:

J (2;1), as he handled a toy elephant, said *a cow, sheep, another cow*

G (1;10) asked *What's that?* about a picture of a toy boat
Adult: *That's a boat*
G: *Eh?*
Adult: *Boat*
G: *Boat*
Adult: *Boat*
G: *Car, choo-choo*

3.2. Lexical structure

I am inclined to believe that most of what I have been discussing in the previous section concerns children's *conceptual* development rather than

their *linguistic* development. It is encyclopaedic knowledge of the world, not knowledge of *English*, that enables us to decide whether *plum* or *peach* is the applicable word when confronted with one of these fruits. All we need to know to be credited with a command of the English meanings of these two words is the 'sense relations' that they bear to other words in the general vocabulary of English (for 'sense relations' see Lyons 1977: ch. 9). Two of the relevant sense relations for *peach* and *plum* are that they are both *hyponyms* of the *superordinate* term *fruit* (and *fruit* itself stands in a *part of* relation to *plant*) and that they are members of a set of *incompatible* terms that includes *apple*, *pear*, etc. The relationship of incompatibility summarizes the fact that speakers of English, whether or not they can recognize peaches or plums on sight, know that if a fruit is a *plum* then it follows that it is not a *peach*, nor a *pear*, nor an *apple* etc. Someone who does not, at least tacitly, have knowledge of these sense relations is lacking in knowledge of English. A person who, on the other hand, is uninformed about the furriness of peach skins or the prototypical colour of plums or the comparative sizes or different tastes of these fruits cannot in these respects be judged deficient in knowledge of the English language.[10]

Vocabularies are not jumbled heaps of words rattling loose; rather, the meanings are interconnected in a mutually defining structure. A person with knowledge of sense relations, and who already has some vocabulary items in a structure, can be given more semantic knowledge through the medium of language. When J (2;2) said *hen* on seeing a picture of a parrot, his mother said *It's not a hen. It's a parrot*, and he echoed the word *parrot*. To the extent that he could understand what his mother had said, he was thereby, in effect, informed that *hen* and *parrot* stand in the relation of incompatibility.

Griffiths (1976: 182–7) offered a cursory examination of lexical structure in the nominal vocabularies of three children, up to 2;6. To a very great extent, their vocabularies of nominals appeared to be only one layer deep, superordinates being absent (see Rescorla 1981 for similar observations). This is not to say that there were no examples of words that are superordinates *in the adult language*. There were a few such, but (with one exception) they were not superordinates in the child's vocabulary. For instance, K had some nominals such as *ball* and *choo choo* for particular types of toy, but they were not hyponyms of *toys* when he began to use the latter word (2;5). *Toys* he applied only to the components of construction toys. In his vocabulary it was therefore another word on the same level as *ball* and *choo choo* and not superordinate to them. The single exception was J's word *food*. He used it, when he was approaching $2\frac{1}{2}$

years old, to label things for which he also used more specific words such as *cake* and *(ba)nana*. *Cake* and *nana* were thus, in his system, true hyponyms of *food*. This suggests that hyponymy (and the hierarchical layering of vocabulary that it introduces) is a phenomenon that enters some considerable time after the appearance of syntax.

Before hyponymy is detectable, and almost certainly in the period up to 1;6, the only sense relation in children's vocabularies appears to be *incompatibility*: 'if something is an X then it is not a Y or a Z or any of the other terms in the set of incompatibles'. (A very limited amount of *synonymy* may be present too. G, for instance, around age 2;0, seemed to use *choo choo* and *train* interchangeably.) That we are indeed dealing with a *structural* relationship between words, namely incompatibility, is strongly suggested by the fact that I found 'many examples of denotata deserting an "overextended" denotation class as soon as a separate lexeme had entered the child's vocabulary to cover them' (Griffiths 1976: 184). This observation – generalization (e) of section 3.1 – has subsequently been more firmly established by Barrett (1978, 1982a).

Why should children in the age range under consideration rely almost exclusively on the sense relation of incompatibility and not group together sets of incompatible co-hyponyms under superordinates? I want to offer the speculation that this is a consequence of what they are able to understand from among the clues about sense relationships provided by adult speech. One possible counterexplanation, that children in their second year are simply cognitively incapable of coping with categories, is ruled out by an elegant, large-scale (150 subjects) experiment conducted by Ross (1980). For a small number of categories (including food, animals and furniture) she demonstrated, using appropriate control comparisons, that 1–2 year olds, having spent some time playing with members of a given category, showed a significant preference for an object from one of the other categories, when given a choice between two objects not previously experienced. To be able to show the preference they must have had mental categories for the objects.

There are two further pointers to the existence of cognitive categories before the appearance of linguistic superordinates that label these categories. Firstly, there is the observation – part of (d) in section 3.1 – that a word 'overextended' in production may cover a set of denotata that is divided between several more specific words in comprehension. The little girl observed by Rescorla (1981) to be distinguishing in comprehension between *car, motorcycle, plane* etc. implicitly grouped these together under the 'overextended' word *car* in production. Secondly, there are the cases mentioned at the end of section 3.1 of children vacillating between proto-

types. When J said a *cow, sheep, another cow* while trying to find a label for an elephant, he was implicitly grouping *cow* and *sheep* together. One of Valentine's children (1942: 412), at age 1;9, exclaimed *tea!* after she had failed several times to pronounce *coffee* at her father's behest.

Bowerman (1978b) reports instances, in the age range 2–5 years, but predominantly towards the end of this period, of her daughters making errors involving intersubstitution within semantically related pairs of words, even when they had for some time previously been using both words of a pair correctly. Bowerman interprets these word selection errors as indications that semantic connections (i.e. structural relationships) were being established between words that had previously been semantically isolated. Bowerman's data are extremely interesting, but I prefer to treat them as symptomatic of increasing automatization of speech production, rather than as the first signs of lexical structure.

Rogers (1978) has opened up a potentially rewarding area of study: the verbal pointers to word meaning contained in parental speech. He focused on size adjectives and noted, for example, that a mother's advice to her 25-month-old child: 'Little tiny bits; not too big' offers a clue that the child could use towards learning that the sense relation of antonymy holds between *big* and *little / tiny*. To use such clues the child has to be able to understand the language in which they are presented. In their second year children certainly have some grasp of negation. Even an understanding of negative as 'rejection' should suffice for a child to infer that incompatibility holds between two words, from hearing, for instance: *No, it's not a horse. It's a cow.* On this point I differ with Gruendel (1977), who sees such communications as likely to hamper development because they repeat the 'wrong' word, *horse* in this case, that the child has proffered.

What would a child have to be able to understand to infer from parental speech that two words stand in a superordinate to hyponym relation? I do not know, but an indication may be derived from the question that Anglin (1977: ch. 2) put to children when he was trying to elicit superordinate terms. Having first requested a name for each object in a set separately, he then asked 'What are they all?' I surmise that if a child could understand, say, *They are all clothes* with respect to socks, shirt and pants that had just been separately named, then that child should be in a position to infer that *socks, shirt* and *pants* are hyponyms of *clothes*. My guess is therefore that comprehension of plural inflection (unlikely before age 2 years), and perhaps of *all*, might be preconditions for the layering of vocabulary into superordinates and hyponyms.

Ann M. Peters

1. Introduction

In the previous edition of this volume, Garman (1979) assembled an impressive array of results from work that had so far been published on early grammatical development, starting just prior to the first word combinations and including developments reported for children as old as 4;6. His account provides a useful integration of information from four, somewhat parallel, strands of development: growth in vocabulary size, the progressive differentiation of word classes (with respect to grammatical function), mean length of utterance (MLU), and emerging types of grammatical constructions. Rather than repeat Garman's synthesis, or merely extend it with such new results as have appeared in the past five years, I will refer the interested reader to Garman's chapter and take a complementary approach in this one.

I will begin, as did Garman, with the period just prior to the first word, but I will only attempt to cover early syntax, specifically productions up to several words in length. Moreover, my focus will be on how the learner approaches the problem of the acquisition of syntax, rather than on comparison of children's stages with adult norms. To this end, we will be looking at learners' strategies as well as at identifiable processes and transitions in syntactic development. Before proceeding, I must first introduce some basic themes that will underlie this approach to early syntax.

1.1. Processes and transitions

The first theme is the focus on the dynamic process of language development as opposed to static stages. On the whole, descriptions of the acquisition of syntax have tended to be organized as reports of disconnected stages. If, however, we are to understand how language *develops*, we must try to describe what sorts of *processes* are going on and how the learner is able to move from one stage to the next. This is the motivation for organizing

this presentation of early syntax in terms of transitions rather than stages, although we will have to begin by describing some aspects of the stage which is the basis for the first transition of interest to us (see also Marshall 1980 for further support for this view).

1.2. Cognition as a driving force

Although there is much debate about both the extent and the degree of modularity[1] of innate mechanisms for learning language (see Gleitman and Wanner 1982 for discussion), it is also increasingly clear that much of the evidence on the course of language acquisition is very compatible with a view of the language learner as an active, cognitively driven processor of language data. By this I mean that, although the child must be born with certain innate mechanisms for processing linguistic data (mechanisms such as ability to make certain phonetic discriminations), many of the processes that we infer the child to be using seem to be indistinguishable from those we infer for other aspects of cognitive development. These processes include: paying attention to perceptually salient stimuli (e.g. those that are frequent, loud, or occurring together with vital activities such as feeding); remembering such stimuli, making discriminatory judgements about these stimuli along a number of biologically salient dimensions (e.g. whether they are the same or different with respect to loudness, pitch, rhythmic patterning, situation of occurrence); and (cross-) classifying these stimuli according to the results of these judgements. Moreover, I see the child as actively using these innate abilities to try to make sense of linguistic stimuli in the same ways that she tries to make sense of stimuli in other cognitive domains. To some extent she is able to make *selective* use of these processes of discrimination and classification. Our observations of such selectivity allow us to account for individual differences in the course of language acquisition through variation in the application of language learning *strategies*. Finally, this view accounts for observable changes in the child's linguistic behaviour through the metaphor of the child as an active hypothesis maker: she is seen as actively looking for patterns (although at an unconscious level); making (unconscious) hypotheses about how certain bits of data are related to others; testing these patterns / hypotheses against new data as it comes in; assimilating new data that fit the hypothesized system; and, when crucial data do not fit, reorganizing the system as necessary. (See Bowerman 1982b; Braine and Hardy 1982; Newport 1982; Slobin 1982, 1985a, for other perspectives on a cognitive view.)

1.3. Item learning and system building

Before a learner can make any hypotheses about systems that could underlie the specific language forms that she has perceived, she must first learn (probably through rote memorization) a certain (critical, but so far unspecified) number of separate (i.e. unlinked) items. This is what I will call the *item learning stage*, after Cruttenden (1981), who presents evidence for the existence of such stages in the learning of phonology, morphology / syntax, and semantics. (See also Nelson 1981b for discussion of such a stage in vocabulary learning.) Once a critical number of such items has been learned, however, it seems to be in the nature of the human mind to try to discover relationships among them. Slobin (1985a) also believes that once some linguistic material has been stored it must be systematized through comparison of acquired material and through establishment of classes of linguistic material. He suggests that 'although we have no direct evidence for the basic strategies for grouping information in linguistic storage, some O[perating] P[rinciple]s can be proposed as at least minimal prerequisites'. In a broad view, salient dimensions for system building include phonological similarity, referential meaning, pragmatic function, and formal patterning (Slobin 1985a develops this theme at length). Such activity thus initiates the period of *system building*, characterized by the kinds of hypothesis making, testing and revision just discussed. Here, of course, we will be concerned with the transition from item learning to system building in the area of syntax.

1.4. The continuity problem

A longstanding controversy in the description of early syntax deals with the theoretical underpinnings of such description. Briefly stated, should children's first word combinations be described in terms of their ultimate target, i.e. in terms of adult syntax? Or should they be described in such terms as semantics, case relations, or pragmatics? The argument against using adult grammatical constructs (e.g. noun phrase, subject of sentence) as a descriptive framework is basically that much grammatical machinery is not needed, and is in fact much too powerful at the early stages, and that semantic relations or case categories fit the data much better (see Brown 1973: 74–147, for a lengthy discussion; also Ewing 1983). On the other hand, the need for the full syntactic machinery to describe *adult* speech poses the following problem for the semantics / case approach: how can we explain the shift from semantically to syntactically organized word combinations? Is there some sort of developmental discontinuity? Such

a discontinuity would demand its own explanation, and in any case no such major discontinuity has yet been observed.

Thus we seem to be caught between two kinds of implausibilities: either we have to use implausibly much descriptive machinery in order to preserve continuity of development (start out and end up with syntax), or we have to accept some sort of developmental discontinuity in order to start out with a plausible descriptive framework (see Gleitman and Wanner 1982; Hill 1983 for further discussion). There may be a way out of this dilemma, but it depends on having a finer-grained, more process-oriented account of syntactic development than any that exists to date. What I would propose is that if the child indeed periodically reorganizes the grammatical system she is building, and if there are enough small reorganizations, no sharp discontinuity will appear in the data and yet, over enough time, a major organizational shift could take place. To give an analogy, if I present you with two photographs, one of my hand palm up and one with it palm down, there is no obvious link between these positions. But, if I present you with an ordered set of pictures showing a series of intermediate stages of me turning my hand over there no longer seems to be a major discontinuity. Following this line of reasoning, it would seem to be worth experimenting with closer time sampling in language acquisition studies in order to see whether it is indeed possible to trace the details of such a series of minor reorganizations for syntactic development. Ewing (1983) presents diary data supporting this view at the earliest stages of word combination, and Hill (1983) presents a plausible model of early language production that successively reorganizes in just such a manner. Such an approach may be an important step in solving the continuity problem. Lacking such a solution, my present bias will be to look at early syntax as much as possible from the child's (rather than the adult's) perspective.

1.5. Strategies and individual differences

The present view of language acquisition is compatible with the notion that there may be different strategies for accomplishing this task, which different children may prefer to different degrees. And in fact, as more and more data on language acquisition accumulate, it is becoming increasingly clear that not all children do proceed in exactly the same manner, even when learning the same language (see Nelson 1973b; Bloom, Lightbown and Hood 1975; Ramer 1976; Peters 1977). We must therefore be wary about generalizing to all children from data collected from only a few. In this chapter 1 will refer to two important early strategies, the *bottom-up* and *top-down* approaches. In brief, when using the bottom-up approach

the learner seems to try to work with chunks that are as small as possible – often only single (usually stressed) syllables of the adult language (extracted from, and taken by observers to correspond to, whole adult words).[2] These small chunks are eventually both filled out (i.e. unstressed syllables are added) and juxtaposed to produce longer utterances. By contrast, users of the top-down approach seem to feel comfortable working with much longer chunks of language (often referred to as *formulae*) which correspond to whole words or phrases of the adult language. These longer chunks are eventually analysed into their constituents which are then combined to form new utterances. Most learners use both these approaches, although particular learners may prefer one approach to the other (see Peters 1983 for further discussion). Since different children may be working with chunks of different sizes (i.e. corresponding to adult syllables or words or phrases) I will use the term *unit* to refer to any chunk that functions as an unanalysed whole for the child. The term *word* will, in general, refer to adult language.

2. Initial item learning

The first important transition in language development is clearly the one from prespeech to speech. Since, however, we are concerned here with early combinations, our first concern will be the move from one unit to two. In order to understand this move, however, we need to take a look at the base from which it proceeds: the one-unit stage. In what ways does this period, during which learners universally seem to be limited to processing only a single unit at a time, serve as a precursor to the ability to combine units? Two of the possible ways can be related to the two strategies we have just discussed: bottom-up and top-down.

In order to pursue either of these strategies the learner must acquire a sufficient amount of material to work with, either enough small chunks (bottom-up) to begin to hypothesize some sort of classificatory system to guide early combinations, and / or enough large chunks (top-down) to perform some sort of preliminary analysis which will yield formulaic slots to be filled.

Looking from this perspective at several studies on early vocabulary development reveals several noteworthy findings. One is that quite regularly a spurt in vocabulary development occurs sometime after 10 and before 50 (productive) items have been acquired, although a small proportion of children start out rapidly and another small proportion acquire vocabulary at a more constant rate (W. Stern 1930; McCarthy 1954; Nelson 1973b;

Corrigan 1978; Benedict 1979; McShane 1979). Nelson summarizes these results as follows:

> the child usually has been speaking only a few words for a number of months (3 to 12) and within the space of a month or so – at around 17 to 20 months – accelerates the rate of acquisition of new words from a rate of around 3 or 4 per month to 30–50 per month. [But] individual differences are the rule here [since] some children spurt very early . . . and some children never spurt at all (1981b: 151–2).

Although researchers such as Nelson tend to describe this spurt in terms of the age at which it occurs, seen in terms of the shift from item learning to system building it might better be thought of in terms of the number of items that have been acquired prior to the spurt. These findings suggest that between about 15 and 40 items constitutes a critical number, in terms of having enough data to hypothesize a rudimentary system that links most of the items semantically, and in terms of allowing the learner to begin to predict new semantic configurations that ought to occur in the language. Moreover, Corrigan's data can also be interpreted to show that first word combinations begin to appear when the children are producing 20 to 30 different vocabulary items, suggesting that 15 to 40 also constitutes a critical range of units for making combinatorial predictions.

Another finding is that individual differences are already showing up in this early period. Some children do prefer to stick to short units, while others are willing to deal with longer ones as well (Nelson 1973b; Peters 1977), thus providing evidence in support of early use of both the bottom-up and top-down strategies.

3. The transition from one unit to two

The move from producing single units to producing a reliable proportion of combinations of units may be more or less rapid. In her study of seven children, Ramer (1976) found that the period needed to move from the appearance of the first combination (MLU 1.0+) to the point where at least 20 per cent of the child's productions were subject + verb + complement (MLU about 2.0) ranged from one-and-a-half to nine months. While one might suppose that a more protracted transition period would offer the observer a better window on the processes involved, Ramer's evidence suggests that her slow developers (three boys who each took more than six-and-a-half months) progressed in ways that were qualitatively somewhat different from her fast developers (four girls who each took less than four-and-a-half months). And Horgan (1976) suspects that late talkers, who

make this transition after age 2;0, may progress quite differently from early talkers, possibly because of differences in their knowledge of semantic relations and word order at the time of the shift. These findings warn us to keep the possible effects of individual differences firmly in mind as we look at this first major move into syntax.

An important distinction to be made at this point is the one between *combination* and *syntax*. It is quite possible that early multi-unit productions are not governed by any ordering constraints that we would wish to call syntactic. That is, such productions may either be unordered (e.g. *byebye Calico, Calico byebye*), or they may have fixed but non-contrasting orders (e.g. *airplane allgone, allgone juice*, where *airplane* always comes first and *juice* always comes second; Braine 1976a: 7). Therefore, until we find evidence in children's productions for contrasting order patterns (e.g. that *byebye Calico* means something different fron *Calico byebye*), we will call them *combinations* rather than *syntactic constructions*.[3]

Once a critical number of single units has been learned, there are two further prerequisites for the production of combinations and a third for syntactic (contrastive word order) productions. First, the child must develop enough productive control to plan and articulate two units in the same utterance. Second, she must have two words that she wants to express about a single situation. For fully syntactic productions she will also have to have perceived that certain kinds of relationships between ideas are regularly expressed through patterns of word order.

How syntactic are early two-unit productions? Many researchers concur that during this transition children seem to express semantic relationships quite reliably (e.g. Bloom 1973; Brown 1973; Dore *et al.* 1976; Horgan 1976; Ramer 1976; Scollon 1976; Ewing 1983). On the other hand, ordering consistencies are harder to find and even harder to justify as syntactic. For instance, variable order to express a single relationship is sometimes found (see Braine 1976a and Ewing 1983 for examples). However, such consistencies as do occur may be fortuitous in that they are noncontrastive, possibly because they are tied to particular words or situations (i.e. they are limited in scope in the sense of Braine 1976a).

3.1. Presyntactic devices

Reports on children making the transition from one to two units indicate that in general this move is not a sudden one, and that children find various ways of easing into it as they develop the necessary skills. Moreover, they seem to be able to advance somewhat independently on several different fronts, acquiring separate skills and eventually integrating them. Dore *et*

al. (1976: 26) call this a *bridging process*. We can identify three major ways in which children progress. The first is by extending a one-unit utterance by adding extra, meaningless phonological material. The second is to memorize multiword formulae and gradually find and make use of substitution points within them. The third is to juxtapose two successive single-unit utterances (each with its own intonation contour and with a detectable intervening pause), but gradually to speed up the articulation and subsume both units within the same contour. The first two of these strategies correspond to the 'fluent' mode of grammatical development proposed by Garman (1979), while the third corresponds to his 'nonfluent' mode.

3.2. Phonological extension

A way of sounding more adult-like, both through increased utterance length and through more effective use of intonation contour, is to extend a one-unit utterance by adding extra syllables. These syllables may be more or less meaningful, as indicated by the following graded list:

(1) Incorporation of a word into otherwise meaningless babble, but usually with adult-like intonation. For examples see Bloom (1970: 102), Peters (1977), Macken (1979). (A number of anecdotal examples of this phenomenon have also been reported to me by various parents of small children.)

(2) Addition of a dummy form with no clear referent, either:
     (a) A single phonetically unstable syllable, for example:
          [dæ] *bottle*, [ma] *bottle*, [te] *bottle*, [wə] *bottle*

          (Dore *et al.* 1976: 21)

          [ɪ] *ball*, [æ] *ball*, [ə] *ball*, [i] *ball*   (Ramer 1976: 54)
          [e] *baby*, [m] *baby*   (Peters 1977: 565)
          (See also Bloom 1970: 102–7; Braine 1976a: 45; Starr 1975: 704, 707.)
     (b) A phonetically stable empty form (which may be multisyllabic). For example, Bloom (1973) reports the occurrence of [widə] and Dore *et al.* (1976: 28) report [ɪdi] occurring both alone and in combination with recognizable words.

(3) Reduplication of a single word under a single intonation contour, without intending to signal plurality or recurrence (see Dore *et al.* 1976; Ramer 1976).

Extension can be seen as allowing the child to practise articulatory skills prerequisite to more sophisticated combinations without requiring her to have to process two different words in the same utterance. This strategy

persists past the two-unit stage, by which time it is reduced to the insertion of single filler syllables. In the transition from two units to more it serves as a way of signalling awareness of the need for an extra unit without having to process it fully.[4] Here are some examples:

Lois ə coming	(Bloom 1970: 75)
Mommy æ more meat	(Ibid.: 55)
hə look for it	(Ibid.: 118)
you put ə finger	(Bloom, Lightbown and Hood 1975: 12)
Mommy stand up ə chair	(Ibid.: 11)

3.3. Rote memorization and segmentation

Another way to sound more adult-like is to try to reproduce whole (unanalysed) phrases and only subsequently to segment them into words and extract structural patterns in the form of frames with fillable slots. This sort of rote memorization of phrases has been noted as a presyntactic device by Dore *et al.* (1976) and MacWhinney (1982), but they do not trace the subsequent fate of such phrases. Segmentation and pattern extraction are discussed by R. Clark (1974, 1977), Braine (1976a), and Peters (1983). (See also Wong-Fillmore 1976, 1979 for an extensive presentation of similar phenomena for second language learners.)

One way in which pattern extraction can take place is for the child to memorize a set of related expressions such as *all clean, all done, all dressed, all dry.* Braine suggests that his subject Andrew, who produced 12 such combinations with *all*, 'had registered the pattern property of *all* in first position and then preferentially registered new phrases of this pattern' but that 'since the pattern is not productive [i.e. since no novel combinations were observed] we have to assume that he also learned each combination individually' (1976a: 9). Braine calls such a pattern a *positional associative pattern.* At such time as the child realizes that a pattern such as *more* + X, which signals recurrence of X, can be abstracted from an associative collection of phrases with *more*, the pattern becomes a *positional productive* one. Evidence that such a step has been taken is the production of novel combinations such as *more car* meaning 'drive around some more' (Braine 1976a: 7). In some cases the child will produce semantically consistent, but variably ordered, combinations with a particular word (e.g. *Calico allgone, allgone juice*). In such cases she may either be combining words in random order or be dealing with competing, but oppositely ordered, patterns (e.g. X + *allgone, allgone* + X). Braine calls such instances *groping patterns*, remarking that they tend to be transient, soon being replaced with positional patterns.

At first such patterns, although 'positional' in the sense of manifesting a fixed order, seem to express semantic rather than syntactic relations. Moreover, their semantic basis tends to be quite limited in scope, in that each pattern seems to be tied to the particular constant word involved (e.g. *all* or *more*) and to express only a narrow semantic relationship. These early patterns tend to exist quite independently of each other (Braine 1976a: 58–61). Eventually, however, these limited scope patterns are combined into more general ones, e.g. *big* + X, *little* + X, *hurt* + X and *old* + X may generalize into PROPERTY + X (Braine 1976a: 33–5; Ewing 1982). (See also Hill 1983 for a computer model of early syntactic acquisition that abstracts limited scope formulae and then generalizes them.)

Rote memorization followed by pattern extraction and segmentation serves to develop several of the skills needed for syntactic productions. On the phonological front these longish phrases help develop articulatory skills for producing long strings without requiring processing of multiple units. (I am assuming that the processing of a stretch of speech as a single unanalysed unit is easier than processing the same stretch of speech as two or more units.) Semantically, they provide simple ways of expressing narrowly defined relationships such as existence, non-existence or recurrence. Presyntactically, they provide an early basis for the abstraction of word classes, e.g. all the words that can occur with *more* (Maratsos 1982). They also provide early information about word order, although there is little evidence that ordering information is being made full use of as yet.

3.4. Juxtaposition

A third way to make the most of limited productive skills is to produce two single-unit utterances that relate to a single situation.[5] A number of studies have been made of successive single-word utterances (SSWs) from different points of view. In general the criteria for one utterance as opposed to two have included the presence of but a single intonation contour and the absence of a detectable pause between the two elements (Bloom 1973: 41; Rodgon 1976: 37; Scollon 1976: 161). Branigan (1979) used spectrographic analysis to distinguish multiple-words (MW: less than 400 ms pause) from SSWs (between 400 and 1100 ms pause) from independent single-word utterances (ISW: greater than 1100 ms pause). He then found that the pitch contours and word lengths of SSWs were more like MWs than like ISWs. These findings lend support to a view of SSWs as a transitional strategy which eases the articulatory burden in the move to combination of units.

There is also evidence that SSWs and MWs are not juxtapositions of

unrelated words, but that they express a fairly well-defined set of semantic relations such as agent + action, action + location, entity + location, entity + attribute, and possessor + possessed (Brown 1973; Wells 1974; Bloom *et al.* 1975; Starr 1975; Scollon 1976). Ewing (1983) uses diary data from his son to trace the emergence of presyntactic semantic relations within the contextual support available to the child at the time that he is beginning to make such combinations. He shows how the child is able to rely on adults to make use of shared knowledge of specific contexts in interpreting his early combinations, 'obviating the need for rules of syntax for the designation of conceptual relations by means of word order' (1983: 1).

The order in which these semantic constituents are expressed seems, on the whole, to be fairly consistent right from the beginning, although there may be a short period of groping for consistent order for a particular pattern (Braine 1976a; Ramer 1976). If, however, these consistently ordered patterns are at first tied to quite specific contexts, as suggested by Ewing, then order of constituents carries no communicative burden, since it is not contrastive. Thus the child is still at a combinatorial stage, and will only move into syntax when she has generalized her patterns out of their limited contexts to the extent that constituent order does carry communicative load. Horgan, too, concludes that in Very Early Stage I (MLU less than 1.2) 'children know something about semantic relations and sometimes, but rarely, express their knowledge syntactically' (1976: 123).

3.5. Strategies and individual differences

Although reports of individual differences in language acquisition tend to give the impression of dichotomous styles (e.g. expressive versus referential, Nelson 1973b; pronominal versus nominal, Bloom *et al.* 1975; gestalt versus analytic, Peters 1977), careful reading reveals that most children are using multiple strategies as they attempt to break into the language system. A multi-strategy approach is supported by the findings of Bretherton *et al.* (1983), who investigated individual differences in the language of 30 children. They find that two strategies, roughly corresponding to a referential / nominal / bottom-up and to an expressive / pronominal / top-down approach, are also highly correlated with each other across children, 'suggesting that two acquisition strategies are developing in parallel. Only for those children who heavily emphasize one strategy can one speak of a distinctive style' (p. 293). Even so, 'many children balance both strategies, none use one to the exclusion of the other' (p. 312). They conclude: 'It may be more fruitful to pursue the relative contributions of both

strategies to language learning in individual children, rather than to attempt to characterize children's acquisition styles as either analytic or holistic' (p. 312).

4. The transition from two units to several

Before trying to account for this transition from the child's perspective, it is perhaps easier to begin from the viewpoint of emerging adult grammar, since many of the changes reported in the literature are couched in terms of notions such as subject, verb, object, noun phrase, verb phrase. In trying to link these two perspectives, we can say that whereas the child at first juxtaposes units which express functional relations, such as agent, action or object, the patterns of these juxtapositions begin to correspond with patterns of adult syntax in which grammatical roles such as subject, verb and object can be differentiated. Developments reported in the literature include (where '+' indicates juxtapositions):

(1)   At the sentence (or clause) level the number of major constituents that the child can handle grows from two (subject + verb, or verb + object) to three (subject + verb + object). For example *Adam + hit* and *Hit + ball* can now be combined into *Adam + hit + ball* (Brown 1973: 183; also Crystal, Fletcher and Garman 1976; Ramer 1976).

(2)   At the major constituent (or phrase) level constituents are also expanding (or 'unfolding', Brown 1973: 183). For example, *Hit + ball* may now be expanded to *Hit + Adam ball*. (See also Bloom 1970; Wells 1974; Crystal *et al.* 1976.) Whether or not there is as yet a hierarchical suborganization into subject + verb phrase is a moot point – see below for discussion.

(3)   At the word level, morphological markers such as *-ing, -ed,* or plural *-s* are beginning to be used in patterned ways (Brown 1973).

(4)   Bloom *et al.* (1975) and Nelson (1975) have identified two major routes to these developments. The top-down 'pronominal' route is characterized by rote-learned phrases, the appearance of adult functors as parts of pattern-frames, many utterances construable as sentences, and many pronouns (half of all nominals are expressed by pronouns according to Nelson's analysis, p. 469). The bottom-up 'nominal' route is characterized by a large vocabulary, including many names for things, many utterances that do not qualify as sentences (e.g. naming), a juxtapositional strategy with concentration on expansion of nominals (adding adjectives or possessives), and many more nouns than pronouns (only about a quarter of all nominals are

expressed by pronouns according to Nelson). While MLU is less than 2.5 their subjects seem to be following one route or the other. By the time MLU approaches 2.5, however, both types of learners have expanded their strategies so that these two approaches are no longer distinguishable.

How can we account for these changes? As the child becomes more skilful at processing two units in the same utterance, certain further developments take place that allow her to make the transition to handling more than two units. The development of the ability to produce three or more units in a single utterance involves overcoming those processing constraints (e.g. articulatory control, short-term memory limitations, lexical and semantic knowledge) which previously limited productions to only two units. Here similar kinds of bridging processes can be observed, namely phonological extension, pattern extraction, and juxtaposition. These new abilities herald two important conceptual shifts: first, the beginnings of what appears to be hierarchical organization of constituents (which is precipitated by simple expansions of the constituents of two-unit utterances); and second, the beginnings of organization and generalization of both limited scope patterns (frames) and word classes (slot fillers). These developments will take us up to utterances of several units in length. We do not have space to trace the emergence of embedding of clauses or 'transformations' such as may be involved in questions or negation.

4.1. Three problems to be solved

In order to be able to handle three or more units in a single utterance, the child must find solutions for three problems, which we will consider in turn:

(1)   How to organize three or more units in an utterance
(2)   How to handle a growing number of limited scope patterns
(3)   How to handle a growing number of word classes associated with such patterns

Finding techniques for solving these problems will move the child ahead in three major ways:

(1)   She will move toward handling constituents hierarchically rather than linearly
(2)   She will generalize patterns into fewer, more widely applicable ones
(3)   She will generalize word classes, both functionally (in terms of case roles) and grammatically (in terms of formal patterning)

Actually, only the move from linearity to hierarchy must be totally new at this stage, since both pattern and word form / class generalization can begin at the two-unit stage. Constituent structure (hierarchy) is only possible, however, when three or more units are involved. This, then, constitutes the major justification for treating this transition as separate from the previous one.

4.2. Linearity or hierarchy?

As soon as a child begins to combine three units in a single utterance, the linguist is faced with deciding whether there is internal organization within the utterance or whether the three units have merely been concatenated in linear fashion. In describing adult grammars, hierarchical devices such as immediate constituent structure analysis have been used to capture generalizations about the substitutability of constituents. The use of such devices to describe children's early combinations is more problematic – it may be an unthinking adult-oriented carryover. For the child, substitutability of constituents may develop only slowly, along with generalization of both patterns and word classes from highly specific (limited scope) to more widely applicable.

Hill (1983) found in her data from 2-year-old Claire a purely linear mechanism which allowed Claire to produce four- and then three-word strings. Hill calls this mechanism 'concatenate and collapse'. Here are two sets of consecutive utterances by Claire, where she first concatenates two two-word expressions and then collapses them into a three-word utterance:[6]

>   more one daddy one
>   more daddy one   (p. 124)
>
>   another bear mommy bear
>   another mommy bear   (pp. 124–5)

Hill points out that Claire's *another mommy bear* refers to 'another bear which was also a mommy bear', but that to an adult this phrase 'means that there are at least two bears who are mommies' (p. 25). In other words, the adult's structure is hierarchical whereas the child's is linear:

Claire	Adult
another mommy bear	another mommy bear

This implies that evidence for the kind of organization the child is using might sometimes be gleanable from the kinds of contexts in which the

structures are used. Hill further suggests (p. 25) that 'presumably at some point the child will discover the discrepancy between his meaning and the adult meaning. Accommodating to this discrepancy could conceivably serve as a trigger for reorganizing the flat grammar into a hierarchical one.'

Braine, too, has noted that what may appear to the adult-oriented linguist to be hierarchically organized structures may not in fact be so, since what appears to be organization may inhere in the semantics of the particular patterns involved, coupled with the fact that the child is learning positional patterns which do not require any higher levels of organization. Thus if the child produces *other cover down there* by combining two patterns *other* + X and X + *down there*: 'X *down there* locates the object or act indicated by the X item; since *other* X defines an object (as being other than the one at hand), it can appropriately serve as the X term of X *down there*' (Braine 1976a: 13). Although this construction does indeed appear hierarchical, is it necessarily so? At the moment I have no suggestions about how to tell precisely when hierarchy appears in a given child's linguistic system, but it is as well to be aware that it may not be *required* for the production of utterances containing three or more units. Perhaps the move from linearity to hierarchy with the addition of a third unit has been taken too much for granted by linguists. This is an area that needs much more careful exploration in order to map out just how and when it is achieved.

4.3. Generalization of limited scope formulae

According to a view of language acquisition as a cognitively driven process, when the child has collected some critical number of limited scope patterns for combining words she will begin to perceive ways of integrating them into a smaller, more manageable number of patterns. She will discover that two similar patterns can be combined into a single, more general one, and she will discover that one pattern can serve as the X term in another pattern. Ewing (1982) calls these processes *vertical* and *horizontal integration*. Vertical integration is accomplished by noticing that two limited patterns such as *big / little* + X and *hot* + X can be combined into a single pattern involving the same number of elements, but where the fixed term is generalized to a limited *class*, e.g. PROPERTY + X. This sort of integration is already possible at the two-unit stage. Horizontal integration involves the realization that or pattern can be added to another to create a longer pattern, e.g. *big / little* + X and *see* + X can be combined into *see* + *big / little* + X, or actor + action and action + object can be combined

into actor + action + object. Here we are directly involved with the move from two units to three or more.

Ewing has been able to use these notions of vertical and horizontal integration to make testable predictions about how word order in three-word utterances could develop out of specific two-word patterns. The results of his analysis then allow him to make inferences about how the children he studied actually proceeded. Ewing's model also makes predictions about cases in which word order may not develop smoothly, for example, in the combination of the formulae $a + b$ and $a + c$. Given only that she has perceived these two patterns, the child does not have enough information to decide whether they should be combined as $a + c + b$ or as $a + b + c$. In such a case one might expect to observe a short period of groping for the correct order, and Ewing does indeed find such evidence in his son Adam's diary data. For instance, Adam evolved a limited scope pattern: *up* + entity-wanted-up, as attested by utterances such as *up dirty*, *up door*, *up Daddy*. He also used the combination *up bed* when trying to get his Daddy out of bed in the morning. How then would he integrate *up bed* and *up Daddy* into a single utterance meaning 'I want Daddy to get up out of the bed'? A limited scope analysis predicts that *up* will come first, but puts no particular constraint on the relative order of *bed* and *Daddy*. As predicted by this model, Adam produced both *up bed Daddy* and *up Daddy bed*, but no productions with *up* in second or third position.

In this view then, the child is driven to try to consolidate her linguistic knowledge by integrating limited scope patterns into more general ones that give her more precision and more control in linguistic expression.

4.4. Generalization of word classes

As the child discovers more and more meaningful patterns for combining linguistic units, whether they involve specific words (frames with fillable slots) or juxtaposition of restricted classes of words, she will need to deal with a growing number of word classes. As with patterns, she will find ways of integrating and consolidating these classes into more general ones. What are the bases for establishing word classes in the first place, and then for generalizing them?

Traditionally, descriptions of adult languages have classed words distributionally, based on their grammatical roles, for example, subject, verb, object, modifier. These classes overlap, in that a given word such as *child* can play more than one (but not all) of these roles (i.e. subject or object but not verb or modifier). A second, cross-cutting, way of classifying words is by the kinds of things they can refer to; for example, nouns refer to

entities, verbs to actions, adjectives to attributes. Again the classes overlap: *dream* may be either a noun or a verb. A third method of classification is by case roles such as agent, action, goal, benefactor, etc.; again a given word can fill more than one role. Descriptions of language acquisition have been presented in terms of each of these methods of classification, tracing the development of traditional word classes (e.g. McNeill 1966b), grammatical roles (e.g. Ramer 1976), or case roles (e.g. Wells 1974).[7] (See also Brown 1973 for discussion.)

If we adopt a child-oriented view that does not assume the pre-existence of these adult categories but tries to trace their development, where does this lead us? Hill points out that the child could either begin with a single undifferentiated class of words which he progressively subdivides until an adult-like partitioning is achieved, or he could 'begin with as many word classes as he has words, having learned his initial words each as an instantiation of an individual concept', gradually grouping words into classes 'according to his own notion of the way in which words can be combined' (1983; 52). In this latter view, the child is expected to start out with an idiosyncratic set of classes since they depend on the particular expressions and combinations which he has learned; but as his knowledge about language grows his classifications will converge with the adult ones. Information about word use will be both distributional and semantic in nature. For instance, all the words that can occur with *more* can be grouped in a distributional class, but they will also share the semantic property of being the kinds of things that can recur. The fact that generalization can proceed along both these lines simultaneously probably accounts for the reasonableness of descriptions of language acquisition along either of these lines.

Maratsos (1982) notes that although semantic knowledge is a useful basis for forming word class categories at the early stages of language acquisition, it will not suffice in the long run. This is because there are some linguistic categories, such as the masculine nouns in German, that can only be described in purely formal terms. The members of such a class share no defining set of semantic or functional properties, but they do share a set of formal properties (such as being associated with the determiner *der* and the pronoun *er*). Even a category that can be fairly accurately defined in formal terms, such as the verb in English, has subcategories defined in functional terms (e.g. all verbs that take *-ed* in the past tense and $-\emptyset$ in the present, except for third person singular *-s*). In Maratsos' view, the child must be able to construct grammatical categories 'by analyzing the groups of grammatical uses or operations that groups of terms tend to take in common, thereby learning how uses in such operations predict each other' (1982: 247). He is sympathetic to the idea of a limited scope beginning for this

process although he does not have much evidence for how it proceeds at the early stages (most of his evidence is for children of 3 years and older).

The point here is that, again, the child is driven to consolidate her growing linguistic knowledge by forming increasingly general, but complexly overlapping, word classes along both semantic and distributional lines.

5. Conclusion

We have reviewed what is known about early syntax from the perspective of what it is that the child must do in order to make the kinds of developmental shifts that have been observed. This contrasts with views of the child's achievements as a series of stages that deviate in decreasing ways from the goal of adult grammar. We have traced the emergence of early word combinations out of an initial stage of item learning during which a critical number of linguistic units is memorized. Presyntactic devices serve in various ways to ease the transitions from one unit to two and from two to more. The evidence is that the child's basis for making early word combinations has a strong semantic component; how soon there is a formal syntactic basis as well is still an open question. The transition to three or more units is distinguished from the earlier one by the new possibility for developing hierarchical organization of constituents, although we do not yet know just when such hierarchies are needed or discovered by the child. Throughout this period, at least up to MLU 2.5, individual differences in preferences for particular processing strategies can make the syntactic development of one child seem quite different from that of another.

Trying to adopt a child-oriented perspective has given us some insights into the nature of the linguistic and cognitive problems that the learner must solve, and it has also pointed up how little we actually know about the *development* of syntax, i.e. what kinds of hypotheses children make about how words can be combined; what sorts of information trigger their revision; what is the balance between minor revisions and major reorganizations; and how individual preferences in mode of processing affect these developmental processes. To be more specific, we need more information in the following areas:

(1)   When do a child's multiword productions acquire hierarchical rather than linear organization? Careful experimental studies looking at evidence about reference may give some clues (Hill 1983).

(2)   Is there an identifiable discontinuous shift in the organization of word combinations from functional/semantic to formal/syntactic? One

way to try to answer this would be to produce descriptions of syntactic acquisition presented as flow charts in which one can trace the emergence and subsequent fate of particular combinatorial patterns (a model for this would be the phone trees in Ferguson and Farwell 1975.) One would expect that a few patterns would be short-lived, while others would merge into increasingly general and powerful patterns. Such dynamic descriptions would also provide a basis for looking for places where a child makes a hypothesis that turns out to need drastic revision, perhaps even triggering a fairly major reorganization of the whole system she has developed.

(3) How far-reaching are the individual differences so far attested, and what are the underlying commonalities in the development of early syntax? The coexistence of different strategies makes it impossible to posit any single well-defined path from one unit to adult syntax. And yet, there are commonalities: at the very least, all children seem to move from one unit to two to several. There probably are only a few basic, and hopefully identifiable, strategies that can be used, although the possibilities for using them in different proportions may lead to the impression of many more. Sorting these out may be a slow and painstaking process.

15. Assessing morphological development

Bruce L. Derwing and William J. Baker

1. Introduction

Traditionally, morphology or 'word-structure analysis' is divided into two broad areas: inflectional and derivational. A morphological construction normally involves the addition of some 'meaning modifying element' (such as a prefix, suffix, infix, or even a separate root) to some 'basic' root or stem element which carries the 'core' meaning of the resulting combination. The construction type (or associated process) is called inflectional if the resulting word is construed to be a mere 'paradigmatic variant' of its base (as when the suffix *-s* is added to the English noun *cat* to yield its inflected form *cats*), but derivational if the result is construed to represent an entirely 'different word' (as when the suffix *-er* is added to the English verb *teach* to yield the derived noun *teacher*), or when compounds are formed out of two or more roots (e.g. *foot + ball = football*).[1]

As it happens, the study of morphology in either of these aspects has long been under-represented in the literature, in language acquisition as in psycholinguistics generally, where attention continues to be devoted mainly to questions of (sentence) syntax and (lexical) semantics. As a consequence, though Brown presented a very long chapter on 'Grammar and the modulation of meaning' in his influential book (1973), the discussion in that chapter is notable for the relative paucity of data upon which it is based (selected findings from Brown's own longitudinal investigation of the famous triumvirate of Adam, Eve and Sarah, supplemented by the main results from Berko's classic '*wug*' study, now a quarter of a century old, and very little else). Even today, although a steady trickle of studies has recently begun to appear, the data base remains distressingly weak from the standpoint of supporting any serious claims or inspiring any dramatic new theories. Moreover, as we shall try to illustrate here, even the work that has been done in this area has generally been encumbered with an age-base bias that has seriously detracted from the tenability of a number of the resultant claims, particularly on matters concerning developmental

326

trends or stages. For this reason, after a brief survey of the major studies and findings on the acquisition of morphology, we shall here focus our main attention on the definition and resolution of this particular analytical problem.

2. Morpheme recognition

Perhaps the most ignored topic in the study of morphological development is, in the last analysis, the most fundamental one: the assessment of the child's ability to recognize morphemes or to make judgements about morphological relationships. Perhaps this avoidance stems at least in part from Bloomfield's early and very pessimistic assessment of the situation:

> One soon learns that one cannot look to the speakers [of a language] for an answer [to the question of how to analyse words], since they do not practise morphologic analysis; if one bothers them with such questions, they give inconsistent or silly answers.   (1933:209)

We must state at the outset that we now have good reason to believe that this thoroughly negative impression does not really square with the facts, and that ordinary speakers (even fairly young children) show at least some understanding of morphological structure, though the answers one gets by systematic investigation obviously do depend critically on how the questions are asked (Derwing 1976). It is nonetheless important to note that had the results turned out otherwise, and had Bloomfield's dictum proved to be correct, the consequence for (formal) linguistic analysis would have been quite devastating. For if ordinary speakers found no *sing* in *singer*, no *act* in *actor* nor *lie* in *liar*, what basis would linguists have for positing a (derivational) rule of *-er* suffixation as part of the 'grammar of English' (any more than in the case of words like *friar, choir* or *tire*)? And what chance would there be for speakers to find the plural marker *-s* in *cats* without also finding the *cat* (cf. words like *oops, copse, lax* and *Fritz*)? The learning of a morphological rule, surely, depends critically on the discovery of at least a small set of words that succumb to a common morphological analysis – and if the child fails to make such discoveries as part and parcel of his acquisition of the language, then what is the point of the linguist-analyst's making them? (In other words, if the linguist's grammar is not learned by ordinary speakers, of what scientific value is it?) Since we have no reason to believe that a language has any sort of entitative existence apart from in the minds of the speakers who learn and use it, any analysis of the language product that does not prove to reflect some aspect of the speakers' acquisition, knowledge or use of a

form is a pure descriptive artifact and of little interest. Does English therefore 'have' rules for deriving such words as *decisive* and *decision* from the 'underlying' root *decide* (à la Chomsky 1964: 90)? The answer depends critically on our success in marshalling evidence which shows that non-linguist speakers, too, have first of all managed to assay the hypothesized morphological connection between such words, and then proceeded to learn such rules.[2]

Fortunately, as already noted above and further elaborated below, we now do have (limited) evidence that children can perform a certain amount of morphological analysis and extract rules of at least some of the kinds illustrated earlier. In addition, a number of the critical variables involved have also proved to be very much in accord with the (sometimes merely implicit) suggestions of the early linguistic analysts. Specifically, in the case of morpheme recognition, for example, it was the factors of similarity in meaning and similarity in form (or sound) that were always thought to play a crucial role, as in the following account of that master stylist, Bloomfield, once again:

> No matter how refined our method, the elusive nature of meanings will always cause difficulty, especially when doubtful relations of meaning are accompanied by formal irregularities. In the series *goose, gosling, gooseberry, gander*, we shall probably agree that the first two forms are morphologically related, in the sense that the [gaz-] in *gosling* is a phonetic modification of *goose*, but the [guwz] in *gooseberry* does not fit the meaning, and, on the other hand, the formal resemblance [g-] of *goose* and *gander* is so slight that one may question whether it really puts the practical relation of meaning into linguistic form. This last difficulty appears also in the pair *duck : drake*, with their common [d . . . k]. (1933: 208)

Early experimental efforts to assess the psychological validity of morphological analysis, therefore, placed special attention on the influence of these two variables, and most especially on the question of the *limits* of variation allowed along either of these two dimensions in order for perceptions of morphological relatedness to be preserved.

The results of this early work appear in Derwing (1976) and Derwing and Baker (1977) and can be succinctly summarized here as follows:

(1) On the basis of independent judgements of semantic and phonetic similarity among selected word pairs, confident judgements of morphological relationship from a majority of adult subjects (university students) generally required a semantic similarity rating of at least 50 per cent and

a phonetic similarity rating of about 30 per cent or more. Thus, while both of these factors played a role in morpheme recognition, as expected, the semantic connection was easily the more critical of the two, and considerable 'slippage' was allowed on the phonetic dimension so long as the semantic relationships were reasonably clear (as in examples such as *lawyer–law*, *shepherd–sheep* and *wilderness–wild*).

(2) Skill at morpheme recognition was found to proceed in a rather slow but consistent way, in the sense that the morphological relationships that were the most transparent for the adult subjects also tended to be the ones most readily identified by the children (as in the examples *teacher–teach*, *quietly–quiet*, and *dirty–dirt*).[3]

(3) Evidence was also found that variables other than semantic and phonetic similarity can and do influence judgements in a morpheme recognition task, though the extent of these various influences has yet to be explored systematically. Among these contaminating variables we must at least include (a) orthographic similarity (yielding abnormally high recognition rates for such pairs as *breakfast–break* and *handkerchief–hand*); (b) educational experience, intelligence and other such subject-specific factors (including knowledge of specific word etymologies, as with *month–moon* and *Halloween–holy*); and even (c) variations in the construction types themselves (such that the judged analysability of a word appears to be influenced not merely by the transparency of the supposed root, but also by such factors as the productivity of the supposed affix added to it). Thus, while all three of the word pairs *wonderful–wonder*, *handle–hand* and *cookie–cook* rate very much the same with respect to both semantic and phonetic similarity, the first, highly productive exemplar receives a much higher set of identification scores than either of the others, in which the supposed affix is either non-productive or inappropriately used.[4] Similarly, the highly productive nominalizing suffix *-er* (as in *flier–fly*) seems to yield a greater amount of morphemic transparency than does the less productive adjectival suffix *-ous* (cf. *numerous–number*).

(4) When care is taken to control for such extraneous variables, the general findings cited in (2) above were in the main preserved over a variety of different methodological approaches (some of which have not yet been reported in print; but see Derwing and Nearey in press). And to this work can now also be added the evidence from the ingenious application of vocabulary testing and paired associate techniques by Freyd and Baron (1982), which highlights the effects of individual differences in analysing words, and underscores the limits under which most subjects operate, even as late as the eighth grade (approximate age 13–14).

3. The learning of morphological rules

The study of the child's learning of morpho(phono)logical rules has a much longer tradition than the study of morpheme recognition *per se*, though even here the quantity (and quality) of the data are far from optimum. Most accounts begin, quite rightly, with the pioneering work of Berko (1958), who demonstrated in one blow the psychological productivity of an impressive list of morphological processes. Subsequent work, therefore, has largely consisted of extending research in directions already indicated by Berko and in polishing up many details, as only so much could have been expected from any one study. One obvious gap concerned rules for derivational morphology, as only the inflectional component of Berko's study yielded anything in the way of definite conclusions (due largely, it would seem, to the rather restricted age range of her subjects, i.e. 4–7 years). After a hiatus of nearly two decades,[5] the experimental study of word-formation rules was taken up again in the mid-1970s along both these unfinished lines: (1) by extending the scope of the investigation to older (and younger) subjects, and (2) by expanding the range of derivation constructions studied to encompass the following six:

(a)   *-er* nominals, both 'agentive' (e.g. *teach* + *-er* = *teacher*) and 'instrumental' (e.g. *erase* + *-er* = *eraser*) in function
(b)   *-ly* adverbs (e.g. *slow* + *-ly* = *slowly*)
(c)   *-y* adjectives (e.g. *dirt* + *-y* = *dirty*)
(d)   the *-ie* 'affectionate-diminutive' (e.g. *dog* + *-ie* = *doggie*)
(e)   noun compounds (e.g. *bird* + *house* = *birdhouse*).[6]

Thanks to the crosslinguistic case study analysis provided by E. V. Clark (1982), we can now add to this list the 'zero derivation' category (see note 1). The results of most of this work were presented in Derwing (1976) and Derwing and Baker (1979a), and can be updated in summary fashion as follows:

(1)   Of the six derivational patterns studied in a Berko-type task, only one (the noun compound) was found to be productively employed by a substantial portion of preschool children (47% of the 15 subjects tested).
(2)   The first derivational affix to be productively mastered was the *-er* suffix, but only under the agent interpretation (63% of the 40 subjects in the 6–8 age group).
(3)   The adjectival *-y* and instrumental *-er* were next added (55% and 45%, respectively, for the 40 subjects in the 9–11 age group).

(4) Last of the derivational affixes to be used productively, for most sub-
     jects, was the adverbial -ly (79% of the 40 subjects in the 12–17 age
     group).[7]
(5) All five of the above constructions showed a steady, positive develop-
     mental trend up through the adolescent period, and all five were
     productive for the majority of both the adolescent and adult subject
     groups (with two minor qualifications for the adults which need not
     concern us here).

No doubt the most interesting (and at the time, surprising) of these
findings was the large difference in performance on the two stimulus frames
used to elicit the -er suffix, namely, the one calling for the 'agent' interpretation (roughly, 'A man who Xs is called a ____ ?') and the one calling
for an 'instrument' (meaning 'the man Xs with a ____ ?'). Was this difference
due to a real difference in the construction type (and its difficulty of acquisition), or merely to some difference in the particular stimulus frames
employed? A recent follow-up study by Clark and Hecht (1982) would
seem to have resolved at least this issue. Though virtually all of Clark
and Hecht's 48 subjects gave clear evidence of understanding both meanings
of -er in an identification (segmentation) task, the typical child acquired
the agent meaning first in production, relying on other forms (e.g. 'associative suppletives' such as scissors for cutter, or shovel for digger) for the
other meaning. Clark and Hecht's results also provide further support for
viewing the noun compound as the earliest derivational construction (of
this set)[8] to be productively mastered, as their youngest subjects created
novel compounds out of familiar elements in order to convey their first
agent and/or instrument nouns (e.g. build-man for builder, or blow-
machine for blower).

On the theoretical front, Clark and Hecht see the following three main
principles underlying these results, and all three call for some comment:

(1) a principle of semantic transparency, based on the early suggestions
     of Slobin (1973), which implies both that the child will prefer familiar
     forms to unfamiliar forms in constructing new combinations (hence
     compounds precede the innovative use of the bound suffix -er), and
     that each new form is first used with only one (consistent) meaning
     – in this case 'agent' alone, rather than both 'agent' and 'instrument'
(2) a principle of productivity, based on much the same notion of (pattern)
     frequency or 'rule strength' outlined in Derwing and Baker (1979a),
     which strongly influences the choice of which construction or meaning
     is acquired first
(3) a principle of conventionality, which essentially serves to give a name

to the still largely mysterious process by which the child eventually abandons his own innovative forms (e.g. *build-man, blow-machine,* 'Don't *broom* my mess') in favour of those forms conventionally used by other members of his speech community to convey the same intended meaning (e.g. *builder, blower,* and the verb *sweep*).[9]

A second gap long left untouched from the legacy of Berko relates to the question of what *particular* rule(s) a child learns. It is one thing to show that a child can produce and/or understand novel word forms (as Berko and her immediate successors surely did), but quite another to ascertain the specific linguistic regularity that the child was exploiting in the process. If a child were to pluralize an unfamiliar, nonsense form like *wug* as *wugs*, for example, was this because the analogy was made to some particular (whole) known word like *bug*, to a set of rhyming words (e.g. *bug, rug, mug,* etc.), to a less homogeneous but larger set of words ending in the phoneme /g/ (including words like *dog, pig, bag, frog,* etc.), or to a still larger and even more disparate set of nouns all ending in voiced, but non-sibilant, obstruents that all were pluralized in the same way? Whichever of these rules the child might have managed to induce (and still others present quite plausible options – see Derwing 1979b for details), all would yield the same response, i.e. *wugs*, and thus would be compatible with (and hence not empirically distinguished by) Berko's results. On the basis of an extended (and continuing) series of experiments, therefore, we have effectively eliminated quite a number of these alternatives as feasible candidates. (For example, we eliminated rhyme-based analogy in the face of data showing that the child – at least by the age of 4 years – not only does not require knowledge of a common rhyming word in order to pluralize a novel stem, but also treats all such (monosyllabic) nonsense stems in the same way, regardless of the vowel, so long as they all end in the same single consonant.)[10] We even appear at long last to be focusing in on a single analysis as the one that best accords with all the available data, and this is the one that treats both the vocalic (/-ɪz/) and voiced (/-z/) allomorphs as distinct in the lexicon (and *not* derived by rule), but which treats the regular voiceless (/-s/) variant as the product of a general rule of voicing assimilation, acquired quite early on.[11] This conclusion is based largely on details of the relatively late developmental pattern associated with the vocalic variant (now buttressed by the extensive longitudinal findings of Gray and Cameron 1980), together with quite clear (though still scanty) evidence which attests to the productivity of a voicing assimilation rule but which argues decidedly against any parallel rule for vowel insertion (see Baker and Derwing 1982 for a partial report). However, even if we could be more certain and unambiguous in our judgement on

this question than we in fact really are at this point, we still have no sound empirical basis whatever for jumping from the plural inflection to an analogous treatment for some of the other English inflections, such as the past tense (see S. R. Anderson 1974: 54–8; Clark and Clark 1977: 189–90, etc.). Such problems still remain as a formidable challenge for the future, from the standpoint both of methodological ingenuity and of analytical technique. (Our current efforts will hopefully shortly yield some useful information with respect to past tense formation, both regular and irregular.)

One final source of information concerning the learning of morphological rules is highlighted in the recent work of Bybee and Slobin (1982), who report on studies dealing mostly with the acquisition of *irregular* word forms. Based on their analysis of the overgeneralization patterns employed by children in producing English past-tense verb forms, Bybee and Slobin on the whole support a multistage model generally much like that proposed by MacWhinney (1978) for the acquisition of morphologically complex words, that is, starting with an unanalysed 'amalgam' and proceeding to amass sufficient lexical raw material on which to base a gradual process of rule extraction.[12] What Bybee and Slobin add to this is the suggestion that between the stage of rote memorization and the stage at which the first morphological rules appear, there is a qualitatively different, new stage in morphological development which involves the learning of what they call morphological 'schemas'. These are generalizations of a relatively 'loose' kind that provide an association or linkage between a particular phonological shape (or set of shapes) and a particular meaning (e.g. 'A past tense verb ends in *t* or *d*'), but without the stipulation of analysing a word form into its base and affix components and indicating how they interrelate. The main evidence cited for this is the widespread observation that children (and even whole languages) exhibit a persistent tendency 'to avoid adding an affix to a word or stem that already appears to contain that affix' (1982: 269). This was noted for nonsense stems as long ago as 1958 (Berko 1958: 172–3), and many times since; but the phenomenon also seems to hold for real stems, as illustrated by the unusual treatment of verbs like *beat*, *cut* and *hit*, with respect to overgeneralization errors, as compared to the other classes of irregular verbs (Bybee and Slobin 1982: 271).

To summarize so far, then, we can find the following general trends illustrated in the most recent research on morphological development:

(1)   A movement away from purely formal modes of description and argumentation in favour of decidedly empirical considerations; this is a definite 'plus' (see Anschen and Aronoff 1981: 63).

(2)   In line with (1) above, a further attempt to integrate the findings

of both naturalistic (observational) and experimental studies, as well as an attempt to validate the latter by treating the method itself as an independent variable (see Rollins 1980 and related comments below); this is also an important step, as both approaches to data collection have their own unique advantages and disadvantages (see Brown 1973: 293).

(3)   The rehabilitation of frequency as a viable, even central, factor in explaining the course of development (albeit in interaction with many other factors), after a brief period of agnosticism engendered by Brown's very pessimistic assessment : 1973: 368; see Moerk 1980, 1981 and Pinker 1981, for some of the more recent exchanges on this particular controversy).[13]

(4)   A continued, regrettable concentration on English as the almost exclusive language for experimental morphological investigation, despite its relatively meagre and unexciting morphological structure, especially as regards inflection (We make the notable exception of Berman 1981a,b, 1982; see also Dingwall and Tuniks 1973).

(5)   The continued heavy preponderance of cross-sectional over longitudinal investigation, for perfectly obvious reasons.

(6)   A virtually exclusive reliance upon age as the sole basis for grouping subjects for analysis and for assessing developmental trends.[14] Taken together with (5) above, this persistent *modus operandi* pinpoints what we consider to be the most thoroughgoing and troublesome shortcoming of the field generally, and therefore the one most in need of remedy if any notable gains in knowledge and understanding are to be expected in the near future.

4.   On quantifying the notion 'stage of language development'

There can be little doubt that the two foremost questions of all developmental linguistic work are these: how does the child's learning of his language develop and change over time – and why? From the standpoint of morphology, to be sure, this is the last and widest gap left unanswered in our heritage from Berko (who herself, despite finding significant differences between her preschool and older subjects, chose to sidestep the issue by pooling all her results in favour of a static set of generalizations about 'children'; see Berko 1958: 159, 172). As noted above, it is not what a child knows or is doing at any particular age or stage that is of most interest to researchers in this field; rather, what course of development he takes, how his strategies change as he matures, and the major steps by which he eventually arrives at his own 'adult' level of language competence.

Now how is any such course of development to be ascertained from the data provided at one single point in time from the cross-sectional study of individual subjects, no matter how varied in age? Whose data are to be pooled with whose, and on what basis, in order to draw conclusions from such data about developmental trends and the intervening levels or 'stages'? Even in longitudinal studies, in which the facts regarding developmental sequencing can at least be determined for the individual subject, on what basis are cross-subject patterns to be grouped and contrasted (that is, how many distinct developmental 'stages', if any, are there, and where do we draw the lines)? These are formidable questions, to be sure, and ones with which we are only beginning to grapple for empirically defensible answers.

It is quite true that subjects are grouped (and developmental trends assessed) on the basis of age (or school grade) categories in all of the studies cited so far here (including most of our own), but this is not, of course, because the investigators involved are unaware of the problems; rather, there has simply been no better means available. In one major study of the 'progress of development' of a linguistic rule, for example, Innes (1974) showed remarkable agreement with Berko's study, to the extent that comparisons were possible ($r = 0.96$ for comparable items and subject ages); but she also encountered vast individual differences within age categories which frustrated the attempt to tease out any kind of sensible developmental picture in terms of age. (Overall, age and performance correlated at $r = 0.414$ in this study, a significant but nonetheless rather pathetic relationship that is by no means atypical in this field.) When Innes reanalysed her results in terms of internally generated 'performance groups', however (based on overall scores for the full set of 24 nonsense stems employed), a rather neat, Guttmanian developmental pattern emerged (as reported in Derwing and Baker 1979a).[15] The actual number of grouped-subject categories still remained quite arbitrary, however, and with it the same old question of where to draw the lines between them.

We have approached this question assiduously in the intervening years, largely because we had our own quite extensive (but now yellowing) set of cross-sectional data (Derwing and Baker 1974, 1976) and no satisfactory analytical means to come to grips with it. Two key observations eventually emerged. The first, a negative, was the realization of the essential untenability of using between-subject data in order to draw within-subject conclusions, although in the past the attempt, at least, has been commonplace. We can illustrate this point with an example from Rollins (1980), a study undertaken, as noted above, to evaluate the Berko nonsense word elicitation technique in comparison with a realistic 'play' situation carried out

under as spontaneous and natural a set of circumstances as could be devised. For purposes of control, this maximally 'free' testing situation (using stuffed animals) was sandwiched in between the two more 'controlled' presentations of Berko's test (using pictures), all on a pluralization task. For our purposes here we need look only at the results for one of these subjects on the 14 items tested. This subject scored 43 per cent correct[16] (6/14) on the first Berko test, 50 per cent (7/14) on the free-play task, then 43 per cent (6/14) again on the repeat of the Berko test. Despite an apparent superficial appeal, note that in fact these percentage figures tell us virtually *nothing* about this subject's comparative performance on the three tasks. What is critically missing is any indication that the correct scores were achieved on the *same items*: if the six items scored correctly on the first task were completely disjoint from those mastered on the second, for example, there would be no positive correspondence in performance whatever! What enabled us to draw a completely different (and much more satisfac- tory) conclusion was a quite different statistic, namely, that this subject (and others like him) gave *identical responses* (whether 'correct' or 'incor- rect') to 13 of the 14 items across all three presentation modes or tasks. In short, we needed measures indicating consistency of treatment of given items across tasks, not simple, undifferentiated counts of 'number correct' within each task, in order to demonstrate that there was a consistent strategy for a given child with respect to all the tasks. And by the same token, in order to draw parallel conclusions about such things as the stems mastered (and hence possible rules learned) by individual subjects, we need more than the kind of 'per cent correct' data that Berko provides (or that anyone else typically provides in such studies) about overall *group* performance *across* stem types. Specifically, we need to know at least that the group totals provided for the stems in question do indeed involve the *same* sub- jects. Whatever analytic technique we might devise to come to grips with the 'stage' problem, therefore, must first of all take due account of each specific subject's inter-item response profile for the set of items, and this must then provide the basis for measures of between-subject similarities for the identification of common strategy groups.

Our second main consideration follows from our understanding of what the notion 'stage of language development' might be intended to entail. Judging from the way the term is used in the developmental literature generally, we have concluded that subjects are viewed as being at the same 'stage' if they are dealing with their language in the same fundamental way, whether conceived in terms of common rules, strategies, organizing principles or whatever (see Garman 1979: 179). As regards their treatment of language forms, therefore, this implies that subjects at a common stage

will group or partition these forms in a common manner, as a function of the particular rule or strategy employed. Our proposed analytical technique must therefore also take *response coincidences*, not merely responses *per se*, into account.

An analytic technique which fully satisfied our requirements was finally developed and applied to Innes' data (Baker and Derwing 1982), where it revealed a remarkably clear delineation of different subject strategy groups which could then be age-ordered to indicate a developmental trend. Examination of how such groups partitioned and treated the inventory of 24 items used in that study provided a strong empirical basis for specifying the rules being employed within each stage, and this was done quite independently of the extent to which the children did or did not honour the putative adult or 'correct' form. In other words, the analysis was carried out completely in terms of what the children actually did, and nothing else.

Briefly, the analysis began by treating a given subject's response vector as consisting of labels which indicated the category into which the child placed each item. For this study, the categories were labelled as $/$-s$/$, $/$-z$/$, $/$-ɪz$/$, Null, Duplication, or Irrelevant. The last category was defined by default for items where the subject failed to articulate the uninflected stem form correctly or otherwise produced an unclassifiable response; there were very few of these.

Next, we needed explicit information on the pattern of common treatment among the subsets of items indicated by the category labels. This was developed by considering all possible pairs of items and indicating for each pair if they were placed in the same category or not – by recording the common category label if they were, or a zero otherwise. The zero was simply a label to indicate that members of the specified pair were treated differently. There are $n(n-1)/2$ such pairs (276 pairs for 24 items) for each subject, and this 'response coincidence' vector contained all of the necessary information as to how each subject partitioned and labelled the items being tested.

Subjects could then be compared directly in terms of these coincidence vectors. A count of the number of mismatches between a given pair of subject vectors, divided by the total possible (here, 276), yields a 'distance' measure approaching zero when subjects are quite similar, or approaching 1.0 when they are quite different in their approach to the total task. When all possible pairs of subjects are so compared, this yields a 'distance' matrix for subjects, which can then be subjected to a cluster analysis (Wishart 1978) for the identification of subject groups. Four quite distinct groups were identified among Innes' subjects.

Within each of the four subject groups, a count of the number of zeros for each item pair, divided by the number of subjects (here, 94), yielded a distance measure which approached zero when most subjects within a group treated the item-pair in a similar fashion, or approached 1.0 when most did not. This procedure yielded a distance matrix for all pairs of items within each subject group which could then be subjected to a cluster analysis to display item subsets; then their associated labels provided an empirical basis for our interpretation of the rules being employed within each group. The original article should be consulted for the details and for a demonstration of how effective the technique has proved to be.

What all this means, finally, is that a statistical technique is now available (based on the full set of *response coincidences* within each subject) which is capable not only of grouping subjects into homogeneous performance groups, independent of arbitrary criteria such as age, but also of providing a reliable statistical estimate of the demarcation lines between groups. This latter point was achieved by incorporating a randomization test to determine bounds on the cluster solution to indicate clustering both more homogeneous than chance relations (to justify pooling of sets of subjects or items), and more heterogeneous (to justify separating groups). Finally, in preserving the qualitative information provided by subjects which is lost in treatments which score responses as either right (1) or wrong (0) with respect to some extrinsic, putative adult rule, our technique has the advantage of revealing the rules which the subjects themselves are employing. With such a powerful tool at our disposal, therefore, we can be nothing short of highly optimistic concerning the prospects ahead.

16. Personal pronouns

Shulamuth Chiat

1. Introduction

The acquisition of personal pronouns entails control of a range of pragmatic, semantic, syntactic and morphological distinctions. Every pronominal form represents a convergence of such distinctions. The pronoun-acquiring child must isolate each pronominal form, must establish that there are conditions under which it is appropriate to identify individuals in terms of their speech role, and must match each pronominal form isolated to the specific speech role it designates. The child must also determine the syntactic distribution of the form, and any further semantic features which it entails. This chapter will consider only certain aspects of this complex process. It will explore the route which the child takes to the set of speech role categories encoded by personal pronouns.

I shall start by looking at the semantic and pragmatic properties of pronouns which have been the basis for predictions about pronoun development and which have directed investigations into children's pronouns. I shall then turn to the kinds of evidence used to test these predictions, and the methods used to collect such evidence. The bulk of the chapter will be devoted to reporting and discussing the findings which have emerged from studies of children's pronouns. It will assess the role of the different factors investigated in pronoun development, and the inferences made about the kinds of concepts the child brings to pronoun development, and will yield some surprising conclusions about the complexity of the child's early notions of perspective.

This chapter will not be concerned with other aspects of the pronoun system, such as the emergence of case, gender and possessive distinctions (Chiat 1981), or anaphora (C. Chomsky 1969; Maratsos 1973; Lust, Loveland and Kornet 1980; Lust 1981; Solan 1981; Tyler 1983).

2. Pronouns and speech roles

We have said that pronouns designate speech roles. Speaker, addressee

and non-participant (one that is neither speaker nor addressee) are the core pronominal concepts. The role of speaker, encoded in the 1st person pronominal forms *I*, *me*, *my*, *mine*, is distinguished from the role of addressee, encoded in the 2nd person forms *you*, *your*, *yours*. Both are distinguished from the 3rd person forms *he*, *him*, *his*; *she*, *her*, *hers*; *it*, *its*, which identify non-participants and which are distinguished from each other in terms of gender or animacy. Plural pronouns encode combinations of these speech roles. The 1st person plural forms *we*, *us*, *our*, *ours* identify any combination of individuals which includes the speaker. The 3rd person plural forms *they*, *them*, *their*, *theirs* identify any combination which includes non-participants only, i.e. includes neither speaker nor addressee. There have been various analyses of these pronominal distinctions in terms of semantic features (e.g. Postal 1966; Ingram 1971) and, as we shall see, developmental studies have sometimes looked to such analyses (e.g. Huxley 1970; Waryas 1973; Deutsch and Pechmann 1978). However, the above understanding of the speech roles encoded by pronouns is adequate for present purposes. Linguistic characterizations of the pronoun system need only concern us in the context of the developmental theories which appeal to them.

Pragmatic constraints require that every reference a speaker makes is specified according to its role in the speech act. Where the referent is the speaker or addressee, or includes one of these, the reference must be pronominal. It is inappropriate for a speaker to use non-pronominal forms in reference to herself or her addressee, i.e. to use proper names or other nominal expressions such as *Mary* or *the woman who is speaking*. Nominal references to self or addressee are only used to achieve certain pragmatic effects, such as taking a non-speaker's perspective, which will be discussed below (see 5.2). References to non-participants, on the other hand, need not be pronominal. They can take the form of a fully specified NP (e.g. *John*, *the boys in the corner*) or a pronoun standing for that NP (e.g. *he*, *they*), depending on the linguistic and extralinguistic context. Thus, 3rd person references are always marked as non-speaker and non-addressee, but this does not depend on their being pronominal (see Benveniste 1966 and Bruner 1975b for further discussion of the difference between 1st and 2nd person pronouns on the one hand and 3rd person pronouns on the other).

The fact that different pronouns designate different speech roles has an effect on their distribution which has been widely noted in the child language literature. This effect is shifting reference (Clark 1978b; Deutsch and Pechmann 1978). Pronominal expressions identify particular individuals in a speech context, but the particular individuals they identify shift

according to who is speaking: *I* refers to self when I speak, but addressee when you speak. Non-pronominal referential expressions, on the other hand, are fixed in reference, identifying the same individual(s) independently of who is speaking: *Mary* and *the woman in the purple hat* have a fixed referent in a particular speech context. The shift between participants in the reference of a pronoun goes hand in hand with a shift in reference for any one participant between comprehension and production. For any one participant, *I* identifies self in production but someone else in comprehension.

It should be noted, however, that these aspects of pronoun distribution which are subsumed under the label 'shifting reference' are merely a function of the categories pronouns encode. Since pronouns encode speech roles, they must shift with a switch in speech role between participants, and hence with a switch in modality for each participant. This understanding of shifting reference is crucial in considering the child's acquisition of pronouns. If shifting reference is treated as a defining feature of pronouns, one would investigate pronoun development in terms of that feature, and predict direct effects on the child's acquisition of pronouns. But if shifting reference is understood as a by-product of the speech role function of pronouns, its effects on the child will depend on the extent and nature of the speech role categories the child has developed.

The key questions posed in studies of children's pronouns are: how do children infer the semantic and pragmatic functions of pronouns on the basis of their exposure to pronouns in context, and what pronominal concepts, i.e. what semantic and pragmatic functions, do they entertain in the process? Most studies have set out from the characteristics which we have observed in the adult pronoun system, and have sought to discover whether these have effects on the acquisition process.

3. Methods of investigation

Studies of children's pronouns have relied on two kinds of data. These have been gathered in naturalistic contexts or experimentally.

One source of information is the order in which different personal pronouns emerge in production and comprehension. Order of emergence data have served as the basis for inferences about the relative complexity of pronouns for the child, on the assumption that an earlier acquired distinction is a less complex one. These data have provided fairly detailed descriptive information about normal pronoun development. However, as we shall see, they throw little light on the kinds of pronominal concepts underlying the child's pronouns during this development.

For this latter question we must look to the other source of evidence: the systematic errors children make in the production and comprehension of pronouns. Children's pronoun errors have been informative in two ways. The absence of errors where one might expect them on the basis of theoretical analysis of the pronoun system indicates that aspects of pronouns which are linguistically complex may not be psychologically complex. This tells us something about the child's construction of pronominal concepts. The errors that the child does make are more specifically informative, for they alone allow us to infer differences between the child's and the adult's concepts, and hence to identify the kinds of concepts which the child constructs. Analysis of pronoun errors, then, goes beyond descriptive data and promises to give us some insight into how pronominal concepts emerge.

4. Order of acquisition

Semantic analysis of pronouns and their shifting reference properties have led to the prediction that children will acquire personal pronouns in the order 1st person, followed by 2nd person, followed by 3rd person (Clark 1978b; Deutsch and Pechmann 1978). How far is this prediction borne out by the data?

4.1. Naturalistic studies

Diary studies have generally found that children employ the 1st person pronoun *I/me* earlier than other personal pronouns (Huxley 1970; Clark 1978b). The 2nd person pronoun follows close on its tail. The order of emergence of the remaining pronouns is less well established: *he, she, we, they* are not clearly ordered with respect to one another. These observations from diary studies are corroborated by Brown's finding (Brown 1973) that the pronouns produced by the three Harvard children at Stage I (MLU 3.75, age about 1;6–2;0) were *I, you, it* and *my*. Brown also points out that these pronouns tended to occur in specific contexts which matched the distribution of corresponding NPs in the child's language, for example *it* tended to appear in the same position as inanimate object NPs. Similarly, Angiolillo and Goldin-Meadow (1982) note that *it* tends to occur in post-verbal position.

These findings also correspond closely to the findings produced by my own longitudinal study of eight children's pronouns (Chiat 1978). These children were observed at least once a week, in naturalistic play situations. Observation started between the ages of 2 and 3 years, and covered periods varying from 7 months to 2 years. The children were in the process of

acquiring pronouns over the period observed. In all but one case, 1st person singular (*I*, *my*, *mine*) and 3rd person inanimate (*it*) pronouns were the first to be used in significant numbers. 3rd person pronouns followed, with the gap between the emergence of these pronouns varying widely: in some cases the emergence of 2nd and 3rd person pronouns was almost simultaneous, while in others there was a discrepancy of 6 months. The one exception to these generalizations was a child who introduced 1st and 2nd person pronouns almost simultaneously, having previously used her name rather than the 1st person pronoun for self-reference.

Though it confirmed earlier observations, this study pointed up certain problems inherent in making these observations. First, it is not the case that a pronoun is absent one day and present the next. Most pronouns occur sporadically for a while, before being used frequently and consistently. It was usual, for example, for a 3rd person animate pronoun [i] to be produced sporadically months before the child started producing a range of 3rd person forms, and in greater numbers. At what point does one attribute the 3rd person pronoun to the child? A further problem is that pronouns, as unstressed elements, may be so reduced phonetically as to be imperceptible, or may be part of unanalysed phrases which the child has acquired as a whole. All the children produced forms such as [antə], [əŋə], [ɜ̃ə], expressing their intention to do something, and [əjə], [jə], [ə], expressing a request to the interlocutor. It is impossible to say whether the child intends the pronouns *I* and *you* in these cases. Does one credit the child with the pronoun whether or not it is clearly segmented? Given these problems, it is simply not possible to identify with certainty the point at which a particular pronoun is established as a separate, productively used form with a pronominal function. Naturalistic studies do not, then, give rise to a clear-cut order of emergence. This means that they cannot provide clear-cut evidence concerning the relative complexity of every pronoun against which predictions based on semantic complexity can be evaluated. One finding has, however, been borne out by various studies: that the 1st person singular forms, the 2nd person singular forms, and *it* are in advance of other pronouns. How can this finding be interpreted?

As Brown points out, the set of Stage I pronouns do not constitute a natural subclass of English pronouns. This rather undermines explanations of pronoun acquisition in terms of semantic feature complexity, which would predict a systematic order of emergence of subclasses of pronouns. In terms of any feature analysis, *it* would be most closely related to *he* and *she* in its feature make-up. All designate non-participants and can refer to the same range of non-participants, whoever is speaking. Yet the emergence of *it* coincides not with *he* and *she*, but with *I*, which has a

different feature make-up and a different pattern of shifting reference. *I* designates the speaker and therefore refers to a different individual according to who is speaking.

The fact that *he* and *she* emerge later than *it* could be due to their greater morphological, syntactic and semantic complexity. While the inanimate pronoun is invariable, the animate pronouns are idiosyncratically marked for gender and case: *it* versus *he, him, she, her*. However, this pattern of emergence could also be due to the child's preference for specifying 3rd person animate referents with non-pronominal NPs. This option is not available for 1st and 2nd person reference in adult English. We have already seen that one subject in my longitudinal study initially used her name in self-reference, and that as a result, the 1st person pronoun emerged at the same time as, rather than in advance of, the 2nd person pronoun. Clearly it is necessary to look at the child's NP system as a whole when considering pronoun acquisition. Even aspects of development which are compatible with a feature analysis could actually be due to pragmatic factors.

Given the difficulty of pinpointing the emergence of particular pronouns in spontaneous output, and the different interpretations to which even the more reliable data are susceptible, observed orders of emergence must be treated with caution. They are not sufficiently rigorous to confirm or refute specific hypotheses. They are at best suggestive. The naturalistic data currently available suggest that semantic complexity does not override other factors in determining acquisition, since the order of acquisition does not correspond to the order of complexity or the pattern of relationships in semantic analyses of pronouns. I have suggested that pragmatic factors may be involved. However, any further exploration of the factors which determine pronoun development requires more sensitive research techniques, in the form of experimental investigation or error analysis.

4.2. Experimental studies

Experiments on the production or comprehension of pronouns overcome the problem of unrepresentative sampling to which spontaneous data are liable, since they can elicit a response for every pronoun. However, other hazards arise in experimental investigations which test small children's control of fine linguistic distinctions. It is difficult to obtain reliable responses which are not experimental artifacts from children at the crucial stages of development (in the case of pronouns, around 2 years for many children). By the time the child responds reliably, the acquisition process may be well advanced, and the experiment may fail to tap it. This would explain

why appropriate usage is often evidenced earlier in spontaneous production than in experiments. It may be that experimental results say more about the experimental situation and the strategies children use in that situation than they say about the child's processing of the particular linguistic forms under investigation.

These points are illustrated by an experiment eliciting pronouns from German children. This experiment was carried out by Deutsch and Pechmann (1978) to evaluate the hypothesis that linguistic complexity accounts for order of acquisition. Fifty-five children in two age groups, 3;5–5;4 and 5;5–6;5, were tested. They were required to complete the sentence *This card belongs to* ____ by filling in the appropriate pronoun, depending on whether the card matched a card belonging to the child's doll (*me*), the experimenter's doll (*you*), a male or female doll (*him/her*), or a combination of these (*you, us, them*). The results are claimed to support most predictions made by the linguistic complexity hypothesis, since children were more successful on less complex pronouns and less successful on more complex ones. In the case of *me* and *you*, no evidence was obtained, as all the children responded to both pronouns correctly. The order of acquisition for the remaining pronouns was inclusive *us*, then exclusive *us*, then *him* and plural *you*, then *her*, then *them*. Given the ages of the subjects, it is not surprising that they had no problem with *me* and *you*. What is surprising is that they were not equally successful with other pronouns, since most 3 year olds use the full range of pronouns spontaneously. However, these findings become less surprising when we consider what 'errors' the children made. Deutsch and Pechmann comment that there were few instances of pronouns which were actually incorrect. 'Errors' mostly involved substituting for the target pronoun a demonstrative pronoun alone or a demonstrative pronoun combined with a personal pronoun; a combination of two singular pronouns; or a name alone or combined with a personal pronoun. It is not surprising, then, that 'errors' occurred only with 3rd person and plural referents, since no such substitutions are available for *me* and *you*. Moreover, these substitutions are not genuine errors. It is quite legitimate to identify individuals using a name or a combination of pronouns, and it may be that younger children prefer such forms of reference. This does not necessarily imply that the children have not yet acquired the other pronoun forms. In fact, spontaneous data from 3 year olds would suggest that they have. It is quite possible that this experiment does not reveal the order in which pronouns are acquired (one might hypothesize that most subjects will have acquired all of the pronouns), but rather, the preferences which children have in making pronominal references. This would further explain why the two age groups showed almost the same

ordering of pronouns, though the younger group did make more 'errors'. Such an experiment, then, may give us information about patterns of pronoun usage, but probably tells us less than spontaneous data about the natural process of pronoun acquisition.

An experiment on pronoun production carried out by Tanz (1980) provides further evidence that pronouns are already controlled by children in the age range investigated by Deutsch and Pechmann. The 22 subjects in the Tanz study were aged between 2;7 and 3;6. They were required to relay an indirect question, such as *Ask Tom if I have blue eyes*, from the experimenter to the question recipient. This entailed the translation of the experimenter's pronoun into the pronoun representing the same individual from the child's point of view. Clearly, this procedure involved greater pragmatic and linguistic complexity than that used by Deutsch and Pechmann, since it depended on an understanding of the instruction *ask* (see C. Chomsky 1969; Warden 1981, for the problems this may pose), the retention and processing of the embedded question, and the translation from the experimenter's perspective to the child's. Yet the children averaged only 5 per cent errors in their recorded responses. Although this error measure ignored failures to respond at all, which were frequent amongst the youngest subjects, it suggests that even children under 3 years rarely make confusions between different speakers' perspectives on each other and pronouns encoding these.

Neither of these experimental investigations has thrown much light on children's pronoun development; they merely underline the lack of pronoun confusions in young subjects and, in the case of Deutsch and Pechmann's study, the possibility that certain forms of reference are preferred for certain persons or person combinations. An investigation by Charney (1980) produced more complex findings and a more revealing analysis. Charney looked at pronoun comprehension and production in 21 subjects, aged 1;6–2;6. The children were visited twice, with a two-month interval between the visits. At each visit, they were given one of two comprehension tasks, depending on their developmental level. In one, the children were required to retrieve a cut-out which lay under a photograph of either the child, her mother, or the experimenter, following the stimulus *It's under my / your / her / picture* (addressee condition with speaker looking at child), or *Mommy / Roz, it's under my / your / her picture* (non-addressed listener condition with speaker looking at other adult). Thus the child had to understand the pronoun, from either an addressee's or non-addressee's point of view, in order to locate the cut-out. This task proved too difficult for some subjects. These subjects were therefore set a simpler task where they were always the addressee and were required to point to body parts,

objects, or pictures, or to carry out an action, following an instruction which contained one of the pronouns *my / your / her*. These comprehension data were supplemented by production data which Charney collected in a free play situation. The production data consisted of at least 500 utterances, or three hours of recording. This combination of production and comprehension data enabled Charney not only to examine order of acquisition of pronouns, but to compare order of acquisition in production and comprehension, i.e. when the child occupied different speech roles. On the basis of this comparison, inferences about the nature of children's early pronominal concepts were made.

Charney's main finding was that the order of acquisition for 1st and 2nd person pronouns differed according to the child's speech role. In each role, the child initially learned the pronoun which referred to herself, i.e. she understood *your* (referring to herself) before *my*, while she produced *my* (referring to herself) before *your*. Furthermore, 1st person pronouns were sometimes produced before being understood, and 2nd person pronouns were always understood when the child was the addressee before they were produced, and before they were understood when the child was not the addressee. In the non-addressed listener condition, there was no difference between *my* and *your*. In all conditions, *her* was the most difficult pronoun. According to Charney, the discrepancy between comprehension and production indicates that initially 1st and 2nd person pronouns are only controlled when they refer to the child as speaker or addressee, i.e. that the child starts out with what she calls 'person-in-speech-role-referring' pronouns. Charney contrasts the child's 'person-in-speech-role-referring' pronouns with the adult's 'speech-role-referring' pronouns, which label speech roles independently of who occupies them. She also contrasts them with 'person-referring' pronouns, which are confined to particular individuals and function as if they were proper names. Such usage would result in reversals of *my* and *your*, with the child producing *my* only in reference to mother, for example, and *your* only in reference to herself. Charney observed few such reversals.

The complex distribution of pronouns revealed by Charney's investigation is surely significant. But I have argued elsewhere (Chiat 1981) that it cannot be significant in quite the way Charney suggests. The first problem is her analysis of children's early production of 1st person pronouns as person-in-speech-role-referring. As Charney points out, the production of *my* without comprehension seems illogical. The children would only be able to produce *my* in self-reference if they had already understood other speakers' use of *my* as self-referring. If the child had not understood *my* as referring to other selves, what basis would she have for using it to refer

to herself? Hence, the child's correct production of *my* implies that she has understood *my* as referring to other selves, which means it is not person-in-speech-role-referring. How then can we account for the discrepancy between comprehension and production in Charney's investigation? Charney herself provides the answer. In the three cases where *my* was produced without comprehension, the children did not pass Charney's 'criterion for syntactic independence' of a pronoun, which required that *my* function as an independent linguistic unit and not only in rote phrases. It seems that at this stage the child is only producing the 1st pronoun in whole, unanalysed phrases, and has not yet segmented it. In this case the child cannot be said to have acquired the pronoun as a form separate from the context in which it occurs. She could not be expected to understand it in phrases other than the unanalysed phrases she herself produces. This explanation undermines a person-in-speech-role-referring analysis, and points to the possibility that 1st person pronouns initially emerge in unanalysed phrases which the child understands and produces as wholes. These phrases would serve as a basis for correct (adult) analysis of pronouns when the child segments them. We will return to this possibility below.

The findings that in 12 cases the 2nd person pronoun was understood though not produced, and that it was understood before the 1st person pronoun, remain to be explained. The discrepancy between production and comprehension is not surprising, since a time lag between comprehension and production in this direction (comprehension before production) is common. It is only surprising when the time lag is in the reverse direction, as was the case for the 1st person pronoun. If the above analysis is correct, it must be concluded that while children produce *my* in unanalysed phrases before they understand it as an independent form, they are less likely to produce *your* in such unanalysed phrases. This could simply reflect a pragmatic bias towards expression of events and states in which they participate. They may already control phrases containing 2nd person pronouns (such as [əjə], cited above), but happen not to employ these, at least in the pragmatic contexts in which Charney observed her subjects.

The finding that *your* was understood before *my* is the only one that does not invite an alternative explanation to Charney's. According to the sequence of development I have postulated, the child acquires *my* in unanalysed phrases, then segments these and starts to use and understand *my* productively. It is not clear why *your* should be understood before the stage when *my* becomes productive. It may be that Charney's analysis does apply in this case: that the child does initially acquire *your* as referring only to herself, i.e. as a person-in-speech-role-referring pronoun. However, if there is no reason to attribute any other person-in-speech-role-referring

pronouns to the child, it would seem odd to do so in just one case. Further investigation into the order in which *your* and *my* come to be understood may indicate that it is determined by pragmatic factors rather than by the child's pronominal concepts.

Although Charney has clearly identified an interesting set of discrepancies in the order of emergence of pronouns, they do not provide strong evidence that the child starts off with person-in-speech-role-referring pronouns. Some of the findings are more plausibly explained in terms of other aspects of development, such as the child's processing of word strings, and the lag between comprehension and production. However, not all the findings lend themselves to such explanation, and there is clearly a need for further exploration of the patterns Charney has uncovered.

4.3. Summary of order of acquisition data

We are now in a position to summarize the order of acquisition data. It seems that:

(1)   The set of personal pronouns do not emerge in a clear-cut order. Children start off with a fairly predictable subset of pronouns which do not constitute a natural class. These are 1st person singular and inanimate 3rd person singular, followed by 2nd person.
(2)   These pronouns tend to occur in specific contexts, rather than in their full adult distribution, e.g. *it* may be confined to, or most typical of, postverbal position.
(3)   The order in which the remaining pronouns emerge is not well established, and is probably not rigid or predictable.
(4)   Sporadic use of pronouns often precedes more systematic and frequent use.
(5)   Pronouns may be produced initially in stereotyped, unanalysed phrases which encode the relationships involved in events and states as a whole.
(6)   Though pronouns may be sporadic or limited in their distribution when they first emerge, confusions between different personal pronouns rarely occur.

These observations together cast doubt on certain conceptions of pronoun development and are suggestive of others. For example, they provide little evidence that the acquisition of pronouns is driven by a hierarchically ordered set of conceptual or linguistic features such as those used to define the structure of the adult pronoun system. Nor is there any clear evidence that children shift from one kind of pronominal category (person-referring

or person-in-speech-role-referring) to another (speech-role-referring). Instead, the findings suggest that pronominal concepts are initially embedded within a whole conceptual relationship, and that pronominal forms are embedded within a whole linguistic structure which encodes that conceptual relationship. The drive behind pronoun development is, then, the set of conceptual relationships which children construct and express in language: actions, events and states, in which inanimate objects may be affected, and in which they and their addressees participate. Children may acquire whole linguistic structures as expressions of these conceptual relationships, in which case pronouns emerge through a process of segmenting the pronominal form within the linguistic structure and identifying the pronominal form with the speech role embedded in the conceptual relationship.

I shall adopt this analysis of pronoun development as a tentative framework, and turn now to our second source of data, children's pronoun errors. These are less ambiguous than order of acquisition data and so allow more definitive conclusions to be drawn.

5. Errors

We have already observed that confusions between different personal pronouns are rare. This was even true in the sort of experimental paradigm employed by Deutsch and Pechmann, where 'errors' generally involved the substitution of alternative NPs rather than person confusion. Given the pragmatic, semantic and morphological complexity of the pronoun system, the rarity of errors is somewhat surprising. Any theory of children's pronoun development must explain the non-occurrence of many errors which linguists and psycholinguists might expect, as well as the particular range of errors which do occur.

Two types of error have been noted and discussed in the literature: one is the substitution of a proper name for a pronoun; the other is the reversal of 1st and 2nd person pronouns.

5.1. Pronominal use of proper names

This is the only error which has been widely observed. For example, in my cross-sectional study of pronouns in 48 children spread over the age range 2;0–4;6, eight children used proper names in self-reference (Chiat 1981). In my longitudinal study of eight subjects, six used proper names in reference to speaker (self) and four in reference to addressee (Chiat 1978). However, all these subjects employed pronouns as well as names, i.e. their 'error' was inconsistent. Sometimes names and pronouns appeared

to be used interchangeably, and occasionally even co-occurred in a single clause:

Trevor: No, wait, *Trevor*'s going to draw *my* money

In fact, names and pronouns are not fully interchangeable for the child, as might at first appear to be the case. Children who use names for pronominal roles do not make the reverse error of using pronouns where names are required, e.g. the child does not use *you* to refer to her mother when talking to a third person. Furthermore, while children understand a single pronoun as referring to different individuals according to their speech role, a name is always confined to a particular individual. These discrepancies between the distribution of names and pronouns indicate that the child has distinguished the two.

What then accounts for the child's use of names in pronominal contexts? One possibility is that adults adopt a similar usage when talking to children (Wills 1977). Durkin, Rutter and Tucker (1982), for example, cite:

I'll wipe *mummy*'s hand up
I think *mummy* might have to blow hers

Unlike many errors the child makes, this one could, then, have its origins in the input the child receives. According to Wills, and Durkin *et al.*, this adult usage is pragmatically based. Durkin *et al.* suggest that mothers use names most typically to command children's attention and direct their behaviour. It may be that children also use names and pronouns in different pragmatic contexts, either reproducing the adult functions or creating their own. We do not yet have the kind of detailed pragmatic analysis needed to distinguish between these possibilities. Certain differences between the adult and child usage of proper names are suggestive. For instance, the examples above indicate that children occasionally use *my* in anaphoric reference to a name, where adults would use *his/her*, for example:

Trevor's going to draw *his* money

On the other hand, the adult examples indicate that *I* and *mummy* can co-refer where the pronoun is not anaphoric. Until we make a systematic comparison of adult and child distributions we cannot say whether the child is constructing novel pragmatic uses or not.

Whatever the factors underlying the differential distribution of names and pronouns, the fact that the child makes this difference shows that it does not represent a misconstrual of pronoun functions. Even the child who uses names for individuals who are speakers or addressees has recognized that pronouns have the exclusive function of identifying speech roles.

In common with all the data reviewed so far, the use of names in pronominal contexts provides no evidence that the speech role function of pronouns is difficult for the child. On the contrary, the evidence that the child distinguishes between names and pronouns suggests that he is extremely sensitive to the different perspectives within the communication situation, as well as to the individual people within it.

Does the second error in pronoun usage, that of reversing pronouns, provide any counterevidence to this claim?

5.2. Pronoun reversal

The phenomenon of pronoun reversal, where the child uses a 1st person pronoun in reference to the addressee and/or a 2nd person pronoun in self-reference, has been noted and discussed in many child language studies (see Clark 1978b for references). Indeed, Clark suggests that some children may approach pronouns with the hypothesis that they are a type of name: that *I* = 'adult' and *you* = 'child'. Yet actual evidence of pronoun reversal is sparse. Group studies of children's pronouns have concluded that pronoun reversal seldom occurs (Shipley and Shipley 1969; Charney 1980). In my cross-sectional study, only a few of the 48 children reversed pronouns on any occasion, and those who did produced only a few instances. No subject provided enough examples of reversal to permit systematic analysis. My longitudinal study again included only isolated examples. Given the numbers of children observed, it can be concluded that pronoun reversal is an extremely rare phenomenon. This suggests that children have no problem with the shifting reference of pronouns, and that the 'pronoun = name' hypothesis is not a normal route into the pronoun system.

Does this imply that the few children who do reverse pronouns have taken an abnormal route, treating pronouns as proper names with fixed reference? I have argued that this is not the case, on the basis of an analysis of available data and a detailed case study (Chiat 1982). These indicated that pronouns are not like names for pronoun-reversing children, and that these children do control the shifting reference of pronouns. They also gave rise to an alternative explanation of pronoun reversal which reinforces the conception of pronoun development emerging from data we have already considered.

The key evidence for this alternative analysis is that pronoun reversal is not consistent. To my knowledge, there are *no* examples of consistent reversal in the child language literature. Amongst the diary studies, reversed pronouns are always noted to occur alongside correct usage (e.g. Cooley 1908; Jespersen 1922). Examples from my own case study illustrate the

point. Matthew, the 2½-year-old subject of this study, used 1st and 2nd person pronouns correctly:

> I'm (child) gonna ask mumum if we can have some scissors
> You (adult) walk in mine (child)

and incorrectly:

> I'll (adult) cry
> You (child) take off my (adult) shoes.

Matthew was sometimes inconsistent even within an utterance:

> I'm (child) gonna chop my (adult) hair off with these

The distribution of pronouns in production was not random, however. Matthew reversed pronouns significantly more often in reference to addressee than to speaker. In contrast to the inconsistent (sometimes correct, sometimes incorrect) distribution of pronouns observed in production, Matthew's comprehension of 1st and 2nd person pronouns was consistently correct. He scored 44/46 in a comprehension test where he was required to point to pictures, body parts, or objects, or to carry out actions, depending on the pronoun in the instruction.

The inconsistency of pronouns in production, together with the discrepancy between production and comprehension, rule out the possibility that Matthew had equated pronouns with names (i.e. that pronouns were person-referring), since names make consistent reference in production and comprehension. The non-random distribution of pronouns in production, alongside consistently correct comprehension, rule out the possibility that Matthew had neutralized the distinction between 1st and 2nd person pronouns and used them interchangeably. Hence, there is no evidence that children who make this error have problems with distinguishing speech roles from the individuals who occupy them, or with identifying pronominal forms with speech roles.

On the contrary, correct comprehension by the pronoun-reversing child suggests that the child does control the speech-role-referring function of pronouns. Inconsistent production of pronouns is compatible with this analysis if the incorrect (reversed) pronouns have a separate function from the correct (unreversed) pronouns which realize the adult speech-role-referring function. The separate function which I have attributed to reversed pronouns is one of shifting perspective: by using the pronoun which would be appropriate if the addressee were speaking, the child represents the addressee's perspective. This would be analogous to the use of names by adults and children to serve different pragmatic functions, as discussed

in section 5.1. It also finds an echo in certain adult uses of pronouns which take a 2nd or 3rd person's perspective on speech roles and which were alluded to in section 2. Examples of these are:

You're an idiot	(referring to self from 2nd person perspective)
I shouldn't blame yourself	(where the 2nd person reflexive has a 1st person antecedent, with the effect of placing the speaker in the addressee's shoes)
Simple, she says, failing miserably	(referring to self from 3rd person perspective)

If this analysis of reversed pronouns is correct, the pronoun-reversing child has not taken an abnormal route into pronouns, but has extended their function so that they not only distinguish different speech roles as they do for adults, but distinguish different perspectives on each speech role as well. The suggestion that children may find expression for functions which adult language does not realize systematically is not unknown in the child language literature. Karmiloff-Smith, in particular, has looked at the referential functions for which children create expressions (Karmiloff-Smith 1979a).

Clearly, the perspective-shifting analysis of reversed pronouns remains speculative. All that we can say with certainty is that existing explanations of pronoun development and of pronominal errors are incompatible with the data. The perspective-shifting analysis requires further elaboration and investigation. It would, for instance, imply that reversed pronouns occur only in certain contexts – where the child is identifying speech roles from another's perspective. This might be investigated by carrying out a detailed pragmatic analysis of the child's pronoun distribution, or by designing judgement or comprehension tasks involving pragmatic variables. The pronoun-reversing child, rare as she may be, is surely one of the most valuable sources of information about this area of development.

6. Conclusion

This survey of children's comprehension and production of pronouns permits at least one firm conclusion. The complexity of personal pronoun distinctions resides more in the head of the psycholinguist than in the head of the child. None of the investigations into the order in which children acquire pronouns or the errors which they make in the process of acquisition have thrown up any evidence that children confuse different persons with

each other or confuse pronominal categories with non-pronominal categories – in other words, that children have any problem with the speech role function of pronouns. Children may initially acquire particular pronouns in a particular subset of contexts or phrases, but this does not imply that they have acquired pronouns with non-adult functions. They may use names where pronouns are obligatory in standard adult English, but the distinct distribution of names and pronouns indicates that the child has not equated person-referring expressions with speech-role-referring expressions. Even children who reverse 1st and 2nd person pronouns give clear evidence of controlling the speech role function of pronouns through their correct comprehension and the inconsistent pattern of their production. One must assume that speech roles constitute such salient categories for the normal child, presumably before the child even begins to use language, that the child expects to find linguistic encoding of these categories and readily identifies them with pronominal forms as she meets these or segments them from whole phrases. If it turns out that the child's use of names and reversed pronouns has specific pragmatic functions, expressing different perspectives on individuals in speech roles, the child's conceptualization of perspective must be even more complex than that which can be expressed systematically in adult language.

Given that the speech role functions of pronouns are entailed by any intentional use of language – since every utterance implies a speaker and an addressee – perhaps it is not surprising that children, whose earliest use of language is intentional, already control the speech roles that implies. Perhaps children's pronoun development is not such a mystery after all. What remains more of a mystery is the child's prelinguistic construction of roles and perspectives which makes pronouns so accessible.

17. Tense and aspect*

Richard M. Weist

1. Temporal systems

The concepts of tense and aspect in child language will be analysed with reference to the development of four temporal systems. The temporal systems of child language will be conceptualized within the framework of Reichenbach's (1947) theory (see Smith 1978; Comrie 1981a, 1985) which has already been skilfully applied to child language by C. S. Smith (1980). Accordingly, three temporal concepts are necessary: speech time (ST) – the time interval of the speech act; event time (ET) – the time relative to ST which is established for a specific situation; and reference time (RT) – the temporal context which is identified. These temporal concepts have the following relationships: simultaneous ($=$), prior to ($\leftarrow$), and subsequent to ($\rightarrow$):

(1)	Hildegard is reading now	(ST = RT = ET)
(2)	Zhenya voted yesterday	(RT = ET ← ST)
(3)	Seppo will lose the race after sunset	(ET → RT → ST)

Sentences (1)–(3) demonstrate three of the many possible configurations of temporal concepts that fluent speakers can express. In sentence (1), the adverb *now* establishes RT at ST and the present tense indicates that ET is simultaneous with ST. The adverb *yesterday* and the past tense of sentence (2) locate RT and ET prior to ST. The adverb *yesterday* specifies the domain (or context) of past time within which the event under consideration occurs. Just as tense has a deictic function relating ET to ST, some time expressions such as *tomorrow* or *yesterday* also have a deictic function relating RT to ST. Prepositions such as *before* and *after* provide an additional relationship between ET and RT. In sentence (3), RT is specified as *sunset*, the preposition *after* places ET subsequent to RT and the future tense establishes both ET and RT subsequent to ST.

It is proposed that children progress through a sequence of four temporal

356

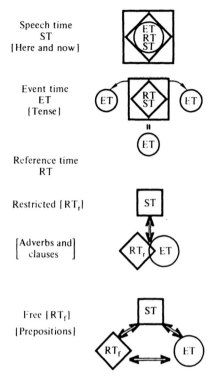

Figure 1. The evolution of temporal concepts and temporal configurations within the proposed systems of child language

systems during the development of the capacity to express increasingly complex configurations of temporal concepts as shown in figure 1. The initial temporal system, called the speech time system, is a (here-and-) now system in which ET and RT are frozen at ST. The second system (or event time system) is characterized by the child's capacity to represent ET prior to and subsequent to, as well as simultaneous with, ST. Smith (1980) has argued convincingly that RT remains frozen at ST during this phase of development. The concept of RT emerges in the child's third temporal system, but this initial reference time system is restricted. When RT is established prior to or subsequent to ST, ET is restricted to the RT context. Finally, ST, ET, and RT can represent three different points in time and can be related freely. The fourth system will be identified as the free reference time system. The symbol ⇔ in figure 1 indicates that all relations (←, →, and =) are available to the child.

1.1. Aspect versus tense

While tense is a relational concept which establishes a relationship between ET and ST, aspect concerns the temporal (or dynamic) properties of situations such as completion, repetition and duration (Comrie 1976). A language is tensed and/or has aspect if these concepts are coded by the inflectional morphology (Majewicz 1982); for example, Mandarin has aspect but not tense and Modern Hebrew has tense but not aspect. Considering the dimension of completion, for example, a situation can begin, continue, end, and produce a result. Languages like Spanish and English have a progressive aspect which identifies the continuative component, and languages like Polish and Serbo-Croatian have a perfective aspect which specifies that a situation is complete (i.e. it has a beginning, continuation and end). The child's understanding of aspect is important in and of itself, but it also has an integral role in the development of the overall temporal system.

2. The speech time system

The initial phase of language development has aptly been described as 'overwhelmingly about the here-and-now, you-and-I, and visible objects in the immediate perceptual field' (Givón 1979: 291), and has been further characterized as having '... no tense, aspect, mood, number or the like' (Brown 1973: 139). During this early period (about 1;0 to 1;6), children make a pragmatic distinction between statements and requests. While acquiring English, at 1;1 Greenfield and Smith's (1976) informant Nicky referred to his mother as *Do(t)* and used the word *mama* in conjunction with reaching and whining behaviours to request desired objects. When two verb forms are involved, children often use an imperative form to obtain action from the listener and an indicative or infinitive form to comment on actions. Typical of children learning Polish, Zarębina's (1965) daughter Hania expressed demands and desires with an imperative form (the 2nd person singular) of verbs at 1;0: e.g. [eś] *weź* 'take' and [uć] or [oć] *chodź* 'come on'; and used an indicative form (the 3rd singular nonpast imperfective) to make statements at 1;3: e.g. [gʰa], *gra* 'plays', and [pχa] *pcha* 'pushes'. At this stage in the acquisition process these are clearly frozen forms, i.e. single unanalysed units, which children do not contrast. Thus, a Polish child is likely to use the perfective imperative form (*daj*) of the verb *dać* 'to give' when demanding something, but at the same time the child will not use other forms such as the nonpast imperfective indicative form *daje* to make a statement. According to Berman

(1985b), children learning Hebrew typically use the imperative form of verbs when they want something done for them and they sometimes use the infinitive form of other verbs when they want to do something themselves. In Japanese, the initial verb forms are the imperative and either the nonpast -ru (Okubo's daughter at 1;6; see Clancy 1985) or the past -ta (Rispoli's 1981 informant Hiroki at 1;6). Hence, the indicative form may even be a past form but it is not used contrastively with other indicative forms such as a present form. Hence child language can still properly be described as tenseless at this phase of development. Erbaugh (1982) has found that child Mandarin is not marked for aspect during the initial phase of development. Hence, Brown's (1973) description of the initial here-and-now phase of child language is confirmed.

While it may be correct to describe early child language as 'overwhelmingly about the here-and-now' it is not *exclusively* about the child's current perceptual environment. At 1;5 Sachs' (1983) daughter Naomi (like other children) began to request objects which were not part of the immediate perceptual field. This observation provides linguistic evidence that Naomi has already achieved object permanence, in that she can now talk about (as well as think about) absent objects. However, this type of utterance, which expanded into a *where + absent objects* construction at 1;8, is tied to the here-and-now, since it expresses the child's speech time wish or desire.

3. Transition from the speech time to the event time temporal system

3.1. The defective tense hypothesis

In languages which mark tense distinctions overtly in the morphology, the simplest hypothesis would be that children can represent a deictic relationship between ET and ST when they can use the tense morphology of their language productively. This simple hypothesis has been challenged by a number of investigators and I have called their alternative hypothesis 'the defective tense hypothesis' (Weist et al. 1984). According to the defective tense hypothesis, the initial tense morphology does not perform its normal deictic function. Instead of coding a deictic relationship, the past tense form codes the aspectual relationship of completion and the future tense form codes intentions. While there were, and still are, a number of advocates (e.g. Bronckart and Sinclair 1973; Aksu 1978; Bloom, Lifter and Hafitz 1980, etc.), Antinucci and Miller (1976) were responsible for the most influential version of the argument. The defective tense hypothesis is particularly interesting because of its potential relevance for the general

course of conceptual development (see figure 2, discussed in section 7). According to Antinucci and Miller, until about 2;6 children use past tense only when prior situations involve a change of state which in turn remains physically present, persisting into the time interval of the speech act.[1] Supposedly, children can use tense morphology only to code the resulting state and they can not specify a situation which is displaced in time as prior to speech time because 'the child lacks an abstract conception of time' (p. 184). Hence, the morphological contrast between past and nonpast represents the distinction between resultative and continuative aspect.

The defective tense hypothesis has three dimensions: semantic, syntactic and temporal. The semantic dimension is based on the claim that only telic verbs will be inflected in the past tense. According to the syntactic dimension, tense distinctions will be redundant and only accompany aspectual distinctions. From the temporal perspective, only references to immediate past situations are expected. Since the semantic dimension of the argument is based on the classification of verbs (evaluated in verb phrase context, Verkuyl 1972), some background remarks are appropriate at this point. Vendler (1967) proposed a classification schema which is particularly sensitive to the temporal contour of situations (cf. Comrie 1976; Lyons 1977, vol. 2; Dowty 1979). Verbs can be partitioned initially into state versus dynamic, with the dynamic set broken down into activity (or atelic) versus telic, and finally telic verbs divided into achievement and accomplishment verbs. Stative verbs refer to situations which remain stable unless something happens to change them: examples are *to be nervous, to love,* and *to know.* In contrast, dynamic verbs refer to situations which must be maintained by continued input. Activity (or atelic) verbs involve pure action, e.g. *to cry, to run, to walk.* In contrast, telic verbs are related to situations which have a well-defined terminal point. With achievement verbs the process is bound to the terminal point, e.g. *to reach, to notice,* or *to find,* while the process leading to the terminal point of an accomplishment verb can be intermittent, as in *to build, to run ten miles, to drink a litre of vodka.* While these situational definitions are useful, the final classification depends on a set of linguistic tests (see, for example, Cochrane 1977; Dowty 1979; Holisky 1981). Some of these linguistic tests can be modified and applied crosslinguistically, for example, the entailment 'If $\emptyset$ is an activity verb, then *X is (now) $\emptyset$ing* entails that *X has $\emptyset$ed*' (Dowty 1979: 57). On the other hand, some of these tests are limited by specific languages: for example the perfective form of stative verbs in Slavic languages has an inchoative meaning (J. E. Miller 1970). Classification based on objective tests which are situationally independent allows one to avoid the circular argumentation which has hindered some investigations of emerging temporal systems.

3.2. The semantic dimension

Antinucci and Miller (1976) found that from about 1;6 to 2;6 Italian children (and one American child) never used activity verbs in the past tense (*passato próssimo* or *imperfetto*) to refer to actual prior situations. From a cross-linguistic perspective, this finding turns out to be relatively unusual. It is more common to find both activity and telic verbs in the past, with the activity verb observed less frequently. For Modern Greek, Stephany (1981) reported that 3 per cent of the activity verbs found were inflected in the past tense as compared to 11 per cent of the telic verbs. Considering only a sample of our data on Polish (Weist *et al.* 1984), the comparable figures for verbs in the past tense are as follows: Marta (1;8) 14 per cent activity, 10 per cent achievement, and 10 per cent accomplishment; Wawrzon (2;2) 8 per cent activity, 12 per cent achievement, and 12 per cent accomplishment; and Agatka (2;8) 13 per cent activity, 11 per cent achievement, and 6 per cent accomplishment. If one pools together achievement and accomplishment verbs, it can be shown that Polish children produce approximately twice as many telic as activity verbs in the past tense. While a similar classification of verbs has not been carried out by other investigators of Slavic languages, examples of activity verbs can be found in the data of Smoczyńska (1978) for Polish, Radulović (1975) for Serbo-Croatian, and Gvozdev (1961) for Russian. Whereas the high frequency categories are present stative and activity verbs and past achievement and accomplishment verbs, investigators have reported some activity verbs in their summaries of past-tense utterances in such diverse languages as Hebrew (Berman, personal communication),[2] Spanish (Eisenberg in preparation), Japanese (Rispoli 1981) and Finnish (Toivainen 1980). Aksu (1978) also observed that Turkish children produce activity verbs in the past tense (for direct experience), but Aksu tried to explain away these examples as either 'ritualized' responses to questions or verbs used after the completion of an activity along with the verb *bitmek* 'to finish'. Whether or not an activity is specified as completed (by some device such as the perfective aspect in Slavic languages or *bitmek* in Turkish) is beside the point (see section 3.3). Hence there are many counterexamples to Antinucci and Miller's argument that children can not make reference to a past activity (completed or not) because pure action leaves no result which can be used as a conceptual or physical link to the past.

3.3. The syntactic dimension

Stephany (1981) reported that when Greek children begin to use the past tense, from 1;8 to 1;11, they use perfective forms and 'imperfective expres-

sions are never past'. Stephany argued that the children used the imperfective form (present stem + present inflection) to code ongoing situations, and the perfective form (aorist stem + past inflection) to code complete situations. The past inflection could thus be viewed as redundant since, according to the argument, only an aspectual distinction was being specified. With the added sensitivity of a diary study however, Dimitra Kontou (personal communication) has found that past imperfective forms are infrequent but not absent from the early period of contrastive tense morphology (see also Stephany 1984). In Slavic languages, imperfective as well as perfective forms are produced from the initial point at which the past tense inflection emerges. In the context of examples from his son at 1;10 and 1;11, Gvozdev (1961) remarked that 'In regard to the past tense ... there are clear cases of the use of both aspects', and furthermore, 'When forms of the future tense emerge they are from the first correctly divided between the simple future of verbs in the perfective aspect ... and the complex future for the imperfective aspect.'[3] For Radulović's (1975) Yugoslavian informant Damir, 30 per cent of the past forms from 2;0 to 2;1 were imperfective. The data from Polish (see Smoczyńska 1985) are quite consistent with Gvozdev's observations on Russian. Hence, the initial argument for redundant tense morphology is not confirmed by a closer look at Greek or by research on Slavic languages.

3.4. The temporal dimension

The idea that the resulting state must be physically present in order for children to make reference to a prior situation has been disconfirmed by data from every language reviewed here, including Italian (Ruth Miller, personal communication). On the other hand, there is some evidence to support the claim that references to the past become progressively more remote. Szagun (1979) has shown that children learning English and German refer to immediate (within a few seconds) events earlier and more frequently than 'remote' (non-immediate) events. In our work on Polish (Weist et al. 1984) we defined moderately remote as requiring an interval of at least two turns in the conversation. Considering all past tense utterances from four 45-minute interactions, the three younger children in our project (ages 1;7–1;9, 1;7–1;8 and 1;9–1;11) produced an average of 32 per cent moderately remote and spontaneous past references, and the older children (ages 2;0–2;3, 2;1–2;3 and 2;2–2;5) produced an average of about 62 per cent. The younger children as well as the older children made reference to events which occurred over two weeks prior to speech time. However, the younger children were likely to express a single proposition, e.g.

Marta (1;7): *towili* '(They) caught/were catching', in reply to her grand-mother's question *A co panowie robili?* 'And what were the men doing?'; while the older children were able to include a number of statements in a description of a prior event, e.g. Kubuś (2;4) used five different verbs in his description of one experience (see Weist *et al.* 1984).

In Finnish, the unmarked past form (imperfect) is one of the first inflectional morphemes to be acquired, and according to Toivainen (1980) the age of acquisition was 1;11 for the median child in his sample. Concerning the remoteness dimension, Toivainen observed that '29 of the 62 past tenses to occur by the age of 1;11 referred to the immediate past, 17 or perhaps 20 to a time still continuing through the moment of speaking, and only 9 to a clearly separate moment in the past' (pp. 66, 69). Hence, moderately remote references to prior situations are conceptually possible for children during the early phase of tense shifting, but they are infrequent. An adequate theory of the development of temporal systems will have to include quantitative as well as qualitative (i.e. →, ←, =) relationships between time concepts, since some languages, e.g. Bantu languages, code various degrees of remoteness (see Comrie 1985: ch. 4). There is very little child language data on this topic (see Burling 1959: 424–7; Brown 1973; 295). In conclusion, the defective tense hypothesis is disconfirmed by the analysis of the semantic, syntactic, and temporal dimensions of child language during the period from 1;6 to 2;6. (See chapter 19 in this volume for a consideration of experimental work on this topic.)

4. Aspect

Aspect has unfortunately been treated primarily as a nuisance which interferes with the detection of deictic relationships. We need to know what temporal properties of situations are coded first in child language, and how these distinctions are related to the development of other aspectual relationships as well as temporally deictic relationships. Erbaugh's (1982) study of the acquisition of Mandarin contains the most interesting observations on aspect. Erbaugh partitioned the acquisition of Mandarin into stages according to the evolution of predicate types. The initial stage of development (the unitary predicate system) represents a prototypical speech time system. Children distinguish between statements and requests but 'there was no marking of aspect, time, or manner' (p. 538). The binary predicate system emerges at about 1;10 and lasts to about 2;4. This stage is characterized by the distinction between stative and dynamic verbs, and the initial coding of perfective aspect with the verb suffix *-le*. Mandarin has an abstract element LE which specifies perfective aspect (PFV) as the verb suffix *-le*,

and a current relevant state (CRS) as a sentence final particle *le*. Children may use LE in the sense of a current relevant state when they want to bring something to the hearer's attention, e.g. Lao Hu pretended to be a robot and said, *wǒ jīgìrén le* 'I robot CRS!' While children make some errors using the perfective *-le* with nouns, imperatives, negations, and future potentials, 'most perfective marking is well-formed and appropriate'. During this stage of development children also indicate completion with the verb complements, *hǎo* 'good' and *-wán* 'finish', in conjunction with *-le*, e.g. *jiǎngwán.le* 'speak-finish-PFV' '(I've) finished speaking'. The perfective aspect is used by Chinese children with activity verbs, e.g. *kū* 'cry' and *fēi* 'fly', as well as telic verbs, e.g. *kāi* 'open' and *lái* 'come'. During the binary predicate stage only a few instances of the progressive aspect were observed, and all instances of progressive aspect were coded 'in the transitive, main story-line, *zài* form, rather than the alternative, *-zhě* background progressive form' (Erbaugh 1982: 568). Hence, the aspectual concepts 'complete' and 'ongoing' are the first to be coded in child Mandarin. Furthermore, during the next stage of development (trinary predicate stage), from about 2;6 to 3;2, 'aspectual marking . . . is still centered around perfectives with duration of an event, iterative, habitual and generic . . . all unmarked' (p. 612). These data are definitely not consistent with claims that the fundamental aspectual distinction in language acquisition (Aksu 1978), as well as in creolization (Bickerton 1975, 1981),[4] is between punctual and nonpunctual.

The distinction between perfective and imperfective aspect is the initial aspectual distinction made by children learning Polish. The distinction is made by prefixation, suffixation, suppletion, and stem alternation (see Weist and Konieczna 1985). In child Polish, this aspectual distinction emerges simultaneously with tense distinctions (Weist 1983; Weist *et al.* 1984). During the initial ST system (pre-aspectual period), children use imperfective verb forms in the present tense, i.e. nonpast imperfective forms (see above, section 2). If the children were simply to specify completion and do nothing with the concept of tense at this point, they would take their nonpast imperfective forms and change them to nonpast perfective forms: e.g. *pisz-e* 'write-nonpast 3rd person singular' would become *na-pisz-e* 'PFV-write-nonpast 3rd person singular' through prefixation, or *kopi-e* 'kick-nonpast 3rd person singular' would become *kop-ni-e* 'kick-PFV-nonpast 3rd person singular' by suffixation. However, this simple change to nonpast perfective forms creates verbs with future meaning, and when children use these forms they have the appropriate tense value. Instead of this incorrect aspect priority scenario, the fact is that children shift from one form (i.e. present imperfective) to four forms (i.e. present

imperfective, past imperfective, past perfective and future perfective). The fifth form of the basic tense–aspect combinations (i.e. the future imperfective) emerges a few months later. All of the evidence (see section 3) indicates that the past tense suffix *-ł* [u̯] has a deictic function and the aspectual affixes such as *po-*, *na-*, *z-*, *-n*, *-ywa*, etc. make the perfective versus imperfective distinction at the point of transition into the ET system. At this point in development, the iterative aspect is not explicitly coded in the morphology. Iterative forms such as *pisywać* 'to write more than once' are not found contrasting with non-iterative forms *pisać / napisać* 'to write', and (though not thoroughly researched) expressions such as *często* 'often' which give imperfective forms iterative meaning, are very rare – if used at all.

We have proposed that during the period of development starting from about 1;6 children are capable of taking an external and an internal perspective on situations (Weist *et al.* 1984). When a situation is conceptualized from an external perspective, properties such as 'complete', 'punctual', and 'resultative' are salient, and when conceptualized from an internal perspective properties such as 'ongoing' ('continuative'), 'durative', and 'incomplete' are prominent. If a child is learning a language where the marked aspect codes the property of completion (e.g. the Polish perfective), or the property ongoing (e.g. the Spanish progressive), the distinction will be coded rapidly in the morphology of the child's language. We do not expect, nor do we find, the early acquisition of tense–aspect combinations which require an internal perspective on situations displaced in time, e.g. the past progressive. The acquisition rate will depend in part on the manner in which aspect is coded in the surface structure of the language. (See Slobin 1985a for a discussion of the relationship between operating principles and the course of acquisition.) In Polish, where verb prefixes and suffixes represent the dominant aspectual coding, the perfective / imperfective distinction emerges rapidly from about 1;6 to 1;9, whereas in Finnish, where perfective versus imperfective aspect is coded by the partitive versus accusative case distinction, it emerges in naturalistic productions somewhat later, at about 2;2 (Toivainen 1980: 185).

5. The event time system

Starting at about 1;8 plus or minus a few months, children are capable of taking internal and external perspectives on situations, and they are able to relate event time to speech time. There is a natural relationship between the internal perspective and speech time events, and between the external perspective and anterior events. It appears to be generally

true that when children break out of the here-and-now constraints of the speech time system, they can make the distinction between ongoing events during the speech time interval and complete events anterior to speech time. In addition, they can independently express their intentions and desires concerning potential subsequent events, i.e. a notion of 'irrealis'. The latter has more to do with modality than tense or aspect (see chapter 18 in this volume). Hence, children are capable of making past/nonpast, continuative/noncontinuative, complete/incomplete, and realis/irrealis distinctions. A concept of deictic future may also be part of the system. During the period from about 1;8 ±0;2 to 2;8 ±0;2 every child language investigated expresses at least the composite notions nonpast-continuative versus past-complete and realis versus irrealis.

Romance child-languages are prototypical of languages with the minimal set of contrasts (see Clark 1985). In French, for example, the event time system contains present, *passé composé*, and an irrealis form *aller* + infinitive. A functionally similar configuration of verb forms emerges during this phase of child Turkish: i.e. *-iyor* present progressive, *-di* direct experience past, and *-sin* modal future (Aksu 1978). In contrast to these languages, child Japanese identifies the deictic ET←ST relation and both of the basic aspectual relations. Before 1;9, Okubo's daughter expressed the following distinctions: past *-ta*/nonpast *-ru*; past *-ta*/completed past *-chatta*; and nonpast *-ru*/progressive *-teru* (see Clancy 1985). These contrasts were also among the earliest found in the Japanese children observed by Clancy and Sanches (see Clancy 1985). In still other languages, children make the past/nonpast distinction and one of the basic aspectual distinctions; for example, perfective aspect is early in Polish, as is progressive in Spanish (see Eisenberg in preparation). If these aspectual distinctions are not explicitly identified in the inflectional morphology of the verb system, they may surface in other ways. Herring (n.d.) has observed that children learning English use locative particles to express the concept of completion, and in Brazilian Portuguese children use the monosyllabic segments /aː/, /oː/, /paː/, and /baː/ also to identify completion; for example, having dropped a deck of cards, Renta 1;6 said *pa* 'pa' and her mother replied *Pa! Caiu, ne?* 'Pa! It fell down, didn't it?' (de Lemos 1981: 64). It is difficult to say when adverbs which specify aspectual properties evolve, given the present research picture; however, there are scattered data which are relevant; for example, we know that *kvar* 'already' is used in an early phase of Hebrew (Berman 1985).

It might be argued that child Mandarin has a functional ET system. During the comparable phase of the development of Mandarin, children use the progressive *zài*, perfective *-le*, and the future potential *huì* 'can'

and *yào* 'want'. Since children seldom use the perfective aspect to identify an event which will be completed subsequent to the speech act (cf. child Polish), the perfective *-le* usually identifies a prior event. Hence, the notion past-complete can be expressed with very little ambiguity.

6. Transition to reference time (RT) systems

6.1. The restricted RT system

It has been argued that RT is frozen at ST during the tenure of the ET system. Cromer (1968) observed:

> after age 4 or $4\frac{1}{2}$ ... we find that there seems to emerge some ability to free oneself from the immediate situation (p. 165)

> a kind of de-centering ... the child seemed to be able to take leave of his own viewpoint in a temporal series and stand outside that series, thereby being able to relate events in new ways (p. 172)

The capacity to vary temporal perspective underlies the evolution of the RT system. The RT system appears to evolve in stages, with the initial stage at about 3;0 ±0;2 and the final stage at about 4;0 ±0;2.

The restricted reference time system is characterized by the onset of temporal adverbs and the use of temporal adverbial clauses. The restricted RT system is characterized further by the absence of the temporal prepositions signifying 'before' and 'after'. In Eve Clark's (1985) lucid review of the acquisition of Romance languages, it is reported that Italian children use temporal adverbs such as *oggi* 'today', *ieri* 'yesterday', and *domani* 'tomorrow' at around 3;0. According to Clark, these adverbs have been found somewhat earlier in French and Spanish, at about 2;6. However, as Clark points out, some investigators have reported a confusion of 'yesterday' and 'tomorrow' in child Spanish which persisted to 3;6. Clancy, Jacobsen and Silva (1976) determined that Italian children produce temporal adverbial clauses with *quando* 'when' at 2;2; e.g. *Quando mamma era piccola on si li lavava i denti!* 'When mamma was little they used to clean her teeth' (p. 77). This type of temporal clause has been found somewhat later in French and Spanish, at about 3;0 and 3;6. Clancy *et al.* compared the acquisition of complex sentences in Italian, English, German and Turkish. In all four languages temporal adverbial clauses which establish RT appear between 2;8 and 3;4, and these constructions always preceded the use of 'before' and 'after' as subordinate conjunctions.

We have just begun an analysis of RT in Polish, and the data that I

will report are based only on a single child. Before 2;6, a few words such as *teraz* 'now' occurred in Wawrzon's speech, but after 2;6 a number of temporal adverbial expressions emerged. During the period from about 2;6 to 2;8, Wawrzon used *dzisiaj* 'today', *jutro* 'tomorrow', *wczoraj* 'yesterday', and *w poniedziałek* 'on Monday'. *Dzisiaj* was used correctly as 'today'. Both *jutro* and *wczoraj* had the meaning 'yesterday', shown in utterances such as: (Wawrzon 2;8) *Co to ja się jutro bawiłem tymi zabawkami* 'Which tomorrow I played with these toys'. *W poniedziałek* had the meaning 'some other day' either in the past or the future. At about 2;8, Wawrzon began to establish reference time with adverbial clauses using *jak* meaning 'when' in this context, as in: (Wawrzon 2;8) *A jak ja urosnę to będę ciągnał za śnur, aż będzie dzwonił dzwon* 'And when I grow up, I will pull the string and the bell will ring!'; and (Wawrzon 3;0) *Bo jak przyszła ciocia to mówie flumbla* 'Because when aunt came, I say flumbla'. By about 3;0 to 3;2, *jutro* 'tomorrow' is used correctly. Wawrzon did not use 'before' and 'after' at this point in development, and event time always corresponded to reference time. Smoczyńska (1985) found temporal adverbs as early as 1;9, but also found that it takes some time before they are used correctly (see also Harner 1975, on English).

According to Mary Erbaugh (personal communication), temporal adverbs occur as early as 2;2 in child Mandarin. Pang, for example, was using adverbial expressions meaning 'earlier', 'in a little while', and 'now' prior to the age 2;2. At 2;3 Pang used *zuótian* 'yesterday', at 2;8 *haǒ jiǔ* 'for a long time', and at 2;11 *míngtiān* 'tomorrow'. In general, the frequency of temporal adverbs increased from 2;2 to 3;2 and could be considered relatively common at 2;8. It is difficult to say if we can consider the initial use of a few temporal adverbs as precocious in Mandarin. The concept of RT appears to be established in Mandarin at a point in development which is similar to that of other languages.

6.2. The free RT system

When children initially establish RT outside of the temporal domain of the speech act, the event that the child is talking about occurs within the RT context. When children progress from the ET system to the restricted RT system, they have demonstrated a measure of the capacity to decentre, but they are still only relating two points in time. Children do not appear to establish RT at some point prior to or subsequent to ST and simultaneously establish ET at yet a third point in time. The emergence of the prepositions 'before' and 'after' represents one important signal that children have developed the added flexibility which permits them to establish

ST, ET, and RT at three related points in time. In English, *before* and *after* are produced (E. V. Clark 1970) and comprehended (Coker 1978) as prepositions prior to their use as subordinate conjunctions. However, most of the research concerning the use of 'before' and 'after' has been concentrated on their function as subordinate conjunctions. Hence, at this point we have to use the evidence concerning their emergence in that function: the crosslinguistic estimate of that point in time is between about 3;5 and 4;0, according to Clancy *et al.* (1976).

The late acquisition of the present perfect in English is also relevant to the development of the free reference time system.[5] For the present perfect, RT is simultaneous with ST and ET is prior to RT. The use of the present perfect appears to require a concept of RT which is independent of ST, and the capacity to establish ET and RT at different points in time. In addition to a complex configuration of time concepts, there are further complications. The present perfect does not merely place ET prior to a RT. The prior situation must also have current relevance. Furthermore, perfect has more than one meaning. Comrie (1976) distinguishes between perfect of result, experiential perfect, perfect of persistent situations, and perfect of recent past. Present perfect has a complex surface realization with variations in the form of the past participle, contracted and uncontracted forms, etc. In addition, there are dialect differences which affect acquisition (Fletcher 1981). Cromer (1974) tried to explain the late acquisition (i.e. 4;0 and older) of the present perfect as a conceptual deficit. According to Cromer, the concept of the continuing relevance of a prior situation is a relatively late cognitive development. Crosslinguistic comparisons make Cromer's argument unlikely. During the phase of development which Erbaugh (1982) calls the trinary predicate system (about 2;6 through 3;2), children learning Mandarin use the perfective -*le* with stative predicates specifying a current state which resulted from a prior situation, and they begin to use the -*guo* suffix which indicates the experiential perfect. A child version of the sentence-final particle *le* meaning current relevant state is used by Chinese children even earlier in their development. Hence, the young American child's failure to use the present perfect should probably not be attributed to a retarded conceptual development (see also Fletcher 1979).

Influenced by its late acquisition in English, the present perfect has been viewed as a temporal configuration requiring the flexibility of the free RT system. This proposition is challenged by some facts about child Finnish. The median child in Toivainen's (1980) study used the perfect (i.e. present perfect) in contrast to the earlier preterite (i.e. simple past) form by 2;4; and 75 per cent of the children used the perfect by 2;5. According to Toivai-

nen, the preterite versus perfect distinction is between the temporal configurations $(ET = RT) \leftarrow ST$ versus $ET \leftarrow (RT = ST)$ respectively. Only two points in time are required and these temporal configurations fall within the domain of the restricted RT system. In contrast to the present perfect, the pluperfect (i.e. past perfect) requires three points in time, i.e. the configuration $ET \leftarrow RT \leftarrow ST$. According to Toivainen (personal communication), the median child added the pluperfect to the preterite and perfect at 4;6. However, about 25 per cent of the Finnish children began to use the pluperfect by 3;8. Clearly the pluperfect requires the relational power of the free RT system, and its emergence in Finnish corresponds to estimates of the development of the free RT system which were based on the use of 'before' and 'after' in other languages.

7. Temporal systems and conceptual development

The development of temporal systems is relevant to the general development of time concepts. When temporal relationships are coded in child language we can infer that certain cognitive developments have evolved in the child's general conceptual development. Linguistic coding is a sufficient condition for drawing this inference, although not a necessary condition. The defective tense hypothesis which was reviewed in section 3 of this chapter made a dramatic claim about conceptual development which is outlined in figure 2, at the top. As the child's overall conceptual development progresses, there is a point at which children are no longer limited to thinking about the here-and-now. At this point, children acquire the property of displacement. When children achieve the capacity for displacement, they can retrieve prior experiences from memory with the understanding that these experiences occurred prior to the interval of the speech act. They can also conceptualize an event which could potentially occur subsequent to the speech act. We can infer that the property of displacement has evolved when child language becomes tensed, but only if the tense morphology codes a deictic relationship. According to Antinucci and Miller's (1976) relatively plausible version of the defective tense hypothesis, displacement could not be inferred until $2\frac{1}{2}$ years or older; but according to a more radical hypothesis, displacement is considered to be delayed much longer (see C. S. Smith's 1980 review). If the argument in section 3 is correct, there is no longer any reason to claim that displacement is deferred, and there are numerous reasons to suppose that displacement is a property of conceptual development at about $1\frac{1}{2}$ years of age.

Slobin (1981) used the term 'cognitive pacesetting' to describe the process whereby children seek linguistic expression for newly emerging concepts.

DEFECTIVE TENSE HYPOTHESIS

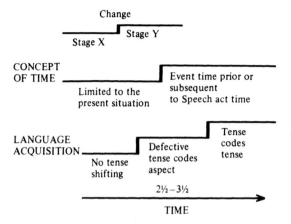

COGNITION and TEMPORAL SYSTEMS

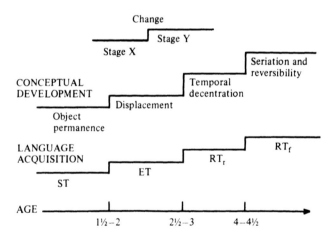

Figure 2. Relationships between conceptual and linguistic development

Although it is difficult to independently specify all the components of the relevant conceptual development, there is some evidence for cognitive pace-setting in the evolution of temporal systems, which is outlined in figure 2. at the bottom. First of all, object permanence is a prerequisite for displacement. Corrigan (1978) used a modified version of the Uzgiris-Hunt scale to measure object permanence. The test of object permanence involved a set of hiding and displacement tasks. There was an overall correlation

between language development scores and the capacity to solve increasingly demanding tests of object permanence. In particular, there was a close relationship between the initial search for invisibly displaced objects and the onset of single-word utterances (at about 1;1), and there was also a correspondence between the point at which children could solve the most demanding test of object permanence and the initial linguistic coding of disappearance and recurrence (at about 1;6).

Piaget has provided some evidence for the capacity to displace prior to the end of the sensorimotor period (see Flavell 1963); but in general there is very little research on memory processes (e.g. Kail 1979) or time concepts (e.g. Friedman 1982) during the critical period from about 1;6 to 2;6 – de Loache's (1980) research on memory for object location is an exception. In this study, de Loache used a hide-and-seek task with children ranging in age from 1;6 to 2;6. The procedure involved hiding a stuffed animal in some location in the home, with the child observing the location. After three to five minutes the children looked for the hidden object, and they were credited with a correct response if they went directly to the correct location. Children ranging in age from 1;6 to 2;0 were 69 per cent correct and from 2;0 to 2;6 they were 84 per cent correct. The results of testing with longer intervals were only reported for the entire group of children and the scores were as follows: 30 minutes – 80 per cent, one hour – 69 per cent, and overnight – 77 per cent. Hence, de Loache has provided us with at least some experimental data which indicate that children in the relevant age range have a sense of displacement.

Cromer (1971a) and Harner (1980) have used a test of decentration which requires that children answer questions about a series of pictures. In Harner's experiment a series of three pictures was presented: for example, a mailman holding a letter, putting the letter in a mailbox, and walking away from the mailbox. The children were asked questions with the present perfect or simple future tense. The general argument was that directions concerning the past, e.g. *Show me the mailman has mailed the letter*, would be easier than future-tense questions, such as *Show me the mailman will mail the letter*, because the child can maintain RT at ST to answer past-tense questions but must shift RT to the beginning of the picture series to answer the future-tense questions. Both Cromer and Harner found that future-tense problems were more difficult for children ranging in age from 3 to 7 and performance improved over the entire age range. Unfortunately, this kind of test does not evaluate temporal decentration independent of linguistic information processing.

The use of 'before' and 'after' as subordinate conjunctions involves the capacity to relate two clauses. As prepositions, their relational function

is limited to two points in time, i.e. ET and RT. While we do not want to equate these functions, research on English which is relevant to the use of *before* and *after* as temporal conjunctions is at least indirectly relevant to the evolution of the free RT system. Trosborg (1982) has shown that there is a close correspondence between the capacity to solve picture arrangement (or seriation) problems and quantity conservation tests of reversible thinking, and the capacity to solve comprehension tests involving acting out sentences with *before* and *after*. Obviously, more research of this type is needed before a good picture of cognitive pacesetting for temporal systems can be presented. Figure 2 outlines a tentative hypothesis of the relationship between cognitive development and the evolution of temporal systems.

While an outline of the course of cognitive development is important, it provides only the general constraints on the development of temporal systems. The transitions from the ST to ET to RT systems can only be predicted from an understanding of the relationship between the way in which languages code the relevant temporal concepts and the way in which children process linguistic information. Slobin's (1973, 1985a) work on 'operating principles' is the best source for an understanding of linguistic information-processing strategies. The need to relate information-processing strategies to linguistic coding of temporal concepts is demonstrated by two observations. When the linguistic mechanisms used to express a time concept are the same across languages, the emergence of the time concept into the evolving temporal systems is stable across those languages. In general, temporal adverbs are used to establish reference time and the onset of the restricted RT system is relatively stable across diverse languages. Within Slavic languages, the configuration of tense–aspect morphology is relatively similar, and children gain access to the ET system at a similar phase in the acquisition process. When the linguistic mechanisms used to express a temporal concept vary, there will be variability in the emergence of temporal concepts. The morphology of tense and aspect varies greatly from one language to the next and there is considerable variability in the emergence of the event time system. In Japanese, where the critical deictic relations and the aspectual relations of completion and continuation are invariantly coded by readily accessible verb suffixes, acquisition is precocious (Clancy 1985). In contrast, in English the important concepts of aspect are confounded with tense and obscured in the surface structure by discontinuous morphology involving auxiliary components and a verb suffix. Furthermore, the auxiliary components have the same form with other functions. As a result, the emergence of the event time system in English is relatively slow.

There are a number of other important problems which are related to the evolution of temporal systems and which provide additional understanding: these include the relationship between discourse functions and temporal configurations, the development of conditionals, and the use of indirect past reference. Unfortunately, these issues are beyond the scope of this paper, where the following arguments were presented:

(1)   Reichenbach's (1947) model provides a useful framework for the analysis of the evolution of temporal systems (though see Comrie, 1981a and 1985, for some reservations and improvements).

(2)   The investigation of tense and aspect is more meaningful if related to the broader context of evolving temporal systems.

(3)   Crosslinguistic perspective is crucial for an understanding of the relationship between conceptual development and the development of temporal systems.

(4)   The final understanding of the acquisition process requires the matching of strategies for acquiring and processing linguistic information with the linguistic coding of temporal concepts.

18. Modality

Ursula Stephany

1. Modality as a language function

From a linguistic point of view, modality is a semantic category expressing concepts such as 'possibility', 'necessity', 'obligation', 'permission', 'intention' and so on. The most important formal devices found in languages for expressing modality are: (1) *modal verbs*, whether main verbs or auxiliaries, e.g. *may, can, must, will*; and (2) *modal inflections*, or *moods*, e.g. imperative, subjunctive, optative, conditional. In this chapter we shall limit ourselves to these forms, since they are the modal categories that have been most systematically studied in linguistics, and (except for intonation in the very early stages of language acquisition) they are the only ones to play a significant role in early child language. Other categories expressing modality, such as adjectives (e.g. *possible, likely, certain*), adverbs (e.g. *possibly, perhaps, maybe*), nouns (e.g. *possibility, likelihood*), derivational affixes (e.g. *-able* in *controllable, governable*), and verbs taking sentential complements (e.g. *believe, doubt*) are almost completely missing from early child language.

The function of modality is to enable the speaker either to qualify the propositions expressed by his sentences with respect to their validity, truth, or factuality (Flämig 1970: 400; Lyons 1977: 797ff; *Grundzüge* 1981: 521) or to indicate obligation and permission 'of acts performed by morally responsible agents' (Lyons 1977: 823) with reference to norms. These types of modality have been called *epistemic* and *deontic*, respectively. While statements of fact such as (1) can be considered as (epistemically) nonmodal (Lyons 1977: 797), the speaker uttering (2) does not categorically assert the proposition expressed by this sentence, but puts it forward as being merely a possibility:

(1) John has left
(2) John may have left

Sentences (1) and (2) may be paraphrased as *I say that it is the case that*

375

John has left and *I think that it is the case that John has left* (or *Possibly / Perhaps John has left*), respectively. In modal logic, sentences like (2) are not interpreted as expressing the speaker's opinion, but rather in terms of the notion of objective possibility bearing on the truth of the proposition. In the ordinary use of language, however, and therefore also in the semantics of modality, it is the subjective epistemic interpretation given above that is much more important.

Whereas sentences like (2) admit only an epistemic interpretation, (3) can be understood either epistemically (*I think that John will leave*) or deontically (*John is allowed to leave*):

(3)   John may leave

Whether a modal expression receives an epistemic or a deontic interpretation depends on a number of factors, such as the tense of the modalized verb, as well as that of the modal verb itself, the subject of the sentence (animacy), verbal agreement (Newton 1979), extrasentential context, and the kind of speech act performed (Pottier 1976; Johnson-Laird 1978; Roulet 1980).

The fact that modal forms typically serve to express epistemic as well as deontic meanings cannot be coincidental. First of all, the notions of obligation and permission are reinterpretable in terms of the notions of necessity and possibility: obligation = necessity to act, permission = possibility to act. While in epistemic modality these notions refer to knowledge of states of affairs (being), in deontic modality they refer to actions (doing) (Greimas 1976; Parisi and Antinucci 1970; Roulet 1980). However, the two modal degrees of necessity and possibility are not of equal importance in the two types of modality. Since one could argue quite plausibly that the origin of deontic modality is to be sought in the desiderative and instrumental functions of language, it should not be surprising for deontic modality to be necessity-based rather than possibility-based, with the converse being true for epistemic modality (Lyons 1977: 801ff).

There are two more notions which are commonly expressed by the modal devices of languages and which thus have to be included in a treatment of modal semantics. These are 'ability' and 'volition'. Although they can be related to both deontic and epistemic modality, they are treated in some studies (on modal logic, von Wright 1963; on modal semantics, Palmer 1979; and on language acquisition, Pea, Mawby and MacKain 1982) as a separate type of modality, *dynamic* modality. As both ability and volition are basically concerned with conditions for action, however, it seems preferable to treat them as deontically modal (see also Shepherd 1981). Volition can then be considered as expressing deontic necessity, as does obligation, but whereas in obligation the source of modality may be some authority

external to the subject, in volition it is the subject itself. Ability expresses deontic possibility and differs from permission in that it qualifies the subject (Greimas 1976) – there is no external source of authority.

As the development of the modalizing function can only be adequately appreciated if it is studied in the context of the grammar of verb forms of the language acquired, I shall treat separately the two languages for which the development of modality has been quite extensively studied. These are Modern Greek, a language with a particularly rich synthetic verb inflection, and English, a language tending towards the analytic morphological type.

2. The development of modality in Greek

The data come from five monolingual, middle-class children (four girls and a boy) living in Athens, Greece, three of whom were studied longitudinally. The speech of the children and their mothers or caretakers was tape-recorded in the children's natural surroundings during activities such as playing, eating, and preparation for bed. The samples were collected during three periods of one or two weeks each. The mean age of the children at the first session of period I (4 subjects) was 1;9:12, of period II (3 subjects) 2;4:2, and of period III (3 subjects) 2;10:2. The transcripts of each child comprise a mean number of 2,000 utterances for period I and 1,220 and 1,430 utterances for periods II and III, respectively. Of these, only interpretable utterances containing a main or a modal verb which were not immediate imitations of adult utterances were included in a study of the development of aspect, tense, and modality (Stephany 1984) on which I largely draw in what follows (for period I see also Stephany 1981). The mean number of verb form tokens analysed for each child was 444 in period I, 550 in period II, and 612 in period III.

The most important formal devices expressing modality in Modern Greek (henceforth MG) are the subjunctive and the imperative mood and the modal verbs *boró* 'can, may' and *prépi* 'must'. The notions of capability, permission, obligation and wish may also be expressed by main verbs such as *kséro* 'know, be able', *epitrépo* 'allow', *anangázo* 'oblige', *θélo* 'want', of which only the latter frequently occurs in child speech. Often permission and obligation are expressed indirectly by stating social norms or habits with the verb in the third person plural of the present indicative, e.g. *ðen léne 'vre'* (literally, 'not they say *vre*' – a currently used vocative considered impolite) 'One doesn't say *vre*'. The periphrastically formed future tense (see below) has a strong modal character in MG and also serves to express

THE DEVELOPMENT OF LINGUISTIC SYSTEMS: GRAMMAR

deontic and epistemic modality. Directives expressed in the subjunctive mood are considered as more polite than commands in the imperative, as the former are interpretable as advice (Babiniotis and Kondos 1967: 181), thus leaving an option to the addressee to comply with the directive or not. In negation, the opposition between the imperative and the subjunctive mood is neutralized, as the modal negative particle *mi(n)* only combines with subjunctive verb forms (e.g. *fíje* imperative, *na fíjis* subjunctive 'go away', *mi fíjis* 'don't go away').

The categories of verb forms expressing mood, aspect, and tense in Greek child language are represented in table 1. Details left aside, the imperative differs from the indicative and subjunctive by a set of inflectional suffixes depending on the morphological class of the verb (e.g. *fíj-e!* 'leave', *krát-a!* 'hold' versus *na fíj-is* 'that you leave', *na krat-ás* 'that you hold'). The indicative differs from the subjunctive by the absence of a modal particle (e.g. *févj-is* 'you leave' versus *na févj-is* imperfective 'that you leave'). The two moods are most often also distinguished either by the stem (*na fíj-is* perfective 'that you leave') or the inflectional ending (*fíɣ-ame* perfective 'we left' versus *na fíɣ-ume* perfective 'let's leave').

Table 1. *Verb forms expressing mood, aspect, and tense in Greek child language*

| Mood | Aspect | |
	Imperfective stem	Perfective stem
Indicative	stem + present inflection	
	stem + past inflection[a]	stem + past inflection
Subjunctive	stem + present inflection	stem + present inflection[b]
Imperative[c]	stem + imperative inflection	stem + imperative inflection

[a] These forms occur only from period II on.
[b] Present indicative and subjunctive inflections coincide in MG.
[c] The opposition of perfective and imperfective aspect is often neutralized in the imperative mood.

Modal particles are used in more than 90 per cent of the obligatory contexts by only one of the three subjects studied in period II and by two of the three subjects studied in period III. Thus, the present tense and imperfective subjunctive will sometimes merge in child language as far as the verb forms are concerned, and can only be told apart by prosodic features (intonation contour and emphatic or non-emphatic mode of speaking) and context. However, the perfective subjunctive, representing the unmarked term of the perfective / imperfective opposition in dynamic verbs

and distinguished from the indicative mood by the verb stem, occurs much more frequently than the imperfective subjunctive in the children's speech (as well as in child-directed mothers' speech). The reason for this is that subjunctive expressions are not about ongoing occurrences but are rather prospective (Seiler 1971). A detailed analysis of the verb forms of all ten transcripts of child speech has shown that perfective and imperfective verb stems are already formally distinguished in more than 90 per cent of all tokens by period I. In contrast to reports on English child language, the percentage of conjugational suffixes lacking in contexts where they are obligatory is extremely low in Greek child language for all three periods studied (3.8% on the average for the verb form tokens of period I and 3.4% for period III). Suffixed verb forms conforming to the norm of MG and appropriately used constitute 87 to 97 per cent of all verb form tokens from period II onwards, with a mean of 81 per cent for three of the four subjects studied in period I and 58 per cent for the fourth, who frequently referred to the speaker by using verb forms in the 3rd person singular.

The verb form categories expressing tense, aspect, and mood (TAM categories) represented in table 1 are not used with equal frequency. In period I, the perfective subjunctive, the indicative present, and the imperative mood occupy the first three positions on the scale ranking the mean frequency of use, preceding the perfective past and the imperfective subjunctive. In period II, the perfective subjunctive and the present tense share the first rank, with the imperative falling back behind the perfective past. In period III, the perfective subjunctive recedes to the second rank behind the indicative present. These predilections for use can be explained as follows. In standard MG, as well as in Greek child language, the subjunctive and imperative moods are the most important formal devices for expressing deontic modality. The high frequency of the perfective subjunctive and the imperative show that modalized utterances play an extremely important role in early Greek child language. The ample use made of the present indicative is due to its functional diversity, which includes modal usage. Nevertheless, the advance of the present tense as well as the perfective past on the scale in the course of language development indicates that nonmodalized descriptive utterances as well as erotetic ones gradually become more important in child speech.

The TAM categories in which verbs are preferentially used depend to a certain degree on their aspectual character (*aktionsart*). The *aktionsart* oppositions of stative/dynamic, durative/punctual, and telic/atelic account for the three most important aspectual verb classes of early child language, namely telic-punctual dynamic, atelic-durative dynamic and stative verbs (referred to in what follows as telic, atelic, and stative – see

chapter 17 in this volume). Only in the case of telic verbs is the perfective subjunctive used more frequently than any other category by all subjects in all periods. In the use of atelic and stative verbs, on the other hand, with the exception of one subject, the present tense already occupies the first position in the rank order scale of TAM categories in period I. The imperfective subjunctive occurs more often with atelic verbs than would be expected from the overall frequency of atelic verb form tokens in the data. As in standard MG, the imperative mood is limited to dynamic verbs in the children's speech. This is because 'a child's early imperatives are all action-oriented ... It would be bizarre if he sought instead to influence the thought-processes and emotions of others by commanding them to want, need, know, etc.' (Bickerton 1981: 157).

A verb form category not included in table 1 is the future tense. In standard MG, the categories of future and subjunctive are solely distinguished by the particle used, *θa* (deriving historically from *θélo na* 'want to') in the case of the future and *na* or *as* in the subjunctive. As indicated above, on the one hand particle use is not yet quite reliable in Greek child language, and on the other, *θa* and *na* are often reduced to their vowel by the children, resulting in homophony of the two categories. As the future and the subjunctive are also functionally closely related, especially when expressing actions under the control of animate subjects, it would in many cases be completely arbitrary to assign a formally ambiguous subjunctive verb form to one category rather than the other in the children's speech. As 'statements made about future occurrences are necessarily based upon the speaker's beliefs, predictions, or intentions, rather than upon his knowledge of "fact"' (Lyons 1968: 310), the future tense could even be called a mood of nonfactivity. Although such an interpretation would not do justice to the structure of standard MG, it is not surprising that in the early stages of Greek language development the future tense should not yet have emerged as a grammatical category distinct from the subjunctive mood (see also section 5).

Preparing the ground for the later development of two separate grammatical categories, that of the future tense and the subjunctive mood, the children's subjunctive forms are already plurifunctional in period I, insofar as they are used to make predictions as well as to express wish or intention. The more temporal, nondeontic use predominates in speech acts describing events posterior to speech time. In typical examples the verb is in the 3rd person, the subject inanimate, and the verb denotes an event not under the control of an agent and often undesirable, making a positive wish pragmatically unlikely. Some of these sentences are uttered as warnings, as in (4):

(4)   (Janna I, commenting on an object)
       a bési 'It's going to fall down'

       = θa   pés-   i
       future particle fall, perfective present 3rd sing.

As predictions are necessarily not statements of fact, they could be considered as precursors to epistemically modalized statements representing
a kind of 'null-degree' of epistemic modality (Pea *et al.* 1982 and section
4 below).

The subjunctive mood mainly serves deontically modal functions in
Greek child language. It is used to state the child's wishes and intentions
to act, as in (5); to make promises, as in (6); to ask for permission, the
addressee's advice concerning an action planned by the child, or to enquire
about the addressee's intentions, as in (7). While the primary illocutionary
force of such utterances, whose subjects generally refer to the speaker
or to speaker and addressee (1st person plural), is representative or erotetic,
the desiderative type especially may be implicitly directive.

(5)   (Spiros I, watching the observer take a picture book out of her bag)
       pìo vavási 'Spiros is going to / wants to read'
       = o   spíros θa / na   ðiavás-   i
       the Spiros future / modal read, perfective present 3rd sing.

(6)   (Mairi II, after being warned by her mother not to break an object)
       əmpáso 'I'm not going to break (it)'

       = ðen θa   to spás-   o
       not future it break, perfective present 1st sing.

(7)   (Mairi I, wanting to take a puzzle representing a squirrel)
       pàri ɣuɣunáki? 'May (Mairi) take the piggy?

       = na   pár-   i   to ɣurunáki
       modal take, perfective present 3rd sing. the piggy

The subjunctive is very frequently used in explicit directives serving to
request an action or the abstention from an action from the addressee
(8) or a third person (9) by introducing a norm:

(8)   (Natali I, asking the nurse Sula to hold something for her)
       i tùla tái 'Sula shall hold (it)'

       = i   súla na   to krat-   ái
       the Sula modal it hold, imperfective present 3rd sing.

(9) (Mairi II, addressing her mother and referring to the observer)
     a mə pài agalíta 'She shall take me in her arms'

     = na   me par-   i   angalítsa
       modal me take, perfective present 3rd sing. embrace

The imperative mood is functionally very similar to the 2nd person of
the subjunctive mood used in directive speech acts. Both are already formally distinguished by period I. The most frequently used imperative forms
are *kíta* 'look', *éla* 'come', *kátse* / *káθise* 'wait, sit down', and *síko* 'get up'.
These constitute half of all imperative form tokens. *Kíta* serves to attract
the addressee's attention to something, *éla* and *kátse* are sometimes used
to urge the addressee either to perform an action or to refrain from it
for a certain time. Prohibitions are expressed by the imperative form *áse*
'leave (it)' or by combining the negative modal particle *mi(n)* (sometimes
preceded by *na* or *as*) with the 2nd person singular of the subjunctive
mood, as in (10):

(10) (Mairi III, addressing a visiting child)
     fíje! na min kitáksis! 'Go away!' 'Don't look!'

     = fíj-   e   na   min
       leave, perfective imperative 2nd sing. modal neg. modal

     kitáks-   is
     look, perfective present 2nd sing.

Explicit directives are much more frequently expressed by the imperative
than by the subjunctive mood. In cases like *kíta* 'look' or *kátse* 'wait',
where it would be impolite to assume a refusal to comply on the part
of the addressee, directives are normally expressed in the imperative mood
in standard MG as well as in child language. There is slight evidence from
period I onwards that at least some of the subjects have begun to grasp
the functional difference between the imperative and the subjunctive mood
mentioned above. The imperative mood is sometimes preferred in addressing persons considered of equal or lower social rank, whereas requests
directed to persons of higher rank are expressed in the subjunctive, as
in (11):

(11) (Spiros I, asking his mother to take a doll out of a recess)
     láli i mamàli . . . típa 'Mummy shall take (it) out of the hole'

     = na   vɣál-   i   i mamá apó tin trípa
       modal take, perfective present 3rd sing. the mummy from the hole

(Spiros I, asking the observer to take off her watch)
lolói! aláto! '(The) watch! 'Take it off!'

= to rolói ja   vɣál-   to
the watch particle take, perfective imperative 2nd sing. it

Considerations of politeness are discarded, however, if the speaker is anxious to see his request fulfilled, as in (10). Generally, the subjunctive will be preferred when the modality derives from objective necessity rather than the speaker's will. In period III, two subjects use it in directives not referring to the immediate future. Sometimes both the imperative and the subjunctive are used during the same interaction in trying to obtain satisfaction either by emphasizing the request (subjunctive followed by imperative) or, on the contrary, by making greater concessions to the addressee's options (imperative followed by subjunctive), as in (12):

(12) (Mairi III, asking her mother to open the wardrobe)
mamá! ànitséto! 'Mummy! Open it!'

= mamá   àniks-   é-   to
mummy open, perfective imperative 2nd sing. it

Mother: he? 'Hm?'

na to anítsis 'Open it'

= na   to aníks-   is
modal it open, perfective present 2nd sing.

In addition to the subjunctive and the imperative mood, the indicative present may convey modal meanings in standard MG as well as in Greek child language. Although subjunctive expressions are much more frequent in these functions, the present tense is occasionally used to express intentions and anticipated or apprehended events, as in (13):

(13) (Janna II, bored with a picture book)
telóni tòra 'It's going to finish now'

= teljón-   i   tóra
end, imperfective present 3rd sing. now

As no examples of inadequate use of the subjunctive mood to convey non-modalized statements can be found in the children's data, it can be concluded that the two categories are not variants of each other in the modalized function. A possible semantic difference which comes to mind is that in the present indicative expressions it is the topicality of the intention, anticipation, or apprehension at speech time that is crucial, while the subjunctive expressions are of a more prospective nature.

A further modal function of the present tense is its occurrence in deontic

statements, i.e. in statements of social norms, whose primary illocutionary force is therefore representative. At least as far as child speech is concerned, they differ from directives in the subjunctive mood, in which the speaker not merely states but usually introduces the norm. Because of their primarily descriptive function, deontic statements do not categorically differ from nonmodalized statements about habitual behaviour, (14):

(14) (Mairi I, when the mother approaches the toy monkey with her foot)
      ze vàzun to póði 'One doesn't put one's foot (there)'

    = ðen váz-   un   to póði
      not put, imperfective present 3rd pl. the foot

Finally, there are a few examples of the present tense rendering the notion of deontic possibility qualifying inanimate subjects, as in (15):

(15) (Natali I, concerning the door of her toy car)
      níi . . . tìto? 'Does this open?'

    = aníj-   i   túto
      open, imperfective present 3rd sing. this

The notion of ability applying to animate subjects is expressed by the modal verb *boró* 'can, may'. Of the two MG modal verbs *boró* and *prépi* 'must' (a defective verb occurring only in the 3rd person singular), only the first is found in all transcripts (with the exception of Spiros I). *Boró*, typically used in conjunction with the negative particle by the children, only expresses ability, and chiefly refers to the speaker, as in (16). In period III there are a few examples of *boró* occurring with a sentence complement, as in (17). There is only one example from period III of a modal use of the verb *kséro* 'know, be able' expressing ability.

(16) (Natali I, trying in vain to open the door of her toy car)
      òbojó 'I can't'

    = ðen bor-   ó
      not can, imperfective present 1st sing.

(17) (Mairi III, concerning a strawberry represented in a book)
      əm borò na do bjáso 'I can't grasp it'

    = ðem bor-   ó   na to
      not can, imperfective present 1st sing. that it

    pjás-   o
    grasp, perfective present 1st sing.

Both *boró* 'can, may' and *prépi* 'must' are restricted to conveying deontic modality in the children's speech. *Prépi* expresses an obligation, the source of which does not reside in the speaker. As the nature of the obligation has to be stated in the complement sentence, examples with *prépi* are rare and occur only from period II on, due to their syntactic complexity (18):

(18) (Maria II, commenting on a neighbour's grandmother)
      pepi a pai: jaja maìa tó
      'Maria's granny must go to the doctor's'

  = prépi na   pái   i   jajá   tis   marías
     must that go, present 3rd sing. the granny of the of Maria

     sto   jatró
     to the doctor

As in other languages, the verb for 'want', *θélo*, is very frequently used by all subjects in the three periods studied, and mainly serves to express the speaker's wishes. As early as in period I, it may occur with an embedded clause (19):

(19) (Spiros I, while trying to turn the taperecorder off)
      sèli . . . klísoo . . . nè: '(Spiros) wants it to be turned off'

  = θéli   na   to klís-   une
     wants that it close, perfective present 3rd pl.

3. The development of modality in English

In contrast to MG, Modern English does not possess separate verb forms for the imperative and subjunctive moods, with certain exceptions. Imperative sentences are therefore usually distinguished from declarative and interrogative ones by leaving the 2nd person subject unexpressed. Due to the marginal role of modal verb form oppositions in Modern English, the main task of fulfilling the modalizing function falls upon the modal verbs.

Brown (1973: 180f) notes the semantic beginnings of the imperative sentence modality in Stage I (MLU 1.5 to 2.0) of the English language development of three children, but finds its formal development, however, only in Stage III (MLU 2.75 to 3.50). The children's ages in Stage I were 1;6 to 1;8 (Eve), 2;3 to 2;5 (Adam), 2;3 to 2;7 (Sarah); and in Stage III, 1;10 to 2;1 (Eve), 2;11 to 3;0 (Adam) and 3;0 to 3;5 (Sarah). In Stage I, imperative sentences cannot yet be identified on purely linguistic grounds as 'there is no really reliable intonational marking' and sentences without an overtly

expressed subject have not been narrowed down to commands. As modal auxiliaries emerge relatively late in English, modalized and nonmodalized utterances are often formally indistinguishable in the early stages of language development, for it is nearly impossible to tell whether or not a modal has been omitted, because 'there are no co-occurring adverbials or other forms to spotlight an omission' in diary or other records of spontaneous speech (Fletcher 1979: 264). As Brown's (1973) selection of modals was restricted by his criterion of acquisition, he 'could only select forms for which it was possible to identify contexts in which the form is obligatory' (p. 12). For this reason he excluded modal auxiliaries such as *can* and *must* and forms like *wanna* and *gonna* from his study. In another study, concerned with the period prior to the productive use of modal auxiliaries in affirmative sentences (age 2;5:21 to 2;7:15, MLU 3.01 to 3.25, i.e. Brown's Stage III), Kuczaj and Maratsos (1975b) compared a boy's spontaneous speech with elicited imitations of both grammatical and ungrammatical declarative sentences containing, in particular, the modal auxiliaries *will* and *can*. They found the child imitated 38 of the 48 grammatical declarative sentences correctly, but none of the 57 ungrammatical ones (with the modal auxiliary either misplaced after the main verb or accompanied by a tensed main verb), which he normalized in various ways. These findings can be taken as evidence that this boy had internalized much of the grammar of these modal auxiliaries before using them in his spontaneous speech.

In tracing the development of English modal verbs, comprising auxiliaries such as *can*, *will* and semi-auxiliaries or quasi-modals such as *going to* / *gonna*, *want to* / *wanna*, and *need to*, I shall base my presentation on reports of children acquiring American and British English. The children acquiring American English are Hildegard (Leopold 1949b,c), Adam, Eve, and Sarah (Klima and Bellugi 1966; Bellugi 1971, 1974), Abe (Kuczaj and Maratsos 1975b; Kuczaj 1977; Kuczaj and Daly 1979), Nina$_1$ (Shepherd 1980, 1981), Nina$_2$ (Pea *et al.* 1982), and six subjects studied by Pea and Mawby (1981). Children's syntactic competence concerning modal constructions has been studied by Major (1974). For British English there are the studies on Daniel (Fletcher 1979) and on 60 children from the Bristol corpus (Wells 1979).

In Stage I (MLU 1.75), the speech of Eve, Adam, and Sarah is still devoid of modal verbs, although there are examples of semantically modalized utterances like *I ride train? Have some?* and *Sit chair?* (Klima and Bellugi 1966). After MLU has reached 2.50 in Stage II, the quasi-modal forms *wanna*, *gonna*, and *hafta* begin to be used. The first modal auxiliary form to emerge is *can't* in Stage III (MLU 2.75), together with *don't* in

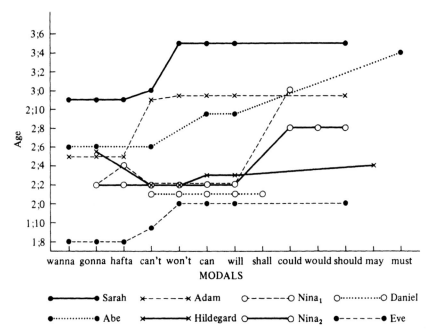

Figure 1. The emergence of English modals

negated imperatives. Modal auxiliaries begin to appear in the children's speech in abundance only after the sentences are longer than 3.50 MLU (Stage IV). Only then do we find *can* separated from its negative element and *will*, *won't*, and *should* occurring. The order of emergence of modal forms in Eve's, Adam's, and Sarah's development is represented in figure 1, together with longitudinal data of five of the other children. The precedence of *can't* over *can*, in Eve's, Adam's, and Sarah's utterances accords with the occurrence of *can't* and *won't* prior to their affirmative forms in both Hildegard's and Abe's speech (Leopold 1949b,c; Kuczaj and Maratsos 1975b; see also Ervin 1964 and Bloom 1970).

There appears to exist considerable variation between subjects concerning the age at which modal forms begin to occur. In part this is, however, due to different criteria used (first appearance versus productive use). Variation could also be reduced if comparison were based on MLU instead of age. The developmental curves of Eve, Adam and Sarah would then coincide. Since MLU calculations were lacking for several children, figure 1 had to be based on age. This, however, does not affect the overall sequence of emergence of modal forms: *wanna*, *gonna*, *hafta* and the affirmative and negative forms of *can* and *will* precede the past forms of the latter,

as well as *shall, should, may,* and *must* (except for *shall* in Daniel's case and for *should* in Eve's, Adam's, and Sarah's cases, which are reported to have appeared in the same period as *can* and *will*). As *might* and *ought to* are missing altogether in the data presented, they emerge even later. The early appearance of *can* and *will* accords with Wells' results (1979), where these are reported to be the two most frequently used modal verbs (negative forms most probably included) in 60 children from the Bristol corpus. Both of these verbs occurred at least once in 50 per cent of the sample by 2;6. This criterion was reached by *going to* at 2;9, by *have got to* at 3;0, by *shall* at 3;3, and by *could* at 3;6. Following the total frequency hierarchy and in the proportion of the sample using the forms, but not reaching the 50 per cent criterion before 3;9, are *have to, must, might, should, would, may, had better,* and *ought to*. The most frequently occurring modal forms in the speech of the six subjects studied by Pea and Mawby (1981), who ranged in age from 2;4 to 2;10 and 2;11 to 3;5 at the beginning and the end of observation, were *gonna, will, have to,* and *can,* with *can't* and *could* following closely, but only one or a few instances of *would, won't, got to, should, had better,* and *might*. Notable omissions in Pea and Mawby's data are *may, must, shall,* and *ought to*.

The only way of gaining some understanding of this piecemeal appearance of modal forms is to cast a glance at the early development of the grammar of verb forms, taking the functions served by main and modal verbal forms into consideration. When quasi-modals began to appear during Stage II, Adam, Eve and Sarah were already inflecting verbs for the present progressive (Brown 1973:271, fig. 14). Sarah was also using past irregular forms. By Stage III, all children had acquired past forms and thus had two non-modal verb form types at their disposal, one for the past and a neutral one which could mark the present or be combined with modal or quasi-modal auxiliaries. The forms *wanna, gonna,* and *hafta* have to be considered as monomorphemic in early child language and can thus not be distinguished from auxiliaries (W. R. Miller and Ervin 1964; Shepherd 1981:100). At least as far as the development of verbal inflection in Adam's and Eve's speech is concerned (but see also the development of Hildegard's verb forms, Fletcher 1979:266), the first division seems to be between nonmodal verb forms describing ongoing actions and processes and intrinsically future-oriented modalized forms. Only after this division of verb forms into modal and nonmodal ones has occurred do the nonmodal forms divide into present and past forms (see chapter 17 in this volume, for discussion of their functions). From what has been said, it seems plausible that modals should be marked for past only after main verbs (Fletcher 1979:273, and figure 1 above).

The importance of modals in child language, once they have emerged, is reflected by their frequency of use. The frequency data presented by Wells (1979) indicate that about 10.8 per cent of the utterances of 60 children from 2;6 to 3;6 contained a modal verb form. This accords almost perfectly with the percentage found by Pea and Mawby (1981) for their six subjects (10 per cent). Shields and Steiner (1972: 103) note a marked increase in the use of modal auxiliaries in their sample of 107 3–5 year olds and characterize this as one of the 'main areas of growth' in language development over this period.

As is also true for main verbs and nonmodal auxiliaries, modal verbs are at first subject to severe morphological, syntactic, and, above all, semantic restrictions. The initial use of negative modal forms by some children long before the respective positive forms emerge is most probably due to pragmatic reasons. It also shows that children may employ fragments of a grammatical system before having analysed it (Kuczaj and Maratsos 1975b). Also, modals have been observed to appear in questions only after having become productive in declarative sentences (Bellugi 1967 for Adam, Eve, and Sarah; Kuczaj and Maratsos 1975b for Abe), in spite of the fact that more than half of the input sentences are questions and imperatives (Newport 1977). This is not at all surprising, however, if language acquisition is seen in an interactive framework, for declarative sentences are just the appropriate type of response to questions and imperatives. Moreover, there is evidence that the use of modals in *yes/no* questions and declaratives is part of a unified system. Although her parents usually contracted *will* in affirmative sentences, Eve used the uncontracted form in declarative sentences and not only in *yes/no* questions, where she had heard it from her parents (Bellugi 1967). Abe, in the experiment referred to above, imitated contracted *'ll* in all six affirmative sentences as *will*, which is evidence for 'a great deal of pre-productive integration of the modal system' (Kuczaj and Maratsos 1975b). When modals became more abundant in questions used by Adam, Eve and Sarah (MLU 3.5 to 4.0), subject and auxiliary were in most cases inverted in *yes/no* questions (e.g. *Will Robin help me?*), while the non-inverted type (e.g. *What you will do?*) predominated with *wh*-questions (Bellugi 1971). Bellugi explains this by the complexity resulting from 'the *combination* of inversion and *wh*-question in a single string' (p. 100).

In an experimental study of 44 subjects aged 5 to 8 years, Major (1974) found that, with few exceptions, the children were able to transform affirmative declarative sentences containing a modal auxiliary into negatives and questions or to add tags. The performance of *may, might,* and *ought to* indicated that these tasks were not yet completely mastered by 8 years

and that these modals are thus acquired later than, for example, *can*. Modals are, however, much more of a semantic than a syntactic problem for children. For this reason, experiments like the one conducted by Major, which do not take the meaning and situational context of sentences into consideration, trying to treat modality as a purely syntactic phenomenon, are unlikely to come to grips with the development of the modalizing function, a conclusion reached by the author herself (Major 1974: 111; see also Fletcher 1975).

As in Greek child language, modalized utterances in early English child language predominantly express deontic meanings. *Can, could*, and *may* are used for deontic, action-oriented possibility and *will, want to, going to, would, shall, have (got) to, must, should, had better*, and *ought to* for deontic necessity. *Can*, the earliest and most frequently used modal, at first occurs only with 1st and 2nd person subjects, stating the child's own ability or social possibility and, above all, his physical inability. It is also used to ask for permission or to request actions from the addressee. *Could*, emerging later than *can*, appears much less frequently in expressions of ability and permission (Wells 1979; Pea and Mawby 1981). While 97 per cent of the Bristol sample used *can* for permission, *may* was used by only 15 per cent in this function (Wells 1979). Of the modals used for expressing deontic necessity, *will, want to, going to*, and *would* are volition-centred and the rest obligation-centred, with *shall* participating in both functions. *Will* is used very early and frequently to announce the child's intentions to act or not to act. *Going to, would*, and *shall* are also used for intentions, but more frequently in other functions (see below). Although *want to / wanna* literally expresses wishes, it is often indirectly requestive (Pea and Mawby 1981). Both obligations which introduce and those which state norms are most often expressed by *have (got) to / hafta*. According to Wells' and Pea and Mawby's analyses, norm stating appears to prevail over norm introducing, i.e. performative use. *Shall* does not occur in Pea and Mawby's data and 50 per cent of the Bristol sample using it performatively did so only after 3;6. *Should, must*, and *had better* are found less frequently in norm stating and norm introducing functions. *Ought to* is missing from Pea and Mawby's data altogether and is used to state obligation by only 3 per cent of the Bristol sample.

The most important class of speech acts that deontically modalized utterances are used for are directives. These have been given special attention in pragmatically oriented research on child language. Imperative sentences, the most important formal device in English for making direct requests, that is commands, appear very early, although, as we have seen, they are

at first not systematically distinguished from declarative sentences on syntactic grounds. Indirectly expressed directives seem to develop later in English than, for instance, in Italian, where interrogative requests were found to develop before 2 years of age (Bates 1976). In English, such speech acts are dependent upon the emergence of modal verbs (Bates 1971). The earliest indirect requests are probably desiderative utterances containing *want (to)* used as a main verb or semi-auxiliary. Menyuk (1969) found that all of the younger children (2;10 to 3;1) in her group used imperative sentences, while the older nursery-school children were using other forms of directives as well (see also Garvey 1975; Dore 1977; Ervin-Tripp 1977; Dore, Gearhart and Newman 1978). Interestingly, Menyuk notes a combination of syntactically interrogative with prosodically imperative requests (e.g. *Would you sit down!*), which shows that 'children are, at this stage, frequently telling you rather than asking you' (1969: 89). While instrumentally used declaratives (*I want / need* X) decline between the ages of 3 and 6 (Bock and Hornsby 1977), when the child has reached the age of 4 both declarative and interrogative directives are still prominent but are used in non-equivalent ways: *I want* is used more often than *Can I?* in re-requests (Wootton 1981). The use of interrogative requests rather than imperatives may also be a function of the addressee (Bock and Hornsby 1977; Mitchell-Kernan and Kernan 1977; James 1978). The interrogatives and declaratives conveying directives indirectly used by children as young as 3 or 4 years old constituted nearly two-thirds of the directives expressed in an experimental situation, although there was no decline in the use of direct, imperative forms up to age 6;6 (Bock and Hornsby 1977). 'Indirect' directives may, however, function independently of their literal meaning for the child and 'in some cases, the literal meaning may grow out of idiomatic uses' (Bock and Hornsby 1977: 80). Thus, interrogative requests for action have been found to precede real questions, i.e. requests for information (Bates 1976; Fletcher 1979). There is controversial evidence on the issue of whether requests for action show a tendency to become less literal with age (Garvey 1975; Bock and Hornsby 1977). In any event, by the age of 6 or 7, children seem to have acquired all the conventional forms that directives may take in standard American English at least, namely statements of need, imperatives, embedded imperatives (*Could you* V?), permission directives (*May/Can I* V?), question directives (*You got a quarter?*), hints (*It's hot out here*), and even elaborate oblique stratagems (*Pretend this was my car*); see Ervin-Tripp (1977), Mitchell-Kernan and Kernan (1977). To a certain extent they also seem to be aware of the situational appropriateness of particular directive forms by that age.

Directives share their forward-looking, future-oriented nature with two

types of utterances having a primarily representative illocutionary force – expressions of intention and predictions. Although *will* and *going to*, as well as *shall*, will eventually be used for both of these functions, intentions, belonging to the domain of deontic modality, precede predictions in English language development (Leopold 1949b: 99; Wells 1979). The fact that future tense forms are significantly better understood by 2–4 year olds in reference to the immediate than to the remote future (Harner 1976) may be attributed to the strongly modal character of the future tense in early child language. According to Harner (1982: 116): 'it seems likely that there is an overlap between immediacy and certainty such that the more immediate the future event, the more certain one can be that it will occur'. These results completely agree with our findings for Greek language development. If it is 'the degree of certainty of the speaker's statement being factual' which influences the choice of a future referent (near versus remote) in 3–5 year olds (p. 123), this is further evidence that epistemic modality develops from the prediction of events not controlled by the child (see section 2 above). While half of the 60 children of the Bristol sample use *will* for intentions at 2;6, this criterion is reached for predictions only at 3;0 (Wells 1979). Unfortunately, Wells does not specify the functions of *going to*, which was being used by half of the sample at 2;9. In Pea and Mawby's (1981) data, 99 per cent of 115 uses of *gonna* and 87 per cent of 55 uses of *will* expressed intention, with most sentence subjects being 1st person. The authors note that relatively few predictive uses of these terms occurred for nonvolitional events in the utterances of children ranging in age from 2;4 to 3;5 (they classify volition as belonging to epistemic modality). While the expression of intention as compared to predictions dominates up to 2;8 in Nina$_2$'s case, the ratio is reversed between 2;8 and 3;4 (Pea *et al.* 1982, who consider intentions and predictions as representing the null degree of dynamic and epistemic modality, respectively).

Shepherd (1980, 1981) found evidence that the distinction between intentions and predictions was lexicalized by Nina$_1$ between 2;5 and 3;0. While she had been using both *will* and *gonna* for volition and intention from 2;2 to 2;5, from then on she reserved *gonna* for events in the immediate future and controlled by herself, usually her own activities, and *will* to refer to the more distant future or to events in the immediate future which she did not control.[1] Evidence for the same kind of semantic distinction between two forms which they do not possess in the standard language comes from Clinton, a 4-year-old boy acquiring Antiguan Creole. He used *go* and *gon*, which are free variants in the standard language, to refer to events controlled by himself and beyond his control, respectively. It must be noted, however, that adult Antiguan Creole differentiates, as does

English, between different degrees of modal value with other modals. The fact that Nina₁ and Clinton went beyond the target languages they were acquiring may be evidence for a trend noted in child language toward one form for one function (Slobin 1973), or more simply, for the child's gradual decentring from his own self (see also Shepherd 1981: 112).

4. The development of epistemic modality

Epistemic modal meanings develop later than deontic ones in language acquisition. As the linguistic forms serving to convey epistemic modality are of the same type as those used to express deontic modality (modal verbs, verbal inflections) and are to a large extent even identical with them, the reason for the later development of epistemically modalized utterances cannot be sought in linguistic complexity but must rather lie in cognitive complexity. As we have seen in section 1 above, epistemically modalized utterances are centrally concerned with the notion of possibility, involving a distinction between reality and some other state of affairs which is based on certain conditions. Studies of cognitive development have shown that the notion of possibility as distinct from reality develops in Piaget's pre-operational stage (from about 2 or 3 to about 7 or 8 years), where possibility is the potential future (see Piéraut-Le Bonniec 1980: 52ff and section 2, above, on predictions). Only at 7 or 8 years do children begin to have some idea of undecidability, and 'the capacity to reason on the basis of hypotheses' (alethic modality) is not acquired until 11 to 12 years of age (Piéraut-Le Bonniec 1980: 76; see also Osherson and Markman 1974/5; Berthoud and Sinclair 1978). The source of the developing notion of possibility may, however, be seen in the child's ability to pretend, emerging as early as Piaget's stage 6 of the sensorimotor period (at about 1;6), when the child first engages in symbolic play (Piaget 1946b; see also Cromer 1974; Bates 1976; McCune-Nicolich 1981b).

In a number of languages, the first use of the imperfective past has been observed to be not a temporal, but a modal one, serving to describe simulated activities and states, and to set the stage and assign character roles in pretend play (Lodge 1979; Kaper 1980). Depending on the language acquired, the conditional, the subjunctive II, and the optative as well as modal verbs may also be used in these functions, as in the following examples:

(20) *Brazilian Portuguese 2;11:19 (de Lemos, workshop notes, Nijmegen 1981)*
Eu era a mãe cabeleireira
'I were the mother hairdresser'

Italian 3;6–4;0 (Bates 1976: 230)
Il sono il marito, e tu eri la mia moglie
'I am the husband, and you were my wife'

Greek 3;0–3;3 (Katis 1983)

eγó píjen-a,   esí
I   go, imperfective-past 1st sing. you

na   oðíγaj-es
modal particle drive, imperfective-past 2nd sing.

'I would be going and you would be driving'

Turkish 2;0–2;6 (Aksu, workshop notes, Nijmegen 1981)
Ayı uyu-du
bear sleep-past
'The bear was sleeping'

Bu anne   ol-sun
this mother be-optative 3rd sing.
'This shall be the mother'

Swedish 3;0–3;3 (Strömqvist, workshop notes, Nijmegen 1981)
Den här va flickan, assa va du pappa å ja va mamma ... då skulle
   dom gå ut
'This one was the girl, and then were you Daddy and I was Mummy
   ... then should they go out'

Flemish 3;11 (Schaerlaekens 1977: 159f)
Gij waart een krokodil, gij was nu dood
'You were a crocodile, you were now dead'

German (Kaper 1980: 213)
Das ist ein Pferd und das wäre der Stall
'This is a horse and this were the stable'

English (Cromer 1974: 220)
Dis'll be the blanket. Dis could be the mother

French (Grevisse, in Kaper 1980: 214)
Jouons au cheval: tu serais le cheval
'Let's play horse: you would be the horse'

In Turkish language development, the evidential (-*miş* past) is used in
the function of setting up the scene in pretend games later than the -*di*
past. It was observed in a boy from 2;9 onwards (e.g. *sen hastay-mış-sın*

you ill (evidential, 2nd person singular) '(let's pretend) you are ill'; Aksu, workshop notes, Nijmegen 1981). With respect to the modal distinction of information directly acquired through perception in contrast to information indirectly acquired through inference, the functional differentiation between the two past inflections takes place around the age of 4;0 to 4;6 in Turkish language development (Aksu 1978). The difficulty of the evidential resides in the cognitive complexity of integrating causal relations of events with anteriority (see also below, on hypothetical reference).

In reference to real states of affairs, epistemic main verbs like *think* and adverbs like *maybe* may precede epistemically modalized statements in which the expression of modality is integrated into the verb phrase in language development (Stern and Stern 1928: 107f; Cromer 1974; Pea *et al.* 1982).

Examples for the expression of epistemic possibility or necessity have been found in many languages, at least from the second half of the third year onwards. While potential mood emerges late in Finnish language development (Toivainen 1980: 31), epistemic modality is expressed by the conditional and by modal verbs much earlier, as in these examples, from Toivainen (1980):

(21) Niina 2;9

ol- isi-   ko-   han   nuo ollut romulaatikossa?
be conditional question particle particle those been in the toy box
'Could they (the pencils) have been (instead of *be*) in the toy box?'

Marko 2;3
taitaa   nämä tulla
may, 3rd sing. they   come, infinitive
'(It is possible that) they may come'

Aksu (workshop notes, Nijmegen 1981) cites examples of the use of the aorist inflection for epistemic possibility in Turkish language development from the first half of the third year onwards, as in (22). Deontic as well as epistemic meanings of the aorist appear to be fully developed around 2;8 to 3;0.

(22) 2;3

düş-er- im   ben
fall aorist 1st sing. I
'I might fall'

> 2;8 (answering a question about why one doesn't throw balls)
> ama vur-ur   gözüne   onun
> but hit aorist his eye (dative) his (genitive)
> 'But it might hit his eye'

Smoczyńska (1981) notes hypothetical reference in her Polish data as early as 1;9 or even 1;7, although, in the early stages, the only formal clue to such meanings is the inappropriate use of past tense forms, the conditional particle *by* being omitted, as in (23):

(23) Basia 2;6 (refusing her friend's invitation to climb a hill)
      ja nie pódje, ja spadłam, moja mamusia płakała
      I not will go I fell   my Mummy cried
      'I will not go. I would fall and my Mummy would cry'

In a longitudinal study of a Greek girl from 2;6 to 4;0, Katis (1983) found a few examples of hypothetical reference from 3;3 on, and of epistemically modalized utterances from 3;9 on:

(24) áma kriv-ómuna   se mia spiljá,
      if   hide mediopassive imperfective past 1st sing. in a   cave,
      θa   me é-   vrisk-   es?
      fut. particle me augmentative find imperfective past 2nd sing.

      'If I hid in a cave, would you find me?'

      borí   ke na fov-   ótane
      it may be also that be afraid mediopassive imperfective past 3rd sing.
      'It may also be that he was afraid'

   In spite of an early example of an epistemically modalized statement from Hildegard at 2;2 (*you might break that spoon* and *baby might break that spoon*, addressing a baby and subsequently her parents), Leopold (1949c: 35) recognizes that 'the world of possibilities is opened' to her only at 2;8. The first epistemically modalized statements have generally been found to occur in the second half of the third year in English language development, about six months later than deontic meanings. Epistemically modalized utterances are at first still extremely rare, however, as compared to deontically modalized ones. Of the 1,766 utterance tokens containing a modal in Nina$_2$'s speech between 1;11 and 3;4, only 7 express epistemic modality and 5 of these were found after 2;8 (Pea *et al.* 1982). Epistemically modalized utterances become more frequent only towards the middle of

the fourth year or even later (Cromer 1968, 1974; Kuczaj 1977). Modal verbs used to express epistemic modality in English child language up to 3;6 are *might, must, may, should, can, could,* and *would* (Kuczaj and Daly 1979; Wells 1979; Pea and Mawby 1981). None of these reached the criterion of occurring at least once in 50 per cent of the Bristol sample by 3;6.

Some of the early examples of epistemic modality are about possible future events or likely present states of affairs (see example (21)). Others refer to unlikely future events (see Hildegard's utterances cited above). A third type of such modalized utterances expresses hypothetical reference involving contingent relations between events (see examples (22) to (24)). While Cromer (1968, 1974) did not find any examples of hypothetical reference in the speech of Adam, Eve, and Sarah up to age 4;6, Kuczaj (1977) found some evidence of such reference in the speech of some 2 and 3 year olds learning English. Using eliciting techniques in natural and experimental situations, Kuczaj and Daly (1979) were able to obtain a number of formally unmarked hypothetical statements in English from age 2;7 onwards, and explicit ones from 2;9 onwards, with the early uses by children up to 3;1 being more often implicit than explicit and other-initiated rather than self-initiated. Reference to isolated hypothetical events occurs prior to reference to a sequence of such events. Hypothetical reference develops first in the future domain, where there is more uncertainty than in the past domain (e.g. *If you would have eated all that turkey, your tummy would have kersploded* from a child at 3;11, p. 575). Kuczaj and Daly's results agree with the finding made in some other languages that the conditional mood is the last verbal inflection to develop, a lateness which is generally attributed to the cognitive complexity of the notions it conveys. More research will be necessary before one can be certain whether the relatively late development of hypothetical reference in English as compared to Polish is due to the structural differences between the two languages, as Smoczyńska (1981) assumes.

While the expression of epistemic modality requires that one make a distinction between factual and possible states of affairs, for hypothetical reference it is necessary to take simultaneously into consideration a nonfactual situation and its relation to some other factual or nonfactual situation. This is what makes hypothetical reference in its complete form so difficult (see also Bates 1976; Jakubowicz 1978).

5. Universal aspects of the development of modality

Assuming cognitive development to be fundamentally the same across cultures, differences in the ontogenesis of languages must to a large extent

be attributable to their structural differences. Language development involves a process of grammaticalization of linguistic devices. In the historical development of languages, grammaticalization has been observed to consist of what, in a simplified account, could be called a process of condensation and coalescence, starting 'from a free collocation of isolating lexemes in discourse' and passing to more and more tightened grammatical constructions through syntacticization and morphologization (Lehmann 1982; see also Givón 1979). Although the ontogenetic process of grammaticalization is not quite parallel to the historical one, syntacticization and morphologization are both important factors of language development in the child. There is evidence from verbal as well as nominal grammar that morphological (synthetic) structural devices are acquired earlier than syntactic (analytic) ones. A comparison of the development of modalized verb forms in the early inflectional stages of English and Greek child language shows that while the Greek child cannot, so to speak, escape the expression of inflectional categories, as they are a part of tightly knit lexical forms in the language he is acquiring, the structure of English makes it possible to concentrate first on the expression of lexical content and to leave modulations of meaning aside. While analytic and synthetic structural devices are generally considered to be isofunctional in the languages of the world, infinitive-like verb forms, as they occur in the early inflectional stages of the development of languages like English, German, and French, do not fulfil the modalizing function to the same degree as, for example, the Greek subjunctive or the Turkish optative. In addition to expressing modality, the latter verb-form categories make distinctions of person, number, and (in Greek) aspect, thereby achieving more differentiated communication, while the former do not. In these languages, this will, of course, sooner or later result in 'a pressure towards the development of new forms which are of a more function-specific character' (Werner and Kaplan 1963: 60).

As we have seen, deontic meanings are expressed before epistemic ones by children acquiring typologically and genetically quite different languages. This must therefore be ascribed to cognitive development with the egocentric 'will-do' being much more basic for the child than the 'will-happen' (Pea and Mawby 1981). As far as the function of linguistic devices for expressing modality is concerned, these provide further evidence for the observation that forms are at first not used with their full range of functions. The imperfective past may in some languages be used to express mood prior to tense. This is especially true of the future tense forms. With an increasing differentiation of temporality and modality from concrete action, the meaning range of the old verb forms will shift, and new, more function-specific, form categories will develop. Thus, in Greek, the old

global category of the subjunctive will divide into the future tense and the subjunctive mood, and in Turkish, evidential and non-evidential past will be separated.

The ontogenetic order of the development of deontic and epistemic modality agrees with evidence from Creole and the history of English (Goossens 1981), where epistemic meanings develop from deontic ones (see Shepherd 1981: 102ff). Another parallel between ontogenetic and historical language development comes from work in Romance languages (Fleischman 1982), the results of which suggest that 'the meanings of futurity may provide an intermediate stage in the progression from deontic to epistemic' modality (Shepherd 1981: 115). While the future categories of the ancient Indo-European languages are described as 'desiderative presents' by Meillet (1937: 215), Humbert (1954: 151) recognizes both a 'virtual' and a 'desiderative' component in the ancient Greek future, the first leading to tense and the second approaching mood. This could be considered as a fair characterization of the category of the future in child language (see also Ferreiro 1971: 238f). In Turkish, the later development of the hearsay function of the evidential past as compared to its inferential function again seems to retrace historical development (Slobin and Aksu 1982: 191).

Studying the comprehension of deontic utterances of different modal degrees (e.g. *must* versus *may*) in comparison to epistemically modalized ones in English-speaking children between 3;0 and 6;6, Hirst and Weil (1982) found that children already appreciate the relative strength of epistemic meanings in the second half of their third year, while relative strength is appreciated with deontic meanings only about a year later. As the authors themselves admit, it cannot, however, be excluded from consideration that this result, which seems to be in conflict with evidence from production data, has a nonlinguistic, sociological cause pertaining to the experimental design. In other respects, Hirst and Weil's study confirms the results of longitudinal research. In accordance with Jakobson's principle of maximal contrast, children first distinguish modals from factuals before differentiating within the modal field, where 'the general rule seems to be: the greater the difference in the strength of the two types of modal propositions the earlier this difference will be appreciated' (Hirst and Weil 1982: 665). On different degrees of modality in English language development, see also Shepherd (1981) and Pea *et al.* 1982.

It may be that the affinities of the ontogenetic and the historical processes of grammaticalization can be explained by an important principle of cognitive development according to which 'new forms first express old functions, and new functions are first expressed by old forms' (Slobin 1973: 184f).

The priority of deontic, as compared to epistemic, modality in the ontogenesis as well as in the history of languages can be considered as indicating the primacy of the social, as compared to the epistemic, function of language.

19. Deixis*

Roger Wales

1. Introduction

What do such diverse expressions as demonstratives, pronouns, adverbs of place, verbs of motion such as *come* and *go*, definite articles, tenses, etc. have in common? They are all held to be *deictic* expressions. *Deixis* is the Greek word for indicating or pointing. It has been taken over as a technical term in linguistics to refer to those terms or expressions which serve this linguistic function. That is, they are all expressions which serve to direct the hearer's attention to spatial or temporal aspects of the situation of utterance which are often critical for its appropriate interpretation. They do this in a way which is particularly interesting, since they serve as a meeting point for syntactic, semantic and pragmatic aspects of language. This is because they are, to use G. Stern's (1964) term, contingent expressions. By this is meant that, to interpret them, the interpreter needs not only context-independent semantic information but also information which is contingent on an actual (or construed) context. They are used to direct the attention of the hearer of a communication toward some object or event. The aspect of the situation/speech event which is critical in this regard is, typically, information about the speaker, but in any case this information must be such as to enable decisions to be made about person and/or place in relation to the utterance. These expressions which we group as 'deictic' introduce an explicitly subjective orientation into linguistic classification. They draw attention to the fact that language is acquired and used by people in real situations. Some useful recent discussions of deixis from a linguistic point of view are contained in Fillmore (1971), Kuryłowicz (1972), Atkinson and Griffiths (1973), Lyons (1977), Jarvella and Klein (1982) and Weissenborn and Klein (1982). There has been of late a flurry of studies of children's language incorporating some reference to deixis, some more enthusiastic than others. These studies involve either an examination of how spatial (and/or temporal) information comes to be encoded in the child's language, or how the attention-directing function of deixis

comes to be incorporated in the child's language use. Some studies have distinguished these aspects more clearly (Clark 1978b) than others (Wales 1974). A sample of studies making reference to deixis in children's language are: Bowerman (1973), Bruner (1975b), Bates (1976), Clark (1978b) and Tanz (1980).

In this chapter, we will attempt to distinguish some of the key issues raised by deixis. To that end we will present some of the empirical cum methodological issues that we must grapple with in order to try and give a profile of this area of the child's linguistic development. Before dealing briefly with some topics covered in other chapters in this book (e.g. pronouns and tense), we will concentrate in more detail on studies of the acquisition of demonstratives and locative adverbs. This is because these terms are in many ways central to any discussion of deixis. This approach to exposition has been taken because that is the way most work in the field has been organized. Later we shall 'step back' and review the field as a whole.

2. *This* and *that*, and *here* and *there*

There are two deictic aspects of these terms which we will look at in particular:

(i)   their attention directing function – roughly, 'look', 'see'
(ii)   their contrastive spatial functions – *this* and *here* usually referring to objects and locations proximal to the speaker, *that* and *there* to objects and locations not proximal to the speaker

Given the latter, speaker-oriented semantic contrast, it is clearly possible that the process of acquisition might be constrained by the child's cognitive egocentricity (as generally proposed by Piaget 1926; Piaget and Inhelder 1956, and explicitly argued in this context by Webb and Abramson 1976 and argued against by de Villiers and de Villiers 1973). It is striking that diarists of early language development have found that at least some of these terms occur in the earliest utterances of young children – sometimes in the first ten words, always (where the data are available) in the first fifty (Nelson 1973b). Perhaps even more striking is that they are used extensively in two-word utterances. Such observations already exist for a wide variety of languages. It seems reasonable in the light of these facts to suppose that both deixis and its early emergence are universal. This universality is seen as particularly important in the light of Lyons' (1975) extensive arguments, centred on these terms, that deixis is the source of linguistic reference. (McGinn 1981 argues a similar position in a more philosophical

framework.) For some indication of the relevance of this to development, note that Cross (1977) has observed that 73 per cent of all mother–child utterances involve immediate reference (i.e. reference to objects and events in the immediate environment).

First, let us look at how the young child, and its mother, use these expressions. A detailed analysis was done of some videotaped recordings of mother–child interactions.[1] The occasion of the use of each of these terms was noted (plus the contrast between definite and indefinite article, and pronouns). Where a term was used, a note was also made of the kind of gesture (or lack of gesture) accompanying it. Ten mother–child pairs in a total of 15 recording sessions (of about half an hour each) were thus categorized. Because of differences in the total amount of speech used, all scores were transformed into percentages. The results of the coded categories are summarized in table 1. It is clear that the terms are used very frequently by both mothers and children and, for both, the dominant strategy for the use of these linguistic 'pointing' expressions is associated with some explicit pointing or handling gesture. Among the more striking details, note the mothers' concentration on the use of *that, there* and *the*, whereas a more even spread of terms was used by the children. Also, the dominant mode of gestural support for these expressions is some form of explicit handling. The pattern of gestural response is clearly geared to attracting and holding the listener's attention to the relevant referential domain, and the handling presumably serves the function of making the gesture as unambiguous as possible. This is consistent with the observation of Shatz (1982) that children below the age of 24 months have yet to learn the conventional relations between language and gesture before the latter can be anything more than attentional devices. Pechmann and Deutsch (1980) have also shown that both children and adults often point at the intended referent when both interlocutors can see it, instead of describing it verbally; they have also shown that the use of gestures seems to affect both the form and content of their descriptions. Our analyses are from children aged 19 months upwards. The basic pattern of use seems fairly constant across all the mothers and children, irrespective of the level of linguistic development of the children. What does change, as a function of the linguistic sophistication of the child, is what the mother puts into the referring expression, not how it is introduced. This is what Bruner (1983) describes as the mother 'formating' her utterances. He also relates this strategy to much earlier, prelinguistic, forms of behaviour between mother and child.

While it is difficult at this point to quantify such behavioural patterns, what seems clear is that the mothers of the linguistically less advanced

Table 1. *Mean percentage scores of mothers' and children's use of demonstratives and locative adverbs with associated gestures (standard deviations in parentheses)*

Utterance type	Mothers	Children
this	4.6 (3.2)	7.0 (5.1)
that	25.5 (5.6)	19.3 (8.4)
here	5.0 (3.3)	16.8 (6.6)
there	14.0 (5.4)	18.3 (11.4)
the	31.9 (6.5)	15.3 (10.4)
a	19.6 (5.1)	21.3 (14.0)
Total number of these utterances	6026	3123
Mean (½ hour) session	402 (166)	208 (165)

Category of associated gestures	Mothers	Children
1. Pointing	7.4 (2.9)	8.7 (6.5)
2. Handling – speaker, throughout	19.5 (8.4)	41.2 (12.1)
3. – speaker, putting down	2.9 (1.6)	4.7 (3.7)
4. – listener, throughout	15.2 (6.1)	4.2 (3.3)
5. – listener, putting down	1.7 (1.6)	0.5 (0.7)
6. – picking up	8.2 (3.4)	9.8 (2.8)
7. After putting down (speaker)	0.7 (0.8)	1.0 (1.0)
8. No handling	21.9 (4.4)	18.1 (7.7)
9. No concrete reference present	22.6 (8.9)	12.3 (10.2)

children (on the measures of Cross 1977) tend to relate only one or two items together semantically – almost as if they impart semantic information by a process of casual chaining. The mothers of the more advanced children, however, are using the same deictic devices to introduce referring expressions which relate to a wider network of semantic relations (e.g. while they placed toy furniture in various rooms of a house, an account of the functions of those rooms was given). It is almost as if the mothers are using the same introductory devices, but tuning their 'tutelage' to the competence of the child. Of course, it is an open question on this evidence as to which is the chicken and which the egg – the children's competence or the mothers' communicative strategy. However that question may ultimately be resolved, it is evident that the child has early mastered the general attention-directing function of these deictic terms, typically with accompanying gesture. There is a real question, however, as to whether they have yet mastered the contrastive aspects of these terms. Many of the utterances used by both mothers and children are difficult to categorize reliably from the videotapes, as either proximal or nonproximal to speaker. In the clear cases (approximately on a third of the utterances), it is obvious that the proximal/nonproximal distinction is not usually utilized by the

children. But then, neither is it by the mothers! The dominant use is simply introducing the referring expression and directing attention to the appropriate spatial domain of the conversational environment by means of the gesture. Now, Fillmore (1971) discusses how, as soon as gestures are used, you can 'override' the proximal/nonproximal contrast between *here* and *there*. It could also be argued that while *here* may be used without gesture and be taken to define a reference close to the speaker, *there* always requires some more information, such as that provided by gesture, to select the domain of reference (i.e. there is one *here* for many *theres*). The children do, however, make use of *this* and *here* when an object is introduced into the environment of discourse (say, a toy being brought out of a box), and *that* and *there* are used when such objects 'disappear'. This result is similar to that reported by Macrae (1976b) for children's use of *come* and *go*. Our result was also anticipated by Griffiths (1974a). Clark and Sengul (1978) discuss a possible contrast children may set up, compatible with these results, where *there* may be taken as an aspectual marker for completion (consistent with disappearance uses) in contrast with purely deictic use of *here*.

What hypotheses and strategies do children employ in order to develop the contrastive use of these expressions? The results of a few simple studies will now be summarized to illustrate some of the empirical issues involved. Similar studies have been reported by de Villiers and de Villiers (1973), Webb and Abramson (1976), Clark and Sengul (1978) and Charney (1979). Our studies start to explore differences in linguistic inferential performance, by getting children to use these expressions without the aid of gesture, in different situations and at different ages. Previous studies have checked on the domain talked about, controlled for distance away (since children may tend to reach for nearer objects) and for the position of the speaker (beside or opposite). They have looked at comprehension in the absence of gesture, because only in its absence can the observer determine that the child is processing the linguistic contrasts we are interested in. We looked at the effect of these different possible constraints with the same set of children. In the studies to be described here, there were 80 children in four age groups: 4, 5, 6 and 7 years old (see Wales 1979 for more details).

Each task consisted of four trials, one each on the deictic words *this*, *that*, *here* and *there*. The order of trials and tasks was randomized. Pairs of identical toys were used (varying with each task), and instructions were of the form: 'Make this pig jump', 'Make the monkey there run' etc. The verb of motion was varied and was always one the children were familiar with. Otherwise, the syntactic structure of each sentence was identical. The tasks are schematically laid out in figure 1 and were as follows:

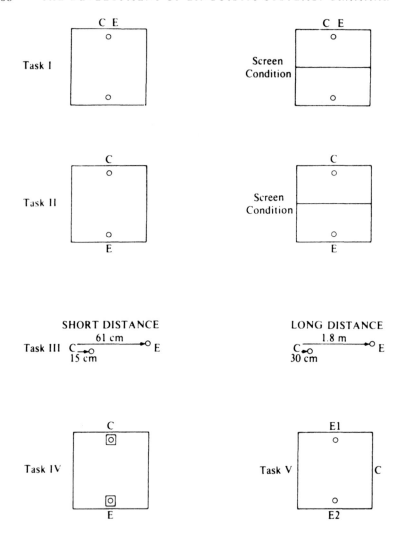

Figure 1.

I.   The child's perspective was the same as the experimenter's; i.e. they sat side by side at a table.
II.   The child and experimenter sat opposite each other, so their perspectives differed.

If the problem of the shifting boundaries associated with deictic reference is what makes for the child's difficulty in interpreting these terms, then

making clear, by demarcation, the areas denoted by each word should facilitate performance. Tasks I and II were therefore repeated with a 15 centimetre high screen across the middle of the table (Screen Condition) as used by de Villiers and de Villiers 1973.

III.   The toys were placed on the floor under two different distance conditions – the 'short distance' being similar to Webb and Abramson's (1976) study of *this* and *that*. This was a different perspective task, as in task II.

IV.   The same as task II, except that the locations for each animal were established before the test itself, and the locations marked with contrasting coloured paper.

V.   A further test of the child's ability to shift perspective, with two experimenters seated opposite each other, and each presenting the four instructions.

A comparison of task I with task II (see table 2) revealed no overall differences. In fact, there was a tendency for performance to be better on the opposite perspective task (II), the effect reaching significance for the youngest group. So much for egocentricity! (The anomaly of arguing for a global application of egocentricity was shown some time ago by Vygotsky 1934/1962, and many of the contradictions in the use of the term were brought out by Donaldson 1978.)

Table 2. *Performance on tasks I and II*

Age	Task I (same perspective)		Task II (different perspective)	
	Mean score	Per cent correct	Mean score	Per cent correct
4 years	1.1500	57.5	1.4750	73.7
5 years	1.2500	62.5	1.4250	71.25
6 years	1.3750	68.75	1.4750	73.7
7 years	1.4250	71.25	1.4500	72.5
Total	1.3000	65	1.4563	72.8

Performance on *here* and *there* (locatives) was better than *this* and *that* (demonstratives), an effect found in most of these tasks (see table 3).

The younger children did not show a difference in performance on the two types of words. Near perspective words (*this, here*) were significantly higher than far perspectives (*that, there*). Because of a position effect (to take the toy nearest the child), there was a significant task by word effect which diminished with age as the children learned to use the words more reliably.

Table 3. *Performance on demonstratives and locatives (tasks I and II)*

Age	Demonstratives		Locatives	
	Mean score	Per cent correct	Mean score	Per cent correct
4 years	1.2750	63.75	1.3500	67.5
5 years	1.2750	63.75	1.4000	70
6 years	1.2500	63.5	1.6000	80
7 years	1.2750	63.75	1.6000	80
Total	1.2688	63.4	1.4875	74.4

Comparing the Screen/No Screen tasks, there was no overall effect for screen, but this factor was involved in a significant word × task × screen interaction. The screen aided performance in the near perspective task but not in the opposite one. This occurred specifically for the demonstratives (the locatives were understood better). Thus when the child and speaker share the same perspective the presence of a distinguishing feature such as a screen aids performance. When the speaker is opposite the child the speaker provides a sufficient spatial cue.

Task III (the distance effect) yielded somewhat similar results, although not achieving significance. In task V, performance on locatives was again better than on demonstratives. An interesting result is that the responses to the experimenter who sat in the position vacated by the child were significantly less correct than those to the other experimenter, suggesting some perseveration from the preceding tasks. (This was confirmed by repeating the task with an independent group who had not had any preceding tasks, where the effect went away.) Comparing tasks IV and II showed no differences.

A further task (VI) was similar to II, except that children were given both a demonstrative and a locative term in the instruction: e.g. 'Make this dog run there' etc. When the terms were contrasted in the instructions (proximal versus nonproximal), the children performed better than when the polarity was noncontrasted. The total scores by items for when the children correctly followed both parts of the instructions were:

this/here 19, *this/there* 25, *that/here* 29, *that/there* 17

This trend was maintained when pooling across individual subcomponents of the instructions. Having two terms in the instructions results in better overall performance, presumably because having two terms helps to highlight the relevant spatial contrast. One odd result here is that, unlike all the earlier results, whether reported above, or by Clark (1978b), the demon-

stratives are significantly better than the locatives. Presumably this is a function of the task. In Clark's studies and those reported above, the locatives were evaluated by *initial* location. In studies such as Wales (1974), the locatives were evaluated in terms of *final* location, but in a context where it may make more intuitive sense to change the locations of the objects. Thus this result may be one more instance of children giving silly answers to silly questions! The answers themselves are not so silly, in that there is a nearly significant age by word effect, which stems from clear improvement of the demonstratives by age.

It seems clear from these results that the children have some notion of how to sort out the relevant deictic contrasts, but that the way in which this limited competence is expressed is situation-specific, often in quite predictable ways. Charney (1979) working with even younger children ($2\frac{1}{2}$ to $3\frac{1}{2}$ years) found that their understanding of *here* and *there* did not start with self reference but rather an inconsistent reference point, before learning that the reference point was the location of the speaker. She also found that *there* was better understood when the perspective of the child was the same as the speaker, or neutral to her, but was worse when the child's perspective was opposite to that of the speaker. Tanz (1980) has shown that by varying the task demands the differences in response with the demonstratives and locatives, and differences in performance on the markedness of each pair of terms, can be made to disappear. We will return to the rationale for these kinds of manipulation of task demands when we consider the verbs of motion.

Another way of looking at these kinds of data is to look at each individual subject and try to work out the strategies being used across the various tasks. As Clark and Sengul (1978) have also suggested, the children fall into three main categories: *no contrast, partial contrast,* and *full contrast.* Clark and Sengul subcategorized the crucial partial contrast set into two; speaker-, or self-orientated, this separation being based on two studies – essentially equivalent to tasks I and II here. Taking as a rule 70 per cent of responses as being necessary for inclusion in any given category, only six of the children in our studies were at all difficult to classify.

I *No contrast stage.* 20 per cent of all subjects showed no evidence of a contrast between proximal and nonproximal. (They might well have had some other contrast, e.g. deictic versus completive aspect, or deictic versus 'out of reach/unobtainable', etc.) They scored 50 per cent, almost invariably having a bias for the object nearest them. There existed an almost perfect correlation between inability to distinguish between contrastive terms, and inability to shift perspective as speaker roles were exchanged in task V.

II *Partial contrast.* 56.25 per cent of the children showed some sign that

a contrast existed. Unlike the suggestions of Clark and Sengul, at least four subcategories were established here:

(a) *Random shifting of focus between the toys* (20% of the children)
(b) *Alternating strategy:* each toy manipulated alternately, although not always correctly (17.5%)
(c) *Egocentric:* either used themselves as the reference point in task II, or performed better on task I than II (11.5%)
(d) *Speaker centred:* these children could only make the contrast successfully when the speaker sat opposite them (7.25%)

III *Full contrast.* 23.75 per cent had mastered the deictic contrast. The distribution of the various strategies is shown in figure 2 and shows a definite improvement in understanding with age. The observation that less than 50 per cent of the 7 year olds had mastered the deictic contrast suggests a tentative link between its acquisition and concrete operations, but our evidence shows that cognitive egocentrism is not involved in this relationship. (The apparent rise in egocentrism by age is simply a function of the rise in number of those using a spatial contrast, and is an effect specific to language.) This is not at all surprising, given the centrality of deixis

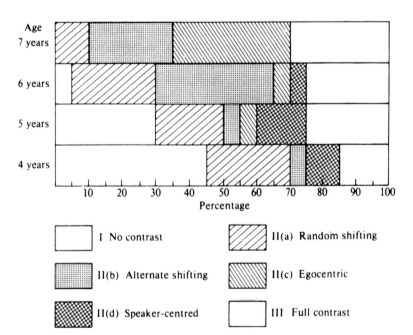

Figure 2. Strategies used by children of different ages

to reference, reference to communication, and communication to social interaction. For even more detailed analyses of individual error patterns, though only for *here* and *there*, see Charney (1979).

Other studies we have conducted have included variation on these types of task: e.g. a 'Gedanken' type of experiment (where 'I am thinking about one of the animals and will tell you something about it. You then try to work out which one I am thinking about'), giving such information as 'I am thinking about *that* one', etc. (without of course revealing the actual animal). When conducted in the same perspective situation, the children performed almost identically to the task II (opposite perspective) results reported earlier. This is presumably because in this task the children are explicitly being required to take the experimenter's viewpoint.

In another version of the 'Gedanken' task, the objects were in pairs on each side of the table and were manipulated so as to 'appear' or 'disappear'. The children focused most of their response choices for the deictic terms on the manipulated object, though this effect diminished with increasing age. This is because, as greater mastery is achieved of the relevant spatial contrast, more choices of a nonmanipulated object come to be made. What was interesting here was that a significantly greater number of 'appearance' choices were for *that* and *there*; and conversely for 'disappearance', there were a greater number of choices for *this* and *here*. That is, it appears to be the converse of the observations on the spontaneous use of these expressions. But note, the task was for the child to indicate which toy the person doing the manipulating was thinking about when using the expression. Thus the children were in fact reversing roles appropriately to take the speaker's point of view, and increasingly doing so by age.

A version of task VI, with both a demonstrative and a locative term in each instruction, was conducted some years ago on children aged 3 and 4 years (ten each) in each of three language groups: English (as spoken by a group of Edinburgh children), Tamil (a Dravidian language), and Lun Bawang (a Malayo-Polynesian language). The English instructions were of the form 'Move this (or that) block here (or there)'. The arrangements for testing are shown in figure 3 where 'this block' is labelled B

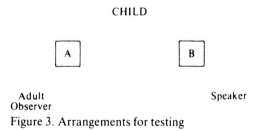

Figure 3. Arrangements for testing

Table 4. *Fully appropriate responses (both demonstrative and locative components simultaneously) in terms of an adult model*

	that/there	this/there	this/here	that/here
Tamil	3	8	6	12
Lun Bawang	0	8	12	19
English	0	3	15	6

and 'that block' A (versions of the results have been reported in Wales 1974 and Garman 1977). Fully appropriate responses are presented in table 4. Performance seems rather low, though looking at individual components obviously improves the picture. The English-speaking (i.e. Scottish) group contained spuriously high scores on *this/here*, due to a general strategy of many of the children of taking the block nearest to the speaker and moving it toward the speaker. If we ignore the results of these strategists for a moment, then it can be said that, overall, for each group *that/there* is hardest and *that/here* is easiest. Furthermore, mixed polarity instructions (relative to the speaker) are easier than nonmixed. The sequential response patterns – 'How many of those subjects who chose the wrong block placed it in the right location?' etc. – are shown in figure 4. (This ignores the

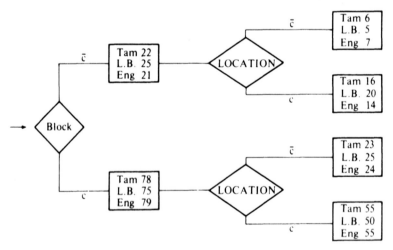

Figure 4. Percent response to all instructions
Tamil (Tam)   Σ = 78
Lun Bawang (L.B.) Σ = 77
English (Eng)   Σ = 29

c = correct; c̄ = not correct

responses of the English 'behavioural strategists'.) It is clear by inspection that the groups are very similar. Subjects are over three times more likely to select the right block than the wrong one, and regardless of which block is selected, are two to three times more likely to place it in the right location. Thus there seems to be much better incipient comprehension of deictic terms than 'fully appropriate' responses reveal. Complicating factors in the various groups and conditions seem to stem from the application of one or other of the following 'naïve' assumptions:

(i)   that proximity of block to speaker implies that speaker will be the agent of any block shifting

(ii)   that a deictic instruction is going to require a change in the deictic specification of the relevant object (it is presumably this principle which makes instructions with terms of similar polarity 'difficult')

It is possible that especially the English group could have been influenced by Block B (in figure 3) being in the direction of gaze of the speaker to child. One way to control for this is to have both objects in the same gaze path, as in figure 5:

SPEAKER   A   B   CHILD

Figure 5.

This study has been done with both English and Tamil 3- and 4-year-old children, who in this situation behave very similarly. The dominant strategy is to move one block from one location (on a stool) to the other, i.e. A to B or B to A. With *this/here* most move B to A; with *that/there* most move A to B; with *this/there* most move A to B; and with *that/here* most move B to A. That is, whenever the choice is between the correct block or the correct final location, the latter tends to win out. This of course fits in well with the general finding that the children are using the locative expressions more easily than the demonstratives.

Yet other studies, one of which will be presented later, have shown that in more overt game-playing situations with a wider set of response options their overall performance can be made to 'improve'. This is neither surprising nor itself relevant. It should be clear that with a wide set of experimental manipulations and a variety of methods of analysis what is of interest is not some absolute level of performance – 'the child's got it', or 'not', as the case may be; rather, they serve to indicate that the acquisition of these terms is a gradual process of putting a system of contrasts together and learning when and how it is appropriate to apply them. The system acquired seems to be roughly as follows:

(i)   A simple 'pointing function' (consistent, incidentally, with the mothers' dominant use of *that* and *there* and consistent with the priority Lyons (1975) gives these as terms of primitive deixis)

(ii)   A recognition that sometimes a contrast of some sort is relevant. This may be hooked into initial 'existence' assumptions like 'appearance' and 'disappearance' relative to the domain of discourse

(iii) The realization that the contrast of (ii) is related to the spatial location of the speaker, and that some spatial cues are helpful in different ways in different situations in determining this. The problem is in general to work out what the appropriate frame of reference relative to the speaker is

(iv)   A 'typical' adult system is developed, though it is perhaps still prone to what may be more sociolinguistic assumptions, like 'proximity of object to speaker implies that the agent of any object shifting will be the speaker', or simply the effects of animacy and agentivity interacting with deixis

At this point, however, we should pause and note a possible problem. It is clear that these expressions are used by children early in the acquisition process and, as Charney has shown, at least *here* and *there* can be interpreted fairly consistently in a formal task without gesture by around age 4 (although she has not shown they are used contrastively at this age). However, taking all the studies to date, there seems to be a sizeable developmental gap of up to 5 years or more between when the child is first able to use these expressions with the benefit of gestural support, and when it can use them to construe the appropriate spatial contrast without the benefit of gesture. This is particularly the case for the demonstratives. This developmental gap is unlikely to be simply a consequence of the early conjunction of gesture and interpretation, and this raises the possibility that something else is entering into the child's interpretations. The latter suggestion has been explored by testing the possibility that children are also using animacy as a ground for making these linguistic contrasts. This relates to a distinction made by Kirshner (1979) who distinguishes 'high' deixis as the use of 'proximal' demonstratives (e.g. *this*) to introduce animate/human referents, and 'low' deixis to introduce (by 'nonproximal' *that*) nonhuman/inanimate referents. The use of both comprehension tasks such as I and II above, and elicitation/production tasks, has served to confirm that children are using animacy as a ground for the use of these deictic expressions (Wales in press). It seems as if the assignment of proximal terms for animate referents and nonproximal for inanimates might be an early basis for a contrast in deictic terms. What this means is not so much that the children are

confounding space and animacy but, rather, using both where interpretable and salient in the environment for contextualizing reference (perhaps an early version of a 'me first' principle). The salience of animacy for young children has been proposed by Gelman and Spelke (1981) as an organizing basis for the development of the concept of object permanence (or constancy). What seems likely is that this strategy is also being applied to the use of deictic expressions. This could well be a ground for the 'appearance/disappearance' patterns reported above.

In all, the process of acquisition seems orderly. It is consistent with the assumptions made about these terms, namely that they have a semantic as well as a syntactic and pragmatic function, which starts off being organized as a general *linguistic* attention-directing device and which subsequently comes to include a more specialized spatial contrastive component (Atkinson 1982 discusses an acquisition model along these lines). Now let us turn to consider briefly studies of the acquisition of some other deictic expressions.

3. Pronouns

Until recently, pronouns have not figured largely in studies of children's language. One rationale for this is given by Brown (1973) in his excellent overview of his own and related work. He indicates that while some pronouns occur early and are used often, they are sufficiently restricted in type that it would require more features than there are pronouns to describe them. On the other hand, statistical studies of Suppes and his colleagues have indicated that pronouns are always in the young child's three most frequently used noun phrase types. Work by, for example, Chomsky (1969), Huxley (1970), Maratsos (1973) and Tanz (1974, 1977) shows that children not only use pronouns early on (typically *I, you, it,* and *mine*), but also observe many of the crucial constraints in their use and comprehension, for example, the distinction between definite and indefinite reference, which the adult use of such pronouns requires.

To give a picture of pronominal usage that fits in with the earlier studies and results, the results of percentage pronoun use by mothers and children is presented in table 5 in the same format as table 1 (from the same population of subjects). A few points are worthy of note: the pronouns used more frequently are *I, you,* (in subject position); *we, he,* (*him, she* and *her* not as often); *it* (in both subject and object position); *they, mine* (by the children); *your* (and *yours*); and *his* (by the mothers). What is most obvious about the associated gesture table is the much larger incidence of 'no handling' behaviour (as compared with the demonstratives and loca-

Table 5. *Mean percentage scores for spontaneous use of pronouns by mothers and children (standard deviations in parentheses)*

Utterance type	Mothers	Children
I	7.99 (2.97)	18.70 (8.19)
me	21.16 (0.57)	8.57 (4.05)
you (subject)	27.28 (6.83)	11.34 (6.33)
you (object)	0.74 (0.50)	1.11 (2.05)
we	8.70 (5.25)	0.44 (0.70)
us	0.53 (0.57)	0.54 (1.42)
he	7.08 (4.68)	5.88 (6.77)
him	2.27 (1.69)	0.73 (1.02)
she	3.12 (2.70)	1.06 (1.22)
her	1.77 (1.47)	0.93 (1.15)
it (subject)	16.92 (6.21)	11.71 (11.53)
it (object)	8.96 (3.76)	17.57 (17.69)
they	5.21 (3.57)	2.19 (3.82)
them	1.91 (1.99)	0.78 (1.33)
my/mine	0.28 (0.43)	15.27 (16.95)
your/yours	2.21 (1.28)	1.50 (2.14)
his	2.27 (1.31)	1.16 (1.36)
her/hers	0.51 (0.17)	0.24 (0.43)
its	0.34 (0.91)	0.00 (0.00)
their/theirs	0.55 (0.68)	0.09 (0.24)

Category of associated gestures	Mothers	Children
1. Pointing	2.01 (2.48)	3.96 (3.26)
2. Handling – speaker, throughout	15.90 (4.96)	30.56 (9.14)
3. – speaker, putting down	1.30 (0.70)	2.15 (1.41)
4. – listener, throughout	16.15 (3.86)	7.03 (5.55)
5. – listener, putting down	0.32 (0.36)	0.59 (1.02)
6. – picking up	1.85 (1.23)	2.47 (1.88)
7. After putting down (speaker)	0.56 (0.38)	0.29 (0.49)
8. No handling	53.47 (8.46)	46.53 (14.19)
9. No concrete reference present	8.44 (2.64)	6.42 (78.63)

tives of table 1). This rise in 'no handling' is directly a product of 'no gesture' being associated with the use of the 1st and 2nd person pronouns. Thus the picture for 3rd person usage, of whatever type, is very similar to that, say, for demonstratives. Thus it seems reasonable to hypothesize that the children learn person deixis, i.e. the use of pronouns to 'point to' persons, initially through the medium of the 'real' personal pronouns *I* and *you*. Indicating persons in the 3rd person (implied by gender distinctions) has gestural support as a typical concomitant, as found with the demonstratives. This suggests that experimental studies of children's use of the 3rd person pronouns might run into similar problems in the children's ability accurately to infer what the reference was when there was no gestural support.

In the earlier version of this chapter (Wales 1979) results were reported supporting this expectation with a wide range of pronouns. More recently a thorough study by Charney (1980) has shown that children's earliest pronoun use (of *my, your,* and *her*) is correct only when referring to the child's own speech role – i.e. when they themselves occupy those roles. Hence *my* and *your* are used 'correctly' earlier than *her*. From her analysis of children's spontaneous errors, Chiat (1981) suggests that the pronoun is only isolated as picking out the referent after it has been acquired in phrases encoding whole situations, i.e. it is initially context-specific in its use. Related to these claims is that of Deutsch (1983), based on a re-analysis of Brown's (1973) data. In looking at early possessive forms he distinguishes between indicating that the possessor is a sort of attribute of the object referred to (Karmiloff-Smith's 1979a 'descriptor function') and picking out one object among several ('determiner function'). Through Brown's stages I to III, descriptor functions are realized by nominal forms, e.g. child's own name, and determiner functions are realized by pronouns. Only at stage IV are both functions realized by pronominal forms. The acquisition pattern, repeated in Karmiloff-Smith's (1979a) study of the (later) acquisition of the determiner system in French, is that forms are initially unifunctional before they become plurifunctional. This would help to account for why, in general, deictic uses are so much earlier than the anaphoric ones (i.e. where pronouns 'refer back' between sentences). In general, the use of pronouns seems to be analogous to, say, the demonstratives, in providing a mechanism for context- (and role-) specific reference before they can be used independently to identify particular individuals. Thus they fulfil their primary deictic function by acting as referential place holders in whole expressions. (See Chiat in this volume, for a fuller discussion of the development of pronouns.)

4. Prepositions and related terms

Locative expressions are likely to play a key role in establishing a spatial context for an utterance. These may be expressed in various ways in different languages, by either pre- or postpositions, and these factors of linguistic form are likely to influence the nature of acquisition (e.g. Slobin 1973 has argued that, all other things being equal, postpositions would be acquired earlier). However, the acquisition process is proceeding within the framework of the child's conceptual development and thus will be influenced by its perception of such relations as containment and support. In studies of English speakers, Clark (1973a) hypothesized that the acquisition of the prepositions *in, on* and *under* would be in that order because

of the influence of such nonlinguistic cognitive constraints. This claim has been qualified on two counts. First, Wilcox and Palermo (1974) indicated that part of the child's response set was determined by functional relations between the nouns (cars normally go on roads, etc.). Secondly, Grieve, Hoogenraad and Murray (1977), using the same physical objects (which thus had the same perceptual relations) construed in different ways (e.g. as a table and chair, or a baby and bath), produced somewhat different patterns of responses to the prepositions. Thus there was an interaction between the interpretation of the preposition as driven by the conceptual bias, and the construal of the nouns being related. The qualifications do not, however, negate the relevance of the nonlinguistic conceptual framework – rather, they suggest that it operates in interaction with other features of the language acquisition process. Similar conclusions may be drawn from Parisi and Antinucci's (1970) observations of the acquisition of locative expressions in Italian.

More recently, Johnston and Slobin (1979) have systematically compared the acquisition of locative expressions in English, Italian, Serbo-Croatian and Turkish. Specifically, they found a general order of development: (1) *in, on, under* and *beside*; (2) *between, back* and *front* with 'featured' objects; (3) *back* and *front* with 'non-featured' objects; this despite the fact that these locative expressions are realized in quite different ways, which in turn resulted in the Italian and Turkish children acquiring the relevant expressions earlier than the English or Serbo-Croatian children. From these results it is clear that both conceptual and linguistic complexity are implicated in the acquisition process. For further data on German and French, plus discussion of the theoretical issues involved in such interpretations, see Weissenborn (1981). What these studies, so far, fail to resolve is precisely when the conceptual and when the linguistic expressions must take precedence in the acquisition process. A very useful contribution to making predictions of this kind more explicit is provided by Clark (1980). She looked at the acquisition patterns for *top, bottom, front* and *back* with objects that were either featured for both horizontal and vertical aspects (e.g. had intrinsic fronts and tops, such as a truck), only featured vertically (e.g. a bottle), only featured horizontally (e.g. a watch), or neither. The expectation was that nonlinguistic strategies involving both the salience of verticality and supportive surfaces would account for the order of acquisition: i.e. *top* and *bottom* before *front* and *back*. They did. However, more work needs to be done to specify just how language-specific acquisitions interact with general conceptual constraints. It is generally assumed that the latter should precede the former, but there are data in, for example, Johnston and Slobin (1979) which are hard to account for in these simple terms.

The ambiguity in the use of *in front of* and *behind* which distinguishes the groups (2) and (3) of expressions in Johnston and Slobin's study is of special relevance in considering the development of deixis. Essentially, the ambiguity is a result of the fact that many ('featured') objects have an intrinsic front. That is, they have a part of them which is characteristically interpretable as 'the front'. (H. Clark 1973 argues that it is from knowing this that one can work out 'the back'.) On the other hand, something may be said to be 'in front of' the speaker. So, in making a judgement as to whether something is, say, 'in front of an aeroplane', the person may have to decide between two conflicting judgements: the one involving the interpretation which uses the intrinsic front of the plane, and the other using the 'egocentric' front of the speaker. (Note again that this speaker orientation is distinct from the Piagetian notion of 'egocentrism'.) Of course, this conflict will only arise as a function of the orientation of the aeroplane and speaker to each other and to the object. Following Fillmore (1971), there has been an interesting study of this issue by Kuczaj and Maratsos (1975a); see also Cohen-Levine and Carey (1982).

Kuczaj and Maratsos found several interesting results with children between the ages of 3 and 4 years: children apparently acquire the notion that *front* and *back* are opposites before they have a general understanding of either term – and they subsequently simultaneously acquire both correctly. *Sides* is a later acquisition. Further, correct use of the terms seems to begin with reference to the self and spreads to objects with fronts. This latter result is in line with results obtained by Hall (1975). The relevant two studies were part of a thesis looking at scanning strategies used by children when evaluating the truth or falsity of particular perceptual arrays. There were three groups of children aged 5, 7, 9, and an adult group, and they were required to evaluate the truth of statements regarding 'in front of' and 'behind' two-dimensional representations of intrinsically fronted objects as seen in profile. The most striking result was that most of the subjects in the younger two age groups judged both true and false sentences as 'false' because the relevant object was not placed between the subject and the array! To follow this up, Hall had subjects place the pictures of objects 'in front of' or 'behind' a specified picture (SP) of a faced (fronted) object, either in a two-dimensional or three-dimensional frame. When the SP extended along a horizontal axis there was a tendency for all subjects from all groups to make 'egocentric' responses, especially on the three-dimensional array. Thus the 'faced' aspect of the SPs tended to be ignored when the SP was placed along a horizontal axis. However, when it came to placing a picture relative to a SP whose front/back corresponded to the vertical axis, even the youngest subjects were able to take note of the front/back cues. In yet other studies, looking at the scanning

eye movements evaluating various instructions relating to faced as opposed to unfaced object pictures, the results indicate that even though the relationships between the pictures were not specified by the instructions, the subjects tended to look in the faced direction of the faced object. Presumably because of this, the visual search performance of young subjects was superior to chance when required to verify sentences requiring faced responses, but not so when handling sentences involving unfaced ones. Taken together, these studies help to add substance to our growing knowledge of how subtle differences in linguistic and spatial information may influence children's (and our) view of the world. It is also relevant to refer to Hall's studies, since they highlight the utility and need to study the relevant parameters of visual search with adequate precision – adequate in the sense that we can be sure that the observations have been accurately made. This minimal level of adequacy is not met by many studies currently making claims about where the mother and child look.

5. *Come* and *go*

The typical interpretation of these verbs involves deixis in that the motion described is conditioned by the relative positions of the speaker and addressee. Thus the addressee moves toward the speaker for *come* and away from the speaker for *go*. Similarly, *bring* may be distinguished from *take*. Although temporal expectations may complicate the picture – for example, on meeting a guest at the garden gate a host may say 'Come into the house and bring your bottle with you' – it is clear that deictic considerations are critical and are as stated. The question is how and under what conditions do children come to make the relevant spatial distinction. To test this, Clark and Garnica (1974) designed a comprehension test in which the children had to use the contrast between *go* and *come*, or between *bring* and *take*, to identify either the speaker or addressee of an utterance. They studied children ranging in age from 6 to 9 years. The youngest children tended to identify both speaker and addressee with the animal at the goal of the movement. Thus when asked which animal can say to the lion 'Go into the garden', when there was a choice between an animal located inside the garden and two outside, the youngest chose the animal inside the garden. This strategy was replaced by one in which the children were able to give the correct identification to the speaker but not the addressee. It was not until the children were over 8 years old that a reasonable success rate was achieved on the task. The children overall found *come* easier than *go*, and *bring* easier than *take*, with the former pair easier than the latter pair of verbs. Somewhat similar results have been obtained by Macrae

(1976a), although she shows that the children's performance is sensitive to small changes in the experimental situation which do not obviously fit into a typical adult framework of interpretation. What Macrae argues is that *come* is easier in some of her studies, and in those of Clark and Garnica's, because its adult interpretation more often matches the strategies the children use in experiments, but that others of her studies suggest that this does not have to be the case. Both Clark and Garnica, and Macrae, argue that the basic strategy used by the children to identify the speaker or the addressee on a particular occasion depends on identifying the goal of the movement rather than its source. However, it may be the case that these results reflect characteristics of the experimental design rather than stages in the development of the verbs. Tanz (1980) failed to find a tendency to choose the goal in her study, in which the goal did not figure as prominently in the instruction as it had in the Clark and Garnica design. Thus when the non-goal is just as available as the goal as a response, the tendency to choose only the goal-oriented interpretation seems to disappear. The basic technique Tanz used was to have a toy 'house' with stairs and some toys inside, and some outside (sometimes upstairs). The child was then given a statement (e.g. 'Come upstairs and take a bath', 'Take a paper clip inside') and was supposed to make one of the dolls say it and make another act it out. We have conducted a study using Clark and Garnica's, and Tanz' procedures on the same set of subjects (four groups ranging in age from 5 to 8 years) to enable a more direct comparison to be made. There were highly significant task differences, but these were not reliably present until age 6, and overall there was a significant interaction between task, speaker/addressee differences, and age. There was no independent effect of speaker/addressee difference. Overall there was a highly significant effect for *come* and *go* versus *bring* and *take*; and for *come and bring* versus *go and take*. Both these main effects also significantly interacted with type of task, particularly the latter. Thus both studies are both vindicated and qualified. The task devised by Tanz, of course, provides more linguistic spatial cues through the use of such terms as *inside* and *upstairs*. It is not surprising, therefore, that it is easier (though not for the youngest children). However, it is not clear why such information should alone serve to eliminate source/goal differences. It seems more likely that that is also the product of requiring the explicit nomination of both speaker and hearer. Hence we seem to have another instanc of complex interaction between conceptual and linguistic factors. Furthermore, given a pronounced tendency for young children to handle directional terms in an allative manner (direction towards – see Garman, Griffiths and Wales 1970; Wales 1974; Macrae 1976b; Freeman, Sinha and Stedmon 1981),

it seems clear that *come* is likely to be given an adult-like response by the children for reasons which do not strictly follow from a grasp of the relevant deictic parameters.

Another complicating factor in these studies is suggested by an observation by Macrae (1976b). Seven 2-year-old children in their spontaneous speech would use either *come* or *go* when an action was carried out in full vision of the child, but they would use *go* to describe the movement of an object or person which disappeared from sight, and *come* for one where something or someone came into view. Note that the experimental studies referred to above were all carried out in full view of the child.

Another interpretation of the source of difficulty in these kinds of study (specifically citing Clark and Garnica) has been proposed by Richards (1976). She argues that these kinds of simple experimental task place too heavy a load on the child's inferential processes, and that a more naturalistic game which 'involved' the children more directly would result in superior performance on the part of the children. Games were constructed where the children had to phone information relevant to the occurrence of fires, or communicate about visiting other houses whose occupants and location were known to the children. These games certainly seem to elicit better performance with these verbs than the earlier studies suggested. Interesting as this is, however, the usefulness of the comparison is only marginal. Not only do the children have many more response options – a factor Macrae (1976a) in particular has shown to be crucial – but Richards' task is a production one. The interest therefore may more properly be that as far as these deictic terms are concerned, it is possible that production is easier to elicit than comprehension. If other results support this, it could be because actions guide this domain of language rather than the converse. This point is consistent with that made above about Tanz' study and the probable help provided to the child in interpretation by having to take on the roles of both speaker and actor.

We have made one attempt to check whether a simple variant of one of Richards' games, taken as a comprehension task, would produce analogous results. There were three chairs in a room: one assigned to the child as his/her 'house', another that of the experimenter, and yet a third 'house'. The child was given a toy 'fireman's hose' and told to follow instructions as to which house needed to have a fire extinguished. Eighty children (20 in each of four groups, 4, 5, 6, and 7 years old) participated with relish. Expressions were of the form: 'Go to the house', 'Come to this house', 'That house is on fire', etc. Expressions varied were *this, that, here, there, come, go, go there, come here, go ... that, come ... this, my, your, come ... my* and *go ... your*. Unlike the earlier comprehension studies reported,

there was often more than one option available to the child as a possible 'correct' response. Not surprisingly, therefore, the impression was of overall better performance. Certainly, performance on the demonstrative and locative deictics was 10 to 15 per cent higher than the norm reported earlier.

Although these were the expected trends, there was no age effect for any analysis. The demonstratives and locatives yielded no significant differences on comparison, nor was there a significant effect for proximity versus nonproximity to the speaker. With both the pronouns, performance was virtually perfect. *Go* was significantly better than *come*; *go* being already sufficiently well handled, there were no significant increases due to further deictic specification of the instruction using *that* or *there*. (The superiority of *go* in this task is obviously at least partially attributable to the greater number of options available as 'correct' responses.) However, with *come* as compared to *come . . . this*, there was a dramatic improvement, as also with *come here*. This result most dramatically illustrates two points:

(i)   the relative priority in performance with *come* and *go* is task dependent, and the children are again sorting out the relevant deictic contrasts on the basis of a preceding semantic interpretation – in this case, directional movement

(ii)   when the opportunity is available, the children have enough knowledge of the deictic system to buttress their interpretations interactively, by pooling information appropriately from more than one linguistic source

6. Temporal deixis

In many languages there is a coincidence of spatial and temporal terms. There are a number of arguments and data which suggest that this coincidence is no coincidence at all. Rather, a case can be made that linguistic expressions regarding time are effectively an extended spatial metaphor. That temporal expressions are often recruited from spatial ones has been discussed by, for example, H. Clark (1973), Miller and Johnson-Laird (1976), Traugott (1978). Notice the range of coincidence of the following English expressions: *before, time was short, the end is near, trouble lies ahead, the worst is behind us*, etc. Most expositors discuss the relationships from the viewpoint of the 'time-line', i.e. the view that the time is interpreted in terms of locations and/or movements on a line, and thus a spatial framework is provided for the interpretation. They differ in terms of the details of the 'time-line' model proposed. Wales (1981) discusses some of the alternatives and presents data of several kinds which lend general

support to the view that temporal expressions are developmentally derived from spatial interpretation. First, it is shown that children will give spatial interpretations for temporal expressions even when adults are disinclined to do so. More particularly, it is shown that they will do so for *before* and *after* only if they appropriately interpret *in front* and *behind*: similarly spatial interpretations for *now* and *then* are contingent on appropriate contrasts between *here* and *there*.

Another result, presented by Munro and Wales (1982), builds on a tradition of studies commenced by Clark (1969, 1971) who had shown that children's understanding of *before* and *after* is critically related to the way in which the real-world sequence of events matches the order of the events in the description. When the orders are the same, the result is much more likely both to be used spontaneously and to be understood by the children. This phenomenon is accompanied by the fact that *before* is often found to be easier than *after*. Changes in the child's use of spatial recoding or linear organizing scheme can be proposed to account for such trends. The details of Clark's basic results have been challenged, for example by Cromer (1971a), Amidon and Carey (1972) and Harner (1975); but these challenges have either to do with the cognitive assumptions behind Clark's interpretation, or with whether verbal tense precedes the acquisition of these expressions. Munro and Wales (1982) answer the former objections within a broader cognitive framework of interpretation. They also show the effects on the interpretation of such terms as *before* and *after* of three types of context: a still-time context (stationary lights) in which motions do not define the temporal duration, and two spatial contexts in which relative motions specify durations – one where the beginnings and ends of the motion are spatially aligned and the other where they are non-aligned. The idea behind using these different contexts was to test the prediction that as the amount of spatial data present increased the use of this in making temporal decisions would increase (and thus mislead the children). The prediction was strongly confirmed.

It is of some interest to see if complementary inferences may be drawn about the possible spatial organization of temporal expressions by direct questioning of subjects regarding their intuitions on the subject. Wales (1981) reports such data for children aged 6 and 9 years, and adults who were asked such questions as 'Can you go to the future?' and 'Can the future come to you?' Not only deictic verbs but also adjectives (e.g. *high*), prepositions (e.g. *behind*), adverbs (e.g. *forwards*), demonstratives (e.g. *this*) were used; and 'state' verbs (*be*) were contrasted with process verbs (*go*). The answers to the questions were analysed in order to try to reveal such regularities as might structure the data, and relate these to alternative models of the 'time-line'. Some of the findings include the following:

(i)   The proximal/distal distinction is general to all groups.

(ii)   For the 9 year olds and the adults front = future and back = past; for the 6 year olds, when they were systematic, past = behind was the prior organizing principle.

(iii)   Both the models of ego moving through time and time moving past ego are represented, though the latter is less fully articulated.

(iv)   While only one dimension is lexicalized in temporal expressions in English, the other dimensions are used by most subjects in all three groups; the younger children are using them more, perhaps because they know the relevance of the spatial metaphor but have yet to work out the appropriate dominant axis.

(v)   The deictic models developed as expressions of the 'time-line' fit the data quite well, except for conceptions of the future. This may be because the latter is more associated with linguistic mood and hence expectation. This view is supported developmentally by Harner (1982) who found that past tense forms were equally well understood by children when referring to either immediate or remote past. However, the future form was better understood in reference to the immediate future than the remote future. The latter are interpreted as lacking the immediacy of action and certainty of occurrence that the former have.

A number of studies in recent years have examined the interaction of tense and aspect in ways which are relevant to the topic of deixis. It is generally held that tense is deictic in being the expression in linguistic form of the relationship between the time of occurrence of a situation and the moment of speaking about it. Since the latter varies in its locus, it is necessary typically to know the speaker's temporal position relative to the temporal situation referred to. Aspect, on the other hand, may be seen as not deictic, since it is concerned not with relating the time of a situation to another time point, but rather with the internal temporal structure of the situation. It is concerned with such aspects of temporal situations as whether they should be viewed as analysable wholes or as having various structures typically concerned with beginnings, middles and ends. In a pioneer study, Bronckart and Sinclair (1973) presented a variety of situations to French-speaking children, 3 to 8 years old, for description. The utterances produced were then analysed to see how tense and aspect were used to describe the differently structured situations. Up to the age of 6 there was a tendency to use the present for imperfective events, i.e. without clear end-points; and the past (*passé composé*) for perfective events, i.e. with clear end-points. Bronckart and Sinclair interpret such data as indicating that the children are using tense to encode aspectual differences.

This, they argue, is a result of their inability to 'decentre' because of their cognitive egocentricity. In systematic replications of Bronckart and Sinclair's procedure, both C. S. Smith (1980) and Wales and Pattison (1982) report data which question the generality of the former's cognitive hypothesis – Smith also supporting her argument with records of spontaneous speech. The patterns of data are that perfective events are most often described using past tense (though that is more true of the older children) and imperfective ones are most often described using progressive tense forms. Wales and Pattison's data suggest that simple past may be acquired first with a neutral aspectual function associated with it. However, a variety of tense forms are used and the variety, not surprisingly, increases with age. Smith provides an interesting reinterpretation of the data, suggesting that there are two main stages in development: initially children can refer to events other than the present but always from the point of view of the present – that being the position of the observer/speaker; later, children can talk about times other than from the present (speaker's) point of view. Thus the developmental course of aspect and tense does not commit us to having to postulate a non-deictic stage of acquisition before a deictic one. This seems to be consistent with the fact that tense and aspect are inextricably interwoven in human languages. (For further discussion of related issues see chapters 17 and 18 in this volume.)

7. Concluding observations

The importance of deixis in the process of language acquisition is that it provides a linguistic mechanism for expressing the domain of joint speaker – hearer attention. This mechanism obviously suggests an extension to naming. Bruner, for example, has argued in a number of publications that the achievement of joint attention may be a crucial framework for the learning of 'names'. The various ways in which such a view can be applied have been illustrated by, for example, Bridges (1978), McShane (1980), Ninio (1980), Gopnik (1982) and Bruner (1983). Although we do not have space here for the systematic evaluation of these studies, it seems clear, if only by their juxtaposition, that there are serious methodological problems yet to be solved in this area. These problems stem particularly from the definition of categories and relations between them, and also the criteria by which data came to be categorized in those ways. (There are also often problems in evaluating the reliability of the data as presented.) Nevertheless, together they also offer some hope for progress. For the latter to be realized, however, a clear distinction will need to be drawn between the indexical/contextualizing function of deictic expressions and the acqui-

sition of naming as a referential tool of communication. On the available data it seems, as Lyons (1975) and McGinn (1981) have argued, that deixis provides the mechanism for reference, which is in turn built upon in the acquisition of 'names'. This view argues against that (e.g. McShane 1980) which would have syntax and semantics develop as a consequence to acquiring names. What seems more plausible is that primitive deixis allows reference, and hence communication, to occur at the outset of language use. The child's development of linguistic competence can then be seen as the progressive differentiation of those distinctions which are conceptually available to the child and which are articulated in his or her language, such that the language-specific forms of these distinctions are progressively mastered. In turn, their use of these skills in a widening arena of discourse situations can then also be progressively observed. This takes the basic developmental progression to be one of operating on 'fused' categories which are progressively differentiated (e.g. into space, time, animacy, etc.). If this is correct, then there are some basic methodological problems of doing research on deixis. Such problems have been alluded to earlier: how can one isolate one aspect of, for example, space, or time, and discuss one in the absence of the other? The organization of this article (and much of the work of the field surveyed) presupposes that it is possible to keep them separate. However, the existence of the problem should qualify too facile an acceptance of any interpretations at this stage.

That deictic devices often enter crucially into children's conversational discourse has been reported by Keenan and Schieffelin (1976). In studies of somewhat more formal language use, both Karmiloff-Smith (1979a) and Hickmann (1980) report that there is a progression across age in the discourse functions that the same linguistic form (e.g. definite article, pronoun or demonstrative) may have. They show that intralinguistic uses of such expressions in the creation of referents (i.e. using them anaphorically, not just deictically) are a relatively late development. Some fascinating recent studies of children's route directions illustrate some of the problems children have to learn to overcome in complex discourse (e.g. Weissenborn 1980; W. Klein 1983). Children were required to describe to another child where something had been hidden elsewhere in a small village. It was clear that children's inability to do so effectively was not because they lacked the relevant spatial knowledge. Observing the changes in the descriptions as a function of age (4 to 10 years old), the difficulties which are progressively overcome include: lack of verbal planning strategies, i.e. what needs to be said first, second etc.; an inability to manipulate *effectively* some deictic expressions; failure to effectively check their own (speaker's) deictic knowledge against the listener's deictic space. In general, developmental progress

seems to be a matter of going from conceptual structure, to restricted situation-specific linguistic use, to functional interactive application.

Overall, the pattern of the development of deixis seems reasonably clear. Recruiting relevant cognitive abilities, deictic expressions contextualize reference, using at first a general 'indicating' function. This is subsequently specialized by person, or by spatial location; the organization of the latter is in turn specialized and extended into the temporal domain. Specific contrasts are only acquired later, and influences on these come from constraints provided by the available conceptual structures, the forms in which they are expressed in a specific language, and the interaction with other domains as a consequence, presumably, of functional overlap in early context-specific uses. The whole system is, of conversational necessity, being elaborated in more and more complex interactive uses which provide their own acquisition problems for communicative competence. While the framework seems reasonably clear, the specifics, particularly regarding the constraints on order of acquisition, still need nore work. Some of the contributors to Weissenborn and Klein (1982) and Denny (1978) suggest a functional and formal relation between the structure of the local deictic system and the natural environment of the speaker of particular languages. Observations of acquisition in such different linguistic and natural environments may help to clarify the specific dependencies in the process of acquiring a system of deixis.

20. A crosslinguistic perspective: morphology and syntax

Ruth A. Berman

1. Introduction

Crosslinguistic research in child language has been motivated by the following kinds of questions. *Universality* – which aspects of language development emerge as universal, by contrast with those which are constrained by the forms or content of the particular language that is learned? *Linguistic specificity* – if such commonality is revealed, can it be attributed to more general cognitive underpinnings, or is it a function of uniquely linguistic knowledge? *Relative difficulty* – across languages, what aspects of linguistic structure and of the relationship between forms and content pose special difficulties for the learner, and how can these be predicted and explained? *Acquisitional principles* – what underlying strategies can be detected across children learning different languages, in the shape of such procedures as the drive towards one-to-one mappings between form and meaning or the use of over-regularization?

Two main approaches have been adopted by studies which address such questions on the basis of data from children learning a variety of mother tongues.[1] One approach is to cull data from a range of studies dealing with different languages, and often differing in aim as well as method, in order to reach generalizations about broader, more universal properties of child language development.[2] An early model which evolved out of this type of study is found in Roman Jakobson's claim of an initial universal phonetic inventory underlying a universal ordering of development in phonemic contrasts (Jakobson 1968). Another is the semantic features hypothesis of Clark (1973b), according to which children acquire word meanings componentially, by adding features to their earlier and partial lexical entries. Rather more comparable speech samples were used in analysing the early word combinations of children from different language backgrounds: Bowerman (1973) specifies possibly universal constraints on a grammar that would account for both the syntactic and semantic features of early child speech, while Braine (1976a) outlines a model of three quite ⁓ific forms of structural patterning in early word combinations.

4.

430   THE DEVELOPMENT OF LINGUISTIC SYSTEMS: GRAMMAR

Another crosslinguistically anchored model based on data from both experimental and other types of studies is MacWhinney's (1978) account of the acquisition of morphophonology as a cyclical process rooted in the three central abilities of rote memorization, analogy, and rule operation. Peters (1981, 1983) proposes a model to account for early segmentation of the stream of speech which relies on such factors as prosodic contours and formulaic routines. In the development of grammatical categories, Levy (1983) reviews findings on the acquisition of gender systems in six different languages, to demonstrate that children as young as age 2 can operate with strictly formal generalizations which do not necessarily correlate with semantic or pragmatic categories.

Of major impact in this type of crosslinguistic investigation have been the operating principles proposed by Slobin (1973) to account for the predispositions underlying children's acquisition of form–meaning relations in a variety of different native tongues. These principles have since been extended and refined on the basis of far richer crosslinguistic data, delineating a complex network of strategies and procedures which children have recourse to as part of their *language-making capacity* (Slobin 1985a).

A somewhat different type of crosslinguistic child language study makes use of similar experimental designs across subjects from different language backgrounds. The largest set of such studies is that of the Berkeley project conducted in the early 1970s with preschool children learning American English, Italian, Serbo-Croatian and Turkish (Slobin 1982). These studies investigated such areas as the processing of causative sentences (Ammon and Slobin 1979), the acquisition of locative terms (Johnston and Slobin 1979), and the mapping of grammatical relations in languages which use inflections and word order respectively (Slobin and Bever 1982). Other studies of comprehension have been conducted on the sentence-processing abilities of English- and Italian-speaking children (Bates *et al.* 1984). One other set of crosslinguistically designed studies, focused on the development of word formation devices in comprehending and producing innovative agent and instrument nouns, is centred at Stanford, with findings currently available for English (Clark and Hecht 1982), Hebrew (Clark and Berman 1984), and Icelandic (Mulford 1983). It may seem surprising that so little has been attempted by way of *a priori* crosslinguistic research into the acquisition of grammar. But such research encounters immense difficulties in principle no less than in practice – a point we return to at the end of this chapter.

The findings of both these major directions in crosslinguistic child language studies form the background to the discussion which follows. Here, the task of learning the morphology and syntax of different mother tongues

is analysed in the context of language development viewed as proceeding through three main phases:[3]

(a) Initial entry into the system is highly context-based and dependent on extralinguistic cues. In this primarily pre-grammatical phase, language learning is driven by general communicative needs.

(b) At the next, structure-based phase of grammaticization of knowledge, linguistic data are analysed, and the learner acquires rules which relate forms to meanings as well as to non-semantically motivated systems of formal alternations (e.g. gender marking on articles or nouns, or the internal constituency of different types of relative clause).

(c) By the third phase, mature language use, the rules of grammar are fully internalized and they can be adjusted to take account of constraints on their application and of conventional usages (e.g. a *cooker* is an object used in cooking, whereas a *baker*, but not a **caker*, is a person who makes cakes). With end-state knowledge, grammatical rules can be flexibly applied and alternated for purposes of communication, enabling speakers to attend to discourse functions and the requirements of particular discourse settings and registers or styles. At this point, speakers can give explicit marking to anaphoric relations; they can balance the flow of discourse between old and new information; and they can deploy grammatical forms to talk about a given event from more than one perspective (e.g. *Johnnie hit me* and also *I got hit*, or *I've been hit*).

From a crosslinguistic perspective, the first phase can be construed in light of Slobin's (1985a) analysis of *Basic Child Grammar*, as largely shared, irrespective of the particular native tongue. The next, structure-dependent phase shows an increasing impact of general structural properties of the mother tongue (e.g. pervasive subject–verb or noun–adjective agreement systems in some languages, pervasive marking of aspect distinctions on verbs in others). And in the third phase, focus is on more language-specific phenomena, governed by the norms of how grammatical devices are deployed in lexical convention and in different modes of discourse in the particular native tongue. This sequence can be charted as follows:

I	II	III
Context-anchored	Structure-dependent	Discourse-sensitive
Pregrammatical	Grammaticized	Grammar + usage
Shared across languages	Attentive to major structural properties of the native tongue	Attentive to specific norms and registers of the native tongue

This schematic representation is clearly artificial. Knowledge of a language develops along a continuum rather than by radical jumps from one phase to the next. Besides, children may be well advanced in one part of the grammar while still pregrammatical or only just starting to generalize in another subsystem (as argued in some detail in Berman 1983b, 1985a). From a crosslinguistic perspective, however, there emerges a gradual narrowing of the broad common basis shared by children learning different native tongues, along with an expansion and deepening knowledge of the patterning of their own particular native tongue.

Against this background we review certain commonalities underlying children's initial entry into the grammar of their native tongue (section 2). These form precursors to an increasing attention to major structural characteristics of the language being learned (section 3). Discussion here relies heavily on work of my own and of colleagues on the acquisition of Hebrew, a language with quite distinct properties in both morphology and syntax (Berman 1985b). We conclude by considering the question of the relative difficulty of the task faced by children learning different native languages, and we suggest possible directions for future research in the crosslinguistic study of grammatical development.

2. Initial shared knowledge

Early child speech, from the one-word stage on to early two- and three-word, is striking for how similar it appears across children learning different languages. Prior to the onset of language-specific rules of grammar, the speech productions of young children evince the following commonalities:

(i)   They make use of initial *units of acquisition*, in both single words and early word combinations, which are very similar in content and function

(ii)   They make the same kinds of basic *semantic distinctions* to start with, as the basis for a full range of form–meaning relations which will find detailed grammatical expression in their language

(iii) They talk about the same overall *types of events* from a quite restricted set of pragmatic points of view

(iv)   They deploy similar kinds of acquisitional and processing *strategies* en route to structure-dependent knowledge of the rules of grammar

Firstly, then, children seem to use the same types of building blocks as the basis for initial construction of their grammars. Thus, a survey of children at the one-word stage learning languages as different as Kaluli, Mandarin Chinese, Japanese, German, English, and Turkish (Gentner

1982), as well as Hebrew (Berman 1978; Dromi 1982) reveals quite broad similarity in division of the vocabulary into noun-like and predicate-like terms, with a small proportion of other, functor-type terms. At this same stage, prior to the onset of grammatically governed inflectional marking, children learning different languages will select imperatives and infinitives as the basic form of verbs, whatever the relative formal simplicity of these items in the particular language (e.g. Berman 1978 for Hebrew; Mulford 1983 for Icelandic, Toivainen 1980 for Finnish). Also, across different languages children's early word combinations express the same kinds of functions, such as locating, requesting, or specifying existence (Slobin 1979: 86–7). Thus to start with, children use the limited linguistic means at their disposal in quite similar ways. Even this early on, they do not make merely random selections out of everything they see and hear. Rather, there seems to be a general, overriding set of factors quite beyond the specific language being learned which gears children at this initial phase to give linguistic expression to some elements or contents rather than to others.

Secondly, children divide up at least some areas of semantic space along similar lines in quite different languages. Thus certain basic, possibly superordinate, semantic distinctions are made early on by children, only later being refined to meet more detailed semantic subcategorization imposed by the lexicon of their language. For instance, children across languages may initially use general purpose terms such as *make*, *go*, or *give* to denote basic activities, only later giving lexical specification to the precise nature of the accomplishment, the movement, or the transfer of property, respectively (Clark 1983). Also in various domains children start by making the same kinds of semantic distinctions, irrespective of the specific forms deployed by the mother tongue. Varying explanations have been suggested to account for such commonalities, including appeal to relative conceptual and/or semantic simplicity (as reviewed from somewhat different perspectives in Carey 1982; Clark 1983); factors of general perceptual and/or pragmatic salience; or innate predispositions to attend to some rather than to other distinctions early on in acquisition (Bickerton 1981).

Whatever the reason, there is good evidence that children from different language backgrounds show similar orders of acquisition with respect to such relatively well documented semantic domains as colour terms (*red*, *blue*, and *yellow* before *green*, *brown*, or *orange*); locative terms (*in* and *on* before terms meaning *under* and *next to*, *behind* or *between* respectively); as well as pairs of dimensional adjectives (*big*/*little* being first, before *long*/*short* which in turn are acquired before such pairs as those meaning *wide*/*narrow* or *deep*/*shallow*). Relatedly, children from varying language backgrounds all apprehend such distinctions as the following early on in their

development. They understand the difference between specific/nonspecific object reference: *I saw a horse* refers to a specific, identifiable member of the class of horses, whereas *I want a horse* might refer to any unspecified member of that class. They understand the difference between state/process types of predicates, such as the inner states expressed by verbs like *want, like,* or *know* compared with the process activities encoded by verbs such as *eat, run,* or *cry*; and punctual/nonpunctual events, so that one-time, resultative types of predicates such as *fall, break,* or *tear up* are generally marked initially by something corresponding to a past tense, whereas verbs which typically describe ongoing durative as well as habitual or iterative events, such as *play, live,* or *kick,* will first occur in something equivalent to an English present tense. Relatedly, across languages children first ask *yes/no* kinds of questions, afterwards *what* questions concerned with object identity and *where* questions concerned with object location, only later asking *why* and *when* questions concerned with the causal or temporal anchoring of events.

As noted, such early distinctions are shared by children despite great differences in the actual forms used by different languages to encode these distinctions. For instance, early locatives take the shape of prepositions in English, postpositions in Turkish, synthetic inflectional forms in Russian, and preposed words and prefixes in Hebrew. And the punctual/nonpunctual distinction is realized in a variety of ways in early child language: by perfective versus imperfective inflections in Slavic languages, by nonprogressive past versus progressive present in English, and by middle voice past tense versus active voice present tense forms in Hebrew. This suggests that these early distinctions may indeed be due to some quite deep-rooted predispositions which children bring to bear on the task of early language learning. They can thus apprehend such basic distinctions irrespective of their morphosyntactic patterning in the particular language being learned.

Thirdly, possibly as a precursor to syntax, children favour certain pragmatic perspectives for talking about events in their experience. Thus Maratsos (1983) summarizes a variety of studies, mainly on English, which show that initially children identify the subject relation with an animate doer or actor, e.g. *baby cry, doggie run*; only later will they abstract this relation to a point where the subject slot can also be filled by an inanimate object, e.g. *pencil write, ball fall*. Relatedly, the object of events will first be confined to inanimate entities, e.g. *bite finger, read book*; only later will it be extended to an animate experiencer, e.g. *kiss Mommy, push Dickie*. My Hebrew data show clearly that, to start with, children relate to canonic types of intransitive events where things happen (e.g. the equivalent of intransitive, verb-initial *fell the bottle, got-broken the ball*) by contrast with

activities in which people perform, or where they perpetrate an action upon an object (encoded by subject–verb strings such as *baby drink, Dickie hit doggie*). Such early perspectives that children adopt in relation to different activity or event types are clearly delineated in crosslinguistic terms by Slobin (1985a). Thus, 'basic child grammar' enables the learner to give linguistic expression to certain prototypical scenes: the *manipulative activity* scene is described from an agentive perspective, with an agent performing some act which brings about a tangible change of state in the patient; a *result perspective* will be adopted with respect to events in which a change of state such as breaking, falling, or spilling is highlighted; and these in turn contrast with the basic *figure–ground* scene, where children talk about objects as located in a place or moving towards a goal.

Again, different languages deploy different morphosyntactic means in encoding these distinctions: by accusative marking on patient-objects, or ergative marking on agent-doers, and/or dative marking on experiencers; by use of active versus passive voice or intransitive, middle voice versus active, transitive verb morphology; or by various combinations of such devices. (Compare, for instance, the Hebrew result perspective of verb-initial intransitive plus dative experiencer in *hitpotsets li ha balon* 'got-burst to-me the balloon' versus the manipulative activity perspective of *ani potsats-ti et ha balon* 'I burst (1st person accusative) the balloon', with SVO ordering).[4] At the early phase of a common, basic child grammar, children will typically opt for one rather than another perspective in talking about a given scene or activity type. Only later will they be able to deploy the morphosyntactic devices of their grammar to selectively adopt contrasting perspectives in relation to any given type of event.

A fourth common property of early child language concerns the kinds of strategies or procedures employed by children prior to the phase where they make structure-dependent grammatical generalizations. Only two of these will be noted here (for further discussion, see Berman 1986). One is the so-called *plausible event* strategy employed by young children in interpreting linguistic strings, including laboratory-type comprehension experiments. The effect of this procedure is such that children will disregard morphosyntactic cues such as word order, or inflectional and other markers of gender, number, or case relations, to interpret input strings in terms of expectations based on what is most familiar, hence most plausible, in real-world terms (for a review of relevant studies, see Cromer 1976b). Another, production-oriented strategy is that of *rote learning*, by means of which items are learned as prepackaged amalgams or memorized as formulae (MacWhinney 1978; Peters 1983). Later on, parts of these formerly unanalysed chunks will be extended to other exemplars to form the

basis of rule acquisition (Berman 1983b, 1985a). Other strategies noted in the literature cannot be said to apply at this, as yet context-dependent, phase since they all imply some measure of structure dependence and an indepedent apprehension of formal properties of linguistic material. Such rather more grammar-directed strategies include, for instance, overregularization of anomalous forms to accord with paradigmatic instances (e.g. English *swimmed* or *mans*) or overextension of a single grammatical marker to inappropriate contexts (such as French *que* or Hebrew *she-* 'that' being used in cases where a lexically specific subordinator meaning 'when' or 'so that' is required).

In this section, the focus has been on patterns shared by children learning different mother tongues. Obviously the child is not totally indifferent to the particular input language being learned even at this early phase of pre-grammar, and the specific properties of this language have an effect from the start in both perception and production. For instance, the task of segmenting the stream of speech into units corresponding to adult *words* is different for children learning a language in which main word stress is predictably located (e.g. Czech or Finnish) compared with a language with variable word stress, such as English or Hebrew. And the task of identifying *parts of words*, divided up into stems and affixes, is different for a child learning an agglutinating language like Turkish where each postposition follows the stem in an invariant, quite distinct fashion, compared with the synthetically fused roots plus affixes of a language like Hebrew, on the one hand, or the tendency for words not to take distinct shapes depending on their grammatical category as in English or Chinese. Besides, 2 year olds learning the New Guinean language of Kaluli put ergative markers on actor nouns, whereas their Russian-learning counterparts mark inanimate object nouns with an accusative inflection, and Hebrew learners mark definite object nouns with a special preposition.[5] From the very start children must, of course, pay attention to different surface markings and to distinct linguistic signs dependent on the particular language they are learning. Evidence is provided by the very different quality of 2 year olds' morphological markings on words in structurally distinct languages such as Hebrew (Dromi and Berman 1982), Quiché Mayan (Pye 1983) and Polish as compared with Finnish (Weist and Konieczna 1985). Moreover, children obviously attach meanings to some linguistic signs right from the one-word stage. However, at this initial phase the language learner has not yet extracted *rules* for relating forms to meanings in a structure-dependent fashion. Nor can the child as yet relate to the same scene in various ways, by making use of grammatical markers to encode different perspectives in order to select from, say, *Johnnie hie me, I got hit, I've been hit*, and

also *It's me that got hit.* It is only in the next phase, as noted below, that children move out of such general, crosslinguistic predispositions into the grammar of their native tongue. And they do so on the basis of the knowledge and experience which they have accumulated during this initial phase of crosslinguistic commonality.

3. Emergence of typological diversification

The next phase of acquisition of grammar is critically affected by the general structural properties of the language being learned – what we shall refer to here as *typology*. This notion does not take account of merely incidental or specific facts of linguistic patterning in a given language, nor of structures limited to quite restricted paradigms or classes of items. Rather, typological features in this context refer to quite generally prevalent properties characterizing the input language. For instance, gender and number agreement are clearly typologically deep-rooted properties of Hebrew, applying across the board in subject–verb combinations and in agreement of adjectives and determiners with the head noun. Compare, for instance, Hebrew:

(1) yeled gadol ze
     boy big this
     'This big boy'
(2) ha yeled ha gadel ha hu
     the boy the big the he
     'That big boy'
(3) ha yelad- im   ha gdol- im   ha hem
     the boy   (pl.) the big (pl.) the they
     'Those big boys'
(4) ha yelad- ot   ha gdol- ot   ha hen
     the boy (fem.) the big (pl.) the they (fem.)
     'Those big girls'

as contrasted with the number distinction in the English demonstratives *this boy/these boys* or *that boy/those boys*, which are merely isolated traces of number agreement within the noun phrase, in no way typologically characteristic of the language today. A typological property of English syntax would be auxiliary verb placement, since this functions critically in a variety of constructions, including matrix and tag questions, emphatic affirmations, as well as negatives. Our claim is that as children move into the grammar of their native tongue they become peculiarly attuned to such pervasive structural properties of their language – and they do so with relative ease and rapidity. Thus, Hebrew-acquiring children have overall command of

subject–verb and noun–modifier agreement by their fourth year, although the system itself is a complicated one, as shown by the fact that quite proficient second language learners of Hebrew make more, as well as different, agreement errors than does the native Hebrew-speaking 4-year old. Similarly, non-native learners of English seem to encounter more protracted difficulties with auxiliary placement than do children, who make few errors in this system by around age 4 (for further such examples and discussion, see Berman 1984).

In general, then, what children come to perceive most critically in the major phase of grammar acquisition, in learning the morphosyntax of their native tongue between the ages of about 2 and 4, is that they must pay selective attention to both how and where information tends to be grammatically marked in their language: around consonants and inside words in a Semitic language like Hebrew, from stems to word endings in Hungarian or Turkish, across and between words and phrases in English.

Consider, for instance, the peculiar structuring of words in a Semitic language, including Modern Hebrew. The bulk of its content vocabulary – all verbs, and most nouns and adjectives – are formed out of root consonants combined with obligatory vowel infixes and optional consonant + vowel prefixes and suffixes. For example, the root *g-d-l* yields verbs like *li-gdol* 'to-grow up', *le-gadel* 'to-raise, bring up', *le-hagdil* 'to-enlarge'; adjectives such as *gadol* 'big, large', *me-gudal* 'overgrown'; and nouns such as *godel* 'size', *gidul* 'growth', *mi-gdal* 'tower', *gdul-a* 'greatness', or *ha-gdal-a* 'enlargement'. Studies of Hebrew child language from early preschool through to grade-school age show a quite consistent pattern in relation to this phenomenon. Initially, Hebrew learners, just like children acquiring other native tongues, pay attention to consonants as having particular weight in carrying form–meaning relations – and this makes sense, since consonants are perceptually very salient, and they vary far more than vowels, which are relatively limited in number. Thus, initial variations across familiar items show that children learning different languages recognize words with the same consonants as semantically related, i.e. as versions of the same element: English *drink/drank* no less than Hebrew *shote/shata* for the same meanings, or *sing/song* and their Hebrew equivalents *shar/shir*. Once a typological bias sets in, however, Hebrew-learning children start to show quite specialized attention to vowel alternations within the same 'consonantal skeleton'; for example, not only *shote/shata* for 'drink/drank' but also *yoshev/yashav* 'sit/sat', *noten/natan* 'give/gave', *bone/bana* 'build/built', *oved/avad* 'work/worked', *ose/asa* 'do/did', etc. (Berman 1983a). Moreover, by age 4 or so, children are already able to extract this consonantal skeleton from new contexts. For instance, given an innova-

tive form like *shavr-an* 'breaker', they will quite readily say that this names a person who 'breaks' (= *shover*); and given *mafzer* 'scatterer' they will recognize that this could name an instrument used 'to scatter' (= *le-fazer*); see Clark and Berman 1984; also Badry 1983. Here, they are displaying a kind of knowledge which is uniquely Semitic: the ability to relate to exclusively consonantal elements as the morphological and semantic core of words in their language. (Only later, with the acquisition of orthography at grade-school age, combined with formal study of historical developments in Hebrew morphophonology, will Hebrew speakers acquire a more abstract grammatically motivated notion of a theoretical underlying consonantal root; see discussion in Berman 1981b.)

A second example is afforded by more general trends manifested by children in learning devices for new-word formation in their language. Thus, Hebrew favours creating new words by affixation or stem-internal changes rather than by syntactic means such as conversion (e.g. English *can cook* versus *a cook, to garden* versus *our garden*) or compounding (e.g. *postman* or *postcard* in English). Initially, children learning such diverse languages as English and Hebrew seem to follow quite universal perceptual strategies, finding stem-external affixes easier than stem-internal markings, and suffixes easier than prefixes (Clark and Berman 1984). As they acquire more knowledge, however, and a larger repertoire of both formal devices and actual instances, children pay increasing attention to the general propensity their language has for using certain kinds of devices for constructing new words. At this phase, then, Hebrew-learning children will make very wide use of morphologically bound affixal forms for interpretting and for deriving new words in their language (Berman and Sagi 1981; Walden 1982).

A third example selected here is a comparison of how children learn to mark causative relations in Hebrew and, say, English. Contemporary English marks causatives in the following ways, listed below as E(i)–E(iv) in approximate descending order of productivity:

Formal	*Examples*
E(i) Syntax: auxiliary verb	Make Mommy mad, Make the doll sing
E(ii) Syntax: NP$_1$ V NP$_2$/ NP$_2$V	You'll stop the noise/The noise will stop
	We shut the door/The door shut
E(iii) Lexicon: suppletive verbs	eat/feed, learn/teach, fall/drop, see/show, come/bring, etc.
E(iv) Morphology:	
vowel changes	lie/lay, sit/set
external affix	dark-en, en-large

As analysed by Bowerman (1974), children early on manifest knowledge of such relations by use of the auxiliary verb *make* with intransitive predicates, making use of the most productive option above, E(i). It is only later in development, and in a way that accords with historical processes in the language, that children come to use other causative marking auxiliaries in English such as *get* or *have* (*Get the dolly to sing, Have someone do this*), as analysed by Baron (1977). At a very young age, children also use intransitive verbs inappropriately in causative contexts with two arguments, e.g. **I'm gonna sing the doll.* Thus, English-learning 2–3 year olds understand the difference between an event in which an agent causes something or someone to perform an action and one in which the event is self-initiated. However, they do not yet know the lexical facts as to which verbs in the language allow which options: thus *dance* but not *sing*, and *move* but not *push* allow the two-place versus one-place intransitive option shown in E(ii).

Hebrew-learning children have a rather different set of options, which we shall try to demonstrate as according well with the overall typological properties of the language. These are illustrated below as H(i)–H(iv), again in relative order of productivity for the different devices.[6]

Formal device   *Examples*

H(i) Morphology: change of verb pattern, different affixes on a shared root

hu *hifsik*   et   ha ra'ash /ha ra'ash *nifsak*
he stopped (acc.) the noise   the noise stopped

hu *potsets* et   ha balon / ha balon   *hitpotsets*
he burst   (acc.) the balloon the balloon burst

H(ii) Syntax: auxiliary verb

asa   she-ima   tich'as
made that Mom will-be-mad

gorem la   buba la shir
cause the doll to sing

H(iii) Lexicon: suppletive verbs

li-shon / *le-hardim*
to sleep to put to sleep

li-shtot / le-hashkot
to drink   to-give water/drink

H(iv) Syntax: NP₁ V NP₂/NP₂ V

ron *hitchil* et   ha mischak / ha mischak *hitchil*
Ron began (acc.) the game   the game   began

As I have tried to show elsewhere, Hebrew-speaking children acquire the semantics of causative relations by their third year, much like their English-speaking counterparts (Berman 1980, 1982; Berman and Sagi 1981). However, they manifest this knowledge very differently indeed. As an initial, immature form, they make use of the periphrastic option of an auxiliary verb meaning 'do, make', as in H(ii): e.g. using childish *hu ose li ko'ev* 'he makes me hurt' instead of the lexical, more standard option of H(i) *hu mach'iv li* 'he hurts (+causative) me'. And they also use the same intransitive verb form both in the appropriate context of a one-place predicate (e.g. *ze yored levad* 'it goes-off/gets-down by-itself') and in ungrammatical, causative contexts (e.g. *ani yored et ze levad* 'I go-off it by-myself', where the verb should be *morid* 'take-off, make-go-down' from the same root). In this, they seem to behave much like the English-speaking children reported by Bowerman (1974) and Lord (1979).

This is, however, a totally implausible solution for Hebrew, in which only a few verbs allow change in transitivity with no change in verb form as in H(iv). By contrast, the same interim strategy when selected by English-speaking children can be taken to constitute a very feasible extension of verbs such as *sing* or *fall down* to the large class of common verbs which do allow this alternation, as shown in E(ii): *move, change, stop, start, open, close, cook, melt*, etc. Consequently, and in a way totally foreign to English-learning children, Hebrew learners soon realize that the optimal way of marking this distinction in their language is by means of verb morphology. Thus, by around the fourth year they begin to extend one specific, often causative verb pattern to lexical items which do not in fact occur in this form in the current lexicon of Hebrew:

Conventional causatives	*Juvenile innovations*
ochel 'eat'/ma'achil 'feed'	shote 'drink'/*mashte 'make-drink'
tsochek 'laugh'/matschik 'make laugh'	boche 'cry'/'make-cry'

rochev 'ride'/markiv 'give a   soche 'swim'/*masche 'give a
   ride to'   swim to'
mit'orer 'wake up'/me'ir 'wake   yashen 'sleep'/*moshin 'put to
   (someone)'   sleep'

Like their English counterparts, children who make such extensions show they do not have full knowledge of lexical usage and conventions in their language. But they choose a typologically very appropriate device for expressing this form–meaning relationship in their language – by means of specific affixal patterns associated with a given consonantal root.

Thus, once Hebrew learners know enough about their language they realize that it uses verb-internal modifications to express the relation of causativeness. And they learn this as part of the general typological thrust of their language, in which changes in verb morphology indicate a wide range of predicate–argument relations (e.g. passives, middle voice, reciprocality, reflexiveness, inchoativeness). This is quite different from the task of an English-learning child, who will use auxiliary verbs or other syntactic means to express these distinctions. We see, then, that *both* groups of children manifest a broadly similar developmental pattern. Initially, at the phase we have characterized as pregrammatical, they are not yet able to give overt morphological or syntactic marking to the causative/noncausative distinction. The intermediate phase of grammaticization is then manifested in overextension of one major device for marking this distinction – a device which is appropriate to the main typological tendency of the language being learnt. Finally, at the phase of what we have termed full end-state knowledge – in the case of causative marking at late preschool or early grade-school age – children reach the point of language knowledge where productive rules of the grammar are constrained by lexical convention and by incidental facts about how certain predicates happen to be given a causative interpretation in the current usage of their language.

One further illustration is afforded by the role of *word order* for children learning different languages. (For crosslinguistic evidence of the impact of mother tongue structures on acquisitional patterning in other areas, such as the perception of anaphoric relations in relative clauses and other complex structures, stress patterns, noun-compounding, passive constructions, see Berman 1984.) Crosslinguistic studies of sentence comprehension suggest that even quite young children pay attention to typologically relevant cues in interpreting relations between parts of a sentence (Slobin and Bever 1982; Bates *et al.* 1984; see also Hakuta 1981). Depending on their mother tongue, children become sensitive to factors of word order, inflectional

and other types of case marking, or gender and number agreement. Less clear is the evidence for how language typology affects children's deployment of word order in production. In the preceding section we noted that initially children favour certain perspectives in talking about experiences – as agent-perpetrated actions, as object-experienced events, or as designating the location or movement of entities. We suggest that subsequently, at the next phase of learning, children come to make typologically appropriate use of word order variation to serve discourse functions such as those of relative focus, of contrast, or foregrounding versus backgrounding. Consider, for instance, the rich use of right-dislocation made by French-speaking children to establish referent identity – as in *Then it flies off, the balloon* – compared with their English-speaking peers describing the same event (Karmiloff-Smith 1981). Relatedly, Hebrew-speaking children at late preschool age make free use of non-subject fronting to establish a discourse topic and to focus on different elements in the clause. This yields the equivalent of strings which sound very strange indeed in English (e.g. *With Rina I won't play* or *To you I can tell everything*) but which are felicitous in the stream of Hebrew discourse. And the Hebrew narratives of early school-age children alternate between subject–verb and verb-initial constructions, depending on the relative topicality or newness of the referent being talked about (Berman 1985). These, too, are devices which are inappropriate to languages like English or French, and as such they are simply not available to children learning these languages by this advanced phase of their development.

The curve which can be observed starts, then, with initial attention to major typologically determined cues deployed by the input language for signalling relations between parts of a sentence. In production there is some evidence that this is accompanied by a preference for rigid adherence to one or two basic, canonic types of word orders. Only later will children learn to deploy typologically appropriate word order alternations to meet a variety of discourse functions. And although there are no crosslinguistic comparative studies available on this question, it seems to be the case that this development, from an earlier invariant use of word order signals to later, discourse-sensitive variation of ordering of constituents, is shared by children learning languages with a quite strictly grammaticized word order (e.g. Chinese, Erbaugh 1980; English, Maratsos 1983; and French, Karmiloff-Smith 1979a) and those acquiring languages with a more pragmatically governed, grammatically freer type of basic word order (such as Hebrew, Berman 1985b; Hungarian, MacWhinney 1985; and Turkish, Aksu and Slobin 1985).

4. Conclusions

Findings from studies of grammatical development in typologically distinct languages suggest, firstly, that 'more' grammar does not necessarily make the task of the language learner harder, just as 'less' does not make it easier (to adapt the title of Erbaugh 1980). Rather, there seems to be a trade-off between the learning load demanded by different languages in relation to different maturational stages. For instance, it has been noted that Turkish-speaking children acquire mastery of the complex, but very regular and clearly marked, system of verb morphology as early as age 2 years (Aksu and Slobin 1985). These children, however, have a hard time with relative clauses as late as age 5, whereas children acquiring, say, English, French or Hebrew produce relative clauses by around age 3. Clearly, 5-year-old Turkish children know what is entailed by object specification (as in English *my new book, that book over there, the book I got from Daddy for my birthday*), but they do not yet have command of the complex nominalizations required to form relative clauses in their language.

Take, as another example, verb morphology. The Hebrew-learning child seems faced with a bewildering array of forms every time he or she uses a verb, since there is an obligatory choice between one of five possible forms:

Root	Infinitive	Imperative	Present	Past	Future
sh-t-y 'drink'	li-shtot	shte	shote	shata	yi-shte
sh-q-t 'quiet'	le-hashkit	hashket	mashkit	hishkit	yashkit

And to this must be added alternations of forms occurring in seven different verb classes (only two of which are illustrated above), as well as marking for number, gender and person on finite verbs. Yet all such formal alternations are mastered basically during the third year (Berman 1983a, 1985b). One explanation is that of the *typological imperative*, in the sense that such markings are so ingrained and pervasive in the language that they must be made in order to speak the language even minimally. Note, however, the trade-off balance referred to earlier. The Hebrew-learning child does not at the same time have to contend with elaborate systems of aspect marking in verbs, such as those required by English and even more so in Russian or Spanish. Thus, for instance, the single Hebrew form (*hu*) *avad* can, out of context, translate any of the following English forms: (*he*) *worked, was working, has worked,* and *had worked, had been working.* In general, while it is true that Hebrew-learning children gain mastery of the bulk of the richly synthetic inflectional morphology of their language (not only in verbs, but in nouns, adjectives, pronouns and prepositions)

by age 3 or so, they achieve this task at a time when they have relatively little to encompass by way of intricate syntactic structuring or complex embeddings.

I argued earlier that children bring the same predispositions to bear on tasks which become increasingly differentiated in accordance with the particular native tongue. This is *not* to say that a particular language makes the overall learning task easier or more difficult for the child. Rather, the learner is able to apply a selective allocation of resources to different subparts of the grammar, and this comes to accord most optimally with the particular language being learned. As children move beyond the universal predispositions of early or basic child grammar, their attention becomes increasingly directed to where things are centred, so to speak, and to how content becomes grammaticized in their own native tongue. And this growing focus on cues appropriate to this language rather than to others frees them from paying time and effort-consuming attention to factors which are irrelevant or merely marginal to the language they are learning. By the time children move into the phase of learning grammar, then, they have become so attuned to their own native tongue that they are uniquely suited to learning its particular grammar, rather than that of any other language. At this stage, English becomes 'easiest' for the British or North American child, Hebrew for the Israeli, or Spanish for the Mexican.

At the outset of this chapter we noted how relatively few studies have been undertaken with a deliberately crosslinguistic perspective. One problem is the methodological issue of ensuring an adequate level of *comparability* across languages, across linguistic subsystems, and across tasks (for further discussion, in relation to different language learning settings, see Berman 1984). Thus, in adapting existent language measures for English to Hebrew, we have found that attention must be paid to both the nature of the target language and the developmental task for the child. For instance, in trying to devise a measure of MLU, we found that because of the richly synthetic, bound Hebrew morphology, there was a danger, unless structural analysis were made subservient to developmental facts, of overrating the child's knowledge; and that unlike a more isolating language, such as English, added morphemic complexity is not mainly a matter of added linear length (Dromi and Berman 1982).[7] Relatedly, in the Stanford study noted in section 1 above, of innovative agent and instrument nouns in English, Hebrew, and Icelandic, although very similar general acquisitional principles were hypothesized (and observed) across children, both input stimulus materials as well as output results were different for the different languages. Again, such designs need to rely on prior, quite rich, naturalistic child language data to ensure that not only structural pro-

perties of the target language are taken into account, but also developmental facts which interact with the end-state grammar.

A rich and diverse, though not always strictly comparable, database is now available on children's acquisition of grammar in numerous typologically quite distinct languages (see note 2 to this chapter, also Slobin 1985b). It seems that the work of scholars with an explicitly *functionalist* approach (e.g. Karmiloff-Smith 1979a; Bates and MacWhinney 1982) may today indicate the most fruitful direction to pursue, with focus on how children learn to deploy a variety of linguistic forms and structures to express different functions in discourse. Current work in the complex area of children's acquisition of temporality, and the expression of tense–aspect distinctions in different languages, indicates that it is not enough merely to isolate specific *forms*, for example, morphological aspect markers on the verb, or lexical connectives and adverbs marking sequential and other temporal relations between clauses such as *before* or *while*.[8] Rather, one needs first to consider the linguistic functions which such markers might serve (by encoding different perspectives on events as foregrounded or backgrounded, or by relating one sequence of events to some other set of events, etc.). In principle, such interactions between forms and functions would be differentially deployed not only by children of different ages but also by speakers involved in different discourse settings, for example, narrating past experiences, negotiating future plans, demonstrating ongoing activities, participating in pretend play, and so forth.

Such an orientation to the crosslinguistic study of emergent grammars would entail *a priori* specification of functional and semantic categories which are taken to apply across any language. For instance, in investigating the development of temporality, one would stipulate such parameters as time orientation (past, present, future, or irrealis, say); basic and secondary types of aspect (perfective versus imperfective, supplemented by features of iterativity, inchoativeness, etc.); interclause relations of sequencing or simultaneity; types of background functions and scene settings; and the nature of the predicate (state versus process, say). In talking about objects rather than events, the question thus becomes not merely at what age and in what order children learning English, Hebrew, or Turkish can understand and/or produce relative clauses in their language. Rather, if such constructions serve as a means of explicit specification of object identity (e.g. *I just saw the kid that moved to Arizona*), or for contrastive isolating of an entity (e.g. *I want the one you took from me*), then relative clauses will be analysed as part of an entire range of formal means which children, and languages, use to express such functions. The emergence of *grammar*, within such an endeavour, would be revealed by analysis of the particular

formal linguistic devices (contrastive stress, affixing, adpositions, word ordering, subordination, etc.) which are deployed by children in learning how to express different discourse functions in keeping with the structural properties of their particular native tongue.

Part IV

LATER LANGUAGE DEVELOPMENT

Introduction

It has been commonly understood, since Carol Chomsky's (1969) ground-breaking study, that language development is not nearly as complete by the age of 5 years as had previously been thought. However, there are two ways of interpreting Chomsky's demonstration of continuing difficulties in comprehension of certain predicate constructions after 5. One way is to see the upper bound of language development as simply being pushed higher; but another is to regard 5 still as a 'frontier age', in Karmiloff-Smith's words (Chapter 21), while changing one's view of what sorts of territory the frontier divides. Karmiloff-Smith suggests that while it would indeed be wrong to continue to interpret it as a demarcation of basic versus complex structures (within the older, exclusively structuralist approach), it does seem to represent a frontier with respect to three other contrasts: surface-behavioural phenomena versus their underlying representations (including here the simpler, more basic categories that used to be thought of as 'acquired' before 5); within-sentence versus between-sentence developments (i.e. discourse structures starting to emerge after 5); and contextualized versus decontextualized mastery of language performance (i.e. the ability to manipulate language in its own right, including the ability to reflect metalinguistically on its formal properties, in an increasingly adult-like fashion).

Karmiloff-Smith reviews a wide range of studies carried out since Chomsky (1969), concentrating on what she refers to as the linguistic challenge to the older view. Pronominalization is a prime example of a structural system that shows surface-behavioural completeness before 5 (part of what she calls the 'basic tools' of language), but whose functions are ill-described within the sentence domain: use of pronouns accordingly is sensitive to the shift from within-sentence to discourse domains of language performance.

She also reviews further work on the sort of predicates (e.g. *easy to see* versus *eager to see*) that Chomsky studied, as well as on passives, reversed temporal order, relative clauses and other complex constructions.

451

Karmiloff-Smith goes on to discuss other functional developments subsequent to surface mastery of the relevant forms, referring particularly to article contrast, which is taken further in her discussion of how such terms are plurifunctional in the adult language but may be acquired unifunctionally by children before age 5. This leads in turn to her discussion of discourse developments, which she sees as possibly the most significant development after age 5.

Karmiloff-Smith's discussion of developmental shifts around age 5 from intra- to intersentential domains, from structures to (additional) functions, and from extra- to intralinguistic abilities, sets the scene comprehensively for the following two chapters, on the development of written language abilities in the child. How far are Karmiloff-Smith's shifts bound up in, affected by, or even determined by, the exposure to written forms of the language at about this frontier age of 5? There is surely more here than a simple mapping of established spoken language abilities onto a new medium.

For the beginning reader, exposure to the written language involves, first and foremost, the decoupling of language processing from the time pressures that are characteristic of the articulatory-auditory channel. The importance of this for the development of contemplative linguistic capacities seems clear – although we should also recognize that nonliterate societies have ways of 'recording' language, involving prodigious feats of memory for voluminous texts, as various 'oral literature' traditions (e.g. Emeneau 1958) testify. Along with this new medium of written language comes the opportunity for the child to encounter the individual sound elements that go to make up words (*cat* versus *sat* versus *mat*) and the word elements themselves (words presented in isolation, spaces between words in text, and contrasts such as *hair* versus *hare*, *by* versus *buy*, where the spelling differences do not mark distinctions of pronunciation but differences between words where 'word' is taken to be a complex of sound and meaning). To some extent also, sentence units (initial capital letter, final punctuation markers) and internal clause and phrase units (where these are set off by punctuation markers) are signalled. And, with growing ability to control the written medium, further and deeper awareness of how written language differs from speech, in vocabulary and style, is achieved (by some fairly small proportion of a literate community). For our purposes, however, we may think of exposure to the written language initially as providing the conditions for a reorganization of the child's *lexical* knowledge – particularly, the way that words have in the first years of language development been stored in long term memory as sound schemas and associated structures in the mental lexicon.

Several issues arise here. First, does reading involve the accessing of these established sound schemas via rules which convert the letters on the page into the relevant sound units? For English, which has an alphabetic spelling system, letter-units, or *graphemes*, map most readily onto *phonemes*, hence *grapheme–phoneme conversion rules* may be postulated. Second, there is the distinction between *pre-access* and *post-access* stages of processing: phonemic-type information may be utilized (as in the grapheme–phoneme conversion hypothesis) as a way of accessing a lexical item; or it may become available only *after* access has been achieved by some other means. (Subvocalization during reading may, in principle, derive from either pre- or post-access phases.) Third, there is the consideration that strategies employed by beginning readers may be rather different from those of mature, fluent readers. Finally, for our purposes, we may ask whether writing and reading call on the same psycholinguistic structures and processes, either in course of development, or in mature use.

The picture that is beginning to emerge from a number of different studies may be characterized as follows: (a) initial reading strategies may be profoundly influenced by teaching methods as well as by the properties of the orthography – phonology relationship; (b) notwithstanding this, at some point the beginning reader of English 'discovers' grapheme–phoneme correspondences (the extent to which 'phonemic awareness' is a favourable precondition for reading – see Liberman *et al.* 1980 – or something which arises from reading, is uncertain); (c) these rules of correspondence are not lost in the mature reader, where they remain available, for example, for reading unfamiliar words; but (d) they cannot by themselves lay the foundation for fluent reading, or writing, since a whole range of symbols in English orthography is either irregular in terms of this system (e.g. *ou*, *gh* in *cough, bough*, etc.) or stand outside it altogether (e.g. logographic symbols such as £, & and the numerals); hence (e) nonphonographic strategies must be used increasingly as exposure to written forms of the language is broadened, leading to the establishment in the mental lexicon of word representations as *visual* schemas, interlinked with their corresponding sound schemas.

Finally, it appears that input processing (reading) may be distinct from output processing (writing) developmentally; there are children who can read better than they can spell (in the sense of writing words), and who cannot read their own distorted spellings of irregular words (Frith 1979) – i.e. they appear to be reading 'by eye' (*words* rather than *letters*), but spelling 'by ear' (with the phoneme-to-grapheme conversions breaking down in the case of irregular words).

If this is anywhere near the mark, then there appears to be a developmen-

tal shift in processing units, roughly from phoneme to (visually-represented) word. But our understanding of such units in mature use is still incomplete; it may be, for instance, that we read words in terms of graphic units that, while larger than the letter/phoneme, are smaller than many words (thus *scout* is handled in terms of *sc-* as in *scarp, scrape, scare* rather than in *scissors*, and *out* as in *sprout, pout, rout, lout* and *out* itself, rather than in *crouton*, or *route*; see Glushko 1979). One implication of such a view is that the units of reading may be essentially variable, and determined by knowledge at various levels (e.g. graphotactic constraints, morphology, the distinction between e.g. German- versus Latin-type words, etc.). Smith (Chapter 22), reviews these issues and others in considerable detail, and concludes that by 7 years the child has moved from the 'declarative' stage (the *what* as opposed to the *how*) but still has a way to go to achieve adult-like maturity in reading, He calls, appropriately, for further investigation of how children change their strategies during the course of developing their reading skills, and points out that genuinely longitudinal studies of reading development are required for this purpose.

Just as reading is much more than deciphering letters on the page, so writing is about composing written text, rather than spelling words and forming letter shapes. Perera (Chapter 23) accordingly concentrates on certain structural properties of written language texts produced by children, at the level of sentence, clause and phrase. Reviewing a number of large-scale studies, she is able to point to a shift from the stage where the child's writing is basically driven by the spoken language to one (around 9–10 years) where it starts to take on its own characteristic properties (some of which may subsequently feed back into certain adult speech styles, e.g. in formal lectures). Like Smith, Perera calls for more refined studies of the developmental course of children's writing abilities, focusing on how individual children develop over the early school years. She also raises the important issue of the relationship between writing and reading, noting that there is some plausibility to the claim that the grammar of the written language is largely acquired first in reading and subsequently deployed in writing. In both reading and writing performance, it seems, knowledge of the whole language system is stimulated, reshaped and deployed – the study of language development has reached the point where it is both possible and necessary to understand how children come to develop this new dimension in knowledge of their language.

21. Some fundamental aspects of language development after age 5*

Annette Karmiloff-Smith

1. Introduction

When, in 1976, I was asked to write a chapter on language after age 5 for the first edition of this volume, I was struck by how many studies concentrated either on the period from 2 to 5 years or from 5 to 10. Far less frequent were studies which specifically bracketed the age span between, say, 3 and 7 years. A check through the major journals publishing developmental psycholinguistics shows that much the same holds true at the time of contributing to this second edition.* Is there something crucial about the frontier age of 5 which makes many researchers either terminate or initiate their studies at this age? Does it simply reflect a focus before 5 on morphosyntactic and lexical problems, and after 5 on the complex sentential ones?

In this chapter I shall argue that 5 can be considered as a frontier age psycholinguistically. However, setting up experiments to concentrate on subjects under 5 years old, as if basic morphosyntactic and lexical acquisition were completed by 5 and the complex sentential only after 5, is questionable. It may stem from misconceptions based on surface *behavioural* mastery which neglect underlying *representational* changes. I shall therefore submit that fundamental changes take place in language development after age 5, not only with respect to complex intrasentential constructions, but also with respect to seemingly simpler categories at the morphologico-lexical level, such as determiners. Early mastery of a linguistic category prior to age 5 is frequently not the end of the developmental picture for that category.

Furthermore, I shall expand in this revised version on the intersentential level of connected spans of discourse. I shall demonstrate that a number of linguistic devices, such as pronominalization and subordination, change their function as the child moves from their use at the *intra*sentential level to their use at the *inter*sentential level. A number of fundamental reorganizations occur to internal linguistic representations after 5 even if, at the

455

phenomenological level of behaviour, output before 5 seems perfect in a particular linguistic category. In general, in this chapter I shall give particular emphasis to the idea that, outside the specific cognitive content of children's utterances and of their communicative intentions, language is for the child at all ages a problem space in its own right. Clearly, language development cannot be explained by cognitive development alone. Children have to come to grips with the intricacies of the linguistic structures themselves, and may spend a number of years organizing linguistic categories into systems of relevant options.

2. Cognitive and linguistic developments

A common assumption held until the late 1960s was that the 5 year old had mastered the syntactic structures of her native tongue, and that later development mainly consisted of the addition of a sophisticated lexicon. Two main psycholinguistic currents were to challenge such assumptions: one was cognition-oriented, the other linguistics-oriented. Whilst the theoretical bases for questioning early mastery were substantially different, both of these currents led to the study of rather similar problem areas.

One of the cognition-oriented currents stemmed from Piagetian developmental psychology. Piaget's studies on various categories of knowledge showed that many crucial cognitive developments took place well beyond the age of 5. As is well known, Piaget stressed that language development is dependent on more general mechanisms governing the child's overall cognitive growth. The fact that many fundamental cognitive changes have still to take place after the age of 5, up to age 14, led psycholinguistic interpreters of Piagetian theory to hypothesize that the child's linguistic competence must also reflect these changes beyond the age of 5.

At the lexical level, Sinclair (1967), for example, maintained that despite the fact that certain terms (e.g. *more than, less than, thicker, longer*, etc.) were present in the young child's lexicon, these were not fully comprehended, nor used, as *relational* terms until the child's corresponding concepts in conservation and seriation were mastered. At the syntactic level, it was argued that any linguistic structure which violates canonical order (e.g. agent of an action not in subject slot of the sentence, temporal order of events described in reverse order, and so forth) would be a candidate for acquisition after 5. Basic cognitive acquisitions which take place around 6 or 7, e.g. the first quantitative invariants with their reversible operations, were invoked to explain children's difficulties with semantic invariants across transformations in word order (Sinclair and Ferreiro 1970).

The linguistics-oriented current to challenge early language mastery was

exemplified by Carol Chomsky's work on the development of complex constructions (Chomsky 1969). Chomsky hypothesized that children first use those linguistic rules which hold for a great number of constructions across a language. The following were considered already to be part of the implicit competence of the under-5 year old: (a) grammatical subject is equivalent to logical subject; (b) word order necessarily reflects canonical order; (c) the implicit subject of a complement verb is the NP most closely preceding it (Minimal Distance Principle), and so forth. Any structures which violated such general principles would be candidates for acquisition after 5. Chomsky's experiments on 5 to 10 year olds' understanding of complex adjectival, verbal and pronominal constructions showed that it was a slow process, extending to the age of 10 before the child became able to refrain from overgeneralizing the above rules to all superficially identical constructions (see Bowerman 1979 for a discussion of the acquisition of complex sentence constructions). Chomsky argued that the only exception to late acquisition was pronominalization, which seemed to be fully mastered around age 5. She explained the earlier and more uniform acquisition of pronominal reference by the fact that pronominalization does not pertain to any specific word or word class, but derives from general principles which cover the structural relationships obtaining for whole sentences. Chomsky drew a distinction between, on the one hand, 'basic tools of language' (e.g. pronominalization), which she maintained were acquired by 5, and, on the other hand, specialized syntactic rules for complex constructions, gradually mastered between 5 and 10. Later in this chapter I shall show that the sentence is the wrong unit of analysis for a deep understanding of pronominalization and that much in this area remains to be acquired after age 5.

Many critical replications from both the cognition- and linguistics-oriented currents were to follow in the 1970s, particularly with respect to structures such as *easy to see* (e.g. for English-speaking children: Cromer 1970, 1972; Kessel 1970; Morsbach and Steel 1976; and for French-speaking children: Cambon and Sinclair 1974; Barblan in preparation). Whilst some of these rebuttals stressed the younger age levels at which success could be obtained if misleading features were removed from the experimental design, others sought alternative or complementary explanations to Chomsky's concept of syntactic complexity. More general cognitive factors were argued to be involved also. One difficulty seemed to stem from the broad semantics of the verb *to see*. Others arose from the need for the child to differentiate between her own perspective and that of others. The early success levels of 5 year olds, found in some of the later studies, could be explained by the tendency of small children to take themselves

as the agent of all verbs (i.e. *easy to see* implies '*I* can see easily'). Successful 8 year olds, on the other hand, really understood the nonspecific agent function of the missing grammatical object (i.e. *easy to see* implies 'easy to see by some'). Problems of decentration, a well-known cognitive phenomenon in spheres outside language, were invoked to explain some of the difficulties encountered by children. However, decentration could not alone account for the child's problems with this construction since, when investigators tested children with a different verb, e.g. 'the doll is easy to *draw*' (Cambon and Sinclair 1974) which is clearly biased towards a correct answer, younger children nonetheless persisted in equating grammatical subject with agent and had the doll pretend to do a drawing.

Other complex categories investigated in over-5 year olds were: the passive voice (e.g. in English: Hayhurst 1967; Turner and Rommetveit 1967; Bever 1970; Sinclair, Sinclair and de Marcelus 1971; Scholnick and Adams 1973; Maratsos 1974; Maratsos and Abramovitch 1974; Baldie 1976; Horgan 1978; in French: Sinclair and Ferreiro 1970; in Swiss-German: Caprez, Sinclair and Studer 1971); also constructions reversing temporal order of events (e.g. in English: Cromer 1971b; Weil 1971; Coker 1978; Weil and Stenning 1978; Trosborg 1982; in French: Ferreiro 1971); as well as relative clauses (e.g. in English: Gaer 1969; H. D. Brown 1971; Sheldon 1972, 1974; Limber 1973; Maratsos 1973; Goodluck and Tavakolian 1982; in French: Kail 1975a,b; in Spanish: Ferreiro 1974).

To take research on the relative clause as an example, it indicated that children's difficulties were not only rooted in the linguistic complexity of relativization, but that other factors were involved. Moreover, the relationship between subordination and co-ordination had to be taken into account. Sheldon (1972, 1974) argued that children interpret relative clauses with a 'parallel function hypothesis' which explains why they can cope with the linguistically complex embedded relative, such as that in example (1a), before they understand the seemingly simpler construction of example (1b):

(1a) The dog that jumps over the pig bumps into the lion
(1b) The pig bumps into the horse that jumps over the giraffe

In example (1b) the horse changes function from patient of the main clause to agent of the subordinate clause, whereas in (1a) there are no changes in function. However tempting it might be to generalize the 'parallel function hypothesis' to several spheres of the over-5 year old's language, Sheldon's subsequent experiment indicated that this only partially accounts for the child's behaviour. Indeed, contrary to the difficulties in interpreting relative clauses, shifts of function caused no problems in dealing with the

co-ordinate structure counterparts to the relative sentences, such as those in example (1c):

(1c) The pig jumps onto the horse and the horse jumps over the giraffe

There are, of course, many nonlinguistic difficulties involved in handling three animals more or less simultaneously, and sentences like (1a–c) above are most atypical of normal language usage. Nonetheless, the difference in the results for the two sentence types does tend to suggest that co-ordination is an earlier linguistic achievement than subordination; that the parallel function hypothesis has some effect on children's behaviour; and that the actual structure of the relative clause is also in part a determinant in children's difficulties.

These and similar studies confirmed that certain aspects of language are still being acquired by over-5 year olds; and that many interacting linguistic and general cognitive problems are involved. Whilst differing in their theoretical explanations and in situating the exact age of successful performance, some studies argued for very early mastery; but most of the studies indicated, as did Chomsky's early work, that the over-5 year old does in some circumstances have difficulty in understanding that the grammatical subject of a sentence need not necessarily be identified with the agent of an action. Over-5 year olds in the studies appeared also to expect word order to reflect the temporal order of events. The over-5 year old therefore continues to work from sound mini-theories about language, which are correct for many constructions but which have not yet been clearly tagged with standby procedures regarding exceptions (see Karmiloff-Smith 1978 for discussion of the cognitive processes involved in the interaction of theory construction and exceptions thereto).

3. Functional developments

Whilst each new study adds a few more pieces to the total language puzzle, I should like to submit that talented investigators will always be able to devise novel techniques and contexts which make it possible to demonstrate that a particular structure is understood either much earlier or much later than previous work had indicated. But this tells us relatively little about the *general nature* of developmental changes or about the *function* a given category may have for the child. Should we continue to revisit specific, old structures with ingenious, new techniques? Will we not discover more about the 5 year old's language if emphasis is placed on *why* a change in experimental design elicits a change in procedure in the 5 year old, whereas by 8 or 9 years, children use the same procedure across a series of situations?

In his comprehensive review of developmental strategies for language, Cromer (1976b) placed particular stress on the fact that at around the age of 6 children appear to enter an intermediate stage of language development lasting for some three years. During this period, children may use, for example, the rule 'grammatical subject implies agent' in interpreting the *easy to see* structure, but do not follow the same rule for interpreting the passive. Moreover, Cromer showed that the intermediate child's behaviour was inconsistent from one day to the next, even across a number of items testing the same structure in identical experimental settings.

Thus changes in procedure are not only elicited by changes in experimental design, but are actually *characteristic* of the over-5 year old's behaviour. As of roughly age 5, the child can be said to have built up a series of juxtaposed procedures for language use and understanding, which now need to be organized into coherent systems of relevant options.

Why is it that over-5 year olds seem to have a wide repertoire of linguistic procedures but are inconsistent in their use of them in experimental tasks, whereas in spontaneous speech they appear to cope with language well? One of the reasons may be deeply interwoven with what I termed 'the experimental dilemma' in a discussion of the thorny issue of distinguishing between *ad hoc*, experiment-generated behaviour and normal language usage (Karmiloff-Smith 1979a). On the one hand, we are all aware that if we design an experiment with all the extralinguistic and discourse clues normally available in language, then the child's understanding may be due to the accumulation of interacting clues and not of the linguistic category under study. Yet if we remove all these clues we cannot be sure that we are not dealing with *ad hoc*, experiment-generated procedures, atypical of the child's everyday behaviour.

Let us very briefly illustrate this point from the field of determiners. Say an experimenter decides to study the 'article contrast'. The very use of the word 'contrast' carries theoretical assumptions that are not necessarily true of the child's representations. How do we know that the articles do actually function as contrastive terms for the small child? In order to set up as clean an experiment as possible, researchers narrow down the task to one linguistic contrast (e.g. *the/a*) and the situational context to one cognitive contrast (e.g. singletons/groups of identical objects). But the *child's* problem in a comprehension task of this kind need not be specifically linguistic at all; rather, she may seek to discover each of two distinctions and then map one pair onto the other. A very small amount of knowledge about one of the terms will suffice to elicit, by exclusion, correct responses for the other term. In this way a child may show very consistent, and thus statistically significant, behaviour across the two-way mapping. However, it should be recalled that *we* have placed the articles in contrastive

functions in an experimental setting. What the child *can* do in an experimental task is not necessarily equivalent to what the child *does do* in language use and understanding. The articles may have quite distinct functions initially for the child. Even when they gradually become part of a common system, it is possible that the child does not let the articles carry such a heavy communicative burden if particular contrasts are to be encoded; instead of *the/a*, the child may add relevant linguistic emphasizers such as *the only X/one of the Xs*. At all events, the behavioural patterns observed in an experiment may be generated on the spot by the child's general problem-solving procedures and do not necessarily allow us to draw conclusions about the child's normal language development.

Let us look at what this might imply in relation to some of the constructions violating canonical order which were singled out as candidates for acquisition after 5. It should be recalled that most investigators of these complex structures explicitly removed from their experimental design all extralinguistic, paralinguistic and discourse clues in order to attain the child's competence solely in respect of the structure under study. However, it is a truism to assert that we do not normally speak in isolated sentences devoid of prosodic features, unless we want to send our addressees to sleep! Understanding is based on many interacting clues from syntax, semantics, pragmatics, intonation, presuppositions, dialogic rules, discourse and situational context. Moreover, linguistic categories have various specific *functions* within a language and children may also be sensitive to this fact. Certain structures which violate canonical order, for instance, have at least one function in common: a syntactic focusing device for highlighting constituents (or information) intrasententially, and simultaneously linking this information intersententially to the overall discourse.

Take, for instance, the reversed temporal order. One good reason for violating the canonical order is that the hearer already knows about the second of two subsequent actions and is being informed by the speaker about the first event which preceded it. Are children really sensitive to this functional aspect of language? In a study of temporal relations in French-speaking children's language, Ferreiro (1971) demonstrated that young children have difficulty in coping with reversed temporal order, as in example (2a), yet spontaneously produce and find it much easier to understand longer, redundant strings also reversing temporal order, as in (2b):

(2a) Before the boy went upstairs, the girl washed the boy
(2b) The boy went upstairs, and before the boy went upstairs, the girl washed the boy

Ferreiro noted similar, spontaneous redundancy in her study of Spanish-

speaking children's use of the relative clause. In my view, the redundancy children introduce in this way makes such isolated sentences 'functionally grammatical': the redundant clause makes it possible to insert a distinction between given and new information, and makes the violation of canonical order meaningful.

Changes in word order are clearly far more than stylistic variations, and their functions carry implicit information of which both speaker and hearer make use (see Hupet and Costermans 1974 for relevant discussion of the passive voice). Now if children are sensitive to information of this kind, and they indeed seem to be so after 5, what happens in an experiment where functional, syntactic, semantic, pragmatic and other clues are purposely excluded? I would suggest that it is here that we may find an explanation for the inconsistent behaviour Cromer and others have observed in the 5 to 8 year old. I would argue that the child's behaviour is experiment-generated from her stock of varied procedures, because the normal interplay of clues is not available. However, from the *consistent* experimental behaviour of the over-8 year old, we can deduce that by that age the child has attained a more abstract level of linguistic competence. This does not imply that over-8 year olds do *always* cope without the functional, semantic and pragmatic clues that are characteristic of their normal language usage, but that a more abstract level of linguistic analysis is now part of their competence. Even if atypical of normal language usage, the fact that by around 8 years children can, if need be, rely solely on a linguistic clue should not be underestimated. It may well be symptomatic of an internal reorganization of linguistic categories and a new phase in development.

Thus far the discussion has centred on the over-5 year old's behaviour *vis-à-vis* complex sentential structures. Does this mean that simpler linguistic categories, e.g. noun determiners, verb inflections, etc., present no problems for the older child? A closer look at the *functions* that these markers have in the growing child's language indicates that this may be an erroneous assumption.

4. Plurifunctionality

One of the basic aspects of many languages is the fact that verb and noun markers are plurifunctional. Take, for instance, the articles in French. *Une femme* marks both indefinite reference ('a woman') and the numeral function ('one woman'). The plural definite article *les* simultaneously marks pluralization (as opposed to the singular *le/la*) and totalization (as opposed to the partitive *des*). The plural possessive adjective *mes* marks possession, pluralization (as opposed to *mon/ma*), totalization of a subclass of pos-

sessed objects, and the partitive (as opposed to *les*). A further example concerns modifiers such as *rouge* 'red', which may be used in its descriptor function, giving information about redness, or in its determiner function, picking out a referent which is red from similar objects of a different colour. Such markers are present early in child corpora, but do they have plurifunctional status from the outset and, if not, is this an important facet of language development after age 5?

In a series of experiments aimed at analysing how French-speaking children cope with various elements of the noun phrase (Karmiloff-Smith 1979a), it was found that children pass through three levels.

The first level stretches between the ages of 3 and approximately $5\frac{1}{2}$ years. During this period, children's use of determiners appeared on the surface to be efficient. However, a deeper analysis of the *functions* children attribute to each determiner during the first phase disclosed several facts. First, although children made frequent use of the plural definite article *les*, its main function in production was to mark pluralization. This was also apparent in comprehension tasks: *les X* did not necessarily imply 'all the Xs present' but any plural amount of Xs. Similar patterns were found in experiments devised to study the child's use of the possessive adjective. Under-5 year olds *used* the plural *mes* correctly in its various functions to mark plural possession. However, they *understood* neither its totalizer function for possessed objects nor its determiner function to distinguish a subordinate class of possessed objects from a superordinate class of similar ones. With regard to the indefinite article, the under-5 year olds did seem in many cases to use it correctly to indicate various functions. Developmental trends apparent at the second level, however, raise questions about the actual functions of the indefinite article earlier. As far as the use of the singular definite article (*le/la*) was concerned, its function *for the child* was clearly deictic initially, even if *for the observer* it sometimes appeared to be functioning anaphorically. This brief description of the functions of determiners for the under-5 year old, in a chapter on later language development, is given to highlight the new behavioural patterns that occur after age 5.

The second level lasts from roughly 5 to 8 years of age. Productions of children then were often agrammatical and full of redundant marking. This, of course, does not mean that the 5 to 8 year old normally speaks agrammatically, but rather that in an experimental setting where special contrasts had to be encoded linguistically, these children behaved very differently from younger subjects.

Each time a new function was understood (e.g. totalization), the over-5 year old first expressed the new function by a separate morpheme (e.g.

tous in the case of totalization), and did not make use of a morpheme already serving another function (e.g. *les* which was already being used to mark pluralization). Thus, whereas smaller children used *les X* in a given situation but only meant to convey pluralization, children of the second level added *tous* in the same situation (*tous les X*) in order to cover totalization also. It was not until the third level that children used *les X* to mark pluralization and totalization *simultaneously*. Many of my results on the acquisition of determiners tend to indicate that initially treating a morpheme as if it were unifunctional is a characteristic feature of the language development of the under-8 year old. This does not mean that one and the same word is not used by the child to convey more than one function in different contexts and its use thus seem to be plurifunctional for the observer. However, from the *child's* point of view, when she wishes to mark several functions simultaneously in the same utterance, at this level she will tend to mark each by a separate morpheme.

Further evidence of the gradual development of a plurifunctional system came from two patterns which had not been apparent in behaviour before 5: the tendency to make multiple overmarking and to create agrammatical forms to distinguish between the dual functions of one marker. First let us look at an example of overmarking, which was particularly clear in children's attempts to make anaphoric reference in a potentially ambiguous situation. Whereas over-8 year olds at the third level made anaphoric reference such as that in (3a) below, children at the second level tended to use multiple overmarking (3b) in the same situation:

(3a)   La fille a poussé un chien et puis le garçon a poussé le chien
       'The girl pushed a dog and then the boy pushed the dog'
(3b)   La fille a poussé un chien et puis aussi le garçon il a repoussé encore le même chien
       'The girl pushed a dog and then also the boy he re-pushed once more the same dog'

In their endeavour to make clear their intention to refer *intra*linguistically, these children behaved as if they did not yet fully understand which of the sentence elements should be marked anaphorically; they therefore opted for multiple marking. Again, it should be stressed that this does not imply that such an exaggerated form is typical of the child's everyday speech, where such potential ambiguity rarely exists. However, it does represent a clue to subtle problems the older child is endeavouring to cope with and which are not apparent in the behaviour of the under-5 year old. In general, small children tended to clarify potential ambiguity by making reference to details of the *extra*linguistic setting, e.g. colour of

objects, temporary spatial location and so forth. It was not until after 5 that in such cases children endeavoured to make use of intralinguistic means such as anaphora, first by overmarking and finally as in adult language.

Other evidence pointing to the gradual construction by over-5 year olds of a plurifunctional system came from children's tendency to create agrammatical forms. As they gradually became aware of new functions, e.g. the numeral functions of the French indefinite article (which they already knew as a counting term when used without a noun), they created a surface distinction which exists in some languages but not in French. Thus, *un mouchoir* was used to imply 'a handkerchief' and the same children at level two used the slightly agrammatical *un de mouchoir* to imply 'one handkerchief'. Similar behaviour could be gleaned from children's distinctions between the descriptor and determiner functions of modifiers and possessive adjectives; *la voiture jaune* was used to convey the descriptor function and the same children created the slightly agrammatical *la jaune de voiture* to convey the determiner function; likewise, children made a distinction between *mes voitures* and *les miennes de voitures*.

The fact that children between 5 and 8 years add redundant markers and create agrammatical strings for contrastive purposes suggests that when younger children of the first phase use these morphemes correctly in various situations they in fact represent for the child a series of *unifunctional homonyms*. The same may hold true for lexical development in the language of the under-5 year old.

Further evidence came from the spontaneous corrections which occur towards the end of the second level. Typical corrections from 8 year olds are illustrated by examples (4a) and (4b):

(4a) Tu as caché toutes les voitures rouges . . . enfin, *les* voitures rouges
       'You hid all the red cars . . . well, *the* red cars'
(4b) Tous les camions de mon côté . . . *mes* camions, quoi
       'All the lorries on my side . . . *my* lorries, I mean'

By contrast, it is interesting to note that children at the third level did not accentuate morphemes to convey plurifunctionality, whereas this was particularly apparent at the end of the second level of development in this area. By the third level, the representational reorganization is complete.

Whilst such spontaneous corrections occur around 7 or 8 years of age, metalinguistic awareness of the plurifunctional status of determiners develops considerably later in the third phase. Prior to this, typical comments from 7 to 8 year olds who were interviewed (and who *correctly use* the plural definite article alone to convey totalization for experimental items) are exemplified in (5):

(5)   Il faut dire '*toutes* les voitures rouges', si tu dis seulement '*les* voitures rouges', on ne saurait pas combien prendre
      'You must say '*all* the red cars', if you just say '*the* red cars' you wouldn't know how many to take'

Clearly such children cannot yet consciously access the rule that they had been using in an earlier part of the experimental session.

The third level covered the period between roughly ages 8 and 12. Almost all redundant marking and agrammatical forms disappeared; markers had by then acquired plurifunctional status. Wherever possible in these tasks, children were economical in their utterances and had one marker carry simultaneously several functions. It also seemed clear that when children had reached the third level, they had organized various determiners into a coherent representational system, in which a hierarchy had been established concerning their presuppositional force. The following (6) is a translated example from an advanced 9 year old:

(6)   My yellow cars must ... euh, *the* yellow cars must go to the petrol station. [Experimenter asks the child why he changed from *mes* to *les*] It's because '*les*' is shorter ... well it's not true for the number of letters, but it's just as if ... I can't quite explain ... well, you can say both, '*les*' or '*mes*', but if there [points to another parking lot] there were some yellow cars then I would have to say '*mes*'; but there aren't any there, so it's better to say '*les voitures jaunes*' ... even if they belong to me

This and other similar examples are a clear indication that there is a tendency by the third phase to avoid overdetermining, i.e. to prefer 'weaker' determiners wherever this is feasible. Has not the over-8 year old finally come to terms with an important Gricean principle?

Examples (7a) and (7b) from 11 year olds illustrate the most elaborate form of metalinguistic awareness regarding the presuppositions that the use of one determiner in preference to another conveys:

(7a) I say '*my* watch' because it's mine, but '*the* watch' because it's the only one present, otherwise you'll think there's another one
(7b) [Experimenter asks the child why he changed from an initial indefinite reference to definite reference] Because if you continue to say '*a*', then it could be any old ring, a small one, a big one ... but here it's not just any ring. '*A* ring', well that belongs to anyone, so you must say '*your* ring'. I have to say '*my* ring' if yours is here, but '*the* ring' if I compare it to all that [pile of objects containing no rings]

Such examples bear eloquent witness to the fact that determiners are finally organized into a system of relevant options.

My experiments on the plurifunctionality of determiners concluded with an exploratory, metalinguistic interview (see Karmiloff-Smith in press a, for detailed discussion). The results highlighted an important linguistic development that takes place around 9 years of age. In a variety of different situations, under-9 year olds tended to make reference to characteristics of the *extralinguistic* context when asked to reflect metalinguistically upon their responses, as can be seen in examples (8a) and (8b):

(8a) I knew you were talking to the boy because he's got only one book
(8b) There are no apples left because there was only one in the basket in the beginning

It was not until after 9 in most cases that children explicitly referred to the *linguistic* clue they had used – see (8c) and (8d):

(8c) I know you're talking to the boy, because you said 'lend me *the* book', and if you'd been talking to the girl, you would have said 'lend me *a* book'
(8d) In the story there was only one, because you were precise, you said '*the* apple', and if there had been several of them you could have said 'one of the apples'

The capacity to refer to the presuppositions implied by the *absence* of a contrastive marker was only present in the oldest children's explanations.

Whilst most of the illustrative data given thus far has been from French-speaking children's utterances, much of the theoretical framework regarding the passage from unifunctionality to plurifunctionality and the representational changes leading to systemic organization equally holds for various aspects of acquisition of English after 5 (e.g. use of determiners, verb inflections). But what about linguistic categories which are specific to certain languages? How, for instance, do French-speaking children come to grips with problems of grammatical gender? Is this something entirely settled by 5, or is gender yet another sphere in which the over-5 year old still has ground to break? It is important to recall that in French, grammatical gender has relatively little to do with natural gender.

In a study of the child's acquisition of gender, another of the functions which French determiners mark, it was shown that well before 5, i.e. as soon as the articles were used consistently, the child had constructed a very powerful, implicit system of phonological rules based on the consistency, but not necessarily the frequency, of phonological changes to word endings (Karmiloff-Smith 1975, 1979a). This phonological procedure was

so strong that neither syntactic clues (i.e. gender of indefinite article furnished by the experimenter) nor semantic clues (i.e. sex of imaginary persons depicted in drawings) were determinant in eliciting gender agreement. Attribution of gender was overwhelmingly based on a phonological procedure from word endings. Whilst the phonological procedure remained dominant even in the over-8 year old's behaviour, the *function* of gender for the child changed considerably between the ages of 4 and 8 years. For the under-7 year old, gender served primarily to mark local lexical concord, initially between determiner and noun, and subsequently between determiner, noun and modifier. For over-7 year olds, by contrast, the discourse function of gender seemed to become relevant; these children used gender to mark cohesion intersententially.

Let us look briefly at the contrast between the younger and older children's output – see (9a) and (9b) below. Given, for instance, two pictures of Martian-like females called 'deux bicrons' (where the nonce term *bicron* is supplied with no gender clue from *deux*), children of all age groups referred to each of the representations of *bicron* spontaneously with masculine gender (e.g. *le bicron vert*), despite the fact that they were referring to a picture of a female. They were clearly basing themselves on the typically masculine ending *-on* of the nonce term (as opposed to the feminine ending *-onne*), and not on natural gender. However, developmental differences became apparent in the use of gender in extended discourse. In telling a story, young children based the gender of the pronoun on the sex of the extralinguistic referent and not on the gender of the noun. Typical stories from under-7 year olds about the female 'bicron' ran as follows (The gender examples are not translated since they are of course not relevant to English, but gender markers have been italicized.):

(9a) ... alors *le* bicron ver*t* est sort*i* ... et ensuite *elle* est al*lée*... et puis c'est *elle* qui a ... [Experimenter intervenes and asks: 'Elle, c'est qui?'] *celle-là, le* bicron ver*t*

From the above, it can be clearly seen that local lexical concord is phonologically-based, whereas pronominal reference and demonstratives are deictic- and semantically-based. Young children thus seem to juxtapose different procedures within the same output.

Over-7 year olds also use a phonological procedure for lexical concord, but extend the *same* procedure to pronominal reference, which is by now clearly intralinguistic. The gender of the pronoun is based on the gender of the noun previously mentioned linguistically. It is no longer based on the extralinguistic referent. These older children's stories about the female 'bicron' ran typically as follows:

(9b) C'est *le* bicron ver*t* qui est part*i* ... ensuite *il* est allé chez ... c'est
     lui qui a trouvé ... [Experimenter intervenes and asks: 'Lui, c'est
     qui?' Child points to the picture] bien, c'est *lui* ... non, non, *elle*,
     je veux dire, *la* bicro*nne* ... *celle* qui est ver*te*

Thus, the older child uses a phonological procedure for gender throughout.
When faced with the conflict between grammatical and natural gender,
older subjects make revealing changes to the noun suffix, leaving the phonological procedure intact. (See Karmiloff-Smith 1975, 1979a for further
details of gender acquisition between ages 3 and 12.) For the purpose of
the more general discussion here on language after 5, it is important to
note from the above examples that *intralinguistic* reference, i.e. truly non-
deictic reference, appears to be an achievement that takes place well after
5 years.

5. Development of extended discourse

This brings me to an area of developmental psycholinguistics which has
been much neglected until recently yet which represents, in my view, the
most significant aspect of language acquisition after 5: that of organizing
spoken text, i.e. long spans of connected utterances. Psycholinguistics has
for a long time focused on the sentence as its unit of analysis. Although
developmental psycholinguistics was early to go beyond the isolated sentence, the work was mainly confined to discourse in the form of single-
utterance interaction between dyads. Yet, it is a truism to state that normal
speaking, particularly after 5 years of age, involves much longer stretches
of language. The narrative (in its broadest sense) is perhaps the most common form of extended discourse.

Whilst the gender experiment discussed above was already an attempt
to analyse some facets of discourse cohesion, it was not at that time the
main focus of my work. Since then, however, I and others (Karmiloff-Smith
1979c, 1980, 1981, 1983; Hickmann 1980, 1985; Tyler 1981) have concentrated on various developmental problems involved in producing and understanding linguistic cohesion in spoken text. Due to space limitations, I
shall here deal only with some aspects of production. The data are selected
from a study of 4 to 9 year olds' narratives generated from picture booklets
with no text. Some of the books had a clear central character, with a subsidi-
ary character of the same sex; some had two characters of different sex;
some had three characters, and some were merely a collection of six pictures
with no obvious connection between the drawings. The design was manipulated so that in some cases pronominal devices would be potentially ambiguous, in other cases there would be no ambiguity, because of natural

gender differences; in some cases the picture contents held the story together, whereas others required the introduction of something extraneous to the picture contents to link them together. The visual stimulus of some pictures purposely led the child into describing the picture in one way, but inserted into the story the identical picture might be described in a different way according to the structure the child imposed on the overall narrative.

I shall take examples from two of the stories which illustrate particularly well how pronouns change function well after their earlier mastery with respect to semantic features such as gender and number. The first examples (10)–(14) are from a story about a boy and a girl fighting over a bucket.

(10) There's a boy and a girl. He's going fishing and she's going to make sandcastles. So he takes her bucket and ... she tries to grab it back and he runs off with it, so she sits there crying by the tree. Now he can do his fishing. He got four fish.

This narrative, from an under-5 year old, appears well constructed, coherent and cohesive, and reflects all the details in the pictures. The syntax is correct, there are no lexical mapping errors, no gender errors, and all the pronominal references are unambiguous. However, I shall argue from data from other stories and from older children's output for this story, that example (10) is generated more as a series of juxtaposed utterances, with correct mapping between linguistic terms and extralinguistic referents, than as a single structured linguistic unit. Example (11) is from the over-5 year old group:

(11) There is a boy and a girl. He's going to catch fish so he takes the girl's bucket and he runs off and catches lots of fish.

Compared to example (10), this narrative is weak on story details, providing a mere summary of the boy's activities and scarcely mentioning the girl. But the essential difference is that (11) obeys what I have termed the 'thematic subject constraint'. The boy is chosen as the thematic subject of the narrative and the grammatical subject slot is pre-empted for reference thereto. The story is a structured linguistic unit, even though it lacks detail.

Gradually, children start to relax the rigidity of the thematic subject constraint, the beginnings of which can be seen in the self repairs in examples (12) and (13). It is noteworthy that neither repair can be explained by local constraints or by potential ambiguity of reference. In both cases, the children could have continued their utterance without the repair. The repairs must therefore stem from the interaction between the thematic

subject constraint which organizes the internal representation of the narrative and the external stimuli of the story details.

(12) There's a boy and a girl playing together. But he wants to go off and fish and so he pinches the girl's bucket. He runs quickly away. So he starts to fish and the girl . . . leaving the girl crying.

(13) This boy and girl are out playing. He's gonna catch some fish but she . . . the girl won't lend him her bucket. So he just takes it and the girl gets real mad.

Finally, by 8 or 9 years, children come to make full use for discourse reference of the systemic organization built up earlier at the lexico-morphological level. The stories generated no longer rigidly obey the thematic subject constraint but make use of *differential* linguistic markers (full NPs, pronouns, zero anaphora), without repairs, to convey the structure of the internal representation, as can be seen in (14). It is important to note that the differential markers are used despite the fact that, because of the gender distinction, two pronouns would have been unambiguous.

(14) There's a girl and a boy. The boy wants to go fishing, so he tries to get the girl's bucket, but the girl won't let him take it, so he grabs it out of her hand and the girl chases after him, but he gets away from the girl and he starts to fish while the girl sits there crying. He goes home smiling with four fish.

From these and data from the other stories, it is clear that there is a more complex developmental story to tell than the mere passage from deictic to anaphoric reference.

One of the other stories, examples of which are discussed below, was designed so as not to differentiate between the sexes of the two referents. It was about a boy and a male balloon vendor. Example (15) is from the youngest age group. It shows that when the extralinguistic stimulus does not happen to differentiate gender, and thereby render unambiguous pronominal reference, it becomes even more striking that the young child is generating a sequence of juxtaposed utterances not related intralinguistically:

(15) There's a little boy in red. He's walking along and he sees a balloon man and he gives him a green one and he walks off home and it flies away into the sky so he cries.

The masculine pronouns used here are potentially ambiguous, referring at times to the boy and at times to the man, with no full NP indicating which. Clearly, the child's pronouns are functioning deictically, just as they

did in example (10). Each utterance is a unit unto itself, and if treated as such, the pronouns are *not* ambiguous. Each pronoun refers correctly to the extralinguistic referent. We, as adult addressees, link the pronouns intralinguistically: the young child, I would argue, does not. It is simply that in the other case the story sounded more structured than it really was, because of gender differences. But in my view, both examples (10) and (15) are generated from similar representations: the child is merely seeking correct mapping between picture and linguistic terms. By contrast, example (16) shows how, in a somewhat older child, the thematic subject constraint predominates in the representation generating the output. The story loses details, but gains in its organizational properties, as was the case with example (11) for the bucket story:

(16) There's a boy going along. He gets a green balloon. He lets go of the balloon and he starts crying.

In another part of the narrative study, another set of subjects of between 4 and 9 years were tested with one of the pictures in isolation, the one depicting the boy getting a balloon from the man. The results showed that, in isolation, the stimulus was preferentially interpreted as a man giving a boy a balloon, i.e. the man was placed in subject slot and the boy in object slot. But this was not the case when, for older children, the identical picture was inserted as one of the six pictures forming a story. Thus, the extralinguistic stimulus favours one linguistic organization whilst the thematic subject constraint from the internal representation favours a different one. Example (17) shows, via the self repair, how older children begin to come to terms, via differential markers, with the interaction between their internally imposed constraints and the externally driven ones:

(17) (Halfway through the balloon story)
He meets a man selling balloons and he gives the boy ... a man selling balloons who gives him a green balloon. He goes off really pleased.

Finally, example (18), like (14) in the bucket story, shows how the oldest children make direct use of *differential* linguistic markers to structure their narrative as a linguistic whole:

(18) A little boy is walking home. He sees a balloon man. The balloon man gives him a green balloon so he happily goes off home with it, but the balloon suddenly flies out of his hand and so he starts to cry.

The data from these and other stories have been analysed more fully

elsewhere, from a linguistic perspective in Karmiloff-Smith (1980, 1981) and from a cognitive processing perspective in Karmiloff-Smith (1983). For our purpose here, it suffices to note the general trend from terms being used in their correct extralinguistically referential function (deixis) to the gradual construction of a system of differential markers to be used in their intralinguistic referential function (anaphora).

In general, experimental work on the over-5 year old needs to be rooted in the normal functions and constraints of extended discourse. Whilst the over-5 year old's language is often superficially correct, important clues to ongoing developments can be gleaned from seemingly minor aspects such as children's pauses and spontaneous repairs. Learning studies may also provide indicators to problems of later acquisition (Cromer 1972; Barblan in preparation). Moreover, apart from Bowerman's well-known analyses of her two daughters' late-occurring errors (e.g. Bowerman 1982a,b), there is still a dearth of naturalistic data on the over-5 year old's everyday language which could usefully complement the, by now plentiful, naturalistic data on the under-5 year old.

6. Conclusions

Clearly, it is impossible in a single chapter to cover all aspects of language acquisition after age 5. Other important areas of later development include, *inter alia*: certain aspects of communicative competence (Shatz 1983); the understanding of metaphor, jokes and riddles (Shultz and Horibe 1974; Fowles and Glanz 1977); the knowledge of presuppositional structures in complex syntax (e.g. Hopmann and Maratsos 1978); and in intonational nuclei (Cruttenden 1974). Obviously, too, the over-5 year old's lexicon becomes far more complex with time (Clark, Hecht and Mulford in preparation).

This chapter has focused on but a small selection of issues regarding later developments. It has been shown that the gradual passage from juxtaposed, unifunctional homonyms to plurifunctional systems of relevant options for modulating meaning is a general feature of development of the noun phrase, and also probably the verb phrase, after the age of 5. Related aspects of later language development include the tagging of general principles with rules for exceptions, the passage from co-ordination to subordination, the gradual capacity to be economical, to avoid overly redundant marking, and above all to gauge the communicative burden that a linguistic category can carry single-handed. Important reorganizational processes have been seen to continue well beyond 5 (e.g. Karmiloff-Smith 1979a,b,c, 1983; Bowerman 1982a,b; Newport 1982) in closed and

open class morphology, in semantics and syntax, at the lexemic, sentential and extended discourse levels. The examination of representational changes to what is already mastered behaviourally before 5 is a most fruitful avenue for considering later language development.

It is my view, nonetheless, that the most fundamental feature of later language development concerns the *change of function* of linguistic categories from the local sentential level to the level of *extended spans of discourse*. This depends crucially on the previous creation of plurifunctional systemic organization in underlying representations. In this chapter this point was illustrated from the category of pronouns and the gradual introduction of differential marking. I have made similar arguments with respect to the discourse organizational function of subordinate clauses (Karmiloff-Smith 1983). Lavendera (1983) has recently discussed the notable textual functions of the conditional structure for Spanish-speaking adults; yet, I feel convinced that such functional changes occur with conditional sentences for children, too. It is never sufficient to ask *when* a particular linguistic category is mastered behaviourally; rather, focus must be placed on the representation of the function a category has initially and how its function(s) evolve and change with time.

I would argue that in general, after the prelinguistic and presystemic periods of language acquisition, children first seem to concentrate on building up what might be termed an 'utterance grammar'. This seems to be mastered around the age of 5. They then go on, until 8 years or beyond, to reorganize its components and to acquire procedures for operating on spans of cohesively related utterances, thereby changing the functions of their earlier mastered categories. This involves fundamental changes in children's underlying representations.

In a recurrent three-phase, process-oriented model of how linguistic and nonlinguistic processes are related (discussed in detail elsewhere, e.g. in Karmiloff-Smith 1983, in press b), I found that the only theoretical framework in which I could couch the linguistic part of the comparison was a functional one. If age 5 does represent the beginning of a new period in language development, in my view it is because of the gradual functional shift from using linguistic categories in processing juxtaposed utterances to their use as organizers of coherent and cohesive text. And if age 8 represents the beginning of a further period, it may be related to the over-8 year old's capacity to cope abstractly with language: i.e. if need be, in the case of contrived tasks, the over-8 year old can deal temporarily *without* the functional underpinning and textual organization so essential to normal linguistic production and comprehension.

22. The development of reading: the acquisition of a cognitive skill

Philip T. Smith

1. Introduction

Our treatment of the acquisition of reading follows the outline for the acquisition of any cognitive skill (Anderson 1982). Such work in its turn has developed from an older tradition of perceptual–motor skill learning whose origins go back to the early years of experimental psychology, in particular to the classic studies of the development of the skills of railroad telegraphers (Bryan and Harter 1897, 1899). In this skills literature it is useful to make a distinction between a *declarative* stage of acquisition 'in which facts about the skill domain are interpreted' and a *procedural* stage 'in which the domain knowledge is directly embodied in procedures for performing the skill' (Anderson 1982). In reading, children need to grasp what the activity of reading consists of, and on what principles the writing system that they are faced with is constructed (declarative stage); they then need to exploit this knowledge to achieve a reading performance that becomes increasingly fluent and error-free and in which many of the component skills involved become increasingly automatic (procedural stage).

2. The declarative stage: what do children need to know about reading?

At the declarative stage of reading development, the key insight for the child has two components: first, that speech consists of units of various sizes (phonemic features, phonemes, syllables, morphemes, words, sentences), and second, that some of these units are in reasonably close correspondence with units in the writing system the child is attempting to read. The extent and depth of this necessary metalinguistic knowledge is debatable, and the nature of the orthography the child is attempting to learn will be crucial. Only Korean systematically represents phonemic *features* in its orthography: the place of articulation of a phoneme is indicated by the shape of the corresponding grapheme, and the manner of articulation (stop, aspirate, etc.) is shown by the addition of diacritics (Taylor 1980). Some shorthand systems that are not taught as 'first languages' also contain

information about phonemic features (Smith and Pattison 1980). In some orthographies the *syllable* is the central unit (e.g. Japanese *kana*), in others the *word* (Japanese *kanji*); but in those systems we call alphabetic the *phoneme* is the primary unit, i.e. there is a rough correspondence between the phonemes of speech and a unit in the orthography, the letter (though other larger units, in particular the word, can usually be distinguished in alphabetic orthographies).

Evidence about the metalinguistic knowledge of Korean and Japanese readers is scant, but there is considerable evidence that children (and adults) learning to read alphabetic orthographies develop at the same time a good grasp of concepts such as phoneme and word. For example, M. M. Clark's (1976) study of 32 children who were reading fluently at exceptionally early ages found them remarkably ordinary with respect to most tests of abilities, but outstanding at 'auditory discrimination', which was assessed by the Wepman (1958) test, a test of discriminating words that differ only in one phoneme (*bum* versus *bomb*). Morais *et al.* (1979) showed that ability to carry out tasks adding or subtracting single phonemes from real words or nonsense words discriminates recently literate from illiterate Portuguese adults; and Bradley and Bryant (1983) have shown that exercises in phoneme manipulation lead to improvements in children's reading. At first sight the stress on phonemic segmentation abilities as prerequisites or concomitants of reading seems unremarkable: after all, grapheme–phoneme correspondences are a central aspect of models of adult reading. But this is to underestimate the intellectual achievement that recognizing phonemes entails. In the historical development of writing, and in the development of the child's conceptions, the first attempts show concern with large sentence-size units, which are gradually refined to word-size, then syllable-size units and so on. In some orthographies, and with some dyslexics, the progression to phoneme-size units is never achieved. As evidence of the prereader's reluctance to view words as sequences of phonemes, Ferreiro (1978) reports that many 4- and 5-year olds believe that each word in a sentence should correspond to a particular noun referent, so that, for example, they might believe that a sentence referring to 'three ships' should contain three words, one for each ship. Arnold (1975, cited in Byrne and Shea 1979) reports the retarded reader who considered that removing the final syllable of *pencil* would leave *half a pencil*. Even the precocious attempts of Paul Bissex to write (Bissex 1980) show syllabic as well as phonemic expectations: RUDF ('Are you deaf?'). (Paul Bissex, an American child, invented and developed his own writing system just after his fifth birthday and prior to any formal schooling; his productions offer a

useful perspective on a child's expectations about written language when these are comparatively undistorted by formal training about spelling.)

The insight that phonemes and graphemes are in rough correspondence is not sufficient for readable language, as many of Paul Bissex' early attempts at writing should make clear (e.g. EFUDOTBSELEIWELGUAPRRZET: 'If you don't be silly I will give you a present', Bissex 1980: 10). Spaces between words make a major contribution to the ease with which adults can read text (see Brady 1981 for a review), and thus some concept of the word will stand the beginning reader in good stead. Just as phoneme–grapheme correspondences are not exact in most orthographies, neither are correspondences between the phonological word (see, for example Chomsky and Halle 1968: 367–70) and the written word: for example, is *Fifth Avenue* one word or two? Different languages make different decisions on this point: English is much maligned as a 'complex' orthography, but at least it does not inflict on its readers such German monstrosities as *Ausnahmegenehmigungsgultigkeitseweierung*. Chomsky and Halle (1968) define phonological words (approximately) as those units that occur between successive word boundaries (these are the units within which, but not between which, various phonological rules, such as stress assignment rules, operate). This has the effect of not giving many 'function' words full status as phonological words: correspondingly, Ehri (1975) finds that prereaders are less able to carry out tasks that require the recognition of function words as words.

Finally, the child at an early stage needs to deal with units of the size of the syllable or the morpheme. In English this is partly because within-word parsing is needed to resolve ambiguities of grapheme–phoneme correspondences (e.g. *ph* can be realized as /ph/ *haphazard* or /f/ *telephone*); but even if grapheme–phoneme correspondences were exact in English, the fact that morphemic structure has phonetic consequences means that *admit* and *vomit* or *digress* and *tigress* should receive different morphemic parsings to correlate with different stress patterns (using notation developed by Chomsky and Halle 1968: 364–70, *admit* and *digress* contain morphemic boundaries (=), blocking the application of certain stress assignment rules (ad=mit, di=gress), *tigress* contains a weaker 'formative' boundary (+) (tigr+ess) and *vomit* contains no boundary at all: it will benefit children if they can recognize that *ad-* and *di-*, but not *ti-* and *vo-*, are letter clusters associated with special stress patterns). Morphemic analysis should also benefit a reader, given that English orthography sometimes chooses to preserve morphemes not phonemes (*-ed* may be realized as /t/, /d/ or /əd/, as in *wished, yearned* and *wanted*).

Many of these features are illustrated by the early writings of Paul Bissex. At 5;6 he wrote (Bissex 1980: 25):

SHAP.ING.LETS	Shopping list
5000 BATLZ.AV.WESKY	5,000 bottles of whisky
AND 100 BATLZ.AV.BER	and 100 bottles of beer
AND 5000 BAGZ.AV.DOG FOD	and 5,000 bags of dog food

Putting aside what this tells us about the unfortunate eating and drinking habits of the Bissex family, note the use of two boundary markers (dot and space), and the recognition of -*ing* as a separate unit, but not plural -*s*. Francis (1973) tested beginning readers' awareness of inflections in an auditory odd-one-out task: the children were presented with three words, two of which contained the same inflection (e.g. *cats, mops, girl*), and they were asked to choose the odd one out and to justify their choice. The children improved dramatically on the task as they moved from beginning readers age 5;9 (7% correct) to novice readers age 7;3 (61% correct). Past (-*ed*), progressive (-*ing*) and plural (-*s*) were tested, with performance on -*s* being superior.

One of the most sensitive methods for identifying differences in the size of units being used in reading is the letter cancellation technique of Corcoran (1966). Subjects are required to cancel every exemplar of a target letter that they encounter, while simultaneously reading a prose passage. Results on adults (e.g. Healy 1976; Smith and Groat 1979; Drewnowski 1981; Smith and Sterling 1982) indicate that if the target letter is contained in letter sequences that are plausible candidates for being handled as units (function words such as *the* and *and*, inflections -*ed*, -*ing*, affixes such as *re*- and -*er*), then the subject is more likely to fail to cancel the target letter. Most of these effects can be demonstrated on beginning readers, in particular *the, and, in,* and -*ing* (Drewnowski 1978, 1981) and *the,* -*ed* and some pronouns (Pattison 1983). Drewnowski (1981) obtains similar effects with aLtErNaTiNg CaSe presentation of material, so the effects are not due to gross visual features such as word shape. Drewnowski also finds the effects larger for good than for poor readers of the same age group; but this is difficult to interpret, since, when Pattison gave her subjects passages appropriate for their respective reading ages, most differences between good and poor readers disappeared. A safe, if somewhat conservative, interpretation of this work is that at a very early stage in reading children employ strategies that treat some function words and inflections as units.

This contrasts with the work of Ehri (1975) and Francis (1973) on prereaders and beginning readers mentioned earlier: these authors showed

that when young children are asked to say how two sentences differ, or which is the exception among a group of words, such tasks are more difficult if the distinguishing elements are not themselves full phonological words but are clitic elements within such words, e.g. function words and inflections. Drewnowski and Pattison have shown, however, that once the child begins to acquire reading ability such elements are soon treated as units, in the sense that they are read directly without full analysis of their component letters.

The main thrust of much of this work, then, is that children's awareness of units in their speech and their ability to identify and exploit corresponding units in print are two mutually supportive developments: morphophonological awareness aids reading, and reading aids morphophonological awareness. It follows that the nature of the orthographies the reader is familiar with is likely to influence the extent to which the reader is aware of different linguistic units, and to influence the types of reading strategy that are employed.

A clear contrast should be apparent if we compare use of a logographic script (Chinese) with use of an alphabetic script (English). Tzeng and Wang (1983) summarize a series of studies that illustrate different reading strategies with the two scripts. For example, consider the Stroop task applied to numerals (Besner and Coltheart 1979): the subject's task is to decide which of two numbers, e.g. 6 and 9, is greater. The speed with which this decision can be made is reduced if, incongruously, the smaller number (6) is *physically* larger than the greater number (9). This interference is present in monolingual English readers when the numbers are presented as Arabic numerals (6,9) but not when they are presented as words (six, nine), suggesting that Arabic numerals have direct access to a semantic system in which attributes such as physical size are also directly coded, whereas alphabetic words are processed by a more abstract route which shares few features with physical attributes. Tzeng and Wang report that the same experiment carried out with Chinese readers and Chinese logographs produces interference, i.e. Chinese readers treat the logographs in a similar way to English readers' handling of Arabic numerals rather than their handling of alphabetic words. Most interesting for our purposes, however, Chinese readers who learnt English after they had learned to read Chinese showed an interference effect with English alphabetic words (i.e. they appeared to be treating them as logographs). This is not an artifact of learning to read English as an adult, since native Spanish speakers with similar histories (but an alphabetic mother tongue orthography) behaved like English readers when reading English. A logographic script, then, induces strategies in the reader that are different from strategies induced

by an alphabetic script, and these strategies may be transferred when the reader comes to read a second script.

More subtle differences can be observed with similar scripts in the same language. Groat (1979) and Smith, Baker and Groat (1982) showed that children taught to read with the initial teaching alphabet (i.t.a.) appeared to use phonological rules different from those used by children taught to read with traditional orthography (t.o.).

The i.t.a. system (Pitman and St John 1969) is intended as a compromise between a fully phonemic alphabet (one-to-one correspondence between graphemes and phonemes) and standard English orthography, such that the child may learn initially to read with a phonemically regular alphabet before transferring to t.o. There are 44 symbols for a 41-phoneme analysis of English, the disparity in numbers occurring because occasionally more than one symbol is used for the same phoneme e.g. *c* in *cat* and *k* in *king*. Where a phoneme in t.o. is normally represented by two graphemes, the single symbol that is used in i.t.a. is usually a blend of the graphemes, e.g. the vowel of *bite* is represented as *i̵e*, a blend of *i* and *e*, thus there are no 'silent' final *e*s: *bite* (t.o.) is spelt *bi̵et* (i.t.a.). Warburton and Southgate (1969) provide an evaluation of this system.

Now one aspect of stress assignment rules in English, which depend in a complex way on grammatical class, morpheme structure and syllable structure, is that there is a small group of apparent exceptions, all of which are spelled with a 'silent' final *e* (*giraffe, grotesque, Neptune:* if the surface syllabic structure is taken into account then *grotesque*, for example, should have the same stress pattern as *damask*, and *Neptune* the same pattern as *balloon*). One solution to this problem (Chomsky and Halle 1968) is to regard such words as having underlying three-syllable forms, from which the final syllable (the 'silent' *e*) has been elided: stress assignment takes place before syllable elision, giving the appropriate stress (e.g. *grotesque* now has the same syllabic structure as *veranda*, and thus receives stress on the second syllable). Children taught to read with i.t.a. and transferring to t.o. at age 7 conform in a significant way to the rule system described above: first they learn in i.t.a. that all vowels, including final *e*, are pronounced, then as they transfer to t.o. they learn to inhibit the pronunciation of final *e* for many words. When tested soon after they have transferred to t.o. these children appear to treat nonsense syllables such as *gevespe* as three-syllable words from which the final *e* has been elided: they are more likely than comparable t.o. children to pronounce *gevespe* as a two-syllable word with stress on the second syllable; in contrast t.o. children, who have learned to ignore final *e*s in many circumstances, treat *gevesp* and *gevespe* in an identical fashion, as if they had not noticed the final

e. In this way quite subtle interactions between phonological and orthographic rules might develop.

In the Smith *et al.* (1982) study, 7 year olds demonstrated a good grasp of quite complex stress assignment rules and their relation to orthography. At this age much detail of the English orthographic system is yet to be learned. Smith *et al.* (1982) speculated that the 7 year old has a 'homogeneous' lexicon as far as stress assignment is concerned: the same rules are applied to all words; in contrast, the adult has a 'heterogeneous' lexicon where subclasses of words have different sets of rules to be applied to them (corresponding roughly to the hybrid principles of English orthography which spell Anglo-Saxon, French and more exotic words in different ways, e.g. the spelling of /g/ in *get, guide* and *ghetto*). College students assigning stress to nonsense words are more likely to assign final-syllable stress to words that look like French words. Orthographic knowledge of this sort is likely to be more idiosyncratic, varying with level of education and predisposition of the child; much of it is probably acquired through an interest in word structure, as is evident at an early stage in the development of a gifted reader, e.g. Paul Bissex' speculation, aged 6;10, that *thunder* came from two words in a different language, *thun* meaning 'noise' and *der* meaning 'loud' (Bissex 1980: 148–9).

The theme of this section has been that once the child has achieved some awareness of linguistic units, particularly of the phoneme and the word, then the task of learning to read alphabetic script is radically simplified. Of course, while such awareness may be necessary it may not be sufficient. Failures in acquisition are more common in reading than in speech, and dyslexia assumes more importance, both practical and theoretical, in discussions of reading acquisition than does dysphasia in comparable discussions of speech acquisition. Whether lack of awareness of the relevant linguistic units is the sole, or even the major, cause of dyslexia is a moot point, and there have been many differing claims about the causal connections between various linguistic and cognitive deficits and dyslexia. Byrne (1981), for example, sees the broader concept of linguistic immaturity as responsible for children's failure to read. Byrne found among second graders (7 year olds) that good readers were better than poor readers at understanding auditorily presented complex syntactic structures. Specifically, good readers were superior in handling sentences of the type *The snake is hard to bite* (where the surface subject *snake* is the deep structure object of the verb *bite*) and 'improbable' embedded sentences (*The horse that the girl is kicking is brown:* 'improbable' because the girl, not the horse, is doing the kicking). Good and poor readers did not differ on sentences of the type *The snake is eager to bite*, where the surface subject

snake is also the deep subject of *bite*, nor on 'reversible' embedded sentences, *The cow that the monkey is scaring is yellow* ('reversible' because an equally plausible sentence is obtained from interchanging *cow* and *monkey*). Poor readers' differential difficulty with some but not all structures argues against a general memory deficit being at the root of their disability. Rather it is the more linguistically complex structures (*The snake is hard to bite*) and those structures where it is necessary to let syntactic information override pragmatic expectation (*The horse that the girl is kicking . . .*) which reflect the difficulties: only a linguistically mature individual, argues Byrne, can handle such structures, and only a linguistically mature individual can construct the sophisticated morphophonemic representations necessary for reading.

Byrne's position would find favour with Vellutino and Scanlon (1982), who address themselves to the particular issue of whether dyslexia is a linguistic deficit or a collection of broader cognitive deficits. They point out that there is a sense in which dyslexia, by definition, must be a linguistic deficit: if a dyslexic child is one who is normal on all measures of intelligence except for reading and reading-related tasks, then no deficit of a function that extends beyond the domain of language (e.g. short-term memory, attention, eye movements) can be responsible, since these nonlinguistic deficits would be reflected in other aspects of performance beyond reading. There is a certain sophistry in this argument: if an issue can be settled by definition then it cannot be a very important issue. Indeed, whatever the practical merits of defining developmental dyslexia as a reading deficit without any other cognitive deficit, such a definition might lead to something of a cul-de-sac theoretically: it might be that dyslexics so defined do have general cognitive deficits but that they have successfully disguised these, as far as the relatively insensitive instruments we call intelligence tests are concerned, by exceptional development of other strategies and skills. A comparable case is that of the hearing-impaired child, who does have a major identifiable perceptual deficit, yet to some extent can compensate for this deficit by using different strategies to read (see the discussion of Pattison's work later in this chapter). It might be more productive for an understanding of reading to identify children with perceptual, cognitive or performance deficits and to see how these deficits are reflected in their reading development, rather than, as with the concept of dyslexia, to use reading deficit as the sole independent variable. Nonetheless, Vellutino and Scanlon (1982) produce an impressive catalogue of semantic, syntactic and phonetic deficits among poor readers.

In a broader context, some scholars have seen the good reader's ability to suspend pragmatic expectation as part of the contrast between literate and nonliterate cultures' handling of abstract and counterfactual informa-

tion. For Olson (1977), for example, the progression from nonliterate 'utterance' to literate 'text' is one of increasing conventionalization of meaning: an utterance may need interpretation, but the meaning of a text is in the text itself. Consider the well-documented reasoning performance in nonliterate cultures, where the subject cannot treat the information in the message separately from normal pragmatic consideration. Problem: 'All Kpelle men are rice farmers. Mr Smith is not a rice farmer. Is he a Kpelle man?' Answer: 'I don't know the man in person. I have not laid eyes on the man himself . . . If I know him in person, I can answer that question, but since I do not know him in person I cannot answer that question' (Scribner 1977). With literacy, argues Olson, comes the ability to regard word and object, spoken word and written word, real-world information and information as conveyed solely in a text as separable entities. It is these fundamental segmentations that people in nonliterate cultures find difficult to grasp, and which seem to develop with the more subtle segmentations involved in identifying phonemes, morphemes and words.

There is recent evidence that this position is oversimplified: 'literacy' is not a unique state of intellectual attainment that is identical across all cultures and whose acquisition automatically confers special powers of abstraction and reasoning upon its possessors. In a painstaking study of the Vai, a Liberian people who use three scripts in their culture (Vai, a syllabary; Arabic and English, both alphabets), Scribner and Cole (1981) found that familiarity with different scripts gave their users different cognitive advantages (e.g. grammatical awareness with Vai, ordered memory ability with Arabic). These cognitive advantages, however, could be derived from the social circumstances surrounding the learning of the script (Vai writing is taught informally, often by Vai writers arguing amongst themselves about the appropriate form of words to be used in a letter, thus fostering grammatical awareness; and Arabic is taught through rote memorization of the Koran, giving students plenty of practice in ordered recall). The most important feature of the Scribner and Cole study is that schooling and the acquisition of literacy are not inextricably confounded, as they are in most Western societies: schools exist, but Vai literacy is acquired out of school, picked up informally from relatives or workmates. In these circumstances Scribner and Cole were able to show that it was schooling, not Vai literacy, that was the primary determiner of success in logic and reasoning tasks.

3. The procedural stage: how are improvements in fluency achieved?

Let us pursue Byrne's notion that linguistic maturity is what characterizes the good beginning reader, and that this maturity is reflected in knowledge

about the segmental structure of language and also in the traditional areas of lexical, syntactic and semantic knowledge. To this declarative knowledge ('knowing that') the beginning reader must add procedural knowledge ('knowing how'): that is, the child must be able to exploit linguistic insights to obtain fluent and efficient performance. Corresponding to the segmental insights, in particular the phonemic insights, we may expect efficient performance in *phonemic discrimination* and *memory* (section 3.1); corresponding to lexical knowledge, we can examine the child's increasing *automaticity* (section 3.2) in handling words; and corresponding to syntactic and semantic knowledge, we can examine the role of *context* (section 3.3) in fluent reading.

3.1. Phonemic discrimination and memory

The previous section has established the likely importance of phonemic processing skills in early reading. While much of the literature supports the idea that deficits in phonemic processing are correlated with retarded reading, the precise loci of these deficits in an information-processing system are a matter of dispute. Some authors stress that phonemic discrimination is bad in poor readers (Godfrey *et al.* 1981; Brady, Shankweiler and Mann 1983); others point to phonological coding deficits in short-term memory (Byrne and Shea 1979; Mann, Liberman and Shankweiler 1980; Katz, Shankweiler and Liberman 1981); others see poor readers as having a deficit in postlexical but not prelexical phonology (Briggs and Underwood 1982); another author finds phonemic discrimination in poor readers satisfactory but cross-modal grapheme–phoneme matching retarded (Snowling 1980); and some studies even find phonological coding in short-term memory is normal in retarded readers (Johnston 1982).

There are several ways in which these apparent contradictions can be resolved. First note that we need not expect that a child will display the same abilities or use the same strategies for all levels of difficulty of a task: a child who is adequate at making an easy discrimination may nevertheless have a high threshold on such tasks that is revealed by a more difficult discrimination; a child with 'normal' short-term memory when overall processing demands are modest may display limited memory capacity when additional processing demands are made; and a child using a 'normal' strategy in easy situations may switch to other strategies in response to a difficult task. Such ideas are not uncommon in the experimental psychology literature. For example, there have been many studies of the finite capacity of immediate memory: most of us can recall a 5-digit telephone number immediately after reading or hearing it, but few of us can carry

out the same task with a 20-digit number. This finite capacity has repercussions in a number of related tasks: Baddeley and Hitch (1974) showed that the requirement to remember a 3-digit number had no influence on a concurrent reasoning task whereas remembering a 6-digit number produced slower performance on the reasoning task. These results could be explained if there existed a small capacity short-term memory mechanism (the articulatory loop) capable of handling 3-digit numbers, with lònger sequences of material requiring the involvement of a larger processing system (the central executive) which would also be required for the concurrent reasoning task: 3 digits would not interfere with the central executive, but trying to remember 6 digits would interfere with this system and slow performance on any concurrent task also using the central executive, in particular the reasoning task. Miller (1956) showed that a 21-digit number (actually, a series of zeros and ones) could be recalled immediately, but only if the subject had special training in strategies to cope with the task. The general point here is that a fundamental limitation in a linguistic or cognitive processing system may reveal itself only when a threshold (the capacity of the system) is exceeded, and even these limitations may be masked by appropriate changes in strategy by the subject.

Thus those studies that have shown phonemic discrimination deficits have been difficult tasks, for example, identification of monosyllabic words in noise (Brady et al. 1983), discrimination of synthetic CV syllables (Godfrey et al. 1981); Brady et al. specifically show that word identification without masking noise, and identification of non-speech stimuli, do not discriminate between good and poor 8-year-old readers.

Pattison (1983) has shown some complex interactions between reading ability, memory capacity and coding strategy. She tested children with normal hearing, children with partial hearing (up to 86 dB hearing loss), and deaf children (greater than 86 dB hearing loss); they were further classified as poor readers (reading ages 7–9 years), medium readers (reading ages 9–12 years) and good readers (reading ages better than 12 years). The normal-hearing children had chronological ages commensurate with their reading ages; the hearing-impaired children were aged 12 to 16, usually with their reading ages lagging substantially behind their chronological ages.

Pattison carried out two experiments on these subjects. One was a 'word span' experiment in which subjects read five words and then attempted to write them down from memory in the correct serial order. The second experiment was a 'sentence span' experiment in which, following Daneman and Carpenter (1980), subjects read five short sentences, marking them as true or false, and then attempted to recall, in the correct serial order, the final word of each sentence. The same words were in both experiments

Table 1. *Percentage correct on Pattison's (1983) memory tasks: the phonologically confusable condition is compared with control*

	Word span			Sentence span		
	Control	Phono-logical	Deficit	Control	Phono-logical	Deficit
Good readers						
Hearing	85	54	31	81	64	17
Partially-hearing	85	61	24	76	60	16
Deaf	88	62	26	81	64	17
Medium readers						
Hearing	72	49	23	87	64	23
Partially-hearing	69	50	19	63	56	7
Deaf	70	52	18	64	62	2
Poor readers						
Hearing	47	28	19	58	40	18
Partially-hearing	45	45	0	45	39	6
Deaf	49	48	1	49	50	−1

and were drawn from a phonologically confusable set (*blue, new, through,* etc.), a semantically confusable set (*big, large, tall,* etc.), or a control non-confusable set (*red, round, alive,* etc.). Table 1 compares control and phonological performance. In the word span experiment there is a large phonological deficit (a deficit in performance with phonologically confusable materials, relative to the control condition) for most subjects, indicating reliance on phonological coding in short-term memory. The sole exceptions are the poor hearing-impaired readers, where the effect is totally absent. This difference in coding between good and poor deaf readers was first demonstrated by Conrad (1970, 1971).

When the results of the sentence span experiment are examined, two further effects emerge: first, medium and poor deaf readers are worse than their hearing counterparts in the control condition (this is not the case in the word span experiment); and second, deficits with phonologically confusable materials are markedly reduced for the medium and poor hearing-impaired readers (whereas only the poor hearing-impaired readers showed reduced deficits with phonologically confusable materials in the word span experiment). These results make the general point that differences between groups of readers that are not apparent on an 'easy' memory task (word span) may appear on a more difficult task (sentence span), and that subjects whose phonological coding skills are somewhat fragile may switch to a nonphonological coding strategy under pressure (medium readers who are hearing-impaired, on the sentence span task). All subjects, in fact, show evidence of semantic coding on the sentence span task. Table

Table 2. *Pattison's (1983) memory tasks: the mean semantic deficit (equals percentage correct control condition minus percentage correct semantically confusable condition)*

	Word span	Sentence span
Good readers		
Hearing	−1	4
Partially-hearing	13	5
Deaf	1	8
Medium readers		
Hearing	6	9
Partially-hearing	−3	8
Deaf	−6	10
Poor readers		
Hearing	−1	7
Partially-hearing	−21	10
Deaf	7	9

2 shows an incoherent pattern for the semantic deficit (control minus semantically confusable conditions) on the word span task, but a regular pattern with all groups showing a deficit, and the hearing-impaired groups showing a larger deficit, in the sentence span task. This demonstrates that all levels of reader show flexibility of coding in short-term memory tasks.

In addition to considerations of memory capacity, the second way in which apparent contradictions may be resolved in the literature on phonological information-processing skills and reading is via a more careful consideration of the age of the child. It is not likely that the child approaches reading fully equipped with a static set of strategies that are preserved from kindergarten to college. Most of the work in this area is concerned with 7 and 8 year olds, and even older, and a study by Alegria, Pignot and Morais (1982) highlights how critical this might be. These authors studied first-grade French-speaking children (6–7 year olds), who were taught either by 'phonic' or 'whole word' methods. In tests of segmentation the children were asked to carry out syllabic reversal (e.g. *radis* [radi] should be transformed to [dira]) and also phonemic reversal (e.g. *seau* [so] should be transformed to [os]). The phonically trained children showed a modest and nonsignificant superiority on the syllabic reversal task (75.3 per cent versus 67.5 per cent correct) but a large superiority on the phonic reversal task (58.3 per cent versus 15.4 per cent). Skill on this latter task correlated significantly with reading in the phonically trained group ($r = 0.65$) but not in the whole-word group.

However, in a short-term memory task (a similar paradigm to that used

by Pattison 1983 and described above) both groups showed similar deficits with phonologically confusable materials, and performance on this task was not correlated with reading ability or performance on the syllabic and phonemic reversal tasks. This shows a degree of independence between phonemic awareness and phonological encoding in short-term memory, and between both these skills and reading ability. Apparently there is a developmental progression where, using phonic teaching methods, phonemic awareness and reading skill go hand in hand, but whole-word teaching methods lead to an initial dissociation of phonemic awareness (which is rudimentary) and reading ability. Indeed, how far a child could progress within a whole-word teaching context without achieving phonemic awareness is a moot point. Rozin, Poritsky and Sotsky (1971) showed that children with reading difficulties in English could learn to read comparatively easily with Chinese characters (logographic script, necessitating a whole-word approach to learning). These same children presumably had made comparable progress with English, treating whole words as logographs, but their reading of English was retarded because they had not mastered the alphabetic principle and acquired the power this principle gives to handle unfamiliar words. The fact that the whole-word group in the Alegria *et al.* study show phonological coding in short-term memory without demonstrating phonemic awareness and without correlation with reading ability shows that phonological coding may be a useful facility to have at second and higher grade levels, where reading of larger chunks of print makes more demand on short-term memory – but its presence in the beginning reader guarantees neither phonemic awareness nor good reading.

3.2. Automaticity and lexical access

Components of a complex skill need to be automatic if performance is to be fluent: the concert pianist and the racing driver do not have time to give full attention to all their actions in the manner of a grade 1 pianist or a learner driver. So it is with the novice reader, whose recognition of letters and words, and whose ancillary skills such as eye movements, need to be sufficiently effortless not to distract the reader from the main business of reading, that is comprehending text. Classic modern treatments of automaticity and reading are provided by LaBerge and Samuels (1974) and Posner and Snyder (1975).

Automaticity is not without its disadvantages; 'absent-mindedness' can be interpreted as the result of the execution of automatic sequences of actions with insufficient conscious control (e.g. boiling a second kettle of water after the tea has been made, getting into a bath with clothes still

on, shutting down the wrong engine in an aircraft: all examples from Reason 1977). Automaticity in reading is also generally measured by its deleterious effects on performance. While some of these effects are found in rather contrived tasks (e.g. the Stroop test), they can also appear in more natural settings, for example the rather surprising dominance of word meaning over contextual meaning. Campbell and Bowe (1977; see Campbell and Macdonald 1983 for a slightly revised version) have shown that 4 year olds have great difficulty in understanding the less dominant meaning of a homophone pair, even in context: thus, after the children were read a coherent story involving *hares* and *buoys* they seemed quite happy to draw pictures illustrating *hairs* running across fields and orange and white striped rubber *boys*. (The point here is not whether children know the meaning of *hares* and *buoys*, but that they are prepared to ignore context totally in interpreting the word: more sophisticated children do not do this and *hare*, for example, if its meaning is not known to the child, might be interpreted as a metaphorical extension of *hair*, e.g. grass.) Browne (1982) has made similar observations with 7- and 8-year-old children reading a story containing homonyms, and Doctor and Coltheart (1980) have shown that beginning readers have a strong tendency to regard as acceptable a sentence containing an inappropriate homophone (*We walk in the would*) even though they know the correct spellings of the *wood/would* pair. Finally, Briggs and Underwood (1982) have shown that in a task involving the naming of pictures to which various, possibly misleading, labels were attached, the presence of a 'heterographic homophone' (e.g. a picture of a whale to which the label *wail* was attached) substantially reduced picture naming time (in comparison with a nonsense label control) for both good and poor 11-year-old readers, and this despite the poor readers being much slower at simple *word* naming. This effect was only marginally greater if identity priming was used (a picture of a whale to which the label *whale* was attached). This leads Briggs and Underwood to distinguish between prelexical phonology (to which good and poor readers have equally rapid automatic access) and postlexical phonology (to which poor readers have less rapid access). In summary, these experiments show that even with beginning readers or poor readers access to word meanings (sometimes via the phonological form of the word) is sufficiently automatic, i.e. not susceptible to conscious control, to override context and the presence of misspellings.

The Stroop test, however, is the paradigm most frequently used to examine automaticity. In this test the child is presented with a stimulus in a particular colour ink and the child's task is to name the colour of the ink. The stimulus may be a word or some other significant visual pattern,

and it has been known for fifty years that the meaning of the stimulus affects the speed with which the subject can name the ink (Stroop 1935) and, in particular, if an incongruent word is presented, e.g. *green* is presented in blue ink, that the subject will take longer to name the colour of the ink: the subject has 'automatically' accessed the meaning of *green*, and this has interfered with the colour naming.

One of the most comprehensive studies of Stroop effects with young readers is by Schadler and Thissen (1981). They tested a range of subjects, from kindergarten non-readers to sixth graders (11–12 years). For a given stimulus colour, e.g. green, they used congruent words (*green*); incongruent words (*blue*); pronounceable nonwords (*mafe*); unpronounceable nonwords (*sbti*); strings of 'symbolic' letters, chosen from *o, x, z*; strings of common letters, chosen from *e, s, t*; strings of uncommon letters, chosen from *k, p, v*; and coloured rectangles containing no alphabetic patterns, this latter condition providing a control against which other conditions could be compared. For the youngest nonreaders symbolic letters provided the greatest interference and other letters more modest interference; no other stimuli interfered. For beginning readers all letters were equally interfering, but words or nonwords had no effects. By the end of first grade (6–7 years), all material produced interference, with pure Stroop (naming green ink when the word is *blue*) producing most interference, and congruent words (naming green ink when the word is *green*) producing facilitation. These effects persist largely unchanged at least until sixth grade, with pure Stroop producing largest interference, nonwords intermediate interference and letters small interference. These results tell us what stimuli 'automatically' seize children's attention, and suggest a developmental hierarchy: only 'symbolic' letters for prereaders, letters for beginning readers, and any word-like stimulus for more experienced readers. The early emergence of pure Stroop (particularly large interference for incongruent words and facilitation for congruent words) points to early automatic processing of meaning over and above the level of these processing effects.

3.3. Context effects

It is well known that predictable material is more easily perceived and remembered than unpredictable (e.g. Miller and Selfridge 1953). In studying reading, then, our initial expectation might be that good readers would be better able to exploit the contextual information that they find in text: such an expectation would be strengthened if we regarded reading in Goodman's (1967) phrase as a 'psycholinguistic guessing game'. There are problems *a priori* with this position: the truly skilled performer is not a slave

to context, and a good ball game player, say, will make rapid adjustments to an unevenly bouncing ball or the feints of an opponent. In reading, expert readers may be more able than novice readers to take the contextually unexpected in their stride.

Once again we need to be wary of making generalizations uniformly for all age groups. There is plenty of anecdotal evidence that the prereader relies almost entirely on context (e.g. the child who turns the pages of a story book 'reading' with a mixture of recall of the previously read story and prompts from the illustrations). The beginning reader appears to move rapidly through a series of different strategies. Biemiller (1970), for example, studied oral reading errors of first-grade children over an eight-month period. Within that time he distinguished three strategies: an early stage where errors often were contextually but not graphemically appropriate, a late stage where graphemic factors played a more important role, and an intermediate transitional stage characterized by an increase in failures to respond. The earliest stage can be regarded as 'an attempt by the child to avoid using graphic information as much as possible' (Biemiller 1970: 75), i.e. the weaker reader is relying more on context.

This is very much the message of the Interactive-Compensatory model developed by Stanovich and his associates (e.g. West and Stanovich 1978; Stanovich, West and Feeman 1981): context is used to compensate for slow or incomplete lexical access with difficult words but not with easy words. Stanovich *et al.* use a Stroop-like paradigm in which congruous or incongruous sentence contexts are used to facilitate or inhibit word naming. From studies of beginning readers to adults a consistent picture emerges of young readers, less skilled readers and difficult words requiring more use of context, and older readers, skilled readers and easy words requiring less use, with what use there is being automatic.

A further level of context use is error detection. The fluent reader needs to know if the text being read makes sense and matches expectations; and if it does not meet these criteria, whether the fault lies with the author, the mechanism of transmission or the reader (with something like the English newspaper *The Guardian*, notorious for its misprints, the task can prove a major intellectual challenge). There are also related reading skills, such as choosing to read at a speed appropriate for the difficulty of a passage.

One of the most insightful treatments of this topic is a study by Harris *et al.* (1981), who gave children sentences that did or did not harmonize with their context, e.g. in a story about a visit to a hairdresser's there is either a sentence *He sees his hair getting shorter* (congruous) or a sentence *Luckily, there are no cavities this time* (incongruous). When reading these stories, 8-year-old Dutch children (reading in Dutch) slowed down at the

incongruous sentence but were often unable afterwards to identify the anomaly. In contrast, 11 year olds slowed down an equal amount but were
more often able to indicate the anomaly, though even here their performance was not outstanding: on a strict criterion for demonstrating they
understood which was the anomalous sentence, 44 per cent of 11 year
olds were successful and 11 per cent of 8 year olds. This leads Harris
et al. to distinguish between use of context via 'constructive processing'
(Markman's 1979 phrase), which both groups of children have and which
they use to make appropriate changes in their reading rates, and 'comprehension monitoring', a higher level awareness of the source of difficulties,
which is present only in older children.

Error detection data can also provide information about reading strategies. Pattison (1983) distorted text in four ways: by altering either function
words or content words, and by making alterations that created words
or nonwords (20 words were changed in coherent passages of about 220
words). Errors were better detected in content words than function words,
and if the error made a nonword. There were no strong developmental
trends among normal hearing readers whose ages ranged from 7 to 15,
but the above effects were much more marked among hearing-impaired
readers with low reading ages, as if these children followed a strategy of
picking out content words they recognized and guessing the rest of the
story. These results further make the point that different subjects may
attain the same reading ages with radically different reading strategies.

4. Summary

The conclusions of this survey are at first sight straightforward. By the
age of 7 the normal child has a basic competence in virtually all the subskills
of reading: access to units of all sizes from the phoneme upwards, automatic
access to meaning, use of phonological and semantic coding in short-term
memory, interactive use of contextual and graphemic information, adjustments of reading strategy to match text difficulty. The differences between
the 7 year old and the adult are largely quantitative, not qualitative.

This bald summary, however, glosses over many of the important issues
about the acquisition of literacy. To say that the 7-year-old reader is equivalent to an adult reader minus fluency is to emphasize the undoubtedly
remarkable achievements of the 7 year old, but without explaining them;
we still know very little about the actual learning process, something that
can be remedied only by genuinely developmental studies of a child's performance on a day-by-day or even hour-by-hour basis. We know that phonemic
awareness is a crucial concomitant of reading acquisition in an alphabetic

system, but we have not firmly established why this is the case. Phonemic awareness does not appear to be inextricably connected with a particular component in an information-processing system (e.g. phonological coding in short-term memory: some young readers show evidence for phonological coding unrelated to reading ability or phonemic awareness, Alegria *et al.* 1982). Nor does phonemic awareness necessarily lead to a revolution in cognitive abilities (schooling, not literacy, has a more profound influence on style of thinking; Scribner and Cole 1981). Given the excellent literacy skills of a minority of profoundly deaf children, the whole concept of phonemic awareness needs further examination. The cautious view must be that phonemic awareness and success in reading are linked via a disappointingly imprecise concept, linguistic maturity.

It is also imprecise to describe the 7 year old as a slow adult, and this review has identified some qualitative differences. Principal among these are skills that can develop only with a larger and more diverse vocabulary: contrast the heterogeneous lexicon of the college student, with different rule systems applied to the pronunciation of different parts of the vocabulary, with the homogeneous lexicon of the 7 year old (Smith *et al.* 1982). We also need to consider metalinguistic skills applied to larger chunks of discourse than the phonemes, syllables and words that have featured so prominently in this review (note here the differences between 8 year olds and 11 year olds in 'comprehension monitoring'; Harris *et al.* 1981).

The last mentioned research should remind us of the other major under-investigated feature of reading acquisition: strategy change and strategy flexibility. The phoneme-by-phoneme reading that is a laudable achievement in the 6 year old is a hindrance to fluency in the 20 year old. Both hearing and hearing-impaired readers show changes in coding strategy as a function of task difficulty (Pattison 1983); early experience with a particular type of script can induce strategy preferences in reading (Chinese readers read English logographically; Tzeng and Wang 1983); and one of the major causes of poor spelling among good readers is inflexibility in the strategies used to read words (Frith 1980). A theory of reading development will include a theory of how reading strategies change with reading ability and how control processes develop to select strategies differentially appropriate to the minute-by-minute changes in the demands that are made upon a reader. Both the 7 year old and the student of reading development have a long way to go to master all that is involved in reading.

23. Language acquisition and writing

Katharine Perera

1. Introduction

It is rather unusual for written language to feature in general studies of children's language acquisition. This is perhaps partly because linguists have repeatedly emphasized the primacy of the oral language; also because, as writing is explicitly taught, its development is felt to be more susceptible than speech to the directive intervention of adults. Furthermore, it is not always possible to be sure of the precise status of children's written texts – a piece of writing might, for example, be a child's own first draft, or an unaided revision, or a final version incorporating a teacher's alterations. Nevertheless, there are at least two sound reasons for viewing the acquisition of written language as an integral part of language development. First, in societies with a reasonably long tradition of literacy, the ability to write is an important aspect of linguistic competence: it seems fair to say that someone who can speak but cannot write has not fully acquired the language.[1] Secondly, the grammatical structures of written language are characteristically different from those of speech, since writing is not simply a transcription of oral language. So, in learning to write, children have to learn to use constructions other than the ones they regularly use in their spontaneous speech. To understand the full extent and complexity of the language acquisition process, therefore, it is necessary to be aware of the development of these more literary constructions.

Some recent books on children's writing have emphasized the fundamental differences between speech and writing (e.g. Kroll and Vann 1981; Kress 1982). Kroll and Vann's volume contains many stimulating articles on the relationships between the two modes (see, in particular, the chapters by Schafer, Kroll, Kantor and Rubin, Olson, and O'Keefe). Kress makes the point that if we are to understand properly the extent to which writing differs from speech then we need to have fuller descriptions than currently exist, not only of those structures that are specifically literary but also of the patterns that are typical of unplanned speech; neither style is truly

reflected in the sets of idealized, decontextualized sentences that form the basis of so many grammatical descriptions. As an example of children's developing differentiation between speech and writing, he gives an account of the growth of hierarchically structured sentences in their writing, contrasting them with the loosely co-ordinated clausal complexes that are characteristic of their speech. Kress believes that there is a strong link between cognitive processes and linguistic forms, both syntactic and textual. It is this belief that leads to one of the most controversial notions in the book – the suggestion that where children's writing is less grammatically complex than adults' it should be seen not as 'underdeveloped' but as embodying a different, but equally valid, conceptual structure.

Kress considers that the differences between speech and writing are most marked at the level of the overall text, so he pays particular attention to the relationships between sentences and between paragraphs. Other recent works which also contribute to the literature on children's development of coherent text structures in writing are the collections of readings edited by Gregg and Steinberg (1980) and by Kroll and Wells (1983). In contrast, this chapter focuses chiefly on grammatical development in writing with regard to sentence, clause and phrase structures, and on the differences between speech and writing at these levels.

2. Grammatical development in writing

To provide a preliminary overview of structures children use in writing, this section presents a brief summary of the findings of several large-scale surveys of grammatical development in the writing of American and British children between the ages of 7 and 18 years (Hunt 1965, 1970; O'Donnell, Griffin and Norris 1967; Harpin 1976; Loban 1976).

As far as clause structure is concerned, three developments are reported. First, clause length increases. Hunt (1970: 9), using figures from two different studies, gives an average written clause length of 6.5 words at the age of 8; of 7.7 at age 13 and 8.6 at age 17 (skilled adult writers have an average clause length of 11.5 words). Secondly, more passive constructions are used. O'Donnell et al. (1967: 73) record a three-fold increase in passives between the ages of 8 and 13 on a writing task that was the same for all the children. Thirdly, the number of sentence adverbials increases (Hunt 1965: 138; O'Donnell et al. 1967: 68).

At phrase level, there are considerable developments in the complexity of the noun phrase. Between the ages of 8 and 13, children use progressively more adjectival premodification, and postmodification by prepositional phrases and nonfinite clauses (Hunt 1965: 113; O'Donnell et al. 1967:

60). Nominal constructions that are used only by older and abler children include: a noun modified by an adverb (O'Donnell *et al.* 1967: 63), appositive phrases (Hunt 1970: 25), and a noun with four or more modifiers (Hunt 1965: 113). In the verb phrase, Hunt (1965: 122) notes the use of a wider range of tense and aspect forms with increasing maturity, and particularly, an expansion in the use of modal auxiliaries. Loban (1976: 67), however, reports, with some disappointment, that he failed to discern any developmental trends in his subjects' written verb phrases.

It is in the way that clauses are combined that some of the most significant developments occur. In general, co-ordination decreases as subordination increases. Hunt (1970: 16), for example, notes a sharp drop in the co-ordination of main clauses between the ages of 9 and 11, while in another study (1966: 733), he records a steady growth in the proportion of subordinate to main clauses throughout the school years, with a further slight rise in the writing of skilled adults. O'Donnell *et al.* (1967: 51) and Harpin (1976: 60) find a similar pattern of increasing subordination in the language of their, younger, subjects. Loban's (1976: 40) findings agree with the others', except that his subjects show no growth in subordination between the ages of 13 and 17. Commenting on this levelling off, he points out that during their teens the abler writers among his subjects produce an increasing number of prepositional phrases and nonfinite clauses – structures which are able to express hierarchical relationships between ideas succinctly, without the redundancy of finite subordinate clauses.

The three major types of subordinate clause – nominal, adverbial and relative – show different patterns of development in children's writing. As a class, nominal clauses do not seem to serve as indicators of linguistic growth, being more sensitive to the writer's topic and purpose than to his linguistic maturity. Nevertheless, when grammatical function is taken into account, it becomes apparent that clauses functioning as subjects occur only in the work of older and abler writers (Hunt 1965: 91; Loban 1976: 55). Adverbial clauses show a considerable increase in overall frequency between the ages of 8 and 10 years (O'Donnell *et al.* 1967: 68); after that, their rate of occurrence depends, like nominal clauses, more on the nature of the topic than on the child's linguistic ability (Hunt 1966: 734). Where linguistic growth continues to be noticeable, however, is in the number of different kinds of adverbial clause that are used and, particularly, in the occurrence of the rarer types, such as clauses of concession. Hunt (1965: 81) and Loban (1976: 57), for example, comment on the rarity of *although* clauses in their data, and Harpin (1976: 69) notes that at the age of 11 his subjects use only one such clause in every two hundred subordinate clauses in their writing. All the studies agree that, of the various subordinate

clause types, it is relative (or adjective) clauses that provide the most clear-cut evidence of a developmental pattern of growth. The researchers all report that these clauses double in frequency, though they assign the increase to different age spans. Harpin (1976: 71) says the doubling occurs between the ages of 7 and 11; O'Donnell *et al.* (1967: 60) between 8 and 10; Hunt (1965: 89) between 9 and 17; and Loban (1976: 49) between 10 and 15. Hunt adds that skilled adult writers use an even higher proportion of relative clauses than 17 year olds.

Several studies suggest that nonfinite constructions are likely to prove useful pointers to linguistic maturity, but at present the amount of information available is disappointingly small, perhaps because such structures have not, on the whole, been subjected to a particularly discriminating grammatical analysis (O'Donnell *et al.* 1967: 58, for example, class together the participles in these expressions: *the falling leaf, the ant rolling the ball*). Even so, it seems clear that there is a significant increase in all structures with nonfinite verbs between the ages of 8 and 13 (O'Donnell *et al.* 1967: 60, 62). Loban (1976: 68) reports that among his 15-year-old writers, the high ability subgroup use nearly twice as many nonfinite verbs as the low ability subgroup. Referring to the 'gerund nominal', Hunt (1965: 111) says, 'No other structure increases so dramatically from grade to grade.' He adds that it is especially rare in subject position, not being used at all by his 9-year-old subjects and by only a third of his 17 year olds.

Grammatical development in writing does not occur in a smooth, steady progression but proceeds in a series of spurts followed by fairly stable periods during which, presumably, newly acquired constructions are being consolidated. Spurts of growth are reported as occurring at about the age of 9 (O'Donnell *et al.* 1967: 94; Harpin 1976: 67) and at 13, and then again at 17 (Loban 1976: 80).

3. Grammatical differentiation between speech and writing

For the great majority of children, learning to write does not begin until a firm foundation of oral language has been established.[2] It seems natural, therefore, that the grammatical structures they write should reflect those that they are already using in their speech. The studies by O'Donnell *et al.* (1967) and Loban (1976) provide evidence that, initially, the structures children use in their writing are very closely related to those they use in speech, though at first they display a lower level of grammatical maturity in their written than in their oral language. In all probability, this is because the physical process of writing is so laborious that it absorbs a great deal of their attention. But when handwriting and spelling reach the level of

automaticity, then children are freed to use more complex linguistic structures. Indeed, before long many reach the stage where their use of grammar is more advanced in their written work than in their speech. (Nevertheless, it is necessary to remember that there are always some children for whom the task of writing is so demanding that even at the age of 15 they are still displaying in writing a grammatical ability that is impoverished in comparison with their oral competence; for example, their written texts may consist almost exclusively of simple and compound sentences, although their speech provides ample evidence of subordination within complex sentences.)

The relationships between grammatical maturity in speech and in writing have been presented by Kroll (1981: 39–54) as a series of four phases, which he labels 'preparation', 'consolidation', 'differentiation' and 'integration'. During the *preparation* phase, children learn the physical aspects of handwriting, and copy words written for them by adults. The *consolidation* phase begins when they can write independently: evidence from Harpin (1976) and Wilkinson *et al.* (1979) suggests that in Britain most children have achieved this independence by the age of 7. During the consolidation phase, children use in their writing structures that they use in speech – and in similar proportions. The *differentiation* phase is when written language no longer simply reflects the patterns of speech but takes on its own characteristic grammatical forms. At least some of the children in O'Donnell *et al.*'s study appear to have reached this stage by the age of 9 or 10. The last phase, *integration*, is probably only ever attained by a minority of writers. Kroll (1981: 39) suggests that at this point, 'speaking and writing are both appropriately differentiated and systematically integrated', so that the mature writer can allow his own tone of voice, personal warmth and so on to imbue his written style when he judges it to be appropriate. Kantor and Rubin (1981: 62) suggest that, 'Many writers, perhaps the majority of high school graduates, remain at a middle level of development, suspended awkwardly between speech and writing.'

The remainder of this chapter will consider some aspects of the differentiation between speech and writing, concentrating mainly on children aged 9 to 12. From a grammatical point of view, writing can be differentiated from spontaneous speech in three ways. First, there are some structures that regularly occur in speech which are not normally used by competent writers (unless, of course, they are intending to produce the effect of spoken language); these will be illustrated in section 4. Secondly, writing contains a higher proportion than speech of constructions widely held to be indicative of grammatical maturity; some of these will be described in section 5. Thirdly, there are some structures that rarely or never occur in spontaneous,

unplanned speech, being typically written forms; some examples will be given in section 6.

4. Structures typical of speech

4.1. Mazes

The most immediately obvious grammatical difference between speech and writing is that speakers often get in a muddle, which becomes apparent in false starts, reformulations, redundant repetitions and ungrammatical strings (collectively called 'mazes' by Loban (1976: 10); some researchers use the term 'garbles'). Some of these features are illustrated in the following extracts from samples of children's oral language, collected, transcribed and marked for prosodic features by Fawcett and Perkins (1980):[3]

(1) Int. Did you go with any of your friends?
     B.   yèah/ a 'girl in my./ wèll/ 'hang ón/ it was a'bout . a gàng
          of us went/ and it 'was her bìrthday/
                              12 years (Fawcett and Perkins 1980, vol. IV: 52)
(2) you 'put you get a 'yellow spóon/ and you 'put a a 'round a . 'red
     báll/ 'on the spóon/
                              12 years (Fawcett and Perkins 1980, vol. IV: 50)
(3) Int. What do you think were some of the best bits?
     D.   wèll/er – when the 'man was er got bìtten/ and it showed blòod/
          and come 'out of his móuth/
                              12 years (Fawcett and Perkins 1980, vol. IV: 159)

It is clear that sequences like these arise from the pressure of producing spontaneous speech. A writer, on the other hand, can plan, reflect and make alterations, so mazes like (1) to (3) almost never occur even in young children's writing.

There are some errors, though, that do appear in writing and that seem to be related to the production process in the same way that mazes are a result of the conditions in which speech is produced. Some young writers frequently omit function words (probably because the mind is racing ahead of the labouring pencil), for example:

(4) There was a fete on the beach weekend and there were a lot of side
     show, and evening there a show put by the Life Guard.
                              12 years (Handscombe 1967b: 49)

(Adult writers omit words too, of course, but usually correct the error when they re-read the text; researchers such as Graves (1979) and Calkins

(1980) have demonstrated that such 'proofreading' is a difficult skill for children to acquire.) Another type of error that occurs, but only rarely, is a switch of structure in mid-sentence, for example:

(5)   She had a friend Sidney Herbert who was secretary of war wrote to Florence asking her if she would take a team of nurses into the Crimea.

15 years (Burgess *et al.* 1973: 153)

It seems that when the writer reaches *war*, he has forgotten how he began the sentence and continues as if *Sidney Herbert* were the subject. In this kind of error the beginning and the end of the sentence are each coherent but the two halves do not fit together. The sentence at (6) is a particularly interesting example because it shows how a writer can be misled by re-reading only the last few words, rather than the whole sentence, before continuing:

(6)   The teacher told me to go a few yards away, put my shoulders under the water, pushed off with my feet and the teacher pulled me in.

12 years (Handscombe 1967b: 70)

Here the problem lies in the irregular verb *put*, which can be either the stem form of the verb, as it is in the first part of the sentence where it is co-ordinated with *go*; or the simple past, which is the way the writer re-interprets it when she continues her sentence by co-ordinating *put* with the past tense form *pushed*.

Despite the occurrence of examples such as (4) to (6), the fact remains that children's written language contains far fewer mazes of any kind than their speech. Taking length of response into account, O'Donnell *et al.* (1967: 40) note that, in their 10 year olds' language, mazes are nine times more frequent in speech than in writing. For the grammatical analyst this difference has the practical consequence that it is much easier to identify sentence boundaries (even if punctuation is bizarre or non-existent), and to analyse constituent clauses exhaustively, in written than in spoken samples.

4.2. Oral grammatical structures

There are a number of constructions that occur quite commonly in speech, which cannot be classified as mazes yet which are not considered normal in written language. They will be exemplified from Fawcett and Perkins' (1980) transcripts, and also from a corpus of children's speech collected by Handscombe (1967c) for the Nuffield Foreign Languages Teaching

Materials Project.[4] It must be emphasized, however, that these constructions are not being regarded as evidence of linguistic immaturity, since they occur also in the spontaneous speech of adults.

Expressions like *well* and *you know* are very frequent:

(7)   *Well* ... I can swim about ... fifteen yards I suppose ... *you know* . : .

                    12 years (Handscombe 1967c, vol. 28: 113)

Then, speakers sometimes complete a clause with a vague expression such as *and that, and all, and everything, or something:*

(8)   ... just as we were going to catch the coach *and everything* it started raining ...

                    12 years (Handscombe 1967c, vol. 26: 16)

(9)   'one girl/'ad to uh 'save a man's life *or something/*

                    12 years (Fawcett and Perkins 1980, vol. IV: 301)

Another common colloquial feature is the use of the definite determiners *this* and *these* in a noun phrase that has not yet been introduced to the listener through either the situational or the linguistic context:

(10)   Er I ... I saw *this* film ... well somebody told me about this film 'One Step Beyond' and er ... *this* man ... he went into an air-raid shelter ...

                    12 years (Handscombe 1967c, vol. 28: 51)

In speech, clauses can be emphasized by the addition of a tag statement (Quirk *et al.* 1972: 971):

(11)   I 'don't like 'Louise Évans/ *Í don't/*

                    12 years (Fawcett and Perkins 1980, vol. IV: 11)

Noun–pronoun pleonasms also occur quite frequently. One type is the recapitulatory pronoun which is 'sometimes inserted, in informal speech, within a clause where it stands 'proxy' for an initial noun phrase ... As a result, the noun phrase is not connected syntactically to the clause to which, in meaning, it belongs' (Quirk *et al.* 1972: 970). There are many examples in the two corpora of children's speech:

(12)   and the witches/. *they* 'all – 'haunted in the houses/

                    12 years (Fawcett and Perkins 1980, vol. IV: 182)

(13)   ... all these ... er ... Deputy Dogs and everything *they* don't hu ... help your learning do they?

                    12 years (Handscombe 1967c, vol. 28: 54)

Sometimes a speaker starts a clause with a noun phrase which is, semantically, a direct object. In this case, the recapitulatory pronoun fills the normal object slot:

(14) Int. What did [the witches] do?
      B.   'everyone (that?) went 'up by the hóuse/ they 'used to 'scare
           them òff/
                              12 years (Fawcett and Perkins 1980, vol. IV: 183)

Another less common kind of pleonasm is the amplificatory noun phrase tag, which expands or clarifies an earlier pronoun:

(15) I was bored to start with . . . and he was always picking on me *the
      master* . . .
                              12 years (Handscombe 1967c, vol. 26: 136)

   On the whole, these oral constructions do not occur in writing, even among children as young as 9 (Perera 1984). Examples like the following (from written texts) are very rare:

(16) *Well*, now she has had a foal.
                                     9 years (Handscombe 1967a: 56)
(17) There was *this* little girl and she had two ugly sisters.
                                     9 years (Handscombe 1967a: 108)

So, generally in their writing children are doing something other than simply recording what they would say.

4.3. Dialect forms

Another indication of children's ability to differentiate between the grammar they use in speech and in writing is found in their use of regional dialect. In a small study of children aged 11 to 14, Cheshire (1982) recorded the oral language of working-class children in Reading, Berkshire, both in the playground and in a classroom discussion with a teacher; she also collected examples of their written work. Commonly occurring nonstandard grammatical forms were: the stem+*s* form of the verb as present tense after all subjects, e.g. *I wants to be a farmer; was* as past tense of the verb *to be* after all subjects, e.g. *We was in bed about one hour;* multiple negation, e.g. *The rescuers couldn't do nothing more; what* as a relative pronoun, e.g. *He said something what he should of not said;* and *come* as simple past tense, e.g. *I come here yesterday.* All these dialect forms occurred in the children's speech more often than the equivalent standard forms. In their writing, however, the use of nonstandard constructions was dramatically lower, with standard forms predominating. For example, the

nonstandard stem+*s* form occurred in rather more than 55 per cent of possible contexts in the children's speech with a teacher, but not at all in their written work. It would be interesting to replicate this study with younger children to discover the age at which those who use nonstandard grammatical forms in speech begin to use the standard equivalents in their writing.

5. 'Mature' structures more frequent in writing than in speech

Studies by O'Donnell *et al.* (1967), Loban (1976) and Yerrill (1977) have compared children's speech and writing in order to discover whether grammatical maturity is more apparent in one mode than the other. There are problems associated with deciding what constitutes this maturity; generally, researchers make certain assumptions – for example, that structures which are used rarely by kindergarten children but more frequently by teenagers are, in some sense, 'advanced' and indicative of linguistic development; that maturity in language can be measured partly by the frequency of occurrence of these advanced structures; and that the use of an increasing variety of constructions implies linguistic flexibility and, therefore, a move towards maturity. This section will focus mainly on O'Donnell *et al.*'s study (with some additional evidence from the other two), since it covers a fairly wide range of grammatical structures and employs a methodology which allows valid comparisons to be made between spoken and written language samples.

O'Donnell *et al.*'s subjects were white, middle-class American children, within the normal range of intelligence. The study spanned the age range from kindergarten to grade 7, with thirty subjects in each age group, but writing samples were collected only from those in grades 3, 5 and 7 (with mean ages of 8;8, 10;10 and 13;0). The children watched animated cartoon films of two of Aesop's fables with the soundtrack switched off, and then both told and wrote the story of the film they had just seen. The written compositions and speech transcripts were analysed grammatically, with most attention being paid to noun phrase structures and patterns of subordination. After presenting detailed comparisons between the language in the two modes, O'Donnell *et al.* (p. 95) summarize their findings as follows:

> Distinct and dramatic differences were found in the syntax of speech and writing in all three grades ... On almost all counts, it was clear that where notable differences appeared in Grade 3 ... they indicated weaker control in writing ... Unexpectedly uniform evidence, however, showed that advances in the control of syntax in Grades 5 and 7 were accelerated far beyond those reflected in speech.

Structures which they found conforming to this crossover pattern – from less frequent occurrence in early writing than in speech to higher frequency in writing by the age of 10 – include a noun modified by a finite relative clause, co-ordinated predicates, verbal complementation with a nonfinite clause, and finite adverbial clauses. Structures which were more frequent in writing than in speech even at the age of 8 include a noun modified by a prepositional phrase, and a noun modified by a nonfinite clause. A high level of main clause co-ordination was regarded as a sign of linguistic immaturity; at the age of 8 their subjects were already using only a third as many of these co-ordinations in their writing as they were in their speech.

As a general finding, they report that from the age of 10 their subjects used more subordination and longer T-units in their writing than in their speech.[5] Loban (1976) also notes a higher level of subordination in writing, though not until the age of 13, but he says that his subjects used T-units of closely similar lengths in both modes. His study employed an 'elaboration index' (p. 17) which took into account not only subordinate clauses but also nonfinite and verbless forms of modification. Using this measure he found that, on average, children gained higher elaboration scores in their writing than in their speech from the age of 13; the ablest subjects achieved this when they were only 9.

These two studies have not identified any constructions that occur exclusively in one linguistic mode; their argument that writing, at some stage, displays the greater grammatical control is based on the fact that it contains not different structures but a higher proportion than speech of those structures that can be considered mature.

Yerrill (1977), in an English study, made some comparisons between the grammar of speech and writing, using data both from adults and from children aged 9 and 12. His central concern was the analysis of what he called 'interrupting parenthetical items' – structures such as non-restrictive relative clauses, prepositional phrases, and appositives, which interrupt the basic structure of the sentence at some point. From his data he was able to calculate a 'parenthetical index' to measure the frequency with which interrupting constructions were used. His results are given in table 1. The figures show not only that the number of parenthetical constructions in children's writing increases as they grow older, but also that, even when they are as young as 9, they use more in their writing than adults do in their informal speech.

A consideration of these three studies suggests that there is a need for an investigation that examines the grammar, in both speech and writing, of individual children rather than of groups. At the moment we know, for example, that the average figures provided by the studies for the occur-

Table 1. *Parenthetical items in speech and writing: number of occurrences per 1000 words**

	9 years	12 years	15 years	Adults
Informal speech (conversation)	0.64	0.42	—	1.04
Formal speech (radio discussion)	—	—	—	2.97
Writing	1.40	1.53	9.35	12.05

* Figures derived from Yerrill (1977: 320).

rence of certain constru..ions at given ages indicate that 13 year olds use more advanced grammar in their writing than in their speech. However, experience suggests that these averages must conceal a wide range within which some children are using written language that is extensively differentiated from their speech, while others are still displaying very similar linguistic behaviour in the two modes, and yet others are continuing to produce writing that is less grammatically mature than their spoken language. Only a longitudinal comparison of the speech and writing of individual children will make possible a detailed analysis of the interaction between the two modes in the process of language acquisition.

6. Structures typical of writing

Although the large-scale studies that have been referred to have shown some interesting things about children's grammatical development in writing and its relationship with oral language acquisition, they are in some ways rather limited in their approach and, hence, in what they can reveal. This is because, typically, the grammatical analysis is wide-ranging rather than selective and may not be sufficiently fine-grained to pinpoint features that could be of interest. For example, O'Donnell *et al.* (1967) show that children progressively use more noun modifiers such as adjectives, participles and prepositional phrases; but each of these modifiers is considered in isolation – there is no account of their co-occurrence within a complex noun phrase. Again, all the studies indicate that maturity in language use can be measured, in part, b; the increased occurrence of relative clauses; however, generally they fail to differentiate both between the various types of relative clause and between their grammatical functions. (Hunt's 1965, 1966, 1970 studies are the richest in grammatical detail, but they concentrate exclusively on written language, making no comparisons with speech.)

In this section I shall present some findings from a comparison between speech and writing, focusing on just a very few constructions which I believe are typical of writing and occur very rarely in children's speech; complex subject noun phrases, some types of relative clause, some word order alterations, and nonfinite and verbless adverbial clauses.

The data come from the following sources:

(i) Transcripts of the speech of 29 monolingual English-speaking 12 year olds from Mid-Glamorgan, Wales, recorded by Fawcett and Perkins (1980) as part of a language development project at the Polytechnic of Wales. Following the design of the Bristol Project (see (iii) below), the 15 boys and 14 girls come from 'four classes of family background'. Each child's speech was recorded in two situations: (a) making a Lego construction with two peers, and (b) talking individually with an adult stranger. The topics in (b) include books read, films and TV programmes seen, games played, holidays and career choice.

(ii) Transcripts of the speech of 24 12 year olds from schools in south-east England and Yorkshire, recorded by Handscombe (1967c) as part of a Nuffield project. The 12 boys and 12 girls are 'of mixed intelligence but roughly similar social background'. They were recorded in groups of three, talking between themselves and with an adult stranger. The topics include books read, films and TV programmes seen, holidays, school subjects and hobbies.

(iii) 89 pieces of writing by 18 9 year olds in Bristol, collected by Kroll and Wells as part of the child language development project at Bristol University.[6] The nine boys and nine girls come from four different social classes. All the children except one produced five pieces of writing: an account of 'My happiest moment'; a story based on a cartoon picture; instructions for playing a specially-designed board game, and two letters.

(iv) 48 pieces of writing from at least 30 9 year olds in south-east England and Yorkshire, collected by Handscombe (1967a) for the same Nuffield project as in (ii).[7] The writing is on the topics, 'My last holidays', 'How I learnt to swim' and 'My favourite story'.

(v) 48 pieces of writing from at least 28 12 year olds in south-east England and Yorkshire, also collected by Handscombe (1967b) for the Nuffield project. Most of the children in this group provided speech samples in (ii) as well. Their writing is on the same topics as the 9 year olds'.

All the data come from large-scale, carefully designed projects on children's language development. There are, deliberately, several topic links between the samples selected from the different corpora; for example, all the children in (i) tell the story of a book they have read or a film they have seen and this has similarities with 'My favourite story' in (iv)

and (v). Even so, there are problems involved in making comparisons between these different sets of material: apart from (ii) and (v), the children are not the same and, except in (iv) and (v), the topics are not completely matched. This means that the findings can only be regarded as suggestive. Nevertheless, they seem worth presenting, since they do indicate areas where fuller studies might profitably be made.

In the examples of children's writing quoted in this chapter, misspellings have been corrected but no other alterations have been made.

6.1. Complex subject noun phrases

Children can produce complex noun phrases after the verb, but it is very rare for them to use complex subjects in speech. (Adults, too, seldom use complex noun phrases as subjects in their spontaneous speech: Crystal, 1980: 164, in a study of such speech, notes that only 10 per cent of preverbal clause elements are expressed by anything more complex than a pronoun.) Therefore, it seemed that it might be fruitful to examine just those noun phrases that functioned as subjects, in order to discover whether children's written language differs from their speech in the type of subject that they use. Accordingly, an analysis was made of the grammatical subjects of all finite clauses in corpora (iii), (iv) and (v), and of approximately one thousand clauses each from (ib) and (ii). The subject noun phrases were labelled as simple or complex, following the criteria provided by Quirk et al. (1972; 933): pronouns, proper nouns and nouns with a closed-system modifier such as a determiner are simple; anything else is complex. Further, a subclass of complex NPs was established, to separate out those that exhibited notable complexity; this subclass included anything other than D Adj N; D N prep NP, and two simple NPs co-ordinated by and. The results are given in table 2. For comparison, Quirk et al.'s results for their corpus of adult data are included in italics.

Overall, the figures show a remarkably steady increase in complex subject NPs through the different language samples. Children aged 12 use fewer complex subjects in their speech than adults, but the speech of both children and adults contains a lower proportion of complex subjects than the writing of 9 year olds. Nevertheless, these young writers use considerably fewer complex NPs than the 12 year olds. (As the Handscombe samples consist of writing on identical themes, the grammatical differences between them cannot arise from differences in the topic.) The last adult sample shows that scientific writing is characterized by a high degree of complexity in subject NPs. Commenting on their figures, Quirk et al. (1972: 934) say, 'Even so coarse-grained a comparison makes clear how sensitive the noun

Table 2. *The structure of subject NPs in speech and writing*

	Percentage of simple NPs			Percentage of complex NPs	
	Pronouns and proper nouns	Determiner + noun	All simple	All complex	Notably complex
12 year olds' speech: Fawcett and Perkins (N = 1,000)	91	6	97	3	1
12 year olds' speech: Hands-combe (N = 1,060)	92	5	97	3	1
Informal adult speech: Quirk et al. * *(N = 2,212)*	88	5	93	7	*3*
9 year olds' writing: Hands-combe (N = 1,019)	83	9	92	8	3
9 year olds' writing: Kroll and Wells (N = 1,065)	74	17	91	9	3
Adult fiction: Quirk et al. (N = 2,431)	*80*	*11*	*91*	*9*	*4*
12 year olds' writing: Hands-combe (N = 1,000)	78	10	88	12	5
Adults' serious talk and writing: Quirk et al. (N = 2,008)	*71*	*13*	*84*	*16*	*6*
Adults' scientific writing: Quirk et al. (N = 1,167)	*39*	*23*	*62*	*38*	*15*

* Figures derived from Quirk *et al.* (1972: 933).

phrase is as an index of style and how responsive it can be to the basic purpose and subject matter of any discourse.' This responsiveness can be illustrated by figures from the Kroll and Wells corpus of 9 year olds' writing. Each child wrote five pieces, which together yield a total of 9 per cent complex subject NPs. Four of the pieces are what could broadly be called 'personal' in style, while the fifth is more impersonal, being a set of instructions for playing a board game. Of the 243 subject NPs in the instructions, fully 17 per cent are complex, with 6 per cent being notably so. These figures compare closely with the equivalent figures of 16 per cent and 6 per cent in Quirk *et al.*'s sample of adults' serious talk and writing.

The differences between the children's spoken and written samples can best be illustrated by giving examples of the various types of notably complex subject NP that they use (excluding nouns modified by a finite relative clause, which will be described in the next section). These NPs are divided into three groups in table 3. Group I consists of those structures that occur both in speech and writing (though with greater frequency in writing).

Table 3. *Notably complex subject NPs in children's speech and writing*

NP structure	12 year olds' speech (Handscombe and Fawcett and Perkins)	9 year olds' writing (Handscombe and Kroll and Wells)	12 year olds' writing (Handscombe)
Group I			
D Adj Adj N	the other two men	a little baby girl	my first swimming stroke
Adj N prepNP	little men on motor cycles	a very very distant cousin of mine	a very funny part in the story
NP + nonfinite clause	a horse called Ginger	a huntsman called Jones	another relation to add to the collection
NP + appositive	my little sister Petta	my friends Roy and Kevin	Flicka, a lovely mare
Group II			
Multiple co-ordination		me, Laura, Jean and John	my cousins and my brother and sister
Group III			
nonfinite nominal clause			(a) trying to swim
			(b) actually swimming some distance
co-ordinated NPs with modification			(c) Their unhappiness and loneliness without their parents
			(d) the baskets of fruit and well-selected collections of fans
NP + clause + clause			(e) a little old man selling lanterns of brass (or a metal which looked similar)

In group II there are multiple co-ordinations, which do not figure in either of the speech samples. The structures illustrated in group III are those that appear only in the writing of the 12 year olds. The examples seem increasingly literary in style.

This analysis of subject NPs shows that in order to highlight any differences between spoken and written language it is necessary both to take account of the grammatical function of the noun phrase and to treat the phrase as a whole. The function is important because it is only in subject position that the complexity of children's spoken NPs is somewhat restricted; they use much longer and more complex NPs as objects. Then, the necessity of considering the phrase as a whole becomes clear from an examination of NP(e) in group III: *a little old man selling lanterns of brass (or a metal which looked similar)*. This phrase contains two premodifying adjectives, a nonfinite clause and a finite relative clause – all structures

that, separately, are found in the 12 year olds' speech. It is the occurrence of all three together, in subject position, that seems to differentiate written from spoken language at this stage of children's linguistic development.

6.2. Some types of finite relative clause

We have seen that a number of studies show that children's language development is marked by a considerable increase in their use of relative clauses. On the whole, though, these studies do not analyse the function and structure of the clauses more closely. A relative clause can modify any NP, whether it functions as subject, object, complement or as part of an adverbial; more rarely, the relative can modify a whole clause or sentence. In speech, where elliptical responses are common, the modified NP may stand alone and not be a clause constituent at all. The occurrence of relative clauses in the five corpora of children's language is presented in table 4, according to the function of the NPs they modify.

Apart from the higher number of relatives in elliptical expressions in speech – a direct consequence of the conversational situation – the most consistent difference between the two modes is that a much larger proportion of NPs functioning as subject are modified by relative clauses in children's writing than in their speech; the average figure for the three writing samples is 22 per cent, which contrasts markedly with the average of 6.5 per cent for the two speech samples. This is clearly an extension of the findings of section 6.1, that notably complex subject NPs are more common in written than in spoken language.

Table 4. *Functions of finite relative clauses in children's speech and writing*

Data	Percentage of clauses modifying NP in:				
	Object/ Complement	Adverbial	Subject	Other	Elliptical/ Incomplete
12 year olds' speech: Fawcett and Perkins (N = 56*)	62	9	7	4	18
12 year olds' speech: Handscombe (N = 121)	58	17	6	9	10
9 year olds' writing: Kroll and Wells (N = 48)	44	21	29	4	2
9 year olds' writing: Handscombe (N = 74)	45	36	16	3	0
12 year olds' writing: Handscombe (N = 87)	48	24	20	7	1

* It is not valid to compare the raw numbers of relative clauses in each sample as the corpora were not matched for length.

In the speech samples, the relative clauses that modify subject NPs are generally short and simple, for example:

(18)   The guns *I like shooting* are 22s
                                        12 years (Handscombe 1967c, vol. 28: 20)

On one occasion, the clause is extraposed so that, although it modifies the subject NP *things in the boat*, it is not introduced until after the verb:

(19)   and . 'things – you kńow/ in the 'boat just 'drifted óut/ *that they really nèeded/* like er harpoòns and/
                                        12 years (Fawcett and Perkins, vol. IV: 158)

This type of extraposition is not a structure which typically occurs in written language. Sometimes when a modified NP looks as if it is going to be the subject, it is, in fact, left syntactically isolated, the subject position being filled by a recapitulatory pronoun, for example:

(20)   . . . one person who everybody hated Mrs. D. . . . *she* was absolutely awful . . .
                                        12 years (Handscombe 1967c, vol. 27: 38)

The following examples illustrate the kinds of subject relative that are found in the children's writing:

(21)   The first thing *I wanted to do* was learn to swim.
                                        9 years (Handscombe 1967a: 84)
(22)   The boy *who touches the hand with the blue bird in* has the blue bird.
                                        Philip, 9 years (Kroll and Wells)
(23)   Each child *who wanted to learn to swim or at least go in the pool* had to contribute some money to the building of the pool.
                                        12 years (Handscombe 1967b: 73)

In each corpus of writing, the majority of the subject relatives are, like (21), no more than four words long, but there are also a few like (22) and (23) that are longer and more complex. Such relative clauses modifying a subject NP are very rare in children's speech (as they probably are in the spontaneous speech of most adults).

It seems likely that it is the slow, uninterrupted process of writing that allows the writer to produce long NPs with complex modification at the beginning of a clause where the speaker finds them particularly difficult to manage successfully. In addition, the writer can re-read what he has written whenever he loses track of the structure he has embarked on, and,

if he gets into a grammatical tangle, he can always make alterations which need not appear in the final version.

In addition to their grammatical function, relative clauses can be considered in terms of the way in which they are linked to their antecedents. In the samples of both speech and writing, *who, that, which, where* and zero are widely used. There are just two relative pronouns that appear exclusively in the children's writing – *whose* and *whom*, which are each used only once, and only by the 12 year olds:

(24) One of the girls, *who's* [sic] *name was Josephine but they called her Jo for short*, first saw Laurie looking out of a window.

> 12 years (Handscombe 1967b: 88)

(25) My teacher was a Mr. C. *whom a* [sic] *considered very good.*

> 12 years (Handscombe 1967b: 62)

Another notably formal construction is the fronted preposition preceding a relative pronoun. There is a solitary instance in the 12 year olds' speech:

(26) ... they have their own dinner room *in which the dinners are cooked on the premises* ...

> 12 years (Handscombe 1967c, vol. 26: 208)

In contrast, there are several examples in the writing of both 12 and 9 year olds, for instance:

(27) Each man had a small metal tag *on which a number was stamped.*

> 12 years (Handscombe 1967b: 87)

(28) There was a large battle *in which the Trojans were so sleepy that the Greeks won easily.*

> 9 years (Handscombe 1967a: 109)

The children's written relative clauses are not error-free. Some display a lack of agreement between the relative pronoun and its antecedent:

(29) Soldiers *which had been hidden inside* let down a ladder to climb down it.

> 9 years (Handscombe 1967a: 109)

Others show that the co-ordination of two relative clauses can cause the young writer problems:

(30) So we set out at half-past one for the Emanuel Church *where Mummy and Daddy got married and I was christened there.*

> 9 years (Handscombe 1967a: 56)

In addition, the fronted preposition can induce errors:

(31) I have a basket *of which I can remember my gay holiday in China.*

> 12 years (Handscombe 1967b: 45)

Some young writers seem to be attracted by this construction, perhaps feeling that it lends weight to their style. Certainly, other collections of children's writing also provide examples of errors in its use:

(32) In reference to the accident *of which you gave a statement* . . .

> 11 years (Sutton 1981: 39)

(33) This year it is Pirates of Penzance *in which I'm in.*

> 12 years (Yerrill 1977: 179)

All these errors can be seen as signs of growth, as children try out new constructions and extend their linguistic repertoire.

6.3. Some word order alterations

The large-scale studies of writing development do not, on the whole, refer to alterations in the order of constituents within the clause, presumably because they happen so infrequently that they do not reach a level of statistical significance. Nevertheless, it seems worth considering the types of word order alteration that children make in their writing, because it is one of the areas where there is a noticeable difference between spoken and written language. What is of particular importance is the effect of the alteration within the sentence or paragraph. In other words, these stylistic variants are not a desirable end in themselves, but only in so far as they serve to express the writer's meaning more clearly, effectively or elegantly than could be achieved by the canonical word order. Within a sentence, alterations of word order can prove successful in creating suspense. They can also enable the introduction of new or lengthy material to be delayed until after the verb, thus satisfying the preference, in English, for end-focus and end-weight (Quirk *et al.* 1972: 938–44). Within a paragraph, word order alterations can assist in the creation of a text that displays both thematic continuity and thematic variety. However, in presenting examples of children's use of such alterations, it is not being suggested that they are consciously aware of these reasons for choosing to depart from the normal word order.

Where the predicate of a clause consists of a verb phrase containing part of the verb *to be* plus a participle, followed by an adverbial, the participle and adverbial can be fronted and the subject moved to the end of the clause:

(34) The beach was just across the garden and *tied to the lobby* was *a boat in which you could row.*

9 years (Handscombe 1967a: 52)

Here, the alteration of word order allows the information that is most important to the writer to occur in a prominent position at the end of the sentence. The same effect is seen in the next example, which also provides a good illustration of thematic continuity in the fronted element:

(35) The characters who have the main mention are John, Susan, Titty and Roger Walker and Nancy and Peggy Blacket. *Also mentioned quite a lot* is Captain Flint alias – Jim Turner.

9 years (Handscombe 1967a: 102)

This structure does not occur at all in the two corpora of 12 year olds' speech.

Another type of word order alteration is where a place adverbial is fronted, with subject–verb inversion, giving an AVS clause structure instead of the more usual SVA. Although this construction is briefly mentioned by O'Donnell *et al.* (1967: 72–3), they make no distinction between the AVS constructions that occur in speech and those that are more characteristic of written language. The following examples are typical of the adverbial fronting that the 12 year olds use in their speech:

(36) 'here's a bús stop/

12 years (Fawcett and Perkins 1980, vol. IV: 65)

(37) 'here's a líttle one/

12 years (Fawcett and Perkins 1980, vol. IV: 58)

This form, *here's* plus a noun phrase, is quite common in the 'running commentary' speech that the children use as they play with Lego. It can be contrasted with the structures that are found in the written texts:

(38) Aberhaben beach is very long. There are only very few pebbles, but many shells. *Behind the beach* is a curved sea wall.

9 years (Handscombe 1967a: 67)

(39) There was a beach about a mile down the road *about three miles down the road* was a little town called Sea Palling.

12 years (Handscombe 1967b: 50)

(40) We stayed at a small cottage on the side of a hill. ... *Opposite the cottage* was a parking space with a field of horses behind it.

12 years (Handscombe 1967b: 54)

Each fronted adverbial repeats a noun phrase from earlier in the discourse

so that thematic continuity is maintained. (If the subject had been placed at the beginning of the sentence, in every case it would have constituted a new theme. A succession of new themes in writing produces a jerky and disjointed text.) In (40), the fronting also achieves a sentence with end-weight, as the subject is particularly long. In these written sentences, there is no use of the formulaic *here's*; rather, the adverbial element is realized by a phrase. In (39) and (40), the verb *to be* is in the past tense – a form that is likely to occur in written rather than in spoken AVS constructions.

These two sets of AVS examples from speech and writing highlight the need to make linguistic comparisons between the modes at more than one grammatical level. With the AVS construction, for example, it is necessary to take simultaneous account of discourse structure, clause structure and the phrase-level realization of clause constituents.

6.4. Nonfinite and verbless adverbial clauses

There is one type of nonfinite adverbial clause that is used in speech by quite young children – that is, the adverbial clause of purpose, as in:

(41) we 'had to 'call into an'other càmp/ to 'spend the 'one níght/
                                            6 years (Fawcett and Perkins 1980, vol. I: 85)

Other kinds of nonfinite and verbless adverbial, however, seem to be restricted to the written language, amongst children aged 9 to 12. The following examples of written nonfinite adverbials have no counterparts in the speech data:

(42) *Looking to our right* we saw hundreds of tall green trees and mountains.
                                            9 years (Handscombe 1967a: 52)
(43) *Having done that* I was soon able to iron out my fault.
                                            12 years (Handscombe 1967b: 61)
(44) I tried the same *after hesitating* and I could do it too.
                                            12 years (Handscombe 1967b: 73)

Similarly, the speech corpus does not contain verbless adverbials like these:

(45) They folded up during the daytime *when not in use*.
                                            12 years (Handscombe 1967b: 56)
(46) We arrived in Ostend at 11 o'clock G.M.T. *Once in Ostend* we had about 1¼ hours, so we looked around, had some chips and then went back to the coach.
                                            12 years (Handscombe 1967b: 42)

The use of these constructions enables a writer to reduce redundancy and achieve the compression of meaning that is favoured in writing.

This section has focused on structures that are particularly literary and that seldom or never occur in the *speech* of children aged 12. In the large-scale studies of language development such constructions are either ignored or given only a fleeting mention because, numerically, they are not significant. Even so, the single occurrence of one such construction in the work of a younger writer reveals some important things about his or her language development. It means that the writer must have met the structure (probably in reading) and must have internalized it as part of his or her own linguistic repertoire. It also suggests that, without being able to talk about it, the child has some awareness of the special effects that can be achieved – effects such as emphasis, balance, continuity, variety and succinctness. Finally, it proves that the child is substantially differentiating the written from the spoken language. After all, it is quite possible to produce an acceptable piece of writing simply by using the structures of speech and omitting the mazes, colloquial constructions and dialect features that were illustrated in section 4. This kind of writing could be called 'edited speech'. Quite different is the kind where the use of more literary grammatical structures allows ideas to be presented and related to each other in new and effective ways.

7. Acquiring the grammar of the written language

It is clear that some children, at least, are using in their writing constructions that they do not use in speech. As these constructions – the formal relative clauses, word order alterations and nonfinite adverbial clauses – are particularly literary, it seems unlikely that children hear them regularly, even in the speech of adults. This raises the question of how they acquire them. The obvious explanation is that they learn them by reading. In an article that summarizes more than thirty studies of correlations between reading and writing behaviour, Stotsky (1983: 636) concludes: 'the correlational studies show almost consistently that better writers tend to be better readers … that better writers tend to read more than poorer writers, and that better readers tend to produce more syntactically mature writing than poorer readers'. Although so many studies show positive correlations between high ability in reading and maturity in writing, it cannot be assumed that the link is a causal one: both skills could derive independently from some higher order linguistic ability. Even so, it seems intuitively plausible that children learn to use the grammar that is more typical of writing than of speech not by listening but by reading.

A study that supports this view is one by Eckhoff (1983). She analysed two series of books used to teach 7 year olds to read, and found considerable grammatical differences between them. She then analysed the writing produced by two groups of children who had each read one of the series. The analysis revealed that the grammatical differences between the two groups' written work mirrored the differences between the two series of reading books.

8. Conclusion

Although children's written language initially grows out of their spoken language, by the time they are aged 9 or 10 it can differ from their spontaneous speech in three ways. First, their writing is largely free of mazes and colloquial constructions such as tag statements, vague clause completers and recapitulatory pronouns. Second, in comparison with their speech, their writing may contain a lower proportion of co-ordinated main clauses, and a higher proportion of subordinate clauses and structures such as interrupting parenthetical items. Third, it may include some constructions that do not normally occur in 12 year olds' spontaneous speech; these include: nonfinite nominal clauses as subject, relative clauses introduced by *whose* or *whom*, structures with a fronted lexical verb or adverbial phrase, and nonfinite and verbless adverbial clauses (apart from those of purpose). Not all the children in the samples studied, however, provided evidence of all three types of differentiation in their writing. Broadly, most children achieved the first, some the second and very few the third. It would be interesting to know whether, by the time they leave school, the majority of children can use the grammar of the written language, when appropriate, or whether they remain at the stage of writing 'edited speech'.

So far this chapter has contrasted written language with informal, spontaneous speech. But there are other less common kinds of speech that are more formal and more planned. These include speeches, lectures, interviews, and so on. It seems likely that some of the structures that have been described here as being typical of the written language also occur in these more oratorical styles of speech. A slight piece of evidence for this can be found in Yerrill's (1977) analysis of interrupting parenthetical constructions. The figures given in table 1 show clearly not only that these constructions are far more frequent in writing than in speech but also, significantly, that adults are three times more likely to use them in a radio discussion than in an informal conversation. We can speculate that the more literary grammatical constructions are first met in reading, are then practised and acquired in writing, and that subsequently they can be added to the oral repertoire. Writing is certainly an ideal mode for the acquisition

of a psycholinguistically complex construction because it allows the language user to deliberate, to review and to correct, without pressure from conversational partners. As well as permitting grammatical complexity, writing requires grammatical variety, because it lacks the prosodic and paralinguistic features that enliven speech. Therefore, in terms of children's language acquisition, writing is not simply a reflection of oral language abilities but is, in its own right, a potent agent in the process of language development.

This chapter has shown that throughout the school years there are grammatical developments in children's writing. For example, the following are all reported as increasing until adulthood: relative clauses, parenthetical constructions, clause length and subject NP complexity. Furthermore, it is clear that at the age of 12 children are still making errors in some 'advanced' constructions, such as relative clauses with a fronted preposition. Finally, it has been tentatively suggested that many 12 year olds have still not begun to use in their writing those constructions that are more characteristic of the written than the spoken language. Therefore, we have to conclude that if the written language constitutes a part of what has to be learnt during the process of language acquisition, then it is not possible to agree with Slobin's (1971: 40) assertion that the child 'masters the exceedingly complex structure of his native language in the course of a short three or four years'.

Notes to chapters

1. Psychosocial aspects of language acquisition

* I am grateful to James V. Wertsch for his comments on an earlier draft of this chapter.

1. Vygotsky's writings do not touch directly on many aspects of the theory developed by Piaget and his followers over the years, including, for example, research on moral reasoning. Only some aspects of the contrast between Vygotsky and Piaget can be found explicitly in their writings, particularly those concerned with their interpretation of 'egocentric speech'. I am inferring others on the basis of contemporary writings in a Vygotskian framework and on the basis of an interpretation of the writings left by Vygotsky, whose premature death prevented him from fully developing his theory.

2. I am using the term 'sign' here in its most general sense. To avoid terminological confusions, it is useful to note that Piaget uses distinct terms in French (not always distinguished in translations) to refer to different types of sign. For example, in his terminology, the French term *symbole* referes to iconic signs, i.e. those which have a relation of resemblance to their object. The term *signe* refers specifically to linguistic signs, which he describes mostly as having an arbitrary relation to their object, following a semiotic framework inspired by Saussure (see below).

3. As should become clear below, 'thought' is not the same concept in Piaget's and Vygotsky's writings. Generally speaking, Piaget focuses on the structural properties of cognitive schemata, especially after the sensorimotor period, whereas Vygotsky focuses on thinking as a goal-directed activity throughout development. The term 'thought' refers here to what Vygotsky calls 'verbal thinking', which would include the logico-mathematical skills described by Piaget. Vygotsky recognized that not all forms of thought are mediated by language. In addition, although Vygotsky was mostly interested in the interaction between thought and language, he was also interested in other sign systems.

4. The term 'process approach' is, however, more general than the term 'functional approach'; for example, some information-processing approaches, including neo-Piagetian ones, have focused on process without necessarily invoking any kind of functionalism.

2. Language acquisition and cognition

* I am grateful to the Max Planck Gesellschaft for providing me with facilities

and resources for the period in which this paper was written and to my erstwhile colleagues at the Projektgruppe für Psycholinguistik for stimulation and support. By a happy coincidence, this revised version was also completed at the Nijmegen MPI during a brief visit in 1983. In revising, I resisted the urge to destroy and have made only some structural changes with the goal of securing better comprehension,

1. I would like to acknowledge an especial debt to Bowerman's (1976) review. In addition, Bloom (1973) and Brown (1973) contain many useful sections.

2. For some discussion, see Campbell (1981).

3. With respect to the modified position attributed to Chomsky, there is a different fundamental question, i.e. what criteria determine the attribution of 'cognizing'?

4. Escape from this paradox is not easy. The suggestion is sometimes offered (see, e.g., Brunswik 1956) that whereas errors of perception – illusions – are incorrigible, mistakes of reasoning can be corrected. But this is fallacious, since mistakes of reasoning are corrected only by further reasoning.

5. Henceforth, unless otherwise indicated, the term 'cognitive' will be used in this restricted sense.

6. See also Kirkpatrick (1908), which is acknowledged by Claparede as a source.

7. Even here the needed basis lacks an immediate empirical justification. Some preliminary work has been carried out by Golinkoff (1975; Golinkoff and Kerr 1978).

8. It seems quite remarkable that Chomsky (1975; 1980a,b) persists with the notion that linguistic research can reveal innate constraints governing language acquisition, in the face of (a) profound and growing disagreement about how the most studied language – English – should be described; (b) gross differentiation of the concept 'human language' (see the recent clarification of the nature of pidgins, creoles and dying languages), with consequent weakening of the notion 'empirical linguistic universal'; (c) cogent and very early criticisms of his hypotheses by, for example, Lyons (1966a) and Putnam (1967); (d) a stubborn concern amongst students of child language for independent empirical justification of descriptive categories; and (e) the failure of the hypothesis to attract direct empirical support or to inspire interesting research.

9. This seems to be the most effective use for results like Gold's, namely to apply them to the activities of linguists rather than to the activities of children, since these formal results cannot readily be interpreted in the context of language acquisition (see Levelt 1975 for discussion).

10. Of course (see section 2 of this chapter), Chomsky's definition of cognitive psychology is different; 'cognizing' is constitutive in his framework, thus processes involving tacit knowledge are included.

11. Braine (1976a) has made a valiant attempt to do just this. However, the requirement of independent analysis of message and utterance corpora calls for new techniques on both fronts. While Braine has certainly improved on older ones, there still seems a long way to go.

12. A particularly interesting example of this principle at work can be seen in Bunuel's film *The Obscure Object of Desire* (the intentional object!), in which

a leading part is taken by two quite different actresses. Despite gross differences in physical appearance and behaviour, the viewer has no difficulty in perceiving 'them' as a single individual.

13. See Dennett (1980) for a similar objection to Chomsky's innateness hypothesis. A second consequence of Fodor's analysis is that there is no genuine concept development. I have attempted to refute this argument in Campbell (1982), using the framework developed here.

14. The earliest formulation of this notion appears in Vygotsky (1934/1962; and see now Kemler and Smith 1979). While the discussion of 'family resemblance' in Wittgenstein (1953) poses the problem (which stereotypes solve), it is not until Putnam (1970) and Ziff (1972) that the notion is once more clearly expressed. It is now, of course, pervasive.

15. Incidentally, this finding shows that the similarity space is nonmetric, which scotches the formal model proposed by Osherson and Smith (1981).

16. There is an excellent and conclusive demonstration of this point in Bowerman (1978a).

17. That is, *loss* of awareness may be as important for acquisition as growth. People who wear inverting spectacles manage to stay on their bicycles just so long as no one asks them whether they see the world the right way up or not!

18. What I have in mind here is the tendency, common to these writers, to resist the easy identification of the conceptual basis of an utterance with its semantic basis (in their terms). Of course, in my terms the former is a phenic structure and the latter is cryptic so that such an identification becomes impossible.

19. Readers who are not convinced are referred to the excellent discussion by Chomsky (1980a: 5ff).

3. Language acquisition and linguistic theory

* Work on this paper was supported in part by funds from the Graduate School Research Committee of the University of Wisconsin, and in part by a grant from the Spencer Foundation through the School of Education at the University of Wisconsin.

1. It should not be inferred from this discussion that non-configurational languages do not involve rule systems of a complexity comparable to those of configurational languages. Hale (1983) suggests that many constraints governing configurational languages may be realized in non-configurational languages at levels of representation other than the hierarchical structuring of the word string.

2. This definition derives from Reinhart's definition of the relation c-command (Reinhart 1981). Reinhart was the first to articulate in detail the pronoun principle given below in terms of this relation.

3. The reader may notice that the definition of relative height as given above classifies a node A as 'higher' than another node B when in fact the two nodes are at the same height on the tree (i.e. when the same branching node is immediately above both A and B, as with NP_1 and VP in the example); this is irrelevant to the examples discussed below.

4. It should be noted that Chomsky cast her principle as a perceptual (recognition)

principle, thus leaving open the question of whether the principle exactly corresponded to the child's rule(s) of grammar for *tell* sentences and other constructions, or was a partially independent perceptual principle. The principle has nonetheless been widely discussed in the literature in terms of the rules of the child's grammar. (For discussion of the problems of pulling apart the effects of perceptual devices and rules of grammar, see, among others, Shipley, Gleitman and Smith 1969; Slobin 1973; Goodluck and Tavakolian 1982;

5. There is no space here to discuss in any detail the studies on the development of complementation, although it is worth observing that some of the results to date pose an interesting challenge for the 'no wild grammars' mandate. For example, the rule that determines that the missing subject of an adverbial clause be interpreted as referring to the main clause subject (*the man* and not *the judge* is made the subject of *walk out* in a sentence such as *the man criticized the judge before walking out of the room*) is the norm in languages of the world, regardless of language type. Yet this rule is slow to develop in children, and is often not mastered until the child is aged 6 or older (Goodluck 1981; Hsu, Cairns and Fiengo 1985).

6. Studies that came to my attention after this chapter was in press suggest other lines of analysis; see, for example, Culicover and Wilkins 1984; Manzini and Wexler 1984.

5. Learnability

1. This conforms to what many may see as the most straightforward construal of language learning. The learner is provided with a class of grammars which can be seen as comprising the only legitimate hypotheses available to him. Confronted with a datum, he guesses one of the grammars that generates this datum (among others). Further data may be consistent with this grammar, in which case it will be maintained; or they may not, leading the learner to guess another grammar from the antecedently given set which generates all data to which he has been exposed so far (among others). If the class of grammars in question is identifiable in the limit, this means that there is some finite time at which the learner guesses the 'correct' grammar and his guess will not be modified by subsequent data. In the text, I talk about classes of *languages* being identifiable in the limit, rather than classes of *grammars*, and this simply reflects Gold's lack of concern with descriptive adequacy, in the sense of Chomsky (1965). For Gold, as for Wexler and Culicover, a 'correct' grammar is an observationally adequate one, and this means that we can equivalently talk about classes of languages.

2. The class of primitive recursive languages is that class of languages each of which is the range of some primitive recursive function. It is more restricted than the class of recursive languages, which, in turn, is more restricted than the class of recursively enumerable languages. This last class is the largest class of languages such that each of its member languages consists of an enumerable set of sentences, i.e. those languages for which a grammar of any description exists. If we consider more restricted classes than the class of primitive recursive languages, we find, in order of increasing restrictiveness, context-

sensitive languages, context-free languages, finite state or regular languages and finite cardinality languages (see figure 1).

3. The class of finite cardinality languages is simply the class of languages each of which contains a finite number of well-formed sentences. Obviously, observationally adequate grammars for such languages are supplied by lists of well-formed sentences.

4. An enumeration procedure provides a mechanism for determining the order in which a learner guesses grammars. We assume that the relevant grammars are listed:

$$G_1, G_2, \ldots, G_n, \ldots$$

G_1 is guessed for the first datum to which the learner is exposed. If it generates this datum, it is maintained as the learner's guess for the next datum; if it does not, the learner guesses G_2 and so on. On the assumption that the 'correct' grammar appears in the list, it will eventually be guessed and, thereafter, will be maintained by the learner. It should be clear that other, more efficient, guessing procedures might be devised in certain cases – heuristic procedures – but the failure to *guarantee* success by enumeration will entail failure to guarantee success by any other method.

5. It is important to point out here that I am not taking issue with a familiar claim from theoretical linguists that we do not have prior insight into the set of data to be accounted for, and that we can only be clear about these data when we have constructed a theory. In the argument in the text, assumptions about *data available to the learner* are being used in constructing theories which are intended to account for *a totally different set of data*, and it is this latter set to which we cannot claim privileged access before the construction of the appropriate theory. This may seem an obvious point, but it has been the subject of some misunderstanding.

6. Variation in child language

1. Templin's method of obtaining her speech data, which she claims was as nearly as possible a replication of that used by McCarthy, is described as follows: 'Children were taken into a room with an adult examiner and, after rapport was established, fifty remarks of the child, usually consecutive, were taken down.' (1957; 15). It is worth remembering, also, that 'taken down' means taken down in writing on the spot.

2. For a fuller account of this study see Wells (1981: Introduction; 1984).

3. Interestingly, Fraser and colleagues (Fielding and Fraser 1978; Fraser and Brown n.d.) have found variation in adult behaviour on a dimension that has a preference for nouns as one extreme. Perhaps significantly, however, they see this as a form of variation that is as much situationally determined as resulting from a difference between speakers.

7. Prespeech segmental feature development

* This work was supported in part by a grant no. NS 09628 from the National

Institute of Neurologic Diseases, Communication Disorders and Stroke and in part by a grant no. HD 11970 from the National Institute of Child Health and Human Development.

1. This objection does not apply to the Truby and Lind features. These investigators present cineradiographic data which do yield direct evidence of vocal tract gestures.
2. This section is quoted, with permission, from Stark (1985).

8. Prosodic development

1. One awaits the demonstration that tone-unit sequences operate generally and systematically (cf. paragraphs), though some interesting suggestions along these lines have already been made (e.g. Fox 1973).
2. A single-word polysyllable in principle allows for a contrast, e.g. DÀ*ddy* versus *dad*DỲ. There is no evidence of such forms at this stage (Atkinson-King 1973).
3. A compound-tone, such as this, is in fact singled out by Du Preez (1974) as an important transitional stage.

11. Speech perception and the emergent lexicon: an ethological approach

* I am indebted to Linda Locke, Michael Smith, and Kristine MacKain for their comments on the manuscript.
1. That the child might be sufficiently attuned to the motor–phonetic level for such to be true is suggested by research showing that by 6 months of age infants are aware of phonetic discrepancies between heard and seen speech (see Kuhl and Meltzoff 1982; MacKain *et al.* 1983).
2. Though it is not my purpose here to deal with the child's role in phonological change, my discussion here (and elsewhere, see Locke 1982) has an obvious bearing on this subject.

12. Phonological development: a crosslinguistic perspective

1. The imprimatur given language acquisition by Chomsky (1965) had further-reaching effects on the growth of the field than did Jakobson (1968), but only the latter provided an empirically testable model. Chomsky's theory is now generally argued as isolating the logical problem of acquisition yet remaining neutral with respect to the substance of the process.
2. 'Prosodic theory' here refers to an approach to phonology currently being developed at several US universities. It appears to be largely independent of British prosodic theory but there are notable parallels.
3. 'Typologist' might appear on first glance a misnomer (in that a typology requires differences between languages), but typologists have also considered themselves universalists (see Greenberg 1975).
4. The dots within brackets stand for the other phonetic elements that belong in each set, of which there are many.
5. This three-way division does not handle breathy voice consonants as in Hindi, nor one of the Korean voice contrasts. Korean has both a voiceless unaspirated

stop (mean VOT of +10 ms) and a voiceless aspirated stop (+90 ms) and a third type which is quite unusual in that it falls between the other two (+35 ms); this latter one is called a tense unaspirated stop (Kim 1965).

6. The Spanish contrast is cued mainly by the presence or absence of low-frequency periodicity preceding the stop release and thus may be more directly constrained by the temporal order phenomenon discussed by Pisoni.

7. The Kikuyu data are complicated, in that the infants were tested on [baːpa] while Kikuyu has only a voiced labial (frequently nasalized) and no [p]; however, Kikuyu has the relevant voicing contrasts at the dental and velar places of articulation.

8. Categorical perception, one of the most widely studied topics in perception, has been shown in recent work to be affected by a number of factors (e.g. under proper task conditions, adults can make certain within-category discriminations).

9. It is generally claimed that the infant data show that infants discriminate phonetic categories; however, this is an inference based on the similarity between infant and adult discrimination.

10. The mechanism is crucial. Debate rages over whether it is special to speech or is a general auditory mechanism (note that chinchilla 'discrimination' is very similar to that of infants). If it is a simple transducer then no real analysis is taking place, and the contribution of the infant data to the problem of phonetic categorization is considerably weakened.

11. Experience must play a role, because infants must of course learn which particular categories a given language uses (of those universally available) and the boundaries of those categories, since the locations of boundaries vary by language.

12. We use 'lower-level' to mean the acoustic–phonetic match-up and 'higher-level' to mean both phonological patterning and units larger than the segment. We thus delineate 'bottom-up' and 'top-down' *within* the phonological component. 'Higher-level' and 'top-down' also can refer to syntactic, semantic and pragmatic sources of information.

13. The phenomenon has important consequences for the analysis of children's language (e.g. the 'errors' the analyst makes in using phonetic and phoneme perceptual categories to discover the child's system) and theories of language acquisition (e.g. those that would require adults to shape and reinforce contrasts that they apparently cannot hear). See Macken (1980a), Macken and Barton (1980a).

14. Note that the nasal and obstruent clusters in question fall across syllable boundaries in both the Spanish and Telugu data.

13. Early vocabulary

1. In Griffiths (1979: 109f) I had begun to realize this, but not wholeheartedly so: I was then still inclined to focus exclusively on *adult* interpretations of child utterances and to regard such interpretations as mainly of value because they were *evidence* that the researcher could use to support guesses about

children's communicative intentions. Reading MacLure (1981) has persuaded me that it is the display of interpretations by both child and adult that puts meaning into the system in the first place.

2. See E. Bridges (1951: 36) for an account of how ostensive definition can fail even between adults. He gives a very plausible explanation for how two places in South America came to bear as their names, on our maps, Yahgan expressions that signified 'I don't understand what you mean' and 'otter'.

3. Leopold (1949b: 119n) inveighs against 'the pernicious practice of too many authors to take nouns at face value at too early a stage'. This is certainly a hazard to beware of. Because a child's expression has a form that is based on an adult noun is no guarantee that it 'means' in the same way as an adult noun. Griffiths and Atkinson (1978) report a study of some children for whom *door* was initially an 'action word'.

4. The other contributors to redundancy are the restriction to the 'here-and-now' mentioned under constraint (5), and the existence of rituals before the onset of verbal language. See Bruner (1975a), Ferrier (1978) and Lock (1978) for the latter.

5. Clark's overall position has, in subsequent publications (e.g. 1979), been modified.

6. R is the child whose answers and questions, over a longer period of time than is represented in table 2, form the topic of Griffiths (1980). See that paper for details of data collection.

7. What become prototypes filed under a given 'label' and what expressions are acquired as 'labels' will depend also on the ways in which parents perform ostensive definition (Ninio 1980) and on their object-naming predilections (Anglin 1977: ch. 3).

8. Griffiths (1976: 122–31) suggested a combination of visual fourier analysis and mental holography as a possible mechanism for the comparison process, to avoid the postulation of a homunculus in the brain viewing the 'videotapes' and making the decisions about similarity.

9. Leopold (1949b: 103) says: 'the belief that any words have sharp, logical, unified, unvarying meanings in the developed language is a superstition which has been exposed for a long time, but which is slow to die'. Criterial attributes theories are a prime manifestation of this 'superstitition'.

10. The line that I am adopting in this paragraph derives from the notion of *natural kinds*, an idea that has been recently revived and revised in philosophy. See J. D. Fodor (1977) and Lyons (1981) for introductory explanation and further references.

14. Early syntax

* I am grateful to Susan Fischer, Michael Forman, Robert Hsu, Jacquelyn Schachter, and the editors of this volume for their comments and suggestions on an earlier version of this chapter.

1. In the context of language acquisition, the notion of modularity refers to a capacity (or set of capacities) of the human mind that has specifically evolved

to deal with language, and which is quite separate from other cognitive capacities. (See Chomsky 1980a: 28, 40–6.) Since, however, the kinds of abilities that concern us here, namely hypothesis making and testing, seem to be available for both language acquisition and other kinds of cognitive development, it does not really matter for the purposes of this chapter whether or not these processes spring from a separate 'module' of the brain. Therefore I feel no need to take a stand on the degree of modularity of these particular processes.

2. Evidence for this strategy abounds in the acquisition of English, where stressed syllables are word-internal (see, for instance the discussion in Gleitman and Wanner 1982: 17–21). Evidence for such a strategy is even more remarkable in the acquisition of languages where morpheme boundaries and syllable boundaries fail to coincide much of the time. In such languages (e.g. Quiché Mayan as reported in Pye 1983, or Mohawk as reported in Mithun 1982) the strategy of extracting stressed syllables often leaves the child with a linguistic unit that is meaningless in the adult language, since it contains only the final part of one morpheme and the initial part of another. Nevertheless, children acquiring these languages seem to be able to build outward from these extracted syllables and move into the adult morphological system. For more discussion of the possible effects of language structure on early language learning strategies, see Peters (1981).

3. My discussion here is restricted to observation about English, which is a morphologically poor language in which word order is extremely important. In languages with richer morphological systems, where word order is used as a means of indicating pragmatic focus rather than sentential relations, first combinations may be of morphemes rather than words (see Burling 1973; Slobin 1982).

4. It is interesting to note that the use of this strategy has also been observed in morphologically more complex languages, where the units being combined are morphemes rather than words. For instance, Slobin and Aksu (1980: 10) state that in Turkish, 'at very early stages of development (below age 2;6 or so), verbs are sometimes pronounced with extra meaningless syllables between the stem and the final person-number affixes. Early on, it seems that the child attempts to retain some rhythmic picture of complex verbs, uncomprehendingly inserting [syllables] that sound like passive and causative particles.'

5. The units to be juxtaposed can consist of more than one adult word. See R. Clark (1974, 1977), and Peters (1983) for examples and discussion.

6. Although Hill presents neither a discussion of criteria for recognizing Claire's utterance boundaries, nor any kind of detailed prosodic evidence for the presence or absence of such boundaries, she does state (p. 28) that 'I relied very heavily on intonation for the process of transcription . . . Sentence boundaries were . . . clear from her intonation.' Lacking more precise prosodic evidence, we must view Hill's claims about utterance boundaries as suggestions which need further substantiation.

7. A fourth hypothesis for the basis of early classification is that the child becomes aware of functional roles such as topic and comment (see Bates and MacWhinney 1982).

15. Assessing morphological development

1. It is also common for words of one form class (such as nouns) to be directly adapted for use as members of a different class (such as verbs), as in the case of *(the) salt* versus *(to) salt*. Such part-of-speech 'conversions' can also be viewed as derivations, albeit without the use of any overt morphological marker ('zero derivation').

2. See Householder (1971: 21), who notes our lack of evidence on the extent to which language use is in fact rule-governed, and Bolinger (1976), who provides several indications that the amount of generalization may be far less than most contemporary linguists have been wont to think.

3. Some of the younger children, however, did show a certain tendency to be unduly influenced by a very high similarity along just one of these dimensions, whether semantic (as in the case of *puppy–dog*) or phonetic (*bashful–bash* and *eerie–ear*).

4. Note that the word *cookie* does not denote a 'diminutive cook', as the form might suggest, but rather a 'thing cooked'; this meaning, however, is inconsistent with the form, as the *-ie* suffix is appended to noun roots in English, not to verb roots.

5. The extended duration of this gap, so close on the heels of Berko's very promising start, can only be explained in terms of the need to accommodate the once highly-acclaimed 'Chomskian revolution' in linguistics, during which time interest in that field was sharply diverted from any temptation to become involved in experimental psycholinguistic investigation by a renewed, near-total preoccupation with philosophical debate and with purely formal considerations for grammar evaluation – and by the attendant willingness of a few influential psychologists to follow the linguists' misdirected theoretical lead during this period (see Derwing 1973, 1979a for details). It is still a useful object lesson to reflect now on how little of the results of the wanton theorizing engaged in during this period are any longer seriously entertained today, even by generative grammarians (who, with little change in their methods, have by now moved on to almost completely new worlds of imaginative speculation, apparently unmoved by the abysmal failure of the many strong claims so rashly advanced the last time around). Incidentally, the generative grammarians' focus on syntactic description also had the effect of putting even the formal descriptive treatment of morphology on the back burner for about as long a time (Aronoff 1976).

6. Early research was limited to these six constructions on the grounds that available samples of spontaneous child speech suggested that they were the only ones that occurred with sufficient frequency to afford any prospect of rule learning by preschoolers.

7. The sixth, 'diminutive' construction was only marginally productive for even the oldest group (including the adults), but this particular finding was undoubtedly the result of a faulty stimulus frame and should not be taken seriously (see Derwing 1976 for details).

8. The derivationally unmarked denominal verb construction (see note 1) must now also be considered as a strong candidate for this honour.

9. Observe that having a convenient label for this phenomenon does not in itself come to terms with the challenge that Brown formulated as follows: '[W]e do not presently have evidence that there are selection pressures of any kind operating on children to impel them to bring their speech into line with adult models' (1973: 412). The question is not *whether* the child abandons his own forms in favour of the adult ones (we know that this happens, at least in general), but just *why* he does so. One possible answer might, of course, involve relating this linguistic issue to some more general tendency on the part of the child to 'conform' socially, but for all the *prima facie* plausibility and intuitive appeal of such a view, the fact remains that (to our knowledge) no such connection has yet been demonstrated empirically.

10. Consonant clusters do, of course, make a difference, and many more variables enter the picture, as well, than can possibly be treated here, even in summary fashion. For brief descriptions of what (relatively small) portions of this research have been reported so far, see especially Derwing and Baker (1977, 1979b; a full treatment will appear in Derwing and Baker in preparation).

11. Despite the implication apparently suggested here, this particular (tentative) conclusion should not be taken to indicate our belief that representation in the mental lexicon and synthesis by rule must necessarily be mutually exclusive sources for a form (as intended by most generative accounts). Quite the contrary, we see good reasons for positing *both* a memory store and a (potential) rule source for many word forms (in humans as well as in practical computer models).

12. In fact, MacWhinney (like E. V. Clark 1982) actually opts for an intervening stage of 'analogy' (based on isolated word comparisons) between a purely rote 'amalgam' period and the stage at which the child begins to learn more general 'rules'. In our own work, however, we have used the terms 'analogy' and 'rule' as terminological equivalents and speak simply of the learning of rules (or the drawing of analogies) of greater or lesser degrees of generality, on the grounds that both appear to be based on the same fundamental notion, namely, the child's extraction of various kinds of true surface generalizations (see Derwing 1973: 200ff for a fuller characterization, and Derwing and Baker 1977 for a rule taxonomy based upon it). Since little more than a terminological issue seems to be at stake, we shall therefore persist in our former usage here.

13. A related observation that practically leaps out of the literature is the long overdue need for a new, up-to-date frequency count of children's speech (with form class labels supplied for once, as long as we are at it), for we find that counts made well over half a century ago continue to be relied on for data of this kind (Derwing and Baker 1977: 96; Clark and Hecht 1982: 9).

14. Though Brown carries through with the use of the MLU in his own work (1973: 270–3), it is widely known that this device introduces significant new problems of its own and affords few real advantages, particularly insofar as the fine details of morphological development are concerned (see especially, Crystal 1974; Griffiths 1974b).

15. Clark and Hecht (1982) attempt a similar analysis based on performance groups for derivational forms, but then mysteriously revert to their original age-based framework in reporting their results (p. 14).

16. In this study, a response was judged 'correct' (for purposes of comparison only) if it conformed to the predictions of one or another of the various formulations for the presumed 'regular rule' for the plurals (i.e. /-ɪz/ after stem-final sibilants, /-s/ after voiceless non-sibilants, and /-z/ elsewhere).

17. Tense and aspect

* Research contributing to this chapter was supported by NSF grant No. BNS 8121133 and the Kościuszko Foundation. A short version of this paper was presented at the 15th Annual Meeting of Societas Linguistica Europaea in Athens, 1982. I would like to thank the following people for going out of their way to share information about their child language data with me: Ruth Berman, Patricia Clancy, Mary Erbaugh, Ruth Miller, Ursula Stephany, Dan Slobin and Jorma Toivainen.

1. Ruth Miller (personal communication) has changed her position somewhat. Miller points out that some situations involve a past process and a present moment end-state which are related by an effectual relationship. This relationship is not an abstract temporal sequence but a necessarily asymmetrical sequence. Miller argues that the development of a deictic tense relationship is mediated by the concrete effectual relationship existing between a past process and resulting end-state.
2. Berman (personal communication) has found that activity verbs with general usage such as the general motion verb *la-lexet* 'to go', the general action verb *la-asot* 'to do/make' as well as other general usage verbs such as the transfer-of-location verbs *la-tet* 'to give' and *la-sim* 'to put' were used in the past as well as other tenses and nonfinite forms. However, some activity verbs such as *sixek* 'play' and *baxa* 'cry' did not occur in the past during the age period from 1;9 to 2;0.
3. I thank Dan Slobin for his translation of this section of Gvozdev (1961: 424–7).
4. The process of creolization is relevant to language acquisition since children are inventing a language in the context of parents who do not speak the Creole. On the issue of aspect, Muysken (1981) argues that Bickerton has oversimplified matters and 'we often find the perfective/imperfective or completive/incompletive distinction in the aspectual system, next to, or instead of, the punctual/nonpunctual distinction' (p. 197). According to Bickerton (1981) nonpunctual means 'progressive-durative plus habitual-iterative'. Hence, particles like *a* in Guyanese Creole and *stei* in Hawaiian Creole English code the property nonpunctual, and in some Creole languages, e.g. Jamaican Creole, *a* has a purely continuative meaning (Bailey 1966). If the properties durative and/or iterative are part of the fundamental tense–modality–aspect (TMA) system of Creole languages, then the Creole system differs from the child language system. If these properties are not part of the basic Creole TMA system, then Creole languages, like child languages, specify the properties completive and/or continuative in the aspectual component of the TMA system, i.e. the properties completive and continuative are at the 'roots of language'.
5. The acquisition of 'perfect' forms will depend in part on how they are integrated

into the overall tense–aspect system. In German, for example, where the perfect is the most general (or the only) past form, the perfect emerges first in child German (without the auxiliary) prior to the simple past form (see Mills 1985).

18. Modality

1. Nina$_1$ is reported to have made a similar distinction between *can* and *could*, referring to her own ability and to the ability of others, respectively. Illocutionary force should be taken into consideration here, however. The use of *could* to refer to the ability of others may follow from the common way of making directives more polite by employing the past form of *can* in standard as well as in child American English. Some of Nina's examples of *could* cited by Shepherd (1981: 93f) are conditional.

19. Deixis

* I am grateful to many friends and colleagues who have had a direct hand in some part or other of the contents of this chapter, especially Jane Breekveldt and Michael Garman; also, to the Australian Research Grants Scheme for support. This chapter was revised while visiting the Max-Planck Institut für Psycholinguistik, Nijmegen. I am grateful to Eve Clark, Wolfgang Klein, Suzanne Romaine, Lee Ann Weeks and Jim Wertsch for comments. However, only I should be blamed for it.
1. I am grateful to Toni Cross for making her videotapes available to me for re-analysis.

20. A crosslinguistic perspective: morphology and syntax

1. Discussion here devolves on research aimed at comparing data from children learning two or more languages, rather than on studies of isolated languages which happen to be other than English. I also disregard for present purposes studies concerned primarily with linguistic universals in the sense of the abstract, formal principles underlying the class of possible grammars for natural languages. The view taken here is closer to the approach espoused by scholars such as Comrie (1981b), for whom the study of language universals is anchored in detailed comparative investigation of as rich and diverse a database as possible.
2. Studies on which such generalizations are based can be found, for instance, in the collections of Bar-Adon and Leopold (1971) and of Ferguson and Slobin (1973). A more cohesive set of studies, organized largely around a common set of guiding questions, e.g. typical errors, error-free acquisitions, precocious and delayed acquisitions, is provided by the chapters in Slobin (1985b) on the acquisition of English, French and other Romance languages, German, Hebrew, Hungarian, Japanese, Kaluli, Polish, Samoan, and Turkish. Yet in this context, too, most chapters rely on very mixed data sources, including

laboratory-type experiments as well as naturalistic diary studies and a range of intermediate types of elicitation and interview procedures.

3. The term 'phase' is used here in a sense close to that of Karmiloff-Smith (1983) – as referring to generalized, recurrent processes which characterize how children interact with different problems across different domains (including language), and at various ages. A developmental perspective such as the one I take here is thus very different from that of scholars concerned primarily with language acquisition in relation to general linguistic theory and the formal properties of end-state grammars. Such an orientation would favour focusing on the formal properties of structures and properties which remain invariant across development in different cognitive domains, including the grammar of natural languages (as proposed, for instance, in Keil 1981).

4. Hebrew forms are cited in this chapter in a way that retains English-like orthography wherever possible. Thus what is here written as *ts* is more usually represented by *c*; *ch* is used here instead of *x* (the voiceless velar fricative) as in *Bach*, and *sh* instead of *š* (for the voiceless postalveolar fricative) as in *bush*. Additionally, the apostrophe ' represents a glottal stop.

5. These differences entail no claim as to whether certain tasks or acquisition in general are facilitated by one rather than another type of native tongue. We return to this in section 4.

6. This ordering in terms of relative productivity for both sets of devices is intuitive and tentative. On the difficulty of characterizing what constitutes a *productive* mechanism for speakers in general, and for language-learning children particularly, see Clark and Berman (1984).

7. Other, more clinically oriented measures which have been adapted for use with Hebrew-speaking children are the Fluharty (1974) screening test (Rom, Berman and Guralnik in preparation) and the language assessment and sampling procedure adapted from Crystal, Fletcher and Garman (1976), as described in Berman, Rom and Hirsch (1982).

8. These ideas have been critically influenced by working with Dan Slobin and other colleagues in the following contexts: a seminar on crosslinguistic child language studies held at the Linguistic Institute at the University of New Mexico, July–August 1980; workshops on language acquisition held at the Max-Planck Institut für Psycholinguistik, Nijmegen, Holland, August–September 1981 and June–July 1984; and a project funded by the United States-Israel Binational Science Foundation for examining the development of tense–aspect in Hebrew-speaking children, currently underway at Tel Aviv University. Neither Slobin nor his and my other associates are to be held responsible for details of the claims made here, however.

21. Some fundamental aspects of language development after age 5

* This revised chapter was prepared during one of the author's sojourns at the Max-Planck Institut für Psycholinguistik, Nijmegen. Their facilities are most gratefully acknowledged. I should also like to thank Dr Hilary Johnson for her assistance with the literature search.

23. Language acquisition and writing

1. 'To write' here means to compose a written text, not to form letter shapes and spell words. The argument of this chapter, that the grammatical structures of writing differ from those of speech, applies regardless of the instrument used to record them – be it pen, wordprocessor or Braille typewriter.
2. There are a very few reported instances of deaf or language-disordered children who acquire some competence in writing before they are able to communicate through speech or signing, but these are highly exceptional.
3. I am very grateful to Robin Fawcett and Michael Perkins for allowing me to make extensive use of their large corpus of data. An explanation of their conventions of transcription is given on pp. xi–xii of the introduction in each of their four volumes of transcripts.
4. I am indebted to Richard Handscombe and to the Nuffield Foundation for their permission to quote from this corpus and from the parallel collections of children's writing.
5. 'T-unit' is an abbreviation of 'minimal terminable syntactic unit', a term coined by Hunt (1965) to label a main clause and any subordinate clauses attached to it. Loban uses the term 'communication unit'.
6. I am most grateful to Barry Kroll and Gordon Wells for supplying me with copies of their unpublished written texts and for allowing me to quote from them. Their account of this phase of the Bristol project appears in Kroll and Wells (1983).
7. As the children are not individually identified, and as most of them provided writing on several different topics, it is not possible to be certain how many were responsible for the 48 pieces of writing selected. The minimum figure given is derived from the school and section code that labels each piece.

Bibliography (and citation index)

Note: Publications with up to three authors are listed in alphabetical order; publications with four or more authors follow, in *chronological* order.

Adams, N. 1972. Unpublished phonological diary of son Philip from 1;7 to 2;3. p. 226

Adlam, D. S. 1977. *Code in context.* London: Routledge and Kegan Paul. pp. 130, 131

Aitchison, J. 1972. Mini-malapropisms. *British Journal of Disorders of Communication* 7: 38–43. p. 249

    and Chiat, S. 1981. Natural phonology or natural memory? The interaction between phonological processes and recall mechanisms. *Language and Speech* 24: 311–26. p. 249

    and Straf, M. 1981. Lexical storage and retrieval: a developing skill? *Linguistics* 19: 751–95. p. 249

Aksu, A. A. 1978. Aspect and modality in the child's acquisition of the Turkish past tense. Unpublished doctoral dissertation, University of California, Berkeley. pp. 359, 361, 364, 366, 395

    and Slobin, D. I. 1985. Acquisition of Turkish. In Slobin (1985b). pp. 443, 444

Alegria, J., Pignot, E. and Morais, J. 1982. Phonetic analysis of speech codes in beginning readers. *Memory and Cognition* 10: 451–56. pp. 487, 493

Allen, G. D. 1983. Linguistic experience modifies lexical stress perception. *Journal of Child Language* 10. p. 191

    and Hawkins, S. 1978. The development of phonological rhythm. In A. Bell and J. B. Hooper (eds.) *Syllables and segments.* Amsterdam: North-Holland. p. 191

    1980. Phonological rhythm: definition and development. In G. H. Yeni-Komshian, J. F. Kavanagh and C. A. Ferguson (eds.) *Child phonology,* vol. 1. *Production.* New York: Academic Press. p. 191

Amidon, A. and Carey, P. 1972. Why five-year-olds cannot understand *before* and *after. Journal of Verbal Learning and Verbal Behavior* 11: 417–23. p. 424

Ammon, M. S. and Slobin, D. I. 1979. A cross-linguistic study of the processing of causative sentences. *Cognition* 7: 1–17. p. 430

Andersen, E. 1977. Learning to speak with style: a study of the sociolinguistic skills of children. Unpublished dissertation, Stanford University. pp. 23, 28

    and Johnson, C. E. 1973. Modifications in the speech of an eight-year-old to younger children. *Stanford Occasional Papers in Linguistics* 3: 149–60. p. 71

Anderson, H. 1973. Abductive and deductive change. *Language* 49: 735–93. p. 249

Anderson, J. R. 1982. Acquisition of cognitive skill. *Psychological Review* 89: 369–406. p. 475

535

Andersen, S. R. 1974. *The organization of phonology*. New York: Academic Press. p. 333

Angiolillo, C. and Goldin-Meadow, S. 1982. Experimental evidence for agent–patient categories in child language. *Journal of Child Language* 9: 627–43. p. 342

Anglin, J. M. 1977. *Word, object, and conceptual development*. New York: Norton. pp. 295, 296, 298, 300, 301, 302, 306, 526n

Anschen, F. and Aronoff, M. 1981. Morphological productivity and phonological transparency. *Canadian Journal of Linguistics* 26: 63–72. p. 333

Antinucci, F. and Miller, R. 1976. How children talk about what happened. *Journal of Child Language* 3: 167–89. pp. 359, 361, 370

Argyle, M. 1975. *Bodily communication*. London: Methuen. p. 174

Arnold, L. 1975. *Word analysis skills in retarded readers*. Unpublished BA honors thesis, University of New England. p. 476

Aronoff, M. 1976. *Word formation in generative grammar*. Cambridge, Mass.: MIT Press. p. 528n

Aslin, R. N. and Pisoni, D. B. 1980a. Effects of early linguistic experiences on speech discrimination by infants: a critique of Eilers *et al*. 1979. *Child Development* 57: 107–12. p. 260

    1980b. Some developmental processes in speech perception. In G. H. Yeni-Komshian, J. F. Kavanagh and C. A. Ferguson (eds.) *Child phonology*, vol. 2. New York: Academic Press. pp. 172, 203, 260

Aslin, R. N., Pisoni, D. B. and Jusczyk, P. W. 1983. Auditory development and speech perception in infancy. In M. Haith and J. Campos (eds.) *Infancy and the biology of development*, vol. II of *Carmichael's manual of child psychology*, 4th edn. New York: Wiley. p. 220

Atkinson, K., MacWhinney, B. and Stoel, C. 1970. An experiment on the recognition of babbling. *Stanford Papers and Reports on Child Language Development* 1: 71–6. pp. 180, 261

Atkinson, M. 1979. Prerequisites for reference. In E. Ochs and B. B. Schieffelin (eds.) *Developmental pragmatics*. New York: Academic Press. p. 288

    1982. *Explanations in the study of child language development*. Cambridge: Cambridge University Press. pp. 98, 104, 289, 295, 415

    1983. FLATs and SHARPs: the role of the child in language acquisition research. In J. Durand (ed.) A Festschrift for Peter Wexler: *University of Essex Department of Language and Linguistics Occasional Papers:* 27. p. 90

    and Griffiths, P. 1973. Here's *here's, there's, here* and *there*. *Edinburgh Working Papers in Linguistics* 3: 29–73. p. 401

Atkinson-King, K. 1973. Children's acquisition of phonological stress contrasts. *UCLA Working Papers in Phonetics* 25. pp. 184, 191, 524

Babiniotis, G. and Kondos, P. 1967. *Sugkronike grammatike tes koines neas ellenikes: theoria, askeseis*. Athens. p. 378

Baddeley, A. D. and Hitch, G. J. 1974. Working memory. In G. H. Bower (ed.) *The psychology of learning and motivation* vol. III. New York and London: Academic Press. p. 485

Badry, F. 1983. Acquisition of lexical derivation rules in Moroccan Arabic. Unpublished doctoral dissertation, University of California, Berkeley. p. 439

Bailey, B. 1966. *Jamaican Creole syntax*. Cambridge: Cambridge University Press. p. 530n

Baker, C. L. 1979. Syntactic theory and the projection problem. *Linguistic Inquiry* 10: 533–81. pp. 98, 104, 106

1981. Learnability and the English auxiliary system. In Baker and McCarthy (1981). p. 98

and McCarthy, J. (eds.) (1981). *The logical problem of language acquisition*. Cambridge, Mass.: MIT Press. p. 68

Baker, W. J. and Derwing, B. L. 1982. Response coincidence analysis as evidence for language acquisition strategies. *Applied Psycholinguistics* 3: 193–221. pp. 332, 337

Baldie, B. I. 1976. The acquisition of the passive voice. *Journal of Child Language* 3: 331–48. p. 458

Bar-Adon, A. and Leopold, W. F. (eds.) 1971. *Child language: a book of readings*. Englewood-Cliffs, NJ: Prentice-Hall. p. 531n

Baran, J. A., Laufer, M. Z. and Daniloff, R. 1977. Phonological contrastivity in conversation: a comparative study of voice onset time. *Journal of Phonetics* 5: 339–50. p. 247

Barblan, I. In preparation. Facile à voir? Vers l'analyse des conditions de réalisation de l'apprentissage d'une structure syntaxique complexe par l'enfant. Unpublished doctoral dissertation, University of Geneva. pp. 457, 473

Bard, E. G. and Anderson, A. H. 1983. The unintelligibility of speech to children. *Journal of Child Language* 10: 265–92. p. 247

Barnes, S. B., Gutfreund, M., Satterly, D. J. and Wells, C. G. 1983. Characteristics of adult speech which predict children's language development. *Journal of Child Language* 10: 65–84. pp. 76, 81, 113, 134, 136

Baron, N. 1977. *Language acquisition and historical change*. Amsterdam: North-Holland. p. 440

Barrett, M. D. 1978. Lexical development and overextension in child language. *Journal of Child Language* 5: 205–19. pp. 296, 297, 301, 305

1982a. Distinguishing between prototypes: the early acquisition of the meaning of object names. In S. A. Kuczaj (1982). pp. 295, 296, 297, 301, 305

1982b. The holophrastic hypothesis. *Cognition* 11: 47–76. p. 40

Barton, D. P. 1976. The role of perception in the acquisition of speech. Unpublished PhD thesis, University of London. pp. 201, 206

1980. Phonemic perception in children. In G. H. Yeni-Komshian, J. F. Kavanagh and C. A. Ferguson (eds.) *Child phonology*, vol. 2. New York: Academic Press. pp. 201, 262

Bates, E. 1971. The development of conversational skill in 2, 3 and 4 year olds. Unpublished Masters thesis, University of Chicago. (Reprinted in *Pragmatics Microfiche* 1975, 1(2), Cambridge University). p. 391

1975. Peer relations and the acquisition of language. In M. Lewis and L. A. Rosenblum (eds.) *Friendship and peer relations: the origins of behaviour*, vol. III. Chichester: Wiley. p. 83

1976. *Language and context: the acquisition of pragmatics.* New York: Academic Press. pp. 17, 74, 162, 391, 393, 394, 397, 402

1979. *The emergence of symbols.* New York: Academic Press. p. 38

and MacWhinney, B. 1982. Functionalist approaches to grammar. In Wanner and Gleitman (1982). pp. 446, 527n

Bates, E., MacWhinney, B., Caselli, C., Devescove, S., Natale, F. and Vanza, V. 1984. Cross-linguistic study of the development of sentence interpretation strategies. *Child Development* 55: 341–54. pp. 430, 442

Bellinger, D. 1979. Changes in the explicitness of mothers' directives as children age. *Journal of Child Language* 6: 443–58. p. 79

1980. Consistency in the pattern of change in mothers' speech: some discriminant analyses. *Journal of Child Language* 7: 469–87. p. 79

Bellugi, U. 1967. The acquisition of negation. Unpublished doctoral dissertation, Harvard University. p. 389

1971. Simplification in children's language. In R. Huxley and E. Ingram (eds.) *Language acquisition: models and methods.* New York: Academic Press. pp. 386, 389

1974. Some aspects of language acquisition. In T. A. Sebeok (ed.) *Current trends in linguistics,* vol. XII. The Hague: Mouton. p. 386

Benedict, H. 1979. Early lexical development: comprehension and production. *Journal of Child Language* 6: 183–200. pp. 279, 281, 291, 312

Benveniste, E. 1966. *Problèmes de linguistique générale.* Paris: Gallimard. p. 340

Berko, J. 1958. The child's learning of English morphology. *Word* 14: 150–77. pp. 330, 333, 334

Berko-Gleason, J. and Weintraub, S. 1978. Input language and the acquisition of communicative competence. In K. Nelson (ed.) *Children's language,* vol. I. New York: Gardner Press. p. 288

Berman, R. A. 1978. Early verbs: comments on how and why a child acquires her first words. *International Journal of Psycholinguistics* 5: 21–39. p. 433

1980. Child language as evidence for grammatical description: preschoolers' construal of transitivity in the verb system of Hebrew. *Linguistics* 18: 667–701. p. 441

1981a. Regularity vs. anomaly: the acquisition of Hebrew inflectional morphology. *Journal of Child Language* 8: 265–82. p. 334

1981b. Language development and language knowledge: evidence from the acquisition of Hebrew morphophonology. *Journal of Child Language* 8: 609–26. pp. 334, 439

1982. Verb-pattern alternation: the interface of morphology, syntax and semantics in the Hebrew child language. *Journal of Child Language* 9: 169–91. pp. 334, 441

1983a. Establishing a schema: children's construals of verb-tense marking. *Language Sciences* 5: 61–78. pp. 438, 444

1983b. From non-analysis to productivity: interim schemata in child language. Paper presented to the Tel-Aviv Workshop on Human Development: Stage and Structure, Tel-Aviv University, October. pp. 432, 436

1984. Cross-linguistic first language perspectives on second language acquisition

research. In R. Anderson (ed.) *Second languages*. Rowley, Mass.: Newbury House. pp. 438, 442, 445

1985a. A step-by-step model of language acquisition. In I. Levin (ed.) *Stage and structure: reopening the debate*. Norwood NJ: Ablex. p. 366

1985b. Acquisition of Hebrew. In Slobin (1985b). pp. 359, 432, 443, 444

1986. Cognitive components of language development. In C. Pfaff (ed.) *First and second language acquisition processes*. Rowley, Mass.: Newbury House. p. 435

and Sagi, Y. 1981. Word-formation processes and lexical innovations of young children. *Hebrew Computational Linguistics Bulletin* 18: 36–62 (in Hebrew). pp. 439, 441

Berman, R. A., Rom, A. and Hirsch, A. 1982. Working with HARSP: Hebrew adaptation of the LARSP language assessment, remediation and screening procedure. Tel-Aviv University internal publication, February. p. 532n

Bernstein, B. 1960. Language and social class. *British Journal of Sociology* 11: 261–76. p. 128

1965. A sociolinguistic approach to social learning. In J. Gould (ed.) *Penguin survey of the social sciences*. Harmondsworth: Penguin Books. p. 128

1971. *Class, codes and control*, vol. I. London: Routledge and Kegan Paul. pp. 110, 128, 129

Bernstein, N. E. 1982. An acoustic study of mothers' speech to language-learning children: an analysis of vowel articulation characteristics. Unpublished doctoral dissertation, Boston University. p. 247

Berthoud, I and Sinclair, H. 1978. L'expression d'éventualités et de conditions chez l'enfant. *Archives de Psychologie* 179: 205–33. p. 393

Berwick, R. C. 1981. Computational analogues of constraints on grammars: a model for the acquisition of syntactic knowledge. In J. Pustejovsky and V. Burke (eds.) Markedness and learnability. *University of Massachusetts Occasional Papers in Linguistics* 6. p. 103

and Weinberg, A. J. 1982. Parsing efficiency, computational complexity and the evaluation of grammatical theories. *Linguistic Inquiry* 13: 165–91. p. 94

1983. *The grammatical basis of linguistic performance: language use and acquisition*. Cambridge, Mass.: MIT Press. p. 103

Besner, D. and Coltheart, M. 1979. Ideographic and alphabetic processing in skilled reading of English. *Neuropsychologia* 17: 467–72. p. 479

Bever, T. G. 1961. Prelingual behavior: a systematic analysis and comparison of early vocal and general development. BA honors thesis, Harvard University. p. 149

1970. The cognitive basis for linguistic structures. In J. R. Hayes (ed.) *Cognition and the development of language*. New York: Wiley. p. 458

Bickerton, D. 1975. *Dynamics of a Creole system*. Cambridge: Cambridge University Press. p. 364

1981. *Roots of language*. Ann Arbor, Mich.: Karoma. pp. 364, 380, 433, 530n

Bickhard, M. 1980a. On models of knowledge and communication. In M. Hickmann (ed.) *Proceedings of a working conference on the social foundations of language and thought*. Chicago: Center for Psychosocial Studies. p. 20

1980b. *Cognition, convention, and communication.* New York: Praeger. p. 20

Biemiller, A. 1970. The development of the use of graphic and contextual information as children learn to read. *Reading Research Quarterly* 6: 75–96. p. 491

Bissex, G. L. 1980. *Gnys at wrk: a child learns to write and read.* Cambridge, Mass.: Harvard University Press. pp. 476, 477, 478, 481

Blasdell, R. and Jensen, P. 1970. Stress and word position as determinants of imitation in first-language learners. *Journal of Speech and Hearing Research* 13: 193–202. p. 191

Bloch, O. 1913. Notes sur le langage d'un enfant. *Mémoires de la Société Linguistique de Paris* 18: 37–59. pp. 227, 228, 232

Bloom, L. 1970. *Language development: form and function in emerging grammars.* Cambridge, Mass.: MIT Press. pp. 23, 38, 314, 315, 318, 387

1973. *One word at a time: the use of single word utterances before syntax.* The Hague: Mouton. pp. 39, 280, 283, 291, 292, 295, 298, 313, 314, 316

Bloom, L. 1974. Talking, understanding and thinking. In R. L. Schiefelbusch and L. L. Lloyd (eds.) *Language perspectives: acquisition, retardation and intervention.* London and Basingstoke: Macmillan; Baltimore, Md: University Park Press. p. 39

Bloom, L., Capatides, J. B. and Tackeff, J. 1981. Further remarks on interpretive analysis. *Journal of Child Language* 8: 403–11. p. 39

Bloom, L., Lifter, K. and Hafitz, J. 1980. Semantics of verbs and the development of verb inflection in child language. *Language* 56: 386–412. p. 359

Bloom, L., Lightbown, P. and Hood, L. 1975. *Structure and variation in child language.* Society for Research in Child Development Monographs 40. pp. 119, 310, 315, 317, 318

Bloom, L., Rocissano, L. and Hood, L. 1976. Adult–child discourse: developmental interaction between information processing and linguistic knowledge. *Cognitive Psychology* 8: 521–52. p. 39

Bloomfield, L. 1933. *Language.* New York: Holt, Rinehart and Winston. pp. 327, 328

Blount, B. G. 1977. Ethnography and caretaker–child interaction. In Snow and Ferguson (1977). p. 138

and Padgug, E. J. 1977. Prosodic, paralinguistic and interactional features in parent–child speech: English and Spanish. *Journal of Child Language* 4: 67–86. pp. 69, 192

Bock, J. K. and Hornsby, M. E. 1977. How children ask and tell: a speech act analysis of children's requests. *Stanford Papers and Reports on Child Language Development* 13: 72–82. p. 391

Bohannon, J. N. and Marquis, A. 1977. Children's control of adult speech. *Child Development* 48: 1002–8. p. 80

Bohannon, J. N., Stine, E. L. and Ritzenberg, D. 1982. The 'fine-tuning' hypothesis of adult speech to children: effects of experience and feedback. *Bulletin of the Psychonomic Society* 19 (4): 201–4. p. 80

Bolinger, D. L. 1964. Intonation as a universal. In *Proceedings of the IXth International Congress of Linguists, Boston, 1962.* The Hague: Mouton. p. 177

1972. Accent is predictable (if you're a mind-reader). *Language* 48: 633–44.
p. 176

1976. Meaning and memory. *Forum Linguisticum* 1: 1–14. p. 528n

Bonvillian, J. D., Raeburn, V. P. and Horan, E. A. 1979. Talking to children:
the effects of rate, intonation and length on children's sentence imitation.
Journal of Child Language 6: 459–67. p. 196

Bosma, J. F. 1972. Form and function in the infant's mouth and pharynx. In J. F.
Bosma (ed.) *Third Symposium on Oral Sensation and Perception: the mouth
of the infant.* Springfield, Ill.: Thomas, pp. 163, 164

1975. Anatomic and physiological development of the speech apparatus. In D. B.
Tower (ed.) *Human communication and its disorders,* vol. III. New York:
Raven Press. pp. 163, 167, 168

Bosma, J. F., Truby, H. M. and Lind, J. 1965. Cry motions of the newborn infant.
In J. Lind (ed.) *Newborn infant cry.* Acta Paed. Scan. Supplement. Uppsala:
Almquist and Wiksells. p. 163

Bower, T. 1974a. *Development in infancy.* San Francisco: Freeman. p. 36

1974b. Repetition in human development. *Merrill-Palmer Quarterly* 20: 303–18.
p. 35

Bowerman, M. 1973. *Early syntactic development: a cross-linguistic study with
special reference to Finnish.* Cambridge: Cambridge University Press. pp. 75,
402, 429

1974. Learning the structure of causative verbs: a study in the relationship of
cognitive, semantic, and syntactic development. *Stanford Papers and Reports
on Child Language Development* 8: 142–87. pp. 440, 441

1976. Semantic factors in the acquisition of rules for word use and sentence
construction. In D. M. Morehead and A. E. Morehead (eds.) *Normal and
deficient child language.* Baltimore, Md.: University Park Press. pp. 30, 41,
295, 298, 520n

1978a. The acquisition of word meaning: an investigation into some current
conflicts. In N. Waterson and C. E. Snow (eds.) *The development of
communication.* Chichester: Wiley. pp. 45, 296, 302, 521n

1978b. Systematizing semantic knowledge: changes over time in the child's
organization of word meaning. *Child Development* 49: 977–87. p. 306

1979. The acquisition of complex sentences. In P. Fletcher and M. Garman (eds.)
Language acquisition. 1st edn. Cambridge: Cambridge University Press. p. 457

1982a. Starting to talk worse. In S. Strauss (ed.) *U-shaped behavioral growth.*
New York: Academic Press. pp. 47, 473

1982b. Reorganization processes in lexical and syntactic development. In
Wanner and Gleitman (1982). pp. 68, 308, 473

1983. How do children avoid constructing an overly general grammar in the
absence of feedback about what is not a sentence? *Stanford Papers and
Reports on Child Language Development* 22, p. 68

Bradley, L. and Bryant, P. 1983. Categorising sounds and learning to read – a
causal connection. *Nature* 301: 419–21. p. 476

Brady, M. 1981. Towards a computational theory of early visual processing in
reading. *Visible Language* 15: 183–214. p. 477

Brady, S., Shankweiler, D. and Mann, V. 1983. Speech perception and memory coding in relation to reading ability. *Journal of Experimental Child Psychology* 35: 345–67. pp. 484, 485

Braine, M. D. S. 1959. The ontogeny of certain logical operations: Piaget's formulation examined by non-verbal methods. *Psychological Monographs: General and Applied* 73 (5). p. 12

1962. Piaget on reasoning: a methodological critique and alternative proposals. In W. Kessen and C. Kuhlman (eds.) *Thought in the young child.* Society for Research in Child Development Monographs 27. p. 12

1963. The ontogeny of English phrase structure: the first phase. *Language* 39: 1–14. p. 23

1976a. *Children's first word combinations.* Society for Research in Child Development Monographs 41. pp. 313, 314, 315, 316, 317, 321, 429, 520n

1976b. Review of N. V. Smith. *The acquisition of phonology. Language* 52: 489–98. pp. 146, 262

In press. Modeling the acquisition of linguistic structures. In Y. Levi and I. M. Schlesinger (eds.) *Perspectives on language acquisition theory.* p. 87

and Hardy, J. A. 1982. On what case categories there are, why they are, and how they develop. In Wanner and Gleitman (1982). p. 308

Brainerd, C. J. 1973. Judgements and explanations as criteria for the presence of cognitive structures. *Psychological Bulletin* 79: 172–79. p. 12

1978. The stage question in cognitive-development theory. *Behavioral and Brain Sciences* 1: 173–82. p. 162

Branigan, G. 1977. Some early constraints on word combinations. Unpublished doctoral thesis, Applied Psycholinguistics Program, Boston University. pp. 119, 203, 206, 211

1979. Some reasons why successive single word utterances are not. *Journal of Child Language* 6: 411–21. p. 316

Braun-Lamesch, M. M. 1972. *La comprehension du langage par l'enfant: la role des contextes.* Paris: Presses Universitaires de France. p. 46

Bresnan, J. W. 1971. Sentence stress and syntactic transformations. *Language* 47: 257–81. p. 176

1982a. Control and complementation. In Bresnan (1982b). p. 62

(ed.) 1982b. *The mental representation of grammatical relations.* Cambridge, Mass.: MIT Press.

and Kaplan, R. 1982. Grammars as mental representations of language. In Bresnan (1982b). p. 56

Bretherton, I., McNew, S., Snyder, L. and Bates, E. 1983. Individual differences at 20 months: analytic and holistic strategies in language acquisition. *Journal of Child Language* 10: 293–320. pp. 118, 125, 293, 317

Brice Heath, S. 1982. What no bedtime story means: narrative skills at home and school. *Language and Society* 11: 49–76. p. 138

Bridges, A. 1978. Directing two-year-olds' attention: some clues to understanding. *Journal of Child Language* 6: 211–26. p. 426

Bridges, E. L. 1951. *Uttermost part of the earth.* London: Readers Union. p. 526n

Briggs, P. and Underwood, G. 1982. Phonological coding in good and poor
    readers. *Journal of Experimental Child Psychology* 34: 93–112. pp. 484, 489
Brimer, M. A. and Dunn, L. 1963. *English Picture Vocabulary Test.* Slough:
    NFER. pp. 110, 111, 123
Broen, P. A. 1972. *The verbal environment of the language-learning child.*
    Monograph of the American Speech and Hearing Association 17, December.
    p. 70
Bronckart, J. P. and Sinclair, H. 1973. Time, tense and aspect. *Cognition* 2: 107–30.
    pp. 359, 425
Bronckart, J.-P. and Ventouras-Spycher, M. 1979. The Piagetian concept of
    representation and the Soviet-inspired view of self-regulation. In
    G. Zivin (ed.) *The development of self-regulation through private speech.* New
    York: Wiley. p. 17
Brown, H. D. 1971. Children's comprehension of relativized English sentences.
    Child Development 42: 1923–6. p. 458
Brown, R. 1958. How shall a thing be called? *Psychological Review* 65: 14–21.
    p. 44
    1973. *A first language: the early stages.* London: Allen and Unwin; Cambridge,
    Mass.: Harvard University Press. Also published 1976 by Penguin Books,
    Harmondsworth, Middx. pp. 23, 39, 57, 79, 110, 116, 117, 189, 292, 293, 309,
    313, 317, 318, 323, 326, 334, 342, 358, 359, 363, 385, 386, 388, 415, 417, 520n,
    529n
    1977. Introduction. In Snow and Ferguson (1977). p. 194
    and Bellugi, U. 1964. Three processes in the child's learning of syntax. *Language
    and learning* (special issue of *Harvard Educational Review*) 34: 133–51. p. 81
    and Hanlon, C. 1970. Derivational complexity and order of acquisition in child
    speech. In J. R. Hayes (ed.) *Cognition and the development of language.* New
    York: Wiley. pp. 76, 105
    and Hildum, D. O. 1956. Expectancy and the perception of syllables. *Language*
    32: 411–19. p. 206
Brown, R., Cazden, C. B. and Bellugi, U. 1969. The child's grammar from I to
    III. In J. P. Hill (ed.) *Minnesota symposium on child psychology*, vol. 2.
    Minneapolis: University of Minnesota Press. pp. 105, 117
Browne, A. 1982. Young children's attention to textual context when reading.
    Unpublished MA thesis, University of Manchester. p. 489
Bruner, J. 1975a. The ontogenesis of speech acts. *Journal of Child Language*
    2: 1–19. pp. 86, 181, 182, 183, 289, 526n
    1975b. From communication to language: a psychological perspective. *Cognition*
    3: 255–82. pp. 16, 340, 402
    1981. The social context of language acquisition. *Language and Communication*
    1: 2–3, 155–78. p. 16
    1983. *Child talk.* New York: Norton. pp. 403, 426
    and Hickmann, M. 1983. La conscience, la parole et la 'zone proximale':
    reflexions sur les théories de Vygotsky. In M. Deleau (ed.) *Le developpement
    de l'enfant: savoir faire et savoir dire* (collected writings of J. S. Bruner). Paris:
    Presses Universitaires de France. p. 16

Brunswik, E. 1956. *Perception and the representative design of psychological experiments*. Berkeley, Cal.: California University Press. pp. 35, 520n

Bryan, W. L. and Harter, N. 1897. Studies on the physiology and psychology of the telegraphic language. *Psychological Review* 4: 27–53. pp. 46, 475
1899. Studies on the telegraphic language. *Psychological Review* 6: 345–75. p. 475

Bühler, C. 1930. *The first year of life*, trans. P. Greenwood and R. Ripin. New York: John Day. pp. 292, 294

Buhr, R. 1980. The emergence of vowels in an infant. *Journal of Speech and Hearing Research* 23: 73–94. p. 154

Burgess, C., Cartland, L., Chambers, R., Hedgeland, J., Levine, N., Mole, J., Newsome, B., Smith, H. and and Torbe, M. 1973. *Understanding children writing*. Harmondsworth, Middx: Penguin Books. p. 500

Burling, R. 1959. Language development of a Garo and English-speaking child. *Word* 15: 45–68. pp. 363, 527n
1973. Language development of a Garo and English-speaking child. In Ferguson and Slobin (1973). p. 527

Bybee, J. L. and Slobin, D. I. 1982. Rules and schemas in the development and use of the English past. *Language* 58: 265–89. pp. 273, 333

Byrne, B. 1981. Deficient syntactic control in poor readers: is a weak phonetic memory code responsible? *Applied Psycholinguistics* 2: 201–12. p. 481
and Shea, P. 1979. Semantic and phonetic memory codes in beginning readers. *Memory and Cognition* 7: 333–38. pp. 476, 484

Calkins, L. M. 1980. Children learn the writer's craft. *Language Arts* 57: 207–13. p. 500

Cambon, J. and Sinclair, H. 1974. Relations between syntax and semantics: are they easy to see? *British Journal of Psychology* 65: 133–40. pp. 457, 458

Campbell, R. N. 1976. Propositions and early utterances. In G. Drachman (ed.) *Akten des 1. Salzburger Kolloquiums über Kindersprache*. Tübingen: Gunter Narr. pp. 39, 40
1981. Language acquisition, psychological dualism and the definition of pragmatics. In H. Parret, M. Sbisa and J. Verschueren (eds.) *Possibilities and limitation of pragmatics*. Amsterdam. Benjamins. p. 520n
1982. On Fodor on cognitive development. In B. de Gelder (ed.) *Knowledge and representation*. London: Routledge and Kegan Paul. p. 521n
and Bowe, T. 1977. Functional asymmetry in early language understanding. In G. Drachman (ed.) *Akten der 3. Salzburger Jahrestagung für Linguistik*. Salzburg: Wolfgang Neugebauer. p. 489
1978. Functional asymmetry in early child language. In G. Drachman (ed.) *Salzburger Beiträge sur Linguistik* 4. Salzburg: Wolfgang Neugebauer. p. 46
and Macdonald, T. B. 1983. Text and context in early language comprehension. In M. C. Donaldson, R. Grieve and C. Pratt (eds.) *Early childhood development and education*. Edinburgh: Grant McIntyre. p. 489

Campbell, R. N., Donaldson, M. C. and Young, B. M. 1976. Constraints on classificatory skills in young children. *British Journal of Psychology* 67: 89–100. p. 35

Canellada, M. J. 1970. Sobre linguaje infantil. *Filologia* 13: 39–47

Caprez, G., Sinclair, H. and Studer, B. 1971. Entwicklung der Passiveform im Schweizerdeutschen. *Archives de Psychologie* 41: 23–52. p. 458

Carey, S. 1982. Semantic development: the state of the art. In Wanner and Gleitman (1982). p. 433

Carlson, P. and Anisfeld, M. 1969. Some observations on the linguistic competence of a two-year-old child. *Child Development* 40: 569–75. pp. 185, 188

Carr, J. 1953. An investigation of the spontaneous speech sounds of five-year-old deaf-born children. *Journal of Speech and Hearing Disorders* 18: 22–9. p. 241

Carter, A. L. 1974. The development of communication in the sensorimotor period: a case study. Unpublished doctoral dissertation, University of California. pp. 282, 291, 292

  1979. Prespeech meaning relations: an outline of one infant's sensorimotor morpheme development. In P. Fletcher and M. Garman (eds.) *Language acquisition.* 1st edn. Cambridge: Cambridge University Press. p. 162, 282, 292

Cattell, P. 1940. *The measurement of intelligence in infants and young children.* New York: Psychological Corporation. p. 149

Cazden, C. 1965. Environmental assistance to the child's acquisition of grammar. Unpublished doctoral dissertation, Harvard University. p. 81

  1970. The neglected situation in child language research and education. *Journal of Social Issues* 25: 35–60. pp. 110, 120

Chaney, C. 1978. Production and identification of /j, w, r, l/ in normal and articulation impaired children. Unpublished doctoral thesis, Applied Psycholinguistics Program, Boston University. p. 214

Chang, H. and Trehub, S. 1977. Auditory processing of relational information by young infants. *Journal of Experimental Child Psychology* 24: 324–31. p. 179

Chapman, R. S. 1981. Mother–child interaction in the second year of life: its role in language development. In R. L. Schiefelbusch and D. Bricker (eds.) *Early language: acquisition and intervention.* Baltimore: University Park Press. pp. 78, 80, 194

Charney, R. 1979. The comprehension of 'here' and 'there'. *Journal of Child Language* 6: 69–80. pp. 405, 409, 411

  1980. Speech roles and the development of personal pronouns. *Journal of Child Language* 7: 509–28. pp. 274, 346, 352, 417

Cherry, L. 1975. Sex differences in child speech: McCarthy revisited. *Research Bulletin.* Princeton, NJ: Educational Testing Service. p. 122

Chervela, N. 1981. Medial consonant cluster acquisition by Telugu children. *Journal of Child Language* 8: 63–73. pp. 267, 268

Cheshire, J. 1982. Dialect features and linguistic conflict in schools. *Educational Review* 34: 53–67. p. 502

Chevalier-Skolnikoff, S., Galdikas, B. M. F. and Skolnikoff, A. Z. 1982. The adaptive significance of higher intelligence in wild orang-utans. *Journal of Human Evolution* 11: 639–52. p. 32

Chiat, S. 1978. The analysis of children's pronouns: an investigation into the prerequisites for linguistic knowledge. Unpublished doctoral dissertation, University of London. p. 35

  1979. The role of the word in phonological development. *Linguistics* 17: 591–610. pp. 263, 265

1981. Context-specificity and generalization in the acquisition of pronominal distinctions. *Journal of Child Language* 8: 75–91. pp. 339, 342, 347, 350, 417

1982. If I were you and you were me: the analysis of pronouns in a pronoun-reversing child. *Journal of Child Language* 9: 359–79. p. 352

Chomsky, C. 1969. *The acquisition of syntax in children from 5 to 10*. Cambridge, Mass.: MIT Press. pp. 57, 62, 196, 339, 346, 415, 457

Chomsky, N. 1963. Formal properties of grammars. In R. D. Luce, R. R. Bush and E. Galanter (eds.) *Handbook of mathematical psychology*, vol. II. New York and London: Wiley. p. 92

1964. Current issues in linguistic theory. In J. A. Fodor and J. J. Katz (eds.) *The structure of language: readings in the philosophy of language*. Englewood Cliffs, NJ: Prentice-Hall. p. 328

1965. *Aspects of the theory of syntax*. Cambridge, Mass.: MIT Press. pp. 39, 55, 71, 522n, 524n

1968. *Language and mind*. New York: Harcourt Brace Jovanovich. p. 39

1973. Conditions on transformations. In S. Anderson and P. Kiparsky (eds.) *Festschrift for Morris Halle*. New York: Holt, Rinehart and Winston. p. 97

1975. *Reflections on language*. New York: Pantheon; Glasgow: Fontana/Collins. pp. 30, 39, 55, 520n

1980a. *Rules and representations*. New York: Columbia University Press; Oxford: Blackwell. pp. 520n, 527n

1980b. Rules and representations. *Behavioral and Brain Sciences* 3: 1–61. pp. 30, 520n

1981a. *Lectures on government and binding*. Dordrecht, Holland: Foris Publications. pp. 62, 64

1981b. Markedness and core grammar. In A. Belletti, L. Bandi and L. Rizzi (eds.) *Theory of markedness in generative grammar. Proceedings of the 1979 GLOW conference*. Scuola Normale Superiore, Pisa. p. 64

1981c. Principles and parameters in syntactic theory. In Hornstein and Lightfoot (1981). p. 102

and Halle, M. 1968. *The sound pattern of English*. New York: Harper and Row. pp. 189, 192, 252, 477, 480

and Lasnik, H. 1977. Filters and control. *Linguistic Inquiry* 8: 425–504. p. 100

Clancy, P. M. 1985. Acquisition of Japanese. In Slobin (1985b). pp. 359, 366, 373

Clancy, P. M., Jacobsen, T. and Silva, N. 1976. The acquisition of conjunctions: cross-linguistic study. *Stanford Papers and Reports on Child Language Development* 12: 71–80. pp. 367, 369

Claparède, E. 1917. La psychologie de l'intelligence. *Scientia* 361–3. p. 37

1918. La conscience de la resemblance. *Archives de Psychologie* 17: 77ff. p. 37

Clark, E. V. 1969. Language acquisition: the child's spontaneous description of events in time. Unpublished doctoral dissertation, University of Edinburgh. p. 424

1970. How young children describe events in time. In G. B. Flores d'Arcais and W. J. M. Levelt (eds.) *Advances in psycholinguistics*. Amsterdam: North-Holland. p. 369

1971. On the acquisition of the meaning of *before* and *after*. *Journal of Verbal and Learning Behavior* 10: 266–75. p. 424

1973a. Non-linguistic strategies and the acquisition of word meaning. *Cognition*
2: 161–82. p. 417

1973b. What's in a word? On the child's acquisition of semantics in his first
language. In T. E. Moore (ed.) *Cognitive development and the acquisition of
language.* New York: Academic Press. pp. 295, 296, 297, 299, 429

1978. Awareness of language: Some evidence from what children say and do.
In A. Sinclair, R. J. Jarvella and W. J. M. Levelt (eds.) *The child's conception
of language.* Berlin: Springer Verlag. p. 28

1978b. From gesture to word: on the natural history of deixis in language
acquisition. In J. S. Bruner and A. Garton (eds.) *Human growth and
development.* London: Oxford University Press. pp. 340, 342, 352, 402, 408

1979. Building a vocabulary: words for object, actions, and relations. In
P. Fletcher and M. Garman (eds.) *Language acquisition.* 1st edn. Cambridge:
Cambridge University Press. p. 526n

1980. Here's the *top*: nonlinguistic strategies in the acquisition of orientational
terms. *Child Development* 51: 329–38. p. 418

1982. The young word maker: a case study of innovation in the child's lexicon.
In Wanner and Gleitman (1982a). pp. 330, 529n

1983. Meanings and concepts. In P. H. Mussen (Gen. ed.) *Carmichaels' manual
of child psychology,* vol. III. 4th edn. New York: Wiley. p. 433

1985. Acquisition of Romance, with special reference to French. In Slobin
(1985b). pp. 366, 367

and Berman, R. A. 1984. Structure and use in the acquisition of word-formation.
Language 60: 542–94. pp. 430, 439, 532n

and Garnica, O. K. 1974. Is he coming or going? On the acquisition of deictic
verbs. *Journal of Learning and Verbal Behavior* 13: 559–72. p. 420

and Hecht, B. F. 1982. Learning to coin agent and instrument nouns. *Cognition*
12: 1–24. pp. 273, 331, 430, 529n

and Sengul, C. 1978. Strategies in the acquisition of deixis. *Journal of Child
Language* 5: 457–75. pp. 405, 409

Clark, E. V., Hecht, B. F. and Mulford, R. C. In preparation. Coining complex
compounds. p. 473

Clark, H. H. 1973. Space, time, semantics and the child. In T. E. Moore (ed.)
Cognitive development and the acquisition of language. New York: Academic
Press. pp. 419, 423

and Clark, E. V. 1977. *Psychology and language: an introduction to
psycholinguistics.* New York: Harcourt Brace. pp. 40, 333

Clark, M. M. 1976. *Young fluent readers.* London: Heinemann. p. 476

Clark, R. 1974. Performing without competence. *Journal of Child Language*
1: 1–10. pp. 119, 315, 527n

1977. What's the use of imitation? *Journal of Child Language* 4: 341–58. pp. 119,
183, 315, 527n

Clark, R., Hutcheson, S. and Van Buren, P. 1974. Comprehension and production
in language acquisition. *Journal of Linguistics* 10: 39–54. p. 188

Clarke-Stewart, K. VanderStoep, L. and Killian, G. 1979. Analyses and replication
of mother–child relations at 2-years of age. *Child Development* 50: 777–93.
pp. 79, 80

Clements, G. N. 1976. Vowel harmony in nonlinear generative phonology. MS, Harvard University. p. 211
  and Keyser, S. J. 1983. *CV phonology: a generative theory of the syllable.* Cambridge, Mass.: MIT Press. pp. 204, 211
Clumeck, H. 1977. Studies in the acquisition of Mandarin. Unpublished doctoral dissertation, University of California, Berkeley. pp. 212
  1980. In G. H. Yeni-Komshian, J. F. Kavanagh and C. A. Ferguson (eds.) *Child phonology,* vol. I: *Production.* New York: Academic Press. pp. 185, 187
Cochrane, N. J. 1977. Verbal aspect and the semantic classification of verbs in Serbo-Croatian. Unpublished doctoral dissertation, University of Texas. p. 360
Cohen-Levine, S. and Carey, S. 1982. Up front: the acquisition of a concept of a word. *Journal of Child Language* 9: 645–57. p. 419
Coker, C. H., Umeda, N. and Browman, C. P. 1973. Automatic synthesis from ordinary English text. *IEEE Transactions on Audio and Electroacoustics* AU-21: 293–8. p. 248
Coker, P. L. 1978. Syntactic and semantic factors in the acquisition of *before* and *after. Journal of Child Language* 5: 261–77. pp. 369, 458
Cole, M. and Scribner, S. 1974. *Culture and thought: a psychological introduction.* New York: Wiley. p. 16
Cole, M., Gay, J., Glick, J. A. and Sharp, D. W. 1971. *The cultural context of learning and thinking.* New York: Basic Books. p. 16
Cole, M., Hood, L. and McDermott, R. 1978. Ecological nichepicking: ecological invalidity as an axiom of experimental cognitive psychology. Laboratory of Comparative Human Development, Rockefeller University. pp. 15, 16
Cole, R. A. 1981. Perception of fluent speech by children and adults. *Annals of The New York Academy of Sciences* 379: 92–109. p. 263
Comrie, B. 1976. *Aspect: an introduction to the study of verbal aspect and related problems.* Cambridge: Cambridge University Press. pp. 358, 360, 369
  1981a. On Reichenbach's approach to tense. *Papers from the Seventeenth Regional Meeting of the Chicago Linguistic Society.* pp. 356, 374
  1981b. *Language universals and linguistic typology: syntax and morphology.* Chicago: Chicago University Press. pp. 253, 531n
  1985. *Tense.* Cambridge: Cambridge University Press. pp. 356, 363, 374
Conrad, R. 1970. Short-term memory processes in the deaf. *British Journal of Psychology* 61: 179–95. p. 486
  1971. The effect of vocalizing on comprehension in the profoundly deaf. *British Journal of Psychology* 62: 147–50. p. 486
Cooley, C. H. 1908. A study of the early use of self-words by a child. *Psychological Review* 15: 339–57. p. 352
Corcoran, D. W. J. 1966. An acoustic factor in letter cancellation. *Nature* 210: 658. p. 478
Corrigan, R. 1978. Language development as related to stage 6 object permanence development. *Journal of Child Language* 5: 173–89. pp. 3, 312, 371
Cromer, R. F. 1968. The development of temporal reference during the acquisition of language. Unpublished doctoral dissertation, Harvard University. pp. 367, 397

1970. Children are nice to understand: surface structure clues for the recovery of deep structure. *British Journal of Psychology* 61 (3): 397–408. p. 457

1971a. The development of the ability to decenter in time. *British Journal of Psychology* 62: 353–65. pp. 372, 424

1971b. The development of temporal reference during acquisition of language. Prepared for T. G. Bever and W. Weksel (eds.) *The structure and psychology of language.* New York: Holt, Rinehart and Winston. p. 458

1972. The learning of surface structure clues to deep structure by a puppet show technique. *Quarterly Journal of Experimental Psychology* 24: 66–76. pp. 457, 473

1974. The development of language and cognition: the cognitive hypothesis. In B. Foss (ed.) *New perspectives in child language.* Harmondsworth, Middx: Penguin Books. pp. 369, 393, 394, 395, 397

1976a. The cognitive hypothesis of language acquisition and its implications for child language deficiency. In D. M. Morehead and A. E. Morehead (eds.) *Normal and deficient child language.* Baltimore, Md.: University Park Press. p. 30

1976b. Developmental strategies for learning. In V. Hamilton and M. D. Vernon (eds.) *The development of cognitive processes.* London and New York: Academic Press. pp. 30, 435, 460

Cross, T. G. 1977. Mother's speech adjustments: the contribution of selected child listener variables. In Snow and Ferguson (1977). pp. 78, 135, 403, 404

Cross, T. G. 1978. Mother's speech and its association with rate of linguistic development in young children. In N. Waterson and C. Snow (eds.) *The development of communication.* Chichester: Wiley. pp. 78, 80, 81, 135, 136

Cruttenden, A. 1970. A phonetic study of babbling. *British Journal of Disorders of Communication* 5: 110–17. p. 153

1974. An experiment involving comprehension of intonation in children from 7 to 10. *Journal of Child Language* 1: 221–31. pp. 196, 473

1981. Item-learning and system-learning. *Journal of Psycholinguistic Research* 10: 79–88. pp. 298, 300, 309

1985. Intonation comprehension in 10-year-olds. *Journal of Child Language* 12. p. 196

Crystal, D. 1969. *Prosodic systems and intonation in English.* Cambridge: Cambridge University Press. pp. 174, 178, 189, 193

1974. Review of R. Brown, *A first language. Journal of Child Language* 1: 289–306. pp. 110, 529

1975. *The English tone of voice.* London: Edward Arnold. pp. 174, 175, 176, 178, 179, 196

1980. Neglected grammatical factors in conversational English. In S. Greenbaum, G. Leech and J. Svartvik (eds.) *Studies in English linguistics for Randolph Quirk.* London: Longman. p. 507

1981. *Clinical linguistics.* Vienna: Springer Verlag. p. 196

Crystal, D., Fletcher, P. and Garman, M. 1976. *The grammatical analysis of language disability.* New York: Elsevier; London: Edward Arnold. pp. 318, 532n

Culicover, P. W. and Wexler, K. 1977. Some syntactic implications of the theory of language learnability. In P. W. Culicover, T. Wasow and A. Akmajian (eds.) *Formal syntax*. New York and London: Academic Press. p. 90

   and Watkins. 1984. *Locality in linguistic theory*. New York and London: Academic Press. p. 522n

Cullen, J. K., Fargo, N., Chase, R. A. and Baker, P. 1968. The development of auditory feedback monitoring, I: Delayed auditory feedback studies on infant cry. *Journal of Speech and Hearing Research* 11: 85–93. p. 243

Cutler, A. 1976. Phoneme-monitoring reaction time as a function of preceding intonation countour. *Perception and Psychophysics* 20: 55–60. p. 196

Davis, M. 1958. *Computability and unsolvability*. New York: McGraw Hill

Daneman, M. and Carpenter, P. A. 1980. Individual differences in working-memory and reading. *Journal of Verbal Learning and Verbal Behavior* 19: 450–66. p. 485

de Boysson-Bardies, B., Sagart, L. and Bacri, N. 1981. Phonetic analysis of late babbling: a case study of a French child. *Journal of Child Language* 8: 511–24. pp. 153, 261

de Boysson-Bardies, B., Sagart, L. and Durand, C. 1984. Discernible differences in the babbling of infants according to target-language. *Journal of Child Language* 11. pp. 153, 180

de Boysson-Bardies, B., Bacri, N., Sagart, L. and Poizirt, M. 1981. Timing in late babbling. *Journal of Child Language* 8: 525–39. p. 153

Delack, J. P. and Fowlow, P. J. 1978. The ontogenesis of differential vocalization: development of prosodic contrastivity during the first year of life. In N. Waterson and C. Snow (eds.) *The development of communication*. Chichester: Wiley. p. 187

Della Corte, M., Benedict, H. and Klein, D. 1983. The relationship of pragmatic dimensions of mothers' speech to the referential-expressive dimension. *Journal of Child Language* 10: 35–44. pp. 137, 293

de Lemos, C. 1981. Interactional processes in the child's construction of language. In W. Deutsch (ed.) *The child's construction of language*. New York: Academic Press. p. 366

de Loache, J. S. 1980. Naturalistic studies of memory for object location in very young children. In M. Perlmutter (ed.) *New directions for child development*. San Francisco: Jossey-Bass. p. 372

Dennett, D. C. 1978. *Brainstorms*. Hassocks, Sussex: Harvester Press. pp. 32, 33

   1980. Passing the buck to biology. *Behavioral and Brain Sciences* 3: 19. p. 521n

   1981a. Three kinds of intentional psychology. In R. Healey (ed.) *Reductionism, time and reality*. Cambridge: Cambridge University Press. p. 33

   1981b. True believers. In H. Heath (ed.) *Scientific explanation*. Oxford: Oxford University Press. p. 33

   1983a. Intentional systems in cognitive ethology. *Behavioral and Brain Sciences* 6: 343–90. p. 33

1983b. Styles of mental representation. *Proceedings of the Aristotelian Society* LXXXIII: 213–25. p. 33

Denny, J. P. 1978. Locating the universals in lexical systems for spatial deixis. *Papers from the parasession on the lexicon.* Chicago: Chicago Linguistic Society. p. 428

Derwing, B. L. 1973. *Transformational grammar as a theory of language acquisition: a study in the empirical, conceptual and methodological foundations of contemporary linguistics.* Cambridge: Cambridge University Press. pp. 21, 528, 528n

1976. Morpheme recognition and the learning of rules for derivational morphology. *The Canadian Journal of Linguistics* 21: 38–66. pp. 327, 328, 330, 528n

1979a. Against autonomous linguistics. In T. A. Perry (ed.) *Evidence and argumentation in linguistics.* Berlin and New York: de Gruyter. p. 528n

1979b. English pluralization: a testing ground for rule evaluation. In G. D. Prideaux, B. L. Derwing and W. J. Baker (eds.) *Experimental linguistics: integration of theories and applications.* Ghent: Story-Scientia. p. 332

and Baker, W. J. 1974. Rule learning and the English inflections. Final report to the Canada Council (File no. S72-0332). p. 335

1976. On the learning of English morphological rules. Final report to the Canada Council (File no. S73-0387). p. 335

1977. The psychological basis for morphological rules. In J. Macnamara (ed.) *Language learning and thought.* New York: Academic Press. pp. 328, 529n

1979a. Recent research on the acquisition of English morphology. In P. Fletcher and M. Garman (ed.) *Language acquisition.* 1st edn. Cambridge: Cambridge University Press. pp. 330, 331, 335

1979b. Rule learning and the English inflections (with special emphasis on the plural). In G. D. Prideaux, B. L. Derwing and W. J. Baker (eds.) *Experimental linguistics: integration of theories and applications.* Ghent: Story-Scientia. p. 529n

In preparation. *The acquisition of the English inflections: experimental studies.* p. 529n

and Nearey, T. M. In press. A decade of experimental linguistics at the University of Alberta. In J. J. Ohala and J. J. Jaeger (eds.) *Experimental phonology.* New York: Academic Press. p. 329

Deutsch, M. 1965. The role of social class in language development and cognition. *American Journal of Orthopsychiatry* 35: 78–88. pp. 128, 131

Deutsch, W. 1983. Language control processes in development. In H. Bouma and H. Bouwhuis (eds.) *Attention and performance, x: Control of language processes.* Hillsdale, NJ: Erlbaum. p. 417

and Koster, J. 1982. Children's interpretations of sentence-internal anaphora. *Stanford Papers and Reports on Child Language Development* 21. p. 60

and Pechmann, T. 1978. Ihr, dir, or mir? On the acquisition of pronouns in German children. *Cognition* 6: 155–68. pp. 340, 342, 345

1982. Social interaction and the development of definite descriptions. *Cognition* 11: 159–84

Deville, G. 1890–1. Notes sur le développement du langage. *Revue de Linguistique et de Philologie Comparée* 23: 330–43, 24: 10–42, 128–43, 242–57, 300–20. p. 225

de Villiers, P. A. and de Villiers, J. G. 1973. On this, that and the other: nonegocentrism in very young children. *Journal of Experimental Child Psychology* 18: 438–47. pp. 402, 405, 407

Dingwall, W. O. and Tuniks, G. 1973. Government and concord in Russian: a study in developmental psycholinguistics. In B. B. Kachru *et al.* (eds.) *Issues in linguistics: papers in honor of Henry and Renee Kahane.* Urbana, Ill.: University of Illinois Press. p. 334

Dittmar, N. 1976. *Sociolinguistics.* London: Edward Arnold. p. 127

Doctor, E. A. and Coltheart, M. 1980. Children's use of phonological encoding when reading for meaning. *Memory and Cognition* 8: 195–209. p. 489

Donaldson, M. C. 1971. Preconditions of inference. In J. K. Cole (ed.) *Nebraska Symposium on Motivation.* Lincoln, Neb.: University of Nebraska Press. p. 35
  1978. *Children's minds.* London: Fontana/Croom Helm. pp. 38, 114, 292, 407

Dore, J. 1973. The development of speech acts. Unpublished doctoral dissertation, City University of New York. p. 162
  1974. A pragmatic description of early language development. *Journal of Psycholinguistic Research* 3: 343–50. p. 119
  1975. Holophrases, speech acts and language universals. *Journal of Child Language* 2: 21–40. pp. 181, 182
  1977. Children's illocutionary acts. In R. O. Freedle (ed.) *Discourse production and comprehension.* Norwood, NJ: Ablex. p. 391
  1978. Variation in children's conversational experience. In K. E. Nelson (ed.) *Children's language,* vol. 1. New York: Gardner Press. p. 126
  1979. Conversational acts and the acquisition of language. In E. Ochs and B. B. Schieffelin (eds.) *Developmental pragmatics.* New York: Academic Press. p. 23

Dore, J., Gearhart, M. and Newman, D. 1978. The structure of nursery school conversation. In K. E. Nelson (ed.) *Children's language,* vol. 1. New York: Gardner Press. p. 391

Dore, J., Franklin, M. B., Miller, R. T. and Ramer, A. L. H. 1976. Transitional phenomena in early language acquisition. *Journal of Child Language* 3: 13–28. pp. 162, 183, 280, 313, 314, 315

Dowty, D. 1979. *Word meaning and Montague grammar.* Dordrecht: D. Reidel. p. 360

Drach, K. 1969. The language of the parent: a pilot study. Working Paper no. 14, University of California, Berkeley. p. 70

Drachman, G. 1973. Some strategies in the acquisition of phonology. In M. J. Kenstowicz and C. W. Kisseberth (eds.) *Issues in phonological theory.* The Hague: Mouton. p. 262

Dresher, B. E. 1981a. On the learnability of abstract phonology. In Baker and McCarthy (1981). p. 92
  1981b. Abstractness and explanation in phonology. In Hornstein and Lightfoot (1981). p. 92

Drewnowski, A. 1978. Detection errors on the word *the*: evidence for the acquisition of reading levels. *Memory and Cognition* 6: 403–9. p. 478

1981. Missing *-ing* in reading: developmental changes in reading units. *Journal of Experimental Child Psychology* 31: 154–68. p. 478

Dromi, E. 1982. In pursuit of meaningful words: a case-study analysis of early lexical development. Unpublished doctoral dissertation, University of Kansas. p. 433

and Berman, R. A. 1982. A morphemic measure of early language development: data from Modern Hebrew. *Journal of Child Language* 9: 403–24. pp. 436, 445

Du Preez, P. 1974. Units of information in the acquisition of language. *Language and Speech* 17: 369–76. pp. 196, 524n

Durkin, K., Rutter, D. R. and Tucker, H. 1982. Social interaction and language acquisition: motherese help you? *First Language* 3: 107–20. p. 351

Eblen, R. 1982. A study of the acquisition of fricatives by three-year old children learning Mexican Spanish. *Language and Speech* 25 (3): 201–20. p. 268

Eckhoff, B. 1983. How reading affects children's writing. *Language Arts* 60: 607–16. p. 517

Edelsky, C. and Muiña, V. 1977. Native Spanish language acquisition: the effect of age, schooling and context on responses to 'dile' and 'preguntale'. *Journal of Child Language* 4: 453–75

Edwards, A. D. 1976a. *Language in culture and class*. London: Heinemann. p. 127

1976b. Speech codes and speech variants: social class and task differences in children's speech. *Journal of Child Language* 3: 247–66. p. 131

Edwards, D. 1973. Sensory-motor intelligence and semantic relations in early child grammar. *Cognition* 2: 395–434. pp. 38, 292

1978. The three sources of children's early meanings. In I. Markova (ed.) *The social context of language*. Chichester: Wiley. p. 39

Edwards, J. R. 1979. *Language disadvantage*. London: Edward Arnold. p. 127

Edwards, M. L. 1974. Perception and production in child phonology: the testing of four hypotheses. *Journal of Speech and Hearing Research* 20: 766–80. p. 262

Ehri, L. C. 1975. Word consciousness in readers and prereaders. *Journal of Educational Psychology* 67: 204–12. p. 477

Eilers, R. E. 1975. Suprasegmental and grammatical control over telegraphic speech in young children. *Journal of Psycholinguistic Research* 4: 227–39. p. 189

1976. Discrimination of synthetic prevoiced labial stops by infants and adults. Paper presented at the 92nd Meeting of the Acoustical Society of America, San Diego. p. 172

and Oller, D. K. 1976. The role of speech discrimination in developmental sound substitutions. *Journal of Child Language* 3: 319–30. p. 207

Eilers, R. E., Gavin, W. and Wilson, W. R. 1979. Linguistic experience and phonetic perception in infancy: a cross-linguistic study. *Child Development* 50: 14–18. p. 260

1980. Effects of early linguistic experiences on speech discrimination by infants: a reply. *Child Development* 51: 113–7. p. 260

Eilers, R. E., Oller, D. K. and Benito-Garcia, C. R. 1983. The acquisition of voicing contrasts in Spanish and English learning infants and children: a longitudinal study. MS, University of Miami. p. 267

Eilers, R. E., Wilson, W. R. and Moore, J. M. 1976. Discrimination of synthetic prevoiced labial stops by infants and adults. *Journal of the Acoustical Society of America*, 60: Supplement 1, S91 (Abstract). p. 199

1977. Developmental changes in speech discrimination in infants. *Journal of Speech and Hearing Research* 20: 766–80. p. 259

Eimas, P. D. 1974. Linguistic processing of speech by young infants. In R. L. Schiefelbusch and L. L. Lloyd (eds.) *Language perspectives, acquisition, retardation and intervention*. London and Basingstoke: Macmillan; Baltimore, Md.: University Park Press. p. 200

Eimas, P. D., Siqueland, E., Jusczyk, P. and Vigorito, K. 1971. Speech perception in infants. *Science* 303–4. pp. 259, 260

Eisenberg, A. R. In preparation. Language development in cultural perspective. Doctoral dissertation, University of California, Berkeley. pp. 361, 366

Eliot, A. 1981. *Child language*. Cambridge: Cambridge University Press. p. xii

Ellis, R. and Wells, C. G. 1980. Enabling factors in adult–child discourse. *First Language* 1: 46–62. p. 136

Emeneau, M. B. 1958. Oral poets of South India – the Todas. *Journal of American Folklore* 71: 312–24. p. 452

Emonds, J. 1976. *A transformational approach to English syntax: root, structure-preserving and local transformations*. New York: Academic Press. p. 98

Engdahl, E. 1978. Word stress as an organizing principle for the lexicon. In D. Farkas, W. M. Jacobsen and K. W. Todrys (eds.) *Papers from the parasession on the lexicon*. Chicago, Ill.: Chicago Linguistic Society. p. 258

and Ejerhed (eds.) 1982. *Readings on unbounded dependencies in Scandinavian languages*. Umeå Studies in the Humanities, vol. 42. Stockholm, Sweden: Almquist and Wiksell. p. 67

Enstrom, D. H. and Stoll, R. 1976. Babbling sounds of Swiss-German infants: a phonetic and spectrographic analysis. Paper presented at the American Speech and Hearing Association Convention, Houston. pp. 153, 161

Erbaugh, M. S. 1980. Acquisition of Mandarin syntax: 'less' grammar isn't easier. Paper presented at meeting of the Linguistic Society of America, San Antonio, Texas, December. pp. 443, 444

1982. Coming to order: natural selection and the origin of syntax in the Mandarin-speaking child. Unpublished doctoral dissertation, University of California, Berkeley. pp. 359, 363, 364, 369

Ervin, S. 1964. Imitation and structural change in children's language. In E. H. Lenneberg (ed.) *New directions in the study of language*. Cambridge, Mass.: MIT Press. p. 387

Ervin-Tripp, S. 1977. Wait for me, roller skate! In S. Ervin-Tripp and C. Mitchell-Kernan (eds.) *Child discourse*. New York: Academic Press. pp. 23, 391

Ewing, G. 1982. Word-order invariance and variability in five children's three-word utterances: a limited-scope formula analysis. In C. E. Johnson and C. L. Thew (eds.) *Proceedings of the Second International Congress for the Study*

of Child Language, vol. I. Washington, DC: University Press of America. p. 316

1983. Presyntax: the development of word order in early child speech. Unpublished doctoral dissertation, University of Toronto. pp. 309, 313, 316, 317, 321

Farwell, C. B. 1975. Aspects of early verb semantics: pre-causative development. *Stanford Papers and Reports on Child Language Development* 10: 48–58. p. 291

1976. Some strategies in the early production of fricatives. *Stanford Papers and Reports on Child Language Development* 12. p. 216

Fawcett, R. P. and Perkins, M. R. 1980. *Child language transcripts 6–12*, vols I–IV. Pontypridd: Polytechnic of Wales. pp. 499, 500, 501, 502, 506, 511, 514, 515

Fee, J. and Ingram, D. 1982. Reduplication as a strategy of phonological development. *Journal of Child Language* 9: 41–54. p. 231

Ferguson, C. A. 1964. Baby talk in six languages. *American Anthropologist* 66 (part 2): 103–14. p. 192

1976. Learning to pronounce: the earliest stages of phonological development in the child. *Stanford Papers and Reports on Child Language Development* 11. Also in F. Minifie and L. L. Lloyd (eds.) *Comunicative and cognitive abilities: early behavioral assessment*. Baltimore, Md.: University Park Press. p. 198

1977. Baby talk as a simplified register. In Snow and Ferguson (1977). pp. 69, 192

and Farwell, C. B. 1973. Words and sounds in early language acquisition: English initial consonants in the first fifty words. *Stanford Papers and Reports on Child Language Development* 6: 1–60. pp. 243, 244

1975. Words and sounds in early acquisition. *Language* 51: 419–39. pp. 119, 145, 204, 216, 232, 238, 263, 294, 325

Ferguson, C. A. and Slobin, D. I. (eds.) 1973. *Studies of child language development*. New York: Holt, Rinehart and Winston. p. 531n

Fernald, A. 1978. Rhythm and intonation in mothers' speech to newborns. Paper presented to the 3rd Annual Boston University Conference on Language Development. p. 193

Ferreiro, E. 1971. *Les relations temporelles dans le langage de l'enfant*. Paris: Droz. pp. 399, 458, 461

1974. Producción, comprensión y repetición de lar proposición relativa. MS, University of Mexico. p. 458

1978. What is written in a written sentence? A developmental answer. *Boston University Journal of Education* 160: 25–39. p. 476

and Sinclair, H. 1971. Temporal relations in language. *International Journal of Psychology* 6: 39–47

Ferrier, L. J. 1978. Some observations of error in context. In N. Waterson and and C. E. Snow (eds.) *The development of communication*. Chichester: Wiley. pp. 289, 291, 292, 526n

Fey, M. E. and Gandour, J. 1982. Rule discovery in phonological acquisition. *Journal of Child Language* 9: 71–81. pp. 145, 267

Fidelholtz, J. L. 1975. Word frequency and vowel reduction in English. *Papers from the Eleventh Regional Meeting of Amsterdam* 7: 61–9. p. 248

Fielding, G. and Fraser, C. 1978. Language and interpersonal relations. In
    I. Markova (ed.) *Language and the social context.* Chichester: Wiley. p. 523n
Fillmore, C. J. 1971. Lectures on deixis. Unpublished MS, Summer Program in
    Linguistics, University of California at Santa Cruz. pp. 401, 405, 419
Fischer, K. W. and Corrigan, R. 1981. A skill approach to language development.
    In R. E. Stark (ed.) *Language behavior in infancy and early childhood.* New
    York: Elsevier/North-Holland. p. 162
Fisichelli, R. M. 1950. A study of prelinguistic speech development of
    institutionalized infants. Unpublished doctoral dissertation, Fordham
    University. p. 151
Flämig, W. 1970. Bedeutungsstrukturen im Bereich der Temporalität und
    Modalität. *Actes du Xe Congrès International des Linguistes, Bucarest,
    28 âout–2 septembre 1967.* Bucarest: Éditions de l'Académie de la République
    Socialiste de Roumanie, vol. II. p. 375
Flavell, J. H. 1963. *The developmental psychology of Jean Piaget.* New York: Van
    Nostrand. pp. 292, 372
Flavell, J. H., Botkin, P. J., Fry, C. L., Wright, J. L. and Jarvis, P. E. 1968.
    The development of role-taking and communication skills in children. New
    York: Wiley. pp. 14, 26
Fleischman, S. 1982. *The future in thought and language: diachronic evidence from
    Romance.* Cambridge: Cambridge University Press. p. 399
Fletcher, P. 1975. Review of Major (1974). *Journal of Child Language* 2: 318–22.
    p. 390
    1979. The development of the verb phrase. In P. Fletcher and M. Garman (eds.)
    Language acquisition. 1st edn. Cambridge: Cambridge University Press.
    pp. 369, 386, 388, 390, 391
    1981. Description and explanation in the acquisition of verb forms. *Journal of
    Child Language* 8: 93–108. p. 369
Fluharty, B. N. 1974. The design and standardization of a speech and screening
    test for use with preschool children. *Journal of Speech and Hearing Disorders*
    39: 75–85. p. 532n
Fodor, J. A. 1966. How to learn to talk: some simple ways. In F. Smith and G. A.
    Miller (eds.) *The genesis of language.* Cambridge, Mass.: MIT Press. p. 70
    1975. *The language of thought.* Hassocks, Sussex: Harvester Press; New York:
    Thomas Y. Crowell. pp. 30, 33, 44, 103
    1980a. The present status of the innateness controversy. In J. A. Fodor (1981).
    pp. 30, 103
    1980b. Methodological solipsism considered as a research strategy in cognitive
    psychology. *Behavioral and Brain Sciences* 3: 63–110. p. 33
    1981. *Representations.* Hassocks, Sussex: Harvester Press. p. 33
    1983. *The Modularity of Mind.* Cambridge, Mass.: MIT Press. p. 30
Fodor, J. A., Bever, T. and Garrett, M. 1974. *Psychology of language.* New York:
    McGraw-Hill. p. 205
Fodor, J. D. 1977. *Semantics: theories of meaning in generative grammar.*
    Hassocks, Sussex: Harvester Press. p. 526n
Fontanella de Weinberg, M. B. 1981. *Adquisicion fonologica en español
    bonaerense.* MS, Universidad Nacional del sur. Bahia Blanca. p. 265

Forster, K. I. 1976. Accessing the mental lexicon. In R. J. Wales and
E. Walker (eds.) *New approaches to language mechanisms.* Amsterdam:
North-Holland. p. 35
   1978. Accessing the mental lexicon. In E. Walker (ed.) *Explorations in the
   biology of language.* Montgomery, V: Bradford Books. p. 258
Fowles, L. and Glanz, M. E. 1977. Competence and talent in verbal riddle
comprehension. *Journal of Child Language* 4: 433–52. p. 473
Fox, A. 1973. Tone-sequences in English. *Archivum Linguisticum* n.s. 4: 17–26.
p. 524n
Francis, H. 1973. Children's experience of reading and notions of units in language.
British Journal of Educational Psychology 43: 17–23. p. 478
   1974. Social class, reference and context. *Language and Speech* 17: 193–98.
   p. 131
Fraser, C. and Brown, P. (n.d.) Nominal and verbal language styles. MS, Social
and Political Sciences Committee, University of Cambridge. p. 523n
Fraser, C. and Roberts, A. 1975. Mothers' speech to children of four different
ages. *Journal of Psycholinguistic Research* 4: 9–16. p. 79
Freeman, N., Sinha, C. and Stedmon, J. 1981. The allative bias in three-year-olds
is almost proof against task naturalness. *Journal of Child Psychology*
8: 283–96. p. 421
Freyd, P. and Baron, J. 1982. Individual differences in acquisition of derivational
morphology. *Journal of Verbal Learning and Verbal Behavior* 21: 282–95.
p. 329
Friedman, W. J. (ed.). 1982. *The developmental psychology of time.* New York:
Academic Press. p. 372
Frith, U. 1979. Reading by eye and writing by ear. In P. A. Kolers, M. E. Wrolstad
and H. Bosma (eds.) *Processing of visible language*, vol. 1. New York: Plenum
Press. p. 453
   1980. Unexpected spelling problems. In U. Frith (ed.) *Cognitive processes in
   spelling.* London: Academic Press. p. 493
Fujimura, O. and Lovins, J. 1978. Syllables as concatenative phonetic units. In
A. Bell and J. B. Hooper (eds.) *Syllables and segments.* Amsterdam: North-
Holland. p. 204
Furrow, D. 1984. Young children's use of prosody. *Journal of Child Language*
11. p. 187
Furrow, D., Nelson, K. and Benedict, H. 1979. Mother's speech to children and
syntactic development: some simple relationships. *Journal of Child Language*
6: 423–42. pp. 76, 79, 111
Furth, H. G. 1966. *Thinking without language: psychological implications of
deafness.* New York: Free Press. p. 12
Gaer, E. P. 1969. Children's understanding and production of sentences. *Journal
of Verbal Learning and Verbal Behavior* 8: 289–94. p. 458
Garcia, E. C. 1975. *The role of theory in linguistic analysis: the Spanish pronoun
system.* Amsterdam: North-Holland. p. 40
Garman, M. 1977. Crosslinguistic study of deixis. Paper presented at the Salzburg
Conference on Language Acquisition. p. 412
   1979. Early grammatical development. In P. Fletcher and M. Garman (eds.)

Language acquisition. 1st edn. Cambridge: Cambridge University Press. pp. 307, 314, 336

Garman, M., Griffiths, P. and Wales, R. 1970. Murut (Lun Bawang) prepositions and noun particles in children's speech. *Sarawak Museum Journal* 20: 1–24. p. 421

Garnica, O. 1973. The development of phonemic speech perception. In T. Moore (ed.) *Cognitive development and the acquisition of language.* New York: Academic Press. p. 200

1975. Some prosodic characteristics of speech to young children. Unpublished PhD dissertation, Stanford University. p. 194

1977. Some prosodic and paralinguistic features of speech to young children. In Snow and Ferguson (1977). pp. 72, 192, 194

Garvey, C. 1975. Requests and responses in children's speech. *Journal of Child Language* 2: 41–63. p. 391

Gazdar, G. 1982. Phrase structure grammar. In P. Jacobson and G. K. Pullum (eds.) *The nature of syntactic representation.* Dordrecht: D. Reidel. pp. 92, 94

Gelman, R. and Spelke, E. 1981. The development of thoughts about animate and inanimate objects: implications for research on social cognition. In J. Flavell and L. Ross (eds.) *Social cognitive development.* Cambridge: Cambridge University Press. p. 415

Gentner, D. 1978. On relational meaning: the acquisition of verb meaning. *Child Development* 49: 988–98. p. 295

1982. Why nouns are learned before verbs: linguistic relativity versus natural partitioning. In S. Kuczaj (ed.) *Language development,* vol. II. *Language, thought and culture.* Hillsdale, NJ: Erlbaum. p. 433

George, S. L. 1981. A longitudinal and cross-sectional analysis of early cranial base growth change. *American Journal of Psychological Anthropology.* p. 154

Gesell, A. and Amatruda, C. S. 1941. *Developmental diagnoses.* New York: P. B. Hoeber. pp. 149, 158

Gesell, A. and Thompson, H. 1934. *Infant behavior: its genesis and growth.* New York: McGraw-Hill. pp. 158, 162

Gilbert, J. H. V. 1977. A voice onset time analysis of apical stop production in three-year-olds. *Journal of Child Language* 4: 103–10. p. 228

Givón, T. 1979. *On understanding grammar.* New York: Academic Press. pp. 358, 398

Gleitman, L. R. and Wanner, E. 1982. Language acquisition: the state of the state of the art. In Wanner and Gleitman (1982). pp. 308, 310, 527n

Gleitman, L. R., Newport, E. L. and Gleitman, H. 1984. The current status of the motherese hypothesis. *Journal of Child Language* 11. pp. 75, 76

Glushko, J. 1979. The organisation and activation of orthographic knowledge in reading aloud. *Journal of Experimental Psychology: Human Perception and Performance* 5: 674–91. p. 27

Godfrey, J. J., Syrdal-Lasky, A. K., Millay, K. K. and Knox, C. M. 1981. Performance of dyslexic children on speech perception tests. *Journal of Experimental Child Psychology* 32: 401–24. pp. 484, 485

Gold, E. M. 1967. Language identification in the limit. *Information and Control* 10: 447–74. pp. 39, 92

Goldin-Meadow, S., Seligman, M. E. P. and Gelman, R. 1976. Language in the two-year old. *Cognition* 4: 189–202

Goldsmith, J. 1976. Autosegmental phonology. Unpublished doctoral thesis, circulated by Indiana University Linguistics Club. pp. 211, 252

Golinkoff, R. M. 1975. Semantic development in infants: the concepts of agent and recipient. *Merrill-Palmer Quarterly* 21: 181–95. pp. 39, 520n

  1981. The case for semantic relations. *Journal of Child Language* 8: 413–37. p. 39

  and Kerr, J. L. 1978. Infants' perception of semantically defined action role changes in filmed events. *Merrill-Palmer Quarterly* 24: 53–62. p. 520n

Goodglass, H., Fodor, I. G. and Schulhoff, C. 1967. Prosodic factors in grammar – evidence from aphasia. *Journal of Speech and Hearing Research* 10: 5–20. p. 196

Goodluck, H. 1981. Children's grammar of complement subject interpretation. In Tavakolian (1981). pp. 61, 522n

  and Tavakolian, S. 1982. Competence and processing in children's grammar of relative clauses. *Cognition* 11: 1–27. pp. 61, 458, 522n

Goodman, K. S. 1967. Reading: a psycholinguistic guessing game. *Journal of the Reading Specialist* 6: 126–35. p. 490

Goossens, L. 1981. On the development of the modals and of the epistemic function in English. Paper presented at the Fifth International Conference on Historical Linguistics, Galway, Ireland. p. 399

Gopnik, A. 1982. Words and plans: early language and the development of intelligent action. *Journal of Child Language* 9: 303–18. pp. 291, 293, 295, 426

Goudena, P. P. 1983. Private speech: an analysis of its social and self-regulatory functions. Unpublished doctoral thesis, Rijksuniversiteit, Utrecht. p. 27

Graves, D. H. 1979. What children show us about revision. *Language Arts* 56: 312–9. p. 499

Gray, V. A. and Cameron, C. A. 1980. Longitudinal development of English morphology in French immersion children. *Applied Psycholinguistics* 1: 171–81. p. 332

Greenberg, J. H. 1975. Research on language universals. *Annual Review of Anthropology* 4: 75–94. p. 524

  and Kuczaj, S. A. 1982. Towards a theory of substantive word-meaning acquisition. In Kuczaj (1982). pp. 295, 296

Greenfield, P. M. 1973. Who is 'Dada'? Some aspects of the semantic and phonological development of a child's first words. *Language and Speech* 16: 34–43. p. 287

  and Smith, J. H. 1976. *The structure of communication in early language development.* New York: Academic Press. pp. 78, 358

Greenlee, M. 1980. Learning the phonetic cues to the voiced–voiceless distinction. A comparison of child and adult speech perception. *Journal of Child Language* 7: 459–68. p. 263

  and Ohala, J. J. 1980. Phonetically motivated parallels between child phonology and historical sound change. *Language Sciences* 2 (2): 283–308. p. 267

Gregg, L. W. and Steinberg, E. R. (eds.) 1980. *Cognitive processes in writing.*
    Hillsdale, NJ: Erlbaum. p. 495
Grégoire, A. 1939. L'apprentissage du language: les deux premières années
    Bibliothèque de la Faculté de Philosophie et Lettres de l'Université de Liège.
    p. 149
Greimas, A. J. 1976. Pour une théorie des modalités. *Langages* 43: 90–107. pp. 376,
    377
Grice, H. P. 1967. William James Lectures. Harvard University. Published in part
    in 1975 as Logic and conversation. In P. Cole and J. L. Morgan (eds.) *Syntax
    and semantics,* vol. III. *Speech acts.* New York: Academic Press. p. 39
Grieve, R. and Hoogenraad, R. 1979. First words. In P. Fletcher and
    M. Garman (eds.) *Language acquisition.* 1st edn. Cambridge: Cambridge
    University Press. p. 280
Grieve, R., Hoogenraad, R. and Murray, D. 1977. On the child's use of lexis
    and syntax in understanding locative instructions. *Cognition* 5: 235–50. p. 418
Griffiths, P. 1974. *That there deixis I: That.* Unpublished MS, University of York.
    p. 405
    1974b. Review of M. Bowerman, *Early syntactic development. Journal of Child
    Language* 1: 111–22. p. 529n
    1976. The ontogenetic development of lexical reference. Unpublished doctoral
    dissertation, Edinburgh University. pp. 296, 298, 299, 301, 302, 303, 304, 305,
    526n
    1979. Speech acts and early sentences. In P. Fletcher and M. Garman (eds.)
    Language acquisition. 1st edn. Cambridge: Cambridge University Press.
    pp. 280, 288, 525n
    1980. Asking and answering. In D. Ingram, F. C. C. Peng and P. Dale (eds.)
    *Proceedings of the First International Congress for the Study of Child
    Language.* Lanham, Md: University Press of America. p. 526n
    and Atkinson, M. 1978. A 'door' to verbs. In N. Watson and C. E. Snow (eds.)
    The development of communication. Chichester: Wiley. pp. 291, 526n
Groat, A. 1979. The use of English stress assignment rules by children taught
    either with traditional orthography or with the initial teaching alphabet.
    Journal of Experimental Child Psychology 27: 395–409. p. 480
Gruber, J. S. 1967. Topicalization in child language. *Foundations of Language*
    3: 37–65. p. 190
Gruendel, J. M. 1977. Referential extensions in early language development. *Child
    Development* 48: 1567–76. pp. 301, 306
Grundzüge einer deutschen Grammatik 1981. By a collective of authors under the
    direction of K. E. Heidolph, W. Flämig and W. Motsch. Berlin: Akademie-
    Verlag. p. 375
Gvozdev, A. N. 1961. *Voprosy izucheniyz detskoy rechi.* Moscow: Izdo-vo
    Akademii Pedagogicheskikh Nauk RSFSR. pp. 361, 362, 530n
Hakuta, K. 1981. Grammatical description versus configurational arrangement in
    language acquisition: Relative clauses in Japanese. *Cognition* 9: 197–236.
    p. 442
Hale, K. 1983. Warlpiri and the grammar of non-configurational languages.
    Natural Language and Linguistic Theory 1: 5–47. p. 521n

Hall. L. C. 1975. Linguistic and perceptual constraints on scanning strategies: some developmental studies. Unpublished doctoral dissertation, University of Edinburgh. p. 419

Halliday, M. A. K. 1975. *Learning how to mean: explorations in the development of language*. London: Edward Arnold. pp. 39, 184, 185, 188, 211, 212, 282, 283, 290

Halsey, A. H. 1972. *Educational priority*, vol. 1. London: HMSO. p. 131

Hamburger, H. 1980. A deletion ahead of its time. *Cognition* 8: 389–416. p. 105

and Crain, S. 1982. Relative acquisition. In Kuczaj (1982) p. 61

and Wexler, K. 1975. A mathematical theory of learning transformational grammar. *Journal of Mathematical Psychology* 12: 137–77. p. 90

Handscombe, R. J. 1967a. *The written language of nine- and ten-year-old children*. Nuffield foreign languages teaching materials project, reports and occasional papers, no. 24. London: The Nuffield Foundation. pp. 502, 506, 511, 512, 514, 515

1967b. *The written language of eleven- and twelve-year-old children*. Nuffield foreign languages teaching materials project, reports and occasional papers, no. 25. London: The Nuffield Foundation. pp. 499, 500, 506, 511, 512, 513, 514, 515

1967c. *The language of twelve-year-old children*. Nuffield foreign languages teaching materials project, reports and occasional papers, nos. 26–28. London: The Nuffield Foundation. pp. 500, 501, 502, 506, 511, 512

Hardy-Brown, K. 1983. Universals and individual differences: disentangling two approaches to the study of language acquisition. *Developmental Psychology* 19: 610–24. pp. 125, 126, 136

Harkness, S. 1977. Aspects of social environment and first language acquisition in rural Africa. In Snow and Ferguson (1977). p. 85

Harner, L. 1975. Yesterday and tomorrow: development of early understanding of the terms. *Developmental Psychology* 11: 864–5. pp. 368, 372, 392, 424

1976. Children's understanding of linguistic reference to past and future. *Journal of Psycholinguistic Research* 5: 65–84. p. 392

1980. Comprehension of past and future reference revisited. *Journal of Experimental Child Psychology* 29: 170–82. p. 372

1982. Immediacy and certainty: factors in understanding future reference. *Journal of Child Language* 9: 115–24. pp. 392, 425

Harpin, W. 1976. *The second 'R'*. London: George Allen and Unwin. pp. 495, 496, 497, 498

Harris, P. L., Kruithof, A., Terwogt, M. M. and Visser, T. 1981. Children's detection and awareness of textual anomaly. *Journal of Experimental Child Psychology* 31: 212–30. pp. 491, 492, 493

Hawkins, P. R. 1969. Social class, the nominal group and reference. *Language and Speech* 12: 125–35. p. 131

Hayhurst, H. 1967. Some errors of young children in producing passive sentences. *Journal of Verbal Learning and Verbal Behavior* 6: 634–9. p. 458

Healy, A. F. 1976. Detection errors on the word *the*: evidence for reading units larger than letters. *Journal of Experimental Psychology: Human Perception and Performance* 2: 235–42. p. 478

Heath, S. B. 1983. *Ways with words*. Cambridge: Cambridge University Press

Heider, F. 1939. Environmental determinants of psychological theories. *Psychological Review* 46: 383–410. p. 35

Herring, S. C. n.d. Tense versus aspect and focus of attention in the development of temporal reference. Unpublished MS, Department of Linguistics, University of California, Berkeley. p. 366

Hess, R. and Shipman, V. 1965. Early experience and the socialisation of cognitive modes in children. *Child Development* 36: 869–86. p. 131

  1968. Maternal influences upon early learning. In R. Hess and R. Beer (eds.) *Early learning*. London: Aldine. p. 131

Hickmann, M. 1978. Adult regulative speech in mother–child interaction. *Quarterly Newsletter of the Institute for Comparative Human Development* 2 (2): 26–30. p. 19

  1980. Creating referents in discourse: a developmental analysis of linguistic cohesion. In *Papers from the Sixteenth Regional Meeting of the Chicago Linguistic Society: Parasession on Anaphora*. Chicago: Chicago Linguistic Society. pp. 24, 427, 469

  1982a. The development of narrative skill: pragmatic and metapragmatic aspects of discourse cohesion. Unpublished doctoral dissertation, University of Chicago. pp. 24, 27

  1982b. Contexte et fonction dans le développement du langage. Paper presented at the conference on 'Communication, développement du langage et competence psychologique chez l'enfant d'âge pré-scholaire'. Université de Haute-Bretagne, Rennes, June 29–30. p. 27

  1985. The implications of discourse skills in Vygotsky's developmental theory. In J. V. Wertsch (ed.) *Culture, communication and cognition: Vygotskian perspectives*. New York: Cambridge University Press. pp. 25, 469

  In preparation. Metapragmatics in child language. To appear in E. Mertz and R. Parmentier (eds.) *Semiotic mediation: psychological and sociocultural perspectives*. New York: Academic Press

  and Wertsch, J. V. 1978. Adult–child discourse in problem solving situations. In *Papers from the Fourteenth Regional Meeting, Chicago Linguistic Society*. p. 19

Hill, J. A. C. 1983. A computational model of language acquisition in the two-year-old. Unpublished doctoral dissertation, University of Massachusetts, circulated by Indiana University Linguistics Club, Bloomington, Ind. pp. 310, 316, 320, 321, 323, 324

Hirst, W. and Weil, J. 1982. Acquisition of epistemic and deontic modals. *Journal of Child Language* 9: 659–66. p. 399

Holisky, D. A. 1981. Aspect theory and Georgian aspect. In P. J. Tedeschi and A. Zaenen (eds.) *Syntax and semantics: tense and aspect*, vol. xiv. New York: Academic Press. p. 360

Hood, L. In press. Pragmatism and dialectical materialism in language development. To appear in K. E. Nelson (ed.) *Children's language*. Vol.5. p. 10

Hooper, J. B. 1977. Substantive evidence for linearity: vowel length and nasality

in English. *Papers from the Thirteenth Regional Meeting, Chicago Linguistic Society*. Chicago, Ill.: Chicago Linguistic Society. p. 267

Hopmann, M. R. and Maratsos, M. P. 1978. A developmental study of factivity and negation in complex syntax. *Journal of Child Language* 5: 295–309. p. 473

Horgan, D. 1976. Linguistic knowledge at early stage I: evidence from successive single word utterances. *Stanford Papers and Reports in Child Language Development* 12: 116–26. pp. 312, 313, 317

   1978. The development of the full passive. *Journal of Child Language* 5: 63–80. p. 458

   1980. Nouns: love 'em or leave 'em. In V. Teller and S. White (eds.) *Studies in child language and multilingualism. Annals of the New York Academy of Sciences* 345. pp. 118, 119, 127

   1981. Rate of language acquisition and noun emphasis. *Journal of Psycholinguistic Research* 10. pp. 111, 119

Hornstein, N. 1981. The study of meaning in natural language: three approaches to tense. In Hornstein and Lightfoot (1981)

Hornstein, N. and Lightfoot, D. (eds.) 1981. *Explanation in linguistics: the logical problem of language acquisition*. London and New York: Longman. pp. 92, 104

Householder, F. W. 1971. *Linguistic speculations*. Cambridge: Cambridge University Press. p. 528n

Howe, C. 1976. The meanings of two-word utterances in the speech of young children. *Journal of Child Language* 3: 29–47. pp. 39, 186

Howell, M., Schumaker, J. and Sherman, J. 1978. A comparison of parents' models and expansions in promoting children's acquisition of objectives. *Journal of Experimental Child Psychology* 25: 41–57. p. 78

Hsu, J. 1981. The development of structural principles related to complement subject interpretation. Unpublished doctoral dissertation, City University of New York. p. 61

Hsu, J., Cairns, H. and Fiengo, R. 1985. The development of grammars underlying children's interpretation of complex sentences. *Cognition* 20: 25–48. pp. 61, 522n

Huang, C. T. J. 1982. Logical relations in Chinese and the theory of grammar. Unpublished dissertation, MIT. p. 103

Humbert, J. 1954. *Syntaxe grècque*. 2nd ed. Paris: Klincksieck. p. 399

Hundeide, K. 1985. The tacit background of children's judgements. In J.V. Wertsch (ed.) *Culture, communication and cognition: Vygotskian perspectives*. New York: Cambridge University Press. pp. 15, 16

Hunt, K. W. 1965. *Grammatical structures written at three grade levels*. Urbana, Ill.: National Council of Teachers of English. pp. 495, 496, 497, 505, 533n

   1966. Recent measures in syntactic development. *Elementary English* 43: 732–9. pp. 496, 505

   1970. *Syntactic maturity in school children and adults*. Society for Research in Child Development Monographs 35. pp. 495, 496, 505

Hupet, M. and Costermans, J. 1974. Des fonctions sémantiques du passif. *Cahiers de l'Institut de Linguistique* 2. University of Louvain. p. 462

Huttenlocher, J. 1974. The origins of language comprehension. In R. L. Solso (ed.) *Theories in cognitive psychology*. Hillsdale, NJ: Erlbaum. pp. 110, 281, 294

Huxley, R. 1970. The development of the correct use of subject personal pronouns in two children. In G. B. Flores d'Arcais and W. J. M. Levelt (eds.) *Advances in psycholinguistics*. Amsterdam: North-Holland. pp. 340, 342, 415

Hyman, L. and Schuh, R. 1974. Universals of tone rules: evidence from West Africa. *Linguistic Inquiry* 5: 81–115. p. 185

Ingram, D. 1971. Toward a theory of person deixis. *Papers in Linguistics* 4: 37–54. p. 340

   1974. Phonological rules in young children. *Journal of Child Language* 1: 49–64. pp. 201, 228, 233

   1975. Surface contrast in phonology: evidence from children's speech. *Journal of Child Language* 2: 287–92. p. 233

   1976a. *Phonological disability in children*. New York: Elsevier; London: Edward Arnold. pp. 215, 223, 249

   1976b. Phonological analysis of a child. *Glossa* 10: 3–27. p. 233

   1976c. Current issues in child phonology. In D. M. Morehead and A. E. Morehead (eds.) *Normal and deficient child language*. Baltimore, Md: University Park Press. p. 233

   1978. Sensori-motor intelligence and language development. In A. Lock (ed.) *Action, gesture and symbol: the emergence of language*. London: Academic Press. p. 292

   1979. Cross-linguistic evidence on the extent and limit of individual variation in phonological development. *Proceedings of the 9th International Congress of Phonetic Sciences*. Copenhagen: University of Copenhagen. pp. 253, 268

   1981. *Procedures for the phonological analysis of children's language*. Baltimore: University Park Press. p. 234

   Forthcoming. On children's homonymy. p. 234

Ingram, D., Christensen, L., Veach, S. and Webster, B. 1980. The acquisition of word-initial fricatives and affricates in English by children between 2 and 6 years. In G. Yeni-Komshian, J. Kavanagh and C. Ferguson (eds.) *Child phonology*, vol. 1. *Production*. New York: Academic Press. p. 226

Inhelder, B. and Piaget, J. 1964. *The early growth of logic in the child: classification and seriation*. London: Routledge and Kegan Paul. p. 45

Innes, S. J. 1974. Developmental aspects of plural formation in English. Unpublished MSc thesis, University of Alberta. p. 335

Irwin, J. V. and Wong, S. P. 1983. *Phonological development in children: 18 to 72 months*. Carbondale, Ill.: Southern Illinois University. p. 208

Irwin, O. C. 1947. Infant speech: consonantal sounds according to place of articulation. *Journal of Speech Disorders* 12: 397–401. p. 244

   and Chen, H. P. 1946. Development of speech during infancy: curve of phonemic types. *Journal of Experimental Psychology* 36: 431–6. pp. 149, 151

   1947. A reliability study of speech sounds observed in the crying of newborn infants. *Child Development* 12: 351–68. p. 151

Ito, K. 1981. Two aspects of negation in child language. In P. S. Dale and D. Ingram (eds.) *Child language*. Baltimore, Md: University Park Press.

Jackendoff, R. 1972. *Semantic interpretation and generative grammar*. Cambridge, Mass.: MIT Press. p. 56

Jacobson, J. L., Boersma, D. C., Fields, R. B. and Olson, K. L. 1983. Paralinguistic features of adult speech to infants and small children. *Child Development* 54: 436–42. pp. 194, 195

Jakobson, R. 1960. Linguistics and poetics. In T. Sebeok (ed.) *Style in language*. Cambridge, Mass.: MIT Press. pp. 18, 24

   1968. *Child language, aphasia and phonological universals*, trans. A. R. Keiler. The Hague: Mouton. First published 1941 as *Kindersprache, Aphasie und allgemeine Lautgesetze*. pp. 64, 145, 149, 198, 251, 429, 524n

   1972. Principles of historical phonology. In A. R. Keiler (ed.) *A reader in historical and comparative linguistics*. New York: Holt, Rinehart and Winston. First published 1931. p. 248

Jakubowicz, C. 1978. Fait actuel ou fait virtuel? La comprehension d'énonces conditionnels chez l'enfant. *l'Année Psychologique* 78: 105–28. p. 397

   In press. On markedness and binding principles. *Proceedings of NELS* 14. Published by the Graduate Linguistics Student Association, University of Massachusetts-Amherst. pp. 57, 60, 66

James, S. L. 1978. Effect of listener age and situation on the politeness of children's directives. *Journal of Psycholinguistic Research* 7: 307–17. p. 391

Jarvella, R. and Klein, W. (eds.) 1982. *Speech, place and action: studies in deixis and related topics*. New York: Wiley.

Jespersen, O. 1922. *Language: its nature, development and origin*. New York: Holt; London: Allen and Unwin. pp. 223, 352

Johnson, J. I., Leder, S. B. and Egelston, R. L. 1980. Influence of intonation on auditory sequential memory skills. *Perceptual and Motor Skills* 50: 703–8. p. 196

Johnson-Laird, P. N. 1978. The meaning of modality. *Cognitive Science* 2: 17–26. p. 376

Johnston, J. R. and Slobin, D. I. 1979. The development of locative expressions in English, Italian, Serbo-Croation and Turkish. *Journal of Child Language* 6: 531–47. p. 418, 430

Johnston, R. S. 1982. Phonological coding in dyslexic readers. *British Journal of Psychology* 73: 455–60. p. 484

Jones, L. G. 1967. English phonotactic structure and first-language acquisition. *Lingua* 19: 1–59. p. 211

Jurgens, V. and Von Cramon, D. 1982. On the role of the anterior cingulate cortex in phonation. A case report. *Brain and Language* 15: 234–48. p. 168

Jusczyk, P. W. 1983. On characterizing the development of speech perception. In J. Mehler and R. Fox (eds.) *Neonate cognition: beyond the blooming, buzzing confusion*. Hillsdale, NJ: Erlbaum. p. 241

   and Thompson, E. 1978. Perception of a phonetic contrast in multisyllabic utterances by 2-month-old infants. *Perception and Psychophysics* 23: 105–9. pp. 179, 259

Kahn, D. 1976. Syllable-based generalizations in English phonology. Unpublished thesis, Linguistics Department, MIT. p. 204

Kahneman, D. 1973. *Attention and effort*. Englewood Cliffs, NJ: Prentice-Hall. p. 32

Kail, M. 1975a. Étude génétique de la réproduction de phrases relatives: réproduction immédiate. *Année Psychologique* 75: 109–26. p. 458

1975b. Étude génétique de la réproduction de phrases relatives: reproduction déférée. *Année Psychologique* 75: 427–43. p. 458

1979. *The development of memory*. San Francisco: Freeman. p. 372

Kantor, K. J. and Rubin, D. L. 1981. Between speaking and writing: processes of differentiation. In B. M. Kroll and R. J. Vann (eds.) *Exploring speaking–writing relationships: connections and contrasts*. Urbana, Ill.: National Council of Teachers of English. p. 498

Kaper, W. 1980. The use of the past tense in games of pretend. *Journal of Child Language* 7: 213–5. pp. 393, 394

Kaplan, E. L. 1970. Intonation and language acquisition. *Stanford Papers and Reports on Child Language Development* 1: 1–21. p. 179

and Kaplan, G. 1971. The prelinguistic child. In J. Eliot (ed.) *Human development and cognitive processes*. New York: Holt, Rinehart and Winston. p. 179

Karmiloff-Smith, A. 1975. Can developmental psycholinguistics provide clues to the historical origins of gender? MS, University of Geneva. pp. 467, 469

1977. More about the same: children's understanding of post-articles. *Journal of Child Language* 4: 377–94. pp. 24, 25, 41

Karmiloff-Smith, A. 1978. The interplay between syntax, semantics and phonology in language acquisition processes. In R. N. Campbell and P. Smith (eds.) *Recent advances in the psychology of language: language development and mother–child interaction*. New York and London: Plenum Press. pp. 46, 459

1979a. *A functional approach to child language: a study of determiners and reference*. Cambridge: Cambridge University Press. pp. 24, 354, 417, 427, 443, 446, 460, 463, 467, 469, 475

1979b. Micro- and macro-developmental changes in language acquisition and other representational systems. *Cognitive Science* 3: 91–118. p. 473

1979c. Language as a formal problem-space for children. Paper presented at the conference 'Beyond Description in Child Language', Max-Planck-Institute for Psycholinguistics, Nijmegen, Holland. pp. 24, 469, 473

1980. Psychological processes underlying pronominalization and non-pronominalization in children's connected discourse. In J. Kreiman and E. Ojedo (eds.) *Papers from the parasession on pronouns and anaphora*. Chicago: Chicago Linguistic Society. pp. 24, 469, 473

1981. The grammatical marking of thematic structure in the development of language production. In W. Deutsch (ed.) *The child's construction of language*. London: Academic Press. pp. 443, 469, 473

1983. Language acquisition as a problem solving process. In *Stanford Papers and Reports on Child Development* 22: 1–22. p. 22, 469, 473, 474, 532n

In press a. Cognitive processes and linguistic representations: evidence from children's metalinguistic and repair data. *Cognition*. p. 467

In press b. Children's problem-solving. In M. Lamb, A. L. Brown and

B. Rogoff (eds.) *Advances in developmental psychology*, vol. III. Hillsdale, NJ: Erlbaum. p. 474

In press c. Structure, concept and process in comparing linguistic and cognitive development. In I. Levin (ed.) *Stage and structure: reopening the debate.* Hillsdale, NJ: Erlbaum. pp. 469, 473

Katis, D. 1983. O paratatikos sti glossiki ekseliksi tu ellinopulu. (The imperfective past in the linguistic development of the Greek child.) Paper read at the 4th Annual Meeting of the Department of Linguistics, Faculty of Philosophy, Aristotelian University of Thessaloniki, May. pp. 394, 396

Katz, J. J. 1977. *Propositional structure and illocutionary force.* Hassocks, Sussex: Harvester Press. p. 39

Katz, R. B., Shankweiler, D. and Liberman, I. Y. 1981. Memory for item order and phonetic recoding in the beginning reader. *Journal of Experimental Child Psychology* 32: 474–84. p. 484

Keenan, E. O. 1974. Conversational competence in children. *Journal of Child Language* 1: 163–83. pp. 182, 183, 184, 185

and Klein, E. 1975. Coherency in children's discourse. *Journal of Psycholinguistic Research* 4: 365–80. p. 28

and Schieffelin, B. B. 1976. Topic as a discourse notion: a study of topic in the conversations of children and adults. In C. N. Li (ed.) *Subject and topic.* New York: Academic Press. p. 427

Keil, F. C. 1979. *Semantic and conceptual development: an ontological perspective.* Cambridge, Mass.: Harvard University Press. p. 292

1981. Constraints on knowledge and cognitive development. *Psychological Review* 88: 197–227. p. 532n

Kemler, D. G. and Smith, L. B. 1979. Accessing similarity and dimensional relations. *Journal of Experimental Psychology – General* 108: 133–50. pp. 45, 521n

Kent, R. D. 1976. Anatomical and neuromuscular maturation of the speech mechanism: evidence from acoustic studies. *Journal of Speech and Hearing Research* 19: 421–47. p. 220

1981. Articulatory-acoustic perspectives on speech development. In R. E. Stark (ed.) *Language behavior in infancy and early childhood.* New York: Elsevier/North-Holland. pp. 163, 167, 261

and Murray, A. D. 1982. Acoustic features of infant vocalic utterances at 3, 6 and 9 months. *Journal of the Acoustical Society of America* 72: 353–65. p. 155

Kerek, A. 1975. Phonological rules in the language of Hungarian children. Paper presented to the Mid-America Linguistics Conference. p. 225

Kessel, F. S. 1970. *The role of syntax in children's comprehension from ages six to twelve.* Society for Research in Child Development Monographs 35 (6). p. 457

Kessen, W., Levine, J. and Wendrich, K. A. 1979. The imitation of pitch in infants. *Infant Behavior and Development* 2: 93–9. pp. 179, 243

Kewley-Port, D. and Preston, M. S. 1974. Early apical stop production: a voice onset time analysis. *Journal of Phonetics* 2: 195–210. pp. 153, 161

Kim, C. W. 1965. On the autonomy of the tensity feature in stop classification. *Word* 21: 339–59. pp. 267, 525n

Kiparsky, P. and Menn, L. 1977. On the acquisition of phonology. In
    J. Macnamara (ed.) *Language, learning and thought*. New York: Academic
    Press. p. 215
Kirk, L. 1973. An analysis of speech imitations by Ga children. *Anthropological
    Linguistics* 15: 267–75. p. 185
Kirkpatrick, P. 1908. The part played by consciousness in mental operations.
    Journal of Philosophy 5: 421ff. p. 520n
Kirshner, R. 1979. Deixis in discourse: an exporatory quantitative study of the
    modern Dutch demonstrative adjectives. In T. Givón (ed.) *Syntax and
    semantics*, vol. xii: *Discourse and syntax*. New York: Academic Press. p. 414
Klatt, D. H. 1980. Speech perception: a model of acoustic-phonetic analysis and
    lexical access. In R. A. Cole (ed.) *Perception and production of fluent speech*.
    Hillsdale, NJ: Erlbaum. p. 259
Klein, E. 1977. Some remarks on the semantics of children's two word utterances.
    Semantikos 2: 37–46. p. 41
Klein, H. 1978. The relationship between perceptual strategies and productive
    strategies in learning the phonology of early lexical items. Unpublished
    doctoral thesis, circulated by Indiana University, Linguistics Club. p. 262
    1984. Learning to stress: a case study. *Journal of Child Language* 11: 375–90.
    p. 191
Klein, R. 1974. *Word order: Dutch children and their mothers*. Publication 9,
    Institute for General Linguistics, University of Amsterdam. p. 75
Klein, W. 1983. Deixis and spatial orientation in route directions. In H. Pick and
    A. Aaredulo (eds.) *Spatial orientation*. New York: Plenum Press. p. 427
Klima, E. S. and Bellugi, U. 1966. Syntactic regularities in the speech of children.
    In J. Lyons and R. J. Wales (eds.) *Psycholinguistic papers*. Edinburgh:
    Edinburgh University Press. p. 386
Kobashigawa, B. 1969. Repetitions in a mother's speech to her child. Working
    Paper no. 14, University of California, Berkeley. p. 70
Kochurova, E. I., Visyagina, A. I., Gordeeva, N. D. and Zinchenko, V. P. 1981.
    Criteria for evaluating executive activity. In J. V. Wertsch (ed.) *The concept
    of activity in Soviet psychology*. Armonk, NY: M. E. Sharpe. p. 23
Koffka, K. 1935. *Principles of gestalt psychology*. New York: Harcourt Brace. p. 35
Kogan, N. 1976. *Cognitive styles in infancy and early childhood*. Hillsdale, NJ:
    Erlbaum. p. 126
Kohlberg, L. 1969. Stage and sequence: the cognitive-developmental approach to
    socialization. In Goslin (ed.) *Handbook of socialization theory and research*.
    Chicago, Ill.: Rand McNally. pp. 14, 17
    1971. From is to ought. In T. Michel (ed.) *Cognitive development and
    epistemology*. New York: Academic Press. pp. 14, 17
    and Wertsch, J. V. In press. Language and the development of thought. In
    L. Kohlberg *Developmental psychology and early education*. London:
    Longman. pp. 10, 12, 20, 27
Kohlberg, L., Yaeger, J. and Hjertholm, E. 1968a. Private speech: four studies
    and a review of theories. *Child Development* 39: 691–736. pp. 10, 27
Konopczynski, G. 1975. Étude experimentale de quelques structures prosodiques

employées par les enfants français entre 7 et 22 mois. *Travaux de l'Institut de Phonetique de Strasbourg* 7: 171–205. p. 184

Koopmans-van Beinum, F. J. and Harder, J. H. 1982/3. Word classification, word frequency, and vowel reduction. *Proceedings from the Institute of Phonetic Sciences of the University of Amsterdam* 7: 61–9. p. 248

Kornfeld, J. 1971. Theoretical issues in child phonology. *Papers from the Seventh Regional Meeting, Chicago Linguistic Society.* Chicago, Ill.: Chicago Linguistic Society. p. 266

Koster, J. 1979. Some remarks on language learnability. Paper presented to Paris Conference on Learnability. pp. 102, 105, 108

Kress, G. 1982. *Learning to write.* London: Routledge and Kegan Paul. p. 494

Kroll, B. M. 1981. Developmental relationships between speaking and writing. In Kroll and Vann (1981). p. 498

and Vann, R. J. (eds.) 1981. *Exploring speaking–writing relationships: connections and contrasts.* Urbana, Ill.: National Council of Teachers of English. p. 494

and Wells, C. G. (eds.) 1983. *Explorations in the development of writing.* Chichester: Wiley. pp. 495, 533n

Kuczaj, S. A. 1977. Old and new forms, old and new meanings: the form–function hypothesis revisited. Paper presented at the Society for Research in Child Development, New Orleans, March. pp. 386, 397

(ed.) 1982. *Language development,* vol. i: *Syntax and semantics.* Hillsdale, NJ: Erlbaum.

and Daly, J. 1979. The development of hypothetical reference in the speech of young children. *Journal of Child Language* 6: 563–79. pp. 386, 397

and Maratsos, M. 1975a. On the acquisition of *front, back* and *side. Child Development* 46: 202–10. p. 419

1975b. What a child *can* say before he *will. Merrill-Palmer Quarterly* 21: 89–111. pp. 386, 387, 389

Kuhl, P. K. 1976. Speech perception in early infancy: perceptual constancy for vowel categories. Paper presented at the 92nd Meeting of the Acoustical Society of America, San Diego. p. 172

1979. Speech perception in early infancy: perceptual constancy for spectrally dissimilar vowel categories. *Journal of the Acoustical Society of America* 66: 1668–79. p. 261

Kuhl, P. K. 1980. Perceptual constancy for speech sound categories in early infancy. In G. H. Yeni-Komshian, J. F. Kavanagh and C. A. Ferguson *Child phonology,* vol. 2. New York: Academic Press. pp. 199, 261

Kuhl, P. K. and Meltzoff, A. N. 1982. The bimodal perception of speech in infancy. *Science* 218: 1138–41. p. 524n

Kuryłowicz, J. 1972. The role of deictic elements in linguistic evolution. *Semiotica* 5: 174–83. p. 401

LaBerge, D. and Samuels, S. J. 1974. Towards a theory of automatic information processing in reading. *Cognitive Psychology* 6: 293–323. p. 488

Labov, W. 1966. *The social stratification of English in New York City.* Washington, DC: Center for Applied Linguistics. p. 247

1970. The logic of non-standard English. In Williams, F. (ed.) *Language and poverty*. Chicago: Markham Publishing Co. p. 128

1972. *Sociolinguistic patterns*. Philadelphia: University of Pennsylvania Press. pp. 113, 125, 130

1977. *Language in the inner city*. Oxford: Blackwell. pp. 114, 115

and Labov, T. 1978. The phonetics of *cat* and *mama*. *Language* 54: 816–52. pp. 241, 244

Langlois, A. and Baken, R. J. 1976. Development of respiratory time factors in infant cry. *Developmental Medicine and Child Neurology* 18: 732–7. p. 163

Lasky, R. E., Syrdal-Lasky, A. and Klein, R. E. 1975. VOT discrimination by four to six and a half month old infants from Spanish environments. *Journal of Experimental Child Psychology* 20: 215–25. p. 260

Lasnik, H. 1981a. Learnability, restrictiveness and the evaluation metric. In Baker and McCarthy (1981). p. 94

1981b. Restricting the theory of transformations: a case study. In Hornstein and Lightfoot (1981). p. 98

Lasnik, H. 1981c. On a lexical parameter in the government-binding theory. In J. Pustejovsky and V. Burke (eds.) Markedness and learnability. *University of Massachusetts Occasional Papers in Linguistics* 6. p. 101

Laufer, M. Z. 1980. Temporal regularity in prespeech. In T. Murry and A. Murry (eds.) *Infant communication: cry and early speech*. Houston: College Hill Press. p. 154.

Lavendera, B. R. 1983. The textual function of conditionals in Spanish. Paper given at the Symposium on Conditionals and Cognitive Processes, Stanford University, December 8–11. p. 474

Leder, S. B. and Egelston, R. L. 1982. The pragmatic processing of intonation and word order in 2- to 4-year-old children. *Psychological Reports* 51: 247–54. p. 187

Lee, B. and Hickmann, M. 1983. Language, thought and self in Vygotsky's developmental theory. In B. Lee and G. Noam (eds.) *Developmental approaches to the self*. New York: Plenum Press. pp. 18, 20

Lee, B., Wertsch, J. V. and Stone, C. A. 1983. Towards a Vygotskian theory of the self. In B. Lee and G. Noam (eds.) *Developmental approaches to the self*. New York: Plenum Press. pp. 20, 27

Lee, L. 1969. *The Northwestern Syntax Screening Test*. Evanston, Ill.: Northwestern University. p. 110

Lehmann, C. 1982. Thoughts on grammaticalization: a programmatic sketch. *akup* [Arbeiten des Kolner Universalienprojekts] no. 48. p. 398

Lenneberg, E. H. 1962. Understanding language without ability to speak: a case report. *Journal of Abnormal and Social Psychology* 65: 419–25. p. 149

1967. *Biological foundations of language*. New York: Wiley. pp. 71, 181

1976. The concept of language differentiation. In E. H. Lenneberg and E. Lenneberg (eds.) *Foundations of language development*, vol. 1. New York: Academic Press. p. 186

Leonard, L. B. 1973. The role of intonation in recall of various linguistic stimuli. *Language and Speech* 16: 327–35. p. 178

and Schwartz, R. G. 1978. Focus characteristics of single-word utterances after syntax. *Journal of Child Language* 5: 151–8

Leonard, L. B., Newhoff, M. and Mesalam, L. 1980. Individual differences in early child phonology. *Applied Psycholinguistics* 1: 7–30. p. 243

Leonard, L. B., Schwartz, R., Folger, M., Newhoff, M. and Wilcox, M. 1979. Children's imitations of lexical items. *Child Development* 49: 19–27. p. 119

Leonard, L. B., Schwartz, R. G., Morris, B. and Chapman, K. 1981. Factors influencing early lexical acquisition: lexical orientation and phonological composition. *Child Development* 52: 882–7. p. 243

Leonard, L. B., Rowan, L., Morris, B. and Fey, M. 1982. Intra-word phonological variability in young children. *Journal of Child Language* 9: 55–69. p. 232

Leont'ev, A. N. 1981. The problem of activity in psychology. In J. V. Wertsch (ed.) *The concept of activity in Soviet psychology*. Armonk, NY: M. E. Sharpe. p. 23

Leopold, W. F. 1939. *Speech development of a bilingual child: a linguist's record*, vol. I. Evanston, Ill.: Northwestern University Press. pp. 280, 281, 282, 284, 285, 286, 288, 291, 294, 295, 298

1947. *Speech development of a bilingual child: a linguist's record*, vol. II: *Sound-learning in the first two years*. Evanston, Ill.: Northwestern University Press. pp. 149, 151

1949a. Original invention in infant language. *Symposium* 3: 66–75. p. 250

1949b. *Speech development of a bilingual child: a linguist's record*, vol. III: *Grammar and general problems in the first two years*. Evanston, Ill.: Northwestern University Press. pp. 279, 280, 282, 283, 284, 285

1949c. *Speech development of a bilingual child: a linguist's record*, vol. IV: *Diary from age 2*. Evanston, Ill.: Northwestern University Press. pp. 386, 387, 396

Levelt, W. J. M. 1974. *Formal grammars in linguistics and psycholinguistics*. The Hague: Mouton. p. 96

1975. What became of LAD? In *Ut videam: contributions to an understanding of linguistics, for Pieter Verburg on the occasion of his 70th birthday*. Lisse: Peter de Ridder Press. pp. 73, 520n

Levy, Y. 1983. It's frogs all the way down. *Cognition* 13. p. 430

Lewis, D. K. 1969. *Convention*. Cambridge, Mass.: Harvard University Press. pp. 39, 150

Lewis, M. M. 1951. *Infant speech: a study of the beginnings of language* 2nd edn. London: Routledge and Kegan Paul; New York: Harcourt Brace. 1st edn 1936. pp. 151, 157, 179

1963. *Language, thought and personality in infancy and childhood*. London: Harrap; New York: Basic Books. pp. 201, 281, 283, 288, 289, 290, 292, 294

Li, C. N. and Thompson, S. A. 1977. The acquisition of tone in Mandarin-speaking children. *Journal of Child Language* 4: 185–99. p. 185

Liberman, I. Y., Shankweiler, D., Camp, L., Blachman, B. and Werfelman, M. 1980. Steps towards literacy: a linguistic approach. In P. Levinson and C. Sloan (eds.) *Auditory processing and language: clinical and research perspectives*. New York: Grune and Stratton. p. 453

Liberman, M. and Prince, A. 1977. On stress and linguistic rhythm. *Linguistic Inquiry* 9 (2): 249–336. p. 253

Lieberman, P. 1980. On the development of vowel production in young children. In G. H. Yeni-Komshian, J. F. Kavanagh and C. A. Ferguson (eds.) *Child phonology*, vol. 1: *Production*. New York: Academic Press. p. 154

Lieberman, P., Harris, K. S., Wolff, P. and Russell, L. H. 1971. Newborn infant cry and nonhuman primate vocalization. *Journal of Speech and Hearing Research* 14: 718–27. p. 156

Lieberman, P., Buhr, R., Keating, P., Hamby, S. V. and Landahl, K. H. 1976. Speech development in infants – vowel production. Paper presented at the 92nd Meeting of the Acoustical Society of America, San Diego. p. 157

Lieven, E. 1978a. Conversations between mothers and young children: individual differences and their possible implications for the study of language learning. In N. Waterson and C. Snow (eds.) *The development of communication* Chichester: Wiley. pp. 82, 83, 119, 121, 125

    1978b. Turn-taking and pragmatics: two issues in early child language. In R. N. Campbell and P. Smith (eds.) *Recent advances in the psychology of language: language development and mother–child interaction*. New York and London: Plenum Press. p. 82

Limber, J. 1973. The genesis of complex sentences. In T. E. Moore (ed.) *Cognitive development and the acquisition of language*. pp. 57, 115, 458

Linares, T. 1981. Articulation skills in Spanish speaking children. In R. V. Padilla (ed.) *Ethnoperspectives in bilingual education research*. Ypsilanti, Mich.: Eastern Michigan University. p. 252

Linell, P. 1979. *Psychological reality in phonology: a theoretical study*. New York: Cambridge University Press. pp. 244, 249

Lisker, L. and Abramson, A. S. 1964. A cross-language study of voicing in initial stops: acoustical measurements. *Word* 20: 384–422. p. 256

Loban, W. 1963. *The language of elementary school children*. Urbana, Ill.: National Council of Teachers of English. p. 128

    1976. *Language development: kindergarten through grade twelve*. Urban, Ill.: National Council of Teachers of English. pp. 495, 496, 497, 499, 503, 504

Lock, A. 1978. The emergence of language. In A. Lock (ed.) *Action, gesture and symbol: the emergence of language*. London: Academic Press. pp. 292, 295, 526n

Locke, J. L. 1980. The inference of phoneme perception in the phonologically disordered child. Part 2: Clinically novel procedures, their use, some findings. *Journal of Speech and Hearing Disorders* 45: 445–68. pp. 240, 249

    1982. Historical and developmental phonology. First Forum Lecture, Linguistic Institute, College Park, Maryland. p. 524n

    1983. Phonological acquisition and change. New York: Academic Press. pp. 241, 242, 243, 248

Lodge, K. R. 1979. The use of the past tense in games of pretend. *Journal of Child Language* 6: 365–9. p. 393

Longhurst, T. and Stepanich, L. 1975. Mothers' speech addressed to one-, two-, and three-year-old normal children. *Child Study Journal* 5: 3–11. p. 79

Lord, C. 1979. 'Don't you fall me down!' Children's generalizations regarding cause and transitivity. *Stanford Papers and Reports on Child Language Development* 17: 81–9. p. 441

Lust, B. 1981. Constraints on anaphora in child language: prediction for a universal. In Tavakolian (1981). pp. 63, 339

(ed.) In press. *Studies in the acquisition of anaphora: defining the constraints.* Dordrecht: D. Reidel. p. 61

Lust, B. and Wakayama, T. K. 1979. The structure of coordination in children's first language acquisition of Japanese. In F. Eckman and A. Hastings (eds.) *Studies in first and second language acquisition.* Rowley, Mass.: Newbury House. p. 57

Lust, B., Loveland, K. and Kornet, R. 1980. The development of anaphora in first language: syntactic and pragmatic constraints. *Linguistic Analysis* 6 (4): 359–92. pp. 59, 339

Lynip, A. W. 1951. The use of magnetic devices in the collection and analysis of the pre-verbal utterances of an infant. *Genetic Psychology Monographs* 44: 221–62. p. 152

Lyons, J. 1966a. Comments on D. McNeill 'The creation of language'. In J. Lyons and R. J. Wales (eds.) *Psycholinguistic papers.* Edinburgh: Edinburgh University Press. p. 520n

1966b. Towards a 'notional' theory of the 'parts of speech'. *Journal of Linguistics* 2: 209–36. p. 295

1968. *Introduction to theoretical linguistics.* Cambridge: Cambridge University Press. p. 380

1975. Deixis as the source of reference. In E. Keenan (ed.) *Formal semantics of natural language.* London: Cambridge University Press. pp. 24, 402, 414, 427

Lyons, J. 1977. *Semantics.* 2 vols. Cambridge: Cambridge University Press. pp. 295, 304, 360, 375, 376, 401

1981. *Language, meaning and context.* London: Fontana. p. 526n

Macaulay, R. S. 1978. The myth of female superiority in language. *Journal of Child Language* 5: 353–63. p. 122

McCarthy, D. 1954. Language development in children. In L. Carmichael (ed.) *Manual of child psychology.* 2nd edn. New York: Wiley. pp. 116, 121, 122, 123, 128, 311

McCarthy, J. J. 1981a. The role of evaluation metric in the acquisition of phonology. In Baker and McCarthy (1981). p. 92

1981b. A prosodic theory of nonconcatenative morphology. *Linguistic Inquiry* 12 (3): 373–418. p. 252

McCawley, J. D. 1979. Language universals in linguistic argumentation. *Studies in the Linguistic Sciences* 8 (2): 205–19. p. 251

McCune-Nicolich, L. 1981a. The cognitive basis of relational words in the single word period. *Journal of Child Language* 8: 15–34. p. 292

1981b. Toward symbolic functioning: structure of early pretend games and potential parallels with language. *Child Development* 52: 785–97. p. 393

McDonald, L. and Pien, D. 1982. Mother conversational behaviour as a function of interactional intent. *Journal of Child Language* 9: 337–58. p. 136

McGinn, C. 1981. The mechanism of reference. *Synthese* 49: 157–86. pp. 402, 427

MacKain, K. S. 1982. Assessing the role of experience on infants' speech discrimination. *Journal of Child Language* 9: 527–42. pp. 247, 260

MacKain, K. S., Studdert-Kennedy, M., Spieker, S. and Stern, D. 1983.

Intermodal perception of speech structure by prelinguistic infants is a left hemisphere function. *Science* 219: 1347–9. p. 524n

Macken, M. A. 1979. Developmental reorganization of phonology: a hierarchy of basic units of acquisition. *Lingua* 49: 11–49. pp. 263, 265, 267, 268, 314

1980a. Aspects of the acquisition of stop systems: a cross-linguistic perspective. In G. Yeni-Komshian, J. F. Kavanagh and C. A. Ferguson (eds.) *Child phonology*. New York: Academic Press. pp. 253, 265, 525n

1980b. The child's lexical representation: the 'puzzle-puddle-pickle' evidence. *Journal of Linguistics* 16 (1): 1–17. p. 262

and Barton, D. 1980a. A longitudinal study of the acquisition of the voicing contrast in American-English word-initial stops, as measured by voice onset time. *Journal of Child Language* 7: 41–74. pp. 214, 261, 525n

1980b. The acquisition of the voicing contrast in Spanish: a phonetic and phonological study of word-initial stop consonants. *Journal of Child Language* 7: 433–58. pp. 265, 267

and Ferguson, C. A. 1981. Phonological universals of language acquisition. *Annals of the New York Academy of Sciences* 379: 110–29

1983. Cognitive aspects of phonological development: Model, evidence and issues. In K. E. Nelson (ed.) *Children's language*. Hillsdale, NJ: Erlbaum. pp. 209, 265, 267, 268

McLane, J. B. 1981. Dyadic problem solving: a comparison of child–child and mother–child interaction. Unpublished doctoral dissertation, Northwestern University. p. 19

MacLure, M. 1981. *Making sense of children's talk: structure and strategy in adult-child conversation*. Unpublished doctoral dissertation, University of York. p. 526n

Macnamara, J. 1972. Cognitive basis of language learning in infants. *Psychological Review* 79: 1–13. p. 77

McNeill, D. 1966a. The creation of language by children. In J. Lyons and R. J. Wales (eds.) *Psycholinguistics papers*. Edinburgh: Edinburgh University Press. pp. 70, 71, 105

1966b. Developmental psycholinguistics. In F. Smith and G. A. Miller (eds.) *The genesis of language*. Cambridge, Mass.: MIT Press. p. 323

1970. *The acquisition of language: the study of developmental psycholinguistics*. New York: Harper and Row. p. 39

Macrae, A. 1976a. Meaning relations in language development: a study of some converse pairs and directional opposites. Unpublished doctoral dissertation, University of Edinburgh. pp. 421, 422

1976b. Movement and location in the acquisition of deictic verbs. *Journal of Child Language* 3: 191–204. pp. 405, 421, 422

1979. Combining meanings in early language. In P. Fletcher and M. Garman (eds.) *Language acquisition*. 1st edn. Cambridge: Cambridge University Press

McShane, J. 1979. The development of naming. *Linguistics* 17: 879–905. p. 312

1980. *Learning to talk*. Cambridge: Cambridge University Press. pp. 426, 427

MacWhinney, B. 1978. *The acquisition of morphology*. Society for Research in Child Development Monographs 43. pp. 333, 430, 435

1982. Basic syntactic processes. In Kuczaj (1982). p. 315

1985. Acquisition of Hungarian. In Slobin (1985b). p. 443

Majewicz, A. 1982. Understanding aspect, II. *Lingua Posnaniensis* 25: 17–40. p. 358

Major, D. 1974. *The acquisition of modal auxiliaries in the language of children.* The Hague: Mouton. pp. 386, 389, 390

Major, D. R. 1906. *First steps in mental growth.* London: Macmillan. p. 299

Malikouti-Drachman, A. and Drachman, G. 1975. The acquisition of stress in Modern Greek. *Salzburger Beiträge zur Linguistik* 2: 277–89. p. 191

Malouf, R. and Dodd, D. 1972. Role of exposure, imitation and expansion in the acquisition of an artificial grammatical rule. *Developmental Psychology* 7: 195–203. p. 81

Mann, V. A., Liberman, I. Y. and Shankweiler, D. 1980. Children's memory for sentences and word strings in relation to reading ability. *Memory and Cognition* 8: 329–35. p. 484

Manzini, R. and Wexler, K. 1984. Parameters and learnability in binding theory. Paper presented at the Conference on Parameter Setting, University of Massachusetts-Amherst, May. p. 522n

Marantz, A. 1983. *On the nature of grammatical relations.* Linguistic Inquiry Monograph Series. Cambridge, Mass.: MIT Press. p. 56

Maratsos, M. P. 1973. The effects of stress on the understanding of pronominal co-reference in children. *Journal of Psycholinguistic Research* 2: 1–8. p. 196

1974. Children who get worse at understanding the passive: a replication of Bever. *Journal of Psycholinguistic Research* 3: 65–74. pp. 61, 62, 458

1979. How to get from words to sentences. In D. Aaronson and R. Reiber (eds.) *Perspectives in psycholinguistics.* Hillsdale, NJ: Erlbaum. p. 106

1982. The child's construction of grammatical categories. In Wanner and Gleitman (1982). pp. 106, 316, 323

1983. Some current issues in the study of the acquisition of grammar. In P. H. Mussen (Gen. ed.) *Carmichael's manual of child psychology*, vol. III. 4th edn. New York: Wiley. p. 434

and Abramovitch, R. 1974. How children understand full, truncated and anomalous passives. *Journal of Verbal Learning and Verbal Behavior* 14: 145–57. p. 458

and Chalkley, M. A. 1980. The internal language of children's syntax: the ontogenesis and representation of syntactic categories. In K. E. Nelson (ed.) *Children's language*, vol. 2. New York: Gardner Press. p. 106

Markman, E. M. 1979. Realizing that you don't understand: elementary school children's awareness of inconsistencies. *Child Development* 50: 643–55. p. 492

Marshall, J. C. 1980. On the biology of language acquisition. In D. Caplan (ed.) *Biological studies of mental processes.* Cambridge, Mass.: MIT Press. p. 308

Marslen-Wilson, W. D. and Welsh, A. 1978. Processing interactions and lexical access during word recognition in continuous speech. *Cognitive Psychology* 10: 29–63. p. 258

Mason, M., Smith, B. and Hinshaw, M. 1976. *Medida espanola de articulatión.* San Ysidro, CA: San Ysidro School District. p. 252

Matthei, E. 1981. Children's interpretation of sentences containing reciprocals. In Tavakolian (1981). pp. 58, 101

576   Bibliography (and citation index)

Mattingley, I. G. 1973. Phonetic prerequisites for first-language acquisition. Status
    Report on Speech Research. SR 341-5 Haskins Laboratories. p. 167
Maxwell, E. and Weismer, G. 1982. The contribution of phonological, acoustic,
    and perceptual techniques to the characterization of a misarticulating child's
    voice contrast for stops. *Applied Psycholinguistics* 3: 29–43. p. 266
Mazurkevich, I. and White, L. 1982. The acquisition of the dative alternation:
    do we need indirect evidence? Paper presented at the Canadian Linguistics
    Association Meeting, Ottawa. p. 68
Mehler, J., Bertoncini, J., Barriere, M. and Jassik-Gerschenfeld, D. 1978. Infant
    recognition of mother's voice. *Percept* 7: 491–7. p. 179
Meillet, A. 1937. *Introduction à l'étude comparative des langues indo-européennes.*
    8th edn. Paris: Hachette. p. 399
Melgar de Gonzalez, M. 1976. *Como dectar al niño con problemas dei habla.*
    Mexico: Editorial Trillas. p. 252
Meltzoff, A. N. and Moore, M. K. 1977. Imitation of facial and manual gestures
    by human neonates. *Science* 198: 75–8. p. 243
Menn, L. 1971. Phonotactic rules in beginning speech. *Lingua* 26: 225–51. p. 215
    1975. Counter example to 'fronting' as a universal of child language. *Journal
        of Child Language* 2: 293–6. pp. 227, 228
    1976a. Pattern, control and contrast in beginning speech: a case study in the
        development of word form and word function. Unpublished doctoral thesis,
        University of Illinois at Urbana-Champaign. Univ. Micro. 76-24, 139. pp. 181,
        182, 184, 185, 201, 211
    1976b. Evidence for an interactionist discovery theory of child phonology.
        Stanford Papers and Reports on Child Language Development 12: 169–77.
        p. 216
    1978. Phonological units in beginning speech. In A. Bell and J. Hooper (eds.)
        Syllables and segments. Amsterdam: North-Holland. p. 211, 215, 263
    1979. Transition and variation in child phonology: modeling a developing
        system. *Proceedings of the 9th International Congress of Phonetic Sciences.*
        Copenhagen: University of Copenhagen. p. 253
    1979b. Towards a psychology of phonology: child phonology as a first step. In
        R. Herbert (ed.) *Applications of linguistic theory in human sciences.*
        Linguistics Department, Michigan State University. p. 209
    1982. Child language as a source of constraints in linguistic theory. In L. K.
        Obler and L. Menn (eds.) *Exceptional language and linguistics.* New York:
        Academic Press
    1983. Development of articulatory, phonetic and phonological capabilities. In
        B. Butterworth (ed.) *Language production,* vol. II. London: Academic Press.
        p. 209
    and Haselkorn, S. 1977. Now you see it, now you don't: tracing the development
        of communicative competence. In J. Kegl (ed.) *Proceedings of the Seventh
        Annual Meeting of the Northeast Linguistic Society.* pp. 211, 212
Menyuk, P. 1968. The role of distinctive features in children's acquisition of
    phonology. *Journal of Speech and Hearing Research* 11: 138–46. p. 150
    1969. *Sentences children use.* Cambridge, Mass.: MIT Press. pp. 110, 196, 391

1971. *The acquisition and development of language.* Englewood Cliffs, NJ: Prentice-Hall. pp. 198, 203

1972. *Speech development.* Indianapolis, Ind.: Bobbs Merrill. pp. 203, 204

1976. Relations between acquisition of phonology and reading. In J. Guthrie (ed.) *Aspects of reading.* Baltimore, Md: Johns Hopkins University Press. p. 204

1977. *Language and maturation.* Cambridge, Mass.: MIT Press. p. 205

and Bernholtz, N. 1969. Prosodic features and children's language production. MIT *Quarterly Progress Report* 93: 216–19. p. 186

Mervis, C. B. and Canada, K. 1983. On the existence of competence errors in early comprehension: a reply to Fremgen & Fay and Chapman & Thomson. *Journal of Child Language* 10: 431–40. p. 301

Miller, G. A. 1956. The magical number seven, plus or minus two: some limits of our capacity for processing information. *Psychological Review* 63: 81–97. p. 485

and Chomsky, N. 1963. Finitary models of language users. In R. Bush, E. Galanter and R. Luce (eds.) *Handbook of mathematical psychology*, vol. II. New York: Wiley. p. 70

and Johnson-Laird, P. 1976. *Language and perception.* Cambridge, Mass.: Harvard University Press. p. 423

and Nicely, P. 1955. Analysis of perceptual confusions among some English consonants. *Journal of the Acoustical Society of America* 27: 338–52. p. 203

and Selfridge, J. A. 1953. Verbal context and the recall of meaningful material. *American Journal of Psychology* 63: 176–85. p. 490

Miller, J. E. 1970. Stative verbs in Russian. *Foundations of Language* 6: 488–504. p. 360

Miller, J. and Eimas, P. 1983. Studies in the categorization of speech by infants. *Cognition* 13: 135–65. pp. 105, 203

Miller, M. 1976. *Zur Logik der frühkindlichen Sprachentwicklung.* Stuttgart: Ernst Klett. p. 40

1979. *The logic of language development in early childhood.* Berlin: Springer-Verlag. p. 23

1982. Learning how to contradict and still pursue a common end: the ontogenesis of moral argumentation. Paper presented at the Tenth World Congress of Sociology, Research Committee on Sociolinguistics. Mexico City, August 16–21. pp. 14, 17, 26

1984. *Kollektive Lernprozesse und Moral.* Habil. Schrift, University of Frankfurt. pp. 14, 15

Miller, W. R. and Erwin, S. M. 1964. The development of grammar in child language. In U. Bellugi and R. Brown (eds.) *The acquisition of language.* Monographs of the Society for Research in Child Development 29 (1): 9–35. pp. 117, 388

Mills, A. 1985. Acquisition of German. In Slobin (1985b). p. 531n

Milner, E. 1976. Central nervous system maturation and language acquisition. In H. Whitaker and H. A. Whitaker *Studies in Neurolinguistics*, vol. 1. New York: Academic Press. p. 170

Mines, M. A., Hanson, B. F. and Shoup, J. E. 1978. Frequency of occurrence of phonemes in conversational English. *Language and Speech* 21: 221–41. p. 246

Mitchell-Kernan, C. and Kernan, K. T. 1977. Pragmatics of directive choice among children. In S. Ervin-Tripp and C. Mitchell-Kernan (eds.) *Child discourse.* New York: Academic Press. p. 391

Mithun, M. 1982. The acquisition of polysynthesis. MS. SUNY, Buffalo. p. 527n

Moerk, E. L. 1976. Processes of language teaching and training in the interactions of mother–child dyads. *Child Development* 47: 1064–78. p. 72

   1980. Relations between parental input frequencies and children's language acquisition: a reanalysis of Brown's data. *Journal of Child Language* 7: 105–18. p. 334

   1981. To attend or not to attend to unwelcome reanalyses? A reply to Pinker. *Journal of Child Language* 8: 627–31. p. 334

   1983. A behavioral analysis of controversial topics in first language acquisition: reinforcements, corrections, modelling, input frequencies and the three-term contingency pattern. *Journal of Psycholinguistic Research* 12: 129–55. p. 106

Moffitt, A. R. 1971. Consonant cue perception by twenty-two twenty-four-week-old infants. *Child Development* 42: 717–32. p. 259

Montes-Giraldo, J. J. 1970. Dominancio de las labiales en el sistema fonologico del habla infantil. *Thesaurus* 25: 487–88. p. 265

   1971. Acerca de la apropriacion por el niño del sistema fonologia espanol. *Thesaurus* 26: 322–46. p. 265

Morais, J., Cary, L., Alegria, F. and Bertelson, P. 1979. Does awareness of speech as a sequence of phones arise spontaneously? *Cognition* 7: 323–31. p. 476

Morsbach, G. and Steel, P. M. 1976. 'John is easy to see' re-investigated. *Journal of Child Language* 3: 443–7. p. 457

Morse, P. A. 1972. The discrimination of speech and nonspeech stimuli in early infancy. *Journal of Experimental Child Psychology* 14: 477–92. p. 179

   1974. Infant speech perception: a preliminary model and a review of the literature. In R. L. Schiefelbusch and L. L. Lloyd (eds.) *Language perspectives: acquisition, retardation and intervention.* London and Basingstoke: Macmillan; Baltimore, Md: University Park Press. p. 199

   1978. Infant speech perception: origins, processes and Alpha Centauri. In F. Minifie and L. L. Lloyd (eds.) *Communicative and cognitive abilities – early behavioral assessment.* Baltimore: University Park Press. pp. 199, 200

Moser, H. 1969. *One-syllable words.* Columbus, Ohio: Charles E. Merrill. p. 243

Mounoud, P. and Bower, T. G. R. 1974. Conservation of weight in infants. *Cognition* 3: 29–40. p. 35

Mountcastle, V. 1978. An organizing principle for cerebral function: the unit module and the distributed system. In G. Edleman and V. Mountcastle (eds.) *The mindful brain.* Cambridge, Mass.: MIT Press. p. 172

Mulford, R. 1983. On the acquisition of derivational morphology in Icelandic: learning about *-ari. Islenskt mál og almenn málfraedi* 5. pp. 430, 433

Muller-Preuss, P. 1978. Single unit responses of the auditory cortex in the squirrel monkey to self-produced and loudspeaker-transmitted vocalizations. *Nerosci. Lett.* Suppl. 1, S.7. p. 169

Munro, J. and Wales, R. 1982. Changes in the child's comprehension of simultaneity and sequence. *Journal of Verbal Learning and Verbal Behavior* 21: 175–85. p. 424

Murai, J. 1960. Speech development of infants: analysis of speech by sonography. *Psychologia* 3: 27–35. p. 157

Muysken, P. 1981. Creole tense/mood/aspect systems: the unmarked case? In P. Muysken (ed.) *Generative studies on Creole languages*. Dordrecht: Foris Publications. p. 530n

Myers, F. L. and Myers, R. W. 1983. Perception of stress contrasts in semantic and nonsemantic contexts by children. *Journal of Psycholinguistic Research* 12: 2327–38. p. 192

Nakazima, S. A. 1962. A comparative study of the speech development of Japanese and American English in childhood (1): a comparison of the development of voices at the prelinguistic period. *Studia Phonologica* 2: 27–46. pp. 150, 157

1966. A comparative study of the speech development of Japanese and American English in childhood (2): the acquisition of speech. *Studia Phonologica* 4: 38–55. p. 153

1970. A comparative study of the speech development of Japanese and American English in childhood (3): the reorganization process of babbling articulation mechanisms. *Studia Phonologica* 5: 20–35. pp. 162, 200

Nakazima, S. A., Okamoto, N., Murai, J., Tanaka, M., Okuna, S., Meda, T. and Shimizu, M. 1962. The phoneme systemization and the verbalization process of voices in childhood. *Shinrigan-Hyoron* 6: 1–48. p. 150

Neisser, U. 1966. *Cognitive psychology*. New York: Appleton-Century-Crofts. p. 258

Nelson, K. 1973a. Some evidence for the cognitive primacy of categorisation and its functional basis. *Merrill-Palmer Quarterly* 19: 21–39. pp. 44, 45

1973b. *Structure and strategy in learning to talk*. Monographs of the Society for Research in Child Development 38 (1–2) ser. no. 149. pp. 43, 81, 83, 110, 118, 119, 121, 125, 135, 137, 162, 204, 215, 279, 291, 293, 310, 311, 312, 317, 402

1974. Concept, word and sentence: interrelations in acquisition and development. *Psychological Review* 81: 267–84. pp. 43, 291, 296, 297, 302

1975. The nominal shift in semantic–syntactic development. *Cognitive Psychology* 7: 461–79. p. 119

1976. Some attributes of adjectives used by young children. *Cognition* 4: 13–30. p. 45

1979. Features, contrasts and the FCH: some comments on Barrett's lexical development hypothesis. *Journal of Child Language* 6: 139–46. p. 298

1981. Individual differences in language development: implications for development and language. *Developmental Psychology* 17: 170–87. pp. 118, 121, 137

1981b. Acquisition of words by first language learners. In H. Winitz (ed.) *Native*

language and foreign language acquisition. *Annals of the New York Academy of Sciences* vol. 379: 148–59. pp. 309, 312, 318

Nelson, K. E. 1977. Facilitating children's syntax acquisition. *Developmental Psychology* 13: 101–7. p. 81

Nelson, K. E., Carskaddon, G. and Bonvillian, J. D. 1973. Syntax acquisitions: impact of experimental variation in adult verbal interaction with the child. *Child Development* 44: 497–504. p. 81

Neu, H. 1980. Ranking of constraints on /t, d/ deletion in American English: a statistical analysis. In W. Labov (ed.) *Locating language in time and space.* New York: Academic Press. p. 246

Newman, J. D. In press. The infant cry of primates: an evolutionary perspective. In B. M. Lester and C. F. Z. Boukydis (eds.) *Infant crying: theoretical and research implications.* New York: Plenum Press. p. 169

Newport, E. L. 1977. Motherese: the speech of mothers to young children. In N. Castellan, D. Pisoni and G. Potts (eds.) *Cognitive theory,* vol. II Hillsdale, NJ: Erlbaum. pp. 73, 78, 389

   1982. Task specificity in language learning? Evidence from speech perception and American sign language. In Wanner and Gleitman (1982). pp. 308, 473

Newport, E. L., Gleitman, L. R. and Gleitman, H. 1977. Mother, I'd rather do it myself: some effects and noneffects of maternal speech style. In Snow and Ferguson (1977). pp. 55, 73, 76, 78

Newton, B. 1979. Scenarios, modality and verbal aspect in Modern Greek. *Language* 55: 139–67. p. 376

Ninio, A. 1980. Ostensive definition in vocabulary teaching. *Journal of Child Language* 7: 565–73. pp. 425, 526n

   and Bruner, J. 1978. The achievement and antecedents of labelling. *Journal of Child Language* 5: 1–15. pp. 24, 44, 72, 86, 87

   and Snow, C. E. In press. Origins of deep structure in function. In Y. Levi and I. Schlesinger (eds.) *Perspectives on language acquisition theory.* p. 74

Nooteboom, S. G., Brokx, J. P. L. and de Rooij, J. J. 1978. Contributions of prosody to speech perception. In W. J. M Levelt and G. B. Flores d'Arcais (eds.) *Studies in the perception of language.* New York: Wiley. p. 179

Ochs, E. and Schieffelin, B. B. 1984. Language acquisition and socialization: three developmental stories and their implications. In R. Shweder and R. LeVine (eds.) *Culture and its acquisition.* New York: Cambridge University Press. pp. 85, 86

Ochs, E., Schieffelin, B. B. and Platt, M. L. 1979. Propositions across utterances and speakers. In E. Ochs and B. B. Schieffelin (eds.) *Developmental pragmatics.* New York: Academic Press. p. 24

O'Donnell, R. C., Griffin, W. J. and Norris, R. C. 1967. *Syntax of kindergarten and elementary school children: a transformational analysis.* Urbana, Ill.: National Council of Teachers of English. pp. 495, 496, 497, 498, 500, 503, 505, 514

Oleron, P. 1963. Discussion of Piaget's paper, 'Le langage et les operations intellectuelles'. In *Problèmes de psycholinguistique. Proceedings of the symposium of the Association de Psychologie Scientifique de Langue Française.* Paris: Presses Universitaires de France. p. 12

Oller, D. K. 1976. Analysis of infant vocalizations: a linguistic and speech scientific perspective. Invited miniseminar given at the American Speech and Hearing Association Convention, Houston. pp. 157, 160, 162, 163, 171

and Eilers, R. E. 1982. Similarity of babbling in Spanish- and English-learning babies. *Journal of Child Language* 9: 565–77

and Smith, B. L. 1977. Effect of final-syllable position on vowel duration in infant babbling. *Journal of the Acoustical Society of America* 62: 994–7. p. 154

Oller, D. K., Weiman, L. A., Doyle, W. J. and Ross, D. 1976. Infant babbling and speech. *Journal of Child Language* 3: 1–11. pp. 152, 157

Olmsted, D. L. 1966. A theory of the child's learning of phonology. *Language* 42: 531–5. pp. 199

1971. *Out of the mouths of babes.* The Hague: Mouton. pp. 145, 198, 208, 251

Olney, R. and Scholnick, E. 1976. Adult judgements of age and linguistic differences in infant vocalization. *Journal of Child Language* 3: 145–56. p. 180

Olsen-Fulero, L. 1982. Style and stability in mother conversational behaviour: a study of individual differences. *Journal of Child Language* 9: 543–64. pp. 135, 136

Olson, D. R. 1977. From utterance to text: the bias of language in speech and writing. *Harvest Educational Review* 47: 257–81. p. 483

Osgood, E. C. 1953. *Method and theory in experimental psychology.* New York: Oxford University Press. p. 149

Osherson, D. and Markman, E. 1974. Language and the ability to evaluate contradictions and tautologies. *Cognition* 3: 213–26. p. 393

and Smith, E. E. 1981. On the adequacy of prototype theory as a theory of concepts. *Cognition* 9: 35–58. pp. 44, 521n

Otsu, Y. 1981a. Opacity condition and syntactic development in children. *Proceedings of NELS XI.* Amherst, Mass.: Graduate Student Linguistics Association, University of Massachusetts-Amherst. p. 57

1981b. Universal grammar and syntactic development in children. Unpublished doctoral dissertation, MIT. pp. 66, 67

Palmer, F. R. 1979. *Modality and the English modals.* Harlow: Longman. p. 376

Parisi, D. and Antinucci, F. 1970. Lexical competence. In G. B. Flores d'Arcais and W. J. M. Levelt (eds.) *Advances in psycholinguistics.* Amsterdam: North-Holland. p. 418

1976. *Essentials of grammar.* New York: Academic Press. p. 376

Pattison, H. M. 1983. *Reading and writing in hearing-impaired children.* Unpublished doctoral thesis, University of Reading. pp. 478, 485, 486, 487, 488, 492, 493

Pea, R. D. and Mawby, R. 1981. Semantics of modal auxiliary verb uses by preschool children. Paper presented at the Second International Congress for the Study of Child Language, Vancouver, BC, August. pp. 386, 388

Pea, R. D., Mawby, R. and MacKain, S. J. 1982. World-making and world-revealing: semantics and pragmatics of modal auxiliary verbs during the third year of life. Paper presented at the Seventh Annual Boston Conference on Child Language Development, October. pp. 376, 386, 395, 396, 399

Pechmann, Th. and Deutsch, W. 1980. From gesture to word and gesture. *Stanford Papers and Reports on Child Language Development* 19: 113–20. p. 403

582   Bibliography (and citation index)

Peirce, C. S. 1932. *Collected papers of C.S. Peirce*, vol. II. Ed. by C. Hartshorne
     and P. Weiss (1931–5). Cambridge, Mass.: Harvard University Press. p. 18
Perera, K. 1984. *Children's writing and reading*. Oxford: Blackwell. p. 502
Peters, A. M. 1974. University of Hawaii study of the beginning of speech.
     Working Papers in Linguistics 6, University of Hawaii, Honolulu. p. 240
     1977. Language learning strategies: does the whole equal the sum of the parts?
     Language 53: 560–73. pp. 119, 293, 310, 312, 314, 317
     1980. The units of language acquisition. *Working Papers in Linguistics*,
     Fol. 12 (1), University of Hawaii, Honolulu. p. 206
     1981. Language typology and the segmentation problem in early child language
     acquisition. *Proceedings of the Seventh Annual Meeting of the Berkeley
     Linguistics Society*. pp. 430, 527n
     1983. *The units of language acquisition*. Cambridge: Cambridge University Press.
     pp. 110, 111, 115, 119, 249, 311, 315, 430, 435, 527n
Phillips, J. 1973. Syntax and vocabulary of mothers' speech to young children:
     age and sex comparisons. *Child Development* 44: 182–5. pp. 70, 78
Phinney, M. 1981. Markedness and the development of COMP. In J. Pustejovsky
     and V. Burke (eds.) Markedness and learnability. University of Massachusetts
     Occasional Papers in Linguistics 6. p. 105
     1981b. Syntactic constraints and the acquisition of embedded complements.
     Unpublished doctoral dissertation, University of Massachusetts-Amherst,
     distributed by the Graduate Student Linguistic Association, University of
     Massachusetts. p. 67
     1981c. The acquisition of embedded sentences and the nominative island
     constraint. *Proceedings of NELS XI*. Amherst, Mass.: Graduate Student
     Linguistic Association, University of Massachusetts-Amherst. p. 67
Piaget, J. 1923. *Le langage et la pensée chez l'enfant*. Neuchatel: Delachaux et
     Niestle. pp. 13, 17, 27
     1924. *Le jugement et le raisonnement chez l'enfant*. Neuchatel: Delachaux et
     Niestle. p. 13
     1926. *The language and thought of the child*. London: Routledge and Kegan
     Paul. p. 402
     1932. *Le jugement moral chez l'enfant*. Paris: Librairie F. Alcan. pp. 13, 17
     1946a. *Le développement de la notion de temps chez l'enfant*. Paris: Presses
     Universitaires de France. p. 26
     1946b. *La formation du symbole chez l'enfant: imitation, jeu et rêve, image et
     représentation*. Neuchatel: Delachaux et Niestle. Translated and published
     1951 as *Play, dreams and imitation in childhood*. London: Routledge and
     Kegan Paul; 1962 New York: Norton. pp. 11, 17, 41, 393
     1952. *The origins of intelligence in children*. New York: Norton. p. 167
     1963. Le langage et les operations intellectuelles. In *Problèmes de
     psycholinguistique. Proceedings of the symposium of the Association de
     Psychologie Scientifique de Langue Française*. Paris: Presses Universitaires de
     France. p. 11
     and Inhelder, B. 1956. *The child's conception of space*. London: Routledge and
     Kegan Paul. p. 402

Piattelli-Palmarini, M. 1980. *Language and learning: the debate between Chomsky and Piaget.* Cambridge, Mass.: Harvard University Press. p. 30

Piéraut-Le Bonniec, G. 1980. *The development of modal reasoning: genesis of necessity and possibility notions.* New York: Academic Press. p. 393

Pinker, S. 1979. Formal models of language learning. *Cognition* 7: 217–83. pp. 77, 87, 94, 98

    1981. On the acquisition of grammatical morphemes. *Journal of Child Language* 8: 477–84. p. 334

    1982. A theory of the acquisition of lexical-interpretive grammars. In Bresnan (1982b). pp. 56, 68, 90

    In press. *Language learnability and language development.* Cambridge, Mass.: Harvard University Press. p. 56

Pisoni, D. B. 1977. Identification and discrimination of the relative onset time of two component tones: implications for voicing perception in stops. *Journal of the Acoustical Society of America* 61 (5): 1352–61. p. 256

Pitman, J. and St John, J. 1969. *Alphabets and reading: the initial teaching alphabet.* London: Pitman. p. 480

Platt, C. B. and MacWhinney, B. 1983. Error assimilation as a mechanism in language learning. *Journal of Child Language* 10: 104–14. p. 106

Ploog, D. 1979. Phonation, emotion, cognition with reference to the brain mechanisms involved. *Ciba Foundation Symposium* 69. pp. 168, 170

Plowden, Lady 1967. *Children and their primary schools.* London: HMSO. p. 131

Polanyi, M. 1968. Logic and psychology. *The American Psychologist* 23: 34–42. p. 37

Posner, M. I. and Snyder, C. R. R. 1975. Attention and cognitive control. In R. L. Solso (ed.) *Information processing and cognition.* Hillsdale, NJ: Erlbaum. p. 488

Postal, P. M. 1966. On so-called pronouns in English. In F. Dinneen (ed.) *Nineteenth monograph on languages and linguistics.* Washington, DC: Georgetown University Press. p. 340

Pottier, B. 1976. Sur la formulation des modalités en linguistique. *Langages* 43: 39–46. p. 376

Press, M. L. 1974. Semantic features in lexical acquisition. *Stanford Papers and Reports on Child Language Development* 8: 129–41. p. 299

Preston, M. S., Yeni-Komshian, G. H., Stark, R. E. and Port, D. K. 1969. Certain aspects of the development of speech production and speech perception in children. *Journal of the Acoustical Society of America* 46: A102. pp. 153, 161

Priestley, T. M. S. 1977. One idiosyncratic strategy in the acquisition of phonology. *Journal of Child Language* 4: 45–66. pp. 235

    1980. Homonymy in child phonology. *Journal of Child Language* 7 (2): 413–27. p. 233

Putnam, H. 1967. The innateness hypothesis and explanatory models in linguistics. *Synthese* 17: 12–22. p. 520n

    1970. Is semantics possible? *Metaphilosophy* 1: 187–201. p. 521n

Pye, C. 1983. Mayan telegraphese: intonational determinants of inflectional development in Quiché Mayan. *Language* 59: 583–604. pp. 436, 527n

and Ratner, N. B. 1984. Higher pitch in BT is not universal: acoustic evidence from Quiché Mayan. *Journal of Child Language*. pp. 194, 195

Quine, W. V. O. 1975. The nature of knowledge. In S. Guttenplan (ed.) *Mind and language*. Oxford: Oxford University Press. p. 45

Quirk, R., Greenbaum, S., Leech, G. N. and Svartvik, J. 1972. *A grammar of contemporary English*. London: Longman. pp. 196, 501, 507, 508, 513

Radford, A. 1979. Notes on *wh*-relatives in Urdu. Unpublished paper, University of Essex. p. 101

Radulović, L. 1975. Acquisition of language: studies of Dubrovnik children. Unpublished doctoral dissertation, University of California, Berkeley. pp. 361, 362

Ramer, A. 1976. Syntactic styles in emerging language. *Journal of Child Language* 3: 49–62. pp. 119, 121, 127, 310, 312, 313, 314, 317, 318, 323

Randall, J. 1982. The acquisition of agents: morphological and semantic hypotheses. In *Stanford Papers and Reports on Child Language Development* 21: 87–94. p. 68

Ratner, N. and Bruner, J. 1978. Games, social exchange and the acquisition of language. *Journal of Child Language* 5: 391–402. p. 86

Read, C. 1975. *Children's categorizations of speech sounds in children*. Research report no. 17. Urbana, Ill.: National Council of Teachers of English. p. 248

Reason, J. T. 1977. Skill and error in everyday life. In M. J. A. Howe (ed.) *Adult learning*. London: Wiley. p. 489

Rees, N. 1972. The role of babbling in the child's acquisition of language. *British Journal of Communication Disorders* 7: 17–23. p. 149

Reich, P. A. 1976. The early acquisition of word meaning. *Journal of Child Language* 3: 117–23. pp. 230, 232

Reichenbach, H. 1947. *Symbolic logic*. Berkeley, Ca.: University of California Press. pp. 356, 374

Reinhart, T. 1981. Definite anaphora and c-command domains. *Linguistic Inquiry* 12: 4. p. 521n

Remick, H. 1976. Maternal speech to children during language acquisition. In W. von Raffler-Engel and Y. Lebrun (eds.) *Baby talk and infant speech*. Amsterdam: Swets and Zeitlinger. pp. 70, 192

Renfrew, C. E. 1966. Persistence of the open syllable in defective articulation. *Journal of Speech and Hearing Research* 38: 304–15. p. 231

Rescorla, L. A. 1980. Overextension in early language development. *Journal of Child Language* 7: 321–35. pp. 279, 280, 291, 298, 299, 301
    1981. Category development in early language. *Journal of Child Language* 8: 225–38. pp. 301, 304, 305

Retherford, K. S., Schwartz, B. C. and Chapman, R. S. 1981. Semantic roles and residual grammatical categories in mother and child speech: who tunes into whom? *Journal of Child Language* 8: 583–608. p. 79

Reynell, J. 1969. *Developmental Language Scale*. Slough: NFER. pp. 110, 111

Rheingold, H. L., Gewirtz, J. L. and Ross, H. W. 1959. Social conditioning of vocalizations in the infant. *Journal of Comparative and Physiological Psychology* 52: 68–73. p. 150

Ricciuti, H. 1965. Object grouping and selective ordering behavior in infants 12–24 months old. *Merrill-Palmer Quarterly* 11: 129–48. p. 45

Richards, M. M. 1976. *Come* and *go* revisited: Children's use of deictic verbs in contrived situations. *Journal of Verbal Learning and Verbal Behavior* 15: 655–65. p. 422

Ringel, R. L. and Kluppel, D. D. 1964. Neonatal crying: a normative study. *Folia Phoniatrica* 16: 1–9. p. 156

Risley, T. R. and Reynolds, N. J. 1970. Emphasis as a prompt for verbal imitation. *Journal of Applied Behavioral Analysis* 3: 185–90. p. 191

Rispoli, M. 1981. The emergence of verb and adjective tense–aspect inflections in Japanese. Unpublished Master's thesis, University of Pennsylvania. pp. 359, 361

Rodgon, M. M. 1976. *Single-word usage, cognitive development and the beginnings of combinatorial speech.* Cambridge: Cambridge University Press. p. 316

Roeper, T. 1981. Introduction. In J. Pustejovsky and V. Burke (eds.) Markedness and learnability. *University of Massachusetts Occasional Papers in Linguistics* 6. p. 68

1982a. The role of universals in the acquisition of gerunds. In Wanner and Gleitman (1982). pp. 61, 103, 105

1982b. On the importance of syntax and the logical use of evidence. In Kuczaj (1982). p. 67

Roeper, T., Bing, S., Lapointe, J. and Tavakolian, S. 1981. A lexical approach to language acquisition. In Tavakolian (1981). p. 68

Rogers, D. 1978. Information about word-meaning in the speech of parents to young children. In R. N. Campbell and P. T. Smith (eds.) *Recent advances in the psychology of language*, vol. 1. New York: Plenum Press. p. 306

Rogoff, B. and Wertsch, J. V. (eds.) In press. *Cognitive growth in children. The zone of proximal development.* San Francisco: Jossey-Bass. p. 16

Rollins, W. C. 1980. Laboratory vs. 'free' testing situations in language acquisition research. Unpublished BA honours thesis, University of Alberta. pp. 334, 335

Rom, A., Berman, R. A. and Guralnik, E. In preparation. A language screening test for Hebrew-speaking preschoolers. p. 532n

Rommetveit, R. 1974. *On message structure: a conceptual framework for the study of language and communication.* London: Wiley. p. 21

1977. On Piagetian operations, semantic competence, and message structure in adult–child communication. In I. Markova (ed.) *The social context of language.* London: Wiley. pp. 15, 16

1979a. On negative rationalism in scholarly studies of verbal communication and dynamic residuals in the construction of human intersubjectivity. In R. Rommetveit and R. Blaker (eds.) *Studies of language, thought and verbal communication.* New York: Academic Press. p. 21

1979b. On the relationship between children's mastery of Piagetian cognitive operations and their semantic competence. In R. Rommetveit and R. Blaker (eds.) *Studies of language, thought and verbal communication.* New York: Academic Press. p. 16

Roulet, E. 1980. Modalité et illocution: pouvoir et devoir dans les actes de permission et de requête. *Communications* 32: 216–39. p. 376

Roussey, C. 1899–1900. Notes sur l'apprentissage de la parole chez un enfant. *La Parole* 1: 870–80; 2: 23–40. pp. 227, 232

Routh, D. K. 1969. Conditioning of vocal responses in infants. *Developmental Psychology* 1: 219–26. p. 151

Rosch, E. H. 1973. On the internal structure of perceptual and semantic categories. In T. E. Moore (ed.) *Cognitive development and the acquisition of language*. New York: Academic Press. pp. 296, 303

Rosch, E. H., Mervis, C. B., Gray, W., Johnson, D. and Boyes-Braem, P. 1976. Basic objects in natural categories. *Cognitive Psychology* 8: 382–439. p. 44

Rose, S. A. and Blank, M. 1974. The potency of context in children's cognition: an illustration through conversation. *Child Development* 45: 499–502. p. 114

Rosenthal, D. M. 1980. The modularity and maturation of cognitive capacities. *Behavioral and Brain Sciences* 3: 32. p. 33

Ross, A. S. C. 1937. An example of vowel-harmony in a young child. *Modern Language Notes* 52: 508–9. pp. 231, 238

Ross, G. S. 1980. Categorization in 1- to 2-year olds. *Developmental Psychology* 16: 391–6. p. 305

Rozin, P., Poritsky, S. and Sotsky, R. 1971. American children with reading problems can easily learn to read English represented by Chinese characters. *Science* 171: 1264–7. p. 488

Rūķe-Draviņa, V. 1981. In P. S. Dale and D. Ingram (eds.) Child language – an international perspective. Baltimore, Md.: University Park Press. p. 185

Ryan, J. 1978. Contour in context. In R. N. Campbell and P. T. Smith (eds.) *Recent advances in the psychology of language: language development and mother–child interaction*. New York and London: Plenum Press. p. 74

Sachs, J. 1977. The adaptive significance of linguistic input to prelinguistic infants. In Snow and Ferguson (1977). pp. 192, 194

  1979. Topic selection in parent–child discourse. *Discourse Processes* 2: 145–53. p. 79

  1983. Talking about the there and then: the emergence of displaced reference in parent–child discourse. In K. E. Nelson (ed.) *Children's language*, vol. 4. Hillsdale, NJ: Erlbaum. pp. 79, 359

  and Devin, J. 1976. Young children's use of age-appropriate speech styles in social interaction and role-playing. *Journal of Child Language* 3: 81–98. pp. 71, 187

  and Truswell, L. 1978. Comprehension of 2-word instructions by children in the 1-word stage. *Journal of Child Language* 5: 17–24. p. 41

Sachs, J., Brown, R. and Salerno, R. 1976. Adult's speech to children. In W. von Raffler Engel and Y. Lebrun (eds.) *Baby talk and infant speech*. Lisse: Peter de Ridder Press. p. 70

Sazaki, C. T., Levine, P. A., Laitman, J. T. and Crelin, E. S. 1977. Postnatal descent of the epiglottis in man. *Arch. Otolaryng.* 103: 169–71. p. 166

Schadler, M. and Thissen, D. M. 1981. The development of automatic word recognition and reading skill. *Memory and Cognition* 2: 132–41. p. 490

Schaerlaekens, A. M. 1977. *De taalontwikkeling van het kind: een oriëntatie in het Nederlandstalig onderzoek.* Groningen: Wolters-Noordhoff. p. 394

Schieffelin, B. B. 1979. Getting it together: an ethnographic approach to the study of the development of communicative competence. In E. Ochs and B. B. Schieffelin (eds.) *Developmental pragmatics.* New York: Academic Press. pp. 23, 85, 138

    1984. *How Kaluli children learn what to say, what to do, and how to feel: an ethnographic study of the development of communicative competence.* New York: Academic Press. p. 85

Schlesinger, J. M. 1971a. Learning grammar: from pivot to realisation rule. In R. Huxley and E. Ingram (eds.) *Language acquisition: models and methods.* London: Academic Press. p. 77

    1971b. Production of utterances and language acquisition. In D. I. Slobin (ed.) *The ontogenesis of grammar.* New York: Academic Press. pp. 23, 39

Schneider, P. In preparation. Discourse skills in formal operations. Doctoral dissertation, Northwestern University. p. 12

Scholnick, E. K. and Adams, M. J. 1973. Relationships between language and cognitive skills: passive voice comprehension, backward repetition and matrix permutation. *Child Development* 44: 741–6. p. 458

Schumaker, J. B. 1976. Mothers' expressions: their characteristics and effects on child language. Unpublished doctoral dissertation, University of Kansas. p. 81

Schwartz, R. and Leonard, L. 1982. Do children pick and choose? An examination of phonological selection and avoidance in early lexical acquisition. *Journal of Child Language* 9: 319–36. pp. 216, 238, 294

    and Terrell, B. Y. 1983. The role of input frequency in lexical acquisition. *Journal of Child Language* 10: 57–64. p. 247

Schwartz, R., Leonard, L., Wilcox, J. and Folger, K. 1980. Again and again: reduplication in child phonology. *Journal of Child Language* 7: 75–88. p. 231

Scollon, R. T. 1976. *Conversations with a one year old.* Honolulu: University of Hawaii Press. pp. 280, 313, 316, 317

Scribner, S. 1977. Modes of thinking and ways of speaking: culture and logic reconsidered. In P. N. Johnson-Laird and P. C. Wason (eds.) *Thinking: readings in cognitive science.* Cambridge: Cambridge University Press. p. 483

    and Cole, M. 1981. *The psychology of literacy.* Cambridge, Mass.: Harvard University Press. pp. 483, 493

Searle, J. R. 1969. *Speech acts.* Cambridge: Cambridge University Press. p. 288

    1980. Rules and causation. *Behavioral and Brain Sciences* 3: 37. p. 33

Sebeok, T. A., Hayes, A. S. and Bateson, M. C. (eds.) 1964. *Approaches to semiotics.* The Hague: Mouton. p. 174

Seiler, H. 1971. Abstract structures for moods in Greek. *Language* 47: 79–89. p. 379

Selman, R. C. 1976. Toward a structural analysis of developing interpersonal relations concepts: research with normal and disturbed pre-adolescent boys. In A. D. Pick (ed.) *Minnesota Symposia on Child Psychology,* vol. 10. Minneapolis. pp. 14, 17

    1980. *The growth of interpersonal understanding: developmental and clinical analyses.* New York: Academic Press. pp. 14, 15, 17

Seuren, P. 1978. Grammar as an underground process. In A. Sinclair, R. Jarvella and W. J. M. Levelt (eds.) *The child's conception of language*. Berlin: Springer-Verlag. p. 40

Shaffer, H. R. and Crook, C. K. 1979. Maternal control techniques in a directed play situation. *Child Development* 50: 989–98. p. 79

Shallice, T. 1972. Dual functions of consciousness. *Psychological Review* 79: 383–93. p. 37

Shankweiler, D., Strange, W. and Verbrugge, R. 1977. Speech and the problem of perceptual constancy. In R. Shaw and J. Bransford (eds.) *Perceiving, acting and knowing: toward an ecological psychology*. Potomac, Md: Erlbaum. p. 255

Shatz, M. 1978. Children's comprehension of question-directives. *Journal of Child Language* 5: 39–46. p. 23

   1981. Learning the rules of the game. Four views of the relation between social interaction and syntax acquisition. In W. Deutsch (ed.) *The child's construction of language*. New York: Academic Press. p. 16

   1982. Influences of mother and mind on the development of communication competence: a status report. In M. Perlmutter (ed.) *Minnesota Symposia on Child Psychology*, vol. 17. Hillsdale, NJ: Erlbaum. p. 403

   1983. Communication. In J. Flavell and E. Markman (eds.) *Cognitive development*. P. Mussen (Gen. ed.) Carmichael's manual of child psychology. 4th edn. New York: Wiley. p. 473

   and Gelman, R. 1973. *The development of communication skills: modifications in the speech of young children as a function of the listener*. Society for Research in Child Development Monographs 38 (5). pp. 28, 71

Sheldon, A. 1972. The acquisition of relative clauses in English. Unpublished doctoral dissertation, University of Texas, Austin. p. 458

   1974. The role of parallel function in the acquisition of relative clauses in English. *Journal of Verbal Learning and Verbal Behavior* 13: 272–81. p. 458

Shepherd, S. C. 1980. Strategies and semantic distinctions in the acquisition of Standard English and Creole modals. Paper presented at the Annual Meeting of the Linguistic Society of America, San Antonio, December. pp. 386, 392

   1981. Modals in Antiguan Creole, child language acquisition, and history. Unpublished doctoral dissertation, Stanford University. pp. 376, 386, 388, 392, 393, 399, 531n

Sheppard, W. C. 1969. Operant control of infant vocal and motor behavior. *Journal of Experimental Child Psychology* 7: 36–51. p. 150

Shields, M. H. and Steiner, E. 1972. The language of three- to five-year-olds in pre-school education. *Educational Research* 15: 97–105. p. 389

Shipley, E. F. and Shipley, T. E. 1969. Quaker children's use of *Thee*: a relational analysis. *Journal of Verbal Learning and Verbal Behavior* 8: 112–7. p. 352

Shipley, E., Gleitman, L. R. and Smith, C. 1969. A study in the acquisition of language: free responses to commands. *Language* 45: 322–42. pp. 71, 74, 80, 522n

Shockey, L. 1973 Phonetic and phonological properties of connected speech. Unpublished doctoral dissertation, Ohio State University

   and Bond, Z. 1980. Phonological processes in speech addressed to children. *Phonetica* 37: 267–74. p. 247

Shugar, G. W. 1978. Text analysis as an approach to the study of early linguistic operations. In N. Waterson and C. E. Snow (ed.) *The development of communication*. Chichester: Wiley. p. 81

Shultz, T. R. and Horibe, F. 1974. Development of the appreciation of verbal jokes. *Developmental Psychology* 10: 13–20. p. 473

Shvachkin, N. 1973. The development of phonemic speech perception in early childhood. In Ferguson and Slobin (1973). p. 200

Siegel, G. M. 1971. Vocal conditioning in infants. *Journal of Speech and Hearing Disorders* 34: 3–19. p. 150

Silverstein, M. 1976. Shifters, linguistic categories and cultural description. In K. Basso and H. Selby (eds.) *Meaning in anthropology*. Albuquerque: University of New Mexico Press. p. 18

    1980. The three faces of 'function': preliminaries to a psychology of language. In M. Hickmann (ed.) *Proceedings of a working conference on the social foundations of language and thought*. Chicago: Center for Psychosocial Studies. pp. 18, 20

Simon, C. and Fourcin, A. J. 1978. Cross language study of speech pattern learning. *Journal of the Acoustical Society of America* 63: 925–35. p. 200

Sinclair, A., Sinclair, H. and Marcelus, O. 1971. Young children's comprehension and production of passive sentences. *Archives de Psychologie* 161: 1–22. p. 458

Sinclair, H. 1967. *Langage et opérations: sous-systèmes linguistiques et opérations concrètes*. Paris: Dunod. p. 456

    and Ferreiro, E. 1970. Étude génétique de la compréhension, production et répétition des phrases au mode passif. *Archives de Psychologie* 40: 1–42. pp. 456, 458

Sinclair-de-Zwart, H. 1967. *Acquisition du langage et développement de la pensée*. Paris: Dunod. p. 12

    1969. Developmental psycholinguistics. In D. Elkind and J. H. Flavell (eds.) *Studies in cognitive development: essays in honor of Jean Piaget*. London: Oxford University Press. p. 12

Sinha, C. and Walkerdine, V. 1978. Conservation: a problem in language, culture and thought. In N. Waterson and C. E. Snow (eds.) *The development of communication*. Chichester: Wiley. pp. 12, 16

Slobin, D. I. 1971. *Psycholinguistics*. 1st edn. Glenview, Ill.: Scott, Foresman and Co. p. 518

    1973. Cognitive prerequisites for the acquisition of grammar. In Ferguson and Slobin (1973). pp. 331, 373, 393, 399, 417, 430, 522n

    1979. *Psycholinguistics*. 2nd edn. Chicago: Scott, Foresman and Co. p. 433

    1981. Operating principles for the acquisition of language. Unpublished report, Department of Psychology, University of California, Berkeley. p. 370

    1982. Universal and particular in the acquisition of language. In Wanner and Gleitman (1982). pp. 308, 430, 527n

    1985a. Crosslinguistic evidence for the language-making capacity. In Slobin (1985b). pp. 277, 308, 309, 365, 373, 430, 431, 435

    1985b. *The crosslinguistic study of language acquisition*. Hillsdale, NJ: Erlbaum. pp. 446, 531n

and Aksu, A. A. 1980. Acquisition of Turkish. Draft of paper to appear in Slobin (1985b). p. 527n

1982. Tense, aspect, and modality in the use of the Turkish evidential. In P. J. Hopper (ed.) *Tense–aspect: between semantics and pragmatics.* Containing the contributions to the Symposium on Tense and Aspect, held at UCLA, May 1979. Amsterdam: Benjamins. p. 399

and Bever, T. A. 1982. Children use canonical sentence schemas. A crosslinguistic study of word order and inflections. *Cognition* 12: 229–65

Smedslund, J. 1970. Circular relation between understanding and logic. *Scandinavian Journal of Psychology* 11: 217–19. p. 38

Smith, B. L. 1982. Some observations concerning premeaningful vocalizations of hearing-impaired infants. *Journal of Speech and Hearing Disorders* 47: 439–40. p. 152

and Oller, D. K. 1981. A comparative study of premeaningful vocalizations produced by normal and Down's Syndrome infants. *Journal of Speech and Hearing Disorders* 46: 46–51. p. 152

Smith, C. S. 1978. The syntax and interpretation of temporal expressions in English. *Linguistics and Philosophy* 2: 43–99. p. 356

1980. The acquisition of time talk: relations between child and adult grammars. *Journal of Child Language* 7: 263–78. pp. 356, 357, 370, 426

Smith, N. 1973. *The acquisition of phonology: a case study.* Cambridge: Cambridge University Press. pp. 65, 201, 225, 228, 262, 263, 267

Smith, P. and Connolly, K. 1972. Patterns of play and social interaction in pre-school children. In N. B. Jones (ed.) *Ethological studies of child behaviour.* Cambridge: Cambridge University Press. p. 122

Smith, P. T. and Groat, A. 1979. Spelling patterns, letter cancellation and the processing of text. In P. A. Kolers, M. E. Wrolstad and H. Bouma (eds.) *Processing of visible language*, vol. I. New York: Plenum Press. p. 478

and Pattison, H. M. 1980. English shorthand systems and abbreviatory conventions: a psychological perspective. In P. A. Kolers, M. E. Wrolstad and H. Bouma (eds.) *Processing of visible language*, vol. II. New York: Plenum Press. p. 476

and Sterling, C. M. 1982. Factors affecting the perceived morphemic structure of written words. *Journal of Verbal Learning and Verbal Behavior* 21: 704–21. p. 478

Smith, P. T., Baker, R. G. and Groat, A. 1982. Spelling as a source of information about children's linguistic knowledge. *British Journal of Psychology* 73: 339–50. pp. 480, 481, 493

Smoczyńska, M. 1978. Wczesne studia rozwoju skladni w mowie dziecka. (The early phase of development of syntax in the speech of children.) Unpublished dissertation, Jagiellonian University, Krakow. pp. 361, 362, 368

1981. Acquisition of Polish. Unpublished MS, Institute of Psychology, Jagiellonian University, Krakow. pp. 396, 397

1985. Acquisition of Polish. In Slobin (1985b). pp. 362, 368

Snow, C. E. 1972a. Mothers' speech to children learning. *Child Development* 43: 549–65. pp. 70, 71

1972b. Young children's responses to adult sentences of varying complexity. Paper presented at 4th International Congress of Applied Linguistics, Copenhagen. pp. 71, 80

1977a. The development of conversation between mothers and babies. *Journal of Child Language* 4: 1–22. pp. 83, 182, 290

1977b. Mothers' speech research: from input to interaction. In Snow and Ferguson (1977). pp. 78, 79, 120, 135

1979. The role of social interaction in language acquisition. In A. Collins (ed.) *Children's language and communication: 12th Minnesota Symposia on Child Psychology.* Hillsdale, NJ: Erlbaum

1981. The uses of imitation. *Journal of Child Language* 8: 205–12. p. 88

1983. Saying it again: the role of expanded and deferred imitations in language acquisition. In K. E. Nelson (ed.) *Children's language*, vol. 4. Hillsdale, NJ: Erlbaum. pp. 86, 88

and Ferguson, C. (eds.) 1977. *Talking to children: language input and acquisition.* Cambridge: Cambridge University Press. p. 133

and Gilbreath, B. J. 1983. Explaining transitions. In R. M. Golinkoff (ed.) *The transition from prelinguistic to linguistic communication.* Hillsdale, NJ: Erlbaum. p. 87

and Goldfield, B. A. 1982. Building stories: the emergence of information structures from conversation. In D. Tannen (ed.) *Analyzing discourse: text and talk.* Georgetown University Round Table on Languages and Linguistics, 1981. Washington, DC: Georgetown University Press. p. 79

1983. Turn the page please: situation-specific language learning. *Journal of Child Language* 10: 551–69. p. 86

Snow, C. E., Dubber, C. and DeBlauw, A. 1982. Routines in parent–child interaction. In L. Feagans and D. Farran (eds.) *The language of children reared in poverty: implications for evaluation and intervention.* New York: Academic Press. p. 83

Snow, C. E., Arlman-Rupp, A., Hassing, Y., Jobse, J., Joosten, J. and Vorster, J. 1976. Mothers' speech in three social classes. *Journal of Psycholinguistic Research* 5: 1–20. p. 78

Snowling, M. J. 1980. The development of grapheme–phoneme correspondence in normal and dyslexic readers. *Journal of Experimental Child Psychology* 29: 294–305. p. 484

Snyder, L. S., Bates, E. and Bretherton, I. 1981. Content and context in language development. *Journal of Child Language* 8: 565–82. pp. 279, 300

Sober, E. 1980. Representation and psychological reality. *Behavioral and Brain Sciences* 3: 38. p. 33

Solan, L. 1981. The acquisition of structural restrictions on anaphora. In Tavakolian (1981). pp. 59, 66, 339

1983. *Pronominal reference: child language and the theory of grammar.* Dordrecht: D. Reidel. p. 59

and Ortiz, R. In press. The development of pronouns and reflexives: evidence from Spanish. In Lust (in press). p. 57

and Roeper, T. 1978. Children's use of syntactic structure in interpreting relative

clauses. In H. Goodluck and L. Solan (eds.) *Papers in the structure and development of child language. University of Massachusetts Occasional Papers in Linguistics.* p. 61

Spring, D. R. and Dale, P. S. 1977. Discrimination of linguistic stress in early infancy. *Journal of Speech and Hearing Research* 20: 224–32. p. 179

Srivastava, G. D. 1974. A child's acquisition of Hindi consonants. *Indian Linguistics* 35: 112–8. p. 268

Staats, A. W. 1967. Emotions and images in language: a learning analysis of their acquisition and function. In K. Salzinger and S. Salzinger (eds.) *Research in verbal behavior and some neurophysiological implications.* New York: Academic Press. p. 198

Stabler, E. P. 1983. How are grammars represented? *Behavioral and Brain Sciences* 6: 391–422. p. 33

Stalnaker, R. 1972. Pragmatics. In D. Davidson and G. Harman (eds.) *Semantics of natural language.* Dordrecht: D. Reidel. p. 39

Stampe, D. L. 1969. The acquisition of phonetic representation. *Papers from the Fifth Regional Meeting of the Chicago Linguistic Society*: 433–44. p. 223
  1973. A dissertation on natural phonology. Unpublished doctoral dissertation, University of Chicago. p. 249

Stanovich, K. E., West, R. F. and Feeman, D. J. 1981. A longitudinal study of sentence context effects in second-grade children: tests of an interactive-compensatory model. *Journal of Experimental Child Psychology* 32: 185–99. p. 491

Stark, J., Poppen, R. and May, M. Z. 1967. Effects of alterations of prosodic features on the sequencing performance of aphasic children. *Journal of Speech and Hearing Research* 10: 844–8. p. 196

Stark, R. E. 1972. Some features of the vocalizations of young deaf children. In J. F. Bosma (ed.) *Third symposium on Oral Sensation and Perception: the mouth of the infant.* Springfield, Ill.: Thomas. p. 169
  1978. Features of infant sounds: the emergence of cooing. *Journal of Child Language* 5: 379–90. p. 165
  1980. Stages of speech development in the first year of life. In G. H. Yeni-Komshian, J. F. Kavanagh and C. A. Ferguson (eds.) *Child phonology,* vol. 1: *Production.* New York: Academic Press. p. 170
  1983. Phonatory development in young normally hearing and hearing-impaired children. In I. Hockberg and M. J. Osberger (eds.) *Speech of the hearing impaired.* Baltimore: University Park Press. p. 169
  1985. Dysarthria in children. In J. K. Darley (ed.) *Speech evaluation in neurology (children).* New York: Grune and Stratton. p. 524n
  and Nathanson, S. N. 1974. Spontaneous cry in the newborn infant: sounds and facial gestures. In J. F. Bosma (ed.) *Fourth Symposium on Oral Sensation and Perception: development in the fetus and infant.* Bethesda, Md.: US Government Printing Press. pp. 156, 163

Stark, R. E., Heinz, J. and Wright-Wilson, C. 1976. Vowel utterances of young infants. Paper presented at the 92nd Meeting of the Acoustical Society of America, San Diego. pp. 154, 157, 158

Stark, R. E., Rose, S. N. and McLagen, M. 1975. Features of infant sounds: the

first eight weeks of life. *Journal of Child Language* 2: 205–21. pp. 155, 156, 179

Starr, S. 1975. The relationship of single words to two-word sentences. *Child Development* 46: 701–8. pp. 119, 314, 317

Stephany, U. 1981. Verbal grammar in Modern Greek child language. In S. Dale and D. Ingram (eds.) *Child language: an international perspective.* Baltimore, Md.: University Park Press. pp. 361, 377

    1984. *Aspekt, Tempus und Modalität: eine Studie der Entwicklung der Verbalgrammatik in der neugriechischen Kindersprache.* Tübingen: Gunter Narr. pp. 362, 377

Stern, C. and Stern, W. 1928. *Die Kindersprache: eine psychologische und sprachtheoretische Untersuchung,* 4th edn. Leipzig: Barth. pp. 149, 238, 395

Stern, D. N., Spieker, S. and MacKain, K. 1982. Intonation contours as signals in maternal speech to pre-linguistic infants. *Developmental Psychology* 18: 727–35. pp. 79, 194

Stern, D. N., Spieker, S., Barnett, R. K. and MacKain, K. 1983. The prosody of maternal speech: infant age and context related changes. *Journal of Child Language* 10: 1–15. pp. 193, 194

Stern, G. 1964. *Meaning and change of meaning.* Bloomington Ind.: Indiana University Press. p. 401

Stern, W. 1930. *Psychology of early childhood.* New York: Holt. p. 311

Stevens, K. N. 1972. The quantal nature of speech: evidence from articulatory-acoustic data. In P. Denes and E. David (eds.) *Human communication: a unified view.* New York: McGraw-Hill. p. 204

    1975. The potential role of property detectors in the perception of consonants. In G. Fant and M. A. A. Tatham (eds.) *Auditory analyses and perception of speech.* London: Academic Press. p. 257

    and Blumstein, S. E. 1981. The search for invariant acoustic correlates of phonetic features. In P. D. Eimas and J. L. Miller (eds.) *Perspectives on the study of speech.* Hillsdale, NJ: Erlbaum. p. 257

Stine, E. L. and Bohannon, J. N. 1983. Imitations, interactions, and language acquisition. *Journal of Child Language* 10: 589–603. p. 80

Stoel-Gammon, C. M. 1974. The acquisition of liquids in Spanish. Unpublished thesis, Stanford University. p. 268

Stone, C. A. and Day, M. C. 1980. Competence and performance models and the characterization of formal operational skills. *Human Development* 23: 323–53. pp. 12, 15, 21, 22

Stotsky, S. 1983. Research on reading/writing relationships: a synthesis and suggested directions. *Language Arts* 60: 627–42. p. 516

Streeter, L. A. 1976. Language perception of 2-month-old infants shows effects of both innate mechanisms and experience. *Nature* 259 (January 1–8): 39–41. p. 260

Stroop, J. R. 1935. Studies of interference in serial verbal reactions. *Journal of Experimental Psychology* 18: 643–62. p. 490

Stross, B. 1973. Acquisition of botanical terminology by Tzeltal children. In M. S. Edmondson (ed.) *Meaning in Mayan languages.* The Hague: Mouton. p. 230

Sullivan, J. W. and Horowitz, F. D. 1983. The effects of intonation on infant

attention: the role of the rising intonation contour. *Journal of Child Language*. pp. 179, 194

Sully, J. 1896. *Studies of childhood*. London: Longman. p. 282

Summerfield, Q. 1982. Differences between spectral dependencies in auditory and phonetic temporal processing: relevance to the perception of voicing in initial stops. *Journal of the Acoustical Society of America* 72 (1): 51–61. p. 257

Sutton, C. (ed.) 1981. *Communicating in the classroom*. London: Hodder and Stoughton. p. 513

Szagun, G. 1979. *The development of spontaneous reference to past and future: a crosslinguistic study*. Institut für Psycholgie, Technische Universität, Berlin. p. 362

Tager-Flusberg, H., de Villiers, J. and Hakuta, K. 1982. The development of sentence coordination. In Kuczaj (1982). p. 57

Tanouye, E. K. 1979. The acquisition of verbs in Japanese children. *Stanford Papers and Reports on Child Language Development* 17: 49–56. p. 291

Tanz, C. 1974. Cognitive principles underlying children's errors in case marking. *Journal of Child Language* 1: 271–7. p. 415

    1977. Learning how 'it' works. *Journal of Child Language* 4: 225–36. p. 415

    1980. *Studies in the acquisition of deictic terms*. Cambridge: Cambridge University Press. pp. 346, 402, 409, 421

Tavakolian, S. (ed.) 1981. *Language acquisition and linguistic theory*. Cambridge, Mass.: MIT Press. p. 104

Taylor, I. 1980. The Korean writing system: an alphabet? a syllabary? a logography? In P. A. Kolers, M. E. Wrolstad and H. Bouma (eds.) *Processing of visible language*, vol. II. New York: Plenum Press. p. 475

Templin, M. C. 1957. *Certain language skills in children*. Minneapolis: University of Minnesota Press. pp. 116, 122, 128, 252, 523n

    and Darley, F. L. 1960. The Templin–Darley tests of articulation. Iowa City: Iowa Bureau of Educational Research and Service. p. 150

    1966. The study of articulation and development in early school years. In F. Smith and G. A. Miller (eds.) *The genesis of language*. Cambridge, Mass.: MIT Press. p. 208

Thiemann, P. A. 1982. Phonetic modification in mothers' speech to children. Unpublished MA thesis, University of Maryland. p. 248

Thomas, E. K. 1981. The use of formulaic speech in father–child conversational interaction. Unpublished doctoral dissertation, Boston University Applied Psycholinguistics Program. p. 206

Thomson, J. R. and Chapman, R. S. 1977. Who is 'Daddy' revisited: the status of two-year olds' over-extended words in use and comprehension. *Journal of Child Language* 4: 359–75. pp. 294, 299, 301

Toivainen, J. 1980. *Inflectional affixes used by Finnish-speaking children aged 1–3 years*. Helsinki: Suomalaisen Kirjallisuuden Seura. pp. 361, 363, 365, 369, 395, 433

Tough, J. 1977. *The development of meaning*. London: Unwin Education Books. pp. 130, 132

Tracy, F. 1893. The language of childhood. *American Journal of Psychology* 6: 107–38. p. 291

Traugott, E. C. 1978. On the expression of spatio-temporal relations in language. In J. Greenberg, C. Ferguson and E. Moravcsik (eds.) *Universals of human language*, vol. III *Word structure*. Stanford, Calif.: Stanford University Press. p. 423

Trehub, S. E. 1973. Infants' sensitivity to vowel and tonal contrasts. *Developmental Psychology* 9: 91–6. p. 259

1976. The discrimination of foreign speech contrasts by infants and adults. *Child Development* 47: 466–72. p. 260

Trevarthen, C. 1977. Descriptive analyses of infant communicative behaviour. In H. R. Schaffer (ed.) *Studies in mother–infant interaction*. London: Academic Press. p. 83

Trosborg, A. 1982. Children's comprehension of 'before' and 'after' reinvestigated. *Journal of Child Language* 9: 381–402. pp. 373, 458

Truby, H. M. and Lind, J. 1965. Cry sounds of the newborn infant. In J. Lind (ed.) *Newborn infant cry*. Acta Paed. Scan. Supplement. Uppsala: Almquist and Wiksells. pp. 155, 156

Tse, J. K.-P. 1978. Tone acquisition in Cantonese: a longitudinal case study. *Journal of Child Language* 5: 191–204. p. 185

Tuaycharoen, P. 1977. The phonetic and phonological development of a Thai baby: early communicative interaction to speech. Unpublished doctoral dissertation, University of London. pp. 185, 187

1978. The babbling of a Thai baby: echoes and responses to the sounds made by adults. In N. Waterson and C. E. Snow (eds.) *Development of communication: social and pragmatic factors in language acquisition*. Chichester: Wiley. pp. 185, 194

Tulving, E. 1972. Episodic memory and semantic memory. In E. Tulving and W. Donaldson (eds.) *Organization of memory*. New York: Academic Press. p. 298

Turner, E. A. and Rommetveit, R. 1967. The acquisition of sentence voice and reversibility. *Child Development* 38: 649–60. p. 458

Tyack, D. and Ingram, D. 1977. Children's production and comprehension of questions. *Journal of Child Language* 4: 211–24. p. 68

Tyler, L. K. 1981. Syntactic and interactive factors in the development of language comprehension. In W. Deutsch (ed.) *The child's construction of language*. London: Academic Press. p. 469

1983. The development of discourse mapping processes: the on-line interpretation of anaphoric expressions. *Cognition* 13: 309–41. p. 339

Tzeng, O. J. L. and Wang. W. S-Y. 1983. The first two R's. *American Scientist* 71: 238–43. pp. 479, 493

Valentine, C. W. 1942. *The psychology of early childhood*. London: Methuen. pp. 279, 281, 282, 294, 306

Van der Geest, T. 1975. *Some aspects of communicative competence and their implications for language acquisition*. Assen/Amsterdam: Royal van Gorcum. p. 74

1977. Some interactional aspects of language acquisition. In Snow and Ferguson (1977). p. 88

Van Kleek, A. and Carpenter, R. L. 1980. The effects of children's language

comprehension level on adults' child-directed talk. *Journal of Speech and Hearing Research* 23 (3). p. 80

Vellutino, F. R. and Scanlon, D. M. 1982. Verbal processing in poor and normal readers. In C. J. Brainerd and M. Pressley (eds.) *Verbal processes in children: progress in cognitive development research*. New York: Springer-Verlag. p. 492

Velten, H. 1943. The growth of phonemic and lexical patterns in infant language. *Language* 19: 281–92. pp. 225, 226, 232

Vendler, Z. 1967. Verbs and times. In Z. Vendler (ed.) *Linguistics in philosophy*. Ithaca, NY: Cornell University Press. p. 360

Verkuyl, H. J. 1972. *On the compositional nature of the aspects*. Dordrecht: D. Reidel. p. 360

Vihman, M. 1971. On the acquisition of Estonian. *Stanford Papers and Reports on Child Language Development* 3: 51–94. p. 225

    1976. From prespeech to speech: on early phonology. In *Stanford Papers and Reports on Child Language Development* 12: 230–44. p. 217

    1978. Consonant harmony: its scope and function in child language. In J. H. Greenberg (ed.) *Universals of human language*, vol. II *Phonology*. Stanford, Ca.: Stanford University Press. p. 209

    1981. Phonology and the development of the lexicon: evidence from children's errors. *Journal of Child Language* 8: 239–64. pp. 233, 294

Vinson, J. 1915. Observations sur le développement du langage chez l'enfant. *Revue de Linguistique* 49: 1–39. p. 225

Vogel, I. 1975. One system or two: an analysis of a two-year-old Romanian-English bilingual's phonology. *Stanford Papers and Reports on Child Language Development* 9: 43–62. p. 230

von Wright, G. H. 1963. *Norm and action: a logical enquiry*. London: Routledge and Kegan Paul. p. 376

Vuorenkoski, V., Lind, J., Wasz-Hockert, O. and Partanen, T. J. 1971. Cry score: a method for evaluating the degree of abnormality in the pain cry response of the newborn and young infant. *Quarterly Progress Report on Speech Research*. Royal Speech Transmission Laboratory. p. 155

Vygotsky, L. S. 1934/1962. *Myshlenic i rech'*. Moscow: Sotsekviz. Trans. E. Hanfmann and G. Vakan and published 1962 as *Thought and language*. Cambridge, Mass.: MIT Press. pp. 12, 18, 27, 31, 45, 407, 521n

    1978. *Mind in society*. Cambridge, Mass.: Harvard University Press. pp. 12, 14, 15, 22

    1981a. The genesis of the higher mental functions. In J. V. Wertsch (ed.) *The concept of activity in Soviet psychology*. Armonk, NY: M. E. Sharpe. pp. 12, 14

    1981b. The development of higher forms of attention in childhood. In J. V. Wertsch (ed.) *The concept of activity in Soviet psychology*. Armonk, NY: M. E. Sharpe. pp. 12, 18

Wahler, R. G. 1969. Infant social development: some experimental analysis of an infant–mother interaction during the first year of life. *Journal of Experimental Child Psychology* 7: 101–13. p. 150

Walden, Z. P. 1982. The root of roots: children's construction of word-formation

processes in Hebrew. Unpublished doctoral dissertation, Harvard University.
p. 439

Wales, R. 1974. The child's language makes sense of the world. In *Problèmes Actuels en Psycholinguistique*. Paris: Éditions CNRS. pp. 402, 409, 412, 421

1979. Deixis. In P. Fletcher and M. Garman (eds.) *Language acquisition*. 1st edn. Cambridge: Cambridge University Press. pp. 405, 417

1981. What's so spatial about time? In A. Nesdale, C. Pratt, R. Grieve, J. Field, D. Illingworth and L. Hogben (eds.) *Advances in child development: theory and research*. Perth, WA: University of Western Australia Press. pp. 423, 424

In press. Children's deictic reference: the role of space and animacy. In S. Kuczaj (ed.) *Discourse development*. New York: Springer-Verlag. p. 414

and Pattison, R. 1982. Children's use of tense and aspect. *Working Papers in Linguistics* 8. Melbourne, Vic.: University of Melbourne. p. 426

Wanner, E. and Gleitmann, L. R. (eds.) 1982. *Language acquisition: the state of the art*. Cambridge: Cambridge University Press. pp. 96, 105

Warburton, F. W. and Southgate, V. 1969. *i.t.a.: an independent evaluation*. London: John Murray and W. R. Chambers. p. 480

Ward, M. C. 1971. *Them children: a study of language learning*. New York: Holt, Rinehart and Winston. p. 85

Warden, D. A. 1976. The influence of context on children's uses of identifying expressions and references. *British Journal of Psycology* 67: 101–12. pp. 24, 26

1981. Children's understanding of *ask* and *tell*. *Journal of Child Language* 8: 139–49. p. 346

Waryas, C. L. 1973. Psycholinguistic research in language intervention programming: the pronoun system. *Journal of Psycholinguistic Research* 2: 221–37. p. 340

Wasz-Hockert, O., Lind, J., Vuorenkoski, V., Partanen, T. J. and Valanne, L. 1968. *The infant cry: a spectrographic and auditory analysis*. New York: Heinemann Medical Books. pp. 155, 156

Waterson, N. 1971. Child phonology: a prosodic view. *Journal of Linguistics* 7: 179–211. p. 262

Webb, P. A. and Abramson, A. 1976. Stages of egocentrism in children's use of 'this' and 'that': a different point of view. *Journal of Child Language* 3: 349–67. pp. 402, 405, 407

Webster, R. L. 1969. Selective suppression of infants' vocal responses by classes of phonemic stimulation. *Developmental Psychology* 1: 410–14. p. 150

Weeks, 1971. Speech registers in young children. *Child Development* 42: 1119–31. p. 188

Weil, J. 1971. The relationship between time conceptualization and time language in young children. Unpublished doctoral dissertation, City University of New York. p. 458

and Stenning, K. 1978. A comparison of young children's comprehension and memory for statements of temporal relations. In R. N. Campbell and P. T. Smith (eds.) *Recent advances in the psychology of language: language development and mother–child interaction*. New York and London: Plenum Press. p. 458

Weir, R. H. 1962. *Language in the crib*. The Hague: Mouton. pp. 181, 185

Weisberg, P. 1963. Social and non-social conditioning of infant vocalizations. *Child Development* 34: 377–88. p. 150

Weissenborn, J. 1980. Children's route directions. Paper given at LSA Summer Meeting, Albuquerque, New Mexico. MS, Max-Planck-Institut für Psycholinguistik, Nijmegen. p. 427

    1981. L'acquisition des prépositions spatiales: problèmes cognitifs et linguistiques. In C. Schwarze (ed.) *Analyse des prépositions*. Tübingen: Max Niemeyer Verlag. p. 26

    and Klein, W. 1982. *Here and there: cross-linguistic studies on deixis and demonstration*. Amsterdam: Benjamins. pp. 401, 428

Weist, R. M. 1983. Prefix versus suffix information processing in the comprehension of tense and aspect. *Journal of Child Language* 10: 85–96. p. 364

    and Konieczna, E. 1985. Affix processing strategies and linguistic systems. *Journal of Child Language* 12: 27–35. pp. 364, 436

Weist, R. M., Wysocka, H. Witkowska-Stadnik, K., Buczowska, E. and Konieczna, E. 1984. The defective tense hypothesis: on the emergence of tense and aspect in child Polish. *Journal of Child Language* 11: 347–74. pp. 359, 361, 362, 363, 364, 365

Wells, C. G. 1974. Learning to code experience through language. *Journal of Child Language* 1: 243–69. pp. 115, 317, 318, 323

    1975. The contexts of children's early language experience. *Educational Review* 27 (2): 114–25. p. 134

    1977. Language use and educational success: an empirical response to Joan Tough's *The development of meaning* (1977). *Research in Education* 18: 9–34. p. 132

    1979. Learning and using the auxiliary verb in English. In V. Lee (ed.) *Language development: a reader*. London: Croom Helm. pp. 386, 388, 389, 390, 392, 397

    1980. Apprenticeship in meaning. In K. E. Nelson (ed.) *Children's language* vol. 2. New York: Gardner Press. pp. 81, 290, 292

    1981. *Learning through interaction: the study of language development*. Cambridge: Cambridge University Press. p. 523

    1982. A naturalistic approach to the study of language development. In C. G. Wells (ed.) *Language, learning and education*. Bristol: Centre for the Study of Language and Communication, University of Bristol. p. 113

    1984. *Language development in the pre-school years*. Cambridge: Cambridge University Press. pp. 7, 110, 115, 116, 117, 120, 121, 122, 131, 134, 135, 136, 523n

    and Robinson, W. P. In press. The role of adult speech in language development. In C. Fraser and K. Scherer (eds.) *The social psychology of language*. Cambridge: Cambridge University Press. p. 81

Wepman, J. M. 1958. *Auditory Discrimination Test*. Slough: NFER. p. 476

Werker, J. F., Gilbert, J. H. V., Humphrey, K. and Tees, R. C. 1981. Developmental aspects of cross-language speech perception. *Child Development* 6: 349–55. p. 260

Werner, H. and Kaplan, B. 1963. *Symbol formation.* New York: Wiley. p. 398

Wertsch, J. V. 1980. The significance of dialogue in Vygotsky's account of social, egocentric and inner speech. *Contemporary Educational Psychology* 5: 150–62

In preparation. *The social formation of mind: a Vygotskian perspective.* Cambridge, Mass.: Harvard University Press. pp. 18, 19, 20

and Hickmann, M. In press. A microgenetic analysis of problem-solving in social interaction. In M. Hickmann (ed.) *Social and functional approaches to language and thought.* New York: Academic Press. p. 22

and Schneider, P. 1981. Variation of adults' directives to children in a problem-solving situation. Paper presented at the joint USA–USSR Conference on Social and Individual Cognition, San Diego. p. 19

and Stone, C. A. 1978. Microgenesis as a tool for developmental analysis. *Quarterly Newsletter of the Laboratory of Comparative Human Cognition* 1: 8–10. pp. 19, 22

Wertsch, J. V., McNamee, G. D., Budwig, N. A. and McLane, J. B. 1980. The adult–child dyad as a problem-solving system. *Child Development* 51: 1215–21. p. 19

West, R. F. and Stanovich, K. E. 1978. Automatic contextual facilitation in readers of three ages. *Child Development* 49: 717–29. p. 491

Westermeyer, R. and Westermeyer, J. 1977. Tonal language acquisition among Lao children. *Anthropological Linguistics* 19: 260–4. p. 185

Wexler, K. 1981. Some issues in the theory of learnability. In Baker and McCarthy (1981). pp. 90, 94

and Culicover, P. W. 1980. *Formal principles of language acquisition.* Cambridge, Mass.: MIT Press. pp. 6, 67, 75, 77, 87, 90, 92, 93, 104

Wexler, K., Culicover, P. W. and Hamburger, H. 1975. Learning-theoretic foundations of linguistic universals. *Theoretical Linguistics* 2: 213–53. p. 90

White, L. 1981. The responsibility of grammatical theory to acquisitional data. In Hornstein and Lightfoot (1981). pp. 101, 102, 107

Whitehurst, G. J., Kedesdy, J. and White, T. G. 1982. A functional analysis of meaning. In Kuczaj (1982). p. 291

Wickelgren, W. A. 1966. Distinctive features and errors in short-term memory for English consonants. *Journal of Acoustical Society of America* 39: 388–98. pp. 203, 249

Wieman, L. A. 1976. Stress patterns of early child language. *Journal of Child Language* 3: 283–6. p. 190

Wilbur, R. B. 1980. Theoretical phonology and child phonology: argumentation and implications. In D. Goyvaerts (ed.) *Phonology in the 1980s.* Ghent: E. Story-Scientia. p. 201

Wilcox, S. and Palermo, D. 1974.'In', 'on' and 'under' revisited. *Cognition* 3: 245–54. p. 418

Wilkinson, A., Barnsley, G., Hanna, P. and Swan, M. 1979. Assessing language development: the Crediton Project. *Language for Learning* 1: 59–76. p. 498

Williams, E. 1980. Prediction. *Linguistic Inquiry* 11: 203–38. p. 62

1981a. Language acquisition, markedness and phrase structure. In Tavakolian (1981). p. 56

600   Bibliography (and citation index)

1981b. A readjustment in the learnability assumptions. In Baker and McCarthy (1981). p. 97

1981c. X-bar features and language acquisition. In Tavakolian (1981). p. 102

Wills, D. D. 1977. Participant deixis in English and baby talk. In Snow and Ferguson (1977). p. 351

Wishart, D. 1978. *CLUSTAN: user manual*. 3rd edn. Program Library Unit, Edinburgh University. p. 337

Wittgenstein, L. 1953. *Philosophical investigations*. Oxford: Blackwell. p. 521n

Wode, H. 1980. Grammatical intonation in child language. In L. R. Waugh and C. H. van Schooneveld (eds.) *The melody of language: intonation and prosody.* New York: Academic Press. p. 196

Wolff, P. H. 1969. The natural history of crying and other vocalizations in early infancy. In B. M. Foss (ed.) *Determinants of infant behaviour*, vol. 4. London: Methuen. pp. 166, 178, 292

Wong-Fillmore, L. 1976. The second time around: cognitive and social strategies in second language learning. Unpublished doctoral dissertation, Stanford University. p. 315

1979. Individual differences in second language acquisition. In C. J. Fillmore, D. Kempler and W. S. Y. Wang (eds.) *Individual differences in language ability and language behavior*. New York: Academic Press. pp. 126, 315

Wood, D., Ross, G. and Bruner, J. 1976. The role of tutoring in problem solving. *Journal of Child Psychology and Psychiatry* 17: 89–100. p. 16

Wootton, A. J. 1981. Two request forms of four year olds. *Journal of Pragmatics* 5: 511–23. p. 391

Wright, C. W. 1979. Duration differences between rare and common words and their implications for the interpretation of word frequency effects. *Memory and Cognition* 7: 411–19. p. 248

Yerrill, K. A. J. 1977. *A consideration of the later development of children's syntax in speech and writing: a study of parenthetical, appositional and related items.* Unpublished doctoral thesis, University of Newcastle upon Tyne. pp. 503, 504, 505, 513, 517

Yonas, A. and Pick, H. L. 1975. An approach to the study of infant perception. In L. Cohen and P. Salatapek (eds.) *Infant perception: from sensation to cognition*. London: Academic Press. p. 36

Zarębina, M. 1965. *Ksałtowanie się systemu Językowego dziecka*. (The formation of the language system of a child.) Krakow: Wydawnictwo Polskiej Akademii Nauk; Wroclaw: Ossolineum. pp. 225, 358

Zemlin, W. R. 1968. *Speech and hearing science: anatomy and physiology*. Englewood Cliffs, NJ: Prentice-Hall. p. 165

Ziff, P. 1972. *Understanding understanding*. Ithaca, NY: Cornell University Press. pp. 40, 521n

Zinchenko, P. I. 1985. The unit of analysis in Vygotsky's account of mind. In J. V. Wertsch (ed.) *Culture, communication and cognition: Vygotskian perspectives*. New York: Cambridge University Press. p. 23

Zipf, G. K. 1932. *Selected studies of the principle of relative frequency in language*. Cambridge, Mass.: Harvard University Press. p. 248

1949. *Human behavior and the principle of least effort.* Cambridge, Mass.: Addison-Wesley Press. p. 248

Zlatin, M. 1975. Explorative mapping of the vocal tract and primitive syllabification in infancy: the first six months. Paper presented at the American Speech and Hearing Association Convention, Washington, DC. pp. 155, 158, 263

Zlatin, M. A. and Koenigsknecht, R. A. 1975. Development of the voicing contrast: perception of stop consonants. *Journal of Speech and Hearing Research* 18: 541–53. p. 200

Zwicky, A. M. 1972. Note on a phonological hierarchy in English. In R. P. Stockwell and R. K. S. Macaulay (eds.) *Linguistic change and generative theory.* Bloomington, Ind.: Indiana University Press. p. 246

General index

Certain entries include italicized headings in parentheses, which indicate a more general heading under which this item is subsumed. Child names are in each case followed by the principal investigator's name in parentheses.

OTHER CAMBRIDGE TITLES
Second Language Acquisition
WOLFGANG KLEIN

This textbook presents an up-to-date account of the main concerns, problems and theoretical and practical issues raised by second language acquisition research. Research in this field has until recently been mainly pedagogically oriented, but since the 1970s linguists and psychologists have become increasingly interested in the principles that underly second language acquisition for the light these throw on how human language processing functions in general. Moreover, it is only through an understanding of these principles that foreign language teaching can become maximally effective. **Hard covers**

Cambridge Textbooks in Linguistics   **Paperback**

The Units of Language Acquisition
ANN M. PETERS

This book considers how children approach the problem of learning language. Ann Peter's thesis is that children's first 'words' may not always be congruent with adult expectations as previous work has assumed: hence the term 'units'. She asks how these units are discovered by children at different stages and what factors are involved in the discovery process.   **Paperback**
Cambridge Monographs and Texts in Applied Psycholinguistics 1

Language Development in the Pre-School Years
GORDON WELLS

After more than a decade of research the Bristol Study of Language Development has now assembled a corpus of data on the language development of children aged one to five years that is representative both in terms of the sample of children studied and of the situations in which their spontaneous speech was recorded. Gordon Wells, who directed the project, presents a detailed account of the common sequence of development that was observed. **Hard covers**
Language at Home and at School 2   **Paperback**

Lightning Source UK Ltd.
Milton Keynes UK
UKOW02f0850030914

237991UK00001B/39/A